THE
EFFICIENT USE
OF STEAM

THE EFFICIENT USE OF STEAM

General Editor: P. M. Goodall
MIMech E, MIEE, FInstE

Westbury House

Published by Westbury House (the books division of IPC Science
and Technology Press Limited). PO Box 63, Bury Street,
Guildford, Surrey GU2 5BH, England.

First published in 1980
Reprinted 1981

© IPC Business Press Limited 1980

ISBN 0 86103 018 4

Typeset by Southern Litho Limited
Printed in Great Britain by Book Press Services Limited / Thomson Litho Limited

Contents

Preface

Sir Oliver Lyle's *The Efficient Use of Steam* has always been one of my favourite textbooks; its freshness of approach singled it out as something special when it was first published. However, it is over thirty years since it first came out, and because of the continuing development of steam engineering and its allied subjects, it was thought that the time had come for a complete revision of the book.

The original intention was to do just that — to take out old material and to introduce new subjects, and modern methods. Like Chaucer's Monk, we wanted 'to let go by the things of yesterday, and take the modern world's more spacious way'. It became clear however that for copyright reasons this could not be done, and the book would have to be rewritten.

There has been no attempt to imitate the original style — it was inimitable; one exception has been made in Chapter 20 where a typical piece of Sir Oliver's analytical style has been introduced.

The original title has been kept; it was a good title and has served the book well during thirty years, but this new book does cover a little more of the subject. It might well be subtitled 'The Steam Engineer's Manual', because we have tried to provide all the necessary information an industrial steam engineer, or designer, would want about the 'steam-water stuff'. In general the book has been produced for engineers operating in the middle range of industrial power, with an upper limit of about 100 MW. An exception has been made in the material supplied by the Central Electricity Generating Board on installations of 500 MW upwards, because their approach to the efficient use of steam and their monitoring of station performance must surely have lessons for all.

I shall not give an account of my indebtedness to the many people who have helped, because I have thanked each of them individually, but I must make one exception, in the case of my typist. Mrs Mandy Smith has managed to decipher the more lurid details of thermodynamics, written in a bad hand, with an astonishing precision. My debt to her is very great.

It should be clear that any mistakes in the book are my responsibility. If such mistakes occur, I must enter the same plea as that used 200 years ago by Dr Johnson. A lady had taken him to task for a flagrantly wrong definition in his dictionary. When she asked him how he could make such a mistake he replied, 'Ignorance, Madam, pure ignorance'.

Philip M. Goodall
Chideock, December 1979

Steam pressures

The usual problems have arisen as to whether to use the gauge or absolute pressure of steam. It has been decided to make it as simple as possible by using absolute pressure *unless otherwise stated.* Clearly in those cases where general considerations of pressure are being discussed, and no calculations are involved, it is unimportant whether absolute or gauge pressures are being mentioned, but in all other cases, unless bar gauge is specially mentioned, pressures are all in bar abs.

Acknowledgements

This book could not have been written without the help of a great number of people and organizations. The publishers and the editor acknowledge gratefully the assistance of:

First the Authors

W. M. Barber	Chap. 10
J. M. Burnett	Chap. 17
F. H. Cass	
D. Handley	
C. McGreavy	Chap. 12, 13, 14, 15
G. Sachs	
H. S. Davies	
R. C. Hodrien	Chap. 16
W. Gardener	Chap. 9
N. Gibson	Chap. 3
W. Goldstern	Chap. 18
P. M. Goodall	Chap. 19, 20
D. Gunn	Chap. 4
R. Harrison	
F. Mosley	Chap. 3
J. D. Nicholson	Chap. 6
L. T. Robinson	Chap. 21
A. I. J. Treanor	Chap. 7
K. A. Tubman	Chap. 1, 2
D. E. Upton	Chap. 5
R. M. de Vial	Chap. 8
R. M. Wagg	Chap. 6
H. Watson	Chap. 11

Next, the engineers and industries who provided all the material for Chapter 20, 'Steam in Industry'.

A. C. Perrins of Laporte Industries Ltd

I.C. White of BP London, Engineering Dept

J.A. Barlow of BP Chemicals Ltd (the information was sent to the editor by J. Bond)

W.M. Lanyon of British Sugar Corporation Ltd

Z.W. Sochaczewski of CEGB Midlands Region

J.E. Somner of Tate and Lyle Ltd (approval to publish this material was given by Mr John O. Lyle and Messrs. Chapman & Hall Ltd)

R.N. Maclean of Scottish Grain Distillers Ltd

R.D. Haigh of UML Ltd

Finally the firms and organizations who supplied photographs, illustrations and other information which appears throughout the book, or who allowed their engineers to contribute to the book:

Babcock-Bristol Ltd
Babcock & Wilcox Ltd
Bestobell Mobrey Ltd
J. Blakeborough & Sons Ltd
British Engine Boiler and Electrical Insurance Co. Ltd
British Gas Corporation
British Standards Institution
Darchem Ltd
GEC Ltd
Health & Safety Executive
Hick Hargreaves Ltd
Honeywell Ltd
Hopkinson Ltd
Imperial Chemical Industries Ltd
Institution of Mechanical Engineers
Introl Ltd
Kennedy & Donkin
Merz & McLellan
National Engineering Laboratory, East Kilbride
National Vulcan Engineering Insurance Group Ltd
Neles International BV
N.E.I. Parsons
Permutit Boby Ltd
Power & Works Engineering
H. Saacke Ltd
Saunders Valve Co
Spirax Sarco Ltd
Wiegand Ltd
Wolstenholme (Radcliffe) Ltd

1

The properties of water and steam

1.1 The chemical and physical properties

In 1712 Newcomen completed the construction of the first practical steam engine, which was a reciprocating (beam) engine used extensively for mine drainage and later adapted for locomotive propulsion. Steam (i.e. water vapour) has therefore been used as a working fluid since the earliest days of the industrial revolution, and it is difficult to appreciate its impact on and importance for the development of that revolution. Today, its use is common throughout industry not only for mechanical power production, but also for many and varied heating and process applications. The advantages of using steam as the working fluid are partly that it can be easily distributed and controlled and also that it can serve as the same working fluid for combined power generation and/or heating and/or process work duties. In addition, water and steam possess the following unusual merits:

1. Water is by far the most common liquid on the earth and is therefore plentiful and cheap. It is also chemically stable and non-hazardous to health.
2. Water is evaporated into steam at temperatures well below the metallurgical limit of boiler steels.
3. Water and steam both act as good heat sponges and the evaporation of water into steam also involves a high heat absorption. Hence, plant sizes and costs are not impracticably large.

In order for these chemical and physical properties of water and steam to be understood, it is necessary to describe the molecular and atomic structure of matter in a general way and then to discuss the particular structure of the water and steam substance.

All chemical substances consist of vast numbers of very small discrete particles called *molecules*. For example, one kilogram of ice, water or steam consists of about 3×10^{25} molecules, each about 2×10^{-10} m in diameter. Molecules are composed of even smaller particles called atoms, but the molecule is the smallest particle of a substance to possess all the chemical properties of that substance, that is, the qualities which enable us to distinguish between water, salt, iron and so on. The molecules are in constant motion and are separated from one another in the bulk substance by empty space. Any substance can exist in three possible physical states or *phases* — solid, liquid or vapour — depending upon the degree of freedom of movement of its molecules.

In the solid phase, the movement of individual molecules is restricted to a vibration about a mean bonded position, and the molecules are very closely packed in a lattice-type structure. The distance separating adjacent molecules is less than the diameter of a molecule. If the solid is heated the molecules vibrate more energetically and at some stage the vibration will be sufficiently energetic for the molecules to break away from their bonded structures, and the solid then melts into a liquid . This phase change requires the absorption of heat to break the lattice bonding and hence the substance does not become hotter during the melting process. The amount of heat required to melt unit mass of the substance is called the *latent heat of melting,* and this value differs from one substance to another depending upon the strength of the lattice bonding that is broken. The reverse process is freezing, and it occurs with the release of the same amount of latent heat to the surroundings.

In the liquid state, the molecules are free to move about, but only within the restricted volume occupied by the bulk substance. This volume is of no fixed shape, but assumes the shape of the containing (solid) vessel. The liquid molecules are still very close to one another (less than one molecular diameter apart) and chance collisions occur frequently. If the liquid is heated, its molecules move faster and collisions become more frequent and energetic. The collisions result in some molecules having above-average speeds for short periods of time, whilst others have below-average speeds. Molecules with above-average speeds and near the liquid surface may overcome the attractive forces of the surrounding liquid molecules, and they will therefore escape from the bulk liquid and will form the vapour envelope above the liquid surface. If more heat is supplied, the average speed of the molecules will eventually equal the escape speed and then the liquid evaporates into a vapour, or in other words boiling occurs. As in melting, this requires the absorption of heat in order to break the mutual attractions of the closely packed liquid molecules, and therefore the substance does not become hotter during the evaporation process. The amount of heat required to evaporate a unit mass of the substance at its boiling temperature is called the *latent heat of evaporation.* The reverse process is *condensation* and occurs with the release of the same amount of latent heat to the surroundings.

The molecules in the vapour state have no mutual attraction and move in random directions with high velocities of up to several thousand kilometres per second. Under atmospheric conditions they are separated from one another by about ten molecular diameters, and the molecules occupy the whole space that is available, the only restriction being the walls of a containing vessel. If the vessel has a movable wall (for example the piston of a reciprocating engine), and this wall is moved so as to increase the available volume, then the vapour will expand to fill the increased volume. The movements of the individual molecules are dictated by the results of chance collisions with one another and with the walls of the containing vessel. If the vapour is heated it will eventually reach a state such that it cannot be forced by compression to change back into a liquid. At and above this temperature the vapour is then called a gas.

This description of the molecular structure of matter applies to the ice, water and steam substance. However, this substance possesses certain additional and unusual properties and we shall now discuss these. First, let us consider why water is the most common liquid on earth and why therefore it is plentiful and cheap. Each molecule of ice, water and steam consists of two atoms of the element hydrogen (of chemical symbol H) bonded together with one atom of oxygen (of chemical symbol O). The resulting chemical compound therefore has the formula H_2O and is thought to be the most common chemical compound in the universe. Out of every 10 000 atoms in the universe, about 9200 are hydrogen, 790 are helium, 5 are oxygen, 2 are neon, 2 are nitrogen and 1 is carbon. All the other elements make up an insignificant contribution. Since helium does not combine with any other elements, it follows that the most common compound-forming elements are hydrogen and oxygen, and the atomic structures of these elements dictate the chemical bonding of the two atoms of hydrogen with one of oxygen. Naturally, H_2O is not common everywhere in the universe. It does not exist in stars (because of break-up of molecules at very high temperatures) and on small planets (because gravitational forces are too weak to trap the molecules). However, the earth's planetary position, size and mean temperature are such as to contain and hold a more representative sample of H_2O, and it is therefore plentiful and hence cheap on the Earth.

The other special properties of H_2O are due to the unusual type of bonding (called the *hydrogen bond*) of the hydrogen and oxygen atoms. This results in H_2O molecules' having extra-strong mutual attractions, and consequently possessing the following unusual properties:

1. Much higher melting and boiling temperatures than would be expected for such a chemical substance. Without the extra-strong bonds, H_2O would be a gas at atmospheric temperatures and life as we know it would not exist on the earth.
2. Water, in all its three phases, absorbs more heat for each one-degree rise in temperature than would be the case if the extra-strong bonding did not exist. Thus, ice, water and steam are all good heat sponges. This results, for example, in only slight variations in ocean temperatures between summer and winter.
3. Water has unusually high latent heats of melting and evaporation owing to the necessity of breaking the extra-strong molecular bonds. Hence, evaporating water into steam is an effective heat sponge process.
4. Water has a maximum density at 4°C (and not at 0°C) and is an extremely good solvent. Again, if water did not have these properties, life as we know it would not exist on the earth.

The chemical and physical properties of the H_2O substance having been described, the rest of this chapter is concerned with its thermodynamic properties. To this end, we shall use a number of terms and concepts, and these are defined and discussed in the next section.

1.2 Terms and concepts

Mass

The *mass*, m, of a substance is a measure of the amount of matter (atoms and molecules) comprising the substance. Thus, 10 kg of steam consists of ten times as many H_2O molecules as 1 kg of steam.

Furthermore, 1 kg of steam contains exactly the same number of molecules as 1 kg of water or 1 kg of ice.

Density and specific volume

The *density*, ρ, of a substance is the mass (m) per unit volume (V) of the substance. The *specific volume*, v, is the volume per unit mass and is therefore the inverse of density. Its units are m^3/kg or dm^3/kg where $10^3 \, dm^3/kg = 1 \, m^3/kg$. Hence

$$\rho = \frac{m}{V} = \frac{1}{v} \tag{1.1}$$

From our discussions on the molecular structure of liquids and vapours we would expect the density of steam to be much smaller than that of water because the steam molecules are more widely separated from one another, and at typical atmospheric conditions the densities of water and steam are

respectively 1000 kg/m³ and 0.6 kg/m³. One kg of steam at atmospheric conditions therefore occupies a volume about 1700 times that of 1 kg of water. This enormous volume difference is appreciated if a kettle of water is left to boil; the resulting steam soon fills the entire room.

Temperature

The *temperature*, t or T, of a substance is a measure of the degree of hotness or coldness of the substance. From our discussion on the molecular structure of matter, the temperature of a substance is seen to be related to the intensity of molecular and atomic motion; the more energetic the motion of the molecules and atoms, the more energetic are the collisions, the hotter is the substance and the higher its temperature.

In SI units, temperature is measured in °C or K units. The *Celsius* (or *centigrade*) °C scale is the one most commonly used by the engineer as it has a convenient (but false) zero corresponding to the freezing temperature of water. The *absolute* (or *Kelvin*) K scale is a similar scale with the same increments, but with a true zero corresponding to the minimum possible temperature of a substance when all molecular and atomic motion has ceased. It is impossible for a substance to consist of molecules and atoms having negative motion, and therefore it is impossible for a substance to be at a negative absolute temperature. The absolute temperature at which water freezes to ice is 273 K, and hence the two scales of temperature are interchangeable according to the relation

$$T \, (\text{K}) = t \, (°\text{C}) + 273° \tag{1.2}$$

For example, at atmospheric pressure water boils into steam at 100°C or 373 K. As both scales have the same increments, a temperature difference of 1°C is the same as 1 K.

Temperature measurement

The mercury-in-glass thermometer is the common instrument for measuring water or steam temperatures. When the instrument is subjected to a change in temperature, the mercury expands or contracts far more than the glass container. The resulting differential volume change is recorded as a change in position of the mercury column up or down a suitably graduated scale.

Another type of commonly used thermometer is the thermocouple. This consists of two insulated wires of different metals, which are joined together at both ends. When the two junctions are at different temperatures there is an electrical potential difference between the junctions that is proportional to the temperature difference. The cold junction is built into the meter, and there is normally a compensating device for variations in meter temperature. The hot junction is subjected to the water or steam temperature which is to be measured. The meter measures the resulting potential difference and indicates it as a reading on a temperature scale.

Force

Newton's first law of motion tells us that a body must be subjected to a force if it is to undergo acceleration or deceleration. Newton's second law relates the force F (in newtons, N) necessary to cause a mass m (kg) to accelerate by an amount a (m/s²) of

$$F = ma \qquad (1.3)$$

Thus, 1 N is the force which must be applied to a mass of 1 kg in order to accelerate it by 1 m/s².

Weight

The *weight* (wt) of a substance is the force of the earth's gravitational pull on that substance. Since all substances falling freely anywhere in the vicinity of the earth are pulled towards the earth with an acceleration g of 9.81 m/s², application of Newton's second law gives

$$wt = mg$$

Thus, 1 kg of any substance on the earth has a weight of 9.81 N.

Pressure

The *pressure*, p, of a vapour acting on the interior walls of its containing vessel is the force acting on a unit area of the walls caused by the multiple impacts of the vapour molecules against the wall. Heating the vapour will result in its molecules becoming more energetic, and their impacts with the wall molecules more frequent and intense. Therefore, heating will result in an increase in both the temperature and pressure of the vapour if the vessel's volume does not change.

A pressure of 1 N/m² is very small because 1 N is not a large force and yet 1 m² is quite a big area. Hence, a more common pressure unit for the practical engineer is the *bar*, defined as 1 bar = 10^5 N/m². The bar is a convenient unit as it is closely equal to the pressure of the atmosphere.

Atmospheric pressure

The earth is surrounded by an atmosphere consisting mainly of about 79% (by volume) nitrogen gas and 21% (by volume) oxygen gas. The atmosphere extends outwards and the further out from the earth's surface, the less dense it becomes. It has no abrupt ending, but at about 800 km the air is so rarefied that the contribution above this altitude can be neglected.

All the molecules of the atmosphere are held in the earth's vicinity by gravitational pull. The earth's surface is pressurized by the weight of the air above, and is therefore subjected to atmospheric pressure. Its magnitude of approximately 1 bar is an appreciable pressure, but we do not notice it because we live within this environment. Atmospheric pressure varies slightly from one day to the next owing to changes in weather affecting the temperature and density of the air near the earth's surface. One *standard atmosphere* is atmospheric pressure at sea-level on a day when the temperature is 15°C. Its value is 1.013 bar.

Types of pressure

Figure 1.1 illustrates four ways of indicating pressure, defined as:

1. The *absolute pressure* (in bar abs) of a vapour is its pressure measured from the datum of a perfect vacuum, i.e. from a datum of zero bar abs. It is impossible for a vapour to have a negative absolute pressure.
2. The *gauge pressure* (in bar g) of a vapour is its pressure above that of the prevailing atmosphere. Thus, gauge pressure equals absolute pressure minus atmospheric pressure.
3. The *vacuum* or *negative gauge pressure* of a vapour is the pressure of the vapour below that of the atmosphere. This term is therefore used only if the vapour has a pressure below that of the atmosphere. A vacuum of zero bar corresponds to atmospheric pressure and a vacuum of 1 bar corresponds to close to a perfect vacuum.
4. A *differential pressure* is simply the pressure difference between any two pressures.

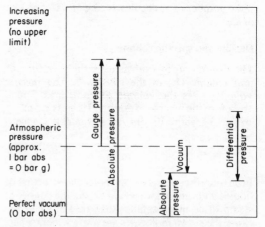

Figure 1.1   Four types of pressure: absolute, gauge, vacuum and differential

Atmospheric pressure measurement — the mercury barometer

The mercury barometer consists of a tube held vertically with its open bottom-end submerged in a mercury bath and with its sealed top-end evacuated. Atmospheric pressure acts on the surface of the mercury bath and forces the mercury to a definite height within the tube. Measurement of the height h of the mercury column enables the atmospheric pressure to be calculated, because

Atmospheric pressure = hydrostatic pressure at the base of the mercury column

$$\frac{\text{mercury weight}}{\text{base area } A \text{ of column}} = \frac{(\text{mercury mass}) (g)}{A}$$

$$= \frac{(\text{mercury density } \rho)(\text{volume})(g)}{A}$$

$$= \frac{(\rho)(A \times h)(g)}{A} = \rho g h \qquad (1.4)$$

For example, if the height h of the mercury column on a particular day is measured as 750 mm, since ρ for mercury is 13.6×10^3 kg/m^3 and $g = 9.81$ m/s^2, the atmospheric pressure on that day is calculated as

Atmospheric pressure $= \rho g h = (13.6 \times 10^3) \times$

$$(9.81)(0.75) \text{ N/m}^2 = 10^5 \text{N/m}^2 = 1 \text{ bar} \qquad (1.5)$$

Steam-pressure measurement using dial Bourdon gauges

The dial pressure gauge is the instrument commonly used for measuring steam pressures above atmospheric, and the dial vacuum gauge is used for pressures below atmospheric. Both measure pressure relative to the prevailing

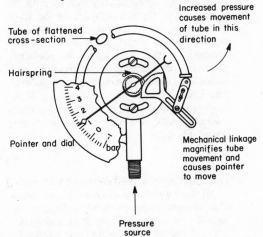

Tube of flattened cross-section

Increased pressure causes movement of tube in this direction

Hairspring

Pointer and dial

Mechanical linkage magnifies tube movement and causes pointer to move

Pressure source

Figure 1.2   The construction of the dial pressure and vacuum Bourdon gauge

atmospheric pressure, and they can be combined into one instrument for measuring pressures both above and below atmospheric. *Figure 1.2* illustrates the construction of these gauges. Atmospheric pressure acts around the outside of a curved, flattened tube and tends to keep the tube flat and curved. The inside of the tube is subjected to the pressure which is to be measured, and if this pressure is greater than atmospheric the tube tends to straighten, and the resulting curvature change causes a pointer to move round a precalibrated scale. If the internal pressure is below atmospheric, the tube becomes more curved and again this is translated into a corresponding movement of the pointer. The gauges are calibrated and their calibration should be periodically checked using dead-weight testers.

Steam pressure measurement using manometers

Steam pressures in the vicinity of atmospheric pressure can be measured accurately using the U-tube manometer, i.e. a glass tube in the shape of the letter U which is partly filled with some fluid, usually mercury. One end of the tube is open to the atmosphere and the other end is connected to a tapping from the steam supply.

Measurement of the differential height of the columns in the two U-tube limbs enables the steam gauge or vacuum to be calculated using the previous hydrostatic pressure equation. For example, if the differential height is 1 m of mercury, then

Steam gauge pressure $= \rho g h$

$$= (13.6 \times 10^3) \ (9.81)(1) \text{ N/m}^2 = 1.33 \text{ bar g} \quad (1.5)$$

Hence, if the barometer reads 750 mm, the atmospheric pressure is 1 bar, and the steam absolute pressure is 2.33 bar abs.

Work

Work is a form of energy transfer. For example, work must be supplied to push a car along a road. The work is supplied to move a force F (counteracting the frictional resistance between tyre and road, and air resistance) through the distance x the car moves. The greater the resistance forces which must be overcome or the greater the distance the car is moved, then the greater must be the work supplied. Hence, work W = force $F \times$ displacement x.

In SI units, one joule (J) is the work required to overcome the resistive force of 1 N over a distance of 1 m. For most engineering calculations, the joule is a small unit and therefore work is usually quoted in kilojoules (kJ), where 1 kJ = 1000 J.

Work must also be supplied to rotate a shaft.

This energy is used to overcome the resistive forces (of bearing friction, coupling load if present, etc.) and to overcome them whilst the shaft rotates through an angular distance. Hence, if r is the shaft radius and θ is the angular displacement (in radians), then

$$
\begin{aligned}
\text{Work } W &= \text{force } F \times \text{displacement } r\theta \\
&= (F \times r)(\theta) \\
&= T \times \theta
\end{aligned}
\tag{1.6}
$$

where T is the torque on the shaft in N m.

Power

Power is defined as the rate of doing work. Consider a young man and an old man both walking along a road. When they reach the end both will have expended the same amount of work. This will have been used in overcoming the resistive forces (of shoe-to-road friction, etc.) and overcoming these forces over the same distance. However, because the young man reaches the end of the road first, his rate of work is greater and hence the power expended is greater, but over a shorter period of time.

Since power is the rate of doing work it is given the symbol $\dot{W}$ just as $\dot{m}$ is the rate of mass flow and $\dot{V}$ is the rate of volume flow. Hence for linear displacement

$$
\dot{W} = \frac{\text{force } F \times \text{displacement } x}{\text{time } t} =
$$

force $F \times$ linear velocity (1.7)

and for rotational displacement

$$
\dot{W} = \frac{\text{torque } T \times \text{angular displacement } \theta}{\text{time } t} = T \times \omega
\tag{1.8}
$$

where ω = angular velocity in rad/s, $= 2\pi N/60$ where N is in rev/min. In both cases the units of $\dot{W}$ are J/s, defined as a *watt* (W). Again, a more practical unit is the kilowatt (kW), where 1000 W = 1 kW.

Heat

Heat, Q, is another type of energy transfer. If two bodies at different temperatures are placed in contact with one another, heat will be transferred from the hotter to the colder until they are both at the same temperature. The units of heat are the same as those of work since both are types of energy. Hence, heat is usually measured in kJ. The rate of heat transfer $\dot{Q}$ is not given a special name, unlike the rate of work transfer (power). Heat transfer can occur in three possible ways: by conduction, convection or radiation. These are discussed in Chapter 12.

Specific heat

The *specific heat, C,* of a substance is a measure of its capacity to absorb heat. It is the amount of heat that must be supplied to a unit mass of the substance in order to cause a unit increase in temperature of the substance, and its units are therefore kJ/kg °C or kJ/kg K. Its value for a particular substance varies both with its temperature and pressure. The high values for both water and steam, as discussed earlier in this chapter, are listed below for atmospheric pressure and temperature:

water	4.19 kJ/kg °C
steam	1.86 kJ/kg °C
air	1.01 kJ/kg °C
mercury	0.14 kJ/kg °C

Energy components of a fluid and enthalpy

We have previously indicated that a fluid does not contain or possess work or heat energy. Rather, it may accept work and/or heat from its surroundings, or reject work and/or heat to its surroundings. Let us now consider what energy components a fluid possesses when it is at a certain condition or state.

The total energy E of a fluid is the sum of the following components:

1. Potential energy (PE), or its energy of position within a gravitational field. Increasing the elevation of the fluid increases its potential energy.
2. Kinetic energy (KE), or its energy of motion. Increasing the velocity of the fluid increases its kinetic energy.
3. Enthalpy H, or its energy due to both the pressure and the temperature of the fluid. The energy due to the pressure is called the *pressure energy* (PrE) and is associated with pressurizing the fluid up to its prevailing pressure and therefore with forcing its molecules into closer proximity to one another. The energy due to the temperature of the fluid is called the *internal energy, U,* and is associated with the kinetic energies of its molecules. Hence

$$
H = \text{PrE} + U
\tag{1.9}
$$

The enthalpy of a fluid therefore increases if its pressure and/or its temperature increases. The specific enthalpy h of a fluid is the enthalpy for unit mass of the fluid, and specific internal energy u is the internal energy for unit mass of fluid.

4. Various other energy components, usually

not of interest to us because their values do not alter during normal thermodynamic processes, for example the chemical energy of the bonding energy of the fluid's atoms into its molecules; atomic energy of the bonding energy of the sub-atomic particles into its atoms; and electrical energy of the movement of charged atoms and charged sub-atomic particles.

All these four components are various forms of energy and therefore each is measured in J or kJ. The specific enthalpy of a fluid is measured in kJ/kg.

Entropy

The entropy S and specific entropy s (i.e. its value for unit mass) of a fluid are difficult concepts to understand. The formal definition of entropy is as follows. If, during a perfectly reversible (i.e. frictionless) process, a small quantity of heat Q is supplied to a fluid, small enough not to change the absolute temperature T of the fluid, then the resultant entropy increase of the fluid is Q/T. The word 'reversible' is important; it implies that if the process is reversed by removing the heat Q no change can be detected in the system or its surroundings. If a large quantity of heat is involved, the temperature of the system will increase and we have to imagine that the process is broken down into a number of small processes. The total change of entropy is then found by adding up all the terms Q/T. Thus, if S_1 is the initial entropy of the fluid and S_2 is its entropy after such a change,

$$S_2 - S_1 = \Sigma \frac{Q}{T} \quad \text{or} \quad s_2 - s_1 = \Sigma \frac{Q}{mT} \quad (1.10)$$

where Σ means 'the sum of all the terms of' and m is the mass of the fluid.

From the above definition, a perfectly reversible process in which $Q = 0$ is a constant-entropy process.

This definition requires clarification. The entropy of a fluid quantifies the degree of orderly or disorderly motion of its molecules when the fluid is at a particular temperature and pressure. Increasing the degree of order of the motions, for example by condensing steam into water, results in a decrease in the entropy of the fluid. Supplying heat to a fluid increases its entropy because its molecules become more agitated, collisions become more frequent and the molecular motions become more chaotic. Although entropy is a property of a fluid, like its pressure and temperature, it cannot be measured directly; there is no instrument capable of measuring the degree of orderly or disorderly motion of molecules.

Instead, it has to be calculated from the other property values of pressure and temperature. From the above definition its units are kJ/K and the units of specific entropy are kJ/kg K.

1.3 The thermodynamic properties of water and steam

Thermodynamic properties

There are six properties of a fluid which are called *thermodynamic properties*. These are specific volume v, temperature t, pressure p, specific internal energy u, specific enthalpy h, and specific entropy s. We have defined and discussed each of these in the previous section. Graphical plots of any one of these against any other for the water and steam substance are of particular interest to the steam engineer because they describe the behaviour of water and steam. Some of the plots reveal the behaviour more clearly than the others and we shall describe these in this section.

The temperature–time and temperature–pressure plots

Suppose we conduct an experiment in which a quantity of ice at –50°C is heated at a pressure of 1 bar. The ice is enclosed in a vertical cylinder fitted with a piston capable of moving vertically up and down and the piston weight is such as to maintain the pressure constant. The supply of heat initially causes the temperature of the ice to increase. At 0°C the ice melts into water and during the melting the temperature remains constant at 0°C. Supplying more heat causes the water temperature to increase from 0°C up to 100°C and then the second phase change occurs in which the water evaporates to form steam. Again, the temperature remains constant until this phase change is completed. Supplying further heat to the steam at 100°C causes the steam temperature to increase.

We can repeat this experiment for different piston weights and hence for different constant pressures. *Figure 1.3* shows the resulting temperature–time curves for five such experiments corresponding to pressures of 0.005, 1, 15.5, 85.9 and 250 bar. The slopes of the near-vertical lines of these curves and the lengths of the horizontal portions are dependent upon the rate of heat supply and are not of importance in this discussion. Rather, we are interested in the number and comparative positions of the horizontal steps. All five curves have steps at 0°C, but only the middle three have second steps and these occur at different temperature levels. Let us relate the shapes of the curves to the changes that occur within the cylinder as heat is supplied. At

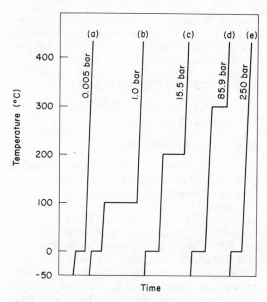

Figure 1.3   The temperature-time curves for ice, water and steam at various pressures

the near-vacuum of 0.005 bar (curve (a)), ice at 0°C does not melt into water, but changes directly into steam. This process is called *sublimation* and seems strange to us because we are unfamiliar with the behaviour of ice at such low pressures. We live within an atmosphere at a pressure of close to 1 bar and therefore we tend to think that the behaviour of substances at atmospheric pressure is 'right' and the behaviour, if different, at very low and very high pressures is 'wrong' or at least strange. Thus, curve (b) of the behaviour at atmospheric pressure is the familiar case of ice melting into water at 0°C and water evaporating into steam at 100°C. Curves (c) and (d) are similar to (b) except that as the pressure is increased, boiling is delayed until a higher temperature is reached. Thus, at 15.5 bar, water does not evaporate to form steam until it reaches 200°C, and at 85.9 bar, until 300°C. This is because increasing the pressure of the water increases the attractive forces of the liquid molecules and therefore increases the resistance to boiling. Hence, boiling is inhibited until a higher temperature is reached. Curve (e) shows that at the high pressure of 250 bar, ice melts into water at 0°C as usual, but the evaporation of water into steam occurs without any abrupt boiling process. It is a gradual phase change occurring with a simultaneous temperature increase. This again seems strange to us, but only because we are unfamiliar with dealing with water and steam at such high pressures.

Figure 1.3 can be used to plot a graph of temperature against pressure, and such a graph is shown in *Figure 1.4*. It is divided into the ice, water

and steam regions. Several terms related to this graph are defined below:

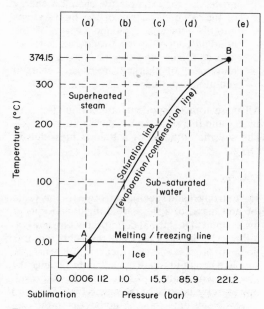

Figure 1.4   The temperature-pressure plot for ice, water and steam showing the constant-pressure lines of Figure 1.3 (not to scale)

1. *Triple point.* The point A is called the 'triple point' as it is the only condition (at 0.01°C and 0.006 112 bar) at which ice, water and steam can all coexist.
2. *Critical point* (CP). The point B is called the 'critical point'. It marks the ending of the abrupt boiling process. Critical-point conditions are 374.15°C and 221.2 bar. Water at any higher (supercritical) pressure has no well-defined boiling point.
3. *Saturation line.* The curve joining the point A to the point B is called the 'saturation line'.
4. *Saturated water and saturated steam.* Water and steam can coexist at any pressure on the saturation line, both being at the boiling temperature. Water and steam at this boiling (or condensing) condition are called 'saturated water' and 'saturated steam'. If saturated steam is not in the presence of saturated water it is called 'dry saturated steam'.
5. *Superheated steam.* Steam at a temperature greater than its saturation temperature for the prevailing pressure is called 'superheated steam'. Its temperature above the saturation temperature is called the 'degree of superheat' of the steam.
6. *Sub-saturated water.* Water at a temperature below the saturation temperature is called 'sub-saturated water'.

The pressure–volume and pressure–enthalpy plots

Figures 1.5 and *1.6* show these plots for the water and steam regions only. *Figure 1.5* has not been

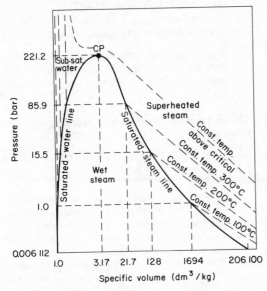

Figure 1.5   The pressure-specific volume plot for water and steam showing various constant-temperature lines (not to scale)

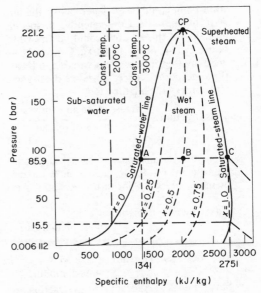

Figure 1.6   The pressure-specific enthalpy plot for water and steam showing various constant-temperature and constant-dryness-fraction lines (to scale)

drawn to scale because of the large range of values of specific volume. *Figure 1.6* is to scale, and it therefore gives a truer representation of the variation of the properties. Both graphs are more complicated than *Figure 1.4* because neither specific volume nor specific enthalpy is constant during the evaporation or condensation process. Consequently the saturation line is broadened into a saturated-water and steam mixture area. Such a mixture is called 'wet steam'.

Several points concerning the plots are noted below:

1. The saturated-water and saturated-steam curves meet at the critical point (CP), there being no step-change in the property values at this point. The two curves should be regarded as being two separate curves having a meeting point at the critical point.
2. The specific volume of saturated water increases only slightly with increasing saturation temperature, and hence with saturation pressure. The behaviour of steam is completely different; its specific volume increases enormously with decreasing pressure, especially in the low-pressure regions. For example, the specific volume of steam at 1 bar is 1694 dm³/kg, but at 0.05 bar (a typical

condenser pressure) it is 28 200 dm³/kg. This has obvious implications for the design of low-pressure steam equipment; such equipment must be of comparatively large size to handle the flow rates.

3. At a constant pressure the specific enthalpy of saturated water is less than that of saturated steam by the specific enthalpy of evaporation or condensation, called the latent heat of evaporation or condensation. The latent heat decreases with increasing pressure, as indicated by the lengths of the upper horizontal steps of curves (b), (c) and (d) of *Figure 1.3*.
4. Only one property value (e.g. saturation temperature or saturation pressure) is required to locate a position on the saturated-water or saturated-steam lines. Thus, as long as we know we are dealing with, for example, dry saturated steam and we know its pressure, then its position (or 'state-point') can be located on these diagrams. To locate a state-point in the superheated-steam, wet-steam or sub-saturated-water regions, two property values must be known. Within the superheated-steam and sub-saturated-water regions the two values are commonly the pressure and temperature. One of these cannot be used for location within the wet-steam region because they are not independent of one another. For example, we know that a wet-steam mixture at 85.9 bar has a temperature of 300°C, but its

state-point could be anywhere along the line ABC of *Figure 1.6*. Consequently, the specific enthalpy of this mixture could be any value between 1341 and 2751 kJ/kg. Obviously we need another independent variable to locate the state-point. Hence, we define the dryness fraction x of the mixture as

$$\text{Dryness fraction } x = \frac{\text{mass of steam in mixture}}{\text{mass of mixture}} \quad (1.11)$$

From this definition, $x = 1.0$ for dry saturated steam; $x = 0.5$ for a 50%–50% mixture by mass, and $x = 0$ for saturated water. Also

$$\text{Mass of steam in mixture} = (x) \times \\ (\text{mass of mixture})$$

and

$$\text{Mass of water in mixture} = (1 - x) \times \\ (\text{mass of mixture})$$

Several lines of constant dryness fraction are shown in *Figure 1.6*. Returning to our earlier example concerning a wet-steam mixture at 85.9 bar, if we are now told that the mixture is a 50%–50% mixture, we can locate the state-point (point B) and we can calculate its specific enthalpy (i.e. enthalpy for unit mass of the mixture) using the equation

Specific enthalpy of mixture = (fractional mass of steam in mixture)(specific enthalpy of saturated steam) + (fractional mass of water in mixture)(specific enthalpy of saturated water) = (x)(specific enthalpy of saturated steam) + $(1 - x) \times$ (specific enthalpy of saturated water) (1.12)

Similar equations can be used to calculate the specific volume, specific internal energy and specific entropy values of a wet-steam mixture.

The temperature–entropy and enthalpy–entropy plots

These plots are shown to scale in *Figures 1.7* and *1.8*. Several points of note are:

1. Both enthalpy and entropy increase during an evaporation process and decrease during a condensation process. These changes are in accordance with our previous definitions and discussions of these terms.
2. The critical point (CP) occurs at peak satur-

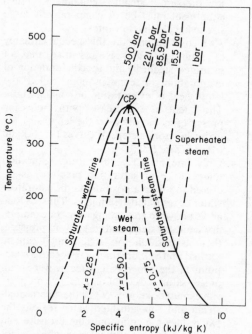

Figure 1.7   The temperature-specific entropy plot for water and steam showing various constant-pressure and constant-dryness-fraction lines (to scale)

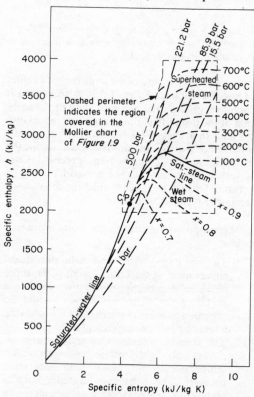

Figure 1.8   The specific enthalpy-specific entropy plot for water and steam showing various constant-temperature, constant-pressure and constant-dryness fraction lines (to scale)

ation temperature and pressure, but not at the maximum saturated-steam enthalpy of *Figure 1.8*. Referring back to *Figure 1.6* shows this to be the case.

3. Large-scale enthalpy–entropy charts are often used for the analysis of steam plant performance. These 'Mollier charts' show only the most useful part of the diagram as indicated in *Figure 1.8*. Mollier charts are described in more detail in the next section.

1.4 Steam tables and charts

Steam tables

Steam tables are no more than the property plots of *Figures 1.4 – 1.8* translated into tabular form. A number of tables compiled by different workers are available and several are listed in the references at the end of this chapter. We shall refer to *Steam Tables in SI Units* produced in 1970 by the National Engineering Laboratory. An abridged version of these tables is provided in Appendix 2 at the end of this book. The publication has three separate tables, corresponding to the abridged versions *Tables 1.1 – 1.3*.

1. *Table 1.1*: Tabulations of property values of saturated water and saturated steam in increments of saturation temperature.
2. *Table 1.2*: Similar tabulations, but for increments of saturation pressure.
3. *Table 1.3*: Tabulations of property values for sub-saturated water and superheated steam in increments of pressure and temperature.

The tables use conventional notations and units of

Pressure	p	bar absolute (not gauge)	
Temperature	t	°C	
Specific enthalpy	h	kJ/kg	
Specific entropy	s	kJ/kg K	
Specific volume	v	dm³/kg $(=10^{-3}\,m^3/kg)$	

In addition, the tables use suffix 's' for the saturation value, suffix 'f' for the saturated-water value, suffix 'g' for the saturated-steam value, and suffix 'fg' for the evaporation or condensation change in value $(f \rightarrow g)$.

Table 1.1 Abridged steam tables: the saturated values in increments of saturation temperature

Temp. (°C)	Abs. press. (bar)	Specific enthalpy (kJ/kg)			Specific entropy (kJ/kg K)			Specific volume (dm³/kg)	
t_s	p_s	h_f	h_{fg}	h_g	s_f	s_{fg}	s_g	v_f	v_g
Triple point									
0.01	0.006112	0.00	2502	2502	0.00	9.16	9.16	1.000	206163
20	0.02337	84	2454	2538	0.30	8.37	8.67	1.002	57838
40	0.07375	167	2407	2574	0.57	7.69	8.26	1.008	19546
60	0.1992	251	2359	2610	0.83	7.08	7.91	1.017	7679
80	0.4736	335	2309	2644	1.08	6.53	7.61	1.029	3409
100	1.013	419	2257	2676	1.31	6.05	7.36	1.044	1673
120	1.985	504	2202	2706	1.53	5.60	7.13	1.061	891.5
140	3.614	589	2144	2733	1.74	5.19	6.93	1.080	508.5
160	6.181	676	2081	2757	1.94	4.81	6.75	1.102	306.8
180	10.03	763	2013	2776	2.14	4.44	6.58	1.128	193.8
200	15.55	852	1939	2791	2.33	4.10	6.43	1.157	127.2
220	23.20	944	1856	2800	2.52	3.76	6.28	1.190	86.04
240	33.48	1038	1765	2802	2.70	3.44	6.14	1.229	59.65
260	46.94	1135	1661	2796	2.88	3.12	6.00	1.276	42.13
280	64.20	1237	1544	2780	3.07	2.79	5.86	1.332	30.13
300	85.93	1345	1406	2751	3.26	2.45	5.71	1.404	21.65
320	112.9	1463	1241	2704	3.45	2.09	5.54	1.500	15.48
340	146.1	1596	1031	2626	3.66	1.68	5.34	1.639	10.78
360	186.8	1764	721	2485	3.92	1.14	5.06	1.896	6.94
374.15	221.2	2107	0.0	2107	4.44	0.0	4.44	3.170	3.170
Critical point									

Table 1.2   Abridged steam tables: the saturated values in increments of saturation pressure

Abs. press. (bar)	Temp. (°C)	Specific enthalpy (kJ/kg)			Specific entropy (kJ/kg K)			Specific volume (dm³/kg)	
p_s	t_s	h_f	h_{fg}	h_g	s_f	s_{fg}	s_g	v_f	v_g
0.01	6.983	29.3	2485	2514	0.11	8.87	8.98	1.000	129 209
0.03	24.10	101	2445	2546	0.35	8.22	8.58	1.003	45 667
0.05	32.90	138	2424	2562	0.48	7.92	8.40	1.005	28 194
0.10	45.83	192	2393	2585	0.65	7.50	8.15	1.010	14 675
0.30	69.12	289	2336	2625	0.94	6.83	7.77	1.022	5229
0.50	81.35	340	2305	2646	1.09	6.50	7.59	1.030	3240
1.0	99.63	418	2258	2675	1.30	6.06	7.36	1.043	1694
3.0	133.5	561	2163	2725	1.67	5.32	6.99	1.074	605.6
5.0	151.8	640	2107	2748	1.86	4.96	6.82	1.093	374.7
10	179.9	763	2014	2776	2.14	4.44	6.58	1.127	194.3
20	212.4	909	1889	2797	2.45	3.89	6.34	1.177	99.54
40	250.3	1087	1713	2800	2.80	3.27	6.07	1.252	49.75
60	275.6	1214	1571	2785	3.03	2.86	5.89	1.319	32.44
80	295.0	1317	1443	2760	3.21	2.54	5.75	1.384	23.53
100	311.0	1408	1320	2728	3.36	2.26	5.62	1.453	18.04
120	324.7	1492	1197	2689	3.50	2.00	5.50	1.527	14.28
140	336.6	1572	1071	2642	3.62	1.76	5.38	1.611	11.50
160	347.3	1651	934	2585	3.75	1.51	5.25	1.710	9.31
180	357.0	1735	779	2514	3.88	1.24	5.11	1.840	7.50
200	365.7	1827	592	2418	4.01	0.93	4.94	2.037	5.88
221.2	374.15	2107	0.0	2107	4.44	0.0	4.44	3.170	3.170

The method of compilation of the tabulated values is beyond the scope of this book, but is described in many thermodynamic textbooks, such as ref. 2. In any case the engineer is interested in using the tables and not in their compilation. However, it should be appreciated that the v_f and v_g values are the absolute (true) values, but those of h and s are based on an arbitrary (but convenient) datum of the values of the saturated water at the triple-point condition. This is the usual datum because the values of ice are not of concern to us. It is perfectly satisfactory to base the h and s values on an arbitrary datum because we are never interested in obtaining the true values. Such differences are the same whatever datum is chosen as long as the datum is fixed.

Let us now look in greater detail at each of the three tables. *Table 1.1* is an abridged version of Appendix 2, *Table A1*. The table lists the values of p_s, h_f, h_{fg}, h_g, s_f, s_{fg}, s_g, v_f and v_g for the corresponding values of t_s for the range from the triple point to the critical-point condition. The table therefore lists the values along the saturated-water and saturated-steam lines of *Figures 1.4 – 1.8*. For example, if you glance down columns two, three and five of the table you will see that the trends correspond with the shapes of the saturation lines of the p–h plot of *Figure 1.6*. As p_s increases, h_f

increases to a maximum of 2107 kJ/kg at the critical point. At this condition $h_f = h_g = 2107$ kJ/kg, and as p_s decreases from 221.2 bar, h_g increases beyond 2107 kJ/kg, reaching a maximum value of 2802 kJ/kg corresponding to $p_s = 33$ bar. Thereafter, h_g decreases slightly, and has a value of 2502 kJ/kg at the triple-point condition. If you repeat this type of exercise, confirming the shapes of the saturation lines of the other figures, any mystery surrounding *Table 1.1* will soon evaporate.

Property values at t_s values between those listed in *Table 1.1* can easily be calculated to a reasonable degree of accuracy using linear interpolation, i.e. by proportionally splitting the difference between values. For example, h_g at 90°C (which we can write as $h_g(90°C)$) is found by looking up the values at 80°C (of 2644 kJ/kg) and 100°C (2676 kJ/kg) and calculating thus:

$$h_g(90°C) = h_g(80°C) +$$

$$\left(\frac{10}{20}\right)[h_g(100°C) - h_g(80°C)]$$

$$\therefore h_g(90°C) = 2644 +$$

$$\left(\frac{10}{20}\right)(2676 - 2644) = 2660 \text{ kJ/kg}$$

Table 1.3 Abridged steam tables: the sub-saturated-water and superheated-steam values

p(bar)	t(°C):	0.01	100	200	300	400	500	600
0.01	h	0.0	2689	2880	3077	3280	3489	3706
	s	0.0	9.51	9.97	10.34	10.67	10.96	11.22
	v	1.0	172187	218352	264508	310661	356814	402965
0.1	h	0.01	2688	2880	3077	3280	3489	3706
	s	0.0	8.45	8.90	9.28	9.61	9.90	10.16
	v	1.0	17195	21825	26445	31062	35679	40295
1	h	0.10	2676	2875	3075	3278	3488	3705
	s	0.0	7.36	7.83	8.22	8.54	8.83	9.10
	v	1.0	1696	2172	2639	3103	3565	4028
10	h	1.02	420	2827	3052	3264	3478	3697
	s	0.0	1.31	6.69	7.12	7.47	7.76	8.03
	v	1.0	1.04	206	258	306	354	401
50	h	5.10	423	854	2926	3198	3434	3665
	s	0.0	1.30	2.33	6.21	6.65	6.98	7.26
	v	0.998	1.04	1.15	45.3	57.8	68.5	78.6
100	h	10.2	427	856	1343	3100	3375	3623
	s	0.0	1.30	2.32	3.25	6.22	6.60	6.90
	v	0.995	1.04	1.15	1.40	26.4	32.8	38.3
150	h	15.2	430	858	1338	2979	3311	3580
	s	0.0	1.30	2.31	3.23	5.89	6.35	6.68
	v	0.993	1.04	1.14	1.38	15.7	20.8	24.9
200	h	20.2	434	860	1334	2821	3241	3536
	s	0.0	1.29	2.30	3.21	5.56	6.15	6.50
	v	0.990	1.03	1.14	1.36	9.95	14.8	18.2
250	h	25.1	438	863	1331	2582	3166	3490
	s	0.0	1.29	2.30	3.19	5.15	5.97	6.36
	v	0.988	1.03	1.13	1.35	6.01	11.1	14.1
300	h	30.1	442	865	1329	2162	3085	3443
	s	0.0	1.28	2.29	3.18	4.49	5.80	6.23
	v	0.986	1.03	1.13	1.33	2.83	8.68	11.4

Similarly, h_g at 92.5°C is calculated:

$$h_g(92.5°C) = 2644 + \left(\frac{12.5}{20}\right)(2676 - 2644) = 2664.0 \text{ kJ/kg}$$

If greater accuracy is desired, then reference can be made to a more comprehensive set of tables, as for example in Appendix 2. *Table A1* of this Appendix shows that $h_g(90°C) = 2660.1$ kJ/kg, and $h_g(92.5°C) = 2664.2$ kJ/kg. Obviously the more comprehensive the tables the more accurate they are and the less the need to use interpolation; on the other hand, the bulkier they are.

Values of h, s and v of wet steam can be calculated using the saturation values of *Table A1* if the dryness fraction x is known. To do so, we use the equations discussed earlier:

$$h_{\text{wet steam}} = (x)(h_g) + (1-x)(h_f)$$
$$s_{\text{wet steam}} = (x)(s_g) + (1-x)(s_f)$$
$$v_{\text{wet steam}} = (x)(v_g) + (1-x)(v_f)$$

Let us consider another example. Suppose we wish to know the specific enthalpy of wet steam at 80°C if the wet-steam mixture consists of 70% by mass of saturated steam and 30% by mass of saturated water, i.e. the mixture has a dryness fraction of 0.7. Using the appropriate equation above,

$$h(80°C, x = 0.7) = (0.7)(2644) +$$
$$(1-0.7)(335) = 1951.3 \text{ kJ/kg}$$

Similarly

$$h(100°C, x = 0.7) = (0.7)(2676) +$$
$$(1-0.7)(419) = 1998.9 \text{ kJ/kg}$$

Let us now look at a more complicated problem. Suppose we wish to know the value of h at 90°C with $x = 0.7$. We now have to use double interpolation. First we have to calculate h at 80°C and $x = 0.7$ (as above), and then h at 100°C and $x = 0.7$ (as above). Finally we have to interpolate between these two calculated values:

$$h(90°C, x = 0.7) = h(80°C, x = 0.7) +$$

$$\left(\frac{10}{20}\right)[h(100°C, x = 0.7) - h(80°C, x = 0.7)]$$

$$\therefore h(90°C, x = 0.7) = 1951.3 +$$

$$\left(\frac{10}{20}\right)(1998.9 - 1951.3) = 1975.1 \text{ kJ/kg}$$

Table 1.2 is an abridged version of *Table A2* from Appendix 2. These tables again list the saturated-water and saturated-steam values, but the primary variable is saturation pressure, and not temperature. *Table 1.2* therefore duplicates the information within *Table 1.1*. If the saturation temperature is known it is easier to look up the saturation values using *Table 1.1*, and if the saturation pressure is known, it is easier to use *Table 1.2*. For example, suppose we wish to find the specific enthalpy of saturated steam at 3 bar. We could use *Table 1.1*, but we would have to interpolate between the values of 2706 and 2733 kJ/kg to obtain the answer. It is much easier to look up the value directly in *Table 1.2*; the value is 2725 kJ/kg.

Table 1.3 is an abridged version of *Table A3* from Appendix 2. It looks more complicated than *Tables 1.1* and *1.2* because it is two separate tables combined into one. It lists the values of h, s and v for sub-saturated water and superheated steam at particular pressures and temperatures. All the values listed to the left of the dividing line are for sub-saturated water, and all those to the right are for superheated steam. Thus, H_2O at 10 bar and 100°C is a sub-saturated water with a specific enthalpy of 420 kJ/kg, a specific entropy of 1.31 kJ/kg K and a specific volume of 1.04 dm³/kg. At

10 bar and 200°C, H_2O is superheated steam with h, s and v values of 2827, 6.69 and 206 respectively. The abrupt changes in the values are because at a pressure of 10 bar, water evaporates into steam at a temperature between 100 and 200°C. Reference to *Table 1.2* shows that the saturation temperature is 179.9°C, and *Table 1.2* lists the corresponding saturation values.

The values listed in *Table 1.3* correspond with the shapes of the curves of *Figures 1.4 – 1.8*. Consider for example the constant-temperature lines within the superheated-steam region (*Figure 1.8*). These lines incline upwards away from the saturated-steam line, and then flatten out. Thus, at a particular temperature, as the pressure decreases the specific entropy increases. The specific enthalpy also increases rapidly at first, but then only very slowly. Inspection of *Table 1.3* confirms this. For example, at 300°C, the p, h and s values are

p (bar)	50	10	1	0.1	0.01
h (kJ/kg)	2926	3052	3075	3077	3077
s (kJ/kg K)	6.21	7.12	8.22	9.28	10.34

The steam (Mollier) chart

Several full-size charts produced by different workers are available as listed in the references at the end of this chapter. *Figure 1.9* shows a simplified small-scale chart. It looks complicated because many lines are shown; the steam saturation line dividing the chart into the superheat-steam and wet-steam regions; constant-pressure lines through both regions; constant-temperature lines in the superheat region; and constant-dryness-fraction lines in the wet-steam region. Constant-temperature lines in the wet region coincide with the constant-pressure lines because saturation temperature is dependent upon saturation pressure. The lines on the chart enable state-points to be located, and if the initial and final state-points of a process are known, the line joining these can represent the process.

A perfect expansion within a steam turbine or a steam engine is represented on the chart by a downward vertical line because it can be shown that it is a constant-entropy and decreasing-pressure process. Also a perfect throttling process across (for example) a partly closed valve in a steam pipeline is a constant-enthalpy and decreasing-pressure process, and can therefore be represented on the chart by a horizontal line running from left to right. These two examples illustrate the advantage of using the chart to analyse steam processes; it provides a pictorial representation of such processes. However, tables must be used if

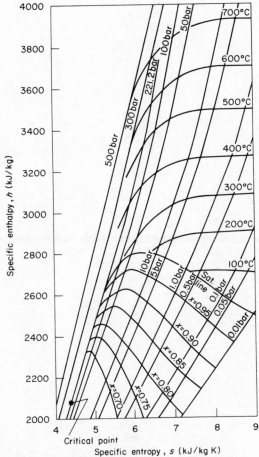

$$\therefore x_2 = \frac{6.21 - 0.48}{8.40 - 0.48} = 0.723$$

and

$$h_2 = x_2\, h_{g2} + (1 - x_2)\, h_{f2}$$
$$= (0.723)(2562) + (0.277)(138) \quad \text{(from } Table\ 1.2)$$
$$= 1890\,\text{kJ/kg}$$

The uses of the tables and the chart are further illustrated in subsequent chapters and particularly in Chapter 2.

References and further reading

On the properties of steam and water

1 Lyle, O. *The Efficient Use of Steam*. 11th impression, Chapters 1, 2 and 26. London: HMSO (1974)
2 Rogers, G. F. C. and Mayhew, Y. R. *Engineering Thermodynamics, Work and Heat Transfer*. 2nd edn (SI units), Chapter 8. London: Longmans (1967)

On steam tables and charts

3 CEGB. *Steam Tables in SI Units*. London: CEGB (1970)
4 NEL. *Steam Tables*. London: HMSO (1964)
5 Urray, S. A. *Steam Tables in Metric Units*. London: Pitman (1962)
6 Mayhew, Y. R. and Rogers, G. F. C. *Thermodynamic and Transport Properties of Fluids*. (SI units.) Oxford: Blackwell (1967)
7 UK Committee on the Properties of Steam. *UK Steam Tables*. (SI units.) London: Edward Arnold (1970)
8 Cooper, J. R. and Le Fevre, E. J. *Thermophysical Properties of Water Substance*. (SI units.) London: Edward Arnold (1969)
9 Keenan, J. H., Keyes, F. G., Hill P. G., and Moore, J. G. *Steam Tables and Mollier Chart* International edition (metric units). New York: John Wiley (1969)
10 UK Committee on the Properties of Steam. *Mollier Diagram for Steam*. (SI units.) London: Edward Arnold (1971)
11 Hickson, D. C. and Taylor, F. R. *Enthalpy–Entropy Diagram for Steam*. (SI units.) Oxford: Basil Blackwell (1967)
12 Electrical Research Association. *Steam Charts*. London: Edward Arnold (1967)

Figure 1.9 The simplified specific enthalpy–specific entropy (Mollier) chart for steam (to scale)

the final state-point of a process lies outside the region covered by the chart. Consider, for example, a perfect expansion of steam from $p_1 = 50$ bar, $t_1 = 300°C$ through a turbine down to $p_2 = 0.05$ bar. In this case, x_2 and h_2 cannot be found using the chart (*Figure 1.9*) because drawing a vertical line downwards from state-point 1 results in state-point 2 at 0.05 bar being off the chart. Instead, the turbine exhaust condition must be found using *Tables 1.2* and *1.3* and using the fact that a perfect expansion is one of constant entropy, i.e. $s_1 = s_2$. Thus

$$s_1 = 6.21\,\text{kJ/kg K} \quad \text{(from } Table\ 1.3)$$
$$= s_2 = x\, s_{g2} + (1 - x_2)(s_{f2})$$
$$= (x_2)(8.40) + (1 - x_2)(0.48) \quad \text{(from } Table\ 1.2)$$

2   Power from steam

2.1 Steam power plant and the laws of thermodynamics

Steam power plant converts heat energy Q from the combustion of a fuel into mechanical work energy W of shaft rotation. Such plant operates on thermodynamic cycles, that is, a closed loop of processes following one another such that the working fluid of steam and water repeats cycles continuously. The design of a plant for a given purpose is determined largely by considerations of capital cost and operating cost; the former depends mainly on the plant size and the latter is primarily a function of the overall efficiency of the plant. In general the efficiency can usually be improved, but only by increasing the capital cost of the plant, hence a suitable compromise must be reached between capital costs and operating costs. Let us consider in turn how we can rate each of these two factors.

The plant capital cost is mainly dependent upon the size of the plant components. These sizes will themselves depend on the flow rates of the steam which is passed through them. Hence, an indication of the relative capital costs of different steam plants is provided by the mass flow rate $\dot{m}$ of the steam required per unit power output, i.e. by the specific steam consumption (s.s.c.). Thus, if W is the net power output from the plant in kW:

$$\text{s.s.c.} = \frac{\dot{m}}{\dot{W}} \frac{\text{kg/s}}{\text{kW}} = \frac{\dot{m}}{\dot{W}} \frac{\text{kg}}{\text{kW s}} = \frac{3600\dot{m}}{\dot{W}} \frac{\text{kg}}{\text{kWh}}$$

$$= \frac{3600}{\dot{W}/\dot{m}} \frac{\text{kg}}{\text{kWh}} \tag{2.1}$$

Next let us consider how we can assess operating costs via the plant's overall efficiency. We shall first have to discuss the first and second laws of thermodynamics and introduce the concept of cycle thermal efficiency. The *first law* is simply the law of the conservation of energy. Applied to a thermodynamic cycle in which the working fluid returns to its initial condition it says that the energy flowing into the fluid during the cycle equals that flowing out of the fluid. We learnt in Chapter 1 that only two types of energy can so flow: heat energy Q and work energy W. Hence, the first law applied to a cycle gives

$$Q_{in} + W_{in} = Q_{out} + W_{out}$$

or

$$\dot{Q}_{in} - \dot{Q}_{out} = \dot{W}_{out} - \dot{W}_{in} \quad (2.2)$$

where $\dot{Q}$ is the rate of heat transfer and $\dot{W}$ is the rate of work transfer, i.e. power.

The first law can also be applied to any individual process of a cycle. In this case, the energy flowing into the fluid minus that leaving must equal the increase in the total energy E of the fluid, i.e.

$$(Q_{in} + W_{in}) - (Q_{out} + W_{out}) = E_{final} - E_{initial} \quad (2.3)$$

Now as noted in Chapter 1,

$$E_{final} - E_{initial} =$$
$$(H_{final} - H_{initial}) + (PE_{final} - PE_{initial}) + (KE_{final} - KE_{initial}) \quad (2.4)$$

where H = enthalpy, PE = potential energy and KE = kinetic energy. For the types of process we shall be analysing later in this chapter changes in PE and KE are negligible. Hence, the first law for such processes becomes

$$(Q_{in} - Q_{out}) + (W_{in} - W_{out}) = H_{final} - H_{initial}$$

or

$$(\dot{Q}_{in} - \dot{Q}_{out}) + (\dot{W}_{in} - \dot{W}_{out}) = (\dot{m}_{fluid})(h_{final} - h_{initial}) \quad (2.5)$$

h being the specific enthalpy.

Let us now consider the second law. So far we know that heat and work are mutually convertible. However, although all of a quantity of work energy can be converted into heat energy (for example, by a friction process), the converse is not true. A quantity of heat cannot all be converted into work. Heat flows by virtue of a temperature difference, and this means that in order to flow, two heat reservoirs must be present; a hot source and a cold sink. During a heat flow from the hot source to the cold sink, a fraction of the flow may be converted into work energy, and the function of a power plant is to produce this conversion. However, some heat must flow into the cold sink because of its presence. Thus, the rate of heat transfer Q out of the cycle must always be positive and the efficiency of the conversion of heat energy into work energy can never be 100%. This fundamental law is known as the *second law of thermodynamics*. It leads us to define a thermo-dynamic efficiency for a cycle η_{th} as a measure of

how well a cycle converts heat into work:

$$\eta_{th} = \frac{\dot{W}_{out\ of\ cycle} - \dot{W}_{into\ cycle}}{\dot{Q}_{into\ cycle}}$$

$$= \frac{\dot{Q}_{into\ cycle} - \dot{Q}_{out\ of\ cycle}}{\dot{Q}_{into\ cycle}} \quad \text{(using the first law)}$$

$$= 1 - \frac{\dot{Q}_{out\ of\ cycle}}{\dot{Q}_{into\ cycle}} \quad (2.6)$$

Such a thermodynamic (or thermal for short) efficiency is concerned only with the efficiency of conversion of heat into work for a particular cycle, and not for a particular power plant operating on that cycle. It therefore does not measure the efficiency of conversion for a complete power plant. Taking a plant with a number of items, we define

$$\eta_{plant} = \eta_{th} \times \eta_{plant\ item\ 1\ external\ to\ cycle}$$
$$\times \eta_{plant\ item\ 2\ external\ to\ cycle} \times \cdots \quad (2.7)$$

From what we have said so far, a power plant must consist of a hot-source reservoir, a plant working on a cycle converting a portion of the input heat energy flow Q_{in} into work energy W_{out}, and a cold-sink reservoir accepting the remaining portion of the input heat energy flow. *Figure 2.1* shows such an arrangement diagrammatically. There are four components of the plant: the boiler, in which the hot-source combustion gases raise steam; the steam reciprocating engine or turbine, which converts a portion of the heat energy into work energy; the condenser, in which heat is rejected to the cold sink; and the condenser extraction pump or the boiler feed pump, which pumps the condensate back into the boiler.

The rest of this chapter will be concerned with describing the thermodynamic cycles of steam power plant. The description and performance of the individual items making up the plant are the subject of several of the later chapters.

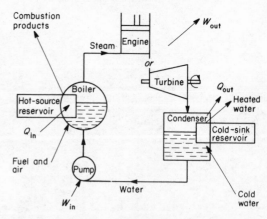

Figure 2.1   The components of a steam power plant

2.2 Steam power plant cycle analysis

The Carnot cycle

The Carnot cycle is an ideal, but non-practical cycle giving the maximum possible thermal efficiency for a cycle operating on selected maximum and minimum temperature ranges. *Figure 2.2* shows that it is made up of four ideal processes:

1 to 2: evaporation of water into saturated steam within the boiler at the constant maximum cycle temperature T_1 ($= T_2$);

2 to 3: ideal (i.e. constant-entropy) expansion within the steam engine or turbine, i.e. $s_2 = s_3$;

3 to 4: partial condensation within the condenser at the constant minimum cycle temperature T_3 ($= T_4$);

4 to 1: ideal (i.e. constant-entropy) compression of very wet steam within the compressor to complete the cycle, i.e. $s_4 = s_1$.

From the definition of entropy in Chapter 1 of $(s_2 - s_1) = Q/mT_1$, where T is absolute temperature, for this cycle:

$$Q_{\text{into cycle}} = (mT_1)(s_2 - s_1) \qquad (2.8)$$

and

$$Q_{\text{out of cycle}} = (mT_3)(s_3 - s_4) \qquad (2.9)$$
$$= (mT_3)(s_2 - s_1)$$

Hence, the cycle thermal efficiency is given by

$$\eta_{\text{th}} = 1 - \frac{Q_{\text{out of cycle}}}{Q_{\text{into cycle}}} = 1 - \frac{(mT_3)(s_2 - s_1)}{(mT_1)(s_2 - s_1)}$$
$$= 1 - \frac{T_3}{T_1} \qquad (2.10)$$

This equation shows that the wider the temperature range, the more efficient is the cycle. However, in practice T_3 cannot be reduced below about 300 K (27°C), corresponding to a condenser pressure of 0.035 bar. This is due to two factors: condensation of the steam requires a bulk supply of cooling water and such a continuous natural supply below atmospheric temperatures of about 15°C is unavailable; and furthermore, if the condenser is to be of a reasonable size and cost, the temperature difference between the condensing steam and the cooling water must be at least 10°C. The maximum cycle temperature T_1 is also limited to about 900 K (627°C) by the strength of the materials available for the highly stressed parts of the plant, such as the boiler tubes and turbine blades. This upper limit is called the *metallurgical limit*. In fact the steam Carnot cycle has a maximum cycle temperature of well below this owing to the properties of steam; it is limited to the critical-point temperature of 374°C (647 K). Hence, modern materials cannot be used to their best advantage with this cycle when steam is the working fluid. Furthermore, because the saturated water and steam curves converge to the critical point, a plant operating on the Carnot cycle with its maximum temperature near the critical-point temperature would have a very large s.s.c., i.e. it would be very large in size and very expensive.

Another major disadvantage of this cycle concerns the compression process 4 to 1. Compressing a very wet steam mixture would require a compressor of size and cost comparable with the turbine, it would absorb work comparable with that developed by the turbine and it would have a short life because of blade erosion and cavitation problems. For all these reasons the Carnot cycle is not practical. It is, however, useful in helping us to appreciate what factors are desirable in the design

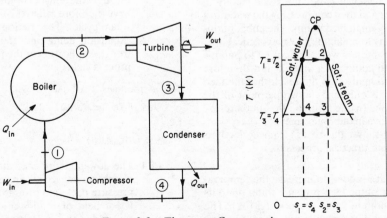

Figure 2.2   The steam Carnot cycle

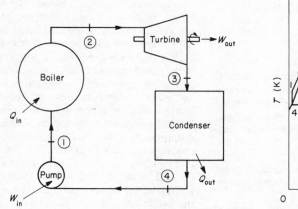

Figure 2.3   The basic steam cycle

of a practical cycle: namely, a maximum possible temperature range, maximum possible heat addition into the cycle at the maximum cycle temperature, and a minimum possible work input into the cycle. The Carnot cycle also helps us to understand the thermodynamic constraints on the design of cycles. For example, even if such a cycle were practicable and even if the maximum cycle temperature could be 900 K, the cycle thermal efficiency would be well below 100%:

$$\eta_{th} = 1 - \frac{T_3}{T_1} = 1 - \frac{300}{900} = 66.7\%$$

A hypothetical plant operating on such a cycle would have a plant efficiency lower than this owing to the inefficiencies of the individual plant items.

The basic steam cycle

The basic steam cycle avoids one of the major problems of the Carnot cycle: that of compressing a very wet steam mixture from the condenser pressure up to the boiler pressure. The problem is avoided by condensing the steam completely in the condenser and then compressing the water in a comparatively small feed pump. The effect of this modification is to make the cycle a practical one. Furthermore, far less work is required to pump a liquid than to compress a vapour and therefore this modification also has the result that the feed pump's work is only one or two per cent of the work developed by the turbine. We can therefore neglect this term in our cycle analysis.

Figure 2.3 shows the basic steam cycle. It is made up of four practical processes:

1 to 2: Heat is added to increase the temperature of the high-pressure water up to its saturation value (process 1 to A). The water is then evaporated at constant

temperature and pressure (process A to 2). Both processes occur within the boiler, but not all of the heat supplied is at the maximum cycle temperature. Thus, the mean temperature at which heat is supplied is lower than that in the equivalent Carnot cycle. Hence, the basic steam cycle thermal efficiency is inherently lower. Applying the first law of thermodynamics to this process gives

$$(\dot{Q}_{in} - \dot{Q}\uparrow_{out}^{=0}) + (\dot{W}\uparrow_{in}^{=0} - \dot{W}_{out}^{=0})$$
$$= (\dot{m}_{fluid})(h_{final} - h_{initial})$$

i.e.

$$\dot{Q}_{in} = (\dot{m}_{fluid})(h_2 - h_1) \qquad (2.11)$$

2 to 3: The high-pressure saturated steam is expanded to a low pressure within a reciprocating engine or a turbine. If the expansion is ideal (i.e. one of constant entropy) the cycle is called the Rankine cycle. However, we shall take into account friction in the flow of steam through the engine or turbine and we have therefore called this cycle 'the basic steam cycle'. The friction results in the expansion being one of increasing entropy. Application of the first law to this process yields

$$(\dot{Q}\uparrow_{in}^{=0} - \dot{Q}\uparrow_{out}^{=0}) + (\dot{W}\uparrow_{in}^{=0} - \dot{W}_{out})$$
$$= (\dot{m}_{fluid})(h_{final} - h_{initial})$$

i.e.

$$\dot{W}_{out} = (\dot{m}_{fluid})(h_2 - h_3) \qquad (2.12)$$

3 to 4: The low-pressure wet steam is completely condensed at constant condenser pressure back into saturated water. The latent heat of condensation is thereby rejected to the condenser cooling water

which, in turn, rejects this heat to the atmosphere. This time, applying the first law gives

$$(\dot{Q}\!\!\uparrow^{=0}_{\text{in}} - \dot{Q}_{\text{out}}) + (\dot{W}\!\!\uparrow^{=0}_{\text{in}} - \dot{W}\!\!\uparrow^{=0}_{\text{out}})$$
$$= (\dot{m}_{\text{fluid}})(h_{\text{final}} - h_{\text{initial}})$$

i.e.

$$\dot{Q}_{\text{out}} = (\dot{m}_{\text{fluid}})(h_3 - h_4) \tag{2.13}$$

4 to 1: The low-pressure saturated water is pumped back up to the boiler pressure and, in so doing, it becomes sub-saturated. The water then re-enters the boiler and begins a new cycle. The first law for this process gives

$$(\dot{Q}\!\!\uparrow^{=0}_{\text{in}} - \dot{Q}\!\!\uparrow^{=0}_{\text{out}}) + (\dot{W}_{\text{in}} - \dot{W}\!\!\uparrow^{=0}_{\text{out}})$$
$$= (\dot{m}_{\text{fluid}})(h_{\text{final}} - h_{\text{initial}})$$

i.e.

$$\dot{W}_{\text{in}} = (\dot{m}_{\text{fluid}})(h_1 - h_4) \tag{2.14}$$

However, as we have said earlier, we can with reasonable accuracy neglect $\dot{W}_{\text{in}}$, and hence we can assume that $h_1 = h_4$. The thermal efficiency of this cycle is given by

$$\eta_{\text{th}} = \frac{\dot{W}_{\text{out}} - \dot{W}_{\text{in}}}{\dot{Q}_{\text{in}}} = \frac{\dot{W}_{\text{out}}}{\dot{Q}_{\text{in}}} = \frac{(\dot{m}_{\text{fluid}})(h_2 - h_3)}{(\dot{m}_{\text{fluid}})(h_2 - h_1)}$$

i.e.

$$\eta_{\text{th}} = \frac{h_2 - h_3}{h_2 - h_1} \tag{2.15}$$

and the specific steam consumption is given by

$$\text{s.s.c.} = \frac{3600}{\dot{W}/\dot{m}} \frac{\text{kg}}{\text{kWh}} = \frac{3600}{h_2 - h_3} \text{ kg/kWh} \tag{2.16}$$

Let us now consider an example. We shall make use of steam tables, which were discussed towards the end of Chapter 1. Suppose we are designing an industrial turbo-alternator plant to generate 1000 kW of electrical power, i.e. 1000 kW(e). Let us assume the plant is to be based on the following information (with all pressures in bar absolute):

1. The steam cycle operates between 10 bar saturated steam at turbine inlet and steam at 0.05 bar and 0.90 dry at turbine outlet.
2. The boiler is fuel-oil-fired, and the fuel oil has a calorific value (CV) of 43 000 kJ/kg, i.e. 1 kg of the oil releases 43000 kJ of heat if it is ideally and completely burned in air.
3. The boiler efficiency η_b is 80%, i.e. only 80% of the heat ideally generated by the combustion of the oil is transferred to the water in the boiler. The remaining 20% is wasted, mainly in the escape of the hot combustion gases through the boiler flue into the atmosphere, and in imperfect combustion of the fuel. Hence

$$\eta_b = \frac{\dot{Q}_{\text{in}}}{(\dot{m}_{\text{fuel}})(\text{fuel CV})} \tag{2.17}$$

where $\dot{m}_{\text{fuel}}$ is the rate of fuel consumption in kg/s.

4. The turbine mechanical efficiency η_{mech} is 95% and the generator efficiency η_{gen} is 97%. The former allows for bearing losses in the turbine shaft. The latter indicates that if the turbine delivers 100 kW of mechanical power to the generator, the generator will convert 97 kW into electrical power, and 3 kW will be wasted in the conversion process as heat dissipation in the electrical windings

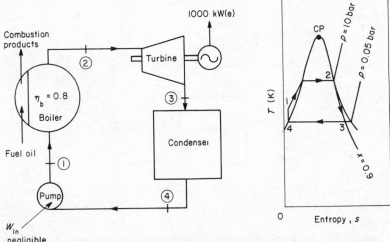

Figure 2.4 The design of a 1000-kW(e) industrial turbo-alternator plant operating on the basic steam cycle

and in the generator rotor bearings.

We wish to calculate the cycle thermal efficiency, the specific steam consumption, the plant overall efficiency and the rate of the boiler fuel oil consumption. *Figure 2.4* shows a diagram of the plant together with the corresponding steam cycle temperature–entropy diagram. Using the steam tables of *Table 1.2* of Chapter 1, or alternatively (but to a lower degree of accuracy) using the Mollier chart of *Figure 1.9*:

$$h_2 = h_g(10 \text{ bar}) = 2776 \text{ kJ/kg}$$

$$h_3 = x h_g + (1 - x) h_f = (0.9)(2562) + (0.1)(138)$$
$$= 2320 \text{ kJ/kg}$$

$$h_4 = h_1 = h_f(0.05 \text{ bar}) = 138 \text{ kJ/kg}$$

Hence,

$$\eta_{th} = \frac{h_2 - h_3}{h_2 - h_1} = \frac{2776 - 2320}{2776 - 138} = \frac{456}{2638} = 17.3\%$$

$$\text{s.s.c.} = \frac{3600}{h_2 - h_3} \frac{\text{kg}}{\text{kWh}} = \frac{3600}{456} \frac{\text{kg}}{\text{kWh}}$$
$$= 7.89 \frac{\text{kg}}{\text{kWh}}$$

$$\eta_{plant} = \eta_{th} \times \eta_{mech} \times \eta_{gen}$$
$$= (17.3)(0.95)(0.97)\% = 15.9\%$$

$$\dot{Q}_{in} = \frac{\dot{W}_{net}}{\eta_{plant}} = \frac{1000}{0.159} \text{ kW} = 6290 \text{ kW}$$

$$\dot{m}_{fuel} = \frac{\dot{Q}_{in}}{(\eta_b)(\text{fuel CV})} = \frac{6290}{(0.8)(43000)} \text{ kg/s}$$
$$= 0.183 \text{ kg/s}$$
$$= 658 \text{ kg/h}$$

Thus we see that in order to generate 1000 kW of electrical power the rate of heat transfer from the combustion of the fuel oil to the water must be over 6000 kW. This is mainly dependent upon the cycle's thermal efficiency and in the following sections we shall discuss a number of ways of improving this. Also, allowing for the inefficiencies in the boiler the rate of fuel combustion must provide a rate of heat energy release of 0.183 × 43000 kW, which is nearly 8000 kW.

The steam cycle with superheat

The main reason why the thermal efficiency was low in the previous example was because the plant operated at a maximum temperature well below the metallurgical limit. This position is improved if the saturated steam is superheated before entry to the turbine. The superheater may be integral with the boiler or it may be a separate unit and separately fired. Superheating the steam has a further important advantage of increasing the dryness fraction at the turbine exhaust. When the steam is wet within the turbine, the water droplets cause gradual erosion of the rotor blades and increase the friction losses, and in practice the dryness fraction at the turbine exhaust is not allowed to fall below about 0.9.

Let us consider the effect of superheating on our previous worked example. We shall assume the plant is the same as before except for three changes: the steam is superheated to 300°C before it enters the turbine; the boiler and superheater are an integral oil-fired unit with an efficiency of 80%; and superheating causes the steam at the turbine exhaust to be dryer, the dryness fraction increasing from 0.90 to 0.95. *Figure 2.5* shows the plant arrangement and the corresponding temperature–

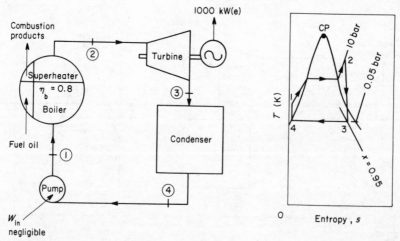

Figure 2.5   The design of a 1000-kW(e) industrial turbo-alternator plant operating on the steam cycle with superheat

entropy diagram.

Using the superheat steam tables of *Table 1.3*, or using the Mollier chart of *Figure 1.9*:

h_2 (10 bar, 300°C) = 3052 kJ/kg

Using the saturation steam tables of *Table 1.2*:

$h_3 = x h_g + (1 - x)h_f = (0.95)(2562) + (0.05)(138)$

$= 2441$ kJ/kg

$h_4 = h_1 = h_f(0.05$ bar$) = 138$ kJ/kg

Hence,

$$\eta_{th} = \frac{h_2 - h_3}{h_2 - h_1} = \frac{3052 - 2441}{3052 - 138} = \frac{611}{2914} = 21.0\%$$

$$\text{s.s.c.} = \frac{3600}{h_2 - h_3} \frac{kg}{kWh} = \frac{3600}{611} \frac{kg}{kWh}$$

$$= 5.89 \frac{kg}{kWh}$$

$$\eta_{plant} = \eta_{th} \times \eta_{mech} \times \eta_{gen}$$

$$= (21.0)(0.95)(0.97)\% = 19.4\%$$

$$\dot{Q}_{in} = \frac{\dot{W}_{net}}{\eta_{plant}} = \frac{1000}{0.194} kW = 5155 \text{ kW}$$

$$\dot{m}_{fuel} = \frac{\dot{Q}_{in}}{(\eta_b)(\text{fuel CV})} = \frac{5155}{(0.8)(43000)} \frac{kg/s}{}$$

$$= 0.150 \text{ kg/s}$$

$$= 540 \text{ kg/h}$$

Thus we see that not only does the thermal efficiency increase, but the specific steam consumption also decreases markedly. Therefore introducing superheat results in several advantages: reduced plant operating costs; reduced wetness of the steam at the turbine exhaust; and reduced mass flow rate of the steam and water circulating around the plant for the same output power of the plant. This latter factor has the effect of reducing the sizes and costs of the boiler, turbine, condenser and feed pump. However, the plant now incorporates a superheater and the sizes of the turbine and condenser will increase since the steam leaves the turbine with a higher dryness fraction. The net effect is an increase in the plant capital cost, but an appreciable reduction in operating costs. Hence, the overall effect for a plant operating almost continuously over many years is a reduction in the cost of each kWh of electrical energy generated.

The steam cycle with superheat and reheat

For the large steam turbines within power stations it is vital to maximize thermal efficiency and minimize specific steam consumption in order to minimize the cost of each unit of electricity generated. Hence, these plants operate on high-pressure steam cycles, but even then superheating to the metallurgical limit will not alone maintain turbine exhaust dryness fractions above 0.9. These plants therefore incorporate reheat. High-pressure superheated steam close to the metallurgical temperature limit enters a high-pressure (h.p.) turbine and expands down to some intermediate pressure. The steam is then reheated at near-constant pressure back to a high temperature, usually the original temperature. Finally the steam is expanded within a low-pressure (l.p.) turbine down to the condenser pressure. The reheater is usually a bank of tubes within an integral boiler–superheater–reheater unit. If the pressure at which reheating takes place is carefully chosen, then reheating has the important extra advantage of slightly but significantly increasing the cycle thermal efficiency as compared with a similar non-reheat cycle.

The following example concerns the design of a power-station turbo-alternator operating on the reheat steam cycle. The design data of the plant are as follows:

1. The plant is to generate 500000 kW (i.e. 500 MW) of electrical power.
2. The steam plant operates on the superheated cycle with a single stage of reheat. The h.p. turbine inlet conditions are 150 bar, 550°C and the exhaust conditions are 30 bar, 350°C. The reheater reheats the steam at a constant pressure to 550°C, and after expansion within the l.p. turbine the steam exhausts into the condenser at 0.05 bar and 0.9 dry.
3. The boiler–superheater–reheater unit is coal-fired and has an efficiency η_{b+r} of 90%. The calorific value of the coal is 28000 kJ/kg.
4. The turbine mechanical efficiency is 99% and the generator efficiency is 99%.
5. The condenser cooling water enters at 15°C, leaves at 25°C, and has a specific heat C (*see* Chapter 1) of 4.19 kJ/kg °C.

We wish to calculate the cycle thermal efficiency, the specific steam consumption, the plant overall efficiency, the boiler coal consumption and the condenser cooling water flow rate.

Figure 2.6 shows the plant diagram together with the corresponding temperature–entropy diagram. We must first calculate the specific enthalpies at each state-point on the diagram. To do so we can use either the steam tables in Appendix 2, or the steam chart of *Figure 1.9*, or the abridged *Tables 1.1, 1.2* and *1.3* of Chapter 1. Again, we shall use the latter tables as it will illustrate the technique of interpolation from the tables. Hence, using *Table 1.3*:

$h_2 = h(150$ bar, 550°C$) = h(150$ bar, 500°C$) +$

$\quad (\frac{1}{2})[h(150$ bar, 600°C$) - h(150$ bar, 500°C$)]$

$\quad = 3311 + (\frac{1}{2})(3580 - 3311) = 3446$ kJ/kg

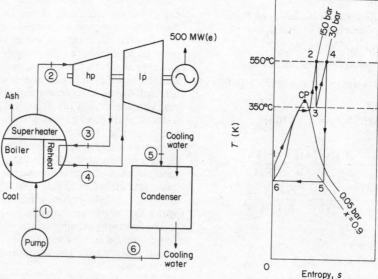

Figure 2.6   The design of a 500-MW(e) power-station turbo-alternator plant operating on the steam cycle with superheat and reheat

The calculation of h_3 at 30 bar, 350°C to a reasonable degree of accuracy involves double interpolation thus:

$h(10 \text{ bar, } 350°C) = h(10 \text{ bar, } 300°C) +$
$(\frac{1}{2})[h(10 \text{ bar, } 400°C) - h(10 \text{ bar, } 300°C)]$
$= 3052 + (\frac{1}{2})(3264 - 3052) = 3158 \text{ kJ/kg}$

$h(50 \text{ bar, } 350°C) = h(50 \text{ bar, } 300°C) +$
$(\frac{1}{2})[h(50 \text{ bar, } 400°C) - h(50 \text{ bar, } 300°C)]$
$= 2926 + (\frac{1}{2})(3198 - 2926) = 3062 \text{ kJ/kg}$

Hence

$h_3 = h(30 \text{ bar, } 350°C) = h(10 \text{ bar, } 350°C) +$
$(\frac{1}{2})[h(50 \text{ bar, } 350°C) - h(10 \text{ bar, } 350°C)]$
$= 3158 + (\frac{1}{2})(3062 - 3158) = 3110 \text{ kJ/kg}$

A similar double interpolation for h_4 at 30 bar, 550°C gives $h_4 = 3569 \text{ kJ/kg}$. From *Table 1.2*:

$h_5 = h(0.05 \text{ bar, } 0.9 \text{ dry}) = x h_g + (1-x)h_f$
$= (0.9)(2562) + (0.1)(138) = 2320 \text{ kJ/kg}$

and

$h_6 = h_1 = h_f(0.05 \text{ bar}) = 138 \text{ kJ/kg}$

Hence

$$\eta_{th} = \frac{\dot{W}_{net}}{\dot{Q}_{in}} = \frac{\dot{W}_{h.p. turbine} + \dot{W}_{l.p. turbine}}{\dot{Q}_{boiler + superheater} + \dot{Q}_{reheater}}$$

$$= \frac{(h_2 - h_3) + (h_4 - h_5)}{(h_2 - h_1) + (h_4 - h_3)}$$

$$= \frac{(3446 - 3110) + (3569 - 2320)}{(3446 - 138) + (3569 - 3110)} = \frac{1585}{3767}$$

$$= 42.1\%$$

$$\text{s.s.c.} = \frac{3600}{(h_2 - h_3) + (h_4 - h_5)} = \frac{3600}{1585} \frac{\text{kg}}{\text{kWh}}$$

$$= 2.27 \frac{\text{kg}}{\text{kWh}}$$

$\eta_{plant} = \eta_{th} \times \eta_{mech} \times \eta_{gen}$
$= (42.1)(0.99)(0.99)\% = 41.3\%$

$$\dot{Q}_{in} = \frac{\dot{W}_{net}}{\eta_{plant}} = \frac{500}{0.413} \text{MW} = 1210 \text{ MW}$$

$$\dot{m}_{coal} = \frac{\dot{Q}_{in}}{(\eta_{b+r})(\text{coal CV})} = \frac{1210000}{(0.9)(28000)} \text{ kg/s}$$

$$= 48 \text{ kg/s} = 173 \text{ t/h†}$$

The first law gives
$\dot{Q}_{out} = \dot{Q}_{in} - \dot{W}_{net} = 1210 - 500 \text{ MW} = 710 \text{ MW}$

Since from the definition of specific heat C:
$\dot{Q}_{out} = [(\dot{m})(C)(t_{out} - t_{in})]_{condenser \, cooling \, water}$

$$\dot{m}_{cooling \, water} = \frac{710000}{(4.19)(25-15)} \text{ kg/s} = 16950 \text{ kg/s}$$

As the density of water is 10^3 kg/m^3, the volume flow rate V of the condenser cooling water is 16.95 m³/s or 1017 m³/min.

This example demonstrates several important points. The plant efficiency is very much higher and the specific steam consumption is very much lower when compared with the previous worked examples. This is due to this power-station plant

† Metric tons (tonnes) per hour.

operating at high pressures and at high peak temperatures near the metallurgical limit. Operating at such high conditions is only worth while for large-scale plants because of their high capital cost. Greater economy of large-scale plants is also due to the boiler, mechanical and generator efficiencies' all being higher because although for a large plant losses are greater in magnitude, proportionally they are reduced. Finally, the example demonstrates the enormous size of modern power-station plant; it is generating 500000 kW of electrical power, enough for the needs of a modern city; the coal consumption is over 170 t/h or over 4000 t each day; and the condenser cooling water flow rate is over 1000 m³/min. A modern power-station usually contains four such plants.

The steam cycle with superheat, reheat and regenerative feedheating

We have emphasized in the last section the importance of minimizing the cost of each unit of electricity generated in power-stations. Large plants operate on the steam cycle with superheat, reheat and regenerative feedheating in order to achieve this. Feedheating involves extracting ('bleeding') steam from one or more positions along the turbine expansion and using this steam to preheat the water in feedheaters prior to its entry into the boiler. This bled steam is therefore used to reduce the heat addition to the water within the boiler, hence the mean temperature of heat addition into the cycle increases and the cycle's thermal efficiency increases. On the other hand, the bled steam has only partly been expanded within the turbine and has therefore only been partly used to develop mechanical power. Thus, the specific steam consumption increases, and the net effect is that the plant capital costs increase and the operating cost decreases. Thus the cost of each kWh of electrical energy generated will be reduced by using some degree of feedheating, but not an excessive amount. Economic-optimization calculations are necessary to calculate the amount of feedheating required to minimize the cost of each unit of electricity generated. Plant reliability must also be taken into account because the greater the number of feedheaters the more complex the plant, and the more prone it is to malfunction. Shutdown of the plant involves not only expense in detection and correction of the malfunction, but also in costly loss of electricity generation revenue. In practice, these economic and reliability factors limit the number of feedheating stages to about seven for a modern large power-station plant.

We shall illustrate the principle of feedheating by considering the plant of our previous example, but we now assume it incorporates one stage of feedheating, with steam bled off at 30 bar, 350°C

before it enters the reheater. We shall assume a sufficient amount of steam is bled off at this point to preheat the boiler feedwater from the condenser extraction condition of saturated water at 0.05 bar up to saturated water at the bled-steam pressure of 30 bar. The bled steam is thereby condensed to saturated water at 30 bar, and mixes with the heated feedwater. *Figure 2.7* shows a diagram of the plant and the corresponding temperature–entropy diagram. For every 1 kg of steam being generated in the boiler and superheater and expanding through the h.p. turbine, it is assumed that the fraction m kg is bled off into the feedheater, and the fraction $(1-m)$ kg is reheated, expanded in the l.p. turbine and is then condensed in the condenser. The $(1-m)$ kg of water is then pumped up to 30 bar in the first feed pump and is mixed with the m kg of bled steam in the feedheater. The resultant mixture of 1 kg of saturated water at 30 bar is finally pumped up to the boiler pressure within a second pump, and the cycle is thereby completed. The cycle is really a combination of two cycles undergone by two different quantities of fluid. Thus, the T–s diagram should be read as one cycle of $(1-m)$ kg undergoing 123456781, superimposed on another cycle of m kg undergoing 12381.

In order to calculate the cycle performance, we must first calculate the fractions m and $(1-m)$. We therefore proceed as follows: The specific enthalpy values around the cycle have been determined in our previous example, viz.

$$h_2 = 3446 \text{ kJ/kg} \quad ; \quad h_3 = 3110 \text{ kJ/kg}$$
$$h_4 = 3569 \text{ kJ/kg} \quad ; \quad h_5 = 2320 \text{ kJ/kg}$$
$$h_6 = 138 \text{ kJ/kg} \quad ; \quad h_7 = 138 \text{ kJ/kg}$$

Also from *Table 1.2*

$$h_8 = h_1 = h_f(30 \text{ bar})$$
$$= 909 + (\tfrac{1}{2})(1087 - 909) = 998 \text{ kJ/kg}$$

The steam conditions into and out of the feedheater are shown in *Figure 2.7* and application of the first law across the feedheater gives

$$(\dot{Q}\!\!\nearrow^{=0}_{in} - \dot{Q}\!\!\nearrow^{=0}_{out}) + (\dot{W}\!\!\nearrow^{=0}_{in} - \dot{W}\!\!\nearrow^{=0}_{out})$$
$$= H_{out} - H_{in}$$

i.e.

$$H_{in} = H_{out}$$

i.e.

$$(1-m)(h_7) + (m)(h_3) = (1-m+m)(h_8)$$
$$\therefore (1-m)(138) + (m)(3110) = (1)(998)$$

$$m = \frac{998 - 138}{3110 - 138} = 0.29 \quad \text{and}$$

$$(1-m) = 0.71$$

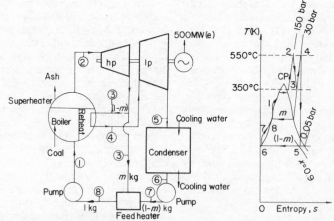

Figure 2.7   The design of a 500-MW(e) power-station turbo-alternator plant operating on the steam cycle with superheat, reheat and one stage of feedheating

Hence

$$\eta_{th} = \frac{\dot{W}_{net}}{\dot{Q}_{in}} = \frac{\dot{W}_{h.p.\ turbine} + \dot{W}_{l.p.\ turbine}}{\dot{Q}_{boiler\ +\ superheater} + \dot{Q}_{reheater}}$$

$$= \frac{(h_2 - h_3) + (1-m)(h_4 - h_5)}{(h_2 - h_1) + (1-m)(h_4 - h_3)}$$

$$= \frac{(3446 - 3110) + (0.71)(3569 - 2320)}{(3446 - 998) + (0.71)(3569 - 3110)}$$

$$= \frac{1223}{2774} = 44.1\%$$

$$s.s.c. = \frac{3600}{(h_2 - h_3) + (1-m)(h_4 - h_5)}$$

$$= \frac{3600}{1223} \frac{kg}{kWh} = 2.94 \frac{kg}{kWh}$$

$$\eta_{plant} = \eta_{th} \times \eta_{mech} \times \eta_{gen}$$
$$= (44.1)(0.99)(0.99)\% = 43.2\%$$

$$\dot{Q}_{in} = \frac{\dot{W}_{net}}{\eta_{plant}} = \frac{500}{0.432} MW = 1157\ MW$$

$$\dot{m}_{coal} = \frac{\dot{Q}_{in}}{(\eta_{b+r})(coal\ CV)} = \frac{1157000}{(0.9)(28000)}\ kg/s$$

$$= 45.9\ kg/s = 165\ t/h$$

$$\dot{Q}_{out} = \dot{Q}_{in} = \dot{W}_{net} = 1157 - 500\ MW = 657\ MW$$

$$\dot{m}_{cooling\ water} = \frac{657000}{(4.19)(25-15)}\ kg/s = 15\ 680\ kg/s$$

$$\dot{V}_{cooling\ water} = 15.68\ m^3/s = 941\ m^3/min$$

Thus, we see in this example that the cycle's thermal efficiency increases by 2% as compared with the similar non-feedheating cycle. This is a marked improvement. It results in a reduction of coal consumption of 8 t/h, or 197 t/d. This reduces not only the fuel cost, but also the associated coal transportation and handling costs and the fuel-ash handling costs. The specific steam consumption increases by 29.5%, indicating an apparent large increase in the sizes of the individual plant items. However, this is offset by the following factors:

1. The boiler heat duty is now lower and the boiler furnace is smaller.
2. Only 71% (i.e. the fraction 1–m) of the working fluid flows through the reheater, l.p. turbine and the condenser, hence the sizes of these items is reduced. As the condenser cooling-water flow rate is reduced, both the cooling-water pumps and the pumping power will be smaller. Furthermore, a reduction in the size of the l.p. turbine is an important advantage, since at the low-pressure end of this turbine the specific volume of the steam is very high and reducing the flow rate eases the design of the long blades near the exhaust.

2.3 Steam power plant appraisal

Improvements in past performance

Table 2.1 shows the past improvements in performance of steam power plant. As discussed earlier in this chapter, they have been brought about by increasing the maximum pressure and temperature of the cycle, lowering the minimum pressure and introducing reheat and feedheating. Most of these are worth introducing only for large plants, and there has therefore been a trend over the years towards commissioning larger and larger steam power-station plants.

Ways of improving plant performance are constantly being investigated, and two of these, by introducing reheat and feedheating, are now

Table 2.1 Approximate performance data of various steam power plant

	Watt's beam engine	1-MW locomotive engine	2-MW marine recip. engine	30-MW turbine for power station	660-MW turbine for power station
Thermal efficiency (%)	2	7	20	35	44
Initial pressure (bar)	1	15	15	40	160
Initial temp. (°C)	100	300	250	450	540
Reheat pressure (bar)					40
Reheat temp. (°)					540
Exhaust pressure (bar)	near 1	1.2	0.1	0.045	0.045
Exhaust condition	wet	near sat.	wet	0.9 dry	0.9 dry
Feedheating stages				4	7

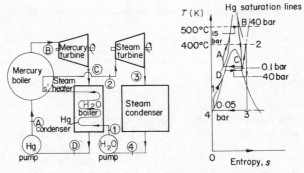

Figure 2.8   The mercury–steam binary vapour cycle and plant showing typical conditions around the cycle

standard practice for the larger plants. Two others that have been tried, but have not been commonly adopted, are worthy of note. They are the mercury/steam binary cycle and the supercritical steam cycle. Both of these are briefly described below.

Figure 2.8 shows the typical conditions of a mercury/steam binary plant. The mercury is evaporated in a mercury boiler and is then expanded within a mercury turbine down to a low pressure. The mercury vapour still possesses a high temperature at the low pressure and during condensation within a heat exchanger the latent heat is used to evaporate water into steam. The liquid mercury is then pumped back into the mercury boiler and the mercury cycle is repeated. The steam generated in the heat exchanger is superheated using the mercury boiler combustion gases and then the steam undergoes an orthodox cycle.

Six such plants were built and operated successfully in the USA between 1928 and 1949. The largest was of 40 MW rated capacity. The thermal efficiencies of these plants are high (about 50%) and mercury fulfils the necessary thermodynamic constraints. However, these plants suffered from having high mercury flow rates (about eight times

the steam rate), because of the low latent heat of mercury. Furthermore, as mercury is both expensive and poisonous the capital costs of the plants were very high and special precautions were necessary to prevent leakage. Thus the mercury binary cycle has not become common. 'Topping' or 'bottoming' the steam cycle with another vapour cycle are sound thermodynamic principles, but to date no completely satisfactory topping and bottoming fluids have been developed.

Figure 2.9 shows the plant arrangement and the T–s diagram for a supercritical steam cycle. Steam is generated in a 'once-through' boiler at a pressure above the critical-point pressure of 221.2 bar. If the plant incorporates reheat and several stages of feedheating there is approximately a 2% gain in thermal efficiency compared with the corresponding subcritical cycle. However, such an improvement is gained only at the expense of increased cost and complexity of the plant. It may have to incorporate double reheat to prevent the l.p. turbine exhaust wetness being excessive, and the boiler unit, the very high-pressure turbine and the boiler feed pumps are all more expensive. Thus, although a number of such plants are operating satisfactorily their popularity is unlikely to increase significantly in the future.

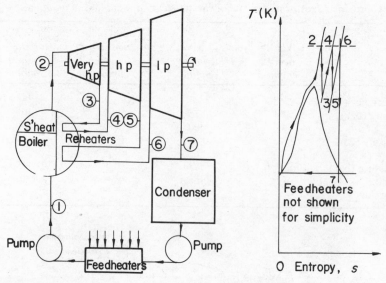

Figure 2.9   The supercritical steam cycle incorporating double reheat and feedheating

Future performance improvements

The continuing use of steam turbine plant for the bulk generation of mechanical power appears to be certain within the foreseeable future; there is no replacement on the horizon. Plant sizes will continue to increase and 1300 MW(e) turbo-generators are likely to be the standard unit sizes in the power-station of AD 2000. Modest perform-ance improvements are therefore expected by virtue of the 'economy of scale' rule. Large im-provements through raising the metallurgical limit are, however, unlikely in the near future because it would seem to involve using prohibitively expensive austenitic steels or using complicated turbine blade cooling methods. Nevertheless, each generation of engineers has thought that the limits have been reached, but has been proved wrong by the succeeding generation. The thermo-dynamic design of the steam cycle for a 1300 MW(e) turbo-generator would not pose any serious problems. The steam conditions through-out the cycle would be similar to those of the present generation of 660 MW(e) sets, but the plant size would be correspondingly larger. Even larger unit sizes of 2000 and 3000 MW(e) have been proposed, but the physical construction and operation of such plants would pose serious problems; in particular, the flexibility of the

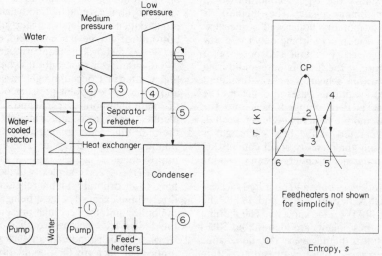

Figure 2.10   The steam cycle associated with the water-cooled nuclear reactor

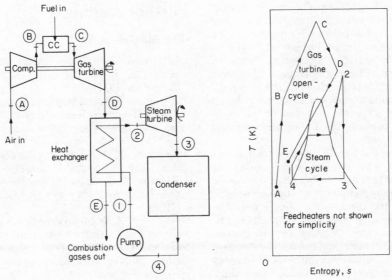

Figure 2.11 The simple combined gas and steam turbine plant

longer rotor shafts, the construction of the huge generator–stator, the effect on the electricity grid system of a sudden outage of one of these very large sets, and the high loss in revenue due to an outage.

Although significant improvements in the steam conditions throughout turbine plant seems unlikely in the near future, major changes in the design of the overall plant are likely through the following:

1. The fossil-fuel boiler will be replaced by a nuclear reactor. Many such plants are already in operation throughout the world. From the steam cycle point of view, nuclear power plants can be divided into two groups: those with water-cooled reactors and those with reactor coolants of some other fluid (e.g. carbon dioxide gas or liquid metal). The latter group incorporate heat exchangers to cool the reactor coolant and thereby generate and superheat steam for the steam plant. Power plants of this type generate and super-heat the steam at conditions similar to those in conventional plants. Hence, the steam plant and cycle and thermal efficiencies are also similar to those of conventional plants. The situation is, however, somewhat different for the water-cooled reactor plants. *Figure 2.10* shows a simplified typical arrangement and the *T–s* diagram for such a plant. The reactor operation limits the conditions at which steam is generated, either directly or more usually indirectly in a heat exchanger. Thus only medium-pressure (about 40 bar)

saturated steam is generated. This steam expands within a medium-pressure wet tur-bine until it is about 12% wet. It then enters a large moisture separator and reheater unit; there the water content is extracted and the saturated steam is reheated using steam bled from the heat exchanger. The low-pressure superheated steam then expands through a low-pressure turbine and is condensed in the condenser. The feedwater is heated in the feedheaters and the cycle is completed by the heated feedwater being pumped back into the heat exchanger. The thermal efficiency of this type of plant is only modest (about 35%) but this is offset by the reactor being of com-paratively simple and compact construction.

2. Topping the steam cycle with a gas cycle using for example a gas turbine. Many variants are possible with such a combined plant. *Figure 2.11* shows one possible simple arrangement. High-pressure, high-temperature combustion gases are produced by compressing air in a compressor (A to B) and then burning fuel in the air within the combustion chamber (B to C). The gases are then expanded within a gas turbine (C to D), but leave it at a high tem-perature. These gases are used to generate and superheat steam within a heat exchanger. Supplementary combustion may be used in the heat exchanger to bring the combustion gases up to a sufficiently high temperature. The steam cycle 1234 is thereafter conven-tional and may incorporate reheat and re-

generative feedheating. The overall efficiency of such a combined plant is about 5% higher than that of a comparable modern steam plant because the gas turbine plant operates at much higher temperatures than the metallurgical limit temperatures of modern steam-turbine plant. However, the combined plant is more expensive and the gas turbine's life span is shorter than that of the steam turbine because of the higher operating temperatures.

3. Designing the overall plant on total-energy concepts. This involves usefully using the low-grade heat rejected from the cycle instead of wastefully dumping it into the atmospheric sink via the condenser cooling water. The heat from large power-station plants can be used for district heating or for market-gardening heating, and the steam exhausting from industrial turbines can be used for factory heating and/or process steam. Such total-energy concepts are not new; industry has been exploiting this principle for many years using back-pressure and pass-out turbines. However, with the current trends towards fuel conservation we are likely to see a growth in the popularity of such schemes. They are described in Chapter 11.

Further reading

On steam plant cycles

1 CEGB. *Modern Power Station Practice*, 2nd edn, Vol. 3, pp 1–4 and 131–226. Oxford: Pergamon (1971)
2 Rogers, G.F.C. and Mayhew, Y.R. *Engineering Thermodynamics: Work and Heat Transfer*. 2nd edn (SI units), Chap. 11. London: Longmans (1967)
3 Kearton, W. J. *Steam Turbine Operation*, 7th edn, Chap. 1. London: Pitman (1964)
4 Kearton, W. J. *Steam Turbine Theory and Practice*, 7th edn, Chaps 4 and 13. London: Pitman (1958)
5 Haywood, R. W. *Analysis of Engineering Cycles*, Chaps 2 and 7. Oxford: Pergamon (1967)
6 Gaffert, G. A. *Steam Power Stations*, 4th edn, Chap. 24. New York: McGraw-Hill (1952)

On nuclear and future power plant

7 CEGB. *Modern Power Station Practice*, 2nd edn, Vol. 3, pp 57–71 and Vol. 8, Chap. 2. Oxford: Pergamon (1971)
8 Haywood, R. W. *Analysis of Engineering Cycles*, Chaps 8 and 9. Oxford: Pergamon (1967)

3   The safe use of steam

3.1 Pressure and temperature hazards

This section deals with the hazards which can arise in steam plant from pressure or temperature. The principal hazard is that arising from overpressure, or failure of pressure parts, but some mention is made of the troubles due to creep which can come from high steam temperatures.

Although nearly all the troubles arise from excess pressure inside the plant, it should not be forgotten that excess external pressure can also cause failure where the outside pressure is atmospheric and a vacuum exists inside. This is unusual, and it generally occurs because steam plant has been shut down without air vents being opened, thus causing a vacuum inside the plant, but it should not be overlooked as a possible cause of failure.

The section refers mainly to steam boilers, since the large size of units, and the added complication of internal and external corrosion, makes this the area where most work has to be done to minimize the likelihood of failure, but in most cases the precautions which have to be taken, and the desirable operating methods, are similar for steam process vessels.

Introduction

Ever since steam boilers were first introduced there has been a continual history of failures and explosions. The investigations into the failures of boilers have in general been in the hands of the specialists, who have been responsible for the periodic inspection of boilers, and therefore a brief historical review of the boiler inspection service may be of interest and also provide the background to the current position.

Since 1882 investigations in the UK into boiler explosions as such have been carried out by engineer surveyors of the Board of Trade, but such investigations have been limited to incidents reported under the Boiler Explosions Act 1882. Over recent years there has been close cooperation between the Board of Trade and the engineering insurance companies. During the first half of the nineteenth century, growing public concern over the increasing number of boiler explosions led a group of mill owners, and leading engineers, to meet in Manchester in 1854 to consider setting up an organization to prevent explosions and to try to ensure safer operation of boilers. In 1855 another public meeting led to the foundation of the Association for Prevention of Steam Boiler Explosions and for Effecting Economy in the Raising and Use of Steam — which eventually became the Manchester Steam Users' Association, generally known as the MSUA. From its inception the MSUA was the recognized world leader not only in the inspection of boilers but in establishing the standards of construction and operation. The magnitude of the problem is best illustrated by quoting from Martin's paper to the Institution of Mechanical Engineers in 1866, when he mentioned 1046 explosions. The MSUA in their reports covering the years 1862–1864 refer to 127 people being killed and 111 injured!

As a result of the MSUA activity, pressure was brought to bear and in 1882 the Boiler Explosions Act was placed on the statute and in 1890 an amendment was added.

The 1901 Factories Act introduced compulsory inspection of steam boilers — again the MSUA exerted great influence — and in 1904 the Quarries Act was brought within the scope of the Factories and Workshops Act; also, the Coalmines Act of 1911 made provision for periodic inspection of steam boilers. The Factories and Workshops Act and others were replaced by the 1937 Factories Act, which was again amended in 1964. The current position is that all this type of legislation has been incorporated in the 1974 Health and Safety at Work etc. Act. At the time of writing, tentative proposals are being considered in respect of pressurized systems under the Health and Safety at Work Act but it may be some time before specific rules are introduced.

Boilers: historical review

A study of the technical literature of the early and mid-nineteenth century indicates many unusual designs of boilers — some most peculiar — but over the years the Cornish boiler became the leader until the introduction of the Lancashire boiler, which has been attributed to Sir William Fairbairn. From the mid-nineteenth century the Lancashire boiler reigned supreme, being the main source of steam production for nearly a century. In the early part of the twentieth century, however, Economic boilers were introduced and became increasingly popular, eventually developing into the modern package boiler which came into greater use after World War II. The main change in construction was the abandoning of riveted construction and its replacement by all-welded boilers.

In the latter part of the nineteenth century, watertube boilers were introduced and these progressed rapidly, particularly where prime movers were involved, to the current boilers where out-

puts of 660 MW are quite common — not to mention working pressures up to critical pressure and the higher final steam temperatures. The main changes in construction of watertube boilers have been the superseding of riveted drums by welding and the use of alloy steels to meet the increasing high temperatures.

Major failures

In the early days, many explosions were due to the boiler's not being of suitable construction to withstand the working pressure, because the basic principles of strength of material and design had not been established at that time. Apart from shortcomings in design and construction it is very clear that the actual operating conditions left much to be desired, as many reports indicated the boiler being full up with sludge, heavy scale deposits and often the safety valves being inoperative.

Boiler explosions due to internal pressure are generally disastrous, often catastrophic, with extensive damage and often injury to personnel. An example of the widespread damage can be seen in *Figure 3.1*. This risk is always present, hence the need for care, attention and proper operation at all times. Quite often remarks are made to the effect that an explosion is 'impossible', but anyone with a lifetime's experience of boiler failures would refute this entirely. Where heat and a fluid are associated there is always the possibility of an explosion — it may be remote, but it is still there.

The foregoing applies to *all* boilers and one must not assume that it is only high-pressure boilers which are at risk, as statistics over many years show that quite a number of people have been killed and injured by the explosion of low-pressure equipment.

Riveted boilers

Reference has already been made to the major changes in manufacture, i.e. replacement of riveted construction by welding, and before the major failures of different types are considered, a few notes on riveted boilers may be of interest as, whilst no more are being made, those in existence may be with us for a few years yet. There have been several disastrous explosions of riveted boilers, both of the shell and watertube type, and whilst in some instances the cause has been construction, in others it has been due to shortcomings in the feedwater treatment, highlighted by caustic embrittlement (*see later*). Experience has shown that if leakage from a riveted seam does not respond to simple caulking then it is essential that a full investigation be made. Often this will

Figure 3.1   An explosion of an all-welded watertube boiler

entail the removal of rivets and carrying out non-destructive testing such as magnetic-particle testing, dye penetrant testing of the rivet holes, or ultrasonic testing (*see* p 35); in addition, checking of the feedwater and boiler water treatment will be necessary since correct feedwater treatment should eliminate caustic embrittlement. When the cause of the leakage has been established, the inspecting authority will be able to determine whether or not repairs can be carried out and if so, the form they are to take. It must not be assumed that caustic embrittlement is the cause of leakage from every riveted seam but any leakage must be viewed with suspicion.

Boiler inspections

Procedure

At this juncture it would be useful to record the procedure for the inspection of steam boilers. Every steam boiler must be prepared at specified intervals for a thorough examination consisting of two parts: (a) an examination with the boiler at rest, and afterwards (b) an examination with the boiler under steam pressure. Both examinations must be carried out to comply with the statutory

requirements. The examinations must be carried out by a competent person and the results of such examinations must be reported on a prescribed form. In the UK practically all examinations of steam boilers are in the hands of the engineering insurance companies, that country being one of the few where such work is handled by non-government bodies. As a matter of interest, safety records in the UK compare favourably with those of countries where the boiler examinations are carried out by government bodies. The current legislation stipulates the period at which steam boilers shall be thoroughly examined, which with specific exceptions is at intervals not exceeding 14 months.

The exceptions are related to watertube boilers used for generation of electricity, mainly through the national distribution system, when the periods between inspection may be extended to 26 or 30 months depending on compliance with regulations as laid down, although the extension of the period is entirely dependent on the person making the examinations.

Safety precautions

It is very important that no person enters a boiler

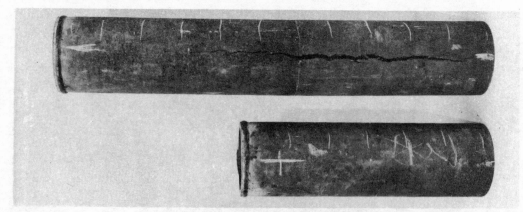

Figure 3.2   Failure of a tube from a gas reformer plant due to creep

until all connections through which steam or water enter have been disconnected or blanked off in a proper manner, also that care is taken to ensure that the boiler is not under vacuum conditions. It is also necessary to take care and follow the correct procedure when coupling up a boiler to the main, in particular to ensure that all drains and traps are open and all condensate removed.

A brief description follows of some of the more common metallurgical terms which may occur during discussions on boiler inspections as an aid to understanding the full implications of inspections and repairs.

Creep

This is the slow and continuous deformation that takes place under stress (below the yield-point value) at elevated temperature. *Figure 3.2* shows the failure of a gas reformer tube resulting from creep. The detailed effects of creep on steam turbines are discussed more fully in Chapter 11.

Hydrogen embrittlement

Hydrogen that is released during corrosion, acid pickling or welding may be absorbed by metals to give rise to a condition of low ductility.

Stress corrosion cracking

As the name suggests, this term relates to the failure under the combined actions of stress and corrosion. The former is usually of the static variety: as induced during manufacture by pressing, tube expansion, welding, etc., rather than that applied externally. The corrosive agent may not be very aggressive and is generally specific for particular metals, for example alkali hydroxides for carbon steels (caustic cracking), ammonia for brass, and chlorides and hydroxides for stainless steels. In carbon steels and brass it is

characterized by intergranular cracking and in stainless steels by transgranular cracking. Stress corrosion cracking differs from corrosion fatigue, in which the stresses are basically of a varying nature and the environment not specific.

Non-destructive testing

Non-destructive testing has already been mentioned in the discussion on riveted boilers. The principal methods are magnetic testing, the use of dye penetrants and ultrasonic testing.

Magnetic

Magnetic methods depend on the application of a magnetic field to the material in such a direction that the principal plane of a suspected fault is across the direction of the flux. This gives rise to flux distortion, and a leakage field is generated in the air immediately adjacent to a defect. Such disturbances may extend some distance from the fault, and, if they affect the external field distribution, the change can be detected by the use of an indicator that is sensitive to variations in field strength.

Cracks in the surface produce well-defined external disturbances and in such cases a suitable detecting medium, such as fine ferrous oxide particles, will show up the details of the crack. The deeper the defect, the more diffuse are the indications, so that even crack-like defects at a considerable depth no longer give rise to well-defined indications. Less sharply defined defects in or near the surface will give similarly diffuse indications. The interpretation of indications from sub-surface defects thus calls for a certain amount of experience on the part of the inspecting personnel.

Penetrants

Cracks, porosity and other surface discontinuities

will permit ingress of a liquid of low viscosity and good wetting properties. Among available proprietary penetrants, the solvent is often a petroleum product or alcohol, and the solute is either an organic dye or a fluorescent material. In one technique the penetrant is a mineral oil.

A penetrant is applied to a specimen depending upon the facilities available and the size of the specimen. An immersion tank may be used, or the penetrant may be merely brushed, swabbed or sprayed over the surface. Heating of the specimen or the penetrant generally assists the penetrating action.

The time required for the test surface to remain in contact with the penetrant may vary over a wide range, depending on the nature of the defect; with fine cracks up to an hour or more may be required. Generally speaking, however, with modern penetrants the total inspection process requires only a few minutes.

The surplus penetrant must then be removed from the surface before the developer is applied. This generally consists of a fine white powder suspended in liquid which is conveniently applied in the form of a fine spray. After application of the developer, a waiting time is usually desirable for development of the optimum flaw indication, before the surface is subjected to final inspection.

Usually a flaw indication will persist over a considerable time, thus readily permitting rechecking and photographing of results if required. Ultimately the intensity will diminish, and blurring of the outlines will occur owing to general spreading of the penetrant by capillary action from the immediate vicinity of the defect.

All parts returned from service, or which may have been in contact with oil, must be thoroughly degreased. Other sources of contamination, such as oxides, corrosion products and solid residues, are less easily dispersed and may completely invalidate the results of a penetrant examination.

Ultrasonics

Ultrasonic waves are mechanical vibrations exhibiting the same characteristics as sound waves, but because of their much higher frequency, they cannot be detected by the human ear.

Materials are inspected for defects by sending ultrasonic energy into them. Since a defect represents a sudden change in the acoustical properties, it results in a proportion of the energy incident upon it being reflected, thus producing an echo. This echo can be detected and displayed and in this way the presence of the defect can be revealed.

The property which renders ultrasonic waves so useful in non-destructive testing is their ability to pass through great thicknesses of most metals without severe absorption or scattering, and their almost complete inability to pass across such defects as cracks, slag inclusions and porosity. Even small defects can be located and in some cases they can also be identified. However, the success or failure of an ultrasonic examination is critically dependent upon the operative.

Shell and watertube boilers

There is quite a distinct difference between the types and causes of failures in shell and watertube boilers, as will be seen in the next two sections.

Shell boilers

General. During the last century, explosions due to overpressure, generally caused by inoperative safety valves, were commonplace, but over recent years there have been very few incidents of this type and over the last two decades the most common explosions as such have been associated with failures of welded seams, in particular those of furnace rings to end-plates and shell to end-plate, the former being more prevalent. The method of failure is common to both and emanates from undercutting of the internal fillet weld. Cracking develops and final failure has been sudden (*Figure 3.3*). If there is evidence of undercutting, the

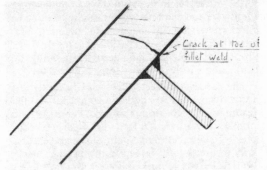

Figure 3.3   Section from a failed boiler drum showing undercutting of fillet weld

application of ultrasonic testing will reveal the extent of any cracking that may be present. The sudden failure of the attachments often coincides with overheating of the furnace rings, owing to shortage of water, and in many cases the reaction from the contents of the boiler being ejected has resulted in the boiler being moved bodily several metres. Similar failures of the shell to end-plate seams have not resulted in such catastrophic damage, as the effects have been somewhat limited owing to the longitudinal stays and tubes. Over recent years the predominant cause of failures in shell boilers has been boilers running short of water with resultant collapse of furnace rings, and often with failure of furnace-shell attachments mentioned in the previous paragraph. Such occurrences have not only resulted in extensive damage but have caused several fatalities.

Practically all modern boilers are provided with automatic controls and at this stage it is as well to consider the position regarding automatically controlled steam boilers. The introduction of the package boiler after World War II brought with it the use of automatic controls, which were necessary as manual controls were not sensitive enough to meet load changes and to maintain good combustion conditions. As a result of this, full-time manual attendance on steam boilers has become to some extent unnecessary provided the controls function properly at all times. Like all equipment, automatic controls can and do fail, and unfortunately when this happens the general result has been boilers running short of water. Such a condition, with a low water level in the boiler but with the burner still operating, results in overheating of the furnace with ultimate collapse.

It was because of this feature that in the UK, the Associated Offices Technical Committee (AOTC) introduced their rules, and even then so many failures occurred that the Department of Employment brought out a leaflet TDN25 — now Health and Safety Executive Guidance Notes PM5 — to highlight the trouble and to indicate to employers and employees what should be done to ensure reliability and achieve safe operation. The introduction of this official leaflet has resulted in a drop in the number of failures and they should be eliminated entirely if the rules are adhered to.

The Associated Offices Technical Committee was formed several years ago and comprises the five leading UK engineering insurance companies. Its primary concern is the technical aspects of engineering plant and to maintain standards, particularly in the field of boilers and pressure vessels. The organization works closely with government bodies both in the UK and overseas and is the recognized authority of the engineering insurance industry on technical matters.

The majority of controls for shell boilers comprise floats working in chambers connected to the boiler by pipes, and any sludge or scale in these chambers can prevent the free action of the floats. If the level of water in the boiler drops, and the float remains at normal level because of sludge or similar deposits, then the burners continue to operate, despite the boiler's being short of water, and furnace collapse is the general result. It is of vital importance to keep sludge from being present in the float chambers and therefore correct feedwater treatment is essential for all package boilers. The removal of possible sludge accumulation from the chambers is the primary reason why the controls must be blown through at regular intervals and at the same time such blowing down tests the controls themselves.

In addition to this, the regulations call for the automatic controls themselves to be overhauled and serviced by competent persons at regular intervals. It is the considered view of many that this service is best put in the hands of the control makers.

Both the PM5 and AOTC rules refer to boilers not under constant supervision, which many assume to mean that the boilers are completely unattended. The issue is quite clear; all automatic controls incorporate alarms of one form or another, and it is no use whatsoever these alarms functioning unless some person is on-site, or is available to attend to the boiler, when the alarms function. Therefore the alarm must be so situated that some personnel are in the vicinity at all times. These controls require testing every shift and there must be some person with sufficient training to carry out this testing, also to attend to the feedwater treatment and, what is very important, to keep the boiler and its surroundings clean. Cleanliness is necessary in all boilerhouses, but more particularly with oil or gas firing, as a high standard of housekeeping is essential to minimize the danger of fire or explosion.

It is desirable to keep a sense of proportion. With single-boiler installations it is not economic to keep a full-time boiler operator, but in larger installations, say, of four boilers, then with the shift testing of controls, feedwater treatment, keeping a log book and general cleaning a strong case can be made out for at least one full-time operator.

Oil- and gas-fired boilers incorporate sophisticated equipment which calls for a high standard of housekeeping with specialized maintenance, bearing in mind that any shortcomings can result in damage to the boiler. Any such damage may result in the boiler's being out of service for several months whilst repairs are being carried out.

Tube attachment troubles. Up to the introduction of the welded packaged boiler, tubes were attached to tube plates by expanding, but this was changed to fillet welding and over recent years the main trouble with modern shell boilers has been leakage and cracking of tube attachments. These features have not resulted in spectacular explosions but have been a major factor in boiler outage, with its attendant considerable costs of repairs. The general pattern has been for radial cracks to develop on the ends of the tubes in the first pass and for the cracks to run longitudinally in the bore — in some cases the cracks extend in the ligaments and in others the cracks are in the fillet welds running circumferentially. The result is, of course, leakage.

In the event of tube end trouble the most obvious cause is the presence of scale or sludge on the water side of the tube plate around the tube necks. Modern boilers have a high heat flux, and any impediment to heat transfer, such as scale, is an obvious cause of overheating. This is another reason why correct feedwater treatment is so essential with all modern shell boilers.

Excessive projection of tubes beyond the tube plate has been a common feature causing tube end cracking, whilst slack tubes in tube holes have also resulted in cracks. Correct burner settings are vital, particularly with gas firing.

It is hoped that the recent amendments to the standard BS 2790: 'Specification for shell boilers of welded construction' will go a long way to eliminating tube end failures but even in spite of this, careful setting up of burners and good combustion operation are still vital if trouble-free service is to be obtained.

Flue gas explosion is a very rare occurrence with shell boilers, which is a tribute to the quality of the controls currently fitted and the standards of maintenance and housekeeping.

Watertube boilers

Watertube boilers developed rapidly between 1958 and 1978, particularly over the years from 1968 to 1978 when sizes of 660 MW and pressures up to and beyond critical were not uncommon.

These extensions in size, pressures and temperatures have brought with them their own troubles, many of which are of great interest to the metallurgist, but the following description deals with major trouble across the board, rather than odd cases of specialized technical interest.

The pattern of failures has been somewhat different and indeed opposite to that of shell boilers in so far as shortage of water is unusual but the number of flue gas explosions gives cause for concern.

Drum explosions. The diminishing number of riveted boilers has brought about a drop in the number of drum explosions, and whilst there are some such boilers still operating they will no doubt be phased out in the near future.

This leads us to consider the position regarding explosion of welded drums. These have been very few and of those known to the author none has been due to failure of a strength-welded seam. *Figure 3.4* shows an explosion of a welded drum but clearly indicates that the main strength weld was intact, and failure actually occurred from a fracture which emanated from slight undercutting at the toe of an internal fillet weld. There are other recorded failures from fillet welds, which would indicate that, if fillet welds cannot be avoided, they should at least be ground to a smooth contour and all undercutting eliminated.

Figure 3.4   Close-up of the top drum of Figure 3.1 showing failure not at welded seam

On-load defects. These are mainly tube failures, either of generator or superheater tubes. Local overheating has often resulted in bulging and subsequent explosion and in other cases creep has occurred or hydrogen embrittlement and oxygen attack, leading to formation of magnetic oxide, but whilst such failures are troublesome in increasing unscheduled outages, repairs to isolated tubes thus affected are relatively simple. The defective portion can be cropped, and a new length of tube welded, *in situ,* by craftsmen to Class I standard, followed by radiography and testing. The apparent simplicity of this description may be misleading as, with a large modern unit, it can take a considerable amount of time to rig scaffolding to gain access to the affected tube. The high final steam temperatures are such that departures from optimum conditions can well lead to overheating, and whilst alloy tubes are used, trouble with creep can still occur, and great care is necessary in operation to ensure that higher temperatures are kept within design parameters.

Flue gas explosions. There is little doubt that watertube boilers operating on pulverized coal, gas or oil are currently vulnerable to flue gas explosion, particularly in the commissioning stages. Start-up and load shedding are sensitive periods, and it is emphasized that a flue gas explosion on a modern large unit can result in extensive damage, and repairs currently can and do run to several million pounds.

In numerous cases investigated, the cause of such disastrous explosions is simply maloperation; that is, someone on-site either ignores warning signs, signals, alarms or deliberately by-passes safety interlocks or circuits, for particular and perhaps obscure reason — often with good intent but with little or no appreciation of the conditions relating to combustion, or the mechanics of a flue gas explosion. In many cases standing orders have been deliberately ignored.

The cause of flue gas explosion is well known. A mixture within the explosive limits of a volatile gas with air, and a source of ignition are all that is required. The explosive limits of some of the more common gases are given in *Table 3.1.* (Natural gas is mainly methane with a small proportion of ethane and higher hydrocarbons.)

In practice, if for some reason ignition is lost and flame-out occurs, the ambient temperatures in the combustion chamber are generally such as to vaporize pulverized coal or oil, and, if the mixture with air is within the explosive limits, then ignition from a 'hot spot' or other source is sufficient. Pulverized fuel is common on large units and to

Table 3.1 Explosive limits of some common gases

Gas	Range of flammability (% v/v in air/gas mixture)
Blast-furnace gas	35.0–74.0
Butane	1.8– 8.5
Carbon monoxide	12.5–74.0
Coal gas	5.3–31.0
Hydrogen	4.0–75.0
Methane	5.0–15.0
Propane	2.0– 9.5

achieve stability it is necessary to maintain the temperature of the combustion chamber by means of auxiliary or start-up oil burners, until the load on the unit is high enough, when combustion of pulverized fuel alone will maintain the requisite temperatures. This means that, when raising steam, it is necessary to operate the boiler on oil burners until a predetermined load is reached, when the combustion chamber temperatures are high enough to ensure stability on the pulverized-fuel burners alone. The actual percentage load will vary on makers' advice, but 50–60% is quite a common figure. Likewise, when shedding load, the oil burners will need to be brought in when load drops to these predetermined limits, and

Figure 3.5   Combustion chamber explosion showing membrane wall distortion

there are cases on record where failure to do this has resulted in very severe flue gas explosions and disastrous damage. In one case alone the cost of repairs was £2 million.

There are cases where loss of flame has occurred and the operator, instead of shutting off the fuel, has tried to obtain reignition on pulverized fuel. With oil fuel the principle is the same and loss of flame has resulted in atomized oil being sprayed into the furnace; the oil becomes volatile and the explosive mixture forms. With all burners, whether for pulverized fuel, oil or gas, there should be a flame failure device which shuts off the fuel immediately flame is lost. When this occurs purging must be carried out in accordance with makers' instructions.

It is not often appreciated that the extensive damage to a modern boiler by a flue gas explosion is in part due to current design and construction, which calls for a gas-tight combustion chamber, usually a membrane wall, and this acts as a pressure casing resulting in high energy release and subsequent extensive damage (*see Figure 3.5*).

Over recent years there have been many instances of implosion on large units. In these cases flame-out has occurred, which means that the air register closes but the induced-draught fans are still running. Under these conditions a partial vacuum has formed in the combustion chamber and the side walls of the combustion chamber have collapsed inwards. When this occurs the damage is considerable; often, many if not all of the buckstays (the girth supports running horizontally around the combustion chamber) collapse and a complete rebuild of the combustion chamber walls is necessary. It is interesting to note that if the combustion chamber were not gas-tight the formation of vacuum would not be so effective, and thus the excellence of construction can be a factor in the trouble. The prevention of this lies in the design, and whilst induced-draught fan characteristics have a bearing, a feasible solution is to construct the combustion chamber so that it will withstand the maximum possible vacuum which could be obtained. This may increase the capital costs, but with a boiler costing £70 million a few thousand pounds will be well spent, rather than run the risk of several thousands of pounds for repairs, coupled with the boiler's being out of service for many months.

Steam process vessels

In many industries, several items of plant work at much lower pressure than do the supply steam boilers, and such pressure vessels are designed and

Figure 3.6 Steam-heated platen damaged as a result of overpressure

constructed only for the lower pressure. In practice this means that it is necessary to install, between the supply boiler and the low-pressure vessels, suitable reducing valves or other appliances and, of great importance, a suitable safety valve to comply with the requirements of the Factories Act.

Many failures of steam process vessels have been due to overpressure, often brought about by an inadequate reducing valve, or even no valve at all, in the steam supply line, or where reducing valves have not functioned and there has been an inadequate valve, or no safety valve, fitted in the supply line, or on the vessel itself. The question is often raised as to what is a suitable safety valve and to the author's mind the issue is quite clear, namely that the safety valve on the low-pressure side of the reducing valve should be set to lift at the correct pressure but also, and this is most important, must be of sufficient capacity to pass to atmosphere all the steam which the reducing valve will pass when in the fully open position. If this procedure is followed then there should be no possibility of overpressure coming on the process vessel. When process plant which is to work at a lower pressure is being installed, then the obvious course is to go to a reputable manufacturer, to specify the capacity of the reducing valve and pressure drop and at the same time order from the same maker a suitable safety valve sized to meet the maximum flow conditions.

The failure of a steam-heated platen arising solely from overpressure is shown in *Figure 3.6*.

Some failures of pressure vessels have been due to the corrosive nature of the processes, but periodic checking with modern aids such as ultrasonic testing should eliminate such occurrences. Water hammer has caused several nasty explosions both in steam pipelines and process equipment, and great care is necessary to ensure that correct and adequate provision is made to ensure condensate removal.

In recent years there have been three disastrous explosions of large autoclaves, and in the UK the Ministry of the Environment has issued a Guidance Note pointing out the necessity of periodic checking of the cover- or door-securing attachments and the various interlocks. The object is to ensure that the door locking mechanisms have not worn to such an extent as to impair their efficiency, and to eliminate the possibility of the door moving whilst the vessel is still under steam pressure.

In the past there have been numerous failures of welds in steam piping caused by rank bad welding. There are now many standards, both in the UK and other countries, which lay down the testing and procedure for welded joints and these should be strictly adhered to. If this is done there should be no more failures from this particular feature.

The Flixborough explosion highlighted some features regarding expansion bellows or expansion joints. The design of steam pipelines is to some extent a specialized field, and should be done only by experienced people who should also contact the specialist manufacturers of expansion joints for full design details.

Cast-iron valves

Occasionally there have been explosions brought about by water hammer, invariably when a boiler is opened up on to a range. The cause has been well known for many years, namely, badly installed pipelines that permit water ponding and have inadequate drainage. The cure is relatively simple: to ensure that the pipelines have a proper fall to drainage points and that adequate drainage with efficient traps is used at such locations. The water hammer effect is of course accentuated when cast-iron valves are in the pipelines, and this is particularly so when the junction valves on steam boilers are of cast iron. British Standard Specification 759 permits the use of cast-iron valves smaller than 8 in (203 mm) bore at pressures not exceeding 13 bar and 220°C, but despite this, where there is a possibility of water hammer or thermal shock, then it would be prudent to give consideration to having such valves made out of cast steel.

3.2 Noise

Basic terminology

Sound

Noise is generally defined as 'unwanted sound' and in order to appreciate the effect of noise and understand methods of controlling it, it is necessary to consider something of the basic physics of sound. Sound is the effect produced at the ear by alternating pressure in the surrounding air. Hence continuous sound is a succession of pressure waves which can be propagated, as vibrations, in any elastic medium. *Table 3.2* gives the velocity of propagation of sound in various materials.

One fundamental property of sound is its *frequency*, which is the number of like waves which pass a fixed point in one second. Previously referred to as cycles per second, the unit of frequency is now the hertz, which has the symbol Hz.

The range of frequencies which are audible to the human ear extends approximately from 20 Hz to 20 000 Hz, but the ear does not respond equally to all frequencies within this range. Below approximately 1000 Hz the ear's sensitivity de-

Table 3.2 Velocity of sound in various materials

Medium	Approximate velocity of sound (m/s)
Air (1 atm pressure)	344
Steam (dry saturated), 1–2 bar	424
Carbon dioxide (STP)	259
Lead	1220
Water	1410
Brick	3000
Wood	3400
Concrete	3400
Glass	4100
Aluminium	5100
Steel	5200
Hydrogen	1265
Nitrogen (STP)	337

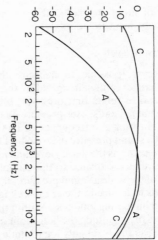

Figure 3.7 Frequency response of A- and C-weighting curves

creases with decrease in frequency, and with advancing age the sensitivity to frequencies above 10 000 Hz also decreases.

Frequency analysis

In order to evaluate noise for noise control purposes it is usual to measure the intensity in bands of frequencies within the audible range. There are a number of instruments available which allow measurements to be made of how much acoustic energy lies within a particular frequency range.

The simplest assessment may be carried out using an instrument equipped with filter circuits that give it a frequency response equivalent to that of the human ear. This type of response is known as 'A-weighting'. By comparing the result obtained using the A-weighted response and that obtained using an instrument which has a linear response with respect to frequency it is possible to determine whether the sound energy is in the higher or lower frequencies or spread evenly throughout the audible range.

It is usual to incorporate both the A-weighting filter and the linear response (or something very close to linear response known as 'C-weighting') within the same instrument with the facility to switch from one to the other. The A and C response curves are shown in *Figure 3.7*.

For a more detailed investigation it is possible to subdivide the curves into narrower frequency bands. The widest band normally used is the octave band in which the upper frequency limit of the band is exactly twice the lower frequency limit. The octave band is usually described by the geometric mean centre frequency of the upper and lower frequency limits of the band. There are internationally agreed octave band limits and the values are shown in *Table 3.3*.

Table 3.3 Preferred frequency bands

Octave band centre frequency (Hz)	Band limits (Hz)
	22
31.5	
	44
63	
	88
125	
	176
250	
	353
500	
	707
1000	
	1414
2000	
	2825
4000	
	5650
8000	
	11300
16000	
	22500

Octave band analysis is usually the limit of analysis possible within a single portable measuring instrument that also has A- and C-weighting networks. Further subdivision is possible using more complex equipment. Bands one-third of an octave wide or even narrower, down to as little as plus or minus 1.5 Hz on the centre frequency are used on occasion.

Loudness

Loudness of noise is a subjective phenomenon that cannot be measured directly.

Sound pressure levels

It is, however, possible to measure the small pressure changes in the air caused by the passage of sound and to relate that pressure to a datum level. The human ear senses pressure change and for normal hearing at a frequency of 1000 Hz can just detect a sound pressure of 20 μbar. This value is therefore taken as the datum level and measured sound pressures are related to this datum. At the other end of the scale a sound pressure of 20×10^6 μbar begins to induce in the ear a feeling of pain rather than increasing loudness. Within this range of six orders of magnitude the behaviour of the ear in detecting sound is roughly logarithmic and it is therefore convenient to use a logarithmic ratio to the datum level. The unit used is the bel or more conveniently the decibel ($= 0.1$ bel) but as this is a ratio of power levels the fact that sound power is proportional to the square of the sound pressure has to be taken into account. Therefore the sound pressure level in decibels (dB) is defined as

$$SPL = 10 \log \left(\frac{P_1}{P_0}\right)^2 = 20 \log \left(\frac{P_1}{P_0}\right) \tag{3.1}$$

where SPL is the sound pressure level in decibels referred to 20 μbar, P_1 is the sound pressure in μbar and P_0 is the reference sound pressure level, 20 μbar. Sound pressure levels range from 0 dB at the threshold of hearing through 40 dB for a quiet room to 120 dB at a distance of 100 m from a jet aircraft on take-off.

Sound power level

Any sound source under steady conditions radiates a constant amount of sound energy or power. Unfortunately no instrumentation exists to allow this power to be measured directly. In practice the sound power of a source is deduced from the measured average sound pressure level over a simple imaginary surface surrounding the source, the sound pressure level at a given distance from the source being proportional to its power. Sound power is expressed in watts and sound power levels can be expressed in decibels with an appropriate reference level, usually 10^{-12} W. Therefore sound power level in decibels is defined as

$$SWL = 10 \log \left(\frac{W_1}{W_0}\right) \tag{3.2}$$

where SWL is the sound power level in decibels referred to 10^{-12} W, W_1 is the radiated sound power and W_0 is the reference power, $= 10^{-12}$ W. The actual sound power of most sources is small. The human voice when shouting generates 0.001 W, the average car 0.01 W and large jet aircraft up to 10^6 W.

Sound propagation

For steam systems it is necessary to consider three types of propagating sound source. The first type is *spherical radiating sources*, where a point source is free to radiate in all directions. Examples of this type of source are high-level steam vents.

For these sources the sound pressure level at a given distance from the source may be calculated from

$$SPL = SWL - 20 \log r - 11 \text{ dB} \tag{3.3}$$

where SPL is the sound pressure level (dB *re* 20 μbar) *r* metres from a source of sound power level SWL (dB *re* 10^{-12} W).

The second type is *hemispherical radiating sources*. These point sources are located close to a large, horizontal reflecting surface, usually the ground, and are hence constrained to radiate into a hemispherical region above that surface. Examples of this are low-level vents, control or pressure-reducing valves. For these sources the sound pressure level at a given distance from the source may be calculated from

$$SPL = SWL - 20 \log r - 8 \text{ dB} \tag{3.4}$$

where SPL is the sound pressure level (dB *re* 20 μbar) *r* metres from a source of sound power level SWL (dB *re* 10^{-12} W).

Finally there are *line sources*, where the sound, instead of radiating from a point source, radiates from a line source in a cylindrical or hemicylindrical manner. Examples of this are elevated pipelines (cylindrical radiation) or pipelines at ground level (hemicylindrical radiation). For elevated pipelines the sound pressure level at a given distance from the source may be calculated from equation (3.4).

For pipelines at ground level when the distance from the source to the point of interest is less than half the length of the line source, the following equation should be used:

$$SPL = SWL - 10 \log r - 5 \text{ dB} \tag{3.5}$$

where SPL is the sound pressure level (dB *re* 20 μbar) *r* metres from a source of sound power level SWL (dB *re* 10^{-12} W). For values of *r* equal to or greater than the length of the line source equation (3.4) should be used.

Directivity

If a sound source does not radiate uniformly in all directions but has marked directional characteristics then an additional term must be included in the foregoing equations.

Enhanced radiation in a particular direction can be allowed for by a simple decibel addition known as a directivity index (DI). This can be defined as

$$DI_\theta = SPL_\theta - SPL_{ave} \qquad (3.6)$$

where SPL_θ is the sound pressure level at a given distance from the source and at angle θ to the axis and SPL_{ave} is the space average sound pressure level (in dB) which would be produced at the same distance by a source that radiated the same amount of acoustic power uniformly in all directions.

Addition of sound levels

It is often necessary to combine the effects of sound from a number of sources. As the units involved are logarithmic ratios their summation is the logarithm of the sum of the antilogs of the various values. This operation can conveniently be carried out by using *Figure 3.8*. It will be noted from this figure that the addition of two equal sound levels increases the total by 3 dB and that for two sound levels more than 10 dB apart the lower sound level has no influence on the total level.

Sound insulation and absorption

When a sound wave strikes a solid barrier some energy will be transmitted through the barrier to be re-emitted on the other side. Some energy will be reflected from the incident side and a small proportion will be absorbed within the barrier material. The ability of the barrier material to resist the transmission of incident sound is referred to as the sound insulation of the material and is directly proportional to its superficial mass. This simple type of barrier acts by reflecting most of the sound energy incident upon it. Hence a barrier material of this type has little ability to absorb sound energy.

If however the sound wave strikes a material of high porosity and low superficial mass, little sound energy will be reflected from it. If the material is thick enough, considerable sound energy will be absorbed by conversion into heat owing to friction of the moving air within the pores of the material. However, because of the low superficial mass, sound energy will still pass through the material and be re-emitted. Thus although it is a good sound absorber it is not a good sound barrier.

By combining a good barrier material with a good absorbing material and presenting the absorbent face to the incident sound, the sound absorbent will minimize sound reflections from the face of the barrier material.

Noise hazard

Hearing conservation criteria

Continued long exposure to high noise levels can produce permanent damage to hearing. In the UK, such damage, if sustained as a result of lengthy employment (20 years) in certain specified industries, is now classified under the National Insurance (Industrial Injuries) Act 1965 as an industrial injury. Noise can also constitute a hazard within the meaning of the Health and Safety at Work etc. Act 1974.

Criteria for work area noise levels and exposure times are laid out in two government codes of practice [1,2]. The recommendations are a maximum exposure of 90 dB(A) for an 8-hour day and an energy-based system which halves the permitted exposure time for each 3 dB(A) increase in noise levels, i.e.

> 90 dB(A) for 8 hours
> 93 dB(A) for 4 hours
> 96 dB(A) for 2 hours

and so on.

In addition there are overriding limits laid down. These are that the unprotected ear should not be exposed to a sound pressure level in excess of 135 dB or an impulsive noise with an instantaneous sound pressure level of 150 dB. Other parts of the body should not be exposed to a sound pressure level in excess of 150 dB.

Other effects

Noise at levels below the hearing conservation criteria may induce stress or fatigue in some individuals. In addition it may also interfere with communication. No widely agreed data exist for noise level limits within this area. Employers in the UK have a general duty under the Health and Safety at Work Act to protect the welfare of the employee and this implies that none of the effects of noise should be ignored.

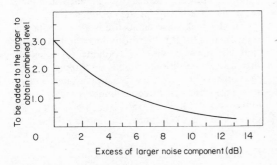

Figure 3.8   Decibel addition chart

Noise nuisance

In the workplace

Other than the general duty referred to above, there is no UK legislation covering noise nuisance in the workplace. However, experience suggests that noise levels of the order given in *Table 3.4* are appropriate for the situations listed. It should be noted that the noise levels quoted are for intrusive noise.

Table 3.4   Background noise levels (offices, etc.)

Type of surroundings	Noise level (db(A))
Control rooms	60
Drawing offices	55
General offices	55
Canteens	50
Private offices	45
Executive offices	40
Conference rooms	35

In the community

Noise at any level, particularly if it contains discrete frequency tones, may give rise to complaints from local residents. The Control of Pollution Act 1974 contains comprehensive provisions for the control of this type of noise within the UK. The implementation of the provisions of the Act is covered in a Department of the Environment circular[3]. Briefly, the controlling authorities have a statutory duty to inspect their area regularly for any noise nuisance which exists, or is likely to occur or recur. Complaints may also be made to the controlling authorities by persons affected. On receipt of such a complaint the controlling authority must carry out an investigation. If as a result of the investigation, or during the inspection referred to above, the controlling authority find such a nuisance they must take steps to secure the abatement of that nuisance. The steps taken may range from informal discussions with the noise producers to the serving on them of a statutory notice requiring the abatement of the nuisance or prohibiting its occurrence or recurrence. The legislation does not contain noise level limits and the decision as to what constitutes a nuisance level must be decided by the controlling authority taking account of local circumstances. Guidance is available in the form of a standard[4], BS 4142. The controlling authorities may also control the noise produced on construction and demolition sites and guidance[5] here is given by BS 5228. Finally the controlling authorities have the powers to create noise abatement zones within which it is an offence to exceed the registered noise levels for particular classes of premises. Details of noise abatement zone procedures are given in the Control of Pollution Act 1974 and various UK government publications[3, 6].

Noise control

Noise control should begin at the source of the noise. Noise should be designed out of any installation by using the lowest-noise-level machinery and layout available. Use may be made of building layout to screen noisy plant items from sensitive areas. Noise sources may be located below ground level and roofed over. Particularly noisy items that could present a potential hazard to hearing should be considered for isolation into structures substantial enough to contain the noise. Steps may then be taken to limit the access of personnel such that the acceptable noise dose under the Government codes[1, 2] is not exceeded. Provision of remote-reading instrumentation may be necessary in order to monitor machinery performance without entering the noisy area.

For large-scale noisy areas, for example turbine halls, it may be appropriate to group the instrumentation into a suitable enclosure within the area. By this means the operators can supervise the area from within the enclosure. It is not proposed to cover the detailed design of enclosures. A British Standard Code of Practice CP 3 is a useful starting point[7]. Proprietary enclosures are also available. The main features of any enclosure must be the provision of adequate sound insulation in the structure and the absence of sound leakage paths. Such leakages can occur through ventilation openings, windows, ill-fitting doors and cable or pipe access points. They can be overcome by fitting suitable silencers to ventilation openings and providing acoustic double glazing[7] (i.e. minimum spacing between panes of 100 mm) and air-lock-type entrances with well-fitting doors and seals. Careful attention must be paid to sealing points where pipes and cables pass into enclosures. One way of achieving a good seal is by running pipes and cables into the enclosure via a sand-filled trench under the enclosure wall.

An efficient noise enclosure is also an efficient heat enclosure. It is therefore important to ensure that adequate cooling is available for enclosed machinery. Additional means of cooling lubrication oil may be necessary, possibly located outside the enclosure. If forced-draught air cooling is employed within or into the enclosure, the possible noise from the ventilation fan should not be overlooked.

Discharges to atmosphere

In order to decide upon appropriate silencing of

atmospheric discharges it is necessary to estimate the noise produced by the discharge.

The following equation[8] will give an approximate value for the sound power level of a free jet:

$$SWL = 60 \log v + 20 \log d + 20 \log \left(\frac{P_1}{P_2}\right) - 4 \text{ dB}$$

$$(3.7)$$

where SWL is the sound power level (dB *re* 10^{-12} W), v is the jet velocity (m/s), d is the jet diameter (m), P_1 is the density of jet fluid (kg/m³) and P_2 is the density of receiving fluid. The sound power spectrum will have a peak frequency given by

$$f_0 = 0.3\frac{v}{d}$$

$$(3.8)$$

where f_0 is the peak frequency (Hz), v is the jet velocity (m/s) and d is the jet diameter (m). Individual octave band sound power levels may be deduced from *Figure 3.9*, the ordinate is the correction to overall sound power level and the abscissa is the ratio of the octave band centre frequency to the peak frequency as calculated by equation (3.8).

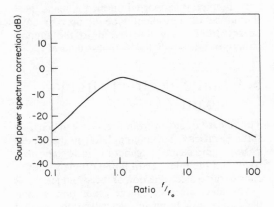

Figure 3.9   Jet spectrum

It should be noted that the above method of calculating jet sound power levels gives only an approximate result ($\pm$ 5 dB).

Jet noise exhibits pronounced directivity and when calculating the sound pressure level at a given point in relation to the jet, allowance must be made for this effect. *Figure 3.10* gives the value of directivity index for an atmospheric jet in terms of the angle between the jet axis and the point of interest.

Thus to calculate the sound pressure level at distance r metres and angle $\theta°$ to the jet, equation (3.3) becomes

$$SPL = SWL - 20 \log r - 11 + DI_\theta$$

$$(3.9)$$

Noise reduction of jets can be achieved by velocity reduction, absorption or a combination of the two.

A method[9] sometimes quoted for reducing the velocity of steam jets is the injection of cold water

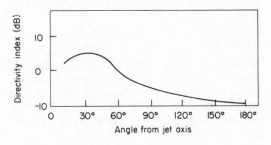

Figure 3.10   Jet directivity

just before the jet orifice. This has the effect of increasing the steam density, by condensation, and hence reducing the jet velocity for a given mass flow, providing the quantity of injected water is small.

Absorption silencers of various types are commercially available. These can be simple cylinders, lined with acoustic absorbent, of a diameter sufficient to give an acceptable exit velocity and of sufficient length to prevent direct sound radiation at angles in excess of 10° on either side of the jet axis. Alternatively a flow diffusion device, for example a perforated pipe with closed end, may be fitted with an absorbent-lined shield. This has the effect of shortening the overall length of the silencer.

In order to prevent the possibility of excessive pressure drop being generated by the perforated pipe it is usual to make the free area of the perforation at least 1½ times the cross-sectional area of the pipe. In addition, although the perforations should be small (*ca.* 5 mm diam.) the possibility of blockage by pipe scale, etc. should not be overlooked. Alternatively slits may be used in place of holes.

Acoustic absorbents are porous and when used on steam duty any condensation that occurs within them will seriously reduce their efficiency. It is therefore important that provision is made within the silencer to allow condensate to drain away. High flow velocities can exist within vent silencers and this can lead to loss of absorbent from the silencer or compaction of the absorbent, thereby reducing its acoustic efficiency. Silencers should therefore contain adequate provision to prevent these occurrences.

Safety valves

Silencers on safety valves, because of their position and the few occasions on which they come into service, should be inspected frequently. They are liable to suffer unnoticed corrosion and possible collapse of internal structures resulting in blockages that prevent the operation of the safety device.

Steam traps

Steam traps are unlikely to give rise to hazardous noise levels but because of the sporadic occurrence of noise considerable community nuisance can occur. The noise can be minimized by drilling perforations in the end of the discharge pipe and submerging the perforations in water.

Steam leaks

Steam leaks can give rise to noise levels which could pose a hearing hazard as well as a possible source of community nuisance.

As a temporary solution, until the leak can be repaired it may be covered with a suitable bandage made of a glass-fibre-filled glass-cloth stocking. These are commercially available or may be improvised. They reduce the noise level but do not reduce the actual leak and hence have a limited life owing to erosion of the bandage by the escaping steam.

Pressure control and reduction valves

Pressure-reduction valves and control valves on steam duty can give rise to high noise levels, 100 dB(A) and above. The noise is generated by the high-velocity jet conditions that occur just downstream of the valve, particularly if sonic flow conditions occur through the valve orifice.

When considering the purchase of reduction or control valves it is important to discuss the question of noise with the potential supplier. The leading valve manufacturers have been active for some time in the area of noise prediction and control for their products. Hence valves with noise-reduced characteristics are now available although in some cases at considerable extra cost. Broadly speaking they rely upon breaking up the single flow path through the valve into a series of multiple paths to reduce the noise generation of the flow.

For relatively simple situations it is possible to achieve a similar effect by means of a perforated pipe fitted directly downstream of the valve, within the pipeline, the dimensions of the perforated pipe being similar to those described above for atmospheric vent noise reduction.

It is worth noting that both multiple-path valves and the perforated pipe system are liable to blockage if pipe scale, etc. is present in the system.

Pipeline noise

Noise generated within a piping system by, for example, a pressure-reduction valve, will travel along the pipe and radiate from the pipe surface. This noise can be controlled by lagging of the pipework and possibly the noise-producing item as well. Normally steam piping will carry a thermal insulation which will help to contain the noise, whilst at the same time acting as thermal insulation.

Such a treatment would consist of a layer of a minimum 50 mm thick mineral wool or other acoustic absorbent, suitable for the pipe surface temperature, covered with an outer skin of metal (aluminium or lead sheet for example) or a cement coating. This outer skin should have a superficial weight of the order of 10–15 kg/m². It should not be applied so tightly as to compress the acoustic absorbent and nullify its acoustic properties. In addition, rigid contact between the outer skin and the pipe should be avoided.

If the pipe is supported on pipe hangers these should be of a resilient type to prevent noise energy from being transferred to the support structure and re-radiated by that structure.

3.3 Static electricity from steam

The release of steam from pressure can generate static electricity. Steam completely in the vapour phase — 'dry steam' — generates little static electricity but the presence of liquid droplets leads to considerable electrification of the steam jet.

The mechanism of charge generation is complex. In general terms the electrification is caused by the movement of droplets in the pipe and by the separation of positive and negative electric charge as each droplet breaks away from the orifice through which the steam is being released. *Figure 3.11* shows a simple model of the process. Immediately prior to a droplet disengaging, the positive and negative charges separate or polarize under the influence of the electric field around the orifice and the droplets carry an excess of charge of one polarity away in the steam jet. The polarity and magnitude of the charge depend on the size and concentration of the droplets entrained with the steam. The process is essentially one of polarization and the presence of impurities — particularly ionic material — can therefore affect both the magnitude and polarity of the electrostatic charge.

Electrification of steam jets is of practical importance in the presence of explosives, flammable

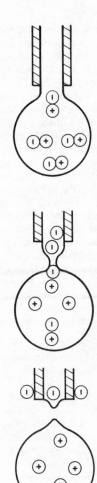

Figure 3.11   Charge separation during droplet formation (schematic)

vapours, gases or dust clouds where the release of electrostatic discharges could ignite the material or atmosphere. For example, an explosion during the injection of steam into a tank containing naphtha to assist cleaning has been attributed to static electricity. The ignition source was a spark discharge from a metal wire on the transfer hose that had become insulated from earth and had collected static electricity generated by the steam jets.

The movement of positively or negatively charged droplets on a jet of steam is analogous to an electric current and has associated with it electric fields and potentials. Electric discharges can originate from a conductor (e.g. metal) insulated from earth onto which the charge transfers from the jet or steam cloud or can be released directly from the dispersed cloud or mist of steam.

Electrification and discharges from conductors

Electrically the separation of the positive and negative charges at the orifice can be considered as the generation of two currents of equal magnitude but opposite polarity, one passing to the orifice surrounding material and the other being carried forward by the steam jet.

If the orifice material has a low electrical resistance to earth (e.g. a hole in a metal pipe) then the charge dissipates quickly to earth. An orifice with a high resistance to earth (e.g. metal nozzle at the end of a rubber hose) retains and accumulates charge and its electric potential increases.

Other conductors in the system can also become charged and attain high voltages. If the steam jet impinges onto a metal object the droplets transfer all or part of their charge to it. Contact between the conductor and steam is not essential for electrification of the former. Objects in the vicinity of the steam can become charged by electrostatic induction.

In the former situation the charge transferred to the conductor depends on the proportion of droplets striking it and in the latter situation it depends on the electric field strength around the conductor and steam.

Metal plant (e.g. pipes, drums, metal cladding on heat insulation) is, in electrical terms, a capacitance and resistance connected to earth, since any electrical inductance is small compared with the capacitance. A conductor receiving a charge from a steam jet has the equivalent electric circuit shown in *Figure 3.12*. The charging current I_c increases the potential V on the object until the current I_L dissipating the charge to earth through the resistance R is equal to the charging current. The maximum potential V_m developed on the metal object is given by

$$V_m = I_c R \tag{3.10}$$

If the electrical capacitance is C, then the maximum energy E_m associated with the metal object is given by

$$E_m = 0.5CV_m^2 = 0.5CI_c^2R^2 \tag{3.11}$$

Typical values of I_c obtained by the release of wet steam through an orifice or nozzle lie in the range 10^{-5}–10^{-7} A. The capacitance of metal plant is a function of its design and location but typical values are in the range 10–500 pF.

For a discharge to occur the potential of the conductor must be raised to 100–1000 V by the retention of the charge. Equation (3.10) indicates that this condition cannot be satisfied if R is less than 10^7–10^8 Ω. If, however, R exceeds this value then a hazardous situation would arise should the maximum energy stored on the conductor be

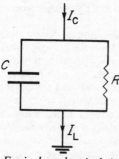

Figure 3.12   Equivalent electrical circuit: electrostatically charged conductor. I_c, charging current in steam jet; R, resistance to earth; I_L, leakage current to earth; C, capacitance of conductor greater than the energy required to ignite the flammable material near the conductor. Typical values for minimum spark ignition energies are:

Explosives (sensitive detonators): 0.001–0.1 mJ

Gases/vapours in air: 0.01–0.2 mJ

Organic dust clouds: 1–5000 mJ

By application of equation (3.11) the risk in any situation can be evaluated. Using typical values: I_c = 10^{-6} A, $C = 100$ pF, $R = 10^{10}$ Ω (resistance through a layer of paint or corrosion), then the energy is 5 mJ, and this energy could ignite a range of flammable atmospheres. The value of R can be several orders of magnitude greater than 10^{10} Ω (e.g. metal insulated by plastic) and the available energy would be correspondingly increased.

The naphtha explosion described above is typical of the hazard that may be present if the metal nozzle or wire reinforcement on a rubber transfer line is insulated from earth. A not uncommon incident is one in which the steam escaping from a pipeline charges the metal cladding covering the electrically non-conducting heat insulation material around the pipe and produces electric discharges from the cladding to a nearby earthed metal support. Such discharges have ignited flammable liquids in the vicinity of the steam leak and also caused fires in oil-soaked lagging. Elimination of this hazard can be achieved by earthing all conductors where steam may be ejected accidentally or intentionally in the presence of explosives or flammable atmospheres. In principle, discharges will not occur if the resistance to earth is less than 10^6–10^8 Ω. For practical reasons however (e.g. ease of earth monitoring), many industries prescribe a resistance to earth of 10–100 Ω. In the selection of a safe earth resistance the earthing requirements for electrical supplies, lightning and cathodic protective systems should be considered.

Electrification and discharges from personnel

A human being is essentially an electrical conductor and, if insulated from earth, can accumulate electrostatic charge when coming into contact with or passing near a steam cloud. Plant operatives electrostatically charged in this manner have received electric shocks when approaching earthed objects such as handrails.

Men wearing footwear with non-leather synthetic soles and heels can have a high resistance to earth (10^{10}–10^{14} Ω) and have attained potentials greater than 20–30 kV from electrified steam jets. The electrical capacitance of a human being is 100–300 pF and hence any resultant discharge can attain energies of the order of 100 mJ. Such discharges can not only ignite flammable gases, vapours and sensitive dusts but can also cause physiological shock. Although such shocks are not fatal to a normal person, involuntary muscular reaction can occur and result in a secondary accident (e.g. fall from a ladder).

Both the ignition and physiological shock risks can be avoided if personnel are earthed by the use of anti-static or conductive footwear.

Electrification and discharges from steam clouds

When steam is released it disperses to form a cloud either unconfined in the atmosphere or contained within a closed volume (e.g. steam cleaning of tanks).

At high levels of steam jet electrification the charge density within the cloud may be such that the associated field strength exceeds the value required to cause electrical breakdown of the atmosphere and discharges occur within the cloud. Discharges of this type have been observed but their ability to ignite flammable atmospheres has not been established. Two factors can combine to minimize the risk of ignition. First, the discharges are of the corona or brush type. The energy density in these discharges is less than that in the spark discharge obtained from conductors and during the release of equal amounts of energy the former are less incendive. The second factor is the reduction in the flammability of the atmosphere that may occur on the injection of the steam. This inerting action cannot be regarded as a means of always ensuring inherent safety because, in the incidents where electrostatically charged conductors initiated the explosion, the steam was present in the tanks.

The hazard associated with electrostatically charged steam clouds is relevant during the steam cleaning of vessels containing flammable atmospheres. Experience to date indicates that, although discharges have been observed in highly charged steam clouds, an ignition is unlikely to occur provided all conductors are earthed. An essential requirement for safety during steam cleaning is the earthing of the injection equipment (e.g. metal nozzles, wire reinforcement in hoses, etc.) and all metal plant. Personnel should be earthed by the use of anti-static or conducting footwear. In situations where the steam condenses or water is sprayed into the vessel (e.g. using a combination of steam and water washing), slugs of water falling from the top of the vessel through the electrostatically charged steam cloud can become electrified and release incendive spark discharges similar to those from metal items. Conventional earthing techniques do not prevent the accumulation of charge on this form of conductor.

For inherent safety in steam cleaning, the flammable atmosphere should be removed prior to the start of the operation. In practice, however, the disturbance of residues at the bottom or on the walls of a tank, can re-establish a flammable atmosphere. To minimize the risk of electrostatic ignition therefore, not only should all conductors be earthed, but dry steam should be used to maintain electrification at low levels.

In electrostatic phenomena associated with steam the important factors may be summarized as follows:

1. Dry steam produces low and hence generally non-hazardous levels of electrification.
2. Wet steam or steam entraining water droplets produces a high rate of charge generation with currents in the range $10^{-5} - 10^{-7}$ A.
3. This electrification can lead to an ignition risk in the presence of explosives, flammable gas, vapours and certain dust clouds.
4. The risk can be virtually eliminated by the earthing of all conductors (metal plant and personnel) and, wherever possible, the use of dry steam.

References and further reading

1　Department of Employment. 'Code of Practice for reducing the exposure of employed persons to noise' (1972)
2　Department of Trade. 'Code of Practice for noise level in ships' (1978)
3　Department of the Environment circular 2/76. Control of Pollution Act 1974. Implementation of Part III – Noise
4　British Standards Institution. *British Standard* 4142:1967 amended 1975. 'Method of rating industrial noise affecting mixed residential and industrial areas'
5　British Standards Institution. *British Standard* 5228:1975. 'Code of Practice for noise control on construction and demolition sites'
6　Department of the Environment booklet. 'Noise abatement zone enquiries, what you need to know'
7　British Standards Institution. *British Standard Code of Practice CP 3.* Chapter III Part 2 1972. 'Sound insulation and noise reduction'
8　Erskine, J.B. *Proc. Brit. Acoust. Soc.* **1** (3), Paper 72 AE 11 (1972)
9　Sharland, I. *Woods' Practical Guide to Noise Control,* p 143. Colchester: Woods (1972)
10　Haase, H. *Electrostatic Hazards: Their Evaluation and Control.* Weinheim and New York: Verlag Chemie (1977)
11　Handley, W. (Ed.) *Industrial Safety Handbook.* London: McGraw-Hill (1977)

4   Shell boilers

4.1 Introduction

This book is concerned with steam, and the subject of shell boilers will be dealt with in the context of those factors which affect the quality, reliability and efficiency of the generation of steam in shell boilers. For detailed description of shell boilers, their components, controls, installation and operation, the reader is referred to the instruction manuals of the makers, many such works being textbooks in themselves.

Shell boilers may be defined as those boilers in which the heat transfer surfaces are all contained within the steam/water drum or 'shell'. In some countries they are referred to as *firetube* boilers, because the products of combustion of the fuel pass through tubes forming the heat transfer surfaces. This distinguishes them from *watertube* boilers in which the steam and water are contained in tubes over which the products of combustion pass. Both types of boiler have their special fields of application, shell mainly for process steam and space heating, watertube for large-scale power production; rarely do these overlap.

Shell boilers are generally much less costly than watertube, by a factor of two or three according to size and specification, but they are limited to transportable dimensions, around 4.27 m diameter in the UK, equivalent to an evaporation of 8 kg/s steam. Because cylinders of large diameter are involved, particularly the furnaces, which are subject to external pressure, the working pressures of shell boilers are limited to about 24 bar, but pressures much less than this satisfy most process needs. Small shell boilers, and certain types of unfired waste-heat boiler, can however be designed for much higher pressures, but such cases are rare.

There is no inherent difference between the efficiencies obtainable from shell and watertube boilers, the basic efficiency in both cases being around 80% of the gross calorific value of the fuel. The actual efficiency obtained will depend on the fuel used, the operating conditions, and whether or not supplementary heating surfaces in the form of economizers and air preheaters are used, which is at present unusual with shell boilers.

4.2 The recent evolution of shell boilers

Until the early 1950s, coal was the basic industrial fuel in many countries, and boilers were naturally designed for this fuel. World War II made severe demands on industry, and in particular coal became scarce and expensive.

The then Ministry of Fuel and Power sponsored a team of experts in a visit to the USA to study fuel utilization in that country. In the team's published report[1], attention was drawn to a new concept in shell boilers, namely the *package* boiler. This was essentially a multitubular shell boiler mounted on a box frame complete with accessories such as combustion appliances, control panel, feed pump, etc., the whole being factory-assembled and easily transportable. All that needed to be done on-site was to connect the boiler to the services, and it could be commissioned immediately.

The fuel used was oil, which had not been extensively used as a boiler fuel in Europe. The rising cost of coal made oil an attractive alternative, not only in price, but also in convenience, cleanliness and the ability to operate automatically, thus greatly reducing boilerhouse labour. Ground space occupied was also much less. At first, package boilers were resisted by both manufacturers and users, but have now replaced the traditional Lancashire and Economic boilers which were basically intended for coal firing.

The change to package boilers has resulted in considerable savings in space and installation cost, also in improved efficiency and running costs. Problems with package boilers have arisen however, and some of these, together with the solutions that have evolved, will now be discussed.

4.3 The process and problems of the generation of steam in shell boilers

Table 4.1 compares some of the dimensions and the performance parameters which derive therefrom, of modern package boilers and the older

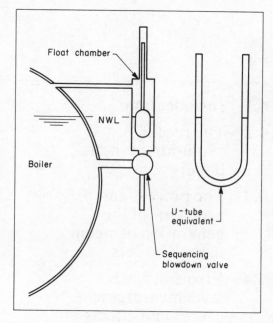

Figure 4.1   External float chamber for measuring and controlling the water level in a boiler, connected via a steam leg and water leg with sequencing blowdown valve. The setup is analogous to a ∪-tube

traditional coal-based boilers. It will be seen that for the same steam output modern boilers are considerably smaller than the older types. One consequence of this is that the rate of steam release from the water surface has almost doubled; in terms of steam quality and boiler control this can create certain difficulties which, however, can be overcome when approached correctly. These difficulties, and their solution, will now be examined in some detail.

The function of a steam boiler is reliably to deliver dry steam, not a mixture of steam and water, to the process. Modern boilers are fully automatic in operation; on receiving a signal, which may be initiated from a fall in boiler pressure or from a time clock, the burner will perform a series of safety checks, ignite at low fire, and, if the signal calls for it, modulate to high fire. The

Table 4.1   Dimensions and performance parameters of various types of boiler

Boiler type	Fuel	Length (m)	Diameter (m)	Rating (kg/s steam)	Efficiency (% of gross CV)	Volumetric heat release rate (kW/m³)	Steam release rate on water surface (kg/m²s)
Lancashire	Coal	9.0	2.75	1.5	74	0.342	0.075
Economic	Coal	6.0	3	1.5	76	0.734	0.127
Modern (package)	Oil	3.9	2.5	1.5	82	2.33	0.213

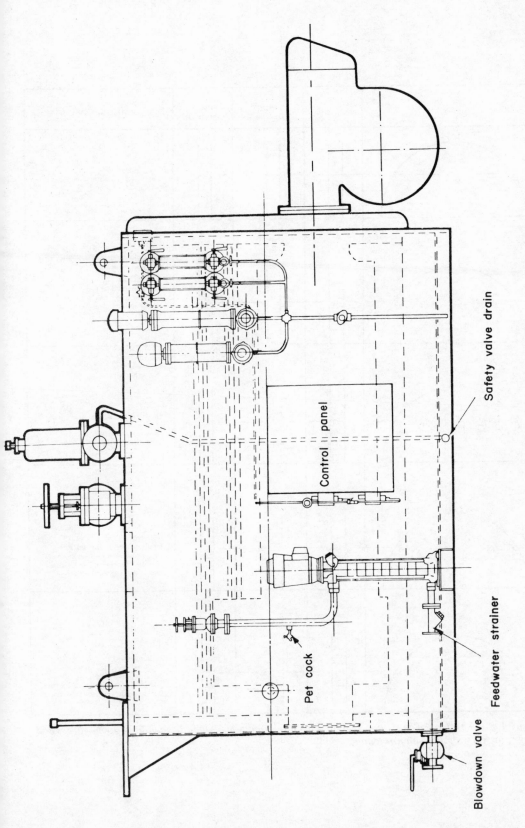

Safety valve drain

Control panel

Pet cock

Feedwater strainer

Blowdown valve

Figure 4.2   Float chamber and gauge glasses mounted at the side of a boiler. (Courtesy of NEI Thompson Cochran Ltd)

54

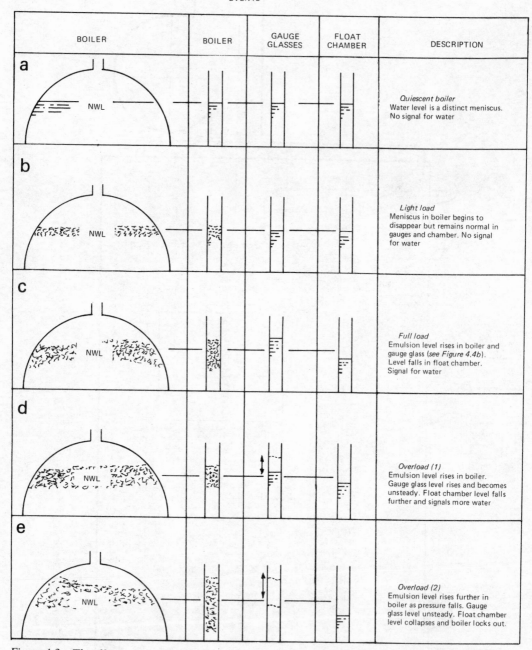

Figure 4.3   *The effects of increasing load on water level conditions and the behaviour of float switches and gauge glasses, without foam formation*

EVENTS

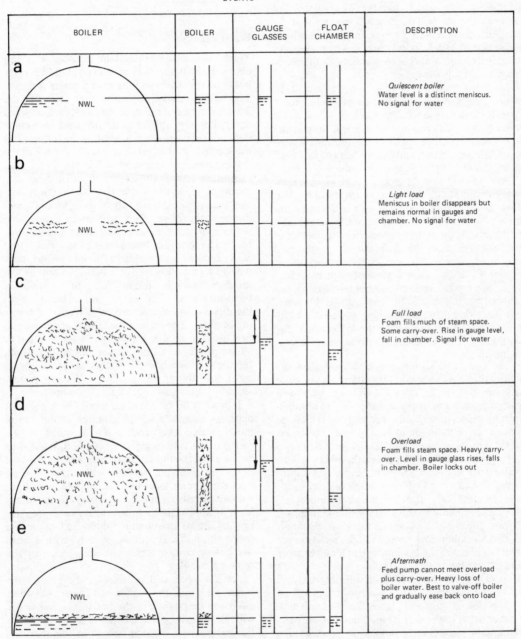

Figure 4.4   The effects of increasing load on water level conditions and the behaviour of float switches and gauge glasses, with foam formation

water level is continuously measured by a float, the movement of which activates a switch or transducer to signal the feedwater system for more or less water according to need. The float is generally contained in a small chamber external to and mounted on the boiler, although in certain of the smaller boilers it is likely to be inside the shell. In some countries, electrical conductivity probes are used instead of floats but their functions and problems are largely the same.

Most boilers are now only partly attended, in which case a second float is used as a mandatory[2] overriding safety device to warn of a low-water condition which could be dangerous. Should the low-water condition persist, the burner is automatically locked out, and cannot be restarted until the water level in the boiler is restored.

An external float chamber is shown diagrammatically in *Figure 4.1,* from which it will be seen that the hydraulic system is like a U-tube, one limb of which is the static head of the water in the boiler above the bottom connection between the boiler and the float chamber, the other limb being the head of water in the float chamber itself. *Figure 4.2* is an external view of float chambers fitted to a typical package boiler. Provided that the density of the water in the two limbs is the same, and that there are no interfering water velocity effects at the connection to the boiler shell, the liquid level will be the same in the float chamber as in the boiler.

The two qualifications made above are important in that if there are density differences or velocity effects, then the float will no longer provide a true measurement of boiler water level. The qualifications also apply to the readings of the gauge glasses. If, as is likely to be the case, the boiler water density is lower than that in the float chamber the level of water in the float chamber will be depressed, and the float will give a premature signal. If there is a high circulation velocity in the boiler water local to the float chamber connection, the static pressure in this locality will be reduced, in turn lowering the level in the float chamber. Both effects therefore result in a false indication of water content of the boiler, both in float chamber and gauge glasses.

At first sight it may appear that floats which are inside the boiler are not subject to this problem. This is not so, however, since the float will sink further in the lower-density medium because of its reduced buoyancy. If the float is in a region of high upward or downward circulation in the boiler, its indication of the water level will be correspondingly affected.

4.4 Errors in water level measurement: causes and effects

Water density

When steam is produced in a boiler it is first evolved well below the water level, at the interface between the water and the heat transfer surfaces. The bubbles may live long enough to rise to the water surface and burst, or they may be short-lived and collapse near their point of formation; much depends on the water temperature and pressure in the vicinity. As heated water rises in the boiler the static pressure is reduced and if the water is at saturation temperature some of it will flash into steam bubbles; the higher they are in the boiler, the greater the rate of ebullition. At any given moment therefore, there will be an appreciable volume of steam beneath the water surface, displacing a mixture of steam bubbles and water, that is, an emulsion, upwards in the shell. Thus there will be a gradation of water density, great at low levels in the boiler and much less in the region of the water level. The water level in fact loses its identity as a meniscus, becoming a mass of bursting bubbles. The greater the rate of steam generation and the smaller the ratio of water content to steam production, the greater will be the effect, the new generation of boilers obviously being more sensitive to the condition than the dimensionally larger Lancashires and Economics.

In what follows, the water level, which does not exist, as such, in a steaming boiler, will be designated 'water level' and in the diagrams will be called the 'NWL' (normal water level). It will thus be seen that the fluid in a working boiler consists of dense water at the bottom, where there are no heat transfer surfaces to cause bubble formation, with an increasing bubble population as the 'water level' is approached. At the 'water level', separation of steam and water occurs, and the steam space should be full of steam only, with a small suspension of droplets which are ejected by the bursting bubbles.

As has been said previously, the greater the steam demand, the higher will the steam–water emulsion be pushed in the boiler, the less dense will the mixture be in the upper regions, and hence the greater the error in the float chamber and gauge glass indications.

Figure 4.3 shows how this effect progresses from zero load to overload. It will be seen that the behaviour of the level in the gauge glasses differs from that in the float chamber, the level rising in the gauge glasses with increasing load but falling in the float chambers. This is because the gauge

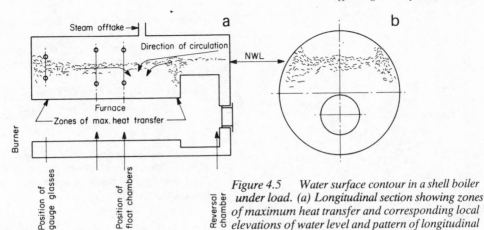

Figure 4.5 *Water surface contour in a shell boiler under load. (a) Longitudinal section showing zones of maximum heat transfer and corresponding local elevations of water level and pattern of longitudinal circulation. (b) Inside view of the front end of a boiler showing heaped steam/water emulsion in the corners*

glasses are placed somewhat differently in the boiler than they are in the float chamber. To be seen they need to be at the front end, where, as will be explained later, there is a powerful upward flow of emulsion, whereas the float chambers which do not need to be seen can be placed elsewhere on the boiler shell where the flow pattern is different. The gauge glass fittings also contain small orifices to limit the discharge of steam in the event of a broken glass; this results in the pressure in the gauge glass being slightly less than the steam pressure in the boiler because there is a steam flow into gauge glass caused by condensation. Gauge glasses are mounted in pairs; one will be in a cooler region than the other and will condense more steam, thus increasing the pressure loss across the orifice. The level in this gauge glass will therefore be higher than that in the other, the difference commonly being 10–15 mm. The events described in *Figure 4.3* are greatly amplified if there are any substances in the boiler water which cause foam formation. *Figure 4.4* shows the effects, which are by no means uncommon.

The main cause of the difference between gauge glass and float chamber levels is shown in *Figure 4.5*. Actual operating boilers have been fitted with quartz windows and the steam spaces illuminated internally, the behaviour of the 'water level' being visually observed and recorded on film[3]. In the case of a horizontal package boiler operating at a full load of 0.56 kg/s steam at 7.0 bar pressure, there were strong upward currents of water rising some 200 mm above the average 'water level' in the boiler. These occurred in the front corners of the boiler where the gauge glasses are normally fitted! As shown in *Figures 4.2* and *4.5*, the float chambers are fitted a little way along the shell from this disturbed region, and may often be in the trough following the peak level although this was

not visible in the experiments.

It will be seen therefore that neither the gauge glasses nor the float chambers provide a true measurement of the quantity of water in the boiler. This can lead to the inconvenient occurrence shown in *Figure 4.3e*; a low 'water level' can be measured by the float, low enough to signal burner lock-out, whereas the gauge glass reading contradicts this!

The causes of low water density

The main cause of low water density has been shown to be the release of steam bubbles below and in the 'water level'. Modern package boilers, operated within their load range, and with correct water conditions, are unlikely to suffer the problems already discussed. If, however, the pressure in a boiler working at or near its full load is for any reason suddenly reduced, trouble can ensue.

A reduction in pressure has a twofold effect. First, the volumes of individual steam bubbles are increased, thus lifting the 'water level', decreasing the water density and amplifying the effect shown in *Figure 4.3d*. Secondly, the water in the boiler is at or near saturation temperature; much of it will flash into steam forming more large bubbles and a great increase in the volume of emulsion in the boiler, still further aggravating the condition shown in *Figure 4.3d* and bringing it to the situation in *Figure 4.3e*. In simple words the boiler primes over.

4.5 Factors affecting boiler pressure

The maximum steam output from a boiler at a given pressure is governed by the rate at which heat can be supplied to and transferred in the

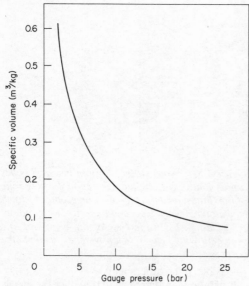

Figure 4.6   The relationship between specific volume and pressure of steam. Note the sharp rise in volume as the pressure falls below about 6 bar

boiler. If the steam demand, from any cause, exceeds this the pressure will fall, and if the reduction is sufficient, the events described above will take place. *Figure 4.6* shows the relationship between the specific volume and pressure of steam. It will be seen that down to a pressure of about 6.5 bar the rate of increase in steam volume with respect to falling pressure is relatively small, but below this pressure the volume rises rapidly. Anything which can cause the boiler pressure to fall below about 6 bar will cause the emulsion level to rise, the float switches to fall, the burner to lock out, and boiling over of the boiler. Such causes include:

1. Cessation of firing resulting from failure of the fuel or air supply or from a component fault.
2. Overload due to excess demands for steam, such as an unscheduled steam user being connected, the failure of another boiler, an incorrect design of steam header, the erratic operation of non-return valves, or to a fracture in the steam distribution system.

Cessation of firing

Cessation of firing could be due to an interruption of the fuel or electricity supply or to an incorrect signal from the flame-failure device on the burner. If the boiler is on full load at the time, the demand of steam can be satisfied only by a fall in boiler pressure. For example, consider a boiler delivering 3 kg/s of steam at 7 bar pressure. Let the water content of the boiler be 20 000 kg and study the conditions after firing has ceased, assuming that the steam demand remains constant at 3 kg/s, neglecting the heat content of the steam, as such, in the boiler:

Initial heat content of boiler water

$$= \text{mass} \times \text{sensible heat at 7 bar}$$
$$= 20\ 000 \times 721.4 \text{ kJ}$$
$$= 14.428 \times 10^6 \text{ kJ}$$

If the burner has locked out it will take about four minutes, after manual resetting, to re-establish full firing rate, during which time the boiler will have lost approximately

$$3 \times 60 \times 4 = 720 \text{ kg of steam}$$

The latent heat to evaporate this amount of steam from the boiler water will be supplied from the sensible heat content of this water.

Latent heat required $= 720 \times 2047.7 \text{ kJ}$
$$= 1.4743 \times 10^6 \text{ kJ}$$

The remaining sensible heat in the boiler water will be

$$(14.428 - 1.4743) \times 10^6 \text{ kJ} = 12.9537 \times 10^6 \text{ kJ}$$

This is equivalent to

$$\frac{12.9537 \times 10^6}{20\ 000 - 720} \text{ kJ/kg} = 671.9 \text{ kJ/kg}$$

This corresponds to a pressure of 5.0 bar, which from *Figure 4.6* is well into the range where boiler instability and carryover will occur. Had the initial pressure been higher, the final pressure would also have been higher, perhaps above the danger level. Most shell boilers are designed for a working pressure at least slightly over 10 bar so that there is everything to be said for operating the boiler up to its pressure limit, and if need be, using a reducing set after the boiler to adjust the pressure to the requirements of the process. The figure of 7 bar was chosen because it is a very common one for operating shell boilers, but users would be well recommended to consider 10 bar instead, which gives more latitude.

The calculation carried out above is approximate, being based for the sake of clarity on a step-change of conditions, whereas in reality the change is continuous. Over the small period of time used, the error is small.

Overload

If the demand for steam exceeds the rate of heat transfer in the boiler the pressure will fall, and if the fall is sufficient, carryover and instability will result. The more obvious causes of overload — excess user plant on-line, failure of another boiler, a gross leakage from the distribution system — will not be discussed, attention being focused on steam

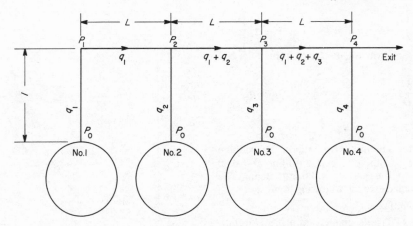

Figure 4.7   Interconnection of four boilers by a steam header. This method is incorrect (see text) *for more than two boilers. Correct methods are shown in Figures 4.9a and 4.9b*

header design, non-return valves and the rate of increase of steam load. It is interesting to note that most package boilers have a modest overload capacity of about 5%.

Steam header design

Shell boilers are made in capacities up to about 8 kg/s of steam. When loads in excess of this are needed two or more boilers are connected in parallel, installation of four or more boilers being not uncommon. The design of the interconnecting steam header is highly important.

Figure 4.7 illustrates a common method of connecting four boilers, a method that is frequently a source of trouble. It will be seen that the outlet from the header is adjacent to boiler No. 4 and remote from boiler No. 1. The operational problem is that boiler No. 4 tends to become overloaded whilst No. 1 rarely delivers its full load. The explanation of this effect is as follows:

Let all the boilers be set to operate at pressure P_0
Let P_1, P_2, P_3 and P_4 be the pressures at their points of connection into the steam header
Let D be the bore of the header, uniform throughout
Let d be the bore of each boiler connection
Let l be the length of each boiler connection
Let L be the length between boiler connections in the header
Let q_1, q_2, q_3 and q_4 be the discharge rates from each boiler

A simple pressure loss formula is

$$\Delta P = \frac{kQ^2L}{D^5} \quad \text{or} \quad Q = \frac{(D^5\,\Delta P)^{1/2}}{kL} \qquad (4.1)$$

where ΔP is the pressure difference between points, Q is the mass flow of the steam, L is the length of pipe, D is the pipe bore, k is a constant

incorporating the acceleration due to gravity, friction factor and steam density. It is not necessary to evaluate k in the following calculation, because it cancels. Applying the formula to the system shown in *Figure 4.7*,

$$P_0 - P_1 = \frac{kl}{d^5}q_1^2 \qquad (4.2)$$

$$P_1 - P_2 = \frac{kL}{D^5}q_1^2 \qquad (4.3)$$

$$P_0 - P_2 = kq_1^2\left(\frac{l}{d^5} + \frac{L}{D^5}\right) \qquad (4.4)$$

Pressure P_2 is lower than P_1, hence there will be a greater pressure difference between boiler No. 2 and the header, than for boiler No. 1 and the header. Boiler No. 2 will therefore discharge more steam, the rate of discharge being

$$q_2 = \left[\frac{d^5}{kl}(P_0 - P_2)\right]^{1/2}$$

$$= \left[\frac{d^5}{kl}kq_1^2\left(\frac{l}{d^5} + \frac{L}{D^5}\right)\right]^{1/2} \qquad (4.5)$$

As will be shown later, the increase in discharge from boiler No. 2 compared with No. 1 is quite small, less than 1%, but the increase becomes progressively greater along the header. The flow between P_2 and P_3 will now be augmented by q_2, which is slightly greater than q_1:

$$P_2 - P_3 = \frac{kl}{D^5}(q_1 + q_2)^2$$

$$P_0 - P_2 = kq_1^2\left(\frac{l}{d^5} + \frac{L}{D^5}\right) \qquad (4.6)$$

$$P_0 - P_3 = \frac{kL}{D^5}(q_1 + q_2)^2 + kq_1^2\left(\frac{l}{d^5} + \frac{L}{D^5}\right)$$

This pressure difference controls the steam discharge from boiler No. 3 as follows:

$$q_3 = \left[\frac{d^5}{kl}\left\{\frac{kL}{D^5}(q_1 + q_2)^2 + kq_1{}^2\left(\frac{l}{d^5} + \frac{L}{D^5}\right)\right\}\right]^{1/2} (4.7)$$

and in the same way the discharge from boiler No. 4 will be

$$q_4 = \left[\frac{d^5}{kl}\left\{\frac{kL}{D^5}(q_1 + q_2 + q_3)^2 + \frac{kl}{D^5}(q_1 + q_2)^2 + kq_1{}^2\left(\frac{l}{d^5} + \frac{L}{D^5}\right)\right\}\right]^{1/2} (4.8)$$

and so on for any number of boilers. To examine the effect quantitatively, let $d = 0.14$ m, $D = 0.30$ m, $l = L = 8.0$ m and $q_1 = 3.0$ kg/s steam. The above formulae give the following figures:

$q_1 = 3.0$ kg/s

$q_2 = 3.035$ kg/s, an increase of 0.8% over q_1

$q_3 = 3.20$ kg/s, an increase of 6.6% over q_1

$q_4 = 3.49$ kg/s, an increase of 16.3% over q_1

and for a fifth boiler it would be

$q_5 = 3.98$ kg/s, an increase of 33%

These figures relate to the value of q_1, l, L, d and D chosen, and the calculation would need to be repeated if other values are used. As has been said previously, most shell boilers can cope with 5% overload, but certainly not 16 or 33%!

Figure 4.8 is a graph of the above figures. If one refers back to the formulae it will be noted that the flow from any boiler other than boiler No. 1, increases with d and L and decreases with D and l. Trouble can be expected with boiler No. 4 if No. 1 is near full rating, and if No. 4 locks out the whole load is thrown on Nos. 1, 2 and 3, but especially No. 3, which in turn may lock out. The risk is therefore that the effect can cascade.

Reducing d and increasing l means, in effect, increasing the resistance of the connecting lines to the boiler. In an existing installation which is troublesome this can be done by fitting orifice plates at the boiler end of the line to provide a pressure drop of, in the first instance, about 1 bar, the exact sizing being adjusted by trial and error to suit the user plant. L, the length between connections, should not be decreased greatly; if the connecting pipes are too close together in the header,

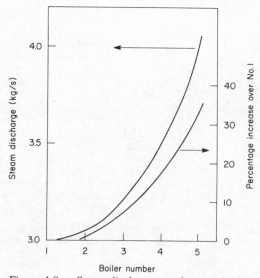

Figure 4.8   Steam discharge rate from each of the five boilers shown in Figure 4.7. Note the escalation in the discharge as the number of boilers increases

their discharge velocities into the header can create disturbances which will make the boilers unstable.

The layouts shown in *Figure 4.9* are recommended for the design of a new header. The header is arranged to discharge from the centre, not at one end. In this way no boiler will be overloaded by the header by more than about 1%. For a six-boiler installation the header discharge could be between boilers 3 and 4, but care must be exercised that the dimensions d, l, D and L are such that no boiler is subject to more than 5% overload. Where more than four boilers are involved it is probably best to connect them by sub-headers, and then to connect the sub-headers, rather like a family tree.

It is emphasized that correct header design in the first place will save much trouble and expense later.

Non-return valves

When two or more boilers are connected into a header, provision must be made so that each boiler can be positively isolated from the header to ensure that there is no chance of steam being discharged

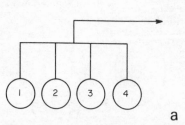

a

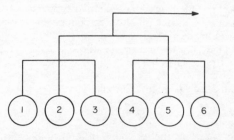

b

Figure 4.9   Correct interconnection of boilers: (a) for three or four boilers, (b) for five or more boilers. These methods avoid the overloading of boilers 3 and 4 that happens in the case shown in Figure 4.7

back from the header, should, for instance, a particular boiler be shut down for repair or inspection. Simple flap-type non-return valves are not suitable for this purpose, for small changes in boiler pressure can cause these to lift and close, resonating with boiler operation and throwing the whole load on to one boiler or the other alternatively; cyclical overloading of the boilers therefore takes place. In more detail the action is as follows in a two-boiler installation: let each boiler be operating at the full rating R, the total load on the installation being $2R$. If the lid of the non-return valve on boiler No. 1 should close, owing to a small temporary excess of header pressure over boiler pressure, the pressure will rise in the boiler and the burner will modulate towards low fire, and may even go out. The load on No. 2 boiler, on a call for more steam, could rise to $2R$ before No. 1 has picked up the load, No. 2 therefore being seriously overloaded and possibly locking out. No. 1 boiler now becomes overloaded and so the swing proceeds. Many cases of carry-over with two-boiler installations are caused in this way.

Screw-down non-return valves or dashpot-controlled valves should always be used.

Rate of increase of load

If the steam demand increases at a greater rate than that to which the boiler can respond, boiler pressure will fall, perhaps far enough to cause trouble. The standard rate of response of a modulating burner control is one minute from low fire to high fire, but controls are available which will operate in a quarter of that time. Nevertheless circumstances which demand this special treatment are rare.

A more frequent source of trouble arises when a boiler plant is on light load and one or more boilers are idle. Should a heavy demand for steam occur suddenly under these circumstances it will take about four minutes for each of the idle boilers to perform its pre-firing cycle, and to begin to pick up its load. During this time those boilers which are firing are seriously overloaded and could lock out.

This condition can best be solved by arranging that the boilerhouse receives sufficient warning of the onset of a load so that boilers can be fired in advance by manual adjustment of the controls. Also, it is another good reason for operating boilers up to their full working pressure.

Thermal storage boilers

To deal with loads of this kind thermal storage boilers are sometimes used. These have a very large water capacity which increases at times of light load, and may be called upon during periods of sudden heavy demand. During this time the feed pump does not operate and hence does not throw extra load on the boiler in having to raise the feedwater to saturation temperature. Thermal storage boilers are often exceptionally large for their normal rated output and special water-level controls are needed. They are particularly suitable where the rate of response of the firing equipment is low, as with coal firing.

These boilers can cater for peak steam demands up to 33% above maximum continuous rating (MCR) for about an hour, meeting lesser peaks for longer periods. As an example, one boiler maker has supplied thermal storage boilers rated at 18 t/h MCR with a peak rating of 23 t/h at a working pressure of 10 bar gauge. Widely fluctuating steam demands can be met without loss of pressure or quality, and the boilers operate at high thermal efficiency because a constant firing rate is maintained. If some pressure drop is acceptable, a greater peak demand can be met for a slightly shorter period.

A thermal storage boiler must have a particularly good feed control system. The principle of this control system is that when a peak demand occurs the feed regulator automatically reduces or stops the flow of feedwater to the boiler. The water level is allowed to fall and the sensible heat stored in the boiler water is given up to increase the rate of evaporation. The firing rate remains constant, maintaining a high thermal efficiency. A drop in the steam demand causes the feed regulator automatically to increase the flow of water to the boiler, so the water level rises. With the constant firing rate maintained, sensible heat is again stored in the boiler water in anticipation of further peak demands. In addition to acting on normal thermal storage principles, the boilers can also be operated as a conventional unit with modulation plus override for bringing in the thermal storage facility when the change in steam demand is in excess of boiler MCR rating.

The boilers can be made for coal, gas, oil or dual firing and provided with automatic fuel/air ratio controls and the necessary safety equipment to guard against maloperation or failure of other equipment.

The thermal storage boiler is thus a conventionally fired boiler but with the ability of steam accumulators to meet peak demands.

Steam accumulators are described in Chapter 18.

Surplus valves

Perhaps the best method of protecting boilers against overload is to use a surplus valve. This is an automatic valve placed in the steam discharge pipe from the boiler. It is actuated by boiler pressure, closing as this falls, so tending to maintain a constant pressure in the boiler however great the

demand for steam may be. In order to avoid dupli-
cating the function of the boiler pressure controls,
with resultant uncertain regulation of the boiler,
the normal pressure controller which reacts on the
burner is moved to a position in the steam discharge main from the boiler downstream of the
surplus valve. This also gives a more sensitive control over boiler pressure, since the signal for more
or less fuel is received by the burner before the
boiler pressure has changed significantly. A surplus valve is shown in *Figure 4.10.*

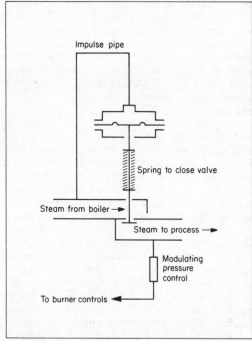

*Figure 4.10   Surplus valve used to protect boilers
from excessive fall in pressure due to overload*

4.6 Control of multiple boilers

There are three possible ways in which a multiple-
boiler plant can be regulated.

1. The installation can be controlled as a whole
   from a master pressure transducer situated
   near the outlet of the steam header which
   interconnects the boilers. This controller
   actuates all burners in unison. This method is
   good when dealing with sudden peak loads
   provided due warning is given, otherwise all
   boilers could be caught in the shut down condition. It is, however, most wasteful to
   operate boilers much below one-third load,
   so from the fuel economy aspect it is better to
   use a baseload boiler at near full load with the
   others shut off until needed.

2. The boilers can be phased to start up or shut
   down in a predetermined sequence, the pressure controller on each boiler being set to
   slightly different values. To avoid a wide
   pressure control band, however, the pressure
   controllers should be of a more sensitive type
   than those normally fitted as standard.
   Special, and rather sophisticated control
   panels are available for phased control and
   these enable the order of firing the boilers to
   be easily changed. This method of operation
   is advantageous when wide, but relatively
   slow fluctuations in demand occur.
3. The ordinary boiler pressure controller can
   be set at the same values and boilers not
   needed shut down manually. This is the
   simplest and most common method of control but requires constant boilerhouse attention if large and irregular load changes occur.

4.7 Boiler water conditions

All water used in all boilers must be treated to
prevent the deposition of scale on the heated surfaces and to prevent water-side corrosion. It is also
essential to prevent excessive concentration of dissolved and suspended solids in the boiler, which
can cause foaming and lead to the events depicted
in *Figures 4.3* and *4.4* escalating.

The treatment of water is complex and specialized, and it is not proposed to discuss the subject in
detail here. There is an elementary guide on the
subject[4] and also a British Standard[5].

To avoid the concentration of solids and consequent foaming, carryover and boiler instability,
three approaches are necessary.

1. Use external rather than internal water
   treatment, i.e. ion exchange and de-aerators.
   These will minimize the introduction of salts
   into the boiler and also reduce the cost of
   chemicals.
2. Make daily tests to determine the solids concentrations, and particularly the alkalinity and
   reserve of oxygen scavenger.
3. As dictated by the results of the tests, blow
   down the boiler to keep the water analysis in
   conformity with BS 2486 and the boiler
   maker's instructions.

Blowdown can be automatic, often a combination
of continuous and intermittent, or it can be
manual; if the latter is used, the blowdown valve
should be opened in a series of short, sharp blasts
in order to disturb and discharge sludge that has
settled in the boiler.

Blowdown is a heavy and sudden thermal load
on the boiler and considerable heat can be lost, as
the following example will show:

Let *F* be the total dissolved solids content of the boiler feed (ppm)
Let *B* be the total dissolved solids content of the boiler water (ppm)
Let B_d be the blowdown required, as a percentage of boiler evaporation

Then $B_d(\%) = \dfrac{F}{B-F} \times 100$ (4.9)

If, in a hard-water area, *F* is 350 ppm and *B* is 3000 ppm, B_d is 13.2%.

If the boiler is working at a saturation temperature of 177°C and the make-up water is at 10°C, the heat loss, assuming no condensate return, is about 3% of the heat input to the boiler; that is, the boiler efficiency, however good it might be in terms of combustion and heat transfer, is reduced by 3%.

As much condensate as possible should therefore be returned to the boiler to reduce the quantity of make-up and it should be reduced further by using external rather than internal treatment. Where these conditions can only partly be satisfied, heat lost in blowdown should be recovered using flash tanks or heat exchangers (*see* Chapter 17).

Boilers should be blown down only at light load, otherwise the overload caused could initiate the events of *Figures 4.3* and *4.4*.

4.8 Superheaters

Superheaters are fitted to shell boilers when the steam produced is used for power generation or when there are long runs of steam mains and pressure and temperature need to be conserved.

Superheaters are heated by gases at a relatively high temperature, so that it is important that the heat received by the tubes shall be absorbed and removed as quickly as possible, otherwise the metal will overheat and eventually fail. When starting a boiler from cold no steam is produced for some time, so that the superheater, being in a hot-gas environment, will overheat unless action is taken to avoid this. Practice varies; steam from another boiler can be used to cool the superheater or it can be flooded with demineralized water, which will evaporate and cool the tubes; alternatively the boiler can be fired on/off very gradually until some steam is produced but in any case the maker's instructions must be strictly adhered to. Whichever method is adopted, skill and patience are needed and during the process the boiler sacrifices its otherwise automatic features.

Unless absolutely essential therefore, the use of superheaters is best avoided, particularly if the final steam temperature needed exceeds about 350°C, in which case watertube boilers should be installed. As has been mentioned previously,

where high-performance steam turbines are used with high-pressure, high-temperature steam, watertube boilers are needed, together with the skill and experience required for their operation.

4.9 Boiler efficiency

The discussion so far has been mainly concerned with the generation and release of steam in boilers, the problems that can arise therefrom, and their solutions. These factors affect overall plant efficiency in the broadest sense; unscheduled shutdown of boiler plant can be very costly both in terms of production and cost of fuel.

The term *efficiency*, however, has a more specific meaning when applied to boilers; it is the ratio of heat output to heat input. The heat output is the heat input minus the sum of the losses, which are:

1. the loss due to sensible heat in the exit gases;
2. the loss due to latent heat in the exit gases;
3. the loss due to incomplete combustion; and
4. the loss from the external surfaces of the boiler.

In addition to these, there is the loss due to blowdown, as previously dealt with. This loss is dependent on feedwater quality and does not affect the discussion which now follows.

Sensible heat in the exit gases

This is the sum of the products of specific heat, mass, and temperature above ambient, of the constituents of the exit gases which consist of nitrogen, oxygen, carbon dioxide, water vapour, sulphur dioxide and perhaps small quantities of products of incomplete combustion such as carbon monoxide and methane. Thus

$L_s = \Sigma (m\,s\,\Delta t)$ (4.10)

where L_s is the sensible heat loss, *m* is the mass of the particular constituent, *s* is the specific heat of the particular constituent and Δt is the true temperature of the gases above ambient. The lower the value of Δt, the lower the value of L_s. Heat transfer conditions dominate Δt, while combustion conditions and boiler load determine the mass and proportions of the various constituents. In practice more oxygen and nitrogen will be present than needed theoretically to burn the fuel; this is because of imperfections, always present, in the combustion appliance. Obviously the lower these can be kept, the lower will be the value of L_s and this is largely under the control of the boiler user.

Latent heat in the exit gases

All fossil fuels contain hydrogen, gas more than oil, and oil more than coal. The hydrogen burns with air to form water vapour, together with its latent heat of evaporation. Unless the water vapour is condensed, which is rarely feasible, it will be discharged up the chimney, complete with its latent heat. The losses from this source, as a percentage of the fuel input to the boiler, are approximately:

Natural gas	11%
Oil	6.6%
Coal	5.5%

This loss cannot be controlled as yet by the user or boiler manufacturer; it is a feature of the fuel, which will have been chosen on grounds of cost, cleanliness and convenience. Hence until satisfactory methods of recovering latent heat become available, the whole of this loss must be added to the sensible heat loss to give the total gas loss.

Total gas loss

Figure 4.11 shows the relationship between total gas loss, boiler exit temperature over ambient, and CO_2, the last being a convenient, inverse measurement of excess air, for the two most commonly used boiler fuels, which are oil and natural gas. The position with coal is rather more difficult to portray owing to its greater variability, and to the usual feature of burning coal, the carbon-in-ash and grit losses which themselves react on the total gas loss.

The exit temperature from a shell boiler is given by[6]

$$t_e = t_m + \frac{t_i - t_m}{\text{antilog}\dfrac{k(L/D)}{(DG)^{0.2}}} \qquad (4.11)$$

where t_e is the exit-gas temperature, t_m is the hot-face temperature of the tubes, t_i is the inlet-gas temperature to tubes, L is the tube length, D is the tube diameter (internal), G is the mass flow rate of the gases through the tubes and k is a constant depending on the units used.

In turn, t_i is given by

$$t_i = k_1 (Q/A)^{0.25} \qquad (4.12)$$

where Q is the heat input to the boiler, A is the heated surface prior to the tube entry and k_1 is a constant depending on the units and fuel used. It will be seen that t_e increases with t_m and t_i and slightly with D and G, but falls as the length to diameter ratio of the tubes increases, while t_i falls as A increases. The factors A, L, D and G are determined by the boiler designer, t_m by the temperature of the heat carrier in boiler, water or steam or both, assuming that the boiler is clean, and Q by the output and designed efficiency of the boiler.

The importance of the equation in the present discussion lies in the dependence of t_e on t_m. If for any reason t_m should rise, t_e and hence the total gas loss will also rise. If for instance the hot face of the

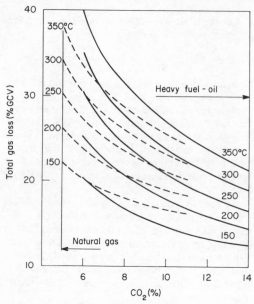

Figure 4.11   Relationship between total gas loss, CO_2, and exit-gas temperature (above ambient), for heavy oil and gas fuels

tubes should become fouled with deposits, the temperature of the hot face of these deposits will become the effective value of t_m. The effect can be serious; a rise in t_e of 17°C means an increase in total gas loss of 1% of the gross calorific value (GCV) of the fuel used, and cases frequently occur when the rise in t_e is well over 100°C. Should the water side of the tube become scaled there is a similar but less marked increase in t_e.

The lesson from this is obvious: both the gas side and the water side of the heat-transferring surfaces in a boiler must be kept clean, and this is up to the user. Gas presents no problems in this respect, but sooty combustion with oil and coal occur, particularly during low-load operation with frequent stops and starts of the burner. The use of an exit-gas temperature recorder to monitor the pattern of change of t_e with time, and so indicate when tubes should be swept, is therefore recommended.

Incomplete combustion

Incomplete combustion can arise from a gross shortage of air or surplus of fuel, generally by accident rather than a continuous operational defect. It usually becomes obvious from the production of smoke, and must be corrected immediately. With gas, the product of incomplete combustion is CO, which is invisible, but in the case of a gross fault the appearance of the flame in the furnace is generally an indication. Carbon monoxide, however, can be a problem with gas firing, and a simple analytical instrument, such as a Draeger tube (rather like a breathalyser), should be kept to hand. On large plant there may be a case for a more sophisticated instrument such as an infra-red analyser, but such instruments are rare in shell boiler applications.

A more frequent cause of incomplete combustion can occur through bad mixing of fuel and air at the burner. Local streams of rich and lean mixture may persist until a change of direction, for example the 180° turn at the reversal chamber, causes them to mix and react, when local combustion will take place. The thermal loss from this source is negligible, but, particularly with gas firing, serious damage to the tube ends may occur. This effect can also result from the chilling of the flame, if it impinges on relatively cool surfaces, thus quenching the reactions until a change of direction forces recombination. Both effects are 'delayed' rather than 'incomplete' combustion, and if there is any suspicion that they are occurring (for example, if there is more than 200 ppm of CO in the reversal chamber) the boiler maker should be asked to investigate.

Unburned solids arise with oil firing. For shell boilers, these by law must not exceed 0.4% of the fuel fired[7] and thermally this is hardly significant.

With coal firing, unburned carbon can be a large loss item. It occurs as grit carryover and carbon-in-ash, and may amount to 2%, or even much more, of the heat supplied to the boiler. Where cases of heavy unburned carbon loss are suspected they should be discussed with the boiler maker and the fuel supplier. Frequently, and with small coal, considerable benefit can be obtained from wetting it to the extent of 1.5 parts of moisture for every 10 parts of coal passing a 3-mm screen. This increases the voidage in the fuel bed, so permitting more air to mix with and burn the coal.

With all fuels, any incomplete combustion which arises is brought about by imperfections in the combustion appliance. These may be faults which can be corrected by the manufacturer, or they may be the result of aerodynamic flow patterns inherent in any flow system, and not capable of easy correction. No combustion appliance is perfect and it is for this reason that, in practice, more air is needed than is theoretically required to burn the fuel.

Surface heat loss

The external surfaces of a shell boiler are hotter than their surroundings and lose heat to them by an amount determined by their area and the difference in temperature between the surface and the surroundings. Most of the external surface of a shell boiler is the insulated shell of the boiler which contains steam and/or water at a substantially constant temperature. The heat loss therefore is mainly a constant quantity of heat irrespective of load.

Thus a surface heat loss of say 1% of the heat input at full load becomes 2% at half load, 4% at quarter, and so on. What was a small item at full load becomes more important at low loads.

Summary of losses

Table 4.2 below summarizes typical losses from a boiler plant operating at full load. These are not maxima or minima but could be taken to represent average practice with modern boiler plant.

The losses for gas firing appear to be higher because of the latent heat loss. In practice this is in part redressed by the cleanliness of this fuel, thus helping to maintain a low exit-gas temperature.

Table 4.2 Average losses from a boiler plant operating at full load

Loss (%)	Fuel		
	Coal	Gas	Oil
Sensible heat	13.0	9.0	11.0
Latent heat	5.5	11.0	6.6
Incomplete combustion	3.0	nil	0.4
Surface loss	1.0	1.0	1.0
Total	22.5	22.0	19.0
Efficiency	77.5	79.0	81.0

The effect of boiler output on efficiency

At zero output the efficiency will be zero; any fuel fired will be used only to supply the losses. Hence as load decreases, efficiency also will tend to decrease, but the position is a little more complex than this simple statement, as down to a certain load, perhaps about one-third, efficiency will increase slightly above the full load value. The factors affecting this are:

1. As load falls, so will the value of the mass flow rate through the tubes. This is G in equation (4.11), from which will be seen that a reduction in G will reduce t_e by a small extent, so reducing the sensible heat loss.
2. Below about half load most combustion appliances need more excess air to burn the fuel completely. This increases the sensible heat loss[8].

3. As discussed above the surface heat loss increases (as a percentage) as load falls.

The net effect of these factors is to produce a load/efficiency curve, shown in *Figure 4.12* for a modern boiler, which also includes a curve for an older-type boiler which for a given output would be physically considerably larger than its modern counterpart. It will be seen that the fall in efficiency begins to become serious below about a quarter load, and if at all possible, operation of boilers below that level should be avoided.

There is therefore an advantage to be gained in splitting the load between several boilers where very variable demands, such as for space heating, are incurred. Robertson, McKenzie and Ravenscroft[9] have studied the optimum number of boilers for different load conditions, and for many situations have found that two boilers of equal size suffice. For loads beyond the maximum unit size of shell boiler, three or more boilers would of course be required.

If existing plant cannot be used in this manner, some alleviation of the problem can be obtained by tuning the burner to meet a low-load period of appreciable length. This can be done, using the advice of the manufacturer, by fitting smaller atomizers and larger diffuser plates.

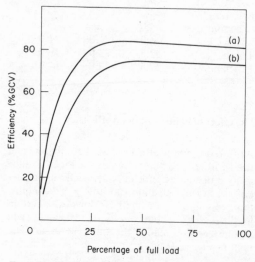

Figure 4.12   Relationship between boiler efficiency and load for (a) a modern package boiler, (b) an old-type Economic boiler

Factors which limit efficiency

When one refers to equation (4.11) it will be seen that the lower t_m is, the lower will be t_e and hence the higher the efficiency. From this it might be argued that advantage would be gained by lowering the temperature of the working fluid in the boiler. There are limits to which this can be done, as follows:

1. The temperature of the working fluid should not be taken to a value lower than that corresponding to the pressure below which the specific volume of steam increases sharply. This is about 6.5 bar, and the consequences of reducing pressure below this were discussed earlier in this chapter.
2. When sulphur-containing fuels are used, some sulphuric acid will be formed and will condense out at temperatures below the acid dewpoint (about 125°C). A typical curve relating corrosion rate due to sulphuric acid with surface temperatures is shown in *Figure 4.13*. It will be seen that above the dewpoint there is no problem, but as the temperature falls there is a peak corrosion rate at about 95°C. Surface temperatures in this range should be avoided, not only in the boiler itself but also in the ducting and chimneys in contact with the gases. Below the peak there is a trough, and though a corrosion hazard is still present, it is much less serious. It is in this region that low-pressure hot-water boilers operate in the range 65–85°C. Below this range copious condensation of water occurs, leaching away the semiprotective products of corrosion, and the deterioration can be very rapid indeed.

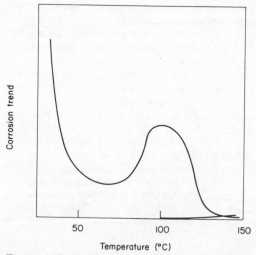

Figure 4.13   Relationship between corrosion rate and surface temperature for the products of combustion of heavy fuel oil burned in a shell boiler

The use of economizers to preheat the feed-water for shell boilers incurs the danger of corrosion in the economizer. In this temperature range the gain in efficiency is only a few percent, but even this may be considered worth while. To combat corrosion in the economizer range magnesia has been found useful when injected into the boiler furnace. It settles out with the acid and neutralizes it. The amount of magnesia necessary is about 1 kg per tonne of oil burned. Corrosion hazards are much less with coal, and non-existent with gas when burned alone. When oil is used as a standby fuel for gas, however, the acid products of corrosion can, when diluted with water from the products of combustion of the gas, prove very aggressive on resumption of gas firing. The use of magnesia will prove beneficial in these cases.

Preheating the combustion air, as is done in the case of large watertube boilers, can be used on shell boilers and could add a further few percent to the efficiency, but the corrosion hazard will still be present. Magnesia should be used and the air entering the preheater should itself be preheated by steam coils so that the air heater surfaces nowhere enter the water dewpoint range. Air heaters on shell boilers are at present rare.

Chimneys serving boilers should always be insulated to maintain the lining above the acid dewpoint under all circumstances, otherwise corrosion and the associated problem of smutting will occur. Ravenscroft and Page[10] and also Gills and Lees[11] have published useful information on this subject.

4.10 Measuring boiler efficiency

Some boiler users require an 'acceptance test' to prove that the makers' claims for boiler efficiency are justified. Codes for the conduct of these tests are contained in BS 845 (ref. 12) and, for large boilers, BS 2885 (ref. 13). The tests involve the measurement of the following quantities: (a) mass of fuel fired; (b) its calorific value, as fired; (c) the thermal output from the boiler, and (d) the heat losses, as discussed above.

A boiler test to these standards is rather in the nature of a ritual, and quite unsuitable for routine checks in a boilerhouse, but the standards should be obtained and studied because they contain useful formulae for gas loss, and helpful advice on various aspects. The following method is suggested as a practical works test.

1. Select the load at which the boiler is to be tested and keep it constant by manipulation of the crown valve on the boiler, venting steam to atmosphere if required. Run the boiler steadily for one hour in this condition.
2. Measure the exit-gas temperature using if possible a suction pyrometer. If this is not available use an ordinary pyrometer or thermometer and add 10% to the reading. The measurement should be made as near as possible to the tube exits and traverses made, taking the average of the readings in the centre of each quarter of the duct area. Deduct from this average the ambient temperature.
3. Measure the CO_2 concentrations at the same station as those used for measuring temperature (a combined probe is useful), and take the average.
4. Check for CO, and if this is found to exceed 50 ppm discuss with boiler or burner maker. Repeat (2) and (3) four times and take the overall average exit-gas temperature and CO_2 level.
5. Work out the total gas losses as follows.

Natural-gas firing

$$L_t = \left(\frac{0.352}{M} + 0.0094 \right) (t_e - t_a) + 10 \qquad (4.13)$$

where L_t is the total gas loss as a percentage of GCV, M is the average CO_2 concentration as a percentage, t_e is the exit-gas temperature (°C) and t_a is the ambient temperature (°C). Add surface heat loss:

Modern package shell boilers: 1% at full load, 2% at half load and *pro rata*

Older Economic, locomotive or Scotch Marine boilers: 2% at full load and *pro rata*

Lancashire boilers: 4% at full load and *pro rata*

Deduct the sum from 100% to give efficiency.

Heavy-oil firing

$$L_t = \frac{98 (2460 + 2.1t_e - 4.2t_a)}{N} + \frac{0.51 (t_e - t_a)}{M} \qquad (4.14)$$

where N is the GCV of the fuel (kJ/kg). Add 0.5% for incomplete combustion, add surface heat loss as above and deduct the sum from 100% to give the efficiency.

Gas-oil firing

$$L_t = \frac{120 (2460 + 2.1t_e - 4.2t_a)}{N} + \frac{0.48 (t_e - t_a)}{M} \qquad (4.15)$$

Add 0.1% for incomplete combustion, add surface heat loss as above and deduct the sum from 100% to give the efficiency.

These are the most commonly used boiler fuels, but there is a reviving interest in coal firing. Because of the greater variability of this fuel and the likelihood of appreciable unburned carbon-in-ash and grit carryover, the test is much more complex and involves the weighing of the fuel into the boiler, the ash out of it, the grit collected in the grit arrestor, riddlings through the grate, and the sampling and analysis of the ash for carbon-in-ash loss. It is hardly a matter for routine checks, and if it is felt that efficiency tests are essential then the methods described in BS 845 or BS 2885 should be used, technical advice being sought from the coal suppliers.

With gas and oil firing, however, the methods suggested for these fuels should provide an efficiency within ± 2% of the real figure. The accuracy called for by most standards is no greater than this.

Steam wetness

Wet steam is, if it occurs, an undesirable product from a boiler, and, if efficiency measurements are conducted by the direct measurement of input and output, can result in a serious error. This is because some water, measured into the boiler and credited with having absorbed latent heat, has absorbed only sensible heat. Where heavy carryover occurs, as described earlier in this chapter, the error can be anything from 2% to 20%. With heavy carryover the flow in the steam offtake is two-phase; that is, water, as such, mostly on the pipe walls, and steam more or less in the core. It is for this reason that sampling techniques are very inaccurate and should not be used. The reader is referred to BS 3812 (ref. 14).

The recording of boiler efficiency

Routine operations should be carried out on all boilers to ensure safe, trouble-free and efficient running. The boiler insurance companies issue log sheets on which the essential safety checks, which should be regarded as mandatory, are recorded daily. Such a log sheet is illustrated in *Figure 4.14*. In addition to these checks it is recommended that CO_2 (or O_2) percentage and the exit-gas temperature be recorded, and also the hourly rate of fuel consumption and steam flow. The recording of draught loss across the boiler can indicate when fouling is taking place and therefore when cleaning is needed. It is particularly useful when certain solid fuels are being burnt. These records should

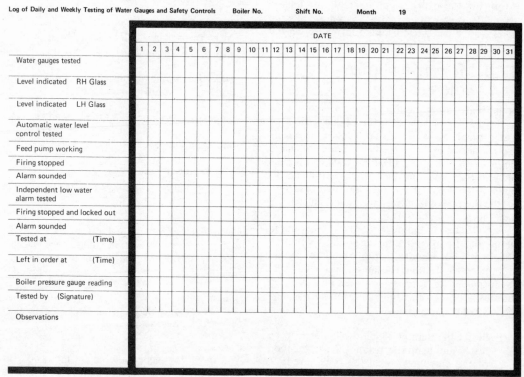

Log of Daily and Weekly Testing of Water Gauges and Safety Controls   Boiler No.   Shift No.   Month   19

	DATE 1	2	3	4	5	6	7	8	9	10	11	12	13	14	15	16	17	18	19	20	21	22	23	24	25	26	27	28	29	30	31
Water gauges tested																																
Level indicated RH Glass																																
Level indicated LH Glass																																
Automatic water level control tested																																
Feed pump working																																
Firing stopped																																
Alarm sounded																																
Independent low water alarm tested																																
Firing stopped and locked out																																
Alarm sounded																																
Tested at (Time)																																
Left in order at (Time)																																
Boiler pressure gauge reading																																
Tested by (Signature)																																
Observations																																

Notes: 1   To be completed by boiler attendant(s) or person(s) responsible for safe working.
2   Tick squares to indicate daily tests completed satisfactorily.
3   Cross squares to indicate weekly tests completed satisfactorily.

Figure 4.14   Insurance company's log sheet for the recording of boiler safety operations. (Courtesy of National Vulcan Engineering Insurance Group Ltd)

be examined daily by a responsible person who can initiate action to investigate and rectify any irregularity.

4.11 Water heaters

The discussion so far has been concerned with steam-generating boilers; many shell boilers are used for heating water which is used as a heat carrier, and in certain cases show advantages over steam.

Water heaters are classified as either low-temperature, low-pressure (i.e. up to about 100°C and 4.5 bar) or high-temperature, high-pressure, (say 200°C and 17 bar). All find their main application for space heating, but high-pressure boilers are sometimes used for process work. The main advantages of hot water compared with steam are:

1. For certain applications the temperature range is more suitable for the process.
2. Return condensate lines and their attendant troubles are absent.
3. Being virtually in a closed system there is no evaporation and water treatment costs are reduced.
4. For a given thermal output the boilers are somewhat smaller.

High-temperature, high-pressure hot water is sometimes referred to as 'superheated water'.

High-temperature, high-pressure boilers

Since the water is well above its boiling point at atmospheric pressure, excess pressure needs to be imposed to maintain it in the liquid state. This can be done either by self-pressurization from a steam blanket on top of a free water surface, or by an externally imposed pressure on a fully flooded boiler with no steam space. The latter means is now more frequently used.

With steam pressurization, the maximum pressure obtainable is that corresponding to the saturation temperature of the water in the boiler. If the pressure in the flow line from the boiler is reduced for any reason some of the water will flash into steam, interfere with flow, and perhaps cause water hammer. A reduction of pressure of this kind could be brought about by the partial closure of a control valve. To overcome this the boiler may be by-passed, to blend cool return water with the flow, so reducing the temperature and providing an anti-flash margin. Also all control valves should be placed on the outlets of the heat users, rather than the inlets. Another problem can arise when boilers are connected in parallel; owing to quite small changes in pressure between the steam spaces of adjacent boilers, there can be a fall in water level in one, and an increase in the water level in the next one. This problem can be overcome by connecting the steam spaces by a generously sized balance pipe, or by fully flooding the boilers and connecting to a common, separate steam drum.

Instead of a steam drum, a more recent development uses a small pressure vessel partly filled with nitrogen, the pressure of which is maintained by nitrogen bottles and a regulating valve. As the water expands with increase in system temperature, the level in the pressure vessel rises, operates a level-sensitive device, and opens a valve to spill excess water to a storage tank. When the system cools the reverse operation takes place. There are many nitrogen-pressurized systems in operation, their main advantage being that the pressure exerted can be considerably higher than and independent of that needed to keep the water in the liquid state.

An alternative method of external pressurization is that of continuous pumping by pumps similar to boiler feed pumps using specially designed spill valves to discharge excess water during the heating-up process. This water is vented to a storage tank, whence the pumps use it to replenish the system during the cooling part of the cycle.

Problems with water heaters

Since there is no release of steam, as such, in a water heater none of the steam release problems discussed earlier in this chapter will occur. However, the fact that there is no free ebullition means that water circulation patterns and the degree of cooling over the heated surfaces of the boiler are altered. The overall circulation through the boiler is likely to be in the streamline region of flow; a velocity of rather less than 2 m/s in the flow and return connections to the boiler becomes very much less than this in the shell itself which is many times the diameter of the pipework. Stratification of temperature in the boiler will therefore occur and this can set up uneven stressing which may lead to leakage at the tube seats. To overcome this, circulation within the boiler should be stimulated by internal or external recirculation in addition to increasing the flow rate within the boiler. Such arrangements also blend hot flow water from the top of the boiler with cool return water, so maintaining a more uniform temperature in the boiler. Page, Simpson and Gunn[15] have discussed this and other aspects of hot-water boiler operation more fully.

4.12 Waste-heat boilers

It has, so far, been assumed that the shell boilers discussed have been directly fired using integral burners or coal-burning grates. There has been a gradual increase over the years in the use of shell boilers, both steam and hot-water, for the recovery of heat from the gaseous products from other plant such as: furnaces, diesel engines, gas turbines, incinerators and chemical processes. With the increasing scarcity of fuel, this trend can only increase. (These boilers can also be of the watertube type, depending on mass flow of gases and steam temperature — *see Figure 4.15*.)

The structure of a waste-heat shell boiler differs very little from that of a fired boiler, and most of the foregoing parts of the chapter apply. The majority of waste-heat shell boilers, however, contain no furnace, which, since this is the main part which limits the practicable maximum operating pressure[16], means that waste-heat boilers without furnaces can be used for considerably higher steam pressures than those so far described, 100 bar being used in certain instances. That said, the majority of shell boilers in operation are in the pressure range 7–24 bar. From equation (4.11), it follows that the lower the pressure (within the limits discussed earlier) the better the heat recovery.

Where high-temperature gases, which may contain depositing substances, are used, it will be best to use a boiler containing furnaces like an ordinary fired boiler. In this way the gases will be cooled somewhat before they impinge on the tube plate. With lower-temperature gases, up to say 1000°C, the gases may be and usually are ducted straight onto the tube plate, the furnace being omitted. Whether a single or double pass of tubes is used depends mainly on the layout of the plant, whether the gases need to exhaust at the end of the boiler remote from their entry (single-pass) or whether they are to be returned to the inlet end (double-pass). Control over heat output from a waste-heat boiler is achieved by motorized dampers activated by pressure or temperature, which by-pass a proportion of the gases when the heat demand is satisfied. When the demand for heat exceeds the supply supplementary firing can be adopted. Where the waste gases can support combustion, for example, the waste gases from a gas turbine, an oil or gas burner may be placed in the entry duct to the boiler. Where the waste gases cannot support combustion, as in the case of waste gases from a furnace using a reducing or neutral atmosphere, or the pulsating exhaust of a diesel engine, a composite construction can be used. In this case the waste gases are passed through a tubular pass, whilst the auxiliary burner fires into a furnace tube, the products of combustion from which pass through a separate bank of convection tubes. Such boilers are quite often used on ships, where the diesel exhaust provides all the heat needed whilst the ship is at sea, the fired portion being used to provide heat services whilst the ship is in port.

The amount of heat recoverable depends on the mass flow of gases and their temperature above the surface metal temperature of the tubes, which latter may be calculated from equations (4.10) and (4.11). *Figure 4.15* shows the heat recoverable in terms of mass flow of gas and their temperature.

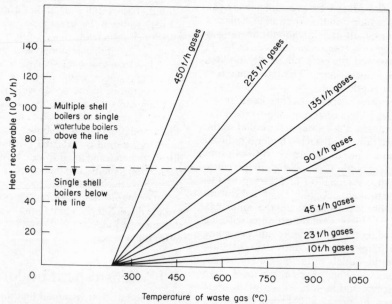

Figure 4.15   Heat recoverable as steam or hot water at various waste-gas mass flow rates (kg/s) and temperatures to a sink at 170°C. Single-shell boilers suffice below the broken line, but multiple-shell boilers or watertube boilers are needed above the line

4.13 The future

Two factors are evident:

1. Oil and gas are in decreasing supply, and their price will rise. More emphasis will be placed on coal as an industrial fuel.
2. Pollution of the atmosphere by noxious products of combustion, such as SO_2, is becoming less and less acceptable in industrial countries.

It therefore follows that, limited though the scope may be, the efficiency of boilers will need to be raised, using economizers and air preheaters to raise present efficiencies in the low eighties into the high eighties. Problems of corrosion with such equipment have been mentioned, and also some guidance given about the solutions that may soon need to be adopted.

A development which is now being fostered energetically is that of fluid-bed combustion. A bed of small refractory particles is made to 'boil' by combustion air passing through at the required flow rate. The bed is heated to a temperature of about 600°C and the fuel (solid, liquid or gaseous, or a mixture of these) is supplied to the bed and combustion becomes self-sustaining. Tubes carrying water or water/steam emulsion are placed in the bed and extract heat from it, the heat transfer coefficient from bed to tubes being particularly high. The products of combustion from the bed then pass through convection tubes (in shell boilers) or over them (in watertube boilers). The bed temperature is usually restricted to 900°C because:

1. At this temperature deposit-forming substances such as sodium undergo very little sublimation.
2. The bed will not sinter.
3. Sulphur-reactive substances, such as dolomite, can be used to fix much of the sulphur in the fuel and prevent its emission as SO_2 or SO_3.
4. The fluid bed will burn a whole variety of fuels mixed if necessary. It is therefore a universal burner.

Fluid beds are now (1979) being operated on a demonstration scale[17] in both shell and watertube boilers and it would appear that they will make a substantial contribution to the fuel-burning technology of the future.

References

1 Department of Energy. Report of a visit to USA in 1952. Anglo-American Council on Productivity 1953
2 'Requirements for automatically controlled steam and hot-water boiler'. Associated Offices Technical Committee, Manchester M60 4DT
3 Research film, 'Boiling in boilers'. Clarke Chapman Ltd, Thompson Cochran Division, Glasgow G32 6BS
4 'The treatment of water for shell boilers'. Association of Shell Boilermakers, Manchester M60 2ED
5 British Standards Institution. *British Standard* 2486. 'The treatment of water for land boilers'
6 McAdams, W. H. *Heat Transmission*, 3rd edn. New York: McGraw-Hill. Equation (4.11) of the text is a transposition of this
7 Clean Air Act 1968. 'Memorandum on Dust and Grit Emission'. London: HMSO
8 Hoggarth, M. L., Pomfret, K. F. and Spittle, P. *Gas Council Communication* GC 196
9 Robertson, P., McKenzie, E. and Ravenscroft, R. P. 'A new approach to the economic sizing and operation of space-heating boiler plant'. *Building Services Engineer*, April 1973
10 Ravenscroft, R. P. and Page, H. A. 'Field investigation and design of insulated chimneys'. *J. Inst. Fuel* **39**, 29 (1966)
11 Gills, B. G. and Lees, B. 'Design and operation of an insulated steel chimney'. *J. Inst. Fuel*, **39**, 29 (1966)
12 British Standards Institution. *British Standard* 845. 'Acceptance tests for industrial-type boilers and steam generators'
13 British Standards Institution. *British Standard* 2885. 'Code for acceptance tests for steam-generating units'
14 British Standards Institution. *British Standard* 3812. 'Recommendations for estimating the dryness fraction of steam'
15 Page, H. A., Simpson, H. M. and Gunn, D. C. 'Steel hot-water boilers'. *Plant Engineer*, May 1969
16 British Standards Institution. *British Standard* 2790. 'Shell boilers of welded construction'. Equations 20 and 21
17 Gibson, J. and Highley, L. 'Fluidised bed combustion'. *J. Inst. Energy* No. 411 (June 1979)

5

Watertube boilers including hot-water and waste-heat boilers

5.1 Design considerations

The introduction and early development of the watertube boiler was intended to provide an alternative to the shell boiler, with advantages in less destructive results from pressure-part failure and the possible reduction in component or total weight. From this beginning the watertube boiler has progressed to the largest units of steam-raising capacity required, and provides the versatility in geometry and arrangement to match particular properties and characteristics of fuels while achieving desired heat exchange performance with efficiency, safety and reliability.

At the outset the designer accepts that the thermal efficiency which can be achieved from heat in the fuel burnt and heat in the steam sent out has a ceiling short of 100%, owing to losses which he strives to reduce but cannot eliminate. These are principally the loss due to incomplete combustion of fuel, the dry-gas loss, the moisture loss and the surface heat loss. These are explained in more detail below.

The aim in the combustion of the fuel is to release as much heat as possible and to avoid waste, such as residual unburnt combustible material remaining in ash, or incomplete combustion of constituents (such as carbon inadequately combining with oxygen to form carbon monoxide, rather than fully burning to carbon dioxide). It is true that in broad terms an over-liberal supply of air for combustion will achieve very good burnout, but a balance must be struck. There will be an increased loss from any air in excess of that theoretically required to match the fuel constituents, because this will carry away heat in the flue gases discharged to the chimney.

The total loss of dry gases, of which that due to excess combustion air is only a part, arises because the flue gases leave at a higher temperature than that of the combustion air and because incondensable gases such as carbon dioxide and sulphur dioxide have been formed in burning the fuel. Not only are the gases hotter but greater in content than the air alone.

The desire of the designer to diminish this loss by cooling the flue gas and contributing to the heat output in the steam must, however, be tempered by other considerations. These are the need for buoyancy in the gas for chimney draught and dispersal in the atmosphere, the capital cost, bulk or weight considerations of progressively lower-performance heat exchange equipment and, by no means least, the risk of corrosion in the cooler regions towards the back of the boiler due to condensation of acidic materials from the gases.

The moisture loss, also associated with the flue gases, is considered separately. This loss, as its name implies, relates to moisture which comes from two sources, either as an initial constituent of the fuel, whether mixed or inherent, or resulting from combustion of hydrogen present in the fuel combining with oxygen in the air. The loss comes about owing to the sensible heat and latent heat of vaporization required to change water at the temperature of the raw fuel to steam at the flue gas temperature. Here again the designer has little room to manoeuvre because of the factors dictating his choice of final flue gas temperature.

The surface heat loss is the loss from all the hot boiler surfaces to the cooler surroundings. This is minimized by thermal insulation applied to the extent judged appropriate (*see* Chapter 6).

Other losses, usually small, may also occur such as the heat carried away in the ash and atmospheric moisture in the air. It is common to treat these minor losses as unaccounted and in the heat balance to combine them with the surface heat loss in an item 'radiation and unaccounted', R & U.

The first step in the design process, having determined the quantity of heat to be released to provide the boiler output at a probable efficiency, is to consider the furnace appropriate to the characteristics of the fuel. A comparison between pulverized coal, oil and gas being fired in a water-cooled furnace may give an indication of the factors involved.

With coal, even when finely pulverized, combustion is taking place between a solid particle and air so that access to the fuel is at the exposed surface of the particle, and some time may be required for progressive burning to proceed. In addition, exposure of the incoming coal particle to the heat of the flame will tend to drive off the volatile constituents which burn as a gas, leaving coke which will burn more slowly and may be hampered by the ash residue masking the combustion material. Thus the furnace must have an adequate volume to contain a large, slow-burning flame, and to give a long residence time within the furnace zone at temperatures required for good burnout of the carbon.

It is a matter of burner design to achieve the necessary intimate mixing of coal and air for combustion. As would be expected, the lower the coal's volatile content, the less readily does it ignite and the more care may be required to give good and stable burning.

The behaviour of the ash has to be considered, to avoid unacceptable and progressive deposition of slag on the furnace walls. This is achieved by having adequate clearance between burners and walls and suitable overall heat release rates.

By comparison, an oil fuel may be expected to burn in a short, bright flame achieved by fine atomization of the fuel coupled with vigorous mixing with air at the burner. Yet care is still needed to allow proper flame development, since premature approach to a cool wall may chill the flame so that combustion is quenched before full burnout is achieved.

Fuel gases, especially those of high calorific value such as natural gas and petroleum gases, burn readily but with larger and less bright flames than oil.

These different behaviours require that the furnace for pulverized coal (PF) should be large compared with that for oil or gas firing to accommodate the flame development needed, to give the necessary residence time, and to avoid slagging problems.

Similarly, because of the high radiation from an oil flame, the heat absorbed in an oil-fired furnace is higher than that with gas.

In the early days of watertube boiler development, furnaces were entirely or largely of refractory construction. Water cooling was progressively introduced so that today furnaces may be completely enclosed in water walls and surfaces, thus directly absorbing a large part of the heat released and contributing substantially to the generation of steam to the point where in very large units very little boiler surface is required after the furnace.

After the furnace the other heat exchange surfaces, which may include superheater, reheater, economizer, and air heater together with any further boiler surface, are arranged to give the best balance of performance to economy and to take up as much heat as possible before the gases are released to the stack. The nature of the fuel has as profound an influence on these other surfaces as it already has had in the furnace. With coal, particularly PF, but also when fired in coarse sizes such as on travelling grates or by spreader stokers, ash particles are entrained in the gases leaving the furnace at a high temperature. This may mean that these particles are sticky or molten and could rapidly adhere to and build up on tube banks in their path. It is necessary therefore to adopt wide pitching between tubes close to the furnace, whether in the water screen or superheater, to avoid bridging between tubes and blockage of the gas path if build-up should take place. In large boilers, widely spaced surfaces of simple geometry may be employed, with the ability to shed molten slag back into the furnace. As the gases give up their heat, tube spacing can be progressively reduced as the fouling risks diminish.

A further consideration is that the ash or dust carried in the gases can cause erosion of tubes and structures so that gas speeds must be kept to levels giving acceptable wear. A typical gas speed for pulverized coal may be 20 m/s, with 30 m/s for oil. Slower speeds such as 15 m/s may be needed for more abrasive fuel ashes such as bagasse and dirty blast-furnace gas. Extreme fuels such as Belgian coals impose limits as restrictive as 9 m/s.

Oil fuels, with much less ash than coal, and giving clean gases, permit much closer pitching between tube surfaces and higher gas speeds as indicated, although deposits must still be taken into account.

Other matters such as high-temperature corrosion by ash deposits on tube surfaces, especially by vanadium in oil ashes, may put a lower limit to superheated steam temperatures. These may have to be reduced to about 540°C, as compared with 565°C for conventional coal burning.

Corrosion and its prevention

An important aspect of boiler design is the minimization of corrosion. Frequent periodic replacement of corroded plant items owing to bad design will involve unacceptably high costs.

High-temperature gas-side corrosion

Some fuel ashes can corrode heating surfaces at high temperature. Vanadium, which is present in varying degree in many fuel oils and high in some such as those from Venezuela, causes corrosion of superheater tubes and supports.

In general, corrosion is progressively more severe as alloying increases from carbon steel to the alloy ferritic steels and then to the austenitic steels. This leads to practical limits to the final steam temperatures adopted for oil-fired units.

Corrosion is also found with coal ashes. Some coals, such as those from the East Midlands field in the UK, contain alkali sulphates and chlorine, and corrosion is found not only at superheater tube temperatures but also on furnace and generating tubes. Corrosion relates to the formation of a sulphate-rich deposit on the tubes but is heavily influenced by furnace atmosphere, being severest where there is general or local reducing atmosphere or where very low-oxygen conditions obtain.

Wastage takes the form of flakes of iron oxide and deposit peeling from the surface of the tube, thus exposing a new surface for attack. This form of corrosion is sometimes not recognized at first because it is mistaken for sootblower erosion since general wastage takes place on the fire face of the tubes, which may be more rapid in areas influenced by sootblowing. The two can be distinguished by observing that wastage is taking place beyond the range of sootblowers and by the flaking corrosion product which would have been dislodged if sootblower action had been the cause.

The cure is to ensure adequate combustion and free oxygen, even if in particular cases this may mean carrying a greater excess of air than would otherwise be required. What is done will depend on circumstances. With travelling-grate or spreader stokers for example, it may be necessary to arrange adequate air entry at the sides of the grate and also proper overfire air to ensure that combustion is not delayed. With pulverized fuel, the burners must be set to give proper mixing and it may be necessary to bias the air to avoid reducing atmosphere around the flame envelope. Long flames licking on walls and general delayed combustion must be prevented.

Low-temperature gas-side corrosion

Low-temperature corrosion is largely due to the sulphur content of the fuel and is particularly significant with oil. Corrosion takes place when metal temperatures or gas temperatures fall below the acid dewpoint or water vapour dewpoint.

There is a limit, therefore, to the amount of heat that can be extracted from the gases in the search for efficiency with an acid dewpoint varying between 130 and 145°C. The quality of combustion has some influence on acid formation since with very low excess air there is not so much oxidation of sulphur dioxide to sulphur trioxide, giving sulphuric acid on condensing with water, as there is with a larger excess of oxygen in the flame. Oil burner development has therefore gone in the direction of minimum excess air. Furthermore, corrosion is least at full-load conditions because then temperatures are highest and because excess air will be at its optimum, being greater at lower loads.

Economizers. Because the heat transfer rate between water and tube is much greater than between gas and tube, the tube surface in an economizer will be very close to water temperature whatever the gas temperature and accordingly, very low feed temperatures result in considerable corrosion risk. Running at part loads will give lower temperature than at full load.

Gas-side deposits forming on heating surfaces will be acidic and since these reduce the heat transfer they will aggravate corrosion. This process is enhanced where deposits bridge between tubes parallel to the gas lanes.

With oil-fired plant it is customary to arrange periodic water washing of the economizer to minimize these difficulties. Extended-surface economizers are less likely to suffer corrosion as they present a slightly warmer surface to the gas than bare tubes and to some extent increase the sacrificial material which can be lost before replacement might be needed.

Air heaters. With air heaters there is a closer match between air and gas-side heat transfer, and accordingly the metal temperature is somewhere midway between the air and gas temperatures so that it is the mean of the two which needs to be related to dewpoint. With tubular air heaters in which air flows through the tubes, this generalization is not always true because the flow turbulence of air at inlet to the tubes will enhance the cooling effect so that close to the inlet there may be an area prone to corrosion. If the inlet tube ends are extended beyond the tube plate into the air box, the turbulent entry zone is kept out of the gas stream and the inlet tube plate should be insulated. Gas-side deposits will also interfere with heat input, which depresses the metal temperature.

Some success has been achieved by use of corrosion-resistant air heater materials such as copper-bearing steels (Corten), vitreous enamelled steel and ceramic coating or ceramic packs in regenerative air heaters. Glass tubes have also had limited application.

Where there might be low air temperatures entering the gas air heater, either in normal running or during start-up and low load, some installations have a steam air heater to boost the inlet air temperature.

Flues and chimneys. Whilst a well-insulated flue will run close to gas temperature, local corrosion may take place where gas flow is sluggish or where there is local cooling, such as an uninsulated access door or region of cold air in-leakage. These points should be looked for during outage inspections and steps taken to minimize the problem.

A flue or chimney which is oversize for its duty will not keep as hot as one correctly sized and for this reason it is particularly important with oil firing to provide each boiler with a separate chimney or individual flue in a big stack with a multi-unit installation. Running at part load will have the same effect.

A particularly troublesome condition is the discharge of acid smuts from the stack. This is more likely to occur with cool flue gas, flues and ducts because of condensation and build-up of acid deposits. In addition to what has been said about flue and stack sizing, the tendency to produce smuts decreases with load so that it is better to carry full load on one of a pair of boilers rather than to split it between the two.

5.2 Construction

The typical watertube boiler comprises an assembly of tube arrays connected either direct to a steam drum alone or to a steam and water drum, or via headers and connecting piping.

The design, materials and workmanship are governed by codes of practice or legislation. In the UK the usual code is BS 1113: 'Watertube steam-generating plant (including superheaters, reheaters and steel tube economizers)'. The materials of construction range from low- and medium-carbon steel, to various alloy steels with better mechanical properties for drums, and with good strength at high temperatures and scaling resistance for superheaters and reheaters. Boiler drums, commonly of riveted or solid forged steel in the past, are now normally of fusion-welded construction, fully stress-relieved.

Traditionally, tube connections to drums and headers are made by expanding and belling the tube end into the tube hole by a roller expander. For thick tube seats the seat may carry one or more grooves to improve the joint, and for very long seats a retractable expander having short rolls, which work progressively over the length of the seat is used rather than the propulsive type which extends a little beyond the full seat length. Tube expanding is not fully successful at high pressures and in superheaters, where the material may be subject to creep at high temperatures, thus relaxing the joint. Economizer tube expandings are subject, especially at the inlet end, to fluctuating temperatures and therefore have limitations.

Welded tube connections are used to overcome these difficulties, often with the drum or header fitted with welded stubs before stress relief, permitting a simpler welding procedure between stub and tube end.

For access to tube ends for expanding and tube replacement, and for mechanical tube cleaning, fitting removable handholes was formerly normal practice. With increased heat transfer ratings and higher pressures, the essential better water conditions avoid the earlier necessity for ready access for cleaning, and permit moving from the disadvantages of removable handhole fittings to welded closures, often used for general inspection rather than giving direct access to individual tubes.

The use of refractories is decreasing with the trend to fully water-cooled furnaces and finned spaced tubes forming the sides of gas passages. The logical development is reached where the tubes are welded together via connecting fins, which eliminates refractories completely and the need for an external gastight casing. This construction ensures complete gas tightness and prevents air in-leakage with balanced draught, so giving more certain control of combustion and the achievement of minimum excess air.

The boiler and economizer pressure-part design is based on the mechanical requirements to carry the pressure and structural loads, making due allowance for corrosion, and the use of minimum material scantlings to ease fabrication.

Fatigue conditions may also need to be considered.

Superheaters and reheaters at the higher temperatures are subject to creep and to scaling. This must be taken into account in deciding the materials of construction, and tube and header thicknesses which will relate to a definite design life expectancy according to appropriate codes or other requirements.

Small and medium-size boilers are bottom-supported with the main structural support provided by the boiler tubes. Large boilers are top-supported and are suspended by slings from a cold overhead steelwork frame carried by cold columns. This construction permits free movement under thermal expansion in the boiler itself, but provision is needed to accommodate differential movements against fixed equipment. Examples are a dip plate in a water trough giving a gas seal at an ash hopper below the furnace, and flexible connections between air ducts and windboxes and at the boiler outlet.

External structural members are provided to give support as required, such as to the furnace walls, and to give strength against possible furnace explosion or external air pressure following on a pressure collapse in the furnace. These structures must accommodate the boiler's thermal movements.

5.3 Steam generation and circulation

Boiler circulation

Natural and assisted circulation

When steam bubbles form in water, the resultant mixture has a much lower density than water alone and it is this density difference which provides the driving force for natural circulation in a boiler. The greatest circulating head is achieved where the water from the steam drum is taken to the inlet of the rising boiler circuit by unheated downcomers, and where the density of the water in the downcomers is not diminished by any entrainment of steam. It may be enhanced if the water temperature is lower than saturation because of the incoming cooler feedwater mixing with recirculated water in the drum.

Resistance to circulation is provided by friction losses in the boiler tubes, headers and return pipes, entry and exit losses and by the drum internal gear.

A fundamental property is that the more heat is received by a tube, the greater is the rate of steam raising, and accordingly the lower the mixture density with corresponding increase in circulating head. This means that the natural-circulation boiler has an inherent tendency for the different circulating systems to be self-adjusting to heat input.

Some boiler designs incorporate pumps to assist the natural circulation, or to impose a pumped-circulation regime. Features of pumped circulation are that there is greater freedom in the disposition of heating surface and that higher-resistance circuits, using smaller tubes, may be employed because of the extra circulating forces available to overcome system resistance or resistance of internal steam separators. Disadvantages are the greater mechanical complexity with added maintenance, the power consumption of the pumps and the fact that the circulation balance does not adjust itself to the heat input pattern.

Once-through boilers

With circulating drum boilers, there is a relatively large volume of water contained in tubes and drum and the proportion of steam to water as the mixture reaches the drum is unlikely to exceed 20% by weight. Once-through boilers, as their name suggests, are arranged for all the incoming feedwater to dry out to steam in its passage along the tubes and to the superheater, without an intermediate separating vessel except probably for start-up. This type of boiler is essential at very high pressures since at or above the critical pressure, 220 bar, there is no density difference between water and steam and above about 185 bar this difference is small, thus there is little natural circulation force. The large once-through boiler requires sophisticated controls and a complementary system to permit pumped circulation at start-up with heat dumping.

Since the water fed to the boiler is all turned to

steam, it is essential that it is of high quality and rigidly controlled.

Coil boilers

Some industrial use is made of coil boilers, which are essentially of the once-through concept, but normally arranged so that only the major part and not the whole of the water is evaporated to steam. There are separating arrangements at the coil outlet, the separated water containing the concentrated solids from the feed, which is then extracted. This is said to permit operation with indifferent feedwater by common watertube boiler standards and to give a good steam purity.

Steam separation

Only in the smallest boilers will the free surface area in the steam drum be large enough to give acceptable separation of steam from water. In addition to the obvious need for the steam leaving the drum to be pure, it is also necessary to avoid steam bubbles being entrained in the water to the circulating system, since this will diminish the head available for circulation and can have other side-effects such as causing cavitation in boiler circulating pumps. Internal equipment is accordingly fitted to the steam drum to improve separation. This will primarily operate on a principle making use of the energy in the steam and water mixture entering the drum from the boiler. Baffle plates may be provided to channel this mixture through simple devices such as downward discharging slots which drive the water down, releasing the steam into the steam space of the drum. More elaborate equipment of higher performance may be necessary such as a cyclone steam separator, which spins out the water by centrifugal action.

In addition to the primary separation of water from steam there may be a secondary device in the form of a dry pipe, or steam scrubber, to encourage removal of the remaining water mist from the steam before it leaves the drum. A general arrangement of the internal fittings is shown in *Figure 5.1.*

Since the steam-separating equipment functions by using some of the energy of circulation it is an important aim in design to keep this to an acceptable level. The pressure head associated with the drum internals is important, and these must be properly installed. This will prevent leak paths which would allow sprays of water into the steam space in the drum, with likely detriment to the steam quality, and possible serious carryover into superheater tubes.

Assemblies should be light-tight and mating faces checked by fine feeler gauge. Where possible, the design should provide for masking

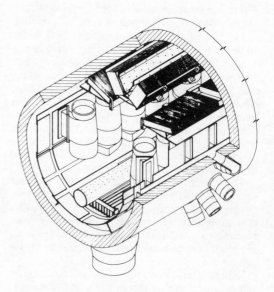

Figure 5.1   Steam drum internals

of joints, at least those facing in a critical direction.

Steam purity

Purity of steam is a basic requirement both for the external load served by the boiler and for the boiler itself. If the steam carries entrained boiler water it is inevitable that solids in the water will be taken into the superheater with the risk of tube overheating. This is due to the build-up of a heat-resisting deposit which in extreme cases will choke the superheater with significant increase in pressure drop and load limitation.

Solids from the boiler water can similarly cause trouble in a turbine owing to build-up on the blades with consequent fall-off in performance.

Carryover for the majority of substances dissolved in the boiler water appears to be by solids dissolved in water droplets in the steam. Silica, however, is carried as vapour in the steam, the amount carried increasing with increased temperature for the same concentration in the boiler water. Strict limits of silica must be observed as pressures, and hence water temperatures, go up. It may be necessary to restrict the pressure at which a boiler is operated, especially in the early steaming of a new unit, if the silica level in the water is too high for the full pressure. The high silica level is due to contamination during erection, leaching out of mill scale, etc. and is overcome by plant clean-up using good-quality feedwater and vigorous blowing down until the desired level is reached.

Consideration must therefore be given to the silica content of the raw water, to determine how it should be treated to achieve an acceptable feedwater.

Determination of steam purity

Although it is not normally necessary to have continuous monitoring of the steam quality, either leaving the drum or at the superheater outlet, it may be desirable to make a test from time to time for routine information, to prove a new installation or to diagnose a problem.

Most determinations of steam purity are made on the basis of measuring solids in the steam rather than by attempting a direct assessment of wetness, because of the much greater accuracy possible and because in most circumstances the water itself does not cause problems while the entrained solids do.

For testing, a steam sample is taken from the boiler, condensed, and tested. From the point of view of carryover from the drum it is preferable to sample before the superheater, since a steam sample at the superheater outlet cannot disclose whether deposits are being laid down in the superheater.

Whilst, ideally, carefully sized and located sampling probes should be used, such as are set out in the standard BS 3285: 'Method of sampling superheated steam from steam-generating units', a gross problem can probably be investigated by simpler methods, even by checking from a drain or vent.

Good results are achieved on the steam leaving a drum having multiple outlets to the superheater by an internal collecting pipe lying along the line of the outlets with one or two small holes facing the oncoming steam in the way of each outlet.

For general investigations, useful information can often be had by determining solids in the condensed sample by measuring electrical conductivity, provided that it is remembered that gases such as ammonia and carbon dioxide in the steam will add to the conductivity measurement and may need to be taken into account. Conductivity of a degassed sample should be 2 conductivity units (microsiemens per centimetre at 25°C), or less. (For measurement of conductivity *see* Chapter 8, while conductivity units are discussed further in Chapter 7.)

A commercially useful and accurate method of determining steam purity is by the sodium ion electrode technique.

Sodium flame photometry also gives a high accuracy and evaporation to dryness may give information such as, for example, iron from a scum which would not be shown by the other methods. Where there is a problem with carryover the drum internals should be checked for correct assembly and fit, and a careful inspection made of water line or deposit markings in the steam space of the drum, which may give clues to irregularities.

Tests may show whether there is a sudden increase in carryover with a sudden load change or with high water level, and this would suggest how the problem can be further explored or operation modified to avoid critical conditions.

The boiler water and feedwater analyses should be carefully assessed. High levels of dissolved or suspended solids will increase the tendency to carryover, as will the presence of organic material which can lead to foaming. Cases have been known where unusual or seasonal conditions in the water supply, such as the effects of drought or changes of reservoir supply, have had a marked influence on behaviour. Oil in the boiler water can lead to trouble both with foaming and with blistering of tubes owing to the heat resistance of a thin film.

5.4 Boiler operation

Safe and reliable operation of boilers, as with all plant, is dependent to a large extent on the skill and attention of the operator. The operator should understand the basic principles, be familiar with the equipment in his charge, and have a background of training and experience. Manufacturers' instruction books should be used, effectively coupled with such specific procedures as may have been established at the time of commissioning by the suppliers' service engineers, or developed by competent persons in the light of experience with the plant.

The supervising engineer should ensure that careful records are kept of boiler performance with particular reference to regular logging of steam flow and temperature, air and flue gas temperatures and gas analysis, air and gas pressure, fuel data and consumption and water temperature, flow and analysis. It is also valuable to record intermediate temperatures of steam and intermediate temperatures and pressure of gases. Charts from recording instruments should be systematically preserved. If relevant, dust and ash should be sampled at regular intervals.

The records should be scrutinized as a routine, to recognize trends of behaviour or to spot departures from the norm, so that these indications can immediately be investigated to discover the cause. The operators should be encouraged to be alert at all times to react to signs of abnormal plant behaviour and, while knowing that senior staff support is available if required, should be trained to take immediate safeguarding action in an emergency.

The operator should have an understanding of the control system and matters such as procedures for changeover from automatic to remote manual control and operation, with various combinations of parts of the control system out of service.

Preparation of a new boiler

A new boiler or one which has extensive repairs should be prepared for service by a process designed to clean out oils, greases and other contaminants such as debris and mill scale arising from the manufacturing and erecting activities.

Boiling out

The basic procedure is to fire the boiler daily over, typically, three days up to a pressure of about half normal working pressure, having filled it with a solution of trisodium phosphate (Na_3PO_4), or if unavailable, soda ash (Na_2CO_3). For every 10 000 kg of water in the boiler there should be 50 kg of crystalline trisodium phosphate ($Na_3PO_4 \cdot 12H_2O$), 22kg of anhydrous trisodium phosphate, which does not dissolve so readily, or 90 kg of soda ash. The chemicals should be mixed outside the boiler and transferred through the open manhole into the drum, which has a level of about 0.6 m of water in it. If the boiler can at the same time be slowly fed with water this ensures a good distribution.

Treatment of the economizer will probably need to be done by introducing chemicals with the feedwater during feeding.

The boiler is allowed to cool each night and each blowdown and drain valve is opened for a brief period to blow out sludge before pressure-raising each day. At the end of the process, when the boiler has cooled, it is emptied while there is still some pressure. A little water is then fed to wash out sludge and the boiler finally completely filled with clean water. The superheater should be carefully flooded over from the drum and then all is emptied for inspection, commencing with the superheater. In this process the alkaline solution degreases and removes protective films, the temperature cycling contributes to the removal of mill scale from the internal surfaces and general debris is loosened and flushed out.

Chemical cleaning

For high-pressure units it is essential and for medium-pressure units often desirable that the internal surfaces are further treated, to ensure complete removal of mill scale and to prepare

the surfaces to initiate the formation of the coherent iron oxide film on which the subsequent successful operation depends. This film provides a barrier between the boiler water and the steel of the pressure parts without which corrosion must take place. Typical cleaning media are inhibited hydrochloric acid and citric acid, often with a wetting agent and sometimes supported by other reagents such as hydrofluoric acid to assist in silica removal.

These processes are usually carried out with hot solutions but careful control is necessary to avoid, say, destruction of an inhibitor as the result of too high a temperature. Although success can be achieved by static 'sit and soak' methods, better control and results are usually had by circulation using temporary pumps or promoted by injection of inert gas. In either case, temporary baffles and restrictions may be arranged in the boiler circulating systems to bring about the required flow paths.

Present (1978) opinion is against the chemical cleaning of large superheaters and reheaters, because of the difficulty of ensuring adequate circulation and flushing owing to the many parallel flow paths. Experience has shown that the after-effects of troubles arising from chemical cleaning may well exceed any benefit.

This whole subject is complex, and to go into detail is beyond the scope of this chapter. Where chemical cleaning is required there are specialist firms to assist and the advice of the boilermaker should be obtained. There are, however, some general points to have clearly in mind.

1. Always add inhibitor before acid.
2. Never fire with acid in the boiler.
3. Prepare for effluent disposal and neutralization before admitting acid.
4. Have a standby circulating pump or certain means of rapid dumping of the boiler contents.
5. Provide full personnel protection against hot chemical hazards.
6. Never permit unacceptable substances to be used where contamination can have disastrous consequences, such as chlorides and hydrochloric acid or caustic soda with austenitic steels, which lead to stress corrosion cracking.

Blowing out steam lines

Before putting a new boiler and pipe system into service, particularly to protect the turbine or other steam user, it is often arranged that the superheater, and reheater if fitted, and the steam mains will be blown through with steam from the boiler to scour out solid debris which would otherwise cause damage.

Temporary discharge piping of adequate size and strength should be arranged at a point local to the turbine steam chest, and the discharge led to a safe locality with unobstructed 'field of fire'. Proper provision is essential to support and guide this pipe and to carry the thrust at discharge. The discharge must not be along the line of a roof or sheeted wall — the steam blow entrains air with it and can lift adjacent surfaces. Any strainers in the system should be removed, and replaced after blowing. The boiler pressure used for blowing out the lines must not exceed the design pressure of the temporary piping and its fittings.

There are two alternatives for blowing out. The first is to raise pressure to just below the permissible pressure, gradually opening the boiler stop valve whilst increasing the firing to maintain pressure, followed by gradual closing of the stop valve. This gives a prolonged blowing period. The second is to raise pressure as before but then to stop firing with the stop valve being quickly opened and then quickly closed, having allowed the pressure to drop by about 15 bar. This method gives a sudden change in pressure and temperature, helping to loosen scale, but subjects the boiler to greater thermal shock. It is advisable not to permit a change in saturation temperature of greater than 40°C. With either method, adequate feedwater must be available to restore the level in the drum, care being taken to avoid an unduly high level, with risk of carryover, or a very low level, when the drum could suffer thermal shock on refilling.

A series of steam blows should be made and after a period when gross debris may be expected to have cleared, a polished target plate or bar can be set up on which the discharge can impinge to give an indication of steam cleanliness and deductions can then be made concerning the need for further steam blows.

When there is a reheater, this and its steam leads should be purged after the superheater and main steam pipe by suitable temporary cross-connecting pipework. This could be from the main steam pipe at the turbine to the cold reheat pipe, with the discharge from the hot reheat pipe. Ideally the cold reheat pipe should be purged alone before connection to the reheater. *Figure 5.2* shows the general arrangement.

Start-up

Before commencing plant start-up, it is highly desirable, if not essential, that the full state of the plant and its auxiliaries is known, particularly in such matters as setting of valves and dampers and availability of supplies. A general check

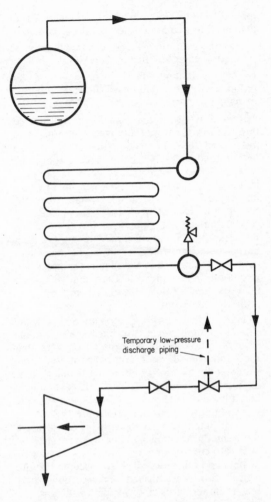

Figure 5.2   Temporary blowout arrangement

should be made to ensure that all is ready for start-up, particularly that access doors are closed. Instrumentation and displays to inform the operator must be ready for service, and all safety interlock systems must be functioning correctly, with simulated check trips made to prove them.

The boiler will be filled with water, usually to a low level in the water gauge to anticipate the volume increase due to thermal expansion as the temperature rises, and air vents and superheater drains opened in preparation for start-up. As start-up proceeds, air vents may be closed once a strong blow of steam and some pressure has been established, and intermediate superheater drains may also be closed. The final superheater drain or vent must remain open at all times until there is sufficient export of steam from the boiler to ensure flow through the superheater. The vent may need to be closed in as pressure increases to achieve the required rate of raising pressure.

Intermediate drains should occasionally be opened to clear any further condensate.

The circulating pumps of a boiler having pump-assisted circulation will be started before firing commences.

Before any source of ignition is introduced into the furnace, especially with gas, liquid and pulverized fuels, an adequate purging of the furnace and the whole boiler setting should be carried out to ensure that there is no accumulation of flammable vapour which might cause an explosion. This purge, usually by air, requires a flow of at least 25% of full-load combustion air maintained for several minutes. A similar purge is essential should the first burner fail to ignite or after any accidental loss of ignition. (Some explosive limits for gases are given on p 38 (Chapter 3).) There may be a purge interlock system to ensure that the purge is properly carried out.

The rate of fuel firing should not be below the safe minimum level for maintaining stable ignition, and fuel flow relatively greater than the available air must not be permitted, thus avoiding the risk of unburnt fuel leading to an explosion. As start-up proceeds, firing should be maintained at a safe level to avoid damage to the plant. Important considerations are the rate of increase in temperature to avoid big temperature differentials, not only in boiler pressure parts but also refractories, and the limits set for superheaters and reheaters which are uncooled before a steam flow is established, and accordingly may reach temperatures close to that of the gas. An acceptable rate of temperature change is 70°C per hour, which has been found to be satisfactory for refractories, and also avoids adverse effects on the pressure parts such as disturbance to expanded tube joints. The temperature rise can be deduced from the saturated steam temperature corresponding to the boiler pressure. In some circumstances, such as with fully welded construction with minimal refractory material, an enhanced firing rate might be established by trial but frequently gas temperature in the superheater will be the limiting factor. With very large or very high-pressure boilers, limits may also be imposed by temperature differentials in the drum, although this is unlikely at drum thicknesses below 100 mm. For superheater protection, the gas temperature must be limited to what the material will permit considering the scaling temperature. Often a limit of 500°C is adopted for carbon steel and 590°C for alloy materials.

Direct measurement of tube metal temperature requires sophisticated equipment, often depending on the accurate life of thermocouples, so that it is generally found better to use a furnace gas temperature measurement in the superheater zone as the guide for control. For a large plant, a mechanically retractable probe may be installed for this purpose, but for smaller units good results can be achieved by a temporary thermocouple inserted at start-ups and a defined procedure may be established during the commissioning of a new plant, which can be followed with confidence in subsequent routine operation.

Operation to control gas temperature may require the intermittent cutting in and out of firing equipment if the low-firing characteristic is too high for continuous use.

Non-drainable superheaters will inevitably contain some water prior to raising pressure, which will prevent a flow of cooling steam; this water is removed by boiling out, which makes control of gas temperature most important. This must give a high enough temperature in the superheater zone for effective drying out, whilst avoiding overheating of tubes through which there is no steam flow. Damage to superheaters has sometimes occurred owing to inadequate dry-out during a protracted start-up with inadequate temperatures, as well as by unwise high firing.

Indications from thermocouples, permanent or temporary, attached to judiciously selected superheater tubes near their outlet, and outside the gas pass, can reveal the progress of boil-out of water since, before a through steam flow is achieved, the temperatures will be at about saturation temperature for the pressure but will move up to show superheat after dry-out.

Attemperators are devices to give control of final steam temperature, by partial cooling of the steam at an appropriate point in the superheater or reheater. Surface-type attemperators consist of tube bundles cooled by boiler water, the steam passing through the tubes, whereas spray-type attemperators work by direct injection of cooling water into the steam. Surface-type attemperators should be by-passed during pressure raising, using the steam side drains periodically to expel condensate. Spray-type attemperators must on no account be used during pressure raising as this would merely flood the superheater.

As pressure raising proceeds, the water level will rise in the gauge glass owing to water expansion, which may necessitate some blowing down to keep the level well in sight. At no time, whether during start-up or ordinary steaming, is it safe to operate without certain knowledge of the water level and it should be axiomatic that firing is to cease if the level passes from sight.

Equipment such as remote water-level indicators and high- and low-water alarms should be brought into use as appropriate in accordance with the maker's instructions.

On-load

To put a boiler on the line, whether the system is cold or a hot range already under pressure, care is required and if there is a by-pass to the main stop valve this should first be opened to warm the system through gradually or to balance pressures. In the case of a range system the boiler will be brought up to or slightly above range pressure before attempting to connect. Where there is no by-pass, the main valve must be cracked open only very gently during the heating or balancing period.

Warming-through a cold system requires adequate drainage of condensate, and hand drains by-passing steam traps should be used.

On a new system there is the likelihood that mill scale will choke the steam traps, which should be given close attention and cleaned as necessary. With the boiler in service, periodic flue gas analyses should be made using the Orsat apparatus or a similar method, to check on the quality of combustion and to show if significant in-leakage of air is taking place. If there is more than a 2% CO_2 drop between boiler outlet and induced-draught fan inlet, unacceptable leakage is probably occurring in the economizer or air heater.

Dampers should be worked away from their normal running position at least once a week, to ensure that they are free to move and that bearings are prevented from seizing.

Boiler water concentration, which will tend to increase as solids are brought in with the feed, is controlled by periodic or continuous blowdown. This should be done through the blowdown systems and in no circumstances, unless an unusually specific procedure has been developed by the manufacturer, should the bottom wall header drains be opened with the boiler on load because of the risk of upsetting the circulation and causing tube overheating.

In the event of the water level being discovered to be very low, and certainly if it has gone out of sight from the gauge glass, firing should immediately be stopped and extreme caution exercised in feeding to restore the level. If there is good reason to suspect that the boiler is grossly short of water and very hot, it is safer to allow it to cool before adding any feedwater, to avoid thermal shock. After a suspected serious loss of water it is advisable to shut the boiler down for inspection for possible overheating damage before returning it to service.

Any leak which may develop in operation should receive attention at the earliest opportunity since even a small leak is likely to increase; often an initial leak, insignificant in itself, can have very serious consequences because of the erosion of adjacent tubes or flange faces by the water or steam jet. This can be particularly damaging in a closely packed surface such as in an economizer, and any leak there should be treated as justifying very prompt action in taking the boiler off.

Shutting down

As the boiler is taken off-load, the fuel should be shut off using the appropriate technique to clean out residual fuel and to leave the system safe and in good order. The forced-draught fan should be stopped before the induced-draught fan to ensure that the setting is purged of gas. The dampers should then be closed to ensure slow cooling of the boiler to minimize temperature stresses. A visible water level should be maintained with occasional feeding of water if necessary during the cooling period. Normal level is not essential.

The superheater drains should be opened to drain condensate. If there is an economizer recirculating line this should also be opened.

Before all the pressure has gone, the air cocks should be opened to make sure that there is no risk of vacuum, which is a safety hazard and could also upset the tightness of joints. It is quite common to drain the boiler whilst some pressure, say under 3 bar, remains, as the pressure draining helps to scour out sludge and the boiler will dry out by the residual heat. If the boiler is to remain off-load but at standby, it will be kept at some intermediate pressure by periodic firing.

It is most important to take precautions against possible explosion by always purging the setting before lighting a burner or, in the case of solid fuel on a stoker, before livening up the fire.

5.5 Control of boiler operation

Automatic control

Automatic control is discussed in more detail in Chapter 8. The basic requirements for boiler automatic control are to control firing to meet the load and to feed in water to match the steam output. The master signal for control is the pressure, either from the individual boiler or from a steam main served by several boilers. A change in pressure is used to signal for a change of firing rate calling for fuel and air changes.

Since over the control range efficiency does

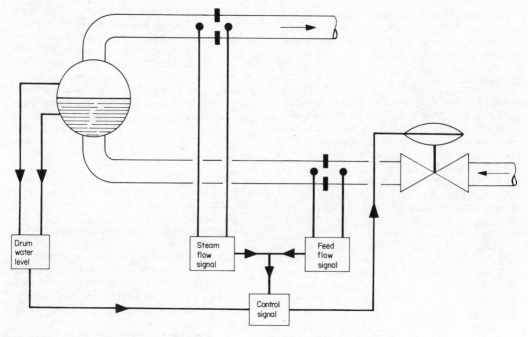

Figure 5.3   Three-element feed regulator

not vary greatly, there is a close relationship between steam flow and air for combustion, so that the classic boiler control sets out to maintain these two quantities in step. This control is set by adjustment against flue gas analysis, while for greater precision it may be trimmed by an additional signal from continuous flue gas monitoring such as oxygen analysis.

Particularly for combustion with a low excess of air, it may be necessary to arrange for air flow to lead fuel flow for rising load, and to lag behind fuel for falling load to ensure that there is always sufficient air for complete combustion. An oil control valve may need to be arranged for slow movement so that it does not get out of step with air flow control, which has a longer reaction time.

Furnace pressure is normally controlled by an independent loop controlling the induced-draught fan and dampers.

Feedwater regulation is required to keep a safe working level of water in the boiler. The simplest type of control uses a single element (water level) alone. However, single-element control is unlikely to be adequate except for small, low-rated boilers since the level at which the control rests varies with load and it will tend to move against longer-term needs as load changes. When load decreases, steam pressure will rise and steam production in the boiler will fall, resulting in less steam volume in the boiler tubes with consequent fall in water level. The

simple control will then call for more water, which is the opposite of the load.

For this reason three-element control (*Figure 5.3*) is common, the three elements being a prime signal for steam flow, to call for feed rate changes, a feedback signal from water flow and a final trimming signal from water level to reach the desired set point. Steam temperature is controlled by an independent loop.

The control of a once-through boiler is different from that for drum boilers. In this case pressure is controlled by feedwater regulation and steam temperature gives the signal for heat input.

Steam temperature control

The majority of superheaters, which see little radiant heat and are mostly subject to heat input by convection, have a characteristic which gives an increasing steam temperature with increasing load. For most purposes the boiler is required to meet a range of load with little change in final steam temperature.

Some change in heat balance between zones in the boiler can be achieved by changing the heat input pattern in the furnace by, say, selection between burners at different levels or by more specialized arrangements such as tilting burners. These may be coarse or slow in response and provision is commonly made for attemperation, which is partial desuperheating between stages in the superheater to absorb the extra heat pickup by evaporation of water. Attemperators may be of the spray type, where condensate-quality water is injected directly into the steam, or of the surface type, where the steam is cooled by passing through a tube bundle either submerged in the boiler drum or in an individual pressure shell which is part of one of the boiler water circuits. An attemperator is shown in *Figure 5.4.*

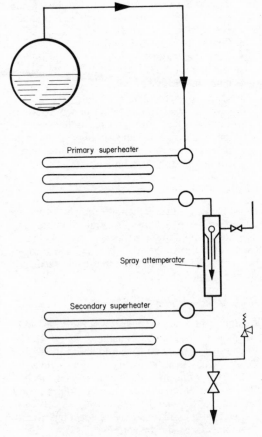

Figure 5.4 Two-stage superheater with attemperator

With spray attemperators it is important to remember that any water not evaporated in the steam will enter the following superheater and can cause waterlogging of individual tubes thus cutting off the steam flow, often leading to overheating and failure. Other risks are stress corrosion and, with gross maloperation, carry-over of water to the turbine. For these reasons spray water must never be admitted during start-up or low-load conditions and also the mixed temperature after the attemperator should not be allowed to approach more closely

to saturation temperature than, say, 30°C.

Surface attemperators are controlled by valve dampers balancing steam flow either through the tubes or to by-pass, and proper drainage is necessary to ensure that the system is not waterlogged during start-up or at loads when attemperation is not required.

Any leak at the tube bundle will contaminate the steam with boiler water likely to have a high solid content, with consequent risk of fouling and damage to superheater and turbine. It is essential therefore that assembly and work-manship are good and the equipment carefully inspected during regular overhauls. A point to keep in mind is that the submerged tube bundle is not designed to withstand full boiler pressure, but probably only a pressure such as 7 bar differential between water and steam, and accordingly no pressure test should be under-taken which would subject only one side to high pressures.

Control of steam temperature is sometimes achieved by gas dampers controlling the amount of gas flow over different tube banks. This method has had considerable vogue in marine boilers between the superheater and generating tube banks, and in large boilers to give temperature control of reheaters, where spray attemperation degrades the steam cycle efficiency. Where the reheater is controlled by dampers, the superheater must be sized to give the required performance when the maximum gas is directed to the reheater, and minimum to the superheater. Excess superheater perform-ance is absorbed by attemperators.

Good reheat control is also achieved without the complication of divided gas passes and proportioning dampers by use of gas recircula-tion, where gas from the back end of the boiler is returned to the bottom of the furnace. This affects heat absorption in the furnace and increases the weight of hot gas passing over the various convective heating surfaces, thus increasing the heat pick-up. Gas recirculation therefore boosts temperature performance and the quantity recirculated is reduced as load increases, to counter the normal convective characteristic. Excess superheat temperature is again controlled by spray water.

Gas recirculation can help with start-up techniques such as good dry-out of flooded superheaters and attaining desired steam temperatures during hot starting.

The amount of excess air influences the total gas flow through the superheater, and accord-ingly, increased excess air will generally increase the superheat temperature. The normal tendency to run at greater excess air at part load than at full load will tend to flatten the steam

which otherwise falls off with load reduction.

Where the feedwater temperature is reduced, as for example with a feedheater out of service, the effect is to burn more fuel for the same steam output. This means that the heat input to the superheater is greater than at normal feed temperature and accordingly the steam temperature will increase.

Control of water level

The boiler *must* be supplied with adequate water to avoid overheating and serious damage, with attendant safety hazards.

Water-level gauge

The basic equipment is the drum water-level gauge or gauges allowing direct observation. Tubular glass gauges are used for low pressures up to 27 bar, flat plate glasses in suitable carriers for medium pressures of 17–95 bar and a series of circular glass 'bull's-eyes' for high pressures from about 82 bar. Apart from considerations of strength, tubular glasses are limited in their pressure range because the boiler water at or near saturation temperature directly wets the glass, and etching and erosion take place with increasing rapidity as pressure increases. Gauge glass erosion is also increased by high alkalinity in the boiler water.

This problem is combated for flat plate and bull's-eye glasses by inserting a mica sheet between glass and water.

In operation, the gauge glass assembly will lose heat to its surroundings, causing a steady condensation of steam and slow return of condensate to the drum through the water connection. The more vigorous this condensation, the more rapid is likely to be the erosion or deterioration of the glass and mica, and this is one reason why it is undesirable for the gauge to be mounted on very long legs from the drum nozzle. For the same reason, water gauges should be protected from draughts.

An internal extension pipe to the water leg may be fitted in the boiler drum, to ensure that the level shown is not distorted by turbulence and other effects of water circulation in the drum.

Another matter to be kept in mind regarding gauge glass performance which becomes significant at the higher pressures, say above 110 bar, is that the column of water in the gauge is at an average temperature lower than the drum water and is accordingly more dense, so that the level of water in the glass is below that in the drum. This can represent several inches at 170 bar.

Gauge glasses should be regularly tested after first ensuring that any other equipment, such as a remote indicator served by the same tappings off the drum, is isolated. Any such equipment must be put back into service after testing the gauge glass. The following test procedure should be followed, taking note of any specific recommendation of the maker:

1. With steam and water connections open to the drum, partly open the drain valve to allow the glass and fittings to reach maximum temperature gradually. Then open the drain wide.
2. Test the steam connection by closing the water valve until satisfied that the steam connection is clear.
3. Open the water connection.
4. Test the water connection by closing the steam valve until satisfied that the water connection is clear.
5. Open the steam valve.
6. Close the drain valve, when the water should return promptly to its level in the gauge glass. Any sluggishness may indicate that the steam or water connection is partly choked and the level may be false.

Remote water-level indication

Remote water-level indication may be provided either to give simply an indication to the operator at his station, or serving also as a signal for level alarm or control. The maker's instructions should be followed in the use and setting of such equipment.

High and low alarms

A high- and low-level alarm is a most desirable addition to direct observation of water levels. The alarm setting points should always be within the range of the water-level gauges or indicators, so that the working of the alarm may be checked at regular intervals by careful raising and lowering of the water level.

External-type alarms may perform incorrectly if unlagged or if the pressure is low. Float chambers require regular blowing through to ensure that the action is not impaired by accumulated sludge.

Safety valves

Safety valves are fitted to safeguard the boiler against overpressure to conform with legal and code requirements. The total capacity of the valves must be fully sufficient to discharge the full potential output of steam whilst not exceeding a permitted rise above working pressure.

Where the boiler incorporates a superheater it is important that a safety valve is provided at the superheater outlet, and that this valve is set so as to lift first, before the drum valves. This ensures that, when the safety valves are called upon to act, a steam flow is maintained through the superheater, thus protecting it from overheating. The setting pressure of the superheater safety valve will relate to the full-load pressure drop through the superheater.

Before a boiler is put into service for the first time, safety valves must be tested for correct lift and reseating at the specified pressures, usually in the presence, and to the satisfaction, of an appropriate witness such as an engineer surveyor from the boiler insurance company or other person called for by regulations.

The valves are 'floated' with the main stop valve closed. At the commencement, all valves except that with the highest lifting pressure are secured by gags to the valve maker's instructions. Starting with the valve set to lift at the highest pressure, each valve is floated separately by raising pressure, removing the gags in sequence. As pressure approaches the lifting pressure, the rate of firing should be increased to lift the valve sharply, and once the valve is fully open the firing rate and air supply is reduced, and water fed as necessary to restore water level. Particular note should be taken of the maker's specific instructions.

After completion of setting and inspection of the valves, guards should be replaced and locked, the keys being put into proper safe keeping.

The reseat pressures should always be above the intended automatic control set point, or the boiler will overfire. It is essential that any part of the steam and water system which is heated, and can be separately isolated, as is sometimes the case for example with the economizer, must be adequately protected with its own relief valve.

Difficulty with safety valves can be caused by undue strains coming onto the valve body, leading to slight distortions. The safety valve discharge should not be restrained by rigid connections to the escape piping unless this is merely a short vent free to move with the valve. Expansion joints with slip plates are common, or sometimes flexible connections are used. With any slip plate arrangement the plate must be free to move and the expansion movement of the valve from its cold position to that at full working conditions should be adequately provided for. A safety valve arrangement is shown in *Figure 5.5*.

Especially where silencers are fitted to the escape pipe, the possibility exists of pressure build-up in the pipe, with risk of steam escape at the expansion joint when the valve lifts. Caution is necessary when first testing valves on a new boiler, and experience may indicate if personnel

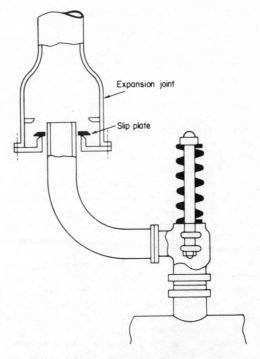

Figure 5.5   Safety valve escape pipe

protection barriers should be provided.

A safety valve with a single offset discharge develops a considerable unbalanced thrust when it lifts. Valves mounted on short nozzles on drums or headers are usually adequately supported, but proper consideration must be given to this thrust if the nozzle is long or on pipework. In any event it is undesirable to locate a safety valve on a long nozzle or pipe leg, lest the local resistance to flow, when the valve is discharging, causes a pressure drop under the valve, encouraging it to reseat only to lift again as flow stops and pressure rises.

Efficiency testing

An efficiency test compares the heat output in the steam with the heat input from the fuel. It is often found impossible to achieve satisfactory tests by this direct method because of the difficulty of accurately determining one of the quantities, usually the heat input, which is likely to become progressively more challenging with increase in size of boilers.

The alternative is to arrive at the required information by determination of the losses, which are described on p 73, coupled with knowledge of, say, the heat output where good accuracy can be achieved in water flow and steam pressure and temperature measurement. It is still necessary to carry out sampling and analysis of the fuel and the gases, as well as the fuel residues, to find the various losses.

The losses, being a relatively small part of the heat account, are proportionally less affected by measurement errors than the major heat account quantities. To complete the heat account a figure arrived at by experience is assumed for the radiation and unaccounted loss.

The conduct of the test requires the boiler to be established on-load under steady conditions, which are carried for a period before the test period commences and continue after it. Conditions should not be disturbed by, say, sootblowing during the test period and the state of the boiler (for example, water level in the drum, thickness of fuel bed on a stoker, and the amount of dust and ash in hoppers) must be the same at the end of the test as at the start.

Whilst an efficiency test will provide an opportunity of recording a wide range of operating data from the installed instrumentation, it is generally found that this instrumentation, while giving useful indications, does not have the accuracy required for contractual tests and for that purpose specially calibrated test instruments and thermocouples are necessary.

Boiler efficiency testing is dealt with in Chapter 4.

5.6 Hazards

Fire and explosion hazards

Chapter 3 deals with explosion hazards, but this section serves to emphasize certain details of boiler operation which will prevent a fuel explosion.

The nature of fuels presents risks which need to be kept in mind and guarded against. Unburnt fuel in any circumstances mixed with air can often burn violently where, for example, an explosive mixture has accumulated and has then ignited. Especially with liquid and gas fuels it is most important that unlit fuel does not seep into an idle boiler owing to leaking valves and bad isolation, and operating practice as well as maintenance procedures should include positive precautions to check that all is well. Gas firing systems should provide venting as well as valve isolation to make certain.

There is a similar risk with solid fuels such as a banked fire in a stoker-fired boiler behaving as a gas producer, where not only may combustible volatiles be released from the fuel bed, but carbon monoxide gas will be formed owing to the restricted amount of air available for reaction with the carbon.

The boiler must be adequately purged before an attempt is made to light it up from cold or to liven up a banked fire and at other times when there may have been a complete loss of ignition. With oil or gas, it is good practice to ensure that dampers at the boiler outlet are not tightly shut off to the stack, but give some permitted leakage to provide venting when off-load. With oil- and gas-fired boilers it is also very much to be preferred, in multiple-boiler installations, that each boiler has its own individual flue to avoid the risk of a spark from a steaming boiler igniting an explosive mixture in an idle unit alongside. This is a real risk with a common flue.

Enclosed dead spaces within the boiler casing are best avoided with oil and gas firing and where they occur, such as the top dead-space chamber of a top-supported boiler, tight durable sealing is necessary, supported by venting to prevent dangerous vapour from accumulating; or they can be pressurized above furnace gas pressure so that any leakage is into the gas stream.

Explosion risk is not confined to flammable mixtures accumulating during shutdown. When on-load, an inadequate air supply will leave some fuel unburnt and sudden air correction could have disastrous results. In the same way there are flammability limits to the ratio of fuel to air outside which combustion will not take place. This property can be put to good account, as for example with PF systems, which run with a rich fuel mixture to avoid an explosion risk.

With natural gas, being largely methane, flammability limits are narrow and flame propagation speed low. This means that tighter operating limits must be observed relative to those with, say, petroleum gases and oil to maintain the flame and to avoid the danger of unburnt gases.

Leakage of fuels from systems should receive immediate attention and catchment by drip trays provided at oil burners, at pumps and in similar locations where spillage may take place. Any spillage should be cleaned up and drip trays regularly emptied.

Hot dust accumulations in the boiler give rise to hazards, either as a possible source of ignition for unburnt fuel or because a sudden disturbance and entrainment of dust, especially when high in combustible matter, could result in an explosive mixture. For this reason sootblowing must be done only with the boiler steaming at a high load with minimum free oxygen in the flue gas or in unusual circumstances at shutdown, and then only if it is certain that dust deposits have cooled completely.

Serious fires resulting in major damage to plant are sometimes experienced at the cold end of a boiler, typically in an air heater where the surface area of tubes or plates is large relative to their weight. These fires have their origin in build-up of combustible deposits, usually finely divided carbon arising from soot from incomplete combustion, and oily deposits from unburnt oil carried over from the furnace. Ignition may take place by spontaneous combustion and a very fierce fire can ensue. There is enough experience for it to be recommended that a fire of this type should be tackled by water only if very good access is possible and copious drenching can be achieved in a short time. Any attempt to put out the fire by steam blanketing or relatively restricted water spraying may well result in setting up a steam/iron combustion reaction making for an even more serious situation. Where a fire of this sort is suspected, all dampers should be shut to discourage through draughts and entry of air. Carbon dioxide blanketing should be applied if possible. Fire hoses, at least at the start, may best be directed to reduce casing temperatures and to localize the effects of the fire.

Prevention being better than cure, poor combustion conditions permitting soot production and carryover of unburnt fuel vapour should not be tolerated and, further, periodic inspections should reveal whether there is a tendency for surface deposits to build up, in which case a routine cleaning cycle should be instituted. It is particularly important to be alert to signs of combustible deposits at times of start-up of new plant and with low-load running.

Access and maintenance hazards

Before attempting entry to a boiler or undertaking maintenance, due consideration must be given to potential dangers so that these can be properly guarded against. A manhole door, plate or flange on a pressure system should never be released without making certain that pressure has been removed by isolation and opening air vents, and that draining is complete. Even after these precautions, items such as a door should only be slackened back, and all retaining nuts kept on until the joint has been broken so as to keep control if there is any residual pressure. Vacuum can be as dangerous as pressure.

Before personnel enter any pressure system it must be completely isolated. The surest way to do this is by physically removing valves or pipe sections, and the ability to remove them should be built into the design where possible. In cases where this is impracticable, full isolation should be ensured by closing valves and chaining and locking them with the keys held in a fully controlled manner. The possibility of back-flow through drain systems should not be overlooked.

Consideration should be given to any possibility of an unsafe atmosphere; a particular case is where a boiler has been stored with nitrogen.

Before entry to the gas side, similar precautions should be taken to secure firing equipment and to isolate fuels from any prospect of leakage. Steps must be taken to immobilize equipment such as fans and rotary air heaters by electrically isolating the motors, again with a formal positive control procedure.

Electrostatic precipitators are provided with elaborate interlocking to prevent direct entry when energized, and care should be taken over any installation where unforeseen danger exists, if entry is even remotely possible via connecting ducts.

Any portable electrical equipment such as hand lamps and power tools should be permitted only if operating on low voltage (not more than 110 V). Air-driven tools are much to be preferred.

Precautions should be taken against falling slag in high furnaces, and dust heaps which may be deceptively cool on the surface but very hot inside. Chambers could also contain dust accumulations of unknown depth.

The normal hazards from height and heavy weights must not be overlooked. If any gallery flooring is removed for access, the opening must be safeguarded by roping off and the posting of warning notices.

Cradles and access platforms are useful in furnace inspection and for light work but often an adequate scaffolding is fully justified and much to be preferred for the greater safety and improved working conditions, and to provide simultaneous access to different areas.

Health hazards may be involved. Asbestos risks are now well recognized (*see* Chapter 6), but hazards may be encountered with other materials including deposits high in vanadium and on occasions with chromates associated with ash constituents or refractories.

As a general policy, men should not enter confined spaces alone and without the knowledge of some responsible person.

5.7 Maintenance and repairs

Gas-side cleaning

Whilst the proportions and arrangements of the heating surface should have been based on the fuel and ash properties, provision has to be made with most fuels to clean the surfaces during operation. Otherwise there will be progressive fouling, which will reduce the output by restricting heat transfer and by increasing the resistance to gas flow, which limits the air and fuel that can be introduced. The topic of corrosion and how it can be minimized was discussed in Section 5.1.

Sootblowers

Steam, and to some extent air, is commonly used for sootblowing. The type of equipment will be influenced by the environment in which it is to work. Sootblowers, where required on furnace walls (which is particularly the case with pulverized fuel), are likely to be of the single-nozzle retractable type which withdraw the nozzle to shelter it from the full furnace heat when not in operation. When working, the nozzle is advanced and rotates to sweep an area of wall. Lance-type retractable sootblowers are used to clean boiler and superheater surface in zones of high gas temperature, often where powerful jets are required.

The principle of operation is for a rotating lance carrying a pair of balanced jets at its leading end to traverse from the side across the tube surfaces and then withdraw to its retracted position. These sootblower lances depend for cooling on the blowing medium and must never be advanced into or left in the gas stream uncooled. Emergency facilities are provided to withdraw the lance in the event of failure of the main drive. These sootblowers are normally located in cavities with appreciable clearance from adjacent tubes both because of the power of the jets and, especially with wide passages demanding long lances, to accommodate droop and gyration. To minimize the effects of droop the sootblower carriage may also be inclined upwards.

In cooler gas zones, and with close tube pitching, multi-jet sootblower elements may be installed permanently across the tube banks, with the jets aligned to blow through the clear lanes between the tubes. The correct setting and periodic checking of this alignment are important to avoid tube erosion. In operation the element is rotated over a prescribed arc to sweep the required areas.

Rake-type blowers are also found in low-temperature zones especially with extended heating surface, such as some types of economizer where a multi-jet element is traversed across the face of the heating surface to be swept.

Except on small units, operation of the sootblowers is by powered actuator drives, and there is a control system to bring each blower or, in a large installation, group of blowers into use.

The frequency and extent of sootblowing must be determined by observation of their effect on the boiler and its performance. Increased draught loss and back-end temperatures are warnings that serious build-up of deposits is developing. It is possible and legitimate to be selective in sootblowing in different zones in the boiler, either because experience shows a particular location to be critical or to modify the relative heat transfer performance between different parts of the heating surface.

As a general rule, sootblowing should be carried out as near as possible to full load, not only to benefit from the gas stream carrying away disturbed deposits, but to avoid any risk of accumulated combustible material being released into a hot gas stream having significant excess oxygen, which could cause sudden ignition or even explosion.

Steam for sootblowing is usually taken from the boiler, either dry saturated or with a moderate degree of superheat. The pressure employed in the sootblower itself is unlikely to be higher than about 25 bar so that even with a flow-restricting device at each sootblower head the system pressure may be well below boiler pressure in a high-pressure unit. In these cases reducing facilities are required although an alternative may be provided for on-load running such as tapping from a reheater.

Damage in the form of severe internal corrosion is sometimes found in the sootblower piping system. This arises when after use the remaining steam in the pipes condenses and, by a combination of leaking sootblower valves and failure of vacuum-breaking devices on the system, flue gases are drawn back into the piping where carbon dioxide and sulphur oxides dissolve in the condensate with subsequent acid attack. This can be prevented by alert maintenance, given a basically sound installation.

Low-pressure purge air is sometimes arranged at the wall box where the sootblower element enters the boiler; it keeps the idle blower nozzle cool and reduces the risk of drawing flue gas back into the steam system. Air sealing is essential with pressure-fired boilers.

Compressed air is an effective blowing medium, avoiding many of the disadvantages of steam but introducing the need for additional mechanical equipment for supplying the air, which often is at a higher pressure than general workshop service air.

It is advisable to increase the furnace suction when sootblowing to avoid puffing of dust and gases into the boilerhouse.

Since the purpose of the sootblower is to disturb deposits on surfaces, a careful watch should be kept, particularly while gaining experience with a new boiler, to avoid erosion of the tubes themselves. Should signs of erosion — such as suspiciously clean surfaces and polishing or measurable metal loss — be found, the blowing movements of the element should be checked and corrected if found faulty and consideration given to adjusting the blowing pressure or the jet capacity itself.

With steam sootblowing it is of first importance that the steam is dry and without entrained water droplets, which are likely to cause erosion damage. The external steam system serving the sootblowers should be properly sized and laid out to ensure adequate draining and the operating cycle should provide for an effective warming through and draining period before the sootblowers operate. Where erosion damage is found, suspicion that it is due to water in the steam may be heightened if the offending sootblower is at the beginning of the sootblowing sequence, or if the steam pipe system arrangements tend to inadequate drainage.

Hand lancing

Hand lancing by compressed air or water is sometimes employed. When hand lancing a steaming boiler, care must be taken to increase the furnace suction to ensure that there is no risk of blowback to the operator.

If water lancing is used, care should be exercised to avoid impingement and quenching on thick components such as headers and the drum which could give thermal shock and potential cracking risks. It is probably advisable to restrict water lancing, if done, to carbon steel tubes.

Shot cleaning

Shot cleaning has had some limited application and success in cleaning compact heating surfaces in lower-temperature zones. The method uses a stream of chilled iron shot which cascades through the heating surface in a vertical gas passage. The dropped shot is separated from the dislodged dust and recycled. Experience shows that better results are had by continuous dropping of shot than by intermittent operation, and this should be commenced on clean surfaces as the plant goes on load rather than after deposits have secured a hold.

Off-load cleaning

The aim of on-load cleaning is to keep the heating surfaces clean enough to give continuous good performance and operation but there may be the need for additional cleaning either for inspection and maintenance purposes, or to overcome a long-term fouling trend. This may be experienced for example with some deposits from oil firing which bond tenaciously on superheater tubes, or there may be accumulation of deposits on low-temperature surfaces of economizers and air heaters, leading to acid corrosion.

Direct hand cleaning has some application, depending on size of plant and other circumstances.

Water washing is widely practised, by drenching for an extended period using fire hoses or high-pressure jets; extremely high pressures can be used if a specialist firm is employed. If possible, alkaline water should be used and wetting agents are beneficial.

Factors to be considered include proper draining and disposal of effluent, which may require special measures to satisfy environmental criteria, and the care and protection of the boiler itself. It may well be necessary to sheet-over areas not to be wetted, for example areas of refractories and constructions such as the Bailey furnace wall *(see Figure 5.6)* where the heat-conducting bond material could be leached out.

It is almost certain that after washing, wetted surfaces and hidden areas will be acidic and

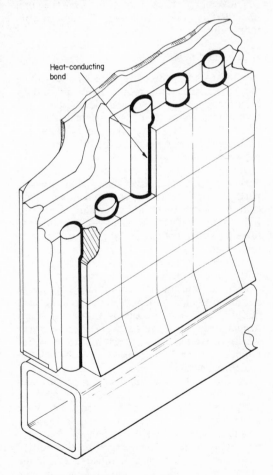

Heat-conducting bond

Figure 5.6   Bailey furnace wall

corrosion damage will ensue if nothing further is done. Water washing should therefore be planned to be followed immediately by lighting the boiler up, if only for a brief period, to ensure that damp pockets are dried out and corrosion risks minimized. Details of the boiler construction should be critically examined to identify possible locations of trouble due to corrosion.

Steam soaking

A technique which has been popular for softening heavy bonded deposits in generating tube banks of boilers, fired by coal on mechanical stokers, is steam soaking. Steam is admitted to the setting for a period, the boiler being cold but water-filled to encourage condensation.

With tenacious deposits a combination of steam soaking and water washing may give good results. The same precautions must be followed as with water washing to protect areas which may be adversely affected and to fire the unit immediately after cleaning to dry it out thoroughly.

Repairs and modifications

Repairs to boiler pressure parts are subject to the same rules and requirements as is new construction, with proper consideration given in addition to the state of the original material. They should be undertaken only with the knowledge and agreement of the inspecting authority and in many cases supported by the advice of the manufacturer.

Welding to the standards required for pressure parts is a highly skilled operation and to keep his skill the welder needs to be regularly exercising it in this class of work. It is unwise and unfair to expect a man not normally practised in it to undertake this work. Many welds require a particular technique including correct pre- and post-heat treatment.

A basic point of first importance is never to permit any sort of unauthorized welding to a major pressure part such as a drum or thick header because of the risks of initiating cracks which could have disastrous results, however tempting it may be to tack on a bracket or something similar.

In the past with simple tube shapes and expanded joints it was normal to make a complete replacement of a failed tube. With more complex tube elements and increase in length, as well as welded attachments, it is often preferable to repair by welding in an insert of new material to replace a defective length. In the same way, complete plugging off of a leaking element in, say, a superheater may mean complete loss of the material with a complicated

exercise required to replace it at a later date. A repair by insert is generally much better. A consideration with plugging and cutting out a tube element is that this will leave an open gas lane which may have the effect of overheating adjacent tubes, especially in a superheater or reheater, and is therefore to be avoided.

When making repairs by tube inserts, as well as making sure that the original material is sound, care is needed to ensure sound welds. Water-side deposits in boiler tubes may contain material such as copper which will lead to risk of cracks in welds if fused in, and in these circumstances cleaning out of the tube bore local to the end is essential.

The integrity of repairs must be proved by hydraulic testing and such other tests as may be prescribed on welds and other repairs.

Protection of idle boilers

When it is known that a boiler is to be out of service for some time, a decision must be taken as to how it is to be cared for. This concerns the gas side of the unit as well as the water side. For the water side the choice lies between dry or wet storage, with dry storage likely to be more suitable for long storage periods. Whichever method is chosen, every care is necessary to clean and dry the gas side of the boiler to avoid corrosion. The boiler, including the air heater, should be thoroughly cleaned and, especially if it is wet-cleaned by water washing, it should be fired for a brief period before final shutdown to dry it out completely.

The setting, including the chimney, should be closed to prevent entry of air from the outside. Periodic inspections should be made to guard against condensation on the surfaces of the pressure parts and subsequent corrosion, particularly with wet storage. It may be necessary to arrange auxiliary heating by coke braziers or electric heaters where there are climatic risks, or as protection against frost.

If the boiler is wet-stored, the water must be chemically treated to give an adequate alkalinity using an oxygen scavenger such as sodium sulphite or hydrazine. This should be checked periodically. With non-drainable superheaters, where it is unwise to introduce solid chemicals, hydrazine and ammonia should be used.

The boiler should have all its valves, drains and vents closed and filled completely to its highest point and be fitted with an overhead surge tank *(Figure 5.7)* arranged from a high vent, to allow for temperature change and as a tell-tale against leakage loss. As an alternative it can be nitrogen-capped above the water line at a low pressure to exclude oxygen.

If the boiler is put into storage it may require

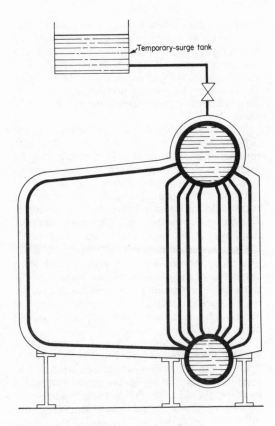

Figure 5.7   Surge tank for wet storage

preliminary water-side cleaning and flushing out to remove deposits and sediments. In any event it should be fired before being stored, and, after firing has ceased and the pressure fallen to 2–3 bar, the water should be drained out with drum blowdowns, aircocks, gauge glass and water wall box drains opened. Superheater drains should be kept closed to minimize the entry of steam with subsequent condensation in the superheater. This is particularly important with non-drainable superheaters. When the boiler has been drained, drum man-doors, water circuit bottom boxes where accessible, and all superheater drains should be carefully opened to encourage an air flow, which can be helped by warm air from portable blowers, to complete the drying out. Trays of desiccant should then be placed in the boiler drum and wall boxes as required but making sure that a good record is kept of their location. The desiccant can be indicating silica-gel or activated alumina at the rate of 60 kg/50 m³ of volume or 1.25 kg/50 m² of heating surface. An alternative is quicklime at four times these quantities. If calcium chloride is used the trays must not be more than three-quarters full to avoid

outflow after moisture has been absorbed. Periodic inspection should be made and desiccants replenished as necessary.

As an alternative, nitrogen may be used for dry storage with the boiler freed from as much water as possible as just described. When the pressure decreases, nitrogen is fed into the drum aircock and the superheater. The boiler may also be purged by nitrogen supplied to bottom drains. Subsequently a slight nitrogen pressure is maintained to exclude air. As an added precaution, once the boiler has cooled, desiccant trays may be put in the drum. Care should be taken against suffocation hazards with nitrogen storage, and breathing apparatus must be used for entry.

Appropriate care should be taken with auxiliary equipment to preserve it during the storage period with general good housekeeping maintenance such as cleaning oil burners, filters and associated items, emptying and cleaning oil-lubricated bearings and gear-boxes and refilling as high as possible with fresh oil. Particular care should be taken that there is no fuel leakage due to defective valves or isolation.

All moving parts, especially equipment with ball and roller bearings, should be rotated once a week to avoid troubles such as brinelling of the bearings, which is a phenomenon where dimpling of the races and balls and rollers occurs under conditions of static vibration by a fretting corrosion mechanism.

The makers' instructions should be consulted and adhered to for all auxiliary items and electrical equipment.

Post-service cleaning

Periodic or occasional chemical cleaning may be required during the life of the boiler to remove undesirable solids. These may be hardness scale deposits arising from inadequate water treatment or control or, with high-pressure units, there may be gradual thickening of the iron oxide coating on the tubes which, although protective when thin, becomes associated with on-load corrosion when massive.

The process and chemical agents employed will be chosen to suit the conditions to be dealt with.

Particularly difficult boiler water deposits are those where there are aluminium and silica in the feedwater, giving risk of a dense, impermeable scale of the mineral analcite type which causes tube blistering owing to its heat insulating property. Along with iron oxide deposits brought in from the feed system, there are likely to be other metals such as copper and nickel from the same source which may call for some special chemical cleaning.

5.8 Waste-heat boilers

As the name implies, waste-heat boilers are ancillary equipment in an installation having a prime purpose other than steam raising. The boiler is provided either to improve the economy of the main process by recovery of useful heat, or to extract heat to satisfy direct process requirements or subordinate requirements such as waste-gas cooling before cleaning and discharge.

Particularly where a waste-heat boiler provides steam for a purpose such as power generation, provision may be made to fire fuel directly on auxiliary burners to give an enhanced total steam output or to fill output troughs due to low waste-heat conditions. An example is a waste-heat boiler heated by gas turbine exhaust (*see* Chapter 20) with auxiliary firing. In such cases the air flow through the turbine does not vary greatly with load but the temperature of the turbine exhaust does.

In many process applications the waste-heat boiler will not receive a disproportionate degree of attention from the plant operators and from the start the boiler design and instrumentation philosophy must rest on this basis.

The particular duty and conditions will decide the general style and arrangement of the boiler and heating surfaces. If it receives gas turbine exhaust which has a large volume of relatively cool and clean gases, extended-surface tubing will probably be employed. For boilers used with metal extraction, such as a copper reverberatory furnace, the tubes will be straight and vertical without attachments or in plain membrane panels to minimize fouling problems. In this service it is common to have two boilers in parallel to the furnace to permit access for cleaning without furnace shutdown.

Tube cleaning may be by steam sootblowers if discharge is to wet scrubbers, or by air blowing or mechanical rapping where moisture is inadmissible, as when the boiler is followed by a sulphur reclamation plant. Steam or air sootblowers must be used consistently from the clean boiler condition at start-up since they are ineffective on heavy deposits once these become established. Good experience is being had with water blowers.

Boilers of the types just described will behave and be operated in much the same way as direct-fired boilers.

In many chemical process applications very high rates of heat flux are experienced which call for excellent feedwater and boiler water conditions to prevent formation of heat-resisting scales. In some processes there is intrinsically a very low thermal inertia as, for example, where

the boiler may follow a catalyst reaction. In this case there is a very rapid change in working temperature as the reaction is established and the process goes on stream. It is essential here that preheat arrangements are provided to bring the boiler up to working pressure and temperature beforehand and pumped circulation must be used.

Where high pressures are encountered in the process stream, round ducts are usual with tubular heat exchangers. Thick tube plates for high pressures give problems with tube connection and high thermal gradients; alternatives, not without their own problems, are either a water-side girder supporting the tube plates or flexible tube plates. In many cases thermal insulation is necessary on the inlet tube plate.

The choice of materials of construction for process application will be heavily dependent on behaviour of the chemical process materials. The start-up and operating procedures may well differ from common direct-fired boiler practice and will need to be adequately communicated to and understood by the operators.

Waste-heat equipment has been applied to various duties in steelworks practice. In the past, open-hearth furnaces have had simple shell and tube boilers for steam generation and heat has been recovered from duties such as the water cooling of the horizontal skids supporting the billets in billet heating furnaces. With basic oxygen steelmaking there is a considerable heat release during the blow, from the heat in the fume and the burning out of carbon monoxide. The fume is cooled and carried to the gas-cleaning plant by a water-cooled hood, essentially of membrane tubular construction which could be arranged for steam production but is commonly used only as a means of carrying the heat away for disposal by air cooling.

In the marine field, extended-surface waste-heat boilers are commonly fitted for main-engine exhaust cooling in diesel ships to provide auxiliary steam. With increasing fuel costs and concern for energy conservation the maximum use of waste heat in this way for, say, driving steam turbine generators is likely to increase.

5.9 High-pressure hot-water boilers

Boilers used for high-pressure hot-water duties (either shell or watertube type according to output and pressure) primarily depend on pumped circulation, usually by the main system pumps. Since they do not generate steam, density differences are slight and natural circulation tendencies have only a minor influence.

System pressure is maintained either by steam pressure in the boiler drum or by gas pressurizing by nitrogen, in which case the pressure will normally be greater than the saturation pressure equivalent to the boiler outlet water temperature.

In theory an enclosed hot-water system will operate with only nominal water make-up requirements and therefore, after initial fill and venting of air, which comes out of solution on heating, it will give little trouble on the water side. Experience is, however, that this ideal situation may not be found and there may have to be considerable feed of water to make up losses by leakage from the whole system, with consequent introduction of foreign matter leading to scale and deposits in the boiler and tube damage by overheating. Care of the boiler accordingly starts with conscientious attention to the total system.

Strainers

However the system is arranged, any foreign matter will gradually be carried to the boiler where it will accumulate. This applies to new systems where mill scale, erection debris and oddments of all kinds may be found, and in old systems after drainage or modification where air entry may have loosened scale. After a few weeks' operation of a new installation it is therefore wise to drain and open the boiler to remove debris and sludge, perhaps assisted by hosing out.

Where strainers are fitted in the main return connections, they should be given close attention during the first few weeks of operation to ensure that the flow to the boiler is not restricted. They should also of course receive regular periodic inspection and cleaning at all times, but particularly after draining of the system and after modifications. Where no permanent strainers are fitted, the boiler should be cleared out perhaps once a year, and on a new system a suitable temporary metal gauze should be fitted between a pair of flanges in the return main near the boiler, preferably in a vertical leg.

Circulation

Particular attention is required to ensure an adequate circulation through the boiler when working, and at no time should it fall below a minimum of 20–25% of full-load circulation. If the heat load falls, with corresponding reduced boiler circulation rates, the heat input should be reduced to avoid steaming which, when due to water shortage, manifests itself by bumping, crackling noises or water hammer. If not corrected this can lead to scaling troubles and

blockages and tube failure as a result of overheating.

Idle boilers serving a common system should not remain in full circulation as a boiler on load has a higher resistance and idle boilers would tend to take more than their share of water.

Oil, grease and scale removal

In most cases a satisfactory treatment for new hot-water boilers is to flush through with clean water or to drain and clean internally after a few weeks' operation.

High-pressure and high-temperature installations should be boiled out for several hours with soda ash.

Gas-side corrosion

Gas-side corrosion is largely due to the sulphur content of the fuel. It can be serious with oil firing but can be minimized by sound operating practice.

Sulphur trioxide formed in combustion combines with water vapour in the flue gas to form sulphuric acid, which can condense on the boiler surfaces when the temperature falls to the acid dewpoint, 130–145°C. Heavy condensation and peak corrosion occurs between 105° and 125°C so that gases cooled to this extent owing to high boiler efficiency will cause the back end to suffer. At or below the water vapour dewpoint of 45–50°C, condensed water vapour will dilute the deposits giving very heavy corrosion.

Since the boiler surfaces will be close to the water temperature, the return water should be above 65°C at all times and gas temperatures at full load below about 220°C are undesirable in boilers operating at a flow temperature of 85°C.

Idle boilers should be kept in partial circulation at not less than 65°C with all dampers shut to prevent air carrying through water vapour.

Burners with a big turndown should be avoided if they are likely to lead to low flue gas leaving temperatures.

As a general rule, multiple-boiler installations should have units of unequal size so that the boiler best suited to the load can be selected, to avoid a big boiler running at low firing and temperature conditions.

The burners should be kept well tuned to run at low excess air, and boilers should be cleaned regularly when working and thoroughly when laid up. Laid-up boilers must be sealed effectively or ventilated after cleaning.

Shutting down a hot-water boiler

For overnight or weekend shutdown the temperature or pressure reduction should be gradual.

Circulating pumps should be run for a short time to allow the boiler to cool evenly and without risk of water hammer.

With a gas-pressurized system the pressure is maintained regardless of temperature. With a steam-pressurized system, arrangements may be made to refire the boiler when the pressure has fallen to a predetermined level.

Where only some of the oil-fired boilers on a system are to be shut down, after firing stops the return valves should be partly closed while the brickwork cools and then left just cracked open enough to ensure sufficient circulation to keep the boiler warm, dry and capable of being easily brought back into operation.

5.10 Special fuels

Watertube boilers having special characteristics are built for a wide variety of special fuels such as wastes and refuses and process residues.

In different parts of the world vegetable refuses are burnt both to dispose of an otherwise waste material and to provide steam for the factory power and process. An example is *bagasse*, the fibrous residue from sugar-cane milling. This is typically burnt by pile-burning in hearths, as in the Ward cell (a firebrick combustion chamber with air ports for admitting preheated air around the fuel pile) in the smaller capacities. Mechanical or air spreader firing with dumping or travelling grates for ash removal is used in larger installations. This type of fuel contains considerable moisture and because of the lightness of the fuel particles appreciable char is carried over from the furnace, and may cause some emission nuisance and give erosion troubles in high-gas-velocity zones and air heaters. The erosion may relate to materials, such as soil and fertilizers, coming with the fuel. As alternative uses for bagasse are developed, such as building board or papermaking, the trend is towards requiring higher burning efficiencies than formerly.

Boilers of this type may have auxiliary firing by another fuel such as oil or coal, partly for lighting up but also to ensure output regardless of bagasse quality and availability where steam is required for other factory purposes such as refining and distilling.

Municipal and industrial refuse are growing in importance as fuels. Development is along the lines of special grates such as roller grates or stepped reciprocating grates which ensure repeated turning of the refuse pile as it traverses through the furnace to encourage heating up to ignition temperature and to give complete burnout. Gas passage and tube layout need to be simple and open because of the quantity of dust carried in the gases and the tendency for deposits and blockage to occur. There are corrosion risks from materials such as hydrogen chloride released by burning plastics wastes. The difficulties are aggravated in reducing atmospheres and care is needed to achieve good air mixing characteristics in combustion.

An example of a specialized boiler related to an industrial process is the soda recovery boiler in the paper pulp industry. In this process, where wood chips are digested in caustic soda, the aqueous process residue is high in chemicals and lignins from the wood. The concentrated residue, black liquor, is sprayed into the specially arranged boiler furnace where it burns in suspension by drying out on the walls and in the pile on the floor under reducing conditions. The chemical ash, or smelt, accumulates in liquid form in a bed at the base of the burning pile. It is run off as molten smelt into a dissolving tank and treated back to caustic soda for the mill requirements. The heat released generates steam for the mill machinery and process purposes.

There is a considerable fume of sublimated saltcake in the flue gases which means care has to be taken in tube surface arrangement and sootblower provision to cope with fouling tendencies. This necessitates adequate gas-cleaning equipment to avoid chemical loss as well as for environmental considerations. Past practice was to take out the main part of the saltcake by wet-scrubbing using diluted liquor and as an aid to concentration by evaporation in the hot gas. This had the disadvantage of the release of obnoxious sulphides, and the trend now is towards electrostatic precipitation to reduce this nuisance.

An especial risk recognized with recovery boilers is that a very severe explosion may result from water entering the liquid smelt bed in the furnace so that emergency procedures for shutdown, boiler water dumping and personnel evacuation are operated if an incident such as a major tube failure occurs.

Reference list of some related codes (*see also* Chapter 21)

BS 845:1972   Acceptance tests for industrial type boilers and steam generators

BS 1113:1969   Watertube steam generating plant (including superheaters, reheaters and steel-tube economizers)

BS 1374:1972   Recommendations on the use of British Standard log sheets for steam and hot-water boiler plants

BS 2885:1974   Code for acceptance tests on stationary steam generators of the power-station type

BS 3285:1960   Method of sampling superheated steam from steam generating units

BS 3812:1964   Recommendations for estimating the dryness of saturated steam

ASME   Boiler and Pressure Vessel Code, Section VII, Recommended Rules for Care of Power Boilers

6

Thermal insulation

6.1 Introduction

The need for efficient thermal insulation has become more important with higher operating temperatures and increased energy costs. The use of wooden lags on boilers in the eras of James Watt and George Stephenson has given way to the present-day use of materials specifically designed and manufactured to conserve energy by minimizing unwanted heat losses. The growth of the insulation industry was very slow when fuel was abundant and cheap. The operating temperatures of steam plants were for many years low enough to permit the use of compositions consisting of waste products, and therefore there was no real incentive to develop new materials.

However, as operating temperatures increased, the cheap compositions containing organic products were no longer suitable and materials were developed to withstand the higher temperatures. Moulded insulation material in the form of slabs for boilers and ducting, and sections for piping, have been available since approximately 1900, but the use of compositions continued as there was an abundance of cheap labour to apply the material. The use of the more efficient preformed insulation increased after 1945 with the general awareness of the need to conserve fuel, and also because of the demand for quicker application to meet the requirements of the construction programme for power-stations, chemical plant and the marine industry.

Materials in general use in the immediate post-war period were 85% magnesia, diatomaceous earth products, asbestos products and fibrous insulations manufactured from glass and blast-furnace slag. These materials were all available as preformed insulation and were used extensively in large projects, but the use of powders which could be mixed with water on-site, mainly composed of magnesia, diatomaceous earth and asbestos, still persisted in the heating and ventilating trade.

Most of the finishing compositions applied over the thermal insulation were clay- or cement-based products reinforced with asbestos fibres. The major change in the insulation industry in the UK occurred in the mid-1960s with the increasing awareness of asbestos-related diseases amongst insulation workers. The

Asbestos Industry Regulation of 1931 applied only to places of manufacture and therefore construction sites, shipyards and maintenance work in power-station, oil, petrochemical and similar plants were excluded from the Regulations, but in spite of this, major user industries would no longer accept insulation materials containing asbestos, and by the time the Asbestos Regulation 1969 became operative in May 1970, asbestos had been virtually eliminated from thermal insulation materials used on steam-raising plant and equipment.

Standards for thermal insulation were non-existent before 1945 and the immediate post-war period saw the first attempt at standardization with the issue of:

BS 1304 (1946): 'Ready to fit thermal insulating materials'

BS 1334 (1947): 'The use of thermal insulating materials for central heating and hot and cold water supply installations'

BS 1588 (1949): 'The use of thermal insulation materials in the temperature range 95°C to 230°C'

BS 1589 (1950): 'Thermal insulating materials plastic composition flexible in loose form'

BS 3533 (1962): 'Glossary of terms relating to thermal insulation'

BS 3708 (1964): 'The use of thermal insulating materials between 230°C and 650°C'

A revision of BS 1334 in 1969 superseded BS 1304 and incorporated BS 1589, while BS 5422 (1977): 'The use of thermal insulating materials' replaced BS 1334, BS 1588 and BS 3708. BS 3958: 'Thermal insulation materials' Parts 1–6 gives requirements for 85% magnesia preformed insulation, calcium silicate preformed insulation, metal-mesh-faced mineral wool matts and mattresses, bonded preformed mineral wool pipe sections, bonded mineral wool slabs and finishing materials respectively.

The British Standard Code of Practice CP 3005 entitled 'Thermal insulating of pipework and equipment in the temperature range –100°F to + 1500°F (−73°C to +816°C)' was published in 1969 and is currently being revised and metricated.

6.2 Reasons for insulation

The production, distribution and use of steam require thermal insulation to ensure that process

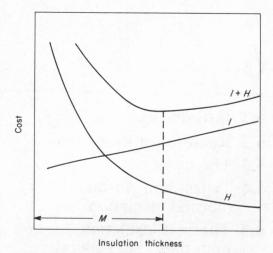

Figure 6.1   *Determination of the economic thickness of insulation material.* I, *thickness of insulation;* H, *cost of heat loss;* I + H, *total cost;* M, *economic thickness*

requirements can be achieved. The first consideration is to ensure that steam generated at the boiler can be delivered to the point of use at the correct temperature and pressure, and correct choice of the thermal insulation system to ensure that energy loss is maintained within design tolerance is essential for this purpose. When the type and thickness of insulation for process requirements have been chosen, and provided the resultant surface temperatures of the insulation meet the requirements for personnel protection — generally 55°C maximum for metal finishes and 60°C maximum for non-metallic surfaces — consideration can then be given to increasing the insulation thicknesses on economic grounds.

The economic thickness of insulation is calculated by the minimum-cost method as demonstrated in *Figure 6.1* to determine the minimum total cost of installed insulation and cost of heat lost over an agreed period of time. Basic information required includes cost of energy (or cost of fuel and boiler efficiency), evaluation period (years and number of hours of operation per year), heat losses and installed costs for a range of thicknesses of insulation. In the absence of specific information the evaluation period is normally taken as 5 years at 8000 h/year for continuous operation and 5 years at 4000 h/year for intermittent working. The usable energy value will vary in any particular plant. For example, at any given temperature and pressure, the energy in main steam to turbines has a greater value per joule than steam to process plant which may eventually exhaust to atmosphere.

Table 6.1 Recommended thicknesses of insulation to BS 5422 — Table 12

Operating temperature (°C):	100	200	300	400	500	600
Thermal conductivity (W/m K):	0.048	0.054	0.061	0.069	0.078	0.088

Pipe o.d. (mm)	Insulation thickness (mm)					
27	30	48	60	73	84	96
34	34	52	66	79	91	104
48	39	59	75	88	102	116
60	42	64	81	95	110	124
89	49	72	91	108	125	141
114	52	77	98	116	134	152
168	58	87	104	130	150	170
219	63	93	118	140	162	183
273	66	98	125	149	172	195
324	69	103	131	156	181	205
406	72	109	138	166	192	218

Table 6.2 Thermal conductivity of insulating materials

Material	Density (kg/m³)	Thermal conductivity (W/m K) at hot-face temperature:						
		50°C	100°C	200°C	300°C	400°C	500°C	600°C
Calcium silicate	210	0.054	0.056	0.060	0.066	0.072	0.079	0.087
Magnesia	190	0.054	0.057	0.059	0.062			
Glass fibre	96	0.033	0.038	0.047	0.058	0.071		
Mineral wool	130	0.038	0.043	0.051	0.061	0.073	0.088	
Mineral wool	96	0.036	0.041	0.051	0.062	0.076	0.090	
Mineral wool	64	0.037	0.043	0.054	0.067			
Aluminosilicate	96	0.033	0.037	0.045	0.053	0.062	0.072	0.083
Magnesia[a]	177–225	0.060	0.062	0.069	0.077			
Calcium silicate[a]	160–320		0.057	0.065	0.073	0.079	0.085	0.092
Mineral wool[a]	50–250	0.041	0.047	0.058	0.071	0.085	0.101	

[a] Requirements of BS 3958

The recommended thicknesses of insulation for process pipework and equipment in BS 5422, for a typical insulating material with thermal conductivity values as shown, are given in *Table 6.1*.

Insulation is applied to flues to maintain required gas temperatures at the chimney and to prevent corrosion and in some cases the emission of acid smuts, by ensuring that the internal face of the flue is above the dewpoint of the gases, and thus insulation of gas flues is designed without any consideration for conservation of energy. On large power-plants the cost of applying insulation to the flue may be in the order of 10–20% of the total insulation cost for the complete station.

Insulation is also used to ensure that heat transfer to traced piping and vessels is achieved in the most efficient manner by minimizing heat loss from the surface. Improved heat transfer to the product is obtained by the use of high-conductivity heat transfer cement and by incorporating reflective foil within the insulation system (*see Figure 6.2*). A typical heat transfer cement would have a thermal conductivity of 14 W/m K, approximately one-third of the k value of mild steel.

6.3 Theory

Thermal insulating materials are non-homogeneous solids which contain a large proportion of gas or air by volume. Heat is

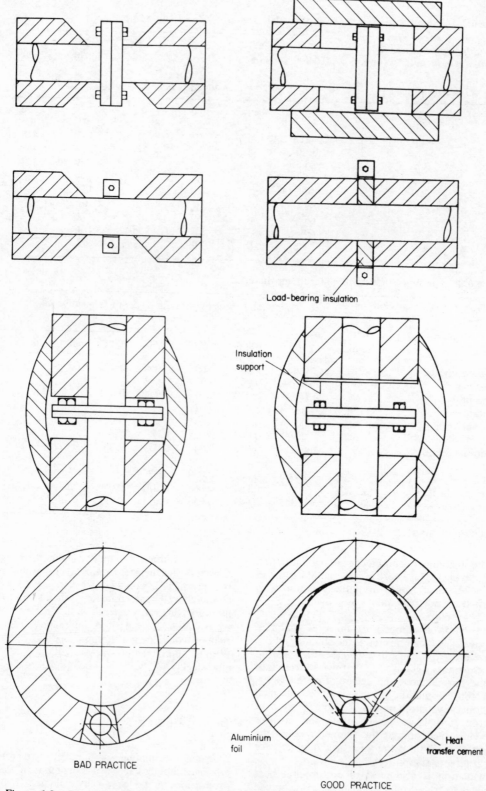

Load-bearing insulation

Insulation
support

Aluminium
foil

Heat
transfer cement

BAD PRACTICE

GOOD PRACTICE

Figure 6.2   Examples of good and bad insulation practice

Table 6.3 Surface coefficients

Insulation surface temperature (°C)	Wind speed (m/s)	Surface coefficient (W/m² K) to ambient air at 20°C		
		Cement or fabric	Galv. mild steel	Aluminium
30	0	9.2	6.7	4.6
30	1	11.8	9.3	7.2
30	5	21.6	19.0	17.0
30	10	33.2	30.6	28.6
40	0	10.0	7.4	5.3
40	1	13.2	10.6	8.4
40	5	24.8	22.2	20.1
40	10	38.6	36.1	33.9
50	0	10.8	8.0	5.8
50	1	14.3	11.5	9.3
50	5	27.1	24.4	22.1
50	10	42.4	39.7	37.4
60	0	11.3	8.5	6.2
60	1	15.1	12.3	9.9
60	5	28.9	26.0	23.7
60	10	45.3	42.4	40.1

Table 6.4 Effect of surface coefficient on heat loss and surface temperature for a 150-mm NB pipe in ambient air at 20°C

Temperature (°C)	Insulation*	Cloth†		Galvanized mild steel†		Aluminium†	
		q	t_s	q	t_s	q	t_s
100	25 mm, k = 0.048	78	31	75	33	70	38
100	50 mm, k = 0.048	47	25	46	27	45	29
300	50 mm, k = 0.061	207	44	202	50	194	59
300	100 mm, k = 0.061	130	32	128	35	126	40
500	100 mm, k = 0.078	283	44	279	50	272	60
500	150 mm, k = 0.078	221	35	219	37	216	46

*k = thermal conductivity (W/m K)
†q = heat loss (W/m); t_s = surface temperature (°C)

transferred through the insulation by one or more of the following modes:

1. solid conduction through matrix or fibres;
2. gaseous conduction;
3. radiation across gas or air spaces;
4. convection across gas or air spaces; or
5. overall convection hot to cold face.

The mechanism of heat transfer through different types of insulation is a complex subject and for the purposes of this chapter the *thermal conductivity* can be taken by definition as the amount of heat transferred in unit time through unit area of unit thickness with unit temperature difference across the faces. Thermal conduc-

tivity of insulation is determined in accordance with the requirements of the British Standard BS 874 and is expressed in watts per metre kelvin (W/m K). Manufacturers' data on thermal conductivity values of insulating materials used in steam-generating and process industries are shown in *Table 6.2* together with thermal conductivity values required to conform to BS 3958.

Heat conducted through an insulating material is transferred to the surrounding air by radiation and convection. For simplicity the combined effect of radiation and convection heat transfer from the insulation surface is referred to as the *surface coefficient*. The surface coefficient is affected by the velocity of the air passing over the surface (convection), and by the emissivity of the surface, which is the rate of heat transfer by radiation from the surface compared with that from a black body *(see Table 6.3)*. Variation of surface coefficient may make a large difference to the insulation's surface temperature but very little difference to the heat loss *(see Table 6.4)*.

Calculation of heat loss

Plane surfaces

The heat loss from a plane surface is given by

$$q = \frac{(\theta_1 - \theta_2)k}{L} = (\theta_2 - \theta_a)f \qquad (6.1)$$

which can be written as

$$q = \frac{(\theta_1 - \theta_a)}{\frac{L}{k} + \frac{1}{f}} \qquad (6.2)$$

where q is the heat loss (W/m²), θ_1 is the hot-face temperature (°C), θ_2 is the cold-face temperature (°C), θ_a is the ambient temperature (°C), L is the thickness of insulation (m), k is the thermal conductivity of insulation (W/m K) and f is the surface coefficient (W/m² K). The surface temperature can then be calculated from the equation

$$\theta_2 = \frac{q}{f} + \theta_a \qquad (6.3)$$

Cylindrical surfaces

The heat loss from a cylindrical surface is given by

$$q = \frac{(\theta_1 - \theta_a)}{r_1 \left(\ln \frac{r_2}{r_1} \right) \times \frac{1}{k} + \frac{r_1}{r_2} \times \frac{1}{f}} \qquad (6.4)$$

where q is the heat loss (W/m²) from a pipe surface, r_1 is the inner radius of insulation (m) and r_2 is the outer radius of insulation (m). The surface tem-

perature can then be calculated from the equation

$$\theta_2 = \left(\frac{q}{f} \times \frac{r_1}{r_2} \right) + \theta_a \qquad (6.5)$$

The surface temperature of an insulated 150-mm pipe at various hot-face temperatures is given in *Table 6.5*.

Effect of air movement over bare and insulated surfaces

Increased air movement has a much greater effect on the heat loss from bare piping than from insulated piping and the better the pipe is insulated the less will be the effect of air movement. By substituting different values of f with constant values of L/k in equation (6.2) it can be shown that the insulation surface temperature is affected much more than is heat loss. *Table 6.6* shows the effect of air movement on heat loss from bare and insulated surfaces.

Thermal conductivity

Thermal conductivity of any material will vary with density, porosity, pore size and (in the case of fibrous materials) fibre diameter and shot content (i.e. non-fiberized particles of rock or glass). The k values acceptable in BS 3958 Parts 1–5 allow for variation in product quality, and heat losses calculated using these values are probably more accurate than those based on manufacturers' declared values of thermal conductivity obtained from laboratory tests that make no allowance for variation in product quality, or—more important—the dimensional tolerance and accuracy of fit on application. Allowable thermal conductivity values in BS 3958 for materials in common use on steam-generating and process plant are shown in *Table 6.2*.

Table 6.5 Surface temperature of insulation for a 150-mm NB pipe insulated with calcium silicate in ambient still air at 20°C

Hot-face temperature (°C)	Surface temperature (°C)				
	25 mm	50 mm	75 mm	100 mm	125 mm
100	31	26	24	23	22
200	47	34	30	27	25
300	64	43	36	31	29
400	82	53	43	36	33
500	101	65	51	42	37

Table 6.6   Effect of wind velocity on heat loss

Wind velocity (m/s)	Heat loss (W/m)				
	Bare	25 mm	50 mm	75 mm	100 mm
0	3970	325	200	150	124
1	4880	340	205	154	128
5	8240	365	212	158	130
10	12200	375	215	160	131

150-mm NB pipe at 300°C (ambient temp. 20°C).
Insulation $k = 0.06$ **W/m K. Finish: galvanized mild steel.**

Table 6.7   Forms of thermal insulation

Form	Description	Examples
Preformed	Fabricated in such a manner that at least one surface conforms to the shape of the surface being insulated, this shape being permanently maintained	Rigid slabs and sections of calcium silicate, magnesia, mineral wool, cork
Plastic composition	Insulation in loose dry form which is prepared for application by mixing with water	**Magnesia, calcium silicate, diatomaceous earth**
Loose fill	Insulation in the form of powder, granules, loose or pelleted fibres	Silica aerogel, perlite, vermiculite, mineral wool
Flexible	Insulation material which, lacking rigidity, tends to drape or conform to the shape of the surface against which it is laid	Low-density mineral wool, flexible polyurethane
Textile	Insulation in the form of rope, cloth, etc.	Asbestos, glass fibre and ceramic fibre rope and fabrics
Mattress	Flexible insulation faced or totally enclosed with fabric, wire netting, expanded metal, etc.	Wire netted mineral wool mattress, asbestos and glass cloth mattresses
Reflective	Insulation comprising numerous layers or random packing of low-emissivity foils	Aluminium foil, stainless-steel foil
Spray applied	Insulation applied by machine in the form of spray. Insulation may be fibrous or granular material mixed with water at the nozzle or formed by the action of two or more chemical compounds	Vermiculite or perlite concrete Polyurethane Sprayed mineral fibre Sprayed ceramic fibre
Foam *in situ*	Filling of cavities with premixed reactants	Polyurethane, urea formaldehyde

6.4 Types and forms of thermal insulation

Thermal insulation materials can be divided into four types: (a) granular, (b) fibrous, (c) cellular and (d) reflective. Granular, fibrous and cellular types rely on enclosed air or gas and minimum solid conduction paths for their thermal properties.

Granular materials such as calcium silicate and diatomaceous earth (kieselguhr), i.e. siliceous particles composed of skeletons of diatoms, contain air entrained in the matrix. Fibrous materials such as mineral wool and refractory fibres contain air between the fibres, and cellular materials such as cellular glass and foamed plastics contain small air or gas cells sealed or partly sealed from each other. Reflective insulation consists of numerous layers of spaced thin sheet material of low emissivity, such as aluminium foil.

It is possible to have a combination of the above types. For example, calcium silicate, whilst of a granular structure, has fibre added to give increased strength, and low-density fibrous materials may be interleaved with aluminium foil

Table 6.8   Typical thermal insulation materials

Insulation	Type	Availability*	Density (kg/m^3)	Approximate limiting temp. (°C)
1. Cellular glass	Cellular	a b	150	450
2. Asbestos	Fibrous	e f	80 – 250	600
3. Glass fibre	Fibrous	a b d e f	10 – 150	550
4. Rockwool and slagwool	Fibrous	a b d e g	20 – 250	850
5. Calcium silicate	Granular	a b c	200 – 600	850
6. Magnesia	Granular	a b c	200	300
7. Diatomaceous	Granular	a b c j	250 – 500	1000
8. Silica	Fibrous	d e f	50 – 150	1000
9. Aluminosilicate	Fibrous	d e f g	50 – 250	1200
10. Aluminosilicate	Granular	j	500 – 800	1200
11. Aluminium	Reflective	h	10 – 30	500
12. Stainless steel	Reflective	h	300 – 600	800
13. Vermiculite	Granular	a b c d g j	50 – 500	1100

* (a) slabs, (b) sections, (c) plastic, (d) loose-fill, (e) mattress, (f) textile, (g) sprayable, (h) reflective, (j) insulating bricks

to minimize radiative heat transfer and thereby to obtain a lower thermal conductance.

The four types of thermal insulation have varied physical characteristics and as insulation is required for a wide range of services they are produced in many forms as shown in *Table 6.7*.

6.5 Thermal insulation materials in general use

Typical thermal insulation materials for use in the temperature range 50–1000°C are listed in *Table 6.8*. Their properties are as follows:

1. Cellular glass, although suitable for use at temperatures up to 450°C, is used primarily as a load-bearing insulation for the base of low-temperature storage tanks and, owing to its impermeability, is also used on piping and equipment subject to spillage of flammable liquids.
2. Asbestos, the most versatile of the insulation materials, was formerly available in almost every form possible. Owing to the associated health hazard its use as an insulating material has been virtually discontinued. It is still available in textile form (i.e. cloth) and is used for mattress making.
3. Glass fibre, originally produced as a spun glass with a fibre diameter of approximately 20 μm and supplied in mattress form with wire mesh, is now supplied mainly as slabs and sections bonded with resin. The average fibre diameter of current production is approximately 6 μm.

4. Production of rockwool and slagwool in the UK is primarily of rockwool having an average fibre diameter of approximately 6 μm. Rockwool is used as slab and sectional insulation when bonded with resins, or in wire mesh mattresses, and is also incorporated in sprayable insulation for irregular surfaces and for fire protection of structural steel.
5. Calcium silicate, originally reinforced with asbestos fibre, has been produced in asbestos-free form since 1967 and this is now the only type made. It is available as moulded slabs and sections and as a plastics composition.
6. Magnesia, originally reinforced with asbestos fibre, was introduced as an asbestos-free product in 1966 and is now available only in that form, either as moulded slabs and sections or as a plastics composition.
7. Diatomaceous products are not now in general use in the UK for thermal insulation of piping although some fired materials in brick or slab form are used as back-up insulation behind refractories in furnace construction.
8. Silica fibres manufactured from glass by the leaching out of other elements to leave pure silica are used primarily in textile form at temperatures above the limit for glass textiles. The silica fibres have a diameter of 5–10 μm and are available as cloth, tape, sleeving, yarn and rope in addition to the felted form for insulation mattresses.

Table 6.9   Insulation materials used between 1945 and 1965

Generic type	Proprietary brands
Asbestos	Caposil*, Caposite*, Limpet*
Calcium silicate	Calsil*, Caposil*, Nadinsulan*, Newtherm*, Paratemp*
Diatomaceous	Dextramite*, Meta-dextramite*, Newtempheit*
Glass fibre	Fibreglass, Versil
85% Magnesia	Darlington*, Newalls*
Rockwool	Banroc, Basalan, Centritex, Rocksil, Rockwool
Slagwool	Eldorite, Stillite

* Contained asbestos fibres.

Table 6.10   Insulation materials in current use

Generic type	Proprietary brands
Calcium silicate	Caposil 16, Newtherm 800, Paratemp AF
Magnesia	Super Magnesia 66
Mineral wool	Banroc, Centritex, Eldorite, Fiberoc, Fibreglass, Lapinus, Rocksil, Rockwool, Stillite, Superglass
Ceramic fibres	Fiberfrax, Kerlane, Refrasil, Saffil, Triton

9. Aluminosilicate fibres are used as insulation of low thermal mass in furnaces and for general applications above the limit for mineral wool fibres. They are also processed into boards and paper. The fibre diameter is 2–3 μm.
10. Light-weight aluminosilicate bricks are used as back-up insulation behind refractories in furnace construction.
11. Aluminium foil is used as reflective insulation, generally at ambient temperatures. Its value as a thermal insulant is due to the low emissivity of aluminium.
12. Stainless-steel foils are used extensively for the internal insulation of nuclear reactors and for the insulation of primary circuits in nuclear environments where compatibility with the reactor system is essential.
13. Vermiculite in slab form is used for the fire protection of structural steel and behind refractories in furnace construction. It is also available as a sprayable material for fire protection and acoustic absorption, and is used extensively as loose-fill insulation.

Typical proprietary materials used between 1945 and 1965 for thermal insulation of boilers, pipework and equipment are shown in *Table 6.9* In addition there were numerous compositions manufactured, most of which included asbestos fibre as reinforcement.

Since 1965 the use of asbestos in thermal insulation materials has decreased owing to awareness of the health hazards, and asbestos-free insulation is now available for the whole range of temperatures encountered in steam-raising plant. Materials in current use are shown in *Table 6.10*.

6.6 Desirable properties of thermal insulating materials

Low thermal conductivity is a prime requirement for thermal insulating materials but a number of other requirements are necessary to ensure that insulating materials will give satisfactory performances for the lifetime of the plant. Thermal insulation, correctly designed and applied, has an indefinite life and removal and replacement should be required only during maintenance or modification to the plant.

When a thermal insulating material is chosen, the following properties should be considered:

1. It should be suitable for continuous use at maximum operating temperatures without degradation of its physical properties.
2. It should have adequate flexural strength and impact resistance to permit transportation and application without breakages.
3. It should have adequate compressive strength, as manufactured and also after exposure to operating temperatures, to resist local loads imposed by foot traffic,

scaffolding boards, ladders, etc.

4. It should be non-corrosive to plant and pipework if inadvertently wetted by rainwater or leaking steam during application or when in service.

5. It should not be permanently damaged if contaminated with water. Insulation which is saturated with water will have a heat transfer rate four to five times higher than in its dry state, and where contamination is liable to occur, insulation materials which regain their physical properties when dry should be used.

6. Insulating material should be non-combustible when tested to BS 476 Part 4. The finishing material should meet surface spread of flame requirement to Grade P of BS 476 Part 7.

7. Insulating material should present no hazard to health during application, under operating conditions or during subsequent removal.

6.7 Application of thermal insulation

There are two important points to remember:

1. All hot surfaces at temperatures above 60°C including valves, flanges, pipe hangers, etc. should be insulated, as heat loss from uninsulated surfaces is many times greater than the loss from insulated surfaces (*see Table 6.6*).

2. The insulation must be correctly applied and finished with impact- or wear-resistant finish to maintain thermal and physical properties. From the requirement of minimum heat transfer through an insulation system it is better to have a material of medium conductivity correctly applied than a low-conductivity material badly applied. The heat losses from surfaces left uninsulated, or with open joints in the insulation, metallic connections between hot surface and metal cleading, and incorrectly supported insulation which may allow subsequent movement to expose hot surfaces, outweigh any benefit from theoretically more efficient insulation.

The insulation system should be considered at the design stage to enable all necessary supports to be fitted, adequate clearance and access allowed for men and materials and the choice made on the basis of technical rather than financial considerations. Maximum use should

be made of off-site fabrication to speed erection time.

The skill of the thermal insulation engineer will have more effect on the thermal performance of an insulation system than any deviation from the manufacturer's claimed values for thermal conductivity of the insulating material. Small samples of flat slabs of insulating material are tested in the horizontal plane for thermal conductivity to BS 874, but to date there is no satisfactory method for measuring performance of insulation *in situ* except where the overall heat loss from a long pipeline can be determined from steam flow and inlet and exit temperatures and pressures. In steam-raising and process plant the loss of heat through the insulation is a very small percentage of the total amount of energy consumed and it is therefore very difficult to assess accurately the efficiency of the thermal insulation. If as an example we consider main steam piping from a power-station boiler to the turbine we may obtain the following:

(a)	Length	100 m
(b)	Pipe size	230 mm NB
(c)	Temperature	540°C
(d)	Pressure	166 bar
(e)	Heat content	3405 kJ/kg
(f)	Steam flow	400 t/h
(g)	Total heat passing $\dfrac{400 \times 3405}{3600}$ =	378 MW
(h)	Heat loss if uninsulated (100 m × 20 000 W/m) =	2 MW
(j)	Heat loss with 125 mm insulation (100 m × 350 W/m) =	35 kW
(k)	Heat loss with 150 mm insulation (100 m × 320 W/m)	
(l)	Incremental saving $\dfrac{(35-32)}{378\ 000}$ =	0.0008%

The application of thermal insulation is not an exact science but it does require a common-sense approach to ensure good value for money. *Figure 6.2* gives examples of good and bad thermal insulation practice.

The BS Code of Practice 3005 (1969) gives guidance on the use of thermal insulating materials.

Insulation of boilers

Boilers of modern design for power generation and the major industries have membrane walls or skin casings where thermal insulation is applied directly to the walls without the need for any refractory protective materials. The maximum temperature to which the boiler wall insulation is subjected is the saturated-steam condition, which would not normally exceed 350°C. The insulation of large boiler walls is usually achieved by the application of mineral fibre slabs applied in two layers, secured to studs and finished with either galvanized mild steel or aluminium. The insulation material should be of a type and density which will not permit overall convection within the insulation and will be sufficiently resilient to accommodate relative thermal expansion between boiler wall and outer metal finish.

Package boilers are usually insulated at the maker's works with mineral fibre slabs or mattresses and with an outer protection of sheet metal.

Piping

Before any thermal insulation is applied to piping it is essential to ensure that pipe hangers are correctly installed and preferably insulated from the pipe *(see Figure 6.2)*. Insulation supports should be provided on vertical piping and should be fitted above each bend, flange or valve. The supports, which may be angles, flat bar or studs, should be welded to the pipe and should extend to within 15 mm of the outer surface of the insulation. Supports should be fitted above flange and valves in a position which will allow mechanical maintenance to be carried out without disturbing insulation on adjoining pipework.

Thermal insulation should be applied in sectional form with a double-layer application where the thickness of insulation exceeds 63 mm. The sections should be applied with joints staggered and expansion joints provided at approximately the following spacing:

5-m intervals up to 200°C
4-m intervals in range 200–300°C
3-m intervals in range 300–400°C
2-m intervals for piping above 400°C

Expansion joints should also be provided at 1 m from either side of bends.

The expansion joint may take the form of a saw cut completely through the insulation with the joint covered by either glass cloth bandage, mattress or sheet metal.

The finish over the insulation may be one of the factory-applied finishes supplied with many thermal insulating materials, or where protection from mechanical damage is required, sheet metal or hard-setting finishes are preferable. Insulation on external pipework should be adequately protected against ingress of water.

Theoretically, flanges and valves should be insulated to the same thickness as the insulation on the adjacent pipework but restricted space often prevents this. It is preferable to use a reduced thickness of insulation on flanges and valves to ensure that the insulation can be fitted correctly rather than to manufacture a valve or flange box with the full thickness of insulation and then to discover that it cannot be fitted correctly, causing a consequent increase in heat loss. The heat loss from uninsulated flanges and valves is approximately equal to that from 0.5 m and 1 m of bare piping respectively. The heat loss from an uninsulated flange may equal that from several metres of insulated piping and it can readily be shown that a piping system with bare flanges may have twice the theoretical heat loss compared with a fully insulated system. The effect of leaving piping, flanges and valves uninsulated can be seen from *Table 6.11*.

Insulation on piping should also be designed to resist damage which may occur from access by personnel, supports for scaffolding boards, ladders, etc. Insulation on piping in areas liable to spillage of organic liquids should be protected from the risk of spontaneous combustion, either by providing an outer impervious surface which is resistant to the liquids or by the use of a non-absorbent thermal insulation such as foamed glass. Piping carrying organic liquids presents a risk at flanges and valves where leakages occur, and it is good practice to prevent the insulation from being contaminated by sealing the edges of the insulation against ingress of liquid at either side of the flanges or valve.

Turbines

Large steam turbines of over 200 MW capacity are normally insulated by the use of sprayed mineral fibres, as the shape of the casings does not permit a satisfactory application of pre-formed insulation or mattresses. Reinforcing studs, or nuts to which threaded rods can be fitted, are welded to the turbine casings and the sprayed insulation is applied and held in place with stainless-steel wire mesh secured to the studs with spring washers.

The thicknesses of insulation for turbine application are higher than for other equipment operating at similar temperatures in order to provide a resilient insulation which will allow the turbine to expand and contract without cracking the finish applied over the sprayed insulation. The finish is usually self-setting cement, which is then treated with an oil-resistant paint to prevent the risk of fire from spontaneous combustion if oil from leaks in adjacent pipework contaminates the insulation.

Table 6.11   Equivalent fuel wastage from uninsulated surfaces

	Litres of fuel oil per metre of uninsulated pipe					
Pipe o.d. (mm)	*50°C*	*100°C*	*150°C*	*200°C*	*250°C*	*300°C*
34	35	120	230	370	545	760
42	43	145	280	450	670	940
48	48	160	315	510	755	1060
60	57	200	385	625	925	1300
89	82	280	550	895	1330	1880
114	105	355	695	1130	1670	2080
168	150	515	1000	1640	2450	3460
219	190	660	1300	2120	3160	4480

Calculation based on:
(a) 8000 h operation per year
(b) Average ambient 20°C
(c) Still air conditions
(d) Boiler efficiency 80%
(e) Calorific value 43 000 MJ/t
Heat loss from uninsulated flange is approximately equal to that from 0.5 m of uninsulated pipe.
Heat loss from uninsulated valve is approximately equal to that from 1 m of uninsulated pipe.

Gas flues

Gas flues are insulated to maintain the required gas temperatures at the chimney and to prevent corrosion by maintaining the temperature of the flue wall above the dewpoint of the gases. The vertical sides and bottom of the flue may be insulated with low-density insulation supported on studs and reinforcing mesh, but the tops of the flue, which may be liable to foot traffic, should be insulated with material of sufficient resistance to compression to withstand imposed loads. The tops are normally insulated with calcium silicate or with heavy-density mineral wool.

Care should be taken to avoid heat bridges and cold spots giving rise to condensation of gas on the inner face of the flue. Expansion joints in gas flues should be insulated to prevent acid deposition.

Open-top tanks

Open-top tanks containing hot fluids lose energy by evaporation. Heat losses can be appreciably reduced by floating a layer of polypropylene (or similar) spheres on the surface of the liquid. Manufacturers claim a reduction in heat loss of 70% by floating a layer of 45-mm diameter balls on the surface of liquid at 90°C.

Avoidance of stress corrosion cracking of austenitic stainless steel

Insulated austenitic stainless-steel surfaces
operating at temperatures above 70°C are liable to external stress corrosion cracking in the presence of chlorides. As most thermal insulating materials contain chlorides when manufactured, and may also pick up chlorides from the atmosphere, it is necessary to take precautions when insulation is applied to stainless-steel piping and equipment.

It is recommended that a barrier be placed between the insulation and the stainless steel to prevent chlorides that may be leached out from the insulation from being deposited on the stainless steel. The usual practice is to apply and fit aluminium foil, not thinner than 0.06 mm, before the insulation is applied.

Painting treatments may also be applied to the stainless steel before the insulation is applied but these methods are labour-intensive and it is not as easy to ensure that 100% cover has been achieved.

It is essential that insulation applied to stainless steel is adequately weatherproofed to prevent ingress of water.

The chapter so far has dealt with the general properties and application of thermal insulation. In view of the amount of work which has been carried out recently on medical aspects of asbestiform materials, the following section has been included to give the present-day position on these materials.

6.8 Safe use of asbestos thermal insulation

Types of asbestos

Asbestos is a general term applied to certain inorganic silicate minerals that occur naturally and have a distinct fibrous crystalline structure. They are distinguished from man-made mineral fibres such as rockwool and glass wool by this true crystalline structure and by the extreme fineness of the fibres and fibrils.

There are three main types of asbestiform minerals, belonging to two main groups with specific crystalline structures, as follows:

Amphiboles	Serpentines
Amosite (grey-brown) Crocidolite (blue asbestos)	Chrysotile (white asbestos)

The individual fibre diameters are generally less than 1μm, with minimum diameter of approximately 0.02μm for fibrils of chrysotile and 0.1μm for amosite and crocidolite.

Properties

The heat and chemical resistance of asbestos and its fibrous nature are the principal properties which have led to its extensive use as a thermal insulant. All types of asbestos progressively break down when heated to temperatures of between 400°C and 1000°C but this decomposition is never complete and residual fibrous asbestos will always remain even if the asbestos insulation has been subject to high temperatures. The thermal insulating properties of asbestos are not affected by this partial decomposition but resistance to erosion and vibration would be reduced.

Crocidolite and amosite have greater thermal stability and chemical resistance and consequently have been more commonly used for high-temperature insulation or where chemical resistance is also required.

Industrial application

Asbestos has been used in a number of ways for thermal insulation materials. Most commonly, amosite and to some extent crocidolite have been bonded and compressed into slabs or rigid sections. Their fibrous properties have also been utilized to reinforce calcium silicate and magnesia compositions to provide slabs and rigid sections for thermal insulation purposes. Crocidolite, amosite and chrysotile fibres have been mixed with cement and applied as a sprayed insulation for plant and equipment, such as turbines. They had the advantage of ease of application, particularly where a contoured surface was required. They were also used for fire protection of steelwork. Crocidolite and chrysotile asbestos can be successfully spun and woven into yarns and cloth and in the past both have been used, as ropes and fabrics, for insulation of pipes and in the manufacture of insulating mattresses. The use of crocidolite for textile material stopped some years ago, but chrysotile fabrics may still be used for covering sectional insulation providing mechanical protection, particularly in situations where there is continuous vibration such as ships' boiler-rooms.

Currently, all insulation products manufactured in the UK are asbestos-free with the exception of textile materials. For most applications, woven glass or ceramic fibre products are suitable alternatives for textile materials. In view of the very stringent hygiene standard applicable to crocidolite, asbestos products containing this fibre are no longer used or indeed available.

The use of spray applications containing asbestos is discouraged, and it has been informally agreed with the spray contractors that no new work will be undertaken which involves using asbestos. It is expected that legislation will be introduced to regularize this position.

Health hazards

Materials containing asbestos present a hazard only when asbestos fibres are released and dispersed to the atmosphere so that they may be inhaled. If asbestos dust is inhaled it is the fine fibres, which are too small to be seen by the naked eye, that are deposited in the lungs and may eventually cause damage.

Prior to the mid-1960s, when a campaign to have mesothelioma registered as an industrial disease led to an increasing awareness of the health hazards associated with asbestos, little interest had been shown in establishing safe working conditions during the application of insulation materials. The level of asbestos during the application and removal of insulation was found to be many times higher than what would now be considered acceptable levels, especially when asbestos was being sprayed or plastic compositions mixed. It was particularly evident in ship construction, where insulation was often applied in confined spaces and many tradesmen other than thermal insulation engineers were exposed to high levels of asbestos dust. Many cases of mesothelioma have been diagnosed in the UK in areas where Admiralty ships were built and repaired, and this is related to the quantities of crocidolite used for insulation and fire protection in naval vessels.

The problems associated with the application of asbestos insulating materials were finally recognized by insulation manufacturers, contractors and by the major users, who issued instructions that no insulation materials containing asbestos should be used on their plants. Manufacturers produced asbestos-free materials which were tested and approved by the major users leaving as the only problem the removal of asbestos prior to reinsulation or the removal of insulation from plant being demolished. Removal of insulation containing asbestos from plant will almost invariably result in dust concentrations that necessitate the use of respiratory protection for personnel. Codes of practice and methods adopted by contractors together with the improved respirators available ensure that asbestos can now be removed without any risk to personnel.

It must be emphasized that asbestos in thermal insulation installed on piping and equipment does not *necessarily* constitute a hazard to health. There is nothing poisonous, toxic or radioactive about asbestos and there is no need to remove insulation from piping and equipment simply because it contains asbestos. If the outer surface is in good condition, no asbestos fibres will be liberated into the atmosphere except during removal for maintenance purposes. There are a number of materials available which can be trowelled, brushed or sprayed on to the surface of insulations that contain asbestos to provide a finish which will protect the insulation and seal the surface against egress of asbestos dust. Suitable materials are asbestos-free hard-setting or self-setting cements, PVA paints with glass cloth membrane, PVC spray or metal cleading.

The diseases associated with asbestos are as follows:

Asbestosis

Asbestosis is a thickening and scarring of lung tissue which usually occurs after many years of exposure to high concentrations of asbestos dust. The disease may become apparent only some years after first exposure or even after occupational exposure has ceased. The degree of risk associated with the development of asbestosis would appear to be related to the duration of exposure and to the level of asbestos dust in the occupational environment. The characteristic symptom of asbestosis is a progressive breathlessness and an unproductive cough. Thickening of the surface of the lung may also sometimes be seen in those exposed to asbestos dust.

Cancer of bronchus or lung

It has been demonstrated that there is an increased incidence of lung cancer among persons who already have asbestosis. It is, however, by no means certain whether asbestos can contribute to cancer of the lung when asbestosis is not already present. There is evidence to indicate that the combined risk of lung cancer from exposure to asbestos dust and from cigarette smoking is greater than the sum of the two risks separately, and therefore cigarette smoking is more than ordinarily dangerous for someone who works in an atmosphere containing asbestos dust.

Mesothelioma

A mesothelioma is a tumour of the lining of the chest, or in some cases of the lining of the abdominal cavity, which is rare in comparison with other cancers in the general population. Whilst it is usually associated with heavy and prolonged exposure to blue asbestos it has sometimes occurred among people exposed much less extensively. Mesothelioma has also been associated with exposure to other forms of asbestos but the risk is thought to be greater for crocidolite than amosite, with a lesser degree of risk for chrysotile. There is usually a long interval, often 30–40 years, between first exposure and the development of this type of tumour. There are some cases of mesothelioma which cannot be traced to asbestos exposure and may have other causes.

UK legislation

The Asbestos Regulations 1969

The Asbestos Regulations 1969 (ref. 1) apply to all factories and to other premises to which Part 4 of the Factories Act 1961 applies, including construction sites, electrical stations and ships under construction or repair, etc., where a process involving asbestos is undertaken, except a process in which asbestos dust cannot be given off. 'Asbestos' as defined in the Health and Safety at Work etc. Act 1974 includes crocidolite, amosite, anthophyllite and chrysotile. 'Asbestos dust' is also defined in Regulation 2 as 'dust consisting of or containing asbestos dust to such an extent as is liable to cause danger to the health of employed persons'.

The Health and Safety at Work Act 1974

In work activities where the Asbestos Regulations 1969 do not apply, standards similar to those required by the Regulations should be adopted by persons having duties under the Health and Safety at Work Act 1974, because of their responsibility under this Act to safeguard their employees' health and to avoid exposing them to risk either to their health or to their general safety.

Hygiene standards for asbestos dust

The relationship between the amount of asbestos taken in and the response of the subject is being reviewed (1978) and will be reported on later by the Advisory Committee on Asbestos. At present, until this committee has published its findings and recommendations, the following criteria are used in assessing whether or not there is compliance with the Asbestos Regulations and the Health and Safety at Work Act[2,3]:

1. Exposure to all forms of asbestos dust should be reduced to the minimum that is reasonably practicable.
2. In any case, occupational exposure to asbestos dust should never exceed:

for crocidolite   0.2 fibres/ml when measured over any ten-minute period.

for other types   2.0 fibres/ml when
of asbestos   measurements are averaged over a four-hour period;
                   12.0 fibres/ml when measured over any ten-minute period.

Fibres are defined as particles of length greater than 5 μm, having a diameter of 3 μm or less and having a length to breadth ratio of at least 3 : 1 when observed by transmitted light under phase contrast conditions at a magnification of approximately 500×.

Precautions[4-6]

It is the very fine particles of asbestos dust that are too small to be seen by the naked eye which if inhaled into the lungs may cause ill effects. Because these particles are very small, if they become airborne they remain suspended in the atmosphere for a considerable period and will migrate from an asbestos working area, if permitted to do so, via draughts and convection currents. Similarly, deposits of dust, if allowed to remain, will become airborne and disperse to the atmosphere where they may be inhaled. Precautions must therefore be taken to prevent or minimize the release of asbestos dust and if this cannot be avoided, to take the necessary procedures to prevent the dust from being inhaled and to prevent its spreading to other areas or work situations.

The majority of thermal insulating materials currently being used by industry do not contain asbestos. There may however be some limited use of asbestos rope and cloth for insulation purposes and these will release asbestos dust when cut and manipulated. However, exposure to asbestos dust will most likely occur during the removal or repair of older insulation materials which will invariably contain asbestos. Removal of asbestos insulation is an extremely dusty process; the following asbestos dust concentrations are likely to arise at operations involving removal of asbestos materials.

With thorough soaking
using water   1–5 fibres/ml
With use of water sprays for
dust suppression   5–40 fibres/ml
Dry removal   over 20 fibres/ml

The removal or repair of any asbestos insulation will result in release of asbestos dust, whatever the method of work, and will be subject in the UK to either the Asbestos Regulations 1969 or the Health and Safety at Work Act. It is therefore essential that in every situation where asbestos-containing materials are handled, proper procedures are adopted which will both protect the persons undertaking the asbestos process and prevent the release of asbestos dust to the environment.

Identification

Before stripping commences, the insulation must be examined to determine whether asbestos is present and to identify its type. It is preferable for the owner of the plant to determine the presence and type of asbestos prior to issuing enquiries or contracts for the stripping of the insulation, although it is the responsibility of the contractor engaged in stripping work to ensure that the instructions concerning the presence and type of asbestos advised by the owner are correct.

The presence of and identification of the type of asbestos should be determined by experienced personnel. A thorough sampling and identification procedure is necessary but, unless the outer finish is completely removed to establish uniformity of the underlying insulation, can give only an indication of the presence and type of asbestos. The cork borer technique of sampling, where a sample of diameter approximately 10–15 mm is taken through the composite insulation and finish, is unsatisfactory as the samples may not necessarily be representative.

If crocidolite asbestos is present, the Health

and Safety Executive should be notified 28 days before any stripping takes place. If this is not practicable, acceptance of a shorter notice should be discussed with the Inspector.

Respiratory protective equipment[7]

The type of respiratory protective equipment (RPE) will be determined by the method of work and whether crocidolite is present or not; only RPE approved by the Chief Inspector of Factories[7] should be used for asbestos operations. Where crocidolite asbestos is present then the RPE selected should be suitable for use in unlimited concentrations of asbestos dust, and RPE with a higher protection factor will be required if insulation not containing crocidolite is removed dry or is only partly damped.

The Asbestos Regulations 1969 require that the RPE provided should be properly maintained and that users should be fully instructed in the proper use of the equipment.

Protective clothing

For any process involving asbestos removal, protective clothing must be supplied, used and maintained. Overalls made from man-made fibres are usually the most suitable as asbestos dust will not be readily retained by this type of material. Protective clothing should be close-fitting at the neck, wrists and ankles to prevent contamination of undergarments. Headgear should also be provided, either a close-fitting cap or a hood, and should be of material similar to that recommended for outer clothing. Footwear of a type which can readily be decontaminated should also be provided.

Simple suction cleaning of protective clothing, before personnel leave the asbestos work area, is sufficient to remove loosely adhering dust before doffing RPE and removing clothing. Contaminated clothing must be regularly laundered and where this is not carried out on the premises the contaminated clothing should be placed in impervious bags and marked with the words 'Asbestos-contaminated clothing'.

Changing accommodation

Accommodation should be provided for changing, and for storing protective clothing and equipment. This should have dirty and clean locker areas preferably separated by a wash or shower room. It is most important that heavily contaminated clothing and equipment is decontaminated by suction cleaning before leaving the working area and before removing RPE and protective clothing.

Method of work

Where practicable, all asbestos insulation should be thoroughly saturated with water before removal. Hard-set finishes should be perforated and water injected into the underlying insulation using hollow metal probes. In some situations where dry stripping methods have to be used, a high standard of RPE will be necessary.

Enclosure

It is important to segregate an asbestos working area to prevent any dust escaping from an asbestos delagging operation to other areas of the plant or premises. Where necessary, enclosures should be constructed of properly fitted screens of thick-gauge polyethylene to isolate the asbestos working area, within which the workers must be fully protected with RPE and protective clothing. Good seals must be maintained between the temporary enclosure and the building structure to prevent any escape of asbestos dust, and suitable air-locks should be constructed for access and exit from the enclosure to ensure that dust does not escape and to provide an area for decontamination of working clothing by suction cleaning.

It is clearly not practicable to erect enclosures for every asbestos operation, as with the removal of small areas of insulation from valves or pipework, but the methods of work should be such as to reduce the release of asbestos dust to the absolute minimum, and to keep away unauthorized persons.

Cleaning

All asbestos waste should be placed in impervious containers during the removal, and sealed. If crocidolite is present these containers must be properly marked 'Blue asbestos — do not inhale dust'. After stripping, the area must be thoroughly cleaned and decontaminated using suction cleaning equipment fitted with secondary air filtration equipment.

Disposal of waste[8]

Asbestos waste should be disposed of in such a way that no dust is emitted to the air during transportation or tipping. Precautions must be taken to ensure that full containers removed from the working area are decontaminated before removing to the disposal site, the most important feature of this being that any loose material on the outside of the container should be removed either by suction cleaning, with waste being placed in a second clean liner, or by thorough washing down.

6.9 Non-asbestos thermal insulation

Substitutes

These include calcium silicate and magnesia which no longer contain asbestos but may be reinforced with other fibres. The well-documented health risks associated with asbestos have given considerable impetus to the use of man-made mineral fibres, which have physical properties similar to those of asbestos, as alternative insulation materials. Generally, man-made mineral fibres fall into three categories: mineral wool, glass fibre and ceramic fibre. Insulation products made from man-made mineral fibre are available as slab or rigid section materials, in blanket form and some may be used in spray applications.

Health aspects

These fibres used for thermal insulation can produce skin and eye irritation. Concern has been expressed on the possible effects which might result from inhalation of airborne dust and fibres, since irritation of the nose, throat and upper respiratory tract is experienced when excessive amounts of dust are inhaled. There is no evidence at present to show that man-made mineral fibre as used for thermal insulation produces respiratory or other diseases in man, but laboratory experiments with animals have suggested that certain fibres might present a hazard. However there is as yet no confirmation from animal inhalation experiments, or from human experience. Further national and international research is being undertaken in order to resolve the uncertainty arising from the animal experiments.

The present situation is being reviewed in the UK by the Health and Safety Executive and a subcommittee is considering all the data at present available. In due course it will report its findings and recommendations to the Advisory Committee on Toxic Substances. Nevertheless, in view of the doubts which have arisen, precautions should be taken to avoid inhaling excessive quantities of man-made mineral fibres.

Thus it is important to reduce the concentration of dust which may be inhaled by workers and to ensure that its concentration in the air breathed by an employee does not exceed the nuisance dust TLV* of 10 mg/m³.

The important points to follow are:

1. Careful handling of materials up to the working area and the removal of scrap material in impervious bags.

2. Suction cleaning of the working area during the lagging operation and as soon as the operation is finished.
3. The provision of suitable enclosures and allowing in the area only those workers whose presence is necessary for the operations.

Where the methods of work do not adequately reduce contact with man-made mineral fibre or debris, or exposure to excessive concentrations of airborne dust, personal protective equipment including dust respirators may be required. This will be so where persons are exposed to airborne dust concentrations exceeding the TLV of 10 mg/m³.

Suitable protective clothing should be worn; this may vary with circumstances from the provision of gloves to full protection. Experience has shown that it is better to wear loose clothing, avoiding tight restrictions at neck and wrist which may increase the problem of skin irritation.

As with asbestos materials, suitable accommodation should be provided for storage of protective clothing and provision should be made for removing heavy contamination by suction cleaning when personnel leave the working area.

British Standards relating to thermal insulation (*see also*

Chapter 21)

BS 476:	'Fire tests on building materials and structures'
	Part 4 (1970): 'Non-combustibility test for materials'
	Part 5 (1968): 'Ignitability test for materials' (amended July 1969)
	Part 7 (1971): 'Surface spread of flame tests for materials'
BS 874 (1973):	'Methods of determining thermal properties, with definitions of thermal insulating terms'
BS 2972 (1975):	'Methods of test for thermal insulating materials' (amended March 1978)
BS 3533 (1962):	'Glossary of terms relating to thermal insulation'
BS 3958:	'Thermal insulating materials'
	Part 1 (1970): '85% Magnesia preformed insulation' (amended April 1972)
	Part 2 (1970): 'Calcium silicate preformed insulation' (amended April 1972)

---

* TLV, threshold limit value.

Part 3 (1967): 'Metal mesh faced mineral wool mats and mattresses'
Part 4 (1968): 'Bonded preformed mineral wool pipe sections'
Part 5 (1969): 'Bonded mineral wool slabs (for use at temperatures above 50°C)'
Part 6 (1972): 'Finishing materials; hard setting composition, self-setting cement and gypsum plaster'

BS 3974:   'Pipe supports'
            Part 1 (1974); Part 2 (1978)
BS 4508:   'Thermally insulated underground piping systems'
            Part 1 (1969); Part 2 (1973); Part 3 (1977); Part 4 (1977)
BS 5422 (1977): 'Use of thermal insulation materials' (amended May 1978)
CP 3005 (1969): 'Thermal insulation of pipework and equipment (in the temperature range of −100°F to +1500°F (−73°C to +816°C)' (amended August 1971 and September 1975)
CP 3009 (1970): 'Thermally insulated underground piping systems'

References and further reading

1 The Asbestos Regulations 1969-S1 1969 No. 690
2 'Asbestos' Final report of the Advisory Committee on Asbestos, Vols 1 and 2. London: HMSO (1979)
3 'Asbestos hygiene standards and measurement of airborne dust concentrations'. Guidance Note EH/10
4 'Protective equipment in the asbestos industry'. ARC Control and Safety Guide No 1
5 'Stripping and fitting of asbestos-containing thermal insulation materials'. ARC Control and Safety Guide No. 3
6 'Cleaning of premises and plant in accordance with the asbestos regulations'. ARC Control and Safety Guide No. 9
7 Asbestos Regulations 1969: Respiratory Protective Equipment Technical Data Note 24 (2nd Rev)
8 Asbestosis Research Council: Recommended Code of Practice
9 Malloy, J. F. *Thermal Insulation*. New York: Van Nostrand–Reinhold (1969)
10 Wilson, A. C. *Industrial Thermal Insulation*. New York: McGraw-Hill (1959)
11 Donnelly, R. G., Tennery, V. J., McElroy, D. L., Godfrey, T. G. and Kolb, J. O. *Industrial Thermal Insulation. An Assessment*. Oak Ridge National Laboratory (1976)
12 Wilkes, G. B. *Heat Insulation*. New York: John Wiley (1950)
13 Tye, R. P. *Thermal Conductivity*. London: Academic Press (1969)
14 McAdams, W. H. *Heat Transmission*. New York: McGraw-Hill (1954)
15 Jakob, M. and Hawkins, G. A. *Elements of Heat Transfer*. New York: John Wiley (1957)
16 British Standard CP 3005: 'Thermal insulation of pipework and equipment (in the temperature range of −100°F to +1500°F (−73°C to +816°C)' (1969, amended Aug. 1971 and Sept. 1975)
17 Lomax, Wilmoth & Co. *Insulation Handbook* (1979)
18 Department of Energy *Fuel Efficiency Booklet No. 8*: 'The economic thicknesses of insulation for hot pipes' (1977)
19 Thermal Insulation Contractors' Association 'Standard method of measurement for thermal insulation' (1973)
20 Green, A. K. and Pye, A. M. *Asbestos — Characteristics, Applications and Alternatives*. Fulmer Research Institute (1970)
21 Bradfield, R. E. N. *Asbestos — Review of Uses, Health Effects, Measurement and Control*. Atkins Research & Development (1977)
22 Hunter, D. *Diseases of Occupations*. London: English Universities Press (1969)
23 Asbestos Research Council: Control and Safety Guides
24 Health and Safety Executive Certificate of Approval for Respiratory Protective Equipment (RPE)
25 British Standard BS 2091: 'Respirators for protection against harmful dusts, gases, etc.'
26 British Standard BS 4275: 'Recommendations for the selection, use and maintenance of RPE'
27 Michaels, L. and Chissick, S. S. (Eds) *Asbestos: Properties, Applications and Hazards*. Chichester: John Wiley (1979)

7

Water treatment

Although there are many applications where treated water is necessary, the predominant use, both in terms of quantity used and frequency of use, is in steam-raising boilers. Because of this, the present chapter deals mainly with water treatment for boiler plants. However, the principles are the same, whatever the end-use of the water, although the specification of the final water can vary somewhat.

A summary of all the water treatment processes is given as *Table 7.6* on p 135.

7.1 The purpose of water treatment

The function of a boiler is to transfer heat produced by the combustion of fuel to the water confined within the boiler in order to generate clean, dry steam under pressure. A boiler can function efficiently only if the heat transfer surfaces and other waterways within the boiler are maintained in a clean and intact condition by proper control of the quality of the feedwater and boiler water.

Virtually all natural waters contain impurities in solution and suspension. When introduced into the boiler with the make-up water some of these impurities can produce scale or other deposits which may restrict water circulation or retard the transfer of heat from the tube wall to the water. In consequence the metal of the heat transfer surface may be inadequately cooled and if steps are not taken to remedy this condition the metal may finally become so hot and weakened that it can no longer withstand the operating pressure. (Heat transfer is discussed in Chapter 12.)

Impurities in the feedwater and boiler water may also cause corrosion of the metal in contact with the water unless the quality of the water is adjusted to counteract this effect. Corrosion occurs when the metal reacts with the water and its dissolved constituents and results in part of the metal being taken into solution. The dissolved metal may be precipitated as an oxide or hydroxide at the site of corrosion or it may remain in solution and perhaps precipitate as a deposit elsewhere in the system.

With correctly adjusted water conditions the initial corrosion of the metal results in the formation of a protective oxide layer which prevents any further aggressive reaction. If this protective oxide is not formed, corrosion may continue unabated with consequent progressive reduction in metal thickness and hence in mechanical strength.

Although corrosion is predominantly due to the action of certain soluble constituents in the water, insoluble material which produces scale and deposit on the metal surface, far from protecting the metal from the corrosive constituents in the water, may actively encourage corrosion of the underlying metal by inhibiting the formation of or by destroying the protective oxide layer.

When water is evaporated within the boiler to form steam, the concentration of both dissolved and suspended solids in the boiler water increases owing to the inflow of additional solids with the feedwater. As the steam bubbles separate from the surface of the water in the boiler, small droplets of the boiler water are ejected from the surface. As these droplets contain dissolved solids at the same concentration as the body of water in the boiler they tend to contaminate the steam not only with water but also with solids.

Priming or carryover of boiler water with the steam may also occur sporadically as a result of sudden changes in operating conditions, particularly when the boiler water contains abnormally high proportions of individual impurities such as suspended solids, caustic soda or sodium phosphate, which alter the surface tension of the water. These are dealt with in Chapters 4, 5 and 17. High concentrations of suspended solids in the boiler water can give rise to the formation of stable foam above the water surface. This can lead to a severe form of water carryover in which large volumes of water are intermittently ejected from the boiler with the steam, and the dryness and purity of the steam are severely impaired.

The purpose of water treatment for boilers is to ensure that all parts of the boiler plant in contact with the water remain clean and intact, so that the design efficiency of steam generation and the production of clean, dry steam can be maintained during the working life of the boiler. The prevention of scale or deposit requires that all water entering the boiler plant, via the feed system, must be free from suspended solids, or any substance in solution which may precipitate as solid by concentration or be formed by reaction with other constituents in the boiler water. The prevention of corrosion requires that where possible the aggressive constituents should be removed or neutralized before the water enters the feed system. In addition, and sometimes as an alternative to external treatment, the condition of the boiler water should be adjusted in such a way as to nullify the action of an aggressive impurity in the event of its being present in the boiler water.

In boilers where only part of the water is evaporated, as is usually the case, the water-borne solids may be allowed to concentrate in the residual water within the boiler, the concentration being controlled by blowdown of concentrate.

A further aim of water treatment is to reduce the concentration of all or some of the impurities present in the make-up water so that a safe maximum concentration of solids in the boiler water can be maintained with a practical and economic level of blowdown.

In the case of 'once-through' boilers where all of the water entering the boiler is evaporated and there is no reservoir of water in which dissolved solids may concentrate, it is essential that the feedwater should be completely free from both suspended solids and dissolved solids.

7.2 Common impurities in water

Pure water seldom if ever occurs in nature because it is readily contaminated by other materials present in the environment. Many of the properties commonly attributed to water are in fact related more to the nature of the impurities it contains than to the water itself. Thus the terms soft and hard, acid or alkaline, clean or turbid refer to the characteristics produced by solution or suspension of different materials in water.

Visual examination of a water sample gives little or no indication of the nature of impurities present and therefore cannot be used for assessing the suitability of a water for use as make-up or feed to a boiler plant. This can only be achieved by carrying out a proper chemical analysis of the water in order to determine the concentration of individual impurities present.

Dissolved gases

Since all gases are to some extent soluble in water, natural water contains small amounts of all the gases present in the atmosphere. Of these the most important, in the context of water treatment for boilers, are dissolved oxygen and dissolved carbon dioxide as these gases play an important role in supporting corrosion of various metals.

The concentrations of these gases in rain-water depends upon the proportion in which they are present in the atmosphere, or strictly speaking upon the partial pressure individual gases exert. On this basis, the amount of free carbon dioxide present should be quite small and in the order of only a few milligrams per litre, whereas in practice, many surface and ground waters often contain an appreciable amount of carbon dioxide. This phenomenon is mainly due to solution of carbon dioxide produced by respiration and decay of surface vegetation in the catchment area and also by bacterial decomposition of organic matter within the soil. The carbon dioxide taken into solution as a result of these processes may amount to several hundred milligrams per litre. The carbonic acid resulting from solution of this carbon dioxide enables the water to dissolve large amounts of otherwise insoluble minerals from the ground and therefore has a major effect on the mineral quality of the water.

Other gases may also occasionally be present in waters derived from boreholes and deep wells. Such gases as methane (CH_4) and hydrogen sulphide (H_2S) are also produced by the action of bacteria on organic matter and certain mineral deposits in the ground. Many borehole waters containing large amounts of CO_2, CH_4 and H_2S are anaerobic or devoid of dissolved oxygen, and contain appreciable amounts of iron and manganese in solution. When these waters are withdrawn from the ground and exposed to the air, the dissolved gases are released. The simultaneous absorption and solution of dissolved oxygen causes the iron and manganese to oxidize and hydrolyse to less soluble ferric and manganic hydroxides. These waters, when first withdrawn from the ground are often sparkling clear but rapidly become turbid owing to the precipitation of these metal hydroxides.

Dissolved mineral salts

In addition to dissolved gases, rain-water usually contains some small amounts of dissolved mineral matter from dust particles in the atmosphere. However, by far the greatest proportion of the dissolved impurities in natural waters are materials leached out of the ground. The concentration of these impurities varies considerably from place to place but it is generally greater in ground water such as from springs, wells and boreholes than from surface water in rivers, lakes and reservoirs.

The nature of the impurities to a very large extent depends upon the geology of the ground over which the water has passed or through which it has percolated. The amount of any individual constituent taken into solution depends not only on the geological form of the mineral present in the ground but also on the presence of other salts or gases already in solution. For instance, sparingly soluble calcium carbonate present as chalk or limestone can be converted to highly soluble calcium bicarbonate by the carbonic acid formed in the manner already described. The importance of the role played by the dissolved carbon dioxide in this reaction may be judged from the fact that the solubility of calcium carbonate in pure water is only about 30 mg/l, whereas many natural waters contain calcium bicarbonate equivalent to many hundreds of milligrams per litre of calcium carbonate.

Organic matter

The organic matter contained in surface water and occasionally in ground waters is derived from the decomposition of dead plant material. The decay products are complex organic materials but may broadly be classified as fulvic and humic acids and their salts. These materials are responsible for the stable brown coloration of surface water often found in peaty areas but the absence of visible colour does not necessarily signify the absence of organic material in solution.

Organic matter may impair the operation of the water treatment processes designed to remove mineral impurities from the make-up water or feedwater. Consequently, special treatment may be required to remove organic matter even though the boiler operating conditions may not require it.

Suspended matter

Most surface waters contain material in suspension. The concentration of the suspended matter present is usually expressed on a weight basis, i.e. as mg/l, when the concentration is high, or as a turbidity value when the concentration is too low to measure accurately on a weight basis. The turbidity value is solely a measure of the amount of light that is absorbed by the suspended material when a beam of light is passed through a sample under standardized condition. The numerical value of turbidity is obtained by comparing the absorbance with that produced by stable suspensions of finely dispersed silica particles of known weight concentration. The result is then reported as a number on the silica scale, e.g. Turbidity 14 (silica scale), but does not represent the weight concentration of the actual material present in the sample.

7.3 Interpretation of water analysis

It is impossible to arrive at any sensible and economic decision regarding the treatment of feedwater for boiler operation unless the characteristics of the available water are clearly established. Where the quality of a water supply is subject to seasonal or other variations, samples of water should be examined to ensure that these variations are taken into account.

The *water analysis report* should encompass all the major constituents, salts and those minor components that are significant in relation to boiler operation. The report should present the results in an internally consistent manner, so that, for example, the sum of the individual soluble components agrees with the measured and reported figure for total dissolved solids content and is consistent with the electrical conductivity of the water. The limit of detection appropriate to the analytical method employed should be evident.

When the characteristics of a water of variable composition are reported it is wise to tabulate each analysis separately showing the date and source of each sample. In this way the designer of the water treatment facility can make his own experienced assessment of the effects of each variable. The practice of extracting the maximum and minimum values of each component from the range of analysis and listing them under headings 'maximum', 'average' and 'minimum' is not only not helpful but counter-productive. The values listed under each heading do not collectively represent any real analysis; they will be inconsistent with one other and if used as the basis of design of the water treatment plant may produce an inefficient and uneconomic process.

Cation and anions

The major impurities in natural water result from the solution of mineral salts with which the water has come into contact. When these salts pass into solution they dissociate into positively charged cations and negatively charged anions. When a sample of water is analysed, the concentration of each cation and anion is determined and reported

separately. Unfortunately there is no national or international uniformity in the way these results are presented. Some laboratories state the concentration of each cation or anion in terms of each specific ion, for example mg/l of (cations) Ca^{2+}, Mg^{2+}, Na^+ and (anions) HCO_3^-, SO_4^{2-}, Cl^-, NO_3. Presented in this form, the sum of the concentrations of all the cations and all of the anions will be equal to the total dissolved solids present in the water, if each and every component has been determined accurately. However it is not possible to see at a glance whether something has been missed out or incorrectly measured. This is due to the fact that the components all have different mass and therefore the sum of the weights of the anions does not balance that of the cations.

In practice, therefore, the analyst may apply a factor to each component so that all the cations and anions are expressed in some common form such as milli-equivalents per litre or as equivalent weight concentration of calcium carbonate ($CaCO_3$). This is similar to converting various different currencies into pounds sterling by applying the appropriate rate of exchange in order to state the total value in a common form. *Table 7.1* indicates how the results of analysis may be transformed from one state to another. The SI system does not permit the use of milli-equivalents per litre but this unit is still in use in many parts of the world and has therefore been included for information only. This method of reporting the analytical results has a number of advantages. The sum of the anions should equal that of the cations if the

Table 7.1 Conversion of analytical results to a common form

	Multiply by f		Divide by f		
	As ions (mg/l)	(f)	As CaCO₃ (mg/l)	(f)	Milli-equivalents per litre (meq/l)
Calcium, Ca^{2+}	60	(2.5)	150	(50)	3.0
Magnesium, Mg^{2+}	12.2	(4.11)	50	(50)	1.0
Sodium, Na^+	27.6	(2.17)	60	(50)	1.2
Total cations			260	(50)	5.2
Bicarbonate, HCO_3^-	213	(0.82)	175	(50)	3.5
Sulphate, SO_4^{2-}	19.2	(1.04)	20	(50)	0.4
Chloride, Cl^-	39	(1.41)	55	(50)	1.1
Nitrate, NO_3^-	12.3	(0.81)	10	(50)	0.2
Total anions			260	(50)	5.2
Total alkalinity			175		
Total hardness			200		
Equivalent mineral acidity			85		

analysis is valid. The concentrations of various cations or anions can be expressed by the terms *'total cations'* and *'total anions'* respectively.

Minor constituents of the water and those which are in suspension and therefore not dissociated into cations and anions (i.e. not ionized) may still be reported as the individual ions. Thus 1.2 mg/l Fe represents the concentration of iron whether it is in solution or suspension.

Total alkalinity

The alkalinity of natural water is due to the solution of salts of carbonic acid, which is the weak acid produced when CO_2 gas is dissolved in the water. The main salts are the bicarbonates and carbonates of sodium, calcium and magnesium, and are weak and moderately alkaline salts. The strong bases sodium hydroxide and calcium hydroxide are not normally present in natural water but are used in the treatment of water and may be formed in boiler water owing to decomposition and hydrolysis of the weaker alkalis. The term *total alkalinity* as $CaCO_3$ encompasses all the forms of alkali present.

The analysis report may indicate the concentration of the different forms of alkali present as well as the total alkalinity. Alternatively, it may merely give values of alkalinity M and alkalinity P in mg/l as $CaCO_3$, which represent the measured alkalinity obtained by neutralization with acid using methyl orange and phenolphthalein respectively as pH indicators. These two values can be used to establish the approximate proportions of the alkalis present, using *Table 7.2*.

Table 7.2

P and M value	*Bicarbonate*	*Carbonate*	*Hydroxide*
$P = O$	M		
$P < 0.5M$	$M - 2P$	$2P$	
$P = 0.5M$		$2P$	
$P > 0.5M$		$2(M - P)$	$M - 2P$
$P = M$			P or M

Example: The alkalinities P and M measured using phenolphthalein and methyl orange respectively as indicators gives values of $P=20$ mg/l and $M=50$ mg/l as $CaCO_3$. As the P value is less than $0.5M$, the form and concentration of alkalis present may be deduced from the line $P < 0.5M$.

Thus:

Bicarbonate $= M - 2P = 10$ mg/l as $CaCO_3$

and

Carbonate $= 2P = 40$ mg/l as $CaCO_3$

Total hardness, alkaline and non-alkaline hardness

The so-called hardness of water is due to the solution of calcium and magnesium salts which can produce hard scale on heat transfer surfaces. *Total hardness* is the sum of the concentrations of calcium and magnesium ions present when these are both expressed as $CaCO_3$.

If the water is alkaline, a proportion of this hardness, equal in magnitude to the total alkalinity also expressed as $CaCO_3$, is considered as *alkaline hardness* and the remainder as *non-alkaline hardness*. If the total alkalinity exceeds the total hardness, all of the hardness is considered as alkaline hardness and the excess alkalinity is assumed to be associated with sodium or other non-scale-forming salts.

Equivalent mineral acidity

It must be emphasized that the term *equivalent mineral acidity* (EMA) does not mean that the water contains mineral acids. It is an expression used to denote the sum, expressed as $CaCO_3$, of those ions normally derived from strong mineral acids such as sulphuric, hydrochloric and nitric acid but actually present owing to the solution of neutral salts.

Free mineral acidity

Water containing the anions SO_4^{2-}, Cl^- and NO_3^-, due to the presence of the free acid rather than the neutral salt, has *free mineral acidity* (FMA) equivalent to the sum of these anions where each is expressed as calcium carbonate.

pH value

pH is not a constituent or impurity of water, but merely a number representing the concentration of hydrogen ions ($H+$) present. A detailed explanation of the meaning of pH may be found in many standard chemistry textbooks.

In absolutely pure water, dissociation of the water molecules produces equal concentrations of hydrogen ions ($H+$) and hydroxyl ions (OH^-).

$$H_2O \longrightarrow H+ \quad + \quad OH^-$$

water $\qquad$ hydrogen $\quad$ hydroxyl
$\qquad\qquad\quad$ ions $\qquad\quad$ ions

The concentration of hydrogen ions ($H+$) is approximately 10^{-7} g/l and because this is balanced by an identical concentration of hydroxyl ions (OH^-) the water is neutral. The pH value, obtained by omitting the base 10 and the negative sign, is pH 7. The pH scale extends from 0 to 14. The mid point of this scale, namely pH 7.0, represents the point at which the concentration of $H+$ ions is exactly matched by the concentration of OH^- ions and the solution is said to be neutral.

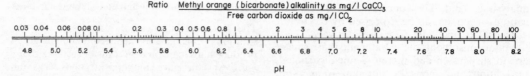

Figure 7.1   Relationship   between   free   carbon dioxide, bicarbonate alkalinity and pH

pH, alkalinity and carbon dioxide relationship

The relationship between pH and the ratio of dissolved carbon dioxide to bicarbonate alkalinity as measured by titration with methyl orange indicator is illustrated in *Figure 7.1*. It will be noted that the pH value is constant for any fixed ratio, irrespective of the concentration of either dissolved CO_2 or bicarbonate alkalinity.

Electrical conductivity

The electrical conductivity of water is frequently used as a means of indicating the presence and approximate concentration of ionized impurities.

Pure water contains no ions except H^+ and OH^- ions formed by the dissociation of the water (H_2O) itself, and is thus a poor conductor of electricity, as illustrated in *Figure 7.2*. Water containing ionized impurities resulting from the solution of salts, alkalis or acids is much more conductive, the magnitude of this conductivity being dependent not only on temperature but also on the nature of the individual ions present. The conductivity of water at 25°C due to solution of various amounts of sodium chloride is shown in *Figure 7.3*.

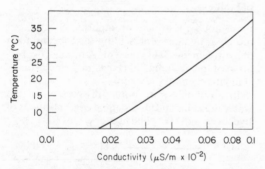

Figure 7.2   Variation of electrical conductivity of pure water with temperature

Using the international system of electrical units (SI units), the electrical conductivity is expressed as microsiemens per metre ($\mu S/m$), but in water treatment it is almost universal practice to use microsiemens per centimetre ($\mu S/m \times 10^{-2}$) since the numerical value of conductivity is then of the same order of magnitude as the concentration of dissolved solids expressed in milligrams per litre. The

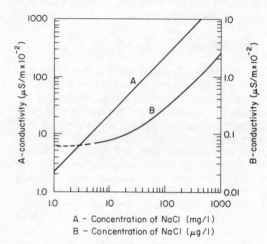

A – Concentration of NaCl (mg/l)
B – Concentration of NaCl (μg/l)

Figure 7.3   Variation of electrical conductivity of water due to concentration of sodium chloride

expression 'micromhos per centimetre' (μmho/cm), which has the same numerical value as $\mu S/m \times 10^{-2}$, is also used in some parts of the world. Conductivity measurement is discussed in Chapter 8.

The measurement of water's electrical conductivity is used extensively in water treatment to indicate the quality of water produced by various treatment processes. It may be used to control automatic treatment plant such as a demineralizer, to monitor variations in both raw and treated water quality and is sometimes used to indicate the concentration of dissolved solids in boiler water and to operate blowdown devices.

7.4   External methods of water treatment

External water treatment covers all the forms of treatment which may be applied to the raw make-up water before it enters the feed system of the boiler in order to remove impurities which are harmful to the boiler and its ancillary equipment. Treatment may involve a single process or a combination of processes used sequentially in order to achieve the desired feedwater quality in the most practical and economic manner.

Factors which may influence the assessment are

the maximum permissible concentration of dissolved solid in the boiler water, the loss of heat due to blowdown, permissible volatile silica concentration in the steam, the type of steam turbine in use (i.e. pass-out or fully condensing), and the availability and cost of recovery of clean condensate from steam-using process plant.

Clarification

Treatment of water to remove suspended matter and colour due to soluble organic matter is frequently necessary when water is drawn directly from rivers, lakes and often reservoirs. The processes of clarification employed depend upon the nature and concentration of the material in suspension and may involve both mechanical and chemical treatment.

The suspended matter normally present in natural water usually consists of small particles carrying negative electrical charge on their surfaces. The particles often tend to remain dispersed and in semi-permanent suspension owing to the mutual repulsion exerted by the surface charges on the individual particles. For them to combine into larger masses which will settle readily, almost complete neutralization of the surface charge must be effected.

Coagulation and flocculation

Coagulation and flocculation are normally achieved by the addition of coagulating chemicals, which may be any of several salts of either aluminium or iron. When they are added to the water under controlled conditions, a precipitate of aluminium or iron hydroxide microfloc is formed. By applying gentle mechanical or hydraulic agitation the microflocs can be flocculated to form large flocs which will settle out of the water under the influence of gravity.

The coagulation process may be used to remove colloidal suspended matter and also certain organic materials which are in solution and often impart colour to the water.

Filtration

The clarified water produced by sedimentation may still contain a small amount of suspended material and require final polishing by filtration. Filtration plants are of the open gravity or pressure vessel type. In most cases the filter bed is composed of fine sand or anthracite.

The depth and grading of the filter media used may vary from one filter design to another. Some filters use layers of coarse anthracite above fine sand to increase the solid-holding capacity and to obtain higher throughput flows. Others operate in

the upflow principle through carefully graded sand so that the water enters the bed through coarse media and passes upwards through progressively finer sands.

When the raw water being treated has a fairly low concentration of suspended solids, it is sometimes practical to omit the flocculation and sedimentation stage and carry out the coagulation process within the filter itself, using the tortuous flow paths within the bed to flocculate the suspended material. In this mode of operation the filter cycles times are usually much shorter than would be the case following prior sedimentation and the quantity of water wasted during cleaning may represent a fairly high percentage of the filtrate produced.

As filtration is normally a batch process, a continuous supply of filtrate requires either a multi-unit installation or adequate storage capacity for filtered water to cater for outage time during backwash cleaning of a filter.

Precipitation softening

Hardness due to calcium and magnesium ions present in raw water can be reduced by the addition of chemicals which cause precipitation of sparingly soluble calcium and magnesium salts.

The chemicals normally used are calcium hydroxide (lime) and sodium carbonate (soda), both of which increase the pH of the water and respectively supply hydroxyl ions and carbonate ions required to precipitate calcium carbonate, magnesium carbonate and magnesium hydroxides.

The treatment process requires that the calcium hydroxide and sodium carbonate are added to the water in amounts which are proportional to the concentration of the calcium and magnesium ions present and also upon the alkalinity and free carbon dioxide content of the raw water.

Lime softening

Where only removal of alkaline hardness due to calcium and magnesium is required, the necessary precipitation can be effected by the addition of calcium hydroxide (lime) alone. In the lime softening process, alkaline hardness salts are caused to precipitate as almost insoluble calcium carbonate and magnesium hydroxide. There is consequently a corresponding reduction in the total dissolved solids content of the water.

Lime soda softening

Non-alkaline hardness cannot be removed by the addition of lime alone and requires the application of either sodium carbonate or sodium carbonate together with lime.

In the removal of non-alkaline hardness by the

addition of sodium carbonate, a corresponding amount of neutral sodium salts is formed and there is no reduction in the total dissolved solids concentration due to these reactions. The residual hardness of the lime-soda-treated water normally corresponds to the sum of the solubilities of calcium carbonate and magnesium hydroxide.

Silica reduction

Where lime softening treatment results in the precipitation of appreciable amounts of magnesium hydroxide, partial removal of soluble silica may also occur by absorption of the silica into the flocculant precipitate.

The degree of soluble silica removal achieved by this absorption depends initially upon the ratio between the concentration of magnesium hydroxide formed and the soluble silica present in the water. In cold water the rate of absorption of the silica is rather slow but increases markedly as the temperature is increased above 80°C.

The absorption capacity of the magnesium hydroxide can be increased by extending the effective contact time by sludge recirculation or sludge blanket operation.

Hot pressure softening

In processes designed to maximize the removal of silica, treatment is often performed in a pressure vessel in which the water can be heated to over 100°C.

Where the raw water is deficient in magnesium hardness, additional magnesium may be added in the form of magnesium oxide with the calcium hydroxide (lime), or dolomitic lime containing natural magnesium carbonate may be used.

Combined treatments

The removal of alkaline hardness, by lime treatment alone, reduces the alkalinity and total dissolved solids (TDS) content of the water. Removal of non-alkaline hardness by the addition of soda does not produce any further reduction in TDS and if excess chemicals are dosed to suppress the residual hardness the treatment will in fact increase the TDS concentration. In cases where reductions in TDS and alkalinity are of prime importance, partial precipitation treatment using lime to remove only the alkaline hardness should be considered. The residual alkaline hardness and non-alkaline hardness must then be removed by some alternative treatment such as ion exchange softening.

Lime softening may also be used as a preliminary treatment ahead of ion exchange demineralization processes when the turbidity of the raw water is too high for direct ion exchange treatment, or

where removal of alkalinity in the lime treatment plant produces an appreciable reduction in the ionic load and hence the operating cost of the demineralization plant.

Ion exchange treatment

An ion exchanger is an insoluble material normally made in the form of small spheres or beads of diameter about 0.5–1.0 mm. The resin beads are porous and hydrophilic, that is, they absorb water. Within the bead structure are fixed ionic groups with which are associated mobile exchangeable ions of opposite charge. These mobile ions can be replaced by similarly charged ions from the salts dissolved in the water surrounding the resin beads.

Ion exchange resins are usually employed in the form of a packed bed consisting of many millions of beads contained within a pressure vessel through which the water to be treated can be passed. Depending upon the active group implanted into the resin bead structure during manufacture, the resin will exhibit cation or anion exchange properties. There are four main types of ion exchanger: weak and strong acid cation, weak and strong base anion.

The weak-acid cation exchanger

In the weak-acid cation exchanger (WAC) the fixed active groups are carboxylic. When the exchangeable cation is H^+, the resin may be considered as an insoluble form of the carboxylic acid, such acids being weak.

When water containing dissolved mineral salts is passed through a bed of this resin, metallic ions such as calcium, magnesium or sodium, in total concentration equivalent to the total alkalinity of the water, will pass into the resin structure and displace an equivalent number of hydrogen ions. As the alkalinity of the raw water is normally due to the presence of bicarbonate ions (HCO_3^-), the hydrogen ions H^+ entering the water in exchange for the metallic ions Ca^{2+}, Mg^{2+} or Na^+ will cause the bicarbonates to become carbonic acid (H_2CO_3) or dissolved CO_2 gas.

Metallic ions in equilibrium with anions derived from neutral salts such as from $CaSO_4$, $MgCl_2$ or $NaCl$ will not pass into the resin and exchange for hydrogen ions.

The exchange reactions of this resin may therefore be illustrated by the following equations in which R^- represents the fixed active groups in the resin.

$$2\,H^+R^- + Ca(HCO_3)_2 \rightarrow Ca^{2+}(R^-)_2 + H_2CO_3$$

| WAC, H^+ form | calcium bicarbonate | WAC, Ca^{2+} form | carbonic form |

This reaction is not reversible because the carbonic acid dissociates only to a limited extent.

$$2\,H^+R^- \; + \; CaSO_4 — no\text{-}reaction$$

WAC,   calcium
H^+ form   sulphate

When the resin is exhausted it may be regenerated or converted back to the original H^+ form by treatment with a dilute solution of a strong mineral acid such as sulphuric acid or hydrochloric acid.

$$Ca^{2+}(R^-)_2 \; + \; H_2SO_4 \; \rightarrow \; 2\,H^+R^- \; + \; CaSO_4$$

WAC,   sulphuric   WAC,   calcium
CA^{2+} form   acid H^+ form   sulphate

Because the reaction is not reversible the regenerant is used at virtually 100% efficiency and the regenerant waste effluent should not contain any unused acid.

The strong-acid cation exchanger

In the strong-acid cation exchanger (SAC) type of resin, the fixed active groups are sulphonic and if the exchangeable ions are H^+, the resin can be regarded as an insoluble form of sulphonic acid, which is a strong acid. It is capable of exchanging its H^+ ions for all metallic ions in the water whether they are present as the result of solution of weak or strong acid salts.

As with the weak-acid exchanger, the replacement of metallic ions in equilibrium with bicarbonate ions (HCO_3^-) results in the formation of carbonic acid. The exchange of H^+ ions for metallic ions in equilibrium with the anions of strong acids converts neutral salts in solution into corresponding acids. Thus

$$2\,H^+R^- + Ca(HCO_3)_2 \rightarrow \; Ca^{2+}(R^-)_2 + H_2CO_3$$

SAC, H^+ Calcium   SAC, Ca^{2+} Carbonic
form   bicarbonate   form   acid

$$2\,H^+R^- \; + \; CaCl_2 \rightleftharpoons Ca^{2+}R^- \; + \; 2\,HCl$$

SAC, H^+ Calcium   SAC, Ca^{2+} Hydrochloric
form   chloride   form   acid

and similar reactions occur for mineral salts of other metallic ions.

An ion with a low affinity for the resin may displace a high-affinity ion from the resin structure only if the concentration of the low-affinity ion is sufficiently high.

When exhausted, the SAC may be regenerated by treatment of the exchange bed with a solution of mineral acid. As the regeneration reactions are reversible, an excess of acid is required to convert the resin adequately to the hydrogen form. The waste effluent of regeneration will thus contain excess acid.

Weak-base anion exchanger

Weak-base anion (WBA) resins have fixed active groups which are tertiary amines. They are capable of absorbing strong mineral acid but will not absorb weak acids such as carbonic or silicic acid. The acid is absorbed into the resin structure by attachment rather than by true ion exchange:

$$R \quad + \quad HCl \quad \rightarrow \quad R\text{–}HCl$$

WBA resin   Hydrochloric   WBA resin
                 acid   hydrochloride

and similar reactions with sulphuric (H_2SO_4) and nitric (HNO_3) acids but

$$R \quad + \quad H_2CO_3 \quad — \quad no\ reaction$$

WBA resin   Carbonic acid

$$R \quad + \quad H_2SiO_3 \quad — \quad no\ reaction$$

WBA resin   Silicic acid

WBA resins may be regenerated with approaching 100% efficiency using sodium hydroxide, sodium carbonate or ammonium hydroxide.

Strong-base anion exchanger

The active groups on strong-base anion (SBA) exchange resins are quaternary ammonium. The resin is normally used in the free-base form so that the mobile counter-ions are hydroxyl (OH^-). The hydroxyl ion can be exchanged for any other anion present in the water whether the anion is derived from a dissolved salt or weak or strong acid.

When reaction occurs with the anion of a salt the process is called 'salt splitting' and results in the formation of the corresponding hydroxide.

$$R^+OH^- \quad + \quad NaCl \rightleftharpoons R^+Cl^- \; + \quad NaOH$$

SBA, OH^- Sodium   SBA, Cl^- Sodium
form   chloride   form   hydroxide

When the reaction occurs with an acid the OH^- ion released combines with the H^+ ion of the original acid to form water. The acid is in effect eliminated and the water thus demineralized.

Because the SBA resin removes both weak and strong acids, it is used wherever it is necessary to remove silica and dissolved CO_2.

SBA resins are normally regenerated by treatment with sodium hydroxide:

$$R^+Cl^- \;+\; NaOH \rightleftharpoons R^+OH^- \;+\; NaCl$$

SBA, Cl^- form	Sodium hydroxide	SBA, OH^- form	Sodium chloride

The reaction is reversible and therefore a substantial excess of regenerant over the theoretical amount is always required.

When silica is removed from the resin structure, some of the silica may immediately polymerize and form insoluble silicates and thus remain on the resin to contaminate the treated water in the subsequent run. This may be minimized by limiting the capacity of the resin used for silica during the treatment cycle, by increasing the regeneration level or by preheating the regenerant to increase the solubility of sodium silicate.

Working capacity of ion exchangers

The true capacity of an ion exchange resin depends upon the number of active groups incorporated into the resin structure during manufacture. However, as many of the treatment cycles and regeneration cycles involve reversible reactions it is seldom possible fully to utilize the theoretical capacity.

The working capacity is normally stated as the mass of ions, expressed as kilograms calcium carbonate, capable of being exchanged by a cubic metre of resin, i.e. kg $CaCO_3/m^3$ resin.

As some ions have greater affinity for a particular exchanger than others, the working capacity is not a fixed quantity but varies depending upon the proportions in which the various ions are present in the water and the ionic form in which the resin is being used.

The manufacturers of ion exchange resins all publish data on the characteristics, regeneration conditions and working capacities of their resins as a guide to the user. Other factors such as the mechanical design of the ion exchange units, specific flow rate through the resin beds, quality and quantity of regenerant chemicals and quality specification of the treated water must also be considered. The interpretation of the published data depends considerably upon the expertise of the manufacturers of ion exchange treatment plant.

Removal of alkaline hardness by ion exchange

The removal of alkaline hardness can be achieved by passing the hard water through an ion exchange column containing a bed of weak-acid cation resin in the hydrogen form. Calcium and magnesium ions, in concentration equivalent to the bicarbonate alkalinity, are exchanged for H^+ ions and these combine with bicarbonate ions (HCO_3^-) to form the weakly dissociated carbonic acid.

The treated water contains only calcium and magnesium due to non-alkaline hardness, a small residual of alkaline hardness, usually 5–10 mg $CaCO_3$/litre, and carbonic acid or dissolved carbon dioxide equivalent to the alkaline hardness removed. On leaving the exchange unit it usually has a low pH of 4.4–5.0 owing to the high CO_2 content and low total alkalinity but removal of the carbon dioxide by degassing, and neutralization of any small residual by application of a very small dose of sodium hydroxide, will increase the pH to 8.5.

When the ion exchange resin is exhausted, the alkalinity of the treated water begins to rise. The service run is usually terminated when the alkalinity reaches about 30 mg/l. This breakthrough of alkalinity causes the treated water's pH to rise above the average treatment cycle value and thus on fully automatic plant pH measurement may be used to initiate the regeneration cycle.

Regeneration is effected by passing a dilute solution of mineral acid through the bed, the quantity of free acid used being equivalent to the calcium and magnesium ions in the exhausted bed. When the process is correctly controlled the waste effluent contains only mineral salts of the acid but no excess free acid. After regeneration the bed is flushed with raw water to displace the products of regeneration before the unit is returned to service. The treatment process was originally called the 'starvation' process, the name being derived from the fact that the quantity of acid used was restricted to the theoretical minimum.

The entire treatment and regeneration operations may easily be fully automated and can handle raw water of varying quality without constant plant operator attendance and chemical control.

An important feature of this process is that by removing the alkaline hardness it also reduces the total dissolved solids content by the same amount.

Removal of total hardness

Removal of all the calcium and magnesium ions as defined by the term 'total hardness' can be achieved by treatment using a strong-acid cation resin in the sodium form. The process is commonly referred to as *base exchange softening* but should really be called sodium ion exchange.

The process merely converts the calcium and magnesium salts in the water into corresponding sodium salts and therefore does not effect any reduction in the total alkalinity or total dissolved solids. It is frequently used for treatment of the make-up to low-pressure boilers for which it is often an entirely satisfactory treatment.

However, it must be pointed out that if the alkalinity of the raw water constitutes a high proportion of the total dissolved solids, the treated water could result in an undesirably high level of hydroxide and carbonate alkalinity in the boiler water. Furthermore the CO_2 produced by the decomposition of sodium bicarbonate in the boiler will be released into the steam and on re-solution in the condensate could cause corrosion in the condensate systems or feed systems.

Regeneration of the sodium ion exchanger is carried out by passing a solution of sodium chloride (common salt) through the bed and then removing the regeneration product by water rinsing. The process is extremely simple to operate, can be easily automated and will handle waters with varying levels of hardness with minimum operator attendance.

Total hardness and alkalinity removal by ion exchange

This process is a combination of the processes described for the removal of alkaline hardness and also total hardness. The treatment is performed in three stages, namely: removal of alkaline hardness in a weak-acid cation exchanger; removal of the carbonic acid in a degassing tower, and finally, removal of non-alkaline hardness and the small amount of residual alkaline hardness in a sodium ion exchanger. A small dose of sodium hydroxide may be applied at the outlet of the degassing stage to raise the pH to 8.5 in order to prevent corrosion of the vessel of the sodium ion exchanger and downstream pipework. If additional sodium hydroxide dosing is required to adjust the ratio between total alkalinity and total dissolved solids in the boiler water it should be applied directly to the boiler feedwater and not at the degasser outlet.

Ion exchange demineralization

Virtually complete removal of all the dissolved solids, or *demineralization,* can be achieved by ion exchange using a combination of cation and anion exchange resins.

The operating principle of all ion exchange demineralizers is the conversion of the mineral salts into their corresponding acid by treatment of the water in a strong-acid cation exchanger and the subsequent removal of the acids by degassing and treatment in an anion exchanger.

In those cases where demineralization of boiler make-up water is required to reduce the overall level of dissolved solids but complete removal of solids is not essential, the anion exchanger may be charged with a weak-base anion (WBA) exchange resin. If removal of silica and the last traces of CO_2 is required, a strong-base anion (SBA) exchanger should be used.

Mixed-bed demineralization

The mixed-bed demineralizer uses an ion exchange bed in which the hydrogen form of strong-cation resin is intimately mixed with a strong-base anion resin in the hydroxyl form. When raw water is passed through the unit it is subjected to repeated two-stage demineralization and thus the treated water leaving the exchange bed is of very high purity. In order to regenerate the resins they must be separated. This is easily effected by fluidizing the bed with an upflow of water.

The cation resin, being of greater density, sinks to the bottom of the column and the anion resin rises to the top of the bed. Regenerant acid is then introduced through a distribution system installed in the column at the interface between the resin layers and passes down through the cation resin. Sodium hydroxide is subsequently fed to the top of the anion bed and having passed through the anion resin is removed via the mid-collecting system (*Figure 7.4*). The separate beds are rinsed with water, after which the resins are intimately remixed by agitation with air and the exchange bed may then be returned to service.

Operating costs of mixed-bed demineralization are usually much higher than for two-stage demineralizers, partly because the anion exchange resin has to be capable of removing all of the carbonic acid produced from the alkalinity of the raw water.

When raw water of high total dissolved solids content is being treated, two-stage ion exchange treatment is often used to remove the bulk of the solids and the treated water polished by a mixed bed to achieve the required final quality.

Removal of organic matter

Anion exchange resins are capable of absorbing not only the anions derived from the solution of mineral acids but also those of organic acids such as fulvic and humic acid — often present in surface waters. Unfortunately some of these larger organic anions have difficulty in penetrating the resin structure and are not completely removed during treatment, whilst others, which are absorbed, become locked into the resin and are difficult to elute during regeneration.

The gradual build-up of organic matter within the resin structure over a number of operating cycles is known as *organic fouling* and reduces the rate of exchange of mineral anions. The symptom of organic fouling is impaired quality of treated

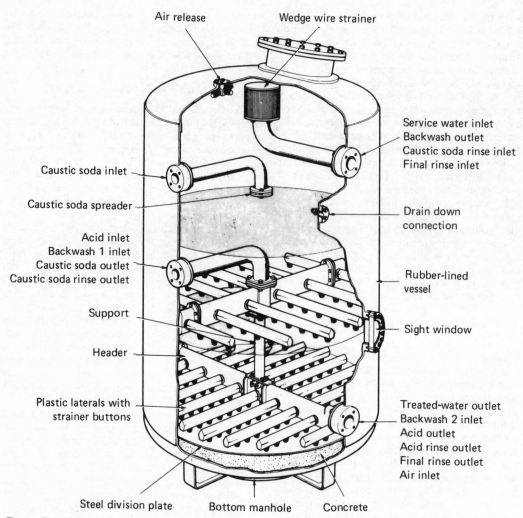

Figure 7.4   Cut-away of mixed-bed ion exchange unit showing collection and distribution system. (Courtesy of Permutit-Boby Ltd)

water, particularly at the beginning of the operating cycle, owing to the retarded diffusion of regenerant from the resin after regeneration.

In some cases the accumulated organic matter may be removed by regular treatment of the anion resin with brine or a mixture of brine and sodium hydroxide, but progressive permanent fouling may occur during the treatment of surface waters in which there is a high ratio between organic and mineral anions.

To overcome organic fouling, anion resins with isoporous or macroporous structure, and resins based on acrylic rather than a polystyrene matrix, have been developed. It is claimed that these resins not only remove the organic matter from the water more effectively during the treatment cycle, but also release the organic matter almost completely when regenerated with sodium hydroxide.

Nevertheless when waters containing appreciable amounts of organic matter are being treated, pretreatment by coagulation and filtration may still be necessary to reduce the organic load.

Degassing and de-aeration

In order to prevent corrosion in boilers and ancillary equipment, it is essential to eliminate both dissolved oxygen and dissolved carbon dioxide from boiler feedwater.

Low concentrations of these cases may often be removed or neutralized by chemical treatment but high concentrations are more effectively and economically removed by physical means.

When water is brought into contact with a mixture of gases, such as air, each gas present exerts a pressure at the surface of the water in proportion to its volume concentration in the air. The pressure exerted by any one component is called the *partial pressure* of that gas. The sum of the partial pressures of all the gases present, including that of water vapour, is equivalent to the total atmospheric pressure.

Owing to the pressure exerted at the surface of the water, the gases contained in the air will transfer and diffuse into the water until an equilibrium is established between the concentration of gas in solution in the water and the concentration in the adjacent air. The equilibrium concentration of any component gas in the water is proportional to the partial pressure of the gas in the adjacent atmosphere divided by a constant which is characteristic of that gas and the water temperature.

Concentration of gas in solution
(expressed as mole fraction)

$$= \frac{\text{partial pressure of the gas}}{H} \qquad (7.1)$$

where H = Henry's law proportionality constant (*see Figures 7.5 and 7.6*). To obtain the equilibrium solubility of the gas in terms of g/m³ of gas (e.g. g/m³ O_2), it is necessary to multiply the equilibrium concentration expressed as a mole fraction by the molecular weight of the particular gas (e.g. $O_2 = 32$) and also by 5.555×10^4 (the number of moles of H_2O in 10^6 g of water).

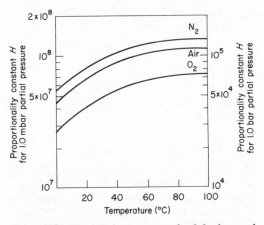

Figure 7.5   *Henry's law constant for 1.0* mbar *and 1.0* bar (10^5 N/m²) *partial pressure* O_2, N_2 *and air*

Example: Water at 20°C is in contact with air at a pressure of 1013 mbar. The air contains 20.95% by volume of oxygen and 0.03% by volume of carbon dioxide. Find the equilibrium solubility of oxygen and carbon dioxide in g/m³ or mg/l.

(a) Partial pressure of oxygen = 1013×0.2095

$$= 212.2 \text{ mbar}$$

From *Figure 7.5*,

$H = 4.1 \times 10^7$ at 1 mbar partial pressure.

Mole fraction concentration O_2 in solution at 212.2 mbar partial pressure

$$= \frac{212.2}{4.1 \times 10^7}$$

$$= 5.176 \times 10^{-6}$$

Equilibrium solubility as g/m³ O_2

$$= 5.176 \times 10^{-6} \times 32 \times 5.555 \times 10^4$$

$$= 9.20 \text{ g/m}^3 \text{ } O_2 \text{ or } 9.20 \text{ mg/l}$$

(b) Partial pressure of carbon dioxide
$$= 1013 \times 0.0003$$
$$= 0.3039 \text{ mbar}$$

From *Figure 7.6*,

$$H = 1.47 \times 10^6$$

Mole fraction concentration CO_2 in solution at 0.3039 mbar partial pressure

$$= \frac{0.3039}{1.47 \times 10^6}$$

$$= 2.067 \times 10^{-7}$$

Equilibrium solubility as g/m³ CO_2

$$= 2.067 \times 10^{-7} \times 44 \times 5.555 \times 10^4$$

$$= 0.5 \text{ g/m}^3 \text{ } CO_2 \text{ or } 0.5 \text{ mg/l}$$

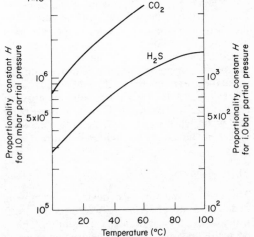

Figure 7.6   *Henry's law constant for 1.0* mbar *and 1.0* bar (10^5 N/m²) *partial pressure* CO_2 *and* H_2S

Removal of dissolved CO_2

Many natural waters and waters that have been treated by ion exchange to reduce alkalinity may contain very high concentrations of dissolved carbon dioxide. This CO_2 can be removed by bringing the water into intimate contact with air in which the concentration and hence the partial pressure of CO_2 is extremely low.

The process is normally carried out in an atmospheric degassing tower containing a randomly packed bed of gas transfer medium. The water to be treated is passed to the top of the tower, is distributed and flows downwards through the packing medium against a forced counter current of air. As the water tends to cling as a film to the extensive surfaces of the packing without actually flooding the bed, the CO_2 rapidly diffuses from the water and is transported to the counter current of air which together with the dissolved CO_2 gas is continually vented from the top of the tower.

Vacuum degassing

The internal design of a vacuum degassing tower is similar to that of the atmospheric degasser but the tower is designed to withstand partial vacuum conditions. The local pressure within the tower is reduced to below atmospheric pressure by fitting either a vacuum ejector or a vacuum pump to the gas vent at the top of the tower and by maintaining a water seal at the bottom.

The vacuum degasser may be used to reduce the concentration of all the gases in solution, but if the water contains a high concentration of dissolved CO_2 it is usually cheaper to use an atmospheric CO_2 degasser ahead of the vacuum tower. Reduction of the air pressure within the tower not only reduces the partial pressure of the gases but also lowers the boiling point of the water and therefore increases the water vapour partial pressure of the atmosphere within the tower. The water vapour may thus be considered as serving the role of a stripping gas and is extracted from the top of the tower together with the dissolved gases.

The vacuum degassing tower is frequently used for the removal of dissolved oxygen from fairly cold water where subsequent treatment makes it undesirable to raise the water temperature.

Thermal de-aerator

The most frequently used device for removing dissolved oxygen (*Figure 7.7*) from boiler feedwater is the thermal or heater de-aerator. This is normally a pressure vessel in which a low-pressure steam is used both as a gas-stripping medium and as a heating medium to raise the temperature of

the water to the saturation temperature of the steam.

Most de-aerators work on the counter-current principle with the incoming steam contacting the already heated and largely de-aerated water first and then passing on to heat the cold oxygen-laden water as it enters the unit. To obtain efficient gas transfer the incoming water must be broken up into droplets. This may be achieved either by use of a water spray system or by allowing the water to pass as rain through a vertical array of perforated trays.

Where very low oxygen residuals are required the de-aerators may also incorporate a scrubbing section where the oxygen-free inlet steam purges the last traces of dissolved oxygen from the essentially de-aerated water leaving the spray or tray section (*Figure 7.8*).

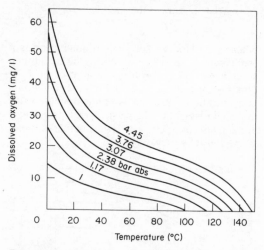

Figure 7.7   Solubility of oxygen in water from air at various pressures and temperatures

7.5 Internal treatment

The borderline between internal treatment and conditioning treatment is often difficult to define. In general, internal treatment covers the addition of chemical substances directly to the boiler in order to prevent scale formation on heat transfer surfaces resulting from hardness salt introduced with the feedwater. The alternative is external treatment, where the hardness salts are removed from the make-up of feedwater before it is delivered to the boiler.

Internal treatment is generally confined to low-pressure boiler operation where there is a large boiler water content relative to steam output. It is not normally recommended for watertube boilers, high-pressure boilers or those designed to operate with high heat flux density. Internal treatment

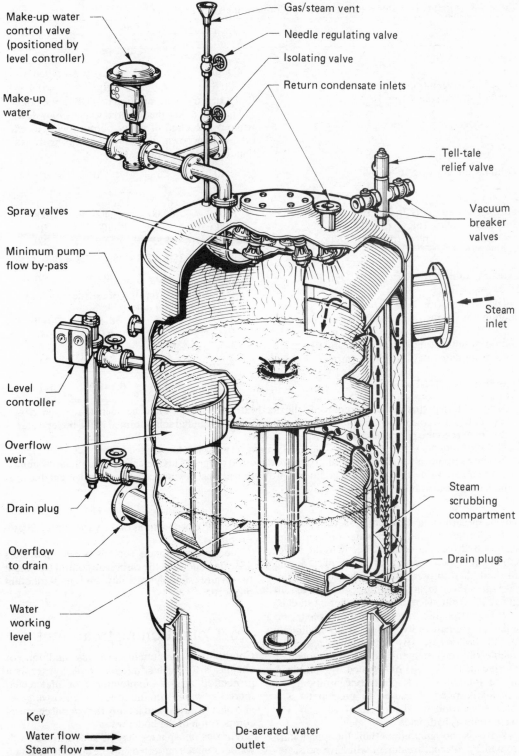

Make-up water control valve (positioned by level controller)

Make-up water

Spray valves

Minimum pump flow by-pass

Level controller

Overflow weir

Drain plug

Overflow to drain

Water working level

Key

Water flow ➡️
Steam flow ➡️ (dashed)

Gas/steam vent

Needle regulating valve

Isolating valve

Return condensate inlets

Tell-tale relief valve

Vacuum breaker valves

Steam inlet

Steam scrubbing compartment

Drain plugs

De-aerated water outlet

Figure 7.8 Cut-away of spray heater–de-aerator incorporating steam scrubber. (Courtesy of Permutit-Boby Ltd)

Table 7.3   Quality of water required for a boiler operating at up to 20 bar

	Group			
	1	2	3	4
Feedwater				
pH	8.2–9.5	8.2–9.5	8.2–9.5	8.2–9.5
Dissolved oxygen (mg/l O$_2$)	<0.5	<0.5	<0.5	<0.5
Total dissolved solids (mg/l)	(Such that the concentration of TDS in the boiler can be kept below the required level by blowdown without reduction of boiler output owing to excessive blowdown, i.e. blowdown normally less than 10% of total evaporation)			
Total hardness* (mg/l CaCO$_3$)	<40	<5	<20	<2
Boiler water				
Total dissolved solids (max) (mg/l)	8000	10 000	3400	2000
Suspended solids (max) (mg/l)	300	<2	100	50
Total alkalinity (max) (mg/l CaCO$_3$)	1800	1800	700	500
or	<40% TDS	<25% TDS	<25% TDS	<25% TDS
Caustic alkalinity (min) (mg/l CaCO$_3$)	350	350	350	200
Silica (mg/l SiO$_2$)	Less than 0.4 of caustic alkalinity			
Total hardness (mg/l CaCO$_3$)	Not detectable			
Sodium phosphate (mg/l Na$_3$PO$_4$) (normal)	30–50	NR†	30–50	30–50
(max)	100		100	100
Sodium sulphite (mg/l Na$_2$SO$_3$) (normal)	30–50	30–50	30–50	30–50
Sodium sulphite (mg/l Na$_2$SO$_3$) (max)	70	70	70	70
or				
Hydrazine (mg/l N$_2$H$_4$)	NA‡	NA‡	0.1–1.0	0.1–1.0

*   When internal treatment is employed, the feedwater hardness should be such that when it is concentrated in the boiler and precipitated, the resulting suspended solids formed in the boiler water do not exceed the permitted level of suspended solids.
†   Not recommended with this type of boiler. Maintain very low hardness in feedwater.
‡   Sodium sulphite is usually employed to remove dissolved oxygen. This increases the sulphate content of the boiler water, thus providing additional protection against possible caustic embrittlement due to high caustic alkalinity.

may be by carbonate control or phosphate control. In the former, sodium carbonate, or sometimes sodium hydroxide, is added directly to the boiler water to maintain a controlled reserve of carbonate alkalinity and to precipitate the hardness salts as calcium carbonate, magnesium hydroxide or silicate in the form of a mobile non-adherent sludge.

With phosphate control, sodium phosphate and sodium carbonate or hydroxide are dosed directly into the boiler water. By maintaining a reserve of soluble phosphate in the boiler water together with a caustic alkalinity of between 10% and 15% of the total dissolved solids concentration, the calcium hardness is caused to precipitate as a calcium phosphate (hydroxyapatite) and the magnesium as hydroxide or silicate.

There is no guarantee that the precipitate formed by internal treatment will have no scale-forming tendencies and will be adequately mobile, since much depends upon the crystalline form and the relative proportions of the various precipitates produced.

Sludge conditioners such as organic polymers are often added to the carbonate control treatment to ensure suitable mobility and non-adherent properties.

7.6 Conditioning treatment

Conditioning treatment involves addition of chemicals to the feedwater or boiler water as a protection against unintentional or undetected ingress of scale-forming solids or corrosive gases and also to adjust and modify the overall chemical composition of the boiler water.

Various phosphates may be added to the feedwater or directly injected into the boiler to maintain a suitable reserve of sodium phosphate in the boiler water to deal with traces of hardness present

Table 7.4 Quality of water required for a watertube boiler operating at 20–60 bar

	Operating pressure		
	30 bar	45 bar	60 bar
Feedwater			
pH	8.5–9.5	8.5–9.5	8.5–9.5
Dissolved oxygen (mg/l O_2)	< 0.05	< 0.02	< 0.01
Total hardness (mg/l $CaCO_3$)	< 2	< 1	< 0.05
Total dissolved solids (mg/l)	(Such that the concentration of each of the		
	constituents in the boiler can be kept below		
Total alkalinity (mg/l $CaCO_3$)	the required level without reduction in		
	boiler output owing to excessive blowdown,		
Silica (mg/l SiO_2)	i.e. blowdown required should not exceed		
	10% of evaporation)		
Oil (mg/l)	Not detectable		
Boiler water			
Total dissolved solids (mg/l)	2000	1500	1200
Suspended solids (mg/l)	50	25	ND*
Total alkalinity (max.) (mg/l $CaCO_3$)	500	400	300
Caustic alkalinity (min.) (mg/$CaCO_3$)	200	160	60
Silica (mg/l SiO_2) (normal)		20	10
(max)	Not greater than 0.4 of caustic alkalinity		
Sodium phosphate (mg/l Na_3PO_4)	30–70	30–70	20–50
Sodium sulphite (mg/l Na_2SO_3)	20–50	20–50	NR†
or			
Hydrazine (mg/l N_2H_4)	0.1–1.0	0.1–1.0	0.1–0.5

* Not detectable. If present, determine origin and apply treatment to eliminate.
† Not recommended at or above this pressure due to decomposition into acid products. Use hydrazine as oxygen scavenger after mechanical de-aeration.

Table 7.5 Quality of water required for a watertube boiler operating at above 60 bar

	Operating pressure		
	80 bar	103 bar	162 bar
Feedwater			
pH*	≮ 8.5	≮ 8.5	≮ 8.5
Dissolved oxygen (mg/l O_2)	< 0.007	< 0.007	< 0.007
Fe + Ni + Ca	< 0.01	< 0.01	< 0.01
Hydrazine (mg/l N_2H_4)	≮ 0.02	≮ 0.02	≮ 0.02
Electrical conductivity† (μS/m × 10^{-2})	< 0.5	< 0.5	< 0.3
Boiler water			
Chloride (mg/l Cl)	≯ 10	≯ 6	≯ 4
Caustic alkalinity (mg/l as $CaCO_3$)	5–10	5–10	3–6
or			
Congruent phosphate control as below			
Phosphate (mg/l PO_4)	5–15	3–10	NR‡
Molar ratio Na^+ : PO_4	2.6 : 1	2.6 : 1	
pH	9.5–9.9	9.3–9.8	
Silica (mg/l SiO_2)	≯ 3	≯ 2	≯ 0.4

* pH attained by combined effect of hydrazine and ammonia.
† At extraction pump after passing through H^+-form strong-acid cation exchange resin column.
‡ Phosphate treatment not recommended

Figure 7.9   Boiler feedwater make-up ion exchange demineralizing plant in a power-station. (Courtesy of Permutit-Boby Ltd)

in the feedwater. Alternatively, chelating* agents such as ethylenediamine tetraacetic acid (EDTA) or nitriolotriacetic acid (NTA) may be dosed continuously at a controlled rate related to the residual hardness in the feedwater to form soluble compounds with calcium and magnesium and prevent them from precipitating.

Sodium sulphite or hydrazine is added to the feedwater to eliminate residual dissolved oxygen and to assist the alkalinity of the boiler water in creating a protective oxide (magnetite) film on the surface of the boiler metal in contact with the boiler water.

Volatile amines such as morpholine or cyclo-hexylamine and ammonia may also be dosed into the feedwater system. As these alkalis are volatile they are carried from the boiler with the steam but redissolve in the steam condensate, imparting alkaline properties to it. In this way they serve to protect the condensate system from corrosion due to carbon dioxide and oxygen which may be

present in the steam or have gained access to the condensate system in the receiving tanks.

7.7 Boiler water characteristics

In order to prevent priming and carryover of boiler water with the steam it is essential to control the overall concentration of dissolved and suspended solids in the boiler water by intermittent or continuous blowdown. It is also necessary to control the concentration of individual dissolved constituents to prevent corrosion or impairment of steam quality.

The quality of the boiler water required in any particular installation depends not only on the operating pressure but also upon the design of the boiler employed. The data given in *Tables 7.3–7.5* are intended solely as a guide to enable the reader to establish the type of make-up water treatment and conditioning treatments that may be required to achieve suitable boiler operating conditions. It is not intended that these data should override any recommendations made by

---

* A chelating agent is an organic substance which can hold in solution otherwise insoluble salts of calcium, magnesium, iron or aluminium or which can make them pass into solution.

Table 7.6 Summary of water treatment processes

Process	Application or objective	Limitations
Sedimentation without chemical treatment	Removal of suspended solids by gravity settling	Suitable for removal of large or dense suspended solids. Not suitable for removal of colloidal suspended solids or soluble organic matter or colour
Coagulation — chemical treatment with inorganic coagulants and/or organic polymers	Destabilization of colloidal suspended particles and organic matter in order to permit them to be flocculated	Frequently requires adjustment of pH. Coagulant dose must be established by laboratory experiments
Flocculation — mechanical or hydraulic controlled agitation to encourage coagulated material to flocculate and form particle clusters of large size	Applied to coagulated water to produce large floc particles which may be removed by sedimentation or filtration	Treatment chemicals must be thoroughly and uniformly mixed into water before flocculation. Condition of agitation must produce collision of particles without excessive shearing
Combined coagulation, flocculation and sedimentation	Used for clarification of waters where the concentration of suspended solids in the raw water, or the quantity of coagulant required produces a concentration of floc which is too great to pass directly onto filtration units	Requires a sedimentation tank specially designed to effect the correct hydraulic and chemical condition for coagulation, flocculation and sedimentation. May be a horizontal-flow, radial-flow or upflow reaction vessel with sludge blanket or sludge recirculation facilities
Filtration without chemical treatment	Removal of suspended solids by filtration through a fixed bed of sand, anthracite or a combination of both. Designs available based on upflow or downflow filtration	Will not tolerate high concentration of suspended solids. Suitable as a roughing stage where high-quality filtrate is not required
Filtration after coagulation	As final polishing stage after coagulation, flocculation and sedimentation or used directly as combined flocculation/filter where level of suspended solids in raw water is low	Filters may be of the open gravity or pressure type. Where used without a pre-sedimentation filter, run times will be shorter and careful control of chemical coagulation conditions essential
Precipitation softening (cold-lime softening)	Used to remove alkaline hardness and reduce total alkalinity and total dissolved solids concentration. Useful where raw water also contains suspended solids	Reaction vessel usually of sludge blanket or sludge recirculation type. Residual alkaline hardness depends upon raw water composition but normally about 30—60 mg/l as $CaCO_3$. Requires subsequent filtration and possible pH correction

Table 7.6 (continued)

Process	Application or objective	Limitations
Precipitation softening (hot-lime softening)	Reduction in soluble silica can be achieved by hot process provided raw water contains sufficient magnesium hardness or magnesium salts are added with lime dose. Lower residual alkaline hardness and faster throughput rates can be achieved by hot operation	To prevent silica pick-up the final filters should be charged with anthracite rather than sand. Waste water from filter backwash and de-sludge of lime softening reaction vessel will be at operating temperature
Precipitation softening (lime-soda)	Largely replaced by ion exchange or lime softening plus ion exchange. Is capable of softening to give residual hardness of about 15 mg/l. Reduction in alkalinity and TDS not as good as with other processes	Requires final filtration as with all precipitation processes; produces waste effluent in the form of sludge which may create a disposal problem. Careful control of chemical dosing required
Sodium ion exchange (base exchange)	Almost complete elimination of hardness. Does not reduce alkalinity or TDS. Simple to operate, can be fully automated. Raw water should not contain suspended solids	Not suitable for boiler make-up if raw water alkalinity forms a high proportion of TDS. Steam condensate may contain appreciable quantities of CO_2 owing to breakdown of bicarbonate in the boiler
Lime softening — filter sodium ion exchange	Lime softener used to clarify water and also reduce alkaline hardness. Ion exchange unit removes remainder of hardness. Reduction in TDS achieved by removal of alkaline hardness	Filtration required between lime softener and ion exchange unit. Reduction in alkalinity by lime softener reduces danger of CO_2 in condensate
Weak-acid cation exchange — base exchange	Suitable for water with low turbidity. Almost complete elimination of alkaline hardness, and corresponding reduction in TDS. Base exchange removes remainder of hardness	CO_2 generated in WAC unit must be removed in degassing tower. Probably the most frequently used process for low-pressure boilers where raw water has high alkalinity. Should be followed by mechanical de-aeration
Strong-acid cation (hydrogen form) blend base exchange	Raw water passed through hydrogen-form SAC and sodium-form SAC units in parallel and the treated water mixed so that the FMA from the former destroys the alkalinity of the latter. The process gives low alkalinity and hardness	The H.1.–Na blend process has higher operating costs than WAC followed by BE. It is usually used where the alkalinity of the raw water is predominantly due to sodium bicarbonate. CO_2 produced should be removed by degassing tower and the feedwater to the boiler should be mechanically de-aerated

Table 7.6 (continued)

Process	Application or objective	Limitations
Demineralization, strong-acid cation, degassing, weak-acid cation	The process removes virtually all dissolved solids except the residual CO_2 after degassing and the silica	Often used as part treatment where demineralized water is blended with base-exchange-softened water to produce a soft make-up with reduced TDS
Demineralization, strong-acid cation, degassing, strong-base anion	Demineralization where removal of silica and residual CO_2 is required	Used for treatment of make-up to high-pressure boilers or where silica limitation must be imposed
Mixed-bed demineralizer	Sometimes used for direct treatment or preceded by base exchange if the raw water is very hard. Normally used as a polishing unit after two-stage demineralizer. Also used for condensate polishing in high-pressure boiler operation	Quality of treated water usually better than obtained by two-stage demineralizer but operating costs higher

Abbreviations
TDS — total dissolved solids
WAC — weak-acid cation
BE   — base exchange
FMA — free mineral acidity

the boiler makers, which may be more or less stringent.

Table 7.3 relates to boilers operating at design pressures up to 20 bar ($2 \times 10^6 \, \text{N/m}^2$). The table is divided into four groups to reflect major differences in boiler design:

1. Single- or double-pass firetube shell boilers with large water content and steam disengagement area relative to steam output.

2. Coil-type steam generator with mechanical steam–water separator.

3. Treble-pass firetube shell boilers.

4. High-output packaged multi-pass firetube boilers operating with high heat flux density; watertube boilers; thermal storage boilers and high heat flux density waste-heat boilers.

Table 7.4 relates to watertube drum-type boilers operating at pressures of 20–60 bar (2×10^6 to $6 \times 10^6 \, \text{N/m}^2$), while *Table 7.5* relates to watertube drum-type boilers operating at pressures above 60 bar ($6 \times 10^6 \, \text{N/m}^2$). As these latter boilers are normally used solely to provide high-pressure steam for turbine operations in electrical generation utilities, the quality of the steam, particularly with regard to silica, is a major consideration. Complete demineralization of make-up water, possibly with condensate polishing, is assumed.

To ensure steam purity and protection from corrosion, control of individual constituents in the boiler water is of greater importance than that of total dissolved solids as such.

7.8 Condensate purification

It is obviously beneficial to recover as much steam condensate as possible from process equipment and turbine condensate provided that it is a suitable quality for reuse as feedwater. Considerable care must, however, be taken if the condensate is likely to contain impurities which could render the feedwater acid or excessively alkaline, or which, owing to decomposition in the boiler, could reduce the boiler water's alkalinity. Care should also be taken to avoid contamination with impurities such as fats and oils, which cause excessive foaming.

A common cause of condensate contamination is ingress of cooling water from process plant or condensers. Where it constitutes a serious problem, that is, an unacceptable increase in the feedwater's total dissolved solids content or hardness, the condensate may be subjected to treatment methods similar to those applied to make-up water. Hardness salts may be removed by sodium ion exchange and other dissolved solids by ion exchange demineralization provided that the temperature of the condensate is reduced to a level acceptable to the ion exchange resins employed.

Condensate is also frequently contaminated by corrosion products resulting from the action of dissolved oxygen and dissolved carbon dioxide on the condensate pipework, etc. Filtration of the condensate may be required and can be effected by use of candle or precoat filters or fixed-bed anthracite filters. In certain circumstances ion exchange beds installed to remove dissolved solids may also serve as filters to remove corrosion products from the condensate.

8   Instruments and controls

The safe and efficient use of steam-generating and steam-utilizing plant demands the availability of accurate and reliable measurement and display equipment, in most cases coupled with some form of automatic or semi-automatic controls. This chapter is a survey developing from basic principles of measurement and transducing, through control techniques and actuation methods, to examples on small and large steam plant. A bibliography for more detailed reading is included.

8.1 Measurement

Flow

The basic principle of flow measurement is either the direct actuation of an in-line mechanism or the inferential method of measuring the differential pressure across an obstruction in the line. In general, methods based on the former principle are cheaper, less accurate and cover the small flow requirements.

Mechanical meters

Examples of mechanical meters are shown in *Figures 8.1, 8.2* and *8.3*. In the rotary piston meter (*Figure 8.1*), a piston with its centre spindle (A) can rotate about the chamber centre spindle (B).

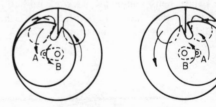

Figure 8.1   Rotary piston meter

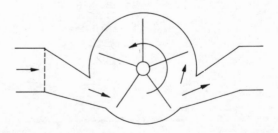

Figure 8.2   Rotary vane meter

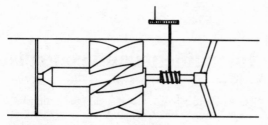

Figure 8.3   Rotary helix meter

The piston is prevented from rotating about its own spindle (A) by a fixed partition which extends into the split wall. As liquid flows into the inlet part, the piston moves in a semi-rotary motion causing the chamber spindle (B) to rotate. This rotary motion is transmitted via gears to an indicator, counter or pulse-transmitting device. Sizes are available from 15 mm to 150 mm, with flows from 0.02 to 100 m³/h, for fluids with viscosities up to 0.012 m²/s, with accuracies between 1% and 2%. They are therefore suitable for both feedwater and oil flow measurement.

In the rotary vane meter (*Figure 8.2*), the incoming fluid impinges on the lower vanes causing the spindle to rotate at a rate proportional to the fluid velocity. Larger versions have a series of tangential entry ports around the circumference of the vane chamber with a similar set of exit ports at a higher level.

The generous clearances of this type of meter make it particularly suitable for water flow where entrained dirt particles are a problem. Sizes are available from 12 to 150 mm, with flows from 0.05 to 100 m³/h, with an accuracy typically of ±2%.

The rotary helix meter has a rotor with helix-shaped vanes that cause it to rotate under the action of fluid flow, with an accuracy of ±2%.

Primary elements

For larger plant the added requirements of higher accuracy and transmission to remote indicators or controls dictate the use of an inferential method of flow measurement. The primary elements, such as orifice plates, flow nozzles and venturi tubes will now be discussed. For methods of transducing the differential pressure they generate, *see* Section 8.2.

Orifice plates. Figure 8.4 shows the characteristics of an orifice plate. The restriction in pipe diameter causes the flow velocity to increase, which reduces the static pressure as shown. By appropriate placing of pressure take-off taps a differential pressure measurement may be obtained, the square root of which can be shown to be proportional to flow. This fundamental aspect of this form of flow measurement limits the useful range of measurement. At 50% flow there is 25% differential and at 10% flow there is only 1% differential with a con-

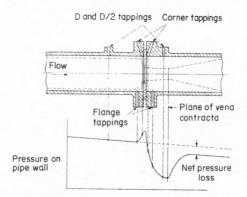

Figure 8.4   Section of square-edged orifice plate showing variation of pressure along the pipe wall

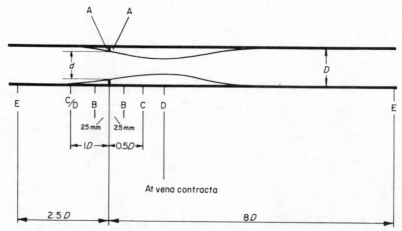

Figure 8.5   Possible positions for pressure take-off connections to an orifice plate. A, corner; B, flange; C, radius; D, vena contracta; E, pipe

sequent loss of accuracy and sensitivity at low flows. Normally a lower limit of 4% differential (20% flow) is used for indication, and 10% differential (33% flow) for control.

There are five possible positions for the pressure take-off connections, as shown in *Figure 8.5*. Ideally the taps should be placed where the differential is high but the change of pressure in the vicinity is low. Position (E) meets the first requirement and position (D) meets both. The pipe connections (E), however, measure only the low permanent pressure loss and, although relatively independent of orifice changes, the measurement is affected by the roughness of the pipe bore.

This method is, however, useful for very large flows. The vena contracta position (D), while being ideal, is dependent on the particular orifice plate dimensions, and the normal compromise is the radius position (C). The main advantage of this position is the extensive data available for calibration purposes. The same comment can be made for the flange position (B), which is the most common standard in the USA. The corner position (A) suffers from being affected by the high turbulence in the area and is somewhat subject to clogging.

The advantages of the orifice plate are the low cost, ready availability in a wide range of materials and the well-established characteristics from many years of application experience. The orifice plate does, however, suffer from the limitation on measurement due to the square-root law, the high permanent pressure loss (*see Figure 8.4*), erosion or corrosion of the sharp edge causing measurement errors, the tendency for the connecting piping to clog or freeze, and the need for a significant length of straight pipe to precede the plate. This last problem depends on the nature of the preceding obstruction to flow and the ratio of the orifice bore *d* to pipe diameter *D*. *Figure 8.6* shows the various standards established in the USA, UK and Germany for the straight length preceding an

orifice plate following a 90° elbow. The use of flow-straightening vanes in the upstream pipe has an increasing effect above a diameter ratio of 0.5,

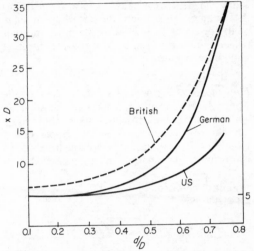

Figure 8.6   *Standards from various countries for the length of straight pipe, expressed in multiples of the pipe diameter, that must precede an orifice plate following a 90° elbow*

with a reduction of 40% at 0.8. A straightening vane is shown in *Figure 8.7*.

Where the water is known to contain solids, or when wet steam is being measured, an eccentric or segmental orifice, as shown in *Figure 8.8*, may be

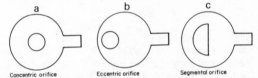

Figure 8.8   *Types of orifice. Shapes (b) and (c) tend to prevent deposition of solid material or condensed water*

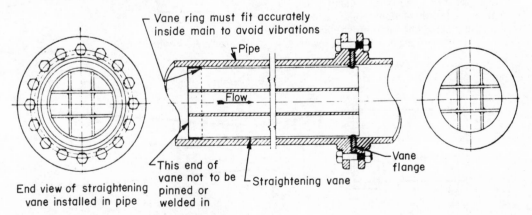

Figure 8.7   *Flange-type straightening vane*

used. This reduces the tendency of the concentric orifice plate to accumulate solids or condensed water on its upstream side with the attendant errors. The taps are usually angled at 90° or 180° to the opening, that is, not on the side where the edge of the orifice is tangential to the pipe. In other respects the non-concentric orifice plates function as do the concentric types.

Flow nozzles. Figure 8.9 shows a flow nozzle where the inlet to the narrow bore follows in an approximate fashion the lines of flow, and has a number of advantages over the simple orifice plate. The flow coefficient is more nearly that of a true venturi (*see below*), which means that for a

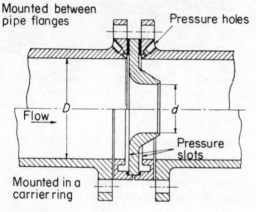

Figure 8.9   Flow nozzle

given diameter and differential pressure drop there is up to 65% greater flow, although the permanent pressure loss is only slightly less than that for an orifice plate. The inlet shape provides a scavenging effect on the flow, so preventing the accumulation of solids or condensate, and is far less affected by erosion than the sharp-edged orifice plate. It is therefore particularly suited to high flow rates and is commonly used for steam flow measurement, where it is preferably installed in a vertical pipe with the flow passing downwards.

The most significant disadvantage of the flow nozzle is the considerably increased cost; it costs more to manufacture owing to the shaping of the inlet, and more to install since a special piece of the pipe must be removable to facilitate periodic inspection.

Venturies. This survey of primary elements is completed by a brief mention of venturies, venturi nozzles and Dall tubes (*Figures 8.10, 8.11* and *8.12*), which are all variations on the classical venturi shape. By following more closely the flow line both upstream and downstream, the flow co-efficient is high and the permanent pressure loss is low (*see Figure 8.13*). They are all, however, even more expensive than the flow nozzle and highly dependent on their particular shape and internal smoothness. They are mainly used where the cost of pumping must be kept to a minimum. The venturi finds particular application in boiler prac-tice, in providing a differential for air flow measurement to be used for air/fuel ratio control, where the shape is constructed in square-section ducting.

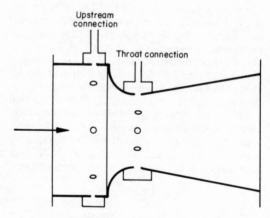

Figure 8.11   Venturi nozzle

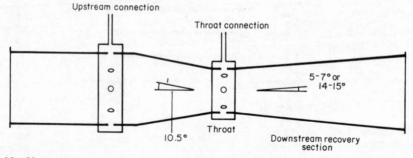

Figure 8.10   Venturi

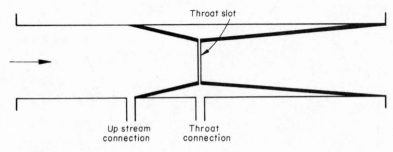

Figure 8.12   *Dall tube*

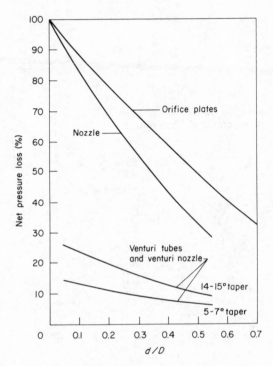

Figure 8.13   Pressure loss across orifice plates, nozzles, venturi tubes and venturi nozzles

Installation. A number of precautions are necessary when installing a primary element, and the associated impulse lines, to ensure the optimum accuracy of flow measurement. The primary element must be installed concentric to the internal diameter of the pipe with the bevel (if there is one) on an orifice plate, facing downstream.

Figure 8 14 shows the typical installation requirements for steam or water flow. Steam, once clear of the lagging around the pipe, will condense and could become a source of error if the height of both impulse lines is not kept equal. This is achieved by bringing the impulse lines to a pair of reservoirs, which are installed at the same height and distance from the pipe. Steam condenses and

fills the lines up to the centre line of the reservoirs, any surplus overflowing into the pipe. Changes in level due to movement of the measuring mechanism are thus minimized, and do not make a significant contribution to the measurement error. Force balance devices, where the volumetric change is negligible, do not need the extra volume of reservoirs, and simple venting tees are sufficient.

Level

Water level may be monitored either directly, by visually or mechanically measuring the height of liquid, or inferentially, by measuring the hydrostatic head of an open tank or differential pressure of a closed tank or drum. The various methods are shown schematically in *Figure 8.15*. All boiler drums are fitted with some form of gauge glass as in *Figure 8.15b*, to give a direct visual indication of the water level within the drum. It should be remembered, however, that owing to temperature difference between the drum and gauge water or steam bubbling in the drum following a sudden steam demand, the gauge may not show the true level. This is explained further in Chapters 4 and 5. Shut-off valves are fitted to isolate the gauge from the boiler to allow for its removal for cleaning or repair. Deposits from the water which gradually coat the inside of the gauge glass and condensing steam on the upper part of the glass can make it difficult to see the actual indicated level. To overcome this, a reflex method is often used, as illustrated in *Figure 8.16*. Light entering the gauge glass from the front strikes the zigzag-shaped rear surface and, in the part not covered by water, is totally reflected back to the viewer, who therefore sees that portion as bright. When water is in contact with the rear surface, the overall refractive index is changed such that the light enters the water and is absorbed in the water tube. The viewer therefore sees this portion as dark, and in this way the level is clearly seen as a division between the light and dark portions.

Where remote transmission for indication or control is required, the type shown in *Figure 8.15c*

144

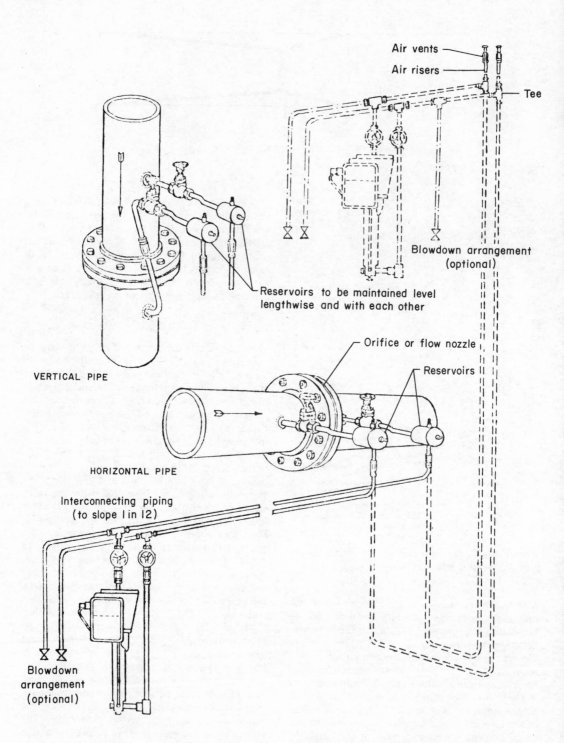

Air vents

Air risers

Tee

Reservoirs to be maintained level
lengthwise and with each other

Blowdown arrangement
(optional)

VERTICAL PIPE

Orifice or flow nozzle

Reservoirs

HORIZONTAL PIPE

Interconnecting piping
(to slope 1 in 12)

Blowdown
arrangement
(optional)

Figure 8.14   Piping diagram for steam or liquid flow transmitters

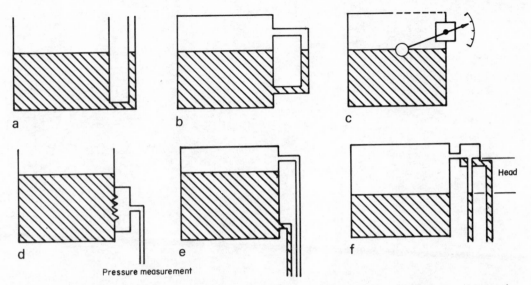

Figure 8.15   Measurement of water level. (a) Open tank, visual reading; (b) closed tank, visual reading; (c) open/closed tank, float mechanism; (d) open tank, hydrostatic head measurement; (e) closed tank, differential pressure measurement; (f) closed tank with a condensing atmosphere, differential pressure measurement

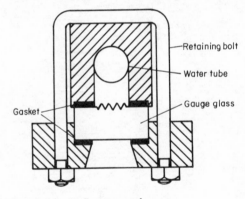

Figure 8.16   Reflex gauge glass

may be used. An example of this is shown in *Figure 8.17* where the float, under the action of changes in water level, causes the magnet to move inside the sealed centre tube. Outside the tube two magnetically operated switches sense when the magnet reaches their level, and change over to enable appropriate valves or pumps to be operated to maintain the water level. *See* Section 8.4 for further discussion of level control.

For remote indication of boiler or drum level the method shown in *Figure 8.15f* can be used. To overcome the problem of head differences due to condensed steam in the lines, a datum column is used which connects between the high- and low-level connections. At the top of this column is a chamber which maintains the condensate in the

upper leg at a constant level. The differential pressure measuring instrument will indicate maximum level when the datum column level equals the upper leg level and the differential pressure is zero. It therefore indicates level as the inverse of differential pressure. An example of a remote drum level indicator is shown in *Figure 8.18*. Other methods of differential pressure measurement are described below.

Pressure

If there is one measurement that is vital to the effective and safe operation of steam plant, it is pressure. Most of the preceding measurements, of flow and level, require in the end the measurement of pressure. The usual ultimate control factor in a boiler is the final steam pressure, and great attention should therefore be paid to the accurate, safe and reliable measurement of all pressures. This will be apparent from the accounts of steam plant failure, caused by overpressure, given in Chapter 3.

Pressure is measured as gauge, absolute or differential. *Figure 8.19* shows schematically the difference between these three forms of measurement. If only the top valve is opened, so that bellows B is open to atmosphere then the indication will be relative to atmospheric pressure, and is *gauge pressure*. If only the middle valve is opened to a vacuum pump then the indication is now relative to zero pressure, at least theoretically, and is said to be *absolute*. Finally, if only the lower

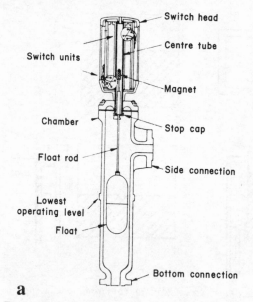

a

Figure 8.17   Mobrey magnetic level controller. NWL, normal water level

valve is opened and a second pressure applied to bellows B then the indication will be of the difference between the two pressures and is the *differential pressure*.

The units of pressure measurement are either those of force per unit area or height of a liquid of known density; thus pressure is referred to as newtons per square metre, or as millimetres of water or mercury. A non-preferred but, in fact, more commonly used unit of pressure is the *bar*, which approximates to one atmosphere. The methods of converting pressure into a movement or force suitable for direct indication or control, or for transducing for remote transmission, reflect these two basic units.

Bourdon tubes

The classical method of pressure measurement is by means of a *Bourdon tube*, originally patented by Eugene Bourdon in 1852, and, like all types

b

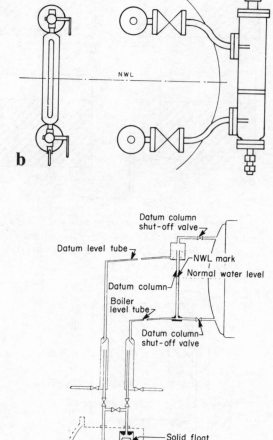

Figure 8.18   Schematic layout of Babcock-Bristol Truscale level indicator

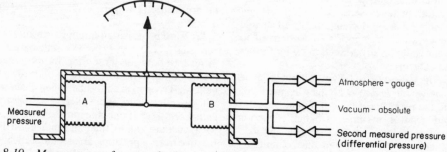

Figure 8.19   Measurement of gauge, absolute and differential pressure

that measure force per unit area, relies on the elastic deformation of the pressure-enclosing material to produce a force or movement. In this case a closed-end flattened tube is bent into a C shape, as shown in *Figure 8.20*, which has the tendency to straighten with the application of pressure. This tip movement, when connected to a simple geared sector and pinion, provides a straightforward indication of pressure or vacuum.

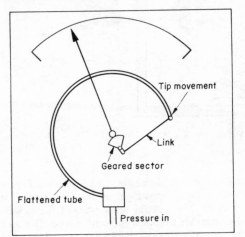

Figure 8.20   C-shaped Bourdon tube

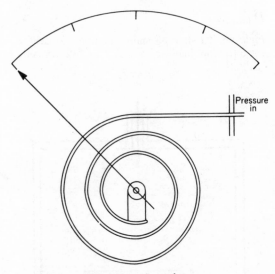

Figure 8.21   Spiral Bourdon tube

Among the many advantages of Bourdon tubes are simple construction, low cost, wide range of pressures, variety of materials of construction and reasonable accuracy. They do, however, suffer from a vulnerability to vibration owing to the long overhang, and poor hysteresis characteristics — the same path is not followed for rising as for

falling pressures. Other types of Bourdon tubes are the spiral (*Figure 8.21*) and helical (*Figure 8.22*) designs, which give far greater tip movement for a given pressure change than the standard shape, and therefore give greater accuracy of measurement. Bourdon tubes are available for pressure ranges from 0.3 to 7000 bar.

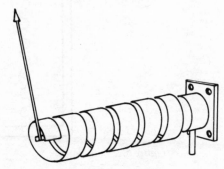

Figure 8.22   Helical Bourdon tube

Bellows

A bellows is essentially a tube which has been formed into convolutions that allow elastic deformation when pressurized. Because of the relatively poor elastic characteristics, it is usually used with a spring whose *rate* — deflection per unit load — is considerably above that of the bellows (*see Figure 8.23*). Alternatively, they may be used in the force balance mode (*see* Section 8.2), where the movement is minimal and no spring is needed. Where good overrange protection is required the nesting construction is used, as shown in *Figure 8.24*. When the convolutions close completely under the action of external pressure, they form a solid mass and no structural damage can occur. By using thin material and large diameter, very low pressures can be measured, the full capability for measurement extending from about 100 mmH$_2$O to over 350 bar. A typical pressure unit providing lever movement with pressure is shown in *Figure 8.25*, and an instrument designed to measure water level as a differential pressure is shown in *Figure 8.26*.

Diaphragm capsules

The simplest form of pressure-responsive element is a flat membrane (*see Figure 8.27a*), which may be made from virtually any deformable material. For measurement of very low air pressures, as in furnace draught, a slack diaphragm is used. An example of this is shown in *Figure 8.28*, which uses a leather or nylon gasket material. For differential measurement a magnetic coupling is used to bring the diaphragm motion onto the indicating mechanism. Such instruments have full-scale ranges down to 25 mmH$_2$O.

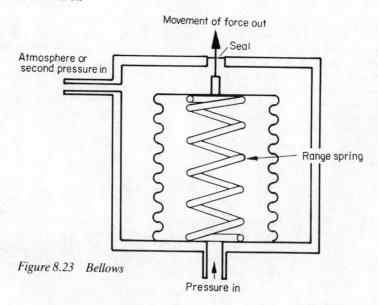

Figure 8.23 Bellows

Metallic diaphragms have very small movements and poor linearity, and are either used in a force balance mode or have a corrugated formation as shown in *Figure 8.27b*. Such diaphragms are often used as seals between two incompatible fluids or for preventing a corrosive fluid from entering a pressure-measuring instrument. When two diaphragms are coupled as in *Figure 8.27c* they form a pressure capsule, and the mating corrugations allow the capsule to survive considerable overrange. A common form of capsule in

pressure-measuring instruments is shown in *Figure 8.27d*, where overrange in both directions is achieved. The central seals prevent the silicon fluid from seeping past the centre connector and damaging the opposite diaphragm. A sophisticated form of such a device is discussed in Section 8.2.

Manometers

Figure 8.29a shows a simple manometer, where the difference in two pressures P_1 and P_2 is directly

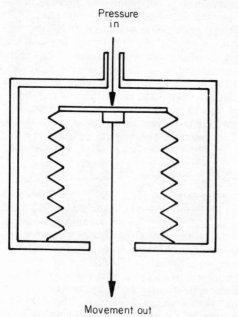

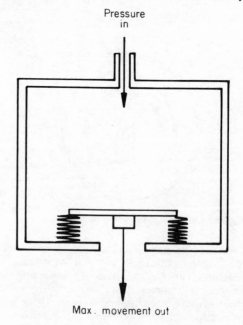

Figure 8.24 Bellows with nesting construction

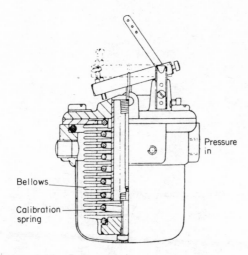

Figure 8.25   Pressure unit

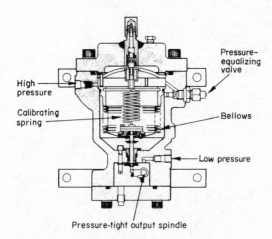

Figure 8.26   Instrument for measuring water level

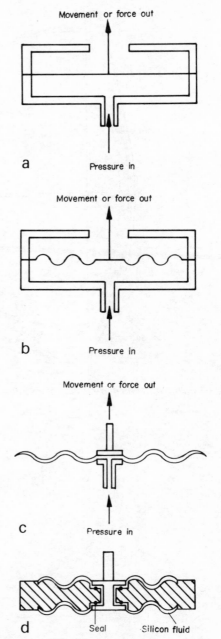

Figure 8.27   Pressure-responsive diaphragms and capsules. (a) Flat membrane; (b) corrugated metallic diaphragm; (c), (d) pressure capsules

proportional to the difference in heights of the two columns and the density of the liquid used. Because of its high density and chemical inertness, mercury is commonly used in manometer-type devices, the scale often being given as millimetres of mercury (mmHg). This is particularly true for vacuum measurements, where P_2 would be reduced to as low a pressure as possible and P_1 connected to the vacuum to be measured.

To provide a mechanical linkage a float is often used as shown in *Figure 8.29b*, with a pressure-tight or magnetic coupling if differential pressures are to be measured. An example of this mechanism was shown in *Figure 8.18*, where the differential pressure of the boiler drum was measured by a mercury manometer arrangement with magnetic

coupling on to the indicator. Condensed steam is taken directly to the mercury surface.

A special application of the manometer principle is the Ledoux bell, shown in *Figure 8.29c*, where the inside of the inverted bell is shaped to conform to a square-root law. The indicator then responds to the square root of the differential pressure. If

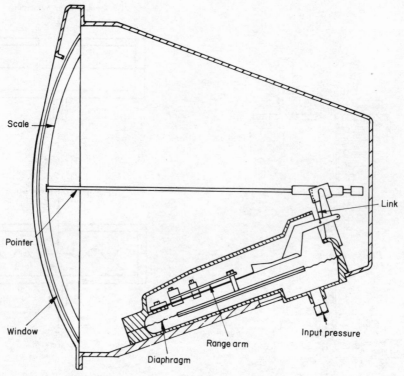

Figure 8.28   Instrument for measuring furnace draught pressure

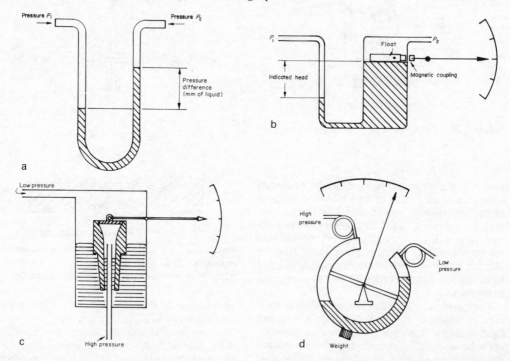

Figure 8.29   Pressure measurement by the use of a manometer. (a) Simple manometer; (b) manometer equipped with float; (c) the Ledoux bell, a special application of the manometer principle; (d) ring balance

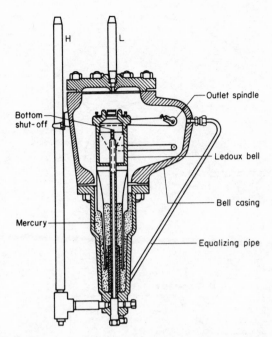

Figure 8.30 Schematic illustration of an instrument based on the Ledoux bell principle

this is derived across an orifice plate or flow nozzle then the indication will be linear with flow. A typical instrument of this type is shown in *Figure 8.30*.

The ring balance, shown in *Figure 8.29d*, can be used for low differential measurement as in furnace draught. The weight of liquid transferred by the pressure differential is counterbalanced by the weight moving in the opposite direction.

Temperature

The measurement of temperature is achieved by one of three methods: the expansion of a fluid in a closed tube, the change in resistance of a metal wire or the thermoelectric effect of a thermocouple.

Expansion of fluid

A standard mercury- or alcohol-in-glass thermometer is an example of this first method and provides a linear visual indication of temperature. An extension of the same principle is the fluid-filled bulb, as shown in *Figure 8.31a*, where the enclosed fluid expands with temperature thus exerting a pressure on the Bourdon tube mechanism, which moves to provide an indication of temperature.

As the pressure change is quite small, a helix-type Bourdon tube is often used and the fluid may be either liquid or gas. This method suffers from the major problem of being sensitive to temperature changes along the length of the capillary and at the indicator itself, which should therefore be located as near as possible to the point of measurement, but it has the outstanding advantage of being self-powered. Examples of different forms of bulb are shown in *Figure 8.32*.

Resistance elements

The resistance element makes use of a fundamental property of some metals, which is to undergo an increase in resistance with increasing temperature. Nickel and copper are sometimes used but, although it has a poorer resistance temperature characteristic, platinum's stability and inertness make it a virtually universal choice. A typical circuit is shown in *Figure 8.31b*, where the resistance element forms one leg of a Wheatstone bridge arrangement. To eliminate the effect of changes in resistance of the interconnecting wires, the arrangement shows how a similar length of wire can be inserted on both sides of the bridge network.

Figure 8.33 shows a simple resistance element construction. A length of platinum wire of approximate diameter 0.4 mm is double-wound, to avoid inductive effects, onto a mica former, with the ends spot-welded onto the terminal strips. Further layers of mica insulation are placed either side of the former and clamped together with stabilizing and thermal conduction springs. After assembly, the unit is annealed to relieve any stresses which would otherwise change the resistance of the wire. The whole assembly is then inserted into a thermometer pocket for protection, the pocket being screwed, bolted or welded into position. An example of a screwed type is shown in *Figure 8.34*, with the terminal housing and access cover. More sophisticated, and therefore more expensive, versions are available where the resistance element is encapsulated in ceramic and then inserted into a steel or alloy sheath packed with granular ceramic. This provides both mechanical rigidity and improved thermal conductivity for a faster response.

A more recent development is that of platinum film elements, where a thin layer of platinum is deposited on an insulating former. The low thermal inertia of the film provides extremely fast response to temperature changes.

Thermocouples

In 1821 T. J. Seebeck discovered the basic phenomenon of the thermocouple. With reference to *Figure 8.31c*, where a junction A exists between two dissimilar metals, a voltage is developed across the junction which is a function of the type of materials and the absolute temperature.

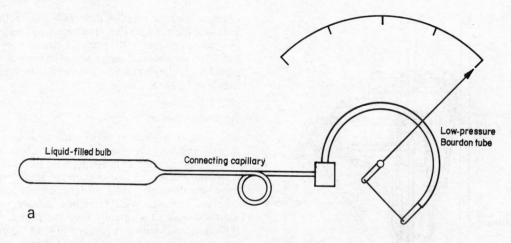

Liquid-filled bulb

Connecting capillary

Low-pressure
Bourdon tube

a

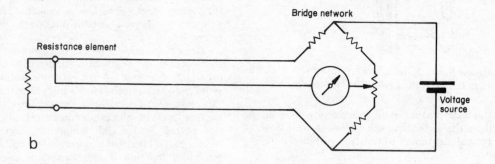

Bridge network

Resistance element

Voltage
source

b

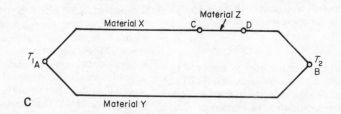

Material Z

Material X   C   D

T_1
A

T_2
B

Material Y

c

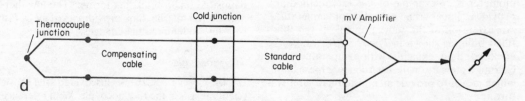

Cold junction

mV Amplifier

Thermocouple
junction

Compensating
cable

Standard
cable

d

Figure 8.31   Temperature measurement. (a) Fluid-filled bulb; (b) electrical circuit for measuring temperature by means of a resistance element; (c) temperature measurement by use of a thermocouple; (d) practical thermocouple circuit

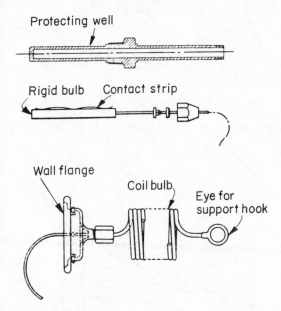

Figure 8.32 *Temperature measurement by means of the expansion of a fluid; different forms of bulb*

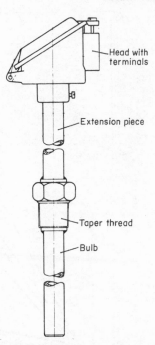

Figure 8.34 *Resistance element with thermometer screwed into position*

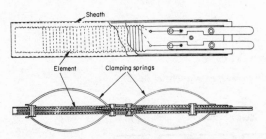

Figure 8.33 *Construction of a simple resistance element*

When the metals are joined at another junction B which is at a different temperature, a net difference in the voltages produced will exist, which causes a current to flow. This is called the *Seebeck effect* and the voltage difference is the *Peltier emf*. A further effect exists, discovered by Lord Kelvin (William Thompson) in 1857, which is that in a single wire with current flowing in it, if a temperature gradient exists along that wire, heat will be transferred. This loss or gain of energy gives rise to the *Thompson emf*, which although small, is a major cause of non-linearity in the thermocouple response. The result is a voltage, the sum of the Peltier and Thomson emfs, which is approximately proportional to the temperature difference between the junctions.

It can be shown that the insertion of another material, 'Z' in *Figure 8.31c*, which gives rise to two more junctions C and D at the same tempera-

ture, will have no overall effect, and from this we have the practical thermocouple circuit shown in *Figure 8.31d*. As thermocouple wire is expensive, the actual temperature element is kept as small as possible, and between the element and the cold junction compensating cable is used, which is a cheaper material having similar thermoelectric properties. At the cold junction, which is often a box containing very many thermocouple junctions, the compensating cable is connected to standard copper cable. As any variation in the temperature of this junction has a direct effect on the voltage developed, it is usually kept some degrees higher than the expected maximum ambient temperature by a thermostatic heater. Alternatively the temperature of the junction is sensed by the amplifier, and variations are electronically compensated. This also applies if the compensating cable is taken directly to the amplifier.

Figure 8.35 shows the voltages generated by various standard thermocouple materials. The precise relationship between temperature and voltage is given in the British Standard BS 4937, where the cold junction is assumed to be 0°C. Where the cold-junction box is at, say, 50°C, then the emf associated with 50°C, in the tables, must be added to that measured at the cold junction to obtain an accurate measure of temperature.

Figure 8.36 shows a simple thermocouple assembly, with the two materials twisted and welded

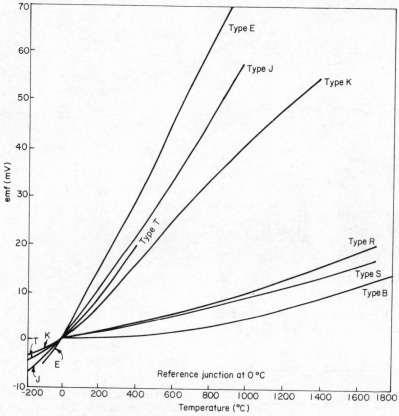

Figure 8.35   Temperature–thermal emf curves for common types of thermocouple

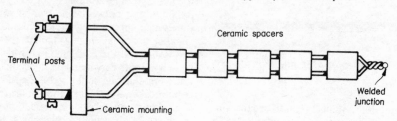

Figure 8.36   Simple thermocouple assembly

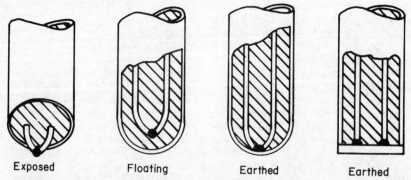

Figure 8.37   Alternative types of thermocouple construction

at the end. They then pass through ceramic spacers, to prevent the wires touching and so forming spurious junctions, and are clamped in the terminal posts. The entire assembly is inserted into a thermometer pocket as with the resistance element.

An alternative construction is shown in *Figure 8.37*, where the thermocouple is encased in a ceramic powder or other suitable oxide within a metallic sheath. The junction so formed may be floating or earthed, as shown.

Conductivity

The water used in steam plant will invariably contain a measure of dissolved salts such as magnesium and calcium chlorides, sulphates and carbonates (*see* Chapter 7). These will tend to deposit out onto the hot surfaces and reduce heat transfer, restrict flow and encourage corrosion. They do, however, lend themselves to a ready means of concentration measurement, and therefore control, as the dissolved molecules will tend to dissociate into ions. An ion is a molecule which has either gained or lost an electron and will therefore have a negative or positive charge. If two electrodes are inserted into the solution with a potential difference across them, then the positive ions will drift towards the negative electrode and the negative ions to-

wards the positive electrode. At the electrode they will gain or lose an electron and become neutral molecules again. The effect is for an electric current to flow in the external circuit of the electrodes, the current being a measure of the ion concentration of the water.

The usual unit of measurement of *conductivity*, which is the inverse of resistance, is the *mho*. As this is a large unit the practical range is in millionths of a mho, or μmho.

Inevitably there are a number of factors affecting the measurement of conductivity, the most serious being polarization. This is where gaseous ions are produced at the electrodes, forming an opposing electrical potential, which in a short time will reduce the current flow to near zero. To overcome this the electrodes are fed with an alternating voltage which, because the direction of travel of the ions is rapidly reversing, prevents the build-up of gaseous ions at the electrodes.

Conductivity varies inversely with the distance between electrodes, directly with their area, and somewhat non-linearly with temperature. It also varies with the type of ions present although for a given installation the variations are likely to be small.

A typical instrument will have platinum elec-

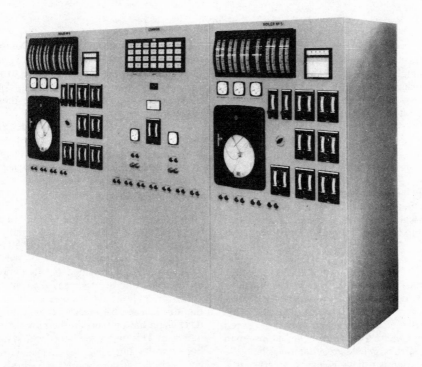

Figure 8.38   Central control panel

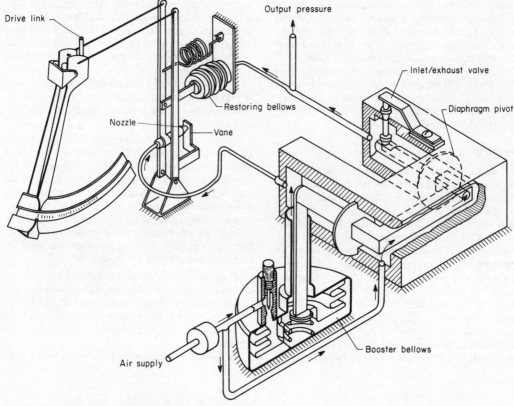

Figure 8.39   Vane/nozzle type of pneumatic transducer

trodes mounted a fixed distance apart in a probe, inserted into the pipe such that the water flows through the probe but the velocity is low to prevent a scouring action on the electrodes. The electrodes form one leg of an a.c. Wheatstone bridge network, with temperature compensation, either by use of a resistance thermometer, or by having a second probe connected to the other leg of the bridge which is mounted adjacent to the measuring probe but sealed with a solution of fixed concentration.

Typically, measurements are taken for steam which has first been condensed and degassed, for feedwater which includes both condensate return and make-up water, or for boiler blowdown.

8.2 Transducers

The previous section discussed various ways of converting flow, level, pressure and even temperature into a movement or force. In many instances this was used directly for indication of the measured variable, but where a number of plant items are in parallel or with larger steam-generating plant, the instrumentation is usually collected together in a central control panel such as that shown in *Figure*

8.38. The same measurements are also used as the measured variable inputs to a control system. For these reasons it becomes necessary to transduce the movement or force into a form that can be transmitted over long distances and then used to actuate displays or control systems.

With one exception the methods described here transduce movement into a *signal*, although when they are used in a force balance type of instrument, that movement is kept to a minimum (*see* p 159).

Pneumatic transducers

Almost universally the pneumatic transducer is the vane/nozzle system. The schematic diagram shown in *Figure 8.39* shows the drive link, which responds to the movement of the bellows, Bourdon tube, Ledoux bell, or other impulse, and moves the vane arm. It may also move a local indicator as shown. If the vane is moved closer to the nozzle it tends to restrict the air flowing from it, causing the pressure in the booster bellows to increase. This pivots the bent-lever system of the booster relay and opens the inlet valve. Air, which has been fed into the booster relay body and then through the pivot lever arm, escapes into the

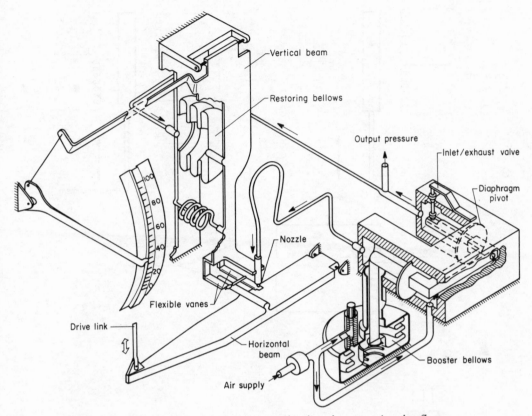

Figure 8.40 Pneumatic transducer in which the signal is directly proportional to flow

connecting piping to the restoring bellows, which causes the nozzle to be moved away from the vane, thus restoring the original balanced position. The output signal is taken from the restoring bellows pressure. By suitable design the output pressure signal can be arranged to be a standard 0.2–1.0 bar or other desired signal range. A variation of the above is shown in *Figure 8.40*, where the use of an instrument that measures differential pressure means that the pneumatic signal is directly proportional to flow.

The drive link is moved in proportion to the differential pressure of the measuring device. A small bar attached to a downward-biased spring bears onto a raised ridge on the horizontal beam, so that it causes the vane to move when the beam moves. Changes in the back-pressure of the nozzle result in changes in the pressure in the restoring bellows as described above. The arrangement is such that the nozzle pivots about a top hinge at right angles to the horizontal beam. As the nozzle motion describes a circular arc relative to the raised ridge of the horizontal beam, the relationship between nozzle and vane is a square-root function and the output pressure, or the restoring bellows pressure, is proportional to the square

root of the drive link motion. The device therefore gives an output which is proportional to flow.

This same vane/nozzle arrangement can be used for control as described under the heading 'Three-term controller' (p 173).

Electric transducers

Electric transducers make use of changes in inductance, reluctance, resistance, impedance or capacitance, as well as using the direct force/voltage effect called the *piezoelectric effect*. These are shown schematically in *Figure 8.41*. In *Figure 8.41a* the moving core alters the reluctance in the a.c. excited bridge network, enabling a proportional output to be generated. An actual arrangement would have the core either within the coil windings or as a disc between the two coils. A somewhat similar arrangement is the linear variable differential transformer shown in *Figure 8.41b*. The induced voltage in either secondary coil is proportional to the core position and of opposite sense. This arrangement gives good linearity over a large range of movement. There are a wide range of other arrangements which work by similar principles, utilizing changes in inductive coupling to

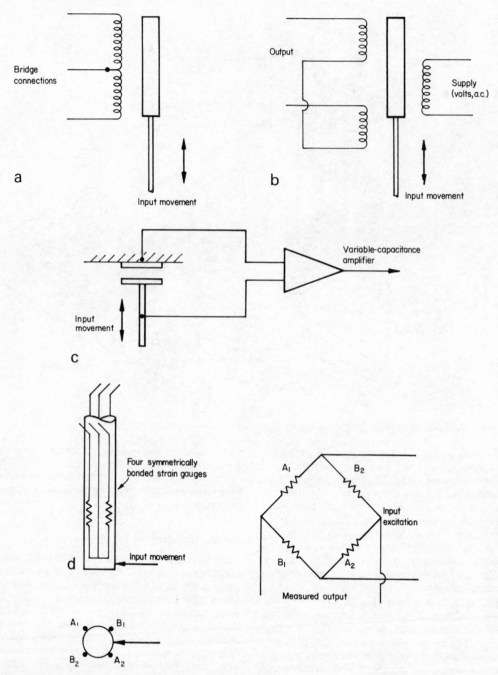

Figure 8.41   Electrical transducers based on (a) variable reluctance, (b) variable inductance, (c) variable capacitance, and (d) strain gauge method

produce a proportional output from the electronic circuitry.

All these techniques have the advantages of being virtually friction-free, giving infinite resolution with no steps in the change in output no matter how small the core movement, and good linearity. They can be arranged where the moving parts are totally sealed off from the electric parts, and are capable of responding to oscillating movements of up to 100 kHz in frequency. An example of a moving-core variable-inductance transmitter is shown in *Figure 8.42*, where the encapsulated

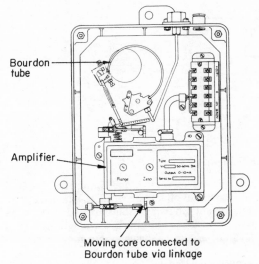

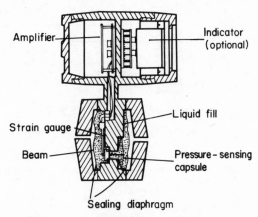

Figure 8.43 *Strain gauge transducer*

Figure 8.42   Moving-core variable-inductance transmitter

amplifier provides a 4–20 mA signal proportional to the pressure-induced movement of the Bourdon tube.

Figure 8.41c shows the variable-capacitance arrangement where movement changes the capacitance between the two sensor plates. This change is measured in the amplifier, which provides a proportional output. This arrangement has many of the advantages of the former methods but cannot be totally isolated from the electrical parts, and suffers from changes in the dielectric constant of the gap due to moisture, or other causes.

The strain gauge method uses the property whereby the resistance of a wire will increase when stretched owing to the reduction in its effective diameter. As the resistance is also affected by temperature, the usual arrangement is to place the gauges as shown in *Figure 8.41d*, so that they form part of a bridge network. By epoxy-bonding the gauges to a beam, as shown, the slight movement of the beam caused by the applied force is translated into resistance change which is measured by the electronic circuitry. Careful selection of material can produce a gauge with high resistance change under strain but which is not greatly affected by temperature. Other arrangements are used in which the gauge is not bonded, but is a length of wire wound round a set of pillars which are caused to move in response to pressure.

A 10–100 times improvement in the strain gauge factor, or change in resistance with stretching, is achieved by the use of semiconductor materials instead of resistance material. These are materials which are half-way between conductors and insulators and whose properties are used extensively in transistor diodes, amplifiers and other electronic components. Unfortunately they also have a considerably greater temperature coefficient, which usually means that additional temperature compensation methods are required.

An instrument which combines the capsule technique described on p 147 and a bonded semiconductor strain gauge is shown schematically in *Figure 8.43*. The two process seal diaphragms are metallic discs with corrugated formations that act as a seal between the process fluid and the fill liquid, which is usually a suitable silicon fluid (or Fluorlube for oxygen service). The nesting sensing capsule acts on the lower end of the beam on which the strain gauges are bonded. The connecting wires are fed through a seal to the electronic amplifier above. A temperature sensor is also mounted in the capsule to enable an electronic temperature compensation to be achieved. The overtravel stops are similar to those described previously.

Force balance techniques

To minimize the problems of non-linearity and hysteresis, inherent in most pressure-measuring devices such as bellows, diaphragms and Bourdon tubes, a force balance technique is often used. In this a null-seeking servo system with a high gain keeps the actual movement of the sensing element to a minimum. One example of the many possible variations of this method is shown in *Figure 8.44*. When the bellows capsule moves slightly in response to a change in differential pressure, this movement is amplified by the beam system and sensed by the detector: in this example, a variable-reluctance device. The mechanically amplified movement is sensed by the oscillator amplifier, which sends a proportional current to the moving coil/magnet force motor. This generates a force which opposes and balances the force produced by the bellows capsule. As the movement of the detector is small, the movement of the bellows

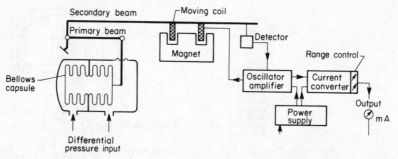

Figure 8.44   Force balance technique of signal transduction

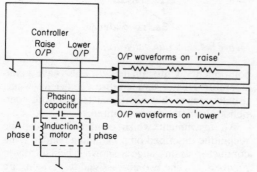

Figure 8.45   Pulse duration actuator circuit

capsule is even smaller and spring rate, linearity and hysteresis effects are virtually eliminated. The coil current can then be transmitted directly as the output or taken through a current converter to facilitate accurate ranging as shown.

Transmitted signals

Transmitted signals used for remote indication or control are, by national and international agreement, restricted to certain ranges. The preferred current range is 4–20 mA, with an option for 0–20 mA, although 0–10 mA is still often used. Other ranges used for local indication and within the

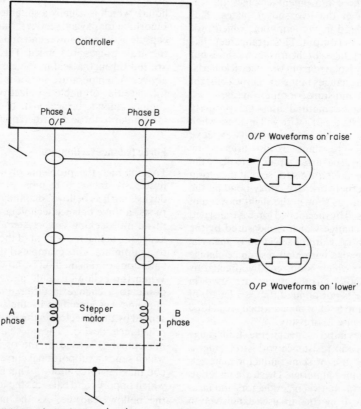

Figure 8.46   Stepper motor actuator circuit

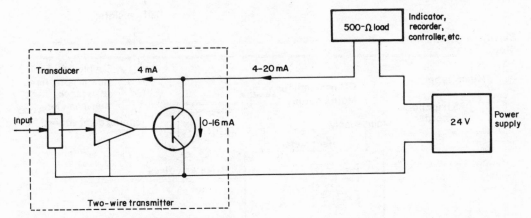

Figure 8.47   Circuit for a two-wire transmitter

control system are 0–5 V, 1–5 V and 0–10 V.

Pneumatic signals are usually 0.2 to 1.0 bar, values higher than these becoming less common. For actuator operation, a pulsed signal is often used, where only the incremental change required is transmitted. When no change is being asked for there is no signal and the actuator remains stationary. This has the particular advantage that in the event of electric-power failure in the controller, the valve or damper does not move to a potentially dangerous position and control of the plant can be readily taken over by the operator using independently generated signals.

Two examples of pulsed signals are 'pulse duration' and 'stepper motor drive' as described below. *Figure 8.45* shows a pulse duration system where the controller output appears as pulses of single-phase a.c. to one phase of an induction motor in the positioner (*see* Section 8.3). The pulses are of fixed duration, typically 200 ms, the number of pulses being proportional to motor rotation and therefore change in actuator position. The direction of rotation of the motor, and hence the movement of the actuator, is determined by which phase the pulses are applied to, the motor moving at a constant speed in the required direction. The length of the pulse limits the minimum incremental movement of the actuator and hence the fine resolution of control.

Figure 8.46 shows a stepper motor drive system which is similar to a pulse duration system. A square wave-form series of pulses are applied to both phases of a stepper motor, one being out of phase with the other. The lead/lag relationship will determine the direction of rotation of the stepper motor and hence the movement of the actuator. This system provides greater resolution and hence more accurate control.

Two-wire transmitters

One of the most significant advantages of using the standard signal range of 4–20 mA is the possibility of having only two wires going out to the transmitter. When the distance is large the savings can be considerable. Such an arrangement is shown schematically in *Figure 8.47*. It is made possible by using the power available from the minimum current of 4 mA to power the transducer and electronic circuitry, which generates the actual variable signal of 0–16 mA in response to the variations in the transmitter input. In the example shown, at the maximum external current of 20 mA the 500-Ω load will drop 10 V of the 24 V available, leaving a minimum of 14 V, and the residual 4 mA, available to power the transmitter. The voltage at the power supply can be increased to accommodate greater loads.

Heat meter

The *heat meter* is an instrument, or more properly a combination of instruments, that utilizes many of the technologies we have been discussing. In a district heating system, or in other applications where hot water is provided for heating purposes, it is necessary for good commercial control to know the quantity of heat being consumed. This is achieved as shown in *Figure 8.48*, where two resistance element thermometers measure the temperature difference between supply and return flow and a flowmeter measures the flow past an orifice plate. These are combined to compute heat difference in the two streams in a bridge network shown in *Figure 8.49*. The flow transmitter output current flows through the bridge arms and the millivolt amplifier senses the imbalance caused by changes in the thermometer resistances. The input to the amplifier is therefore proportional to the flow multiplied by the temperature difference, which is a measure of heat. The amplified signal can then be used for indication, recording or integration.

A feature of this heat meter is the third arm of

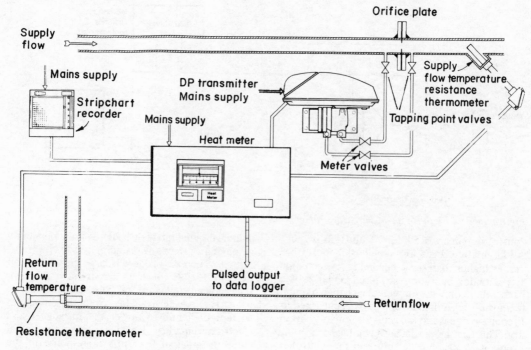

Figure 8.48   Measurement of heat consumption

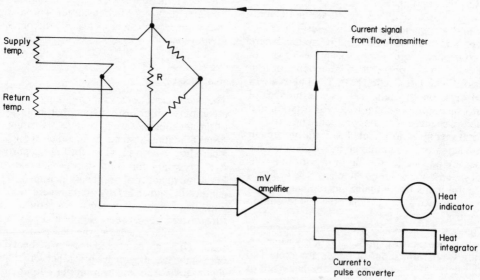

Figure 8.49   Heat meter

the bridge (marked 'R'), which provides a correction for changes in the density of the water flow, and hence the flowmeter calibration, due to an overall temperature change. This provides a greater accuracy than would otherwise be obtained.

8.3   Actuation

We have discussed so far the measurement, transducing and transmitting of flows, levels, pressures and temperatures associated with steam and water.

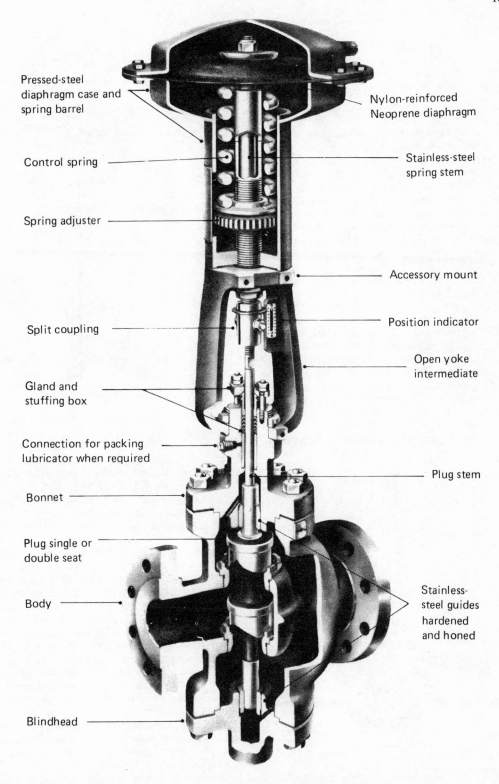

Pressed-steel diaphragm case and spring barrel

Nylon-reinforced Neoprene diaphragm

Control spring

Stainless-steel spring stem

Spring adjuster

Accessory mount

Split coupling

Position indicator

Open yoke intermediate

Gland and stuffing box

Connection for packing lubricator when required

Plug stem

Bonnet

Plug single or double seat

Stainless-steel guides hardened and honed

Body

Blindhead

Figure 8.50   Cut-away of Megaflo double-seated control valve with diaphragm actuator

Equipped with this information, the operator (or the automatic controls) is then in a position to make the adjustments necessary to maintain proper control of the plant. For this he will use actuators that operate control valves or dampers as required.

Valves

There are essentially two broad classes of valves: shut-off valves, designed to be either open or closed; and control valves, designed to regulate the flow passing through them. The ideal control valve will be one which gives good linear adjustment with the minimum 'noise' introduced to the flow, and which is capable of working with the maximum pressure drop across it. It must also resist the erosive effect of high flow velocities and turbulent, cavitating fluids. Associated with the valve itself is the actuator, in the form of a diaphragm/spring arrangement or a piston/screw assembly.

An example of a flow control valve is shown in *Figure 8.50*. Control air pressure is fed to the chamber above the diaphragm which causes a proportional deflection of the control spring together with the plug stem. Note the shaping of the valve plug, which is designed to give a linear relationship between valve movement and flow. The double seat arrangement provides a balancing of the valve stem in the presence of the pressure drop across it.

Where very high pressure drops are encountered,

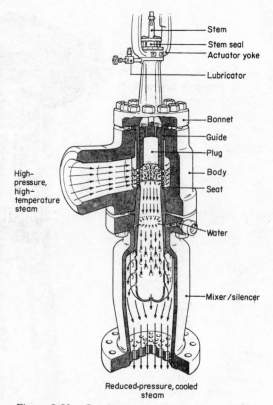

Figure 8.52   Combined pressure-reducing and desuperheating valve

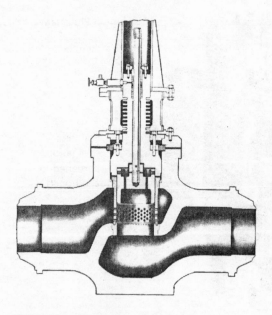

Figure 8.51   Feedwater control valve capable of dealing with very high pressure drops

as in boiler feedwater, and reheat and superheat spray valves, the valve arrangement is usually as shown in *Figure 8.51*. The main fluid stream is broken into a large number of small jets. These jets have a certain amount of their energy reduced by the process of friction during their passage through the perforated section, which causes most of the pressure reduction. The process is completed by the kinetic energy of the jets being converted into heat through the turbulence of the jets as they impinge on each other. The arrangement reduces hydraulic noise and induced vibration. In another arrangement the perforations are in the moving valve plug. A combined pressure-reducing and desuperheating valve is shown in *Figure 8.52*. The pressure reduction section is similar to that described above but an additional section has been bolted to the outlet of the valve. Water is injected in the inlet shown on the right of the valve body to reduce the superheated steam to the required temperature, the flow being controlled by a valve not shown. The water is injected into the steam through a large number of small holes located in the high-velocity steam zone. At this section, and for some distance downstream, the fluid stream is constrained by a stainless-steel liner to withstand

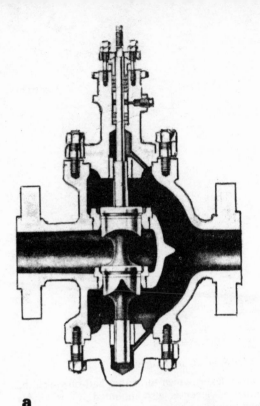

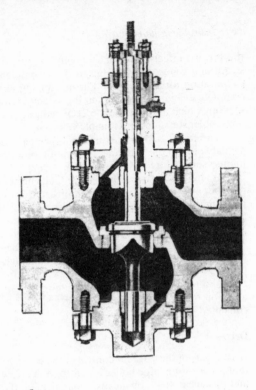

a

b

Figure 8.53 Varieties of valve body style. (a) Globe, double seat, (b) globe, single seat, (c) globe, (d) angle

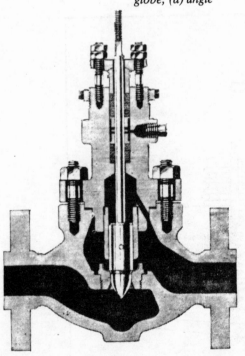

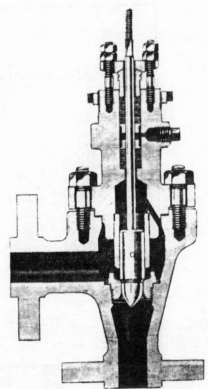

c

d

the erosive effects of a high-velocity mixture of steam and water droplets due to the incomplete evaporation after injection. Further mixing and complete evaporation occurs in the attemperator section, which also has the effect of reducing the now cooler steam to a reasonable velocity.

A variety of body styles and plug shapes are available to suit the particular application requirements, some of which are shown in *Figure 8.53*. Body materials are typically carbon steel, chrome-molybdenum alloy steel, cast iron or bronze, the plug and seats being stainless steel with a facing of Stellite.

The coupling of the pipe to the valve is by screw connection for smaller, low-pressure valves, and by the bolted flange or welding for larger or high-pressure valves. It is essential that the pressure, flow and temperature rating of the valve be suitable for the application; the supplier should be consulted in every case.

Drives

A vital part of the efficient control of the combustion process of a large boiler is control of air flow and furnace draught by means of dampers on the forced- or induced-draught fans. This requirement is met by a control drive such as that shown in *Figure 8.54*. The pneumatic cylinder acts on the

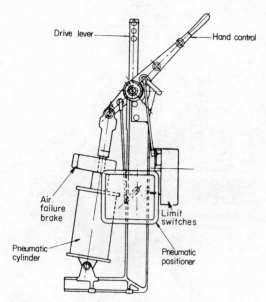

Figure 8.54   Control drive

control lever, which turns the shaft on which the actuation lever is also mounted. Considerable shaft torque can be generated with suitable cylinders and air pressure. An air failure brake may be fitted to lock the drive stationary in the event of a failure

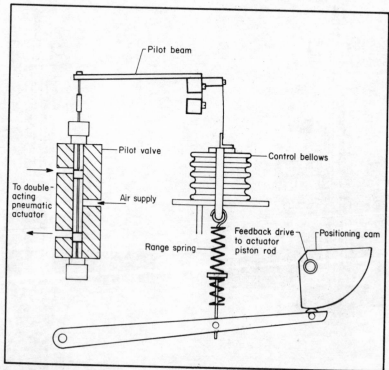

Figure 8.55   Pneumatic positioner

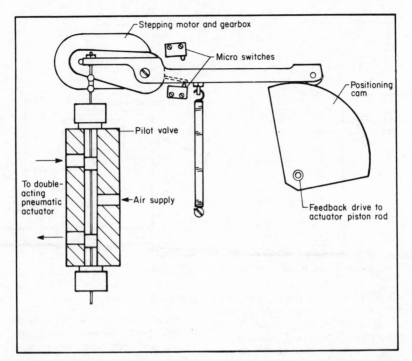

Figure 8.56   Pulse input positioner

in the air supply. Electric motors are also used in these applications.

Positioners

All actuators which are part of a remote or automatic control system require a means of positioning the valve or damper in relation to the output control signal from the controller or hand/auto unit. A pneumatic positioner is shown schematically in *Figure 8.55*. An increase in the control signal is fed to the bellows, which pivots the upper beam and so pushes down the pilot valve. This causes supply air to be fed to the lower connection and allows the upper connection to be vented past the valve stem. If these are connected to either side of the piston in the actuator cylinder or diaphragm, the drive or valve will move. This movement is fed back, via a linkage, to the camshaft which, as it turns, moves the lower beam and stretches the spring, so balancing the pressure in the bellows. As the force equalizes, the pilot valve returns to its central position and the cylinder or valve stops at the desired new position. By using only one connection to the pilot valve a spring-return diaphragm actuator can be controlled. Similarly, by reversing the connections a reverse-acting control can be achieved.

This pneumatic positioner is an example of a force-balance mechanism. A pulse input positioner which works on a movement balance principle is shown in *Figure 8.56*. Incoming pulses from the control system turn the stepper motor shaft and lever. This moves the balance beam and hence the pilot valve. As previously described this moves the valve or damper, which movement is fed back to the camshaft. The cam then moves the balance beam to restore the pilot valve to its central position. In this case the beam takes up a new position for each change in control signal.

By including a cam in the feedback mechanism it is possible to characterize the relationship between the control signal and the valve or damper movement, by choosing how the valve will move for changing control signals. This is particularly important when controlling flow which often has a non-linear relationship to valve position. Alternatively the control signal can be characterized by electronic means and a linear positioner used.

8.4 Control

In the previous pages we have shown how the pressure, level, flow rate and temperature of water and steam may be measured, indicated and a proportional signal transmitted. These are the basic requirements in operating a boiler or steam-using plant but more is needed. To take a simple analogy from the everyday world, the lowest level of steam generation is the humble kettle. Normally

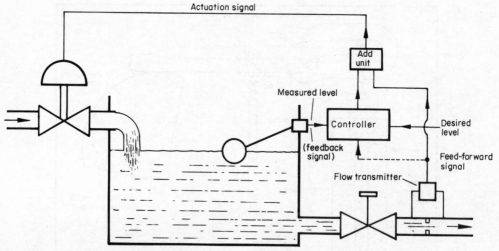

Figure 8.57 Installation equipped with simple on/off control

the visual indication of steam issuing from the spout enables the operator to apply some control action by turning off the source of heat. More freedom is given to the operator if remote indication is used by means of an audible whistle. A significant further step is taken, however, in recognizing the limitations of the operator when an automatic cut-out is used to apply a control action without any involvement of the operator. Both efficiency in fuel consumption and the safety level are increased.

And so it is with the larger world of boilers and steam plant; the demands of efficiency and safety lead to the use of some measure of automatic control. This section therefore first discusses the basic principles of control and then shows these principles in action on small and large boilers.

Basic principles

There are four common types of control action; on/off, proportional, integral and derivative. These, and their combination, will now be described.

On/off control

The simplest form of control, which is entirely suitable for small boilers or larger plant where conditions are very stable, is on/off, or two position, control. To illustrate this and the other forms of control, let us imagine the installation shown in *Figure 8.57.* A controller receives a measured-value signal, and a desired-value signal, and sends an actuation signal to the tank input control valve. A change in flow demand can be effected by opening

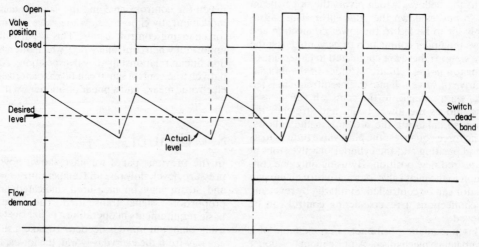

Figure 8.58   On/off control

or closing the output valve. For on/off control the controller is simply a switch, which will open or close the input valve, depending on whether the level is below or above the desired value.

In practice it is necessary, in order to avoid excessive switch wear, to have a 'dead-band' where no changeover occurs. Referring to *Figure 8.58*, at the start of the time chart the input valve is closed and the level is therefore falling. When the level reaches the bottom of the switch dead-band it will change over to open the input valve fully. For effective control this must enable sufficient water to flow in to increase the level rapidly, until the top of the dead-band is reached. The input valve will now close and the level begin to fall again.

If the output valve is now opened further to increase the output flow rate, the effect will be to steepen the graph which shows changes in level. The effect, as shown, is to increase the frequency of switching. It is, of course, essential that a fully open input valve can pass more water than a fully open output valve, or the water level must gradually fall with full demand. The control principle is the same if, instead of the water flowing out through a water valve, it evaporates into steam as in a boiler and passes out to a heating system or turbine.

Although the level stays, on average, at the desired value, it is constantly changing, so this form of control is not suitable where significant load changes are continually occurring.

An example of an on/off controller was described on p 143 under the heading 'Level'.

Proportional control (P)

The lowest level of so-called 'modulating control' is proportional control. In this the controller gives an output that is proportional to the difference between the desired value and the measured value, which is called the *deviation*. This can be expressed as

$$\text{Change in output} = -K \times (\text{deviation}) \qquad (8.1)$$

where K is the proportional band (PB). The PB is usually expressed as a percentage such that *Table 8.1* expresses the relationship between deviation, as a percentage of the maximum, the proportional band and the change in output.

Table 8.1 Relationship between deviation, the proportional band and change in output

Deviation	Proportional band	Change in output
50	50	100
50	100	50
50	200	25
50	1000	5

Figure 8.59 shows what happens to the same tank installation as before but with proportional control. A bias has been added to the output of the controller to hold the valve in mid-position which is, let us assume, the position which provides for the normal flow demand. As, in our example, the actual measured level is equal to the desired level there is no change in position of the valve. When a step change occurs in the flow demand the level will begin to fall, which will cause a deviation that in turn will proportionally open the valve. As the valve opens, the inlet flow rate will increase. As the level falls further, the valve will open further

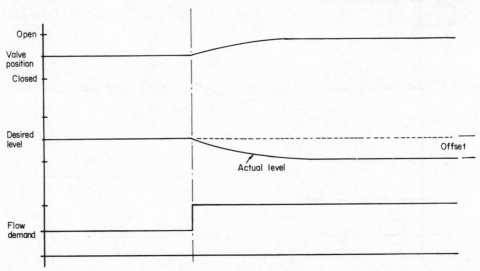

Figure 8.59   Proportional control

until the inlet flow rate exactly equals the outlet flow rate. At that point no further changes will occur until there is another flow demand change. As can be seen, there is a permanent drop in the actual level, called the *offset*, which is a fundamental characteristic of proportional control.

If the proportional band was raised (in percentage) the valve would not open so far and the time taken to stabilize would be longer and the eventual offset would be lower. Conversely if the PB was lowered the valve would open further, causing a shorter stabilization time and smaller offset. Depending on the plant delay times, however, too low a PB can cause overcorrecting and instability.

Where the flow demand, or steaming rate, is usually at a given level and any changes are small, then proportional control is quite adequate. Where larger, more prolonged, load changes are expected then the inevitable offset is undesirable.

Proportional plus integral control (P + I)

To overcome the offset problem, integral action can be added to the proportional control. With this, in addition to the normal proportional output, there is an addition which is proportional to both the deviation (× PB) and the time the deviation exists.

Thus with a deviation of 50% and a PB of 100%, and an integral action time (IAT) of 1 min, the output will immediately change by 50% by proportional control and then increase a further 50% over the next minute. In theory the output will keep increasing while a deviation exists or until full-scale output is reached. Integral action is also expressed as reset rate, in repeats per minute, which is the number of times the proportional change is repeated in a minute.

The effect of this added control function can be seen in *Figure 8.60*. When the flow demand change occurs, the level drops and the valve opens under proportional control, but now the valve opens further by integral action so that not only is the new demand met but the level begins to rise. Even while rising, integral action is still adding to the output of the controller, although now the proportional control will begin to reduce the output. When, because of the increase in input flow, the level returns to the desired value there will be no proportional action and no further change due to integral action. However, because of the accumulated output level, owing to integral action and plant lags there will be a slight oscillation in the level and valve positioning until the level settles at the desired value and the valve is in its new, higher flow position.

The precise characteristic of the curves shown is a function of the proportional band and the integral action time. Because of the effect of returning the measured value to the desired value this form of control is also called *reset*.

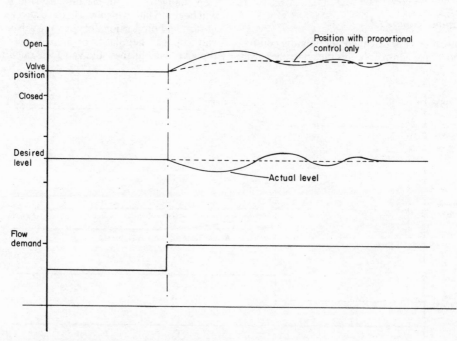

Figure 8.60   Proportional plus integral control

Proportional plus integral plus derivative control (P + I + D)

Where there are significant delays through the plant, as in temperature control loops, both proportional and integral control are a function of the size of the deviation and are therefore retrospective; this can cause unacceptably slow oscillation in the control. Derivative control can be added to speed up the control response and provide a form of anticipatory control. Derivative action will add to the output a signal which is proportional to the rate of change of the deviation. It will therefore give an output even when the deviation is quite small, but, if it is changing rapidly, it will begin to provide a correcting influence sooner than P + I control alone.

The effect is shown in *Figure 8.61*, which shows the shortened time to stable conditions. Because it responds to rate of change of deviation, derivative action is unsuitable for use with noisy signals, that is, signals which oscillate in random fashion about a mean level. These would cause constant, excessive changes in controller output.

Feedback control

The foregoing were all examples of feedback control, where the controller put out an actuation signal to alter the valve position and then received a feedback signal from the level measurement which gave information on the effect of that actuation signal. This is also called 'closed-loop control', as the controller, valve, tank and level measurement form a closed, interactive, loop. This form of control is inherently stable within the limits described in the previous sections.

Feed-forward control

If, instead of the feedback signal from the level measurement, the controller received only a signal from a flow transmitter as shown in *Figure 8.57*, this would be a form of open-loop control. For this control system to work, the precise flow characteristics relative to valve opening would have to be known, and the controller arranged to provide an output proportional to those characteristics, so that for any given output flow rate the precisely correct input valve position could be set. Any change in flow transmitter or controller calibration, or in the valve characteristics, could cause gradual changes in tank level, so this form of control is rarely used on its own.

The feed-forward signal, however, is very useful in providing an anticipatory signal to a feedback control system. In *Figure 8.57*, if we now consider the feed-forward signal from the flow transmitter as being added to the controller output in the 'add unit', then as soon as the output valve is opened the flow transmitter will sense the change in flow, even though the level has not changed significantly. (In a real plant with typical plant delays the delay between flow change and level change could be seconds or even minutes.) Before the controller receives any information of level change, on which it can act, the signal from the flow transmitter begins to open the input valve. The effect is that the drop in level is considerably reduced and more

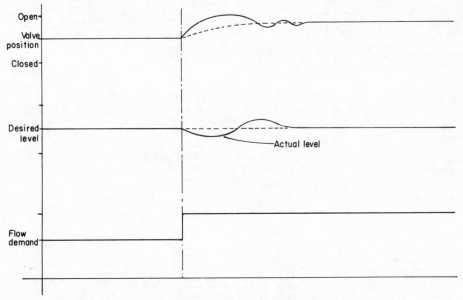

Figure 8.61 Proportional plus integral plus derivative control

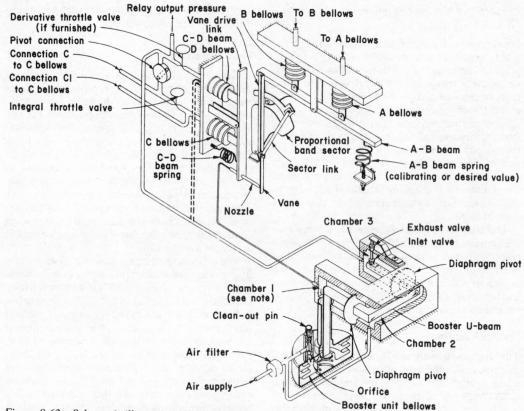

Figure 8.62   Schematic illustration of a pneumatic controller providing up to three-term control. Note: At balance the air pressure in chamber 1 is approximately 240 mbar

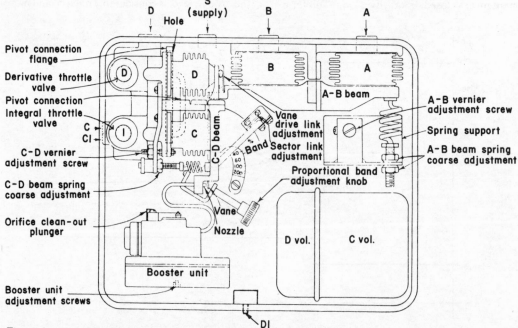

Figure 8.63   Pneumatic controller as illustrated schematically in Figure 8.62

stable control achieved. This form of control can be effectively used where derivative action would cause unacceptable instability.

Three-term controller

An example of a pneumatic controller providing up to three-term control $(P + I + D)$ is shown schematically in *Figure 8.62* with the actual controller shown in *Figure 8.63*. The principle of operation is also achieved by electronic means but can, perhaps, be more readily visualized in this pneumatic example.

For proportional-only action, the pivot connection in *Figure 8.62* is in the isolating position and the upper throttle valve fully open. If two signals are applied to bellows A and B, say the measured and desired value, the A–B beam will move in proportion to the pressure difference and the spring rate of the calibrating spring. This spring could also be used to apply a preset loading or internal desired value. If the A pressure is greater than the B pressure the vane drive link will rise and, by the action of the sector link, pivot slightly clockwise. The pivoting action is governed by the position of the sector link, the upper end of which is moved by the proportional-band sector, which has the effect of altering the gain of the vane movement to A–B beam movement. This is the proportional-band adjustment.

As the vane approaches the nozzle the booster unit output pressure from chamber 3 is increased as described on p 157 under the heading 'Pneumatic transducers'. This pressure is applied to the D bellows, which moves the C–D beam to pull the nozzle away from the vane, until balance is restored. The balance pressure is then the output pressure and is a function of difference in the A and B pressures and the proportional-band setting. This unit also provides for addition and subtraction, as will be shown to be necessary when control loops are discussed below. By using the A, B and C bellows for inputs, and considering the D bellows as output, the instrument gives the formula

$$\text{Change in D} = \frac{100}{PB}(\text{change in A} - \text{change in B})$$
$$+ \text{ change in C} \quad (8.2)$$

where PB is the proportional band expressed as a percentage.

When integral action is required, the pivot connection is turned to the vertical position, the lower throttle valve set as required to restrict the flow of air to the C bellows, and the Cl connection is plugged. When the output pressure rises by proportional action the leakage past the lower throttle valve into the C bellows causes the output to rise further. This will continue until the plant oper-

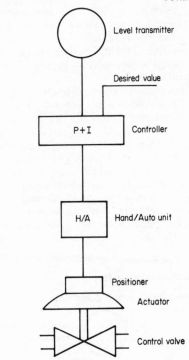

Figure 8.64   Single-element level control

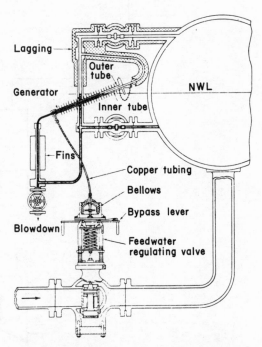

Figure 8.65   Self-acting proportional-only single-element control. NWL, normal water level

ation has restored the A–B beam to balance and the C–D beam is also at balance at the new output pressure. The measured value will then have been reset to the desired value. The time constant of the integral action is governed by the setting of the lower throttle valve.

Derivative action is obtained by changing the D bellows for a double unit, with the small inner bellows connected directly to the booster unit output pressure, shown by a dotted line in *Figure 8.62*. This means that the normal proportional restoring force of the D bellows is considerably reduced (up to 1/7th) and the output caused to be amplified, until air bleeding past the upper throttle returns the C–D beam to its proportional position. The degree and interval of this output pressure amplification depends on the speed at which the pressure changes, and on the setting of the upper throttle valve.

Single-element level control

A single-element level control loop is shown

schematically in *Figure 8.64*. The water level signal is compared with the desired value in the controller which, as described above, provides an output. This output goes to the hand/auto station or unit, allowing the operator to choose either to send the controller output straight on to the positioner and valve actuator, or to cut off the controller output and send out a manual signal, generated from within the unit and set by the operator. The loop would then be under manual control. The desired-value adjustment is often located in the hand/auto unit. In other respects the loop will behave as described in the previous sections.

A self-acting form of proportional-only single-element control is shown in *Figure 8.65*. The generator consists of an inner tube connected to the two drum level connections, and an outer finned tube connected to the bellows of the feedwater-regulating valve. At balance the water level in the inner tube is equal to the condensed water level of the outer tube. If the drum water level drops, the level in the inner tube follows, and the heat from

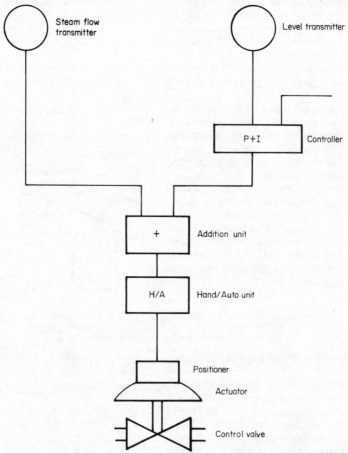

Figure 8.66 Use of a feed-forward signal to provide an increased feedwater flow to accommodate sudden steam demand

the steam in the portion of inner tube, just vacated by water, causes the water in the outer tube to flash into steam. The increased pressure is transmitted to the bellows, causing the control valve to open to admit more water into the drum.

Two-element control

In a boiler shell or drum, the effect of a sudden increase in steam demand will be to lower the pressure and cause bubbles of steam to form. This causes the level to 'swell' temporarily even though the quantity of steam/water is reducing and the level should be falling. This can have the unfortunate effect of the controller responding by closing the inlet feedwater valve when, in fact, more water is required to match the increased steaming rate.

To overcome this problem, a feed-forward signal generated by a steam flow transmitter is added to the controller output, as shown in *Figure 8.66*. When the steam flow changes, a signal is sent straight to the valve to change it by an amount proportional to the change in the steam flow. This provides an immediate increase to accommodate the increased demand, while the P + I controller will subsequently ensure that the water level is restored to the desired value.

Three-element control

A feature of two-element control is that the steam flow signal is always part of the valve-positioning signal. This is eliminated in three-element control, which also provides a feed-forward signal from a feedwater flow transmitter to compensate for any independent changes in feedwater pressure or flow, as shown in *Figure 8.67*. The feedwater flow signal is delayed in a delay unit for a time dependent on the plant lags. When the steam demand is increased the control loop operates in the same way as in two-element control, but the delayed feedwater flow signal will gradually reduce the contribution of the steam flow signal to zero and leave the P + I controller to re-establish the correct level.

The controller is usually placed between the add unit and the hand/auto unit so that the flow signals are also affected by the proportional band and integral action time. Other arrangements of the three signals are also used, with possibly additional signals from spray water flow or drum pressure used.

Steam pressure and combustion control of boilers

The end product of a steam-raising plant is steam flow to meet the demand at a constant pressure and, with superheat boilers, at a controlled tem-

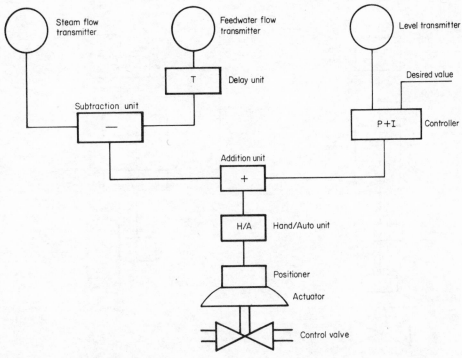

Figure 8.67   Three-element control

perature. (Hot-water plant has the same control philosophy but with water temperature being the master variable.) The product steam with its given flow, pressure and temperature is equivalent to an output of energy from the boiler. To balance this there must be an equivalent input of energy, usually in the form of the chemical energy of the coal, oil or gas being used as fuel.

Increased steam demand causes the pressure to drop. This change is the key variable that is used to increase the firing rate of the burner system by increasing both the fuel flow and the air flow. In addition, for efficiency and safe conversion of the fuel into heat energy the ratio of the air and fuel flows must be carefully controlled, as is described in Chapter 5.

The basic control system of a boiler is shown in *Figure 8.68*. A decrease in steam pressure, which indicates an increased steam flow, causes the fuel valve to open an appropriate amount, acting through the various units shown, and restores the energy balance. Where a number of boilers feed a common steam header then a single pressure signal is used to control them all, usually with a bias facility on the individual boiler masters to compensate for differing boiler characteristics. The fuel valve opening is delayed on increasing firing demand until the pressure control signal has, via the summing unit, opened the forced-draught (FD) fan damper. This ensures smoke-free operation. The FD fan damper positioner is characterized to provide the most efficient air/fuel flow ratio over the range of boiler loads. Final trimming of the air/fuel ratio is achieved by the fuel and air transmitters and the P + I controller. On falling loads the lead/lag unit provides no delay and the fuel valve closes in response to the steam pressure control signal ahead of a reduction in the air flow.

For small boilers, effective control is achieved using the device shown in *Figure 8.69*, which is, in effect, a pressure switch with an adjustable deadband, in conjunction with a linkage mechanism (*Figure 8.70*). A change in pressure beyond the switch dead-band causes a motor to be started.

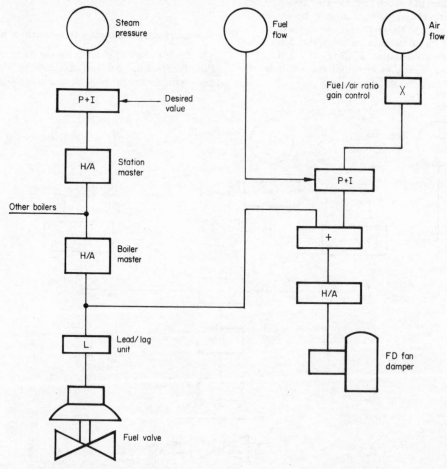

Figure 8.68   Basic control system of a boiler

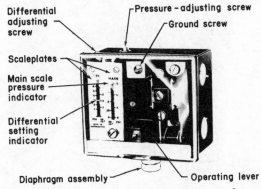

Figure 8.69 labels: Differential adjusting screw, Pressure-adjusting screw, Ground screw, Scaleplates, Main scale pressure indicator, Differential setting indicator, Diaphragm assembly, Operating lever

Figure 8.69 Combustion control system for a small boiler

This motor turns the control shaft, which alters both the fuel flow and the air flow. The characterization of the air/fuel ratio over the boiler load range is by means of the adjustable cam shown in *Figure 8.70*.

On a stoker-fired boiler the control system is

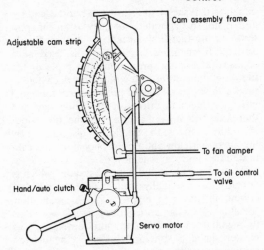

Figure 8.70 labels: Cam assembly frame, Adjustable cam strip, To fan damper, To oil control valve, Hand/auto clutch, Servo motor

Figure 8.70 Control of the air/fuel ratio for boiler combustion by means of an adjustable cam

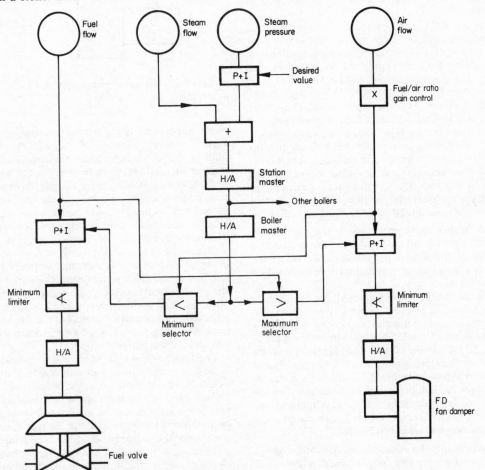

Figure 8.71 Control system for a stoker-fired boiler

similar to that shown in *Figure 8.68* but the lead/lag unit is not incorporated, as there is an inherent delay in the fuel flow variations. As fuel flow is difficult to measure, steam flow is used as a measure of energy throughout in the diagram and replaces the fuel flow transmitter in the diagram. A change in the air flow caused by the pressure control signal has an immediate effect on the firing rate and therefore the steaming rate. As the fuel input gradually changes, the air flow is also altered by the steam/air flow ratio controller until the calibrated fuel/air ratio is achieved.

A more sophisticated control system, which is nevertheless essentially similar to the one just described, is shown in *Figure 8.71*. A steam flow signal is used as an anticipatory signal, as well as the signal from the steam pressure controller. This master signal is split and becomes the desired value inputs to the air flow and the fuel flow P + I controllers, which are part of separate resetting control loops. This technique of using the output of one controller as the desired-valve input to one or more other controllers is known as 'cascade control'.

When the steam flow rises and, subsequently, the steam pressure drops, an increase in fuel flow is required. To prevent a smoking combustion condition from occurring, the increased master signal is prevented from reaching the fuel flow controller by the minimum selector, which passes only the lower of the two input signals. The master signal will, however, pass the maximum selector and cause the air flow controller to raise the air flow through the furnace. As soon as this increased signal is sensed and transmitted by the air flow transmitter, the master signal is freed to pass on to the fuel flow control loop. Similarly, on decreasing loads, the air flow is prevented from being reduced until the fuel flow is lowered.

A further safety precaution is the use of minimum signal limiters, to prevent either the fuel valve or the air damper being closed below the level consistent with minimum safe combustion conditions.

Small firetube package boilers do not normally need furnace draught control, but combustion chambers of larger watertube boilers are usually kept some 25 mmH$_2$O below atmospheric pressure, to prevent the escape of hot furnace gases into the surrounding atmosphere. A simple control loop is shown in *Figure 8.72*, where the induced-draught fan damper is controlled to maintain the furnace at the desired draught. This loop will constantly work to correct the changes brought about by the combustion control system.

Where a boiler is raising superheated steam, a temperature control loop is used. *Figure 8.73* shows a spray attemperator system, although by-

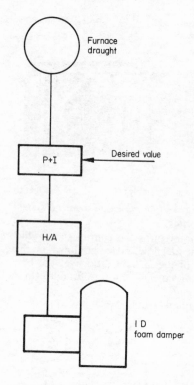

Figure 8.72   Furnace draught control loop for a watertube boiler

pass dampers and tilting burners are also used to vary the energy content of the steam. The large mass of steel in the superheater tubes means there is great thermal inertia in this part of the boiler, with the resultant delay in responding to temperature control action. To help overcome this, a three-term controller with derivative action is used, to provide an increased response to changes in steam temperature. The output of this controller is cascaded to a proportional-only control loop by being added to a temperature measurement from the inlet to the superheater tubes. This signal with the proportional controller and spray valve make up a fast-acting closed loop, which is gradually adjusted by the resetting control of the three-term controller, thus providing a control system which is both accurate and fast-acting.

The final control loop which will be mentioned is that of oxygen trim. Efficient combustion requires that most, if not all, of the oxygen in the air flow is used up in the combustion process. In practice a level of excess air is maintained in a predetermined ratio to fuel. As changes occur in the chemical characteristics of the fuel, temperature and moisture content of the air, or combustion characteristics of the furnace, so will the optimum fuel/air ratio. These changes are generally difficult

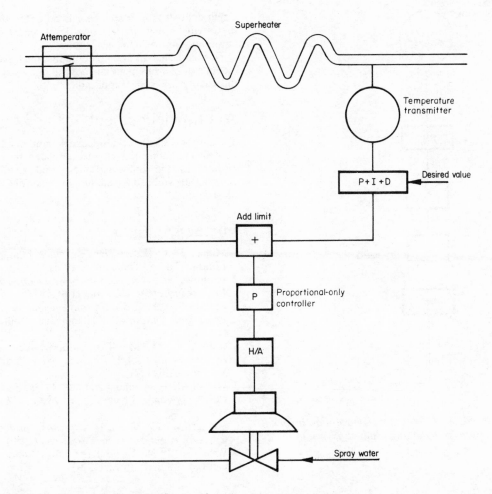

Attemperator

Superheater

Temperature transmitter

P + I + D

Desired value

Add limit

+

P

Proportional-only controller

H/A

Spray water

Figure 8.73 Temperature control loop with spray attemperator

to measure and therefore to incorporate in a control system. Residual oxygen in the flue or stack gases is, however, a good guide to the completeness of the combustion process and, once measured, may be used in a loop such as that shown in *Figure 8.74* to make trimming adjustment to the fuel/air ratio in the combustion control system. Oxygen analysers are available, based on zirconium probes which are inserted directly in the flue or stack to give a fast response to changes in oxygen and enable a small residual level to be maintained.

8.5 Conclusion

Our brief and inevitably incomplete survey of current practice in instruments and controls associated with steam is nearly complete. Mention must, however, be made of the fast-developing technology of computers with its vast potential for

complex, sophisticated control and fast analysis of hundreds of plant variables. In boiler practice more complex and 'intelligent' action can be taken in response to the changes. For instance, adaptive control is more readily achieved. This is where the proportional band, integral action and derivative action times, desired-valve settings and other normally preset values can be altered as the plant load varies to maintain optimum efficient control. Many plant measurements can be rapidly scanned and checked for being in an alarm state, with appropriate action being taken automatically and the information then being printed out for the operator's use. Vast quantities of information can be transmitted in digital form through a two-wire cable which travels in a ring round the various items in the control loops, so drastically reducing installation costs. With the advent of microprocessors bringing intelligent control down to the

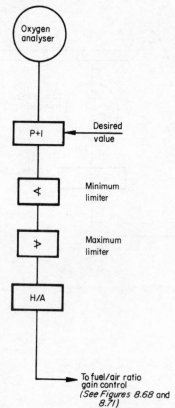

Figure 8.74   Combustion control loop involving provision for analysing residual oxygen in flue or stack gas

single control loop level, there is no doubt that there will be new and exciting developments in automatic control in the near future.

That said, there is also no doubt that the fundamentals of measurement and control discussed in this chapter will still be applicable.

Acknowledgement

The author wishes to acknowledge the considerable help in compiling this chapter provided by the authors of the following books and also to Babcock-Bristol Ltd for the supply of many of the illustrations.

Further reading

1 Miller, J. T. (Ed.). *The Instrument Manual*. London: United Trade Press (1975)
2 Andrews, W. G. *Applied Instrumentation in the Process Industries*. Houston: Gulf (1974)
3 Lipták, B. G. (Ed.). *Instrumentation in the Processing Industries*. Philadelphia: Chilton (1973)
4 Considine, D. M. (Ed.). *Encyclopedia of Instrumentation and Control*. New York: McGraw-Hill (1971)
5 Woodruff, E. B. and Lammers, H. B. *Steam Plant Operation*. New York: McGraw-Hill (1977)
6 Steingress, F. M. *Low Pressure Boilers*. Chicago: American Technical Society (1970)
7 Williams, J. N. *Steam Generation*. London: George, Allen & Unwin (1969)

9   Steam piping systems

9.1 Introduction

When the efficient use of steam is considered, the design of pipework* systems for conveying this and associated fluids must be given the same degree of attention as is accorded the efficient design of the steam-generating equipment and the ultimate user of the heat contained in the steam. So often, expensive measures which can be justified economically are adopted in the design of the steam generator and user whilst the ensuing saving in operating cost due to the improved efficiencies of these units can be partly or even wholly outbalanced by losses through leakage of steam and hot water from a badly designed or erected pipework system. Apart from the loss of heat, it should also be remembered that water suitable for boiler feed is not cheap to produce. Outage of plant for pipework repairs can also cause substantial losses.

As a contributor to the total cost of any power or process plant installation, the pipework should be designed so as to keep an economic balance between installation and operating costs.

Whilst there are often major factors governing the location of the major sections of any plant, one consideration should be the arrangement of the interconnecting pipework. Erection costs for pipework are often a disproportionate portion of the pipework total costs compared with those for the major sections of a plant, therefore ease of erection should be taken into consideration when determining the pipework arrangement.

9.2 Layout of pipework

The major factors governing the layout of a pipework system are:

1. the disposition of other plant to be interconnected;
2. the relative costs of accommodating and supporting pipework including anchoring where necessary;
3. access to valves, pressure-reducing and other equipment which may require access for operation or maintenance;
4. whether provision is to be made for expansion;

---

* The term *pipework* used in this section includes, in addition to the pipes, all of the component parts, eg valves, supports etc.

5. acceptable loading on plant arising from thermal movement of pipework;
6. provision for drainage;
7. avoidance of air or vapour locks;
8. access to pipework joints to ensure their integrity against leakage; and
9. safe design and erection.

During layout of the plant the pipework designers should be consulted for any suggestions that may produce an economic and satisfactory arrangement of pipework without adversely affecting other aspects of the plant.

Pipework inside a building can either be supported from the building structure or accommodated in trenches. The current cost of trenches in the floor and provided with covers can be as high as £300 per cubic metre of trench space compared with £20 per cubic metre of building space. Moreover although trenches would normally be provided with means for drainage it is not unknown for them to become flooded owing to blocked drains, with consequent increased costs due to corroded pipework and additional heat losses due to saturation of the insulation.

Often it may not be necessary to consider any increase in building space to accommodate pipework as the dimensions of the building to accommodate other plant may be the overriding factor. As a rule pipework is arranged above the ground-floor level and supported and anchored from the building steelwork. In some instances where the building structure is of light construction it may be necessary to anchor pipework at ground-floor level.

Pipework external to buildings can be either buried, accommodated in trenches, laid on sleepers at ground level or supported on trestles or bridges constructed of steel or concrete.

Unless there are aesthetic or access reasons for burying or elevating pipework systems, the most economical method is to arrange the pipework at ground level, which simplifies supporting and anchoring. Access to valves for operation and maintenance is also facilitated.

British Standard BS 3974 shows typical methods of supporting pipework[1]. Supports should be placed so as to minimize the effect of the additional loads on the piping imposed by valves and other heavier items of equipment.

9.3 Expansion of pipework

Whilst temperature changes in pipework systems due to ambient conditions can generally be ignored, pipework carrying steam or other high-temperature fluids must include provision for expansion. Carbon and low-alloy steel tubing will expand by approximately 0.13 mm per metre of length for each 10°C temperature increase. In addition, movement of plant due to temperature changes or other causes can increase the pipe movement which has to be accommodated. For example, the action of wind on a large outdoor boiler installation can cause an additional movement of the adjoining pipework which may equal or even exceed the movement due to expansion.

Provision for expansion is provided to limit the bending and torsional stresses in the pipework and also the loads and moments imposed by the pipework on adjoining plant and buildings. Plant manufacturers will usually specify the maximum loads and moments that can be accommodated to maintain any consequent misalignment of the plant within acceptable limits. Care should be taken to ensure that these limits are not set too low as this could lead to excessive pipework costs.

Pipework expansion can be accommodated by the following means:

1. expansion loops or offset bends formed from the same tubing as used for the pipework;
2. bellows expansion pieces;
3. swivel joints; or
4. stuffing box expansion pieces.

The first two methods are not subject to any wear and therefore do not normally require any further attention after installation. Methods (3) and (4) are based on one part being allowed to slide over the other, some form of packing being provided to seal against leaks. Some attention for the adjustment of the seals can therefore be expected.

Expansion loops and offset bends

For a pipework system in which the expansion is accommodated by method (1), it is possible to calculate manually the forces and moments acting on the system due to the expansion's being restrained but these calculations are laborious and time-consuming and it is modern engineering practice to use a computer for all but the simplest pipe configuration.

Nevertheless, it is useful to have some appreciation of the forces and moments that act on a piping system when the temperature changes and an illustration of these is given in *Figure 9.1* for an S bend. The effect of changing the arrangement of piping is also illustrated. The design shown in *Figure 9.1b* is obviously better than that of *Figure 9.1a* as the forces and moments are lower; this should be the preferred scheme if space permits. As the lowest moment occurs at A in *Figure 9.1b* this is the obvious end to which to attach any plant or equipment which could be sensitive to distortion from applied forces and moments.

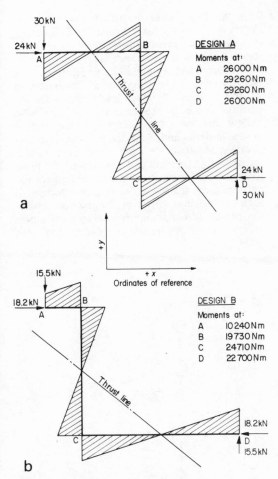

Figure 9.1 Alternative designs for an S bend showing variation in forces and moments

The resultant of forces X and Y acts along the thrust line which passes through the centroid of the pipe centreline, and the bending moment at any point on the pipe is equal to the product of this resultant force and the perpendicular distance from the thrust line. Thus the maximum bending moment occurs at the point furthest from the thrust line. The magnitude and location of the point of maximum stress will usually be given in the printout from the computer and may not occur at the point of maximum bending moment as stress levels can be increased by stress intensification at bends and branches. Values for stress intensification factors are given in British Standard BS 806 (ref. 3).

Hot stresses and forces and moments at the pipe ends can be reduced by making the pipe shorter by a proportion of the calculated expansion and pulling the pipework system into its finally required position during erection, a procedure known as *cold pull*.

The allowable stresses in the pipework may not necessarily be the governing factor in the required degree of flexibility as the end reactions must be within the values that adjoining equipment can safely sustain. Subsequent misalignment of running plant can cause rough running and possible breakdown and the advice of the plant manufacturer must be sought for practical limits to the pipe end reactions where this may occur. Considerable experience is required to establish a design possessing adequate flexibility but this method is limited only by the ability of the pipework material to withstand pressure and temperature and is thenceforth trouble- and maintenance-free.

Bellows expansion pieces

Bellows expansion pieces can be used as an alternative to catering for expansion by using expansion bends and loops. Bellows are formed from sheets of suitable material, rolled to form a tube and welded longitudinally. Convolutions are then formed mechanically or hydraulically to produce a form shown typically in *Figure 9.2*. The result is a section of pipe much more flexible axially and laterally than an equivalent length of ordinary pipe.

If the piping system is straight between two anchor points, an expansion piece as shown in *Figure 9.2* can be used but guides must be provided at the piping on either side of the expansion piece to ensure that the convolutions deform uniformly. Failure to fit guides can result in buckling or squirming as shown in *Figure 9.3*. An alternative method of catering for the expansion of a pipe system as shown in *Figure 9.1* is illustrated in *Figure 9.4* using three bellows expansion pieces. It will be noted that the expansion pieces are tied together to balance the thrust due to pressure on the pipe which, if not restrained, could result in excessive extension of the bellows. The restraint also ensures that each expansion piece deforms by

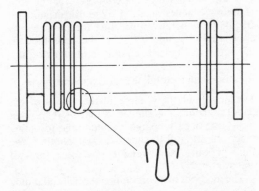

Figure 9.2 Typical bellows expansion piece showing the form of convolution

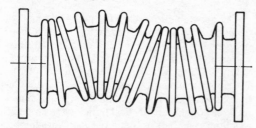

Figure 9.3   Bellows expansion piece showing squirm

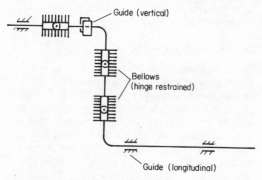

Figure 9.4   Alternative method of absorbing expansion in an S bend using bellows and incorporating guides

a proportionate amount and acts as a hinge.

Bellows are usually formed from stainless steel to resist corrosion, which could otherwise be a problem owing to the retention of water in the convolutions. The convolutions of a bellows are, however, highly stressed and where the working fluid may contain chlorides, nitrates, hydrogen sulphide or caustic alkalis there is a possibility of stress corrosion occurring. Some or all of these corrosive agents may be present in steam from a geothermal source or even in the water used for hydraulic testing. Care should therefore be exercised in the choice of material used for the convolutions. Stainless steel 321S12 to British Standard BS 1449 is generally satisfactory for most bellows applications but steel 310S24 to the same standard has better resistance to chloride stress corrosion.

Rotating, ball and sliding type expansion pieces

The action of these three further types of expansion absorber is similar in that the two main parts, one of each being attached to the adjoining pipe, are allowed to slide over one another, the fluid pressure being retained by some form of gland.

The methods of incorporating the ball and sliding types on a configuration of pipe similar to that shown in *Figure 9.1* are shown in *Figure 9.5a* and

9.5b. An example of the rotating-type joint is shown in *Figure 9.5c* and is capable of absorbing the large movements which occur on parts of steam-heated equipment such as presses.

The forces and movements from piping systems incorporating these three types of expansion absorber are usually much lower than when expansion bends in the pipework or expansion bellows are used but attention is required to ensure integrity and life of the pressure-retaining packing. Moreover the need to use packing limits the operating pressure and temperature for these joints whilst for the two former alternatives the only limits are the properties of the metals used in their construction. However, for practical reasons the operating conditions for bellows expansion pieces are usually restricted to 2 N/mm² and 300°C.

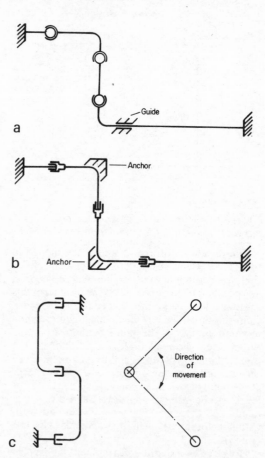

Figure 9.5   Further alternative methods of absorbing expansion on an S bend using (a) ball or (b) sliding joints. (c) Rotating joint for use where large movements have to be absorbed

9.4 Effect of wind and earthquake

Some mention has already been made of the effects of wind on the movements imposed on pipework. On exposed sites the movement due to wind may increase the bending stresses in the pipe so that the combined stress due to bending and pressure exceeds the yield stress and plastic deformation would take place. When the supply of hot fluid is shut off, cooling of the pipework could again result in yielding taking place, and when shutdown is frequent it is most important to consider the effect of wind to avoid fatigue problems.

Earthquakes can also result in excessive movement of pipework and where tremors are likely to occur provision should be made for limiting the movement. Suitably placed absorbers operating on the hydraulic damper system may be used. A typical design is shown in *Figure 9.6*.

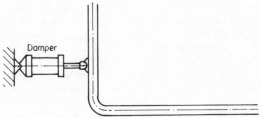

Figure 9.6   Example of the use of a hydraulic damper

It is not necessary to consider wind and earthquake effects occurring simultaneously.

9.5 Drainage

Steam pipes lose heat to the surroundings however well they are lagged. Superheated steam will merely be cooled but if the steam is saturated the cooling causes some of the steam to condense. Since the condensate remains in the presence of steam, the temperature of the water will be the saturation temperature corresponding to the steam pressure. If the wet steam is passed through steam turbines the water, travelling at high velocity relative to the blades and passages of the turbine, will damage the blades by erosion, and particularly if the water drops are large can cause serious damage. Steam flowing over water in a horizontal pipe will produce waves in the water and if the crest of a wave rises to the pipe surface, water can be driven forward in gulps or slugs. If the steam is used in reciprocating steam engines and a slug of water enters the cylinders, and if the volume of water exceeds the clearance volume in the cylinder, then the moving piston will be stopped suddenly and will then try to compress the water. Since water is virtually incompressible the effect is almost the same as hitting a solid. The kinetic energy of the rotating machinery (including the flywheel) can be absorbed by the material of the engine as strain energy, up to a limit, but beyond this limit the kinetic energy will cause the engine to disintegrate, the phenomenon being known as *hydraulic lock* since the water locks the engine and prevents movement. It is essential that condensate should be drained off any pipework to prevent damage by either erosion or hydraulic lock. In process heating vessels the heat supplied to the process is derived from the latent heat of the steam, and so forms condensate, and this also is in the presence of the steam and so is at saturation temperature. It too must be drained off to allow the steam free access to the surface to be heated.

Thus it is essential to ensure adequate drainage of steam mains to avoid:

1. the effects of water hammer and erosion by water accelerated to a high velocity by the steam;
2. the effects of corrosion fatigue due to the water draining back on to surfaces where the metal temperature is substantially higher than the saturation temperature at the operating pressure; and
3. the reduction in heating effect in heat transfer systems by the reduced area of contact between the steam and the heating surfaces.

It is usual where possible to arrange steam mains with a continuous fall in the direction of the steam flow. This ensures that drainage is adequate during the warming up of the pipework and plant when the steam flow will be low and when the drainage rate is usually greatest.

Where condensation of the steam occurs during operation, and not just at start-up, it is necessary to provide means for the continuous removal of drainage water by automatic means such as traps, orifices, etc. and this is dealt with in Chapter 10.

If condensation occurs only at starting up, some economy in cost can be achieved by providing manually operated drain valves only. It must be appreciated, however, that condensation of steam at initial temperatures substantially above saturation can occur if the steam flow is stagnant. This condensed steam draining on to a hotter surface can cause corrosion fatigue by intermittent local cooling. It is essential therefore that each system should be analysed for design and operation to ensure that the drainage is adequate. Typical examples of good and bad drainage practice are shown in *Figure 9.7*.

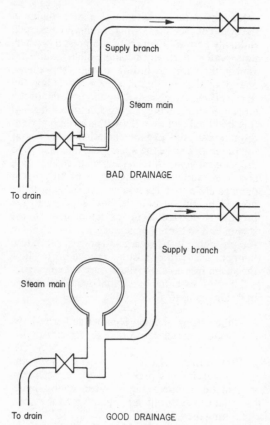

Supply branch

Steam main

BAD DRAINAGE

To drain

Supply branch

Steam main

To drain   GOOD DRAINAGE

Figure 9.7 Examples of good and bad drainage arrangements

With the supply branch from the top of the steam main and the isolating valve closed, steam can condense in the dead leg of the supply branch between the main and the isolating valve. Condensate can then flow back to the steam main and result in local cooling of the higher-temperature surfaces of the steam main. This may cause failure due to corrosion fatigue. In the other example any condensate is led direct to the drainage pot and if the connection to the supply branch is arranged sufficiently far from the main so that the metal temperature at the point of connection to the supply branch is not greater than the saturation temperature corresponding to the pressure then no similar local cooling will occur.

Pipe drainage is best arranged by welding a pot to the underside of the steam main at each low point in the system, and taking the drain pipe from the side of the pot. For saturated steam lines it is good practice to make the pot diameter the same as the pipe being drained; for superheated steam pipes the diameter of the pot may be reduced to 30% of the pipe diameter. The pot is used because it can take a slug of water travelling along the pipe whereas if the comparatively small-bore drain pipe

is just welded onto the steam pipe a slug of water could be carried across the end of the drain pipe. The pot is also useful for catching rust and debris. The drains catch water condensed in the pipe and of course the time when there is most condensation is on start-up from cold. By the use of special start-up drains, or by pipes by-passing traps and blowing direct, the warming-up process can be speeded with economy in time. The start-up drains or by-pass valves must be shut when the pipework is up to temperature and the traps take on their normal duty.

Since the water being drained off is at saturation temperature it is in effect at boiling point, and will boil (flash) either if heat is supplied, which can be prevented, or if the pressure falls below saturation pressure. If water at boiling point flows along a pipe the pressure will fall owing to fluid friction and, unless appropriate steps are taken, part of the water will flash into steam. The rate at which the drain pipe can discharge condensate is determined by the resistance to flow of a mixture of steam and water, and not by the water alone. This discharge rate will be lower than that for water alone. The simplest way of preventing the drain from flashing is to keep it under adequate static pressure, by arranging the drain pipework to have a vertical fall greater than the friction pressure drop before any horizontal section. Where the water passes through a trap there will inevitably be a fall in pressure at the trap itself and, in order to ensure an adequate flow capacity for the trap, it is usual to make the discharge pipe from the trap larger than the upstream pipe.

Where the drainage water is to be recovered, or where the water in flash vessels is to be recovered, it is often necessary to pump the water to some other receiver. If boiling water enters a pump it is liable to flash at the eye of the pump and this may seriously damage the pump by cavitation. In this phenomenon, bubbles of steam, formed when the pressure drops, collapse when the pressure rises again. The water flowing into the bubbles moves at very high velocity and can quickly erode the metal of the pump impeller. Here again is a situation where flashing must be prevented, and this is best done by maintaining an adequate head at the pump, the *net positive suction head* (NPSH), above the vapour pressure corresponding to the water temperature, which will usually be recommended by the pump maker. The NPSH must at the very least exceed the pressure drop corresponding to the kinetic energy needed for the water to flow into the pump, plus pipework and valve friction, etc., and plus a margin adequate to cover any error or change.

Drainage water from traps is at boiling point and proper arrangements must always be made so that the drains do not cause danger.

9.6 Steam separators

Where condensate cannot be dealt with by normal drainage arrangements (for example, when large quantities of water are present), it is usual to provide some form of mechanical separation. The simplest form consists of a vessel larger in diameter than the pipework, in which the direction of steam flow is subject to an abrupt change so that the higher-density water is deflected from the steam flow and collected for drainage. A typical unit is shown in *Figure 9.8*. More sophisticated designs are available employing directional vanes to produce a swirling action of the steam and to separate the water droplets by centrifugal action. It should be borne in mind, however, that all separators introduce additional friction losses and these must be taken into account when assessing pressure losses in the steam system.

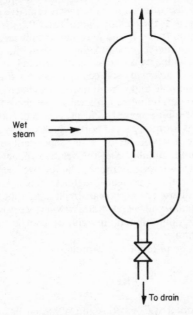

Wet steam

To drain

Figure 9.8 Typical steam separator

9.7 Types and materials for piping

The use of cast iron for pipework systems is confined to those systems where the fluid temperature is less than 220°C but even at these temperatures, for systems where substantial expansion has to be accommodated it is normal to employ steel tubing.

Special care should be taken to avoid cast iron where shock loading, such as may occur with water hammer, could occur.

Seamless steel tubing is manufactured by hot drawing of a pierced billet. To obtain closer tolerances on thickness and outside diameter the tubes may be finally cold-finished.

Welded tubing is formed from plate or strip and welded by one of the following processes:

1. Buttwelding — the longitudinal joint is butt-welded in a furnace as a continuous process.
2. Electrical resistance welding and induction welding — the longitudinal seam is welded by passing an electric current across the seam. No filler metal is used.
3. Submerged arc welding — the seam may be either spiral or longitudinal and is welded by an automatic submerged arc welding process.

Tube sizes are usually classified according to outside diameter (o.d.) and each of these processes results in a close tolerance of approximately ±1% on the o.d. However, other methods of manufacture can involve considerable tolerances of up to ±15% on thickness. Consequently the quoted internal diameter is usually termed 'nominal' as it is dependent on the manufactured thickness.

The materials and methods of construction used in tube manufacture govern the pressures and temperatures for which the tubes can be used and sometimes the life of the tubes under working conditions. All the relevant information on allowable working pressures and temperatures and the related design stresses are detailed in the appropriate British Standards. As quality control of manufacture is developed and experience is gained on the safe working stresses which can be adopted in design, changes are made in the Material and Application Standards and therefore the latest issue of these British Standards should always be referred to before a design exercise is undertaken. However, *Table 9.1* gives general information on the current (1978) values recommended for the maximum pressures and temperatures for the various tube materials and construction.

Although piping carrying hot fluids can be subject to stress due to bending or torsion, these effects are not taken into account in determining the thickness of tube to be ordered. This is established on the basis of the hoop stress, and the minimum thickness t_{min} of tubing is calculated from the equation

$$t_{min} = \frac{pD}{2Se + p} \tag{9.1}$$

where t_{min} is the minimum thickness (mm), p is the design pressure (N/mm^2), D is the outside diameter (mm), S is the maximum permissible design stress at the operating temperature (N/mm^2) and e is a factor varying between 0.9 to 1.0 depending on the quality and construction of the tubes (*see appro-*

Table 9.1   Maximum pressures and temperatures for various tube materials

Material	Tube standard	Construction*	Maximum permissible: pressure (N/mm²)	Maximum permissible: temperature (°C)
Carbon steels	BS 1387	BW	2.1	260
Carbon steels	BS 3601	BW, SAW	2.1	260
Carbon steels	BS 3601	ERW, S	No restriction	380
C and C Mn steels	BS 3602	ERW, S, SAW	No restriction	480
Alloy steels 1% or ½% Mo	BS 3604	S	No restriction	570
2¼% or 1% Mo	BS 3604	S	No restriction	580
½% Mo or ½% Mo, ¼% V	BS 3604	S	No restriction	580

From BS 806 : 1975

* BW, buttwelded; SAW, submerged-arc-welded; ERW, electric-resistance-welded; S, seamless

priate standard). The value calculated is the minimum value acceptable for a straight pipe not subject to corrosion internally or externally. An example is steam and condensate mains which are protected externally and where the condensate is chemically treated to render it inert and also where adequate drainage arrangements are provided. Where these conditions are not met it is usual to provide additional thickness to allow for corrosion. For pipes which are to be bent, a further increase in thickness is required to compensate for thinning during bending.

When the thickness of the tube required to keep the stress within the allowable limit in the appropriate standard has been established, sufficient flexibility must be allowed in the arrangement of the pipework system to ensure that the vector sum of the longitudinal pressure stress and the bending and torsional stresses does not exceed the mean stress which would cause rupture in the design life at the design temperature. In checking this condition it is permissible to take account of any cold pull which can be applied to the piping system when calculating the bending component of the combined stress.

Some pipework application standards also require the maximum stress range and any sustained stress to be checked, and reference should be made to the appropriate code.

9.8 Calculation of pressure losses due to friction

The friction loss in a pipework system is given by

$$P = \left(F\frac{L}{D} + K_s\right)\rho \frac{u^2}{2} \times 10^{-5} \qquad (9.2)$$

where F is the friction factor for a straight pipe, L is the length of straight pipe (m), D is the diameter

of the pipe (m), K_s is the sum of the friction factors K for the fittings, u is the mean velocity of fluid (m/s), ρ is the density (kg/m³) and P is the pressure drop (bar). L and D can be readily measured and the mean velocity is obtained by the rate of flow divided by the cross-sectional area.

There are many sources of values for F and K; considerable experimental work has been carried out to determine suitable values for these factors for various designs of bends, valves, tees and other fittings forming part of normal pipework systems.

The friction factor F is dependent on the Reynolds number and the relative roughness of the pipe's internal surface. The relative roughness is the ratio of a mean roughness height k to the pipe diameter. For commercial steel tubes used for steam and water systems where corrosion is unlikely or inhibited, the value of k can be taken as 0.05 mm.

The semi-empirical formula

$$\frac{1}{F^{\frac{1}{2}}} = -2\log\left(\frac{2.51}{\mathrm{Re}\,(F)^{\frac{1}{2}}} + \frac{k}{3.7D}\right) \qquad (9.3)$$

developed by Colebrook and White can be used to calculate F. However, it is laborious to perform this calculation for each case and values for F can be obtained direct from *Figure 9.9*.

Values of K for bends in commercial pipes are given in *Table 9.2*, and values for globe and gate valves in *Table 9.3*. The K factor for a swing type of check valve may be taken as 1.0.

The friction losses in tees are dependent on the ratio of area of main to branch and also the ratio of flow rate in main and branch and the angle between the main and branch. It is outside the scope of this book to examine all cases but as right-angled tees are common in pipework systems it is appropriate to include some K values for this particular case (*Table 9.4*). These values for K for tees all relate to the velocity in branch 3.

Table 9.2   K factors for bends for various values of R/D ratio of bend radius to pipe diameter and for angles of bend of 30°, 60°, 90° and 180°

	K factor					
Angle of bend	*R/D* *1.0*	*R/D* *1.5*	*R/D* *2.0*	*R/D* *3.0*	*R/D* *4.0*	*R/D* *5.0*
30°	0.09	0.09	0.1	0.11	0.11	0.12
60°	0.22	0.18	0.18	0.18	0.18	0.19
90°	0.36	0.27	0.24	0.22	0.24	0.27
180°	0.5	0.30	0.27	0.33	0.43	0.5

Table 9.3   K factors for various sizes of globe, lift check and gate values with valves fully open

Valve diameter *(m)*	*K factor*	
	Globe valves and *lift check valves*	*Gate*
0.3	3.9	0.07
0.2	4.2	0.08
0.1	4.8	0.10
0.05	4.8	0.18
0.02	9.0	0.4
0.01	15.0	0.55

If the size of branch 3 and therefore the velocity differs from the corresponding values for other sections of the pipework system such as valves, bends, straights, etc. then the friction loss for tees should be calculated separately and added to the friction loss of the remainder of the pipework system.

The equation for friction loss given on p 188 would then become

$$P = \left((F\frac{L}{D} + K_1)\frac{U_1^2}{2} + K_2\frac{U_2^2}{2} \right) \rho \times 10^{-5}$$
$$(9.4)$$

where K_1 is the sum of the K factors for bends, valves and other fittings where the velocities at entry and exit are the same, U_1 is the velocity in straight pipes and fittings with the same velocity at entry and exit, K_2 is the sum of the factors for tees, U_2 is the velocity in the equivalent of branch 3, ρ is the density (kg/m^3) and P is the pressure drop (bar).

Table 9.4   Values of K for combining and dividing of flow in right-angled tees

Values of friction factor K
$K_{1\to3}$ refers to flow from branch 1 to branch 3)

Combining **flow**	Q_1/Q_2 *0.25*	Q_1/Q_2 *0.5*	Q_1/Q_2 *0.75*	Q_1/Q_2 *1.0*
Area ratio A_1/A_3	*Values of $K_{1\to3}$*			
0.25	0.6	4.0	7.0	12.0
0.5	0.5	1.0	2.4	3.5
0.75	0.2	0.6	1.2	1.7
1.0	0.2	0.4	0.85	1.2
	Values of $K_{2\to3}$			
0.25	0.35	0.7	0.95	1.2
0.5	0.35	0.6	0.75	0.9
0.75	0.35	0.52	0.62	0.67
1.0	0.35	0.5	0.52	0.55

Values of friction factor K

Dividing **flow**	Q_1/Q_3 *0.25*	Q_1/Q_3 *0.5*	Q_1/Q_3 *0.75*	Q_1/Q_3 *1.0*
Area ratio A_1/A_3	*Values of $K_{3\to1}$*			
0.25	2.3	6.0	12.0	16.0
0.5	1.15	1.4	1.9	3.5
0.75	0.9	0.97	1.25	1.6
1.0	0.85	0.87	1.1	1.28
All area *ratios*	*Values of $K_{3\to2}$*			
	0	0	0.2	0.4

Q_1, Q_2, Q_3 are the flow rates, K the friction factor

Sizing of pipework

Except where it is desired to dissipate excess pressure by friction loss in the piping system, the sizing of piping is generally determined on an economy basis. A comparison is therefore made between the costs of a range of sizes of piping and the costs of generating the pressure to overcome the friction losses in the pipework system. The following example will illustrate the method:

Example

A pipework system comprising 56 m of straight piping with 8 bends, 1 gate valve and 1 globe valve is required to deliver 330 m³/h of water. Find the most economical size of piping.

It is first necessary to establish the range of piping sizes to be considered. A velocity of 2 m/s is therefore adopted to determine the middle range of piping sizes. Taking a mean velocity of 2 m/s requires a pipe with an internal diameter of

$$D^2 = \frac{Q}{2827 \times V} = \frac{330}{2827 \times 2} \quad \therefore D = 0.24 \text{ m}$$

0.24 m is not a standard size of tube, the nearest standard size according to BS 3600 being 0.225 m. For a bore of 0.225 m the velocity is 2.11 m/s. This suggests that the pipe sizes 0.3, 0.25, 0.225, 0.2 and 0.15 m should be examined.

The friction loss in the 0.225 m bore would be as follows:

$$\text{Velocity head} = \rho \, \frac{V^2}{2} \times 10^{-5} \text{ bar}$$

$$= 10^{-3} \times \frac{2.11^2}{2} \times 10^{-5} = 0.022 \text{ bar}$$

From *Figure 9.9* the friction factor F for a flow of 330 m³/h (91 kg/s) through a pipe of bore 0.225 m is 0.0149. The value of K for bends, gate valve and globe valve is 0.24, 0.08 and 4.2 respectively as shown in *Tables 9.2, 9.3* and *9.4*. The calculation for friction loss is as follows:

Summation of K values

(a) straight pipe $\dfrac{0.0149 \times 56}{0.225}$	= 3.7
(b) 8 bends $= 8 \times 0.24$	= 1.92
(c) 1 gate valve, bore 0.225 m	= 0.08
(d) 1 globe valve, bore 0.225 m	= 4.2
Total	9.9

Pressure drop $= 9.9 \times 0.022 = 0.218$ bar

$$\text{Power requirement} = \frac{\text{mass flow} \times \text{pressure}}{\text{efficiency} \times 10}$$

$$\text{Mass flow} = \frac{330}{3600} \times 1000 \text{ kg/s} = 91 \text{ kg/s}$$

Assuming the overall efficiency is 0.66,

$$\text{Power requirement} = \frac{91 \times 0.218}{0.66 \times 10}$$
$$= 3 \text{ kW}$$

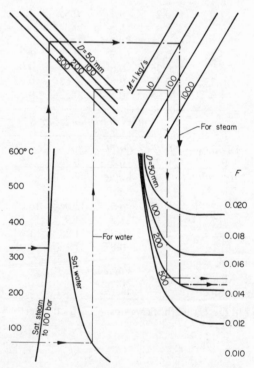

Figure 9.9 *Friction factor F for flow of steam and water in commercial-quality steel pipes, hydraulic roughness 0.05 mm*

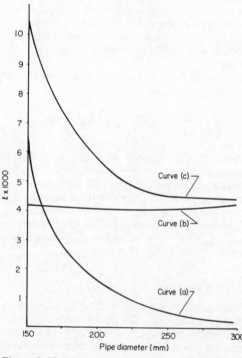

Figure 9.10 *Economical sizing of pipework*

We now have basic figures for comparing overall operating charges. A capitalized value of 1 kW of power is assumed to be £300, which can be adjusted to suit specific installations. Alternatively the cost of the installation for each size of pipe can be debited with the charge made by the power supplier.

Pipe size (m)	Power requirement (kW)	Capitalized value
0.3	0.712	£213
0.25	1.771	£531
0.225	3.0	£900
0.2	5.4	£1620
0.15	22.78	£6834

Pipe size is then plotted against the capitalized value of the power consumed to produce curve (a) in *Figure 9.10*.

The installed costs for the pipework systems based on these various sizes of piping can be assessed as follows, including adjustments for the variation in costs of pumps, motors and cabling to meet the differing duties:

Pipe size (m)	Pipework cost	Cost of pumps, motors, etc.	Total installation cost
0.3	£2228	£2000	£4228
0.25	£1792	£2200	£3992
0.225	£1496	£2500	£3996
0.2	£1275	£2800	£4075
0.15	£917	£3200	£4117

Pipe size is then plotted against total installation to produce curve (b) in *Figure 9.10*.

To determine the most economical size of piping, curve (a) is added to curve (b) to produce curve (c). In this example the choice of pipe size lies between a bore of 0.25 m and one of 0.3 m.

The installation cost of the 0.25 m bore system is less than that for the 0.3 m bore system. The actual choice therefore demands some judgement of possible future trends on loan charges and operating costs to decide whether these are likely to offset the small difference in total installation cost.

The above example is based on costs of low-pressure piping. At higher design pressures the variation in cost of different sizes of piping would be greater. Any insulation and supports for the pipework would tend to be greater in cost as the piping increased in bore. These factors would increase the slope of curve (b) without affecting curve (a), and this trend would therefore tend to favour smaller piping and thus higher velocities.

The optimization of pipework sizes for steam service can be done on a similar basis using a comparison of installation and operating costs.

However the number of items to be considered is much greater and the following should be taken into account:

1. Effect of change in design pressure on the capital cost of the steam generator or steam user due to variation in frictional loss.
2. Additional pumping costs of returned feedwater due to any increase in design pressure of steam generator.
3. Change in enthalpy of steam due to variation in heat loss from pipework. This could affect the output or efficiency of the steam user, which would result in changes in operating costs.
4. Capital cost of pipework installation.

The pressure drop normally adopted in steam services is usually about 5% of the initial steam pressure and this value could be adopted for a first approximation of pipe sizes.

9.9 Velocities in pipework

In some instances the use of proprietary equipment may determine the allowable pressure drop and this will determine the maximum allowable velocity and hence the size of piping. It should, however, be borne in mind that more conservative velocities should be used where erosion of the pipework at bends or changes in direction of flow and through valves and similar equipment can be severe enough over the life of the plant to necessitate replacement.

Erosion can be severe in the case of piping carrying wet steam or where abrasive matter is present in water, but as water used in connection with steam or hot water services is required to be free of abrasive matter, erosion is not a particular problem at the velocities normally adopted.

Sudden closure of a valve in a water pipeline can cause an excessive rise in pressure, normally called *water hammer*, and this pressure rise is directly proportional to the velocity of the fluid for any specific time of closure of the valve. At high velocities this pressure rise can be destructive, particularly if parts of the pipework system have low ductility, and some means such as an air vessel or similar device may be required to protect against fracture of such parts.

It is not being suggested here that water hammer should be a factor in determining the design velocity for the fluid in a pipework system; the idea is merely to draw attention to the effect that the magnitude of the velocity has on the pressures created by this phenomenon. High surge pressures can occur at low initial velocities if the closing of the valve is too sudden and the problem becomes one of arranging a suitable valve closing time.

Cast-iron valves and fittings are particularly liable to failure under the type of shock loading that occurs with water hammer, and this is discussed in Chapter 3.

In pipework systems for space heating, high velocities can cause a noise problem.

Taking account of the above considerations, *Table 9.5* gives a range of velocities normally used.

Table 9.5   Typical velocities of fluids

Fluid	Service	Velocity (m/s)
Water	Space heating	2 – 4
Water	Boiler feed	3 – 6
Saturated steam		30 – 50
Superheated steam		50 – 100

9.10 Supports and anchors

The design and use of supports are important aspects of pipework installations that are often overlooked when the design and arrangements of the pipework system are being prepared. It should be appreciated that the supporting system is an integral part of the pipework system and can influence the safety and efficiency not only of the pipework but of associated plant. Unless provided with a continuous support over its complete length a pipework system is subject to bending moments due to self-weight and the weight of the fluid in the pipe. Pipework systems above ground are not usually continuously supported and therefore the spacing and designs of supports can materially influence the external loading on pipework and plant.

For pipes carrying steam, the weight of the fluid can be ignored but in instances where hydraulic testing is carried out from time to time, the permanent supports must cater for the additional weight of the fluid. Alternatively they must be supplemented by temporary supports suitable for this purpose. A pipework system is usually anchored at its extremities as it is not usually possible to allow the plant to which the pipework is attached at these points to move. Intermediate anchors should be employed sparingly, and should generally be employed only where excessive movements of the pipe would:

1. interfere with the operation of extended spindles on valves owing to the resultant misalignment;

2. cause transmission of forces due to contact with other services, thus also limiting free movement; or
3. cause misalignment of other plant.

Before the advent of computer programs for the analysis of pipework flexibility, intermediate anchors were often introduced to simplify the manual calculations and reduce the time for flexibility analysis. Limitation of pipework movement in a specific direction can often be achieved, however, by substituting a guide for an anchor. Thus movement of the pipework can be allowed in one or both of the other directions, often without increasing the maximum stress in the pipework or jeopardizing the operation of other plant because of increased forces and moments. Guides are therefore preferred to intermediate anchors.

If pipework is arranged just above ground level, intermediate supports can take the form of shoes attached to the underside of the pipes. These shoes rest on bearer plates supported on sleepers at ground level or on some form of stool. The shoes may then slide over the bearer plates.

Care must be exercised in the design of shoes and bearers to ensure freedom of movement in the direction required and it is desirable for an anti-friction material to be placed between the shoe and the bearer. PTFE is a suitable material provided the maximum temperature of the material is not exceeded. Whatever provision is made to minimize friction it is wise to provide stops to prevent movement beyond that calculated for the pipework system. Unequal frictional forces can result in sticking at some supports where the friction is greatest and excessive movement where the friction is least.

Where temperatures are too high for proprietary anti-friction materials because of conduction of heat from the pipe to the shoe, it is common practice for rollers to be placed below the shoes. If the direction of movement has been determined correctly the rollers can be positioned with their axles normal to the direction of movement resulting from the whole of the horizontal expansion. The shoe type of support is also often employed for the support of pipework from trestles on which the pipework has been elevated to provide access underneath and in trenches where vertical space is very limited.

Shoes are also sometimes used to support a vertical pipe but if thermal movement is involved the shoe-type support cannot be used in more than one position unless some automatic means are provided to compensate for expansion at the other points of support of the vertical pipe. By far the commonest and usually the most economical method of supporting pipework is by suspension from adjacent structures. Where no vertical movement of the pipework will occur, this type of support can comprise a rod attached to an overhead structure and provided at the other end with a clip around the pipe. If it is necessary to compensate for vertical expansion then a helical spring with a predetermined compression to suit the pipeload is inserted into the hanger system.

Both of these types of hanger give almost complete freedom of movement in any horizontal direction whilst still maintaining vertical support but it is usual to limit the angularity of the hanger rod to 5° to the vertical.

Where a single spring support is used, expansion of the pipe will modify the initial compression of the spring and as the force which the spring exerts is proportional to the deflection, the supporting force will be different for the hot as compared with the cold condition. It is general practice to limit this variation in supporting force to 25% of the load being supported at that point. Where the variation in supporting force is likely to be greater than 25% of the load being supported, consideration should be given to the fitting of constant-load supports. By employing a system of levers with one or more springs it is possible to arrange for the variation in leverage to compensate for the variation in spring load due to pipe movement and thus attain the ideal of an almost constant supporting force.

The use of constant-load supports ensures that pipe movements and the resulting forces, moments and stresses can be calculated manually with a reasonable degree of accuracy. Where the supporting forces are variable owing to the expansion of the pipework it is advisable that this variation is taken into account during the flexibility calculations, which should preferably be done on a computer using a program that includes factors compensating for these variations in support loads. Failure to take these variations into account can result in moments and forces higher than those calculated. These may not become immediately evident, as yield of the piping material may not result in failure until later in the life of the system. If the system is frequently shut down and started up, the repeated temperature changes on the pipework system together with the associated expansion and contraction could result in failure of the pipework system owing to fatigue. Even if such failure does not occur, the additional forces and moments may cause misalignment of running plant or distortion of flanges with consequent leakage.

Where pipework can be subject to vibration induced either by the fluid or attached equipment or to movement due to wind or seismic action, it is advisable to provide bracing to limit the amplitude of movement. The effects of vibration can often be absorbed by simple bracing to a stationary structure. However, where seismic forces are involved, the structure of the building and usually the plant will move horizontally during an earthquake tremor whereas owing to the inertia effect of the pipework its movement will lag behind the movement of buildings or plant to which the pipework is attached. Subsequent efforts of the pipework to restore the *status quo* result in vibration which, if of sufficient amplitude, can be destructive. Hydraulic or pneumatic damping can successfully prevent failure in these instances.

9.11 Pipe joints

If the pipework system conveys the heating or power medium from the generator to the user with the minimum loss of pressure, temperature and total heat it has performed the duty for which it was designed. Any losses in the properties of the operating medium are readily calculable and are usually determined to give the most economic system from the aspect of combined installation and operating costs. However, it is often assumed that once the arrangement, diameter and thickness of the piping, thickness of lagging and location and design of hangers have been established then it is only necessary to erect the pipework system to ensure trouble-free operation in line with the economics governing the design. This could well be the case if all joints between pipes, and between pipe, valves and other equipment are welded and of guaranteed integrity. Welded joints should always be used if possible.

In a few instances where joints are required to be readily broken to facilitate removal of equipment for maintenance or replacement and where welded joints are not feasible, it is necessary to use flanged or similar joints. The British Standard BS 4504 sets out the scantlings and bolting for flange joints to retain fluids over a range of pressures and temperatures and provided the joints are designed to this standard, a reasonable life free of trouble can be expected under steady pressure and temperature conditions. However, where pressures and particularly temperatures are subject to cyclic variation, considerable trouble with leakage from flanged joints can be experienced. For these conditions all joints should, as far as practicable, be buttwelded. Where it is necessary to use flanged joints to facilitate dismantling, the following precautions can be taken to minimize troubles due to leakage:

1. The flanges should be located:
   (a) If possible at a point where any bending moments or external forces on the pipe-

work are at a minimum. This will reduce external loading on the flange and bolting.

(b) In such a position that access to the bolting is adequate to ensure that all nuts can be properly tightened. Failure to observe this precaution will inevitably result in early leakage of the fluid. It should not be assumed that special spanners requiring the minimum of access will be either available or used, and sufficient space should therefore preferably be allowed so that tightening of nuts can be carried out using standard-length open-jawed spanners.

(c) If possible, remote from areas where fluctuations in temperature and/or pressure can occur such as downstream of an orifice or other flow control device. This is a condition which often occurs in drain systems and *Figure 9.11* indicates a possible arrangement for minimizing trouble. The orifice is placed close to the drain collecting vessel with no flanges downstream.

2. It is important to make the right choice of gasket when the pipework system is being installed. Savings in first cost can sometimes result in incomplete and unsatisfactory sealing where the cost of the loss of energy in the fluid plus the cost of replacing the fluid can far outweigh the extra first cost to obtain a satisfactory gasket. Repairs to joints will often entail costly outages of plant and where an outage has had to be deferred, some dressing of the joint faces may be necessary owing

to scouring by the leaking fluid before a joint can be satisfactorily remade.

3. The faces of the adjoining flanges should be true and flat and also parallel to each other. Springing of pipework to connect adjoining flanges, except where it is included in the design as cold pull to compensate in part for expansion, will only result in unknown forces on the pipework which can affect the pressure exerted on the gasket and thus the effectiveness of the seal. The mating surfaces of the flanges should not be too smooth, a serrated face produced by a continuous spiral groove being preferred; the face should be free of any radial grooving.

For steam and hot water services where the pressure and temperature of the fluids remain almost constant, the fitting of a plain gasket of compressed asbestos or similar material capable of retaining some flexibility under the pressure and temperature conditions obtaining will generally suffice to produce a leak-free joint, providing the other requirements stated for flanged joints have been met.

Where there are periodic major fluctuations in temperature and pressure of the working fluid, a greater degree of gasket flexibility and therefore recovery is required. Spiral-wound gaskets formed by winding a sandwich of thin stainless-steel strip and a strip of asbestos paper or other heat-resisting fabric in the form of a spiral and sealing the ends against unwinding by welding gives a greater degree of recovery. As this type of gasket, owing to its greater flexibility, can be over-compressed some means must be adopted to control the amount of the compression. This can be achieved by positioning the gasket in a recess in one of the pipe flanges of a suitable depth to control the compression or using a gasket fitted with a solid metallic ring, the gasket then being compressed to the thickness of the solid ring. Both of these methods give radial support to the spiral section and also facilitate correct location of the gaskets. Examples are shown in *Figure 9.12*.

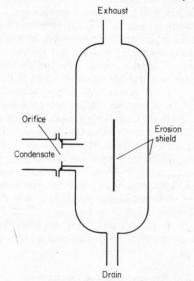

Figure 9.11 Location of orifice in drain line to minimize trouble from flashing

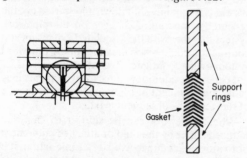

Figure 9.12 Spiral-wound gasket

Some success has also been achieved with gaskets formed from almost pure graphite tape of thickness 0.4 mm used alone or in conjunction with the reclaiming of used spiral-wound gaskets, the tape being applied to both faces of the spiral-wound gasket. Graphite should not, however be used in contact with stainless-steel flanges owing to the possibility of galvanic corrosion.

9.12 Control and distribution of fluid flow

As the rate of flow of a fluid between any two points in a pipework system is directly proportional to the square root of the pressure drop, each part of the pipework system contributes to control of the flow. On the basis that the pressure drop between the two points is a specified value, the most economical system results from sizing the pipework to give the desired drop for the desired flow.

Example

Saturated steam is available from a source at a pressure of 10 bar abs. A flow rate of 10 kg/s is required for a heat exchanger operating at a pressure of 9.5 bar abs. The pipework will have one globe valve, three 90° bends (r/d = 3.0) and 42 m of straight piping. Determine the size of the pipework.

The specific volume of saturated steam at 10 bar is 0.1944 m^3/kg and at 9.5 bar is 0.2055 m^3/kg. Assume a mean of 0.2 m^3/kg. Therefore

Flow $= 0.2 \times 10 = 2.0 \, m^3/s$

Assuming velocity of 50 m/s

Pipe diameter $= \left(\dfrac{2.0 \times 4}{50 \times \pi} \right)^{1/2} = 0.22 \, m$

The nearest standard pipe bore is 0.225 m. This must be checked against pressure drop. Using equation (9.4),

$$P = \left(F\frac{L}{D} + K \right) \, \rho\frac{U^2}{2} \times 10^{-5}$$

From *Figure 9.9* for a flow of 10 kg/s and a bore of 0.22, $F = 0.0143$. For a straight pipe,

$K = \dfrac{FL}{D} = \dfrac{0.015 \times 42}{0.225}$

$= 2.66$

Summating K values,

Straight pipe	$= 2.66$
Three bends $= 3 \times 0.22$	$= 0.66$
One globe valve	$= 4.2$
Total K value	$\overline{7.52}$

$\rho = \dfrac{1}{0.2} = 5 \, kg/m^3$

Velocity head $= \dfrac{5 \times 50^2}{2} \times 10^{-5}$

$= 0.0625 \, bar$

It will be useful to calculate the pressure drop in the individual sections of the pipework to indicate the degree of control of flow exercised by each section.

1. Straight pipe
   2.66×0.0625 $\qquad = 0.166$
2. Bends (three in number)
   0.66×0.0625 $\qquad = 0.041$
3. Globe valve
   4.2×0.0625 $\qquad = 0.263$

   Total $\qquad \overline{0.47}$

This value of 0.47 bar is within the allowance pressue but is based on a nominal bore of 0.225 m, which can be subject to a manufacturing tolerance. As the pressure drop is inversely proportional to diameter[5], then for the margin in pressure drop of 0.03 we could not tolerate the use of tubing with a bore less than the nominal bore of 0.225 m.

The important point to observe in the above example is the effect that the inclusion of a globe valve had on increasing the pressure drop and thus on limiting the flow. Had a gate valve with a K value of 0.08 been substituted for the globe valve, the overall pressure drop would be reduced from 0.47 to 0.212 bar or the flow would increase by 48% if the pressure drop remained the same.

The pressure drop in any pipework system is directly proportional to the sum of the K factors for the individual components multiplied by the velocity head. Therefore each component affects the pressure drop in proportion to the ratio of its individual K value to the K value of the complete system.

Therefore if $K = K_1 + K_2$ and K_1 and K_2 are equal, each has a 50% effect on the pressure drop. If K_1 were eliminated the pressure drop would reduce to 50% of its original value or if the pressure drop remained the same the flow would increase to $(1/0.5)^{1/2}$, i.e. by 44%. If K_1 is reduced only to 50% of its original value the overall pressure drop would reduce to 75% or similarly the flow would increase to $(1/0.75)^{1/2}$, i.e. by 15.5% to give the same pressure drop. The change in pressure drop in any single component must always be treated as a proportional change in the overall pressure drop in estimating the effect on the flow.

9.13 Distribution of flow in parallel circuits

The distribution of flow of fluids in parallel circuits between two vessels so that the pressure drop across each parallel circuit is the same, is governed by the size of pipe used for each circuit and the K value for each circuit.

In the three parallel circuits Nos. 1, 2 and 3 shown in *Figure 9.13*, let the diameters be D_1, D_2 and D_3 respectively and the K values be K_1, K_2 and K_3 respectively. From equation (9.4),

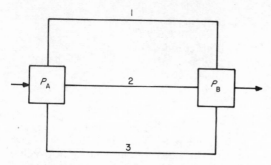

Figure 9.13   Flow in parallel circuits

$$P_A - P_B = \left(F \frac{L}{D} + K_s \right) \rho \frac{U^2}{2} \times 10^{-5}$$

$$\text{for each circuit}$$

Equating $(FL/D) + K_s$ to K, the value of K for each circuit can be determined from *Figure 9.9* and *Tables 9.2, 9.3* and *9.4*. Let the flow through the three circuits be Q_1, Q_2 and Q_3 respectively, then

$$K_1 \frac{Q_1^2}{D_1^4} = K_2 \frac{Q_2^2}{D_2^4} = K_3 \frac{Q_3^2}{D_3^4}$$

$$= \ldots K_n \frac{Q_n^2}{D_n^4} \qquad (9.5)$$

$$Q_2 = Q_1 \frac{D_2^2}{D_1^2} \left(\frac{K_1}{K_2} \right)^{1/2}$$

$$Q_3 = Q_1 \frac{D_3^2}{D_1^2} \left(\frac{K_1}{K_3} \right)^{1/2}$$

$$Q_{\text{total}} = Q_1 + Q_2 + Q_3$$

$$= Q_1 + \frac{Q_1 D_2^2}{D_1^2} \left(\frac{K_1}{K_2} \right)^{1/2} + \frac{Q_1 D_3^2}{D_1^2} \left(\frac{K_1}{K_3} \right)^{1/2}$$

$$\therefore Q_1 =$$

$$\frac{Q}{1 + \left(\dfrac{D_2}{D_1} \right)^2 \left(\dfrac{K_1}{K_2} \right)^{1/2} + \left(\dfrac{D_3}{D_1} \right)^2 \left(\dfrac{K_1}{K_3} \right)^{1/2}}$$

$$(9.6)$$

Example

In *Figure 9.13* the total flow through the three pipework systems is 25 m³/s. The diameters and total K values for each system are as follows:

System	Diameter (m)	K value	Flow
1	0.2	8	Q_1
2	0.23	7	Q_2
3	0.3	5	Q_3

From equation (9.6),

$$Q_1 = \frac{25}{1 + \left(\dfrac{0.23}{0.2} \right)^2 \left(\dfrac{8}{7} \right)^{1/2} + \left(\dfrac{0.3}{0.2} \right)^2 \left(\dfrac{8}{5} \right)^{1/2}}$$

$$= \frac{25}{1 + 1.414 + 2.846}$$

$$= 4.753 \text{ m}^3/\text{s}$$

$$Q_2 = 1.414 \times 4.753 = 6.72 \text{ m}^3/\text{s}$$

$$Q_3 = 2.846 \times 4.753 = 13.53 \text{ m}^3/\text{s}$$

This approximation will often suffice as the accuracy is within the accuracy of assessment of the various friction factors adopted and forming the total K value. A check should, however, be made to ensure that an excessively high velocity does not occur in any of the pipework systems. Should this be so then the pipework diameter should be increased to reduce the velocity to an acceptable value and a flow control device installed in the system in order to regulate the flow to the desired amount by restoring the pressure drop to its original value.

It is, however, wasteful of energy as well as resulting in higher initial cost to resort to flow control devices and the necessary control of flow should, as far as possible, be obtained by correct sizing of pipework.

It may be desired to design parallel pipework systems to pass specified flows at a specified pressure difference $P_A - P_B$. In the previous example let the ratio $Q_1 : Q_2 : Q_3$ be 1 : 2 : 1.5.

Then from equation (9.5),

$$\frac{8 \times 1^2}{D_1{}^4} = \frac{7 \times 2^2}{D_2{}^4} = \frac{5 \times 1.5^2}{D_3{}^4}$$

i.e.

$$\frac{8}{D_1{}^4} = \frac{28}{D_2{}^4} = \frac{11.25}{D_3{}^4}$$

$$\therefore D_2 = \left(\frac{28}{8}\right)^{1/4} D_1$$

$$D_3 = \left(\frac{11.25}{8}\right)^{1/4} D_1$$

If a value is chosen for D_1 to give the required pressure drop, the values of D_2 and D_3 can be readily obtained. Here again it is generally considered that this approximation is usually within the accuracy of the friction factors chosen. The calculation of the pressure drop will reveal the degree of accuracy and allow any necessary adjustment to the pipework diameter to be made.

There is a limit to the amount of adjustment that can be made by choosing an alternative pipe size since tubes are normally manufactured in a range of outside diameters with close tolerance and the bores are determined by the thickness required safely to contain the working pressure. It may not be possible to make the desired adjustment to flow by adopting an alternative pipe size and it becomes necessary to vary the K value by introducing some device to control the flow further.

When the pressure drops are being calculated, the expected bore of the chosen tube should be used. However, the thickness of piping actually used may vary between straight lengths and bent sections and also because of manufacturing tolerances. For example, if a pipe of o.d. 270 mm and nominal thickness 8 mm is chosen as suitable for a particular service, the variation in thickness due to manufacturing tolerances can vary the pressure drop by $+18\%$ and -13% from the value calculated using the nominal bore of 270 mm, and hence vary the flow by between $+8.5\%$ and -6.3% of the calculated value. Further discrepancies in calculated flow rate can also occur owing to changes in fluid density, quality of surface finish of internal surfaces of pipework and inaccuracies in estimating the K values for the various fittings such as valves, bends, tees, etc. comprising the pipework system. It is probable that the rate of flow cannot be forecast within a tolerance of $\pm10\%$ and if a greater degree of accuracy is required then some means of varying the values of K until the required flow is obtained must be installed in the pipework system. Such a device would normally be a valve in which

adjustment of the valve opening is used to vary the K value of the system. It should be borne in mind however that the reduction in flow due to the restriction in area at the valve also applies over the whole of the pipework system in which the same flow is occurring. The pressure drop calculation therefore must be repeated for the complete pipework system using the value of the reduced flow.

Severe restriction of flow through a valve can cause high velocity and erosion of the valve seatings giving subsequent difficulties of tight shut-off. This can lead to loss of steam and increased maintenance costs. Further problems due to excessive throttling can result from noise and vibration. Those from the former are well known but the latter can be the cause of leaking joints and sometimes failure of the pipework system.

It is therefore obvious that careful sizing of pipework to obtain a pressure drop as close as possible to the design value is beneficial not only in reducing the initial capital cost of the installation but also in reduced vibration, noise and attendant troubles.

Pipework sizes are often calculated on the basis of excessively moderate velocities and inaccurate values for pressure drop due to friction, leaving a variable throttling device such as a valve to do more than its fair share of keeping the fluid flow to the required value.

9.14 Valves

The valves used on steam and condensate systems fall generally into two classifications (a) isolation and flow control, and (b) pressure control. Although any valve suitable for flow control will normally also perform an isolating service the reverse does not apply.

Isolation and flow control

The parallel slide and wedge gate type valves shown in *Figure 9.14* are normally used only for isolating purposes and are not generally suitable for controlling flow. In the fully open positions these valves offer very little resistance to flow and some 70% of closure is usually required before any significant throttling becomes evident. The throttling effect is dependent only on the additional friction drop which can be introduced into the system by partial closure of the valve. *Figure 9.15* illustrates a typical increase in K value (*see* p 189) plotted on a logarithmic scale against a linear scale of percentage of valve movement from the fully open position. From curve (a), a 30% movement of a gate valve from the 40% closed position would increase the K value from 1 to 10. This would not, however, increase the friction drop on the pipework system by an amount 10 times the value of the friction at

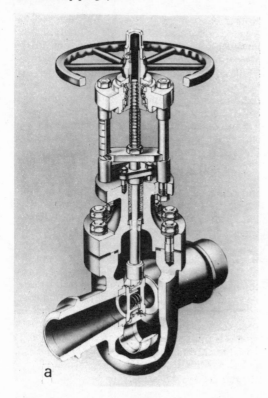

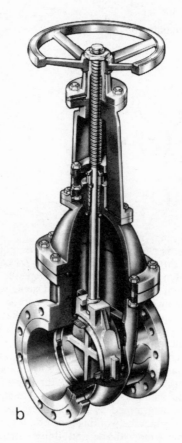

Figure 9.14   (a) Parallel slide and (b) wedge gate valves. (Courtesy of Hopkinson Ltd and Blakeborough Ltd)

40% closure, as the restriction on flow would reduce the friction loss in the rest of the pipework system and the effect of the throttling by the valve would be diminished. The corresponding effect of 70% closure on a butterfly or ball valve would be some 16 times greater than on the gate valve, hence the more obvious choice of the former two types for throttling duty. It should be noted that the principal force acting on a butterfly valve in the partly closed position is the hydrodynamic torque due to the pressure variation over the area of the gate. This torque can vary with the flow conditions, which can be considerably affected by the interactions arising from the proximity of tees, bends and other fittings in the system. This variation in torque can cause a flutter of the gate and the actuator chosen for positioning the gate must be capable of withstanding the consequential effects. The butterfly valve and ball valve are also capable of tight shut-off and examples of these types are illustrated in *Figure 9.16*. Until the development of the butterfly and ball valves for higher-pressure and higher-temperature duty, the globe valve was used in most instances for throttling steam and hot water and is still in common use for this purpose.

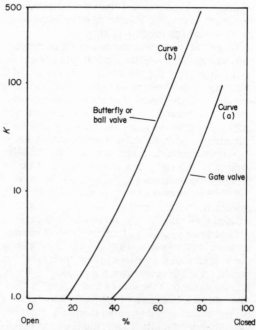

Figure 9.15   Typical valves of friction factor K for varying percentages of closure

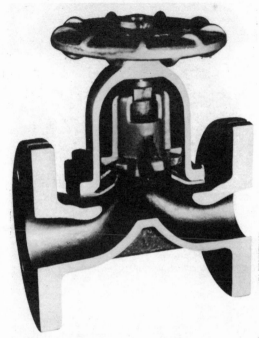

Figure 9.16 Butterfly (above) and ball (below) valves. (Courtesy of Neles International BV)

Figure 9.17 Diaphragm valve. (Courtesy of Saunders Valve Co.)

Figure 9.17 are also used for isolating and flow controlling but the range of pressure and temperature over which they can be used is limited by the material properties of the flexible diaphragm.

It is often necessary to provide against the possibility of reverse flow of the operating fluid or even the influx of a fluid which may cause damage to the operating machinery. This is normally achieved by installing a reflux, check or non-return valve; such a valve is kept open by the fluid flow in the desired direction. Failure of the motive force impelling the fluid through the valve results in automatic closure of the valve and prevents reversal of flow. Examples of this are the the stopping of a pump, the loss of pressure in the flow-sustaining vessel or a build-up of pressure downstream of the non-return valve, such as may occur on a feedheating system if feedwater which is at higher pressure leaks into the steam space. The results of this water flowing back into the turbine via the bled-steam pipes would be disastrous. Two types of non-return valve are illustrated in *Figure 9.18*. The swing type is the more popular as the pressure drop is lower than through the lift type, but it is not however recommended for systems where frequent reversals of flow occur, since these may cause the valve disc to flutter, resulting in noise and ultimately in damage to the seats. Sometimes these valves are

The pressure drop through the globe valve in the fully open position is, however, considerably higher than through the full-bore wedge gate, parallel slide and ball valves and also higher than through the butterfly valve since the bore is partly blocked even where the valve is fully open. The globe valve should therefore be used only where throttling is normally taking place and the wedge gate and parallel slide valves only where the valves are normally fully open or shut. The butterfly or ball valve can be used where either operating condition will occur. It is generally advantageous when choosing a valve for throttling duty to use as small a valve as practicable so that the throttling effect desired is obtained with the valve as fully open as possible. This minimizes erosion and noise problems and also cavitation troubles if water is being handled. It is also the most economical in capital cost. Diaphragm valves as illustrated in

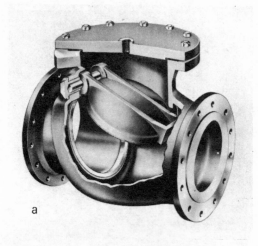

a

Figure 9.18 Swing-type (above) and lift-type (below) non-return valves. (Courtesy of Hopkinson Ltd)

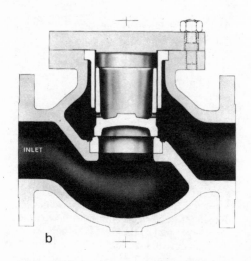

INLET

b

fitted with an external lever and balance weight attached to an extension of the disc spindle which allows the valve to open at a lower differential pressure. The lift-type non-return valve is less susceptible to valve chatter but the design illustrated would be suitable for installation only in a horizontal line.

A different design would be necessary for fitting in a vertical line since it is necessary for the disc spindle to be vertical. The swing-type valve can be fitted on either a horizontal or vertical line.

Pressure control

Pressure control valves function by: (a) control of pressure downstream of the valve, or (b) control of pressure upstream of the valve. Valves in category (a) are termed *pressure-reducing valves* and those in category (b) are termed *pressure relief valves*, the former lifting on reduction in a predetermined pressure downstream and the latter on a rise in a predetermined pressure upstream. The pressure to be controlled is usually fixed by the pre-set compression of a spring, and means should be provided to prevent any further unauthorized adjustment, as a protection against the design pressure of the system being exceeded. The valves are therefore not normally adjusted and are usually provided with means to prevent unauthorized adjustment.

As a precaution against maloperation of pressure-reducing valves, relief valves are mounted downstream of the reducing valves. The fluid discharged from a relief valve should be piped to a point where it does not present a hazard to personnel and plant. It is not usually economic to conserve what should be a very infrequent leakage from the system, but any frequent or continuous discharge from a relief valve should be investigated.

As a valve, by virtue of its design, must be provided with an opening through which the disc can be inserted and also a second opening through which the operating spindle is passed, it automatically becomes a possible source of fluid leakage. If all the joints in the pipework systems are buttwelded then the covers and glands of the valves could be the only possible source of leakage, and it is therefore very important that careful consideration be given to the design of the gland and of the cover joint and also to the choice of packing and gasket materials. Here again the use of cheaper and inferior materials could result in an uneconomic system.

Valves should preferably be located where they can be easily maintained, particularly those which are subject to fluctuating pressure and/or temperature conditions and which are operated frequently.

9.15 Cleaning and commissioning of new pipework systems

The standard of cleanliness required of a pipework system is mainly governed by the requirements of the steam-generating and -using equipment, although parts of the pipework system such as valves and flow-measuring equipment can sustain damage, or blockage owing to the presence of foreign matter which may impair their correct function.

The two methods of cleaning pipework systems

are (a) mechanical and (b) chemical. The quality of water supplied as feedwater to a boiler varies in importance depending on the type and operating pressure of the boiler. Higher-pressure boilers demand more stringent control of the chemical composition of the water, particularly its silica content. Watertube boilers are more susceptible to damage, either from corrosion or from over-heating, due to suspended solids than boilers of the shell type.

Prime movers such as turbines are particularly prone to damage from particles in the fluid, which can attain very high velocities in the turbine pass-ages, but stationary equipment can also sustain permanent damage.

Preliminary cleaning

After fabrication in the works, particularly where welding or hot bending has been applied, pipes are usually shot- or grit-blasted to remove scale and loose materials. This process, if carried out cor-rectly, is usually effective but should not be con-sidered as infallible.

A check should be made immediately after shot-blasting to ensure that all debris, including the shot, is finally removed before the piping leaves the works. Cast-iron shot is often used for blasting and cases have been recorded where shot left in pipes overnight has been cemented by corrosion. Subsequent purging of the piping after erection failed to remove the shot, which had lodged in drain pockets, but this debris was ultimately released by several thermal cycles of the pipework system, and severe damage to turbine blading and diaphragms resulted. Shot-blasting should there-fore be done when the internal surfaces of the pipes are dry and during the shot-blasting operation the pipes should be positioned so that shot will not fall into drain pockets or other places where it may lodge.

When cleaned, the pipe ends should be pro-vided with a temporary seal to protect against further contamination.

Steam purging

After erection, steam piping may be finally cleared by purging the system with steam. This is done by blowing steam through the pipework direct to atmosphere, the steam pressure being chosen so that the velocity and density of the purging steam has a shifting factor greater than the normal steam flow. A shifting factor of 1.5 is normally considered satisfactory and can be determined from the formula

Shifting factor

$$= \frac{(\text{density} \times \text{velocity}^2) \text{ during purge}}{(\text{density} \times \text{velocity}^2) \text{ design flow}} \qquad (9.7)$$

Debris removed during steam purging has included several relatively large objects such as spanners, files and other tools and it is therefore necessary to ensure that the purging steam leaving the system is directed to an area where these objects would not cause injury to personnel or plant.

Chemical cleaning

Boiler feed and condensate systems may be given a chemical clean by circulating a hot caustic solution to remove any oil or grease and any silica which may be present (*see* Chapter 5). Failure to remove the silica could incur the loss of considerable quantities of good-quality water as boiler blowdown. As an example, on a 120-MW boiler installation, nearly 1.4×10^7 l of boiler feedwater had to be blown down to waste before an accept-able level of 2 ppm of silica was reached.

If the pumps are installed before the cleaning process has been carried out then temporary fine strainers may have to be fitted in the suction branches to prevent blockage of pump parts with fine clearances.

Post-erection testing

Pipework systems where the joints are buttwelded may be checked for possible leakage either by applying a hydraulic test pressure or by some form of non-destructive examination of the welded joints. Pipework systems with flanged joints should be hydraulically tested. British Standard BS 806 or other appropriate codes give guidance on testing.

Hydraulic testing should be carried out before flushing or steam purging, so that any contami-nation from the fluid used for testing is removed in the cleaning process. Care should also be taken to ensure that any necessary temporary supports are in position on steam piping before filling it for the hydraulic test, otherwise the permanent spring supports may become overloaded owing to the additional weight of the water, and the resulting damage may cause them to be ineffective for normal use and thus cause overstressing of the pipework. It is important that all temporary sup-ports should be removed after testing and prior to the commencement of commissioning of new mains, as they could restrict the expansion of heated mains and may result in overstressing of the pipework or squirming of any bellows expansion pieces leading to failure.

Commissioning of pipework

Before passing steam to process, heat exchanger or to a prime mover it is essential to ensure that no condensation takes place after the main valves are opened, as any water accelerated to high velocity by the steam can cause severe damage by erosion or vibration. To prevent this the steam piping must be heated to a temperature not lower than the saturation temperature corresponding to the maximum pressure at which the system will be operated. This is generally achieved by opening the drain valves and these should be left open until this saturation temperature has been reached in the pipe wall at the point of extraction of the drainage. If it is not possible to pass the heating steam right up to the end of the pipework system, then it is advisable to provide an additional draw-off point at the end of the main pipework and measure the temperature at that point.

Only when the whole of the pipework has reached the desired temperature as measured at the end of the pipework system, should the steam be considered as suitable for full flow conditions. Whilst this chapter deals primarily with pipework, it is obvious that the unit to be served with steam must undergo a similar process of heating up and in many instances both processes can be simultaneous. However, it is important that the rate of flow of steam during the heating up process can be controlled by the judicious operation of drain valves, otherwise special warming-up by-passes would be required across the main isolating valves to allow this control to be exercised.

Movement of the pipework due to expansion during the process of warming up to the full steam temperature should be checked to ensure that the pipework system still remains correctly supported in accordance with the design conditions. On boiler feed and condensate lines it is necessary to release all air through the vent connections to avoid air locks and also to prevent the air from being passed into the steam-generating plant.

After the system has been raised to the required pressure and temperature, a thorough check should be made for any leaks from joints, valve covers, glands, etc. Leaks allowed to continue almost invariably get worse and should be attended to as early as possible. When one is checking for leaks it should be borne in mind that superheated steam is invisible and the leak may become evident only some distance away from the source after the steam has partly condensed on mixing with the cooler air.

References and further reading

1 British Standards Institution. *British Standard* 3974: 'Pipe hangers, slider and roller supports'
2 Spielvogel, S. W. '*Piping Stress Calculations Simplified*'. New York: McGraw-Hill (1943)
3 British Standards Institution. *British Standard* 806: 'Ferrous piping systems for and in connection with land boilers'
4 Popplewell, P. L. and Hammill, J. *Inst. Mech. Eng. Proc.*, **187**, 181 (1973)
5 British Standards Institution. *British Standard* (draft) 'Selection and application of metallic bellows expansion joints for use in pressure systems'
6 Miller, D. S. *Internal Flow*. Cranfield, Bedford: British Hydromechanics Research Association (1971)
7 Bernhard, H. J. *Inst. Mech. Eng. Appl. Mech. Convention Proc.*, **178** (Part 3J), 22 (1963–64)
8 British Standards Institution. *British Standard* 4504: 'Flanges and bolting for pipes, valves and fittings'. Metric series
9 British Standards Institution. *British Standard* 4865: 'Dimensions of gaskets for pipe flanges to BS 4505'
10 Bernhard, H. J. *Inst. Mech. Eng. Proc.*, **178** (Part 1, No. 5), 107 (1963–64)
11 Donald, M. B. and Salomon, J. M. *Inst. Mech. Eng.*, *Proc.*, **171**, 829 (1957)
12 Jacob, K. B. *Inst. Mech. Eng. Proc.*, **174** (22), 669 (1960)
13 'Code of practice for the cleaning and protection of power station plant.' Central Electricity Generating Board Document No 098/15

10 Steam traps

Condensate is formed whenever steam gives up its enthalpy of evaporation (latent heat). The proper removal of condensate from steam plant of all types is vital if the plant is to work efficiently and this operation is commonly performed by a steam trap.

Frequent causes of unsatisfactory condensate drainage include the choice of the wrong type of steam trap for the application, the use of a trap that is incorrectly sized for the load and pressure conditions, and bad installation. Because any of these factors can seriously reduce plant output, it is worth spending some time studying how steam traps work and their application. Even so, the amount of ground that can be covered in this chapter is necessarily limited and the reader is referred to ref. 1 for additional information.

10.1 What is a steam trap?

A steam trap is an automatic valve capable of distinguishing between condensate and live steam, opening to discharge the former but closing to trap the latter.

The difference between condensate and steam is sensed in several ways. One group of traps detect the difference in density, another group react to a difference in temperature, and a third rely on the difference in flow characteristics.

10.2 Mechanical steam traps

The name 'mechanical steam trap' is usually given to traps that operate on the difference in density between condensate and steam. The operating member is normally a closed float or an open bucket connected to a valve which regulates the discharge.

Float traps

Figure 10.1 shows a simple float trap. The float is a hollow sphere, usually fabricated from stainless steel, mounted on a lever arm pivoted to the body. The lever arm operates a valve, moving it away from or towards a seat orifice in the body as the float rises and falls with the changing level of condensate in the trap.

When steam is first turned on to the plant, the float is in its lowest position and the valve is

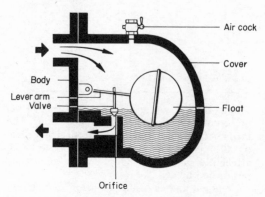

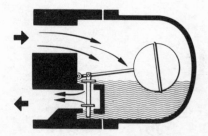

Figure 10.1   *Simple trap*

Figure 10.2   Float trap with double-seated valve

closed. The incoming steam will try to force air in the steam space towards the trap, from which it cannot escape unless the air cock on the top of the body is opened. When condensate, following the air, reaches the trap, it starts to fill the body, covering the valve orifice and then lifting the float and opening the valve.

The float automatically regulates the valve opening to handle condensate at the rate at which it reaches the trap up to the maximum capacity of the valve orifice. If there is no condensate and live steam fills the body, the valve will be closed completely.

The valve is closed by the weight of the float but, once it is on its seat, it is held there by the steam pressure in the trap body. As the water level rises, the buoyancy of the float has to pull the valve off its seat against the force exerted by the steam pressure. Because of this, many float traps use a lever mechanism between the float and the valve to multiply the available effort.

For a float trap of a particular physical size, which effectively determines the force available to unseat the valve, the maximum operating pressure will depend on the size of the valve orifice. A large orifice, giving a high discharge capacity, will limit the working pressure to a value lower than that possible with a smaller, lower-capacity one. Should the pressure rise above the maximum value for a particular orifice, the trap will remain closed because the float buoyancy will not be great enough to open it.

Because of this relationship between capacity and working pressure, it is common practice to make float traps available with a selection of orifices, so that the user can choose one best suited to the actual working load and pressure conditions of his plant.

From time to time, attempts have been made to overcome the limited operating power of the simple float by using some form of trip mechanism. The float then simply acts as a pilot

to release the much stronger force of a weight or spring that operates the valve. Not surprisingly, these more complicated mechanisms have proved unreliable when working in the unfavourable conditions inside a steam trap and have largely been discarded.

A more successful way of obtaining high capacity from a trap of moderate physical size is to use a double-seated valve of the type shown in *Figure 10.2*. Here the forces acting on the two valves are nearly in balance and the float does not have to be very big to operate the mechanism. Because of differential expansion between the valves and seats, it is not possible to get a tight shut-off with this arrangement, but the leak can be made quite small. In any case, this is seldom a problem because the type of plant calling for a high discharge capacity rarely produces a small enough condensate load to allow live steam to reach the trap.

In contrast to the lever-operated float traps, some designs dispense with the lever altogether and make the float itself seat directly on the orifice *(Figure 10.3)*. Although this type has the merit of simplicity, it is clearly not easy to persuade the large fabricated float to seat reliably on the small orifice.

Reference has been made to the need to allow air, forced into the body of the trap, to escape. Unless this is done, condensate would not be able to reach the trap, which would remain permanently closed.

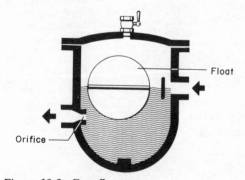

Figure 10.3   *Free float trap*

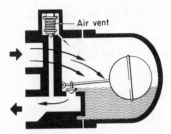

Figure 10.4   Float trap with thermostatic air vent

The hand-operated cock, shown in *Figure 10.1,* is not a very practical way of releasing air because it is unlikely that anybody will be available to open and close it just when needed. It is more usual to fit an automatic air vent as shown in *Figure 10.4.* This consists of a small valve operated by a thermostatic element of the balanced-pressure or bimetallic type, very similar to the corresponding steam traps described later in this chapter. Not only will this air vent discharge air when the plant is being started up, but also it will release any air that reaches the trap during normal running.

To sum up, float traps discharge condensate continuously at steam temperature and work equally well on heavy or light loads. They are particularly suitable for draining plant, such as heater batteries and heat exchangers, that is highly rated for its size and requires the immediate removal of condensate as soon as it forms.

They are not as robust as some other types and can be damaged by water hammer and freezing. If a thermostatic air release is fitted, they should not, as a rule, be used on installations where superheated steam can reach the trap.

Bucket traps

Like float traps, bucket traps also use buoyancy to differentiate between condensate and steam. Instead of a closed float, they are fitted with a bucket open at one end. Open-top bucket traps have the open end of the bucket at the top, whereas inverted bucket traps have it at the bottom. Because the method of operation is quite different, each type will be described separately.

Open-top bucket traps

A typical open-top bucket trap is shown in *Figure 10.5.* Attached to the bottom of the bucket is a spindle carrying the valve at its upper end. Surrounding the spindle and attached to the cover of the trap is a discharge tube. The lower end of the tube reaches almost to the bottom of

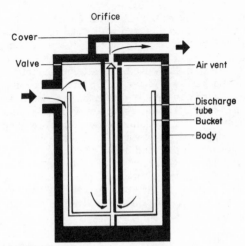

Figure 10.5   Open-top bucket trap

the bucket and the valve orifice is attached to its top.

When the trap is first installed, the bucket, which is empty, rests on the bottom of the body and the valve is open. Steam is then turned on and forces air, followed by condensate, towards the trap. The air enters the bucket, passing up the discharge tube and out through the open valve. Condensate then starts to fill the body of the trap and eventually the bucket floats, shutting the valve. Condensate continues to collect in the body until it reaches the top lip of the bucket, over which it flows. When the weight of water in the bucket is sufficient to overcome the buoyancy and pull the valve off its seat against the steam pressure, the bucket sinks and the trap discharges. Steam pressure forces the water in the bucket up the discharge tube and out through the valve orifice, until the bucket regains its buoyancy, when it floats and shuts the valve again. The cycle then repeats itself.

Once condensate has entered the bucket for the first time, it will seal the bottom end of the discharge tube to prevent the escape of steam and air will no longer be able to get out this way. Just as in the case of the float trap, this air may then stop the trap from working and an alternative means of venting the air must be provided. One method that works well in practice is to drill a small hole across the top of the discharge tube *(see Figure 10.5),* allowing air in the top of the body to pass directly to the valve. But when the trap has to handle large quantities of air, it is better to fit a thermostatic air vent, either inside the body as in the case of the float trap or as a separate unit in a by-pass around the trap.

As in the float trap, the force needed to unseat the valve will depend on the steam pressure and the size of the orifice. Open-top bucket traps are, therefore, also provided with a choice of orifice sizes so they can be matched to the duty required.

Instead of the valve being attached directly to the bucket, as in *Figure 10.5*, a lever can be used to magnify the effort of the bucket. Even so, open-top bucket traps have always been big and heavy and for economic reasons they are going out of use. In some ways this is a pity because, properly chosen and installed, they are very reliable and are capable of working for long periods with the minimum of attention.

Open-top bucket traps have an intermittent, very positive, blast discharge action and handle condensate at steam temperature.

Inverted bucket traps

Figure 10.6 illustrates an inverted bucket trap. Entry is from the bottom into the inside of the bucket, which is attached to a lever carrying the valve. The lever is pivoted to the top cover, which also carries the valve seat orifice. A small vent hole is pierced through the top of the bucket.

Before steam is turned on, the bucket rests on the bottom of the body and the valve is wide open. Steam pressure then forces air, followed by condensate, towards the trap and the air passes slowly through the small vent hole and out through the valve orifice. Condensate then fills the body and the bucket and also flows out through the orifice because the valve is still wide open.

When steam reaches the trap, it enters the bucket and a small amount passes through the vent hole and out through the open valve. Most

of the steam displaces water from inside the bucket and the latter becomes buoyant and floats, closing the valve.

The steam trapped in the top of the bucket will now pass very slowly through the vent hole and condense in the water in the trap body. Condensate at the inlet to the trap will gradually fill the bucket as the trapped steam escapes through the vent hole and, when the buoyancy has been lost, the bucket will drop, pulling the valve off the seat orifice against the steam pressure. The trap will then discharge and the cycle will be repeated. If there is no condensate to be discharged, live steam will replace that which is condensed in the water in the body.

If air reaches the trap during normal running of the plant, it will be discharged through the vent hole and valve orifice when the latter is open. This means that an inverted bucket trap will vent air only slowly. If the vent hole is enlarged to speed up the passage of air, it will also allow more steam to pass and the trap will become wasteful. To try to overcome this, some inverted bucket traps have a second, larger hole in the top of the bucket which is opened and closed by a bimetal thermostat. Unfortunately, the temperature difference available to operate this thermostat is small, so that it is unable to generate much force and closure of the extra vent can become unreliable. When this happens the trap will cycle unnecessarily quickly, waste steam and wear.

If more air has to be removed than the trap can handle, the most satisfactory way of dealing with it is to fit a separate thermostatic air vent in parallel with it.

Should the water seal around the bottom lip of the bucket be lost, steam will pass directly to the outlet, the bucket will not become buoyant and considerable waste of live steam will occur. Loss of water seal or 'prime' can be caused by the hot water flashing off into steam, because of either superheat or a sudden drop in pressure at the trap inlet. It can also occur if the trap is installed above the drain point in such a way that the water siphons out. If any of these things are likely to happen, a non-return valve should be fitted close to the trap inlet. Some inverted bucket traps have a non-return valve fitted to the top of the inlet tube inside the bucket.

Sometimes, with a newly installed trap, particularly if it is a large one, it is difficult to get the water seal to form initially. The cover should then be removed and sufficient water poured into the body to make the seal.

Again, as is the case with float and open-top bucket traps, inverted bucket traps are provided with a choice of valve orifices to match the load and pressure requirements of the plant.

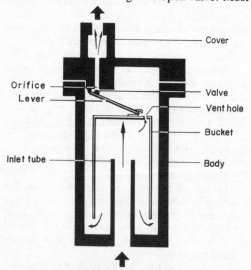

Figure 10.6   Inverted bucket trap

Cover

Orifice
Lever

Valve

Vent hole

Bucket

Inlet tube

Body

Inverted bucket traps discharge condensate at steam temperature. They normally operate intermittently except on very light loads, when they tend to dribble, or when working on full capacity under which conditions they remain wide open. The mechanism is simple and reasonably robust, so they can be used on applications where a certain amount of water hammer is inevitable. They can also be made for fairly high pressures and superheat.

10.3 Thermostatic traps

Thermostatic traps differentiate between steam and condensate by sensing a difference in temperature. When steam condenses, the condensate is initially at the same temperature as the steam. To provide a temperature difference to operate a steam trap, the condensate must lose some of its heat. Therefore, unlike mechanical traps, thermostatic traps must hold back the condensate before discharge while the temperature falls. This is an important factor to be remembered when selecting and installing these traps.

Just as there is a variety of mechanical trap mechanisms, so there are different ways of operating thermostatic traps. These fall into three main groups using vapour pressure, liquid expansion and metallic expansion and each will be considered in turn.

Balanced-pressure traps

Balanced-pressure traps use vapour pressure to operate the valve. The working element can take a variety of forms, a typical example being illustrated in *Figure 10.7*.

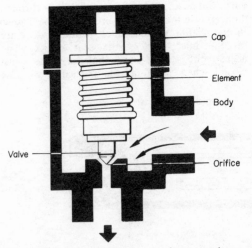

Figure 10.7 Balanced-pressure thermostatic trap

The flexible sealed element expands and contracts lengthwise under the influence of internal and external pressures. It contains a certain amount of liquid, usually alcohol or a mixture of alcohol and water, which boils at a lower temperature than water. In some cases, to lower the boiling point of the filling, the element is evacuated before the filling is introduced. When the element expands, a valve attached to it closes a seat orifice in the body.

When the trap is cold the element is fully contracted and the valve is wide open. Steam is then turned on and forces air, followed by cold condensate, towards the trap, which discharges them freely. As the condensate gets hotter, it heats up the filling in the element, which reaches its boiling point before the condensate rises to steam temperature. This means that the vapour pressure inside the element is higher than the steam pressure outside and the element expands, forcing the valve onto the seat orifice. Live steam cannot escape because the valve will already be closed when it reaches the trap.

Before the valve can open again, condensate surrounding the element must cool down and extract sufficient heat from the vapour inside to condense it and reduce the internal pressure. Once the latter falls far enough below the steam pressure, the element will contract, pulling the valve off the orifice against the pressure of the steam trying to keep it seated. If the steam pressure, and therefore temperature, rises the boiling liquid inside the element will exert a higher vapour pressure to balance the higher external pressure. If the pressure falls the converse will apply.

A filling is chosen having a relationship between pressure and temperature that changes in a similar manner to that of water. This means that the balance of forces acting on the element will remain practically unchanged no matter how the steam pressure varies within the operating range of the particular trap.

Should superheat reach the trap, the balance will be destroyed because the steam temperature is no longer in step with the pressure and a higher pressure will build up inside the element than is needed to balance the outside pressure. Eventually the pressures may become so unbalanced that the element is damaged.

The difference between steam temperature and operating temperature can be varied by choosing an appropriate filling and, at first sight, it would seem best to use one that will allow the trap to work very near to steam temperature. The disadvantage is that the nearer to steam the trap closes, the smaller is the difference in pressure between the inside and the outside of the element. This, in turn, means that the force available to close the valve is reduced and it may not seat very well, particularly if there is dirt present as there nearly always is in practice. Nevertheless, near-to-steam traps are essential on some applications such as wet steaming ovens, used in canteen kitchens, and certain types of hospital sterilizer.

In practice, most balanced-pressure traps operate somewhere between 8 and 14°C below steam temperature. Near-to-steam elements reduce this to about 3°C. For those applications where it is permissible to waterlog the steam space to some extent, traps are available working 20–30°C below steam temperature.

For many years, the elements of balanced-pressure traps were made from a material such as brass, which was easy to form into a flexible bellows with a good fatigue life. Unfortunately, they were readily attacked by corrosive condensate and could be damaged by water hammer. Consequently balanced-pressure traps, at one time by far the most common type, suffered something of an eclipse, despite their obvious advantages of simplicity, small size, relatively low cost and ease of servicing.

Modern developments in forming and welding thin-gauge sheet, made from stainless steel or other corrosion-resistant alloys, have given balanced-pressure traps a new lease of life. Elements can make use of bellows that are fabricated by welding or hydraulically formed, or consist of a flexible diaphragm mounted in a suitable case. They are available fitted into bodies made from steel, iron or brass so that modern balanced-pressure traps will meet a wider range of conditions than ever before.

Many balanced-pressure traps work with a pronounced blast discharge followed by a period when the valve is closed, but some settle down on light loads to give a continuous flow of condensate. Because they hold back condensate until it cools down below steam temperature, balanced-pressure traps should be fitted to a short length of unlagged pipe to act as a cooling leg, unless waterlogging of the steam space does not matter.

Liquid expansion traps

The next type of thermostatic trap to be considered makes use of the expansion of a liquid instead of a vapour to close the valve. Liquid expansion traps are a development of the old metallic expansion type in which the valve was attached to the end of a metal tube. To achieve a reasonable amount of valve movement, the tube and, therefore, the trap had to be excessively long. By substituting a liquid, with a much greater coefficient of expansion, for the metal tube the size of the trap can be very greatly reduced. *Figure 10.8* illustrates the principle. The thermostatic element consists of an outer tube sealed at one end to make a cylinder. A piston rod, carrying the valve, slides through the other end with a bellows forming a flexible gland between piston rod and cylinder. The space between the cylinder and the bellows is filled with a suitable oil. The element is attached to the body of the trap in such a way that it can be moved axially for adjustment purposes by means of a nut and screw thread. A spring is interposed between the element and the body to prevent damage should rising temperature continue to expand the oil after the valve has contacted the seat orifice.

When steam is turned on, air and condensate will be forced towards the trap and pass freely through the orifice, which is wide open because the oil in the element is cold. As the condensate warms up, it will transfer heat to the oil as it passes over the outside of the element, causing it to expand. This expansion will force the piston out of the cylinder and move the valve towards the seat orifice.

In this type of trap the valve is normally on the outlet side of the valve seat. This is done to prevent steam from blowing should the pressure vary. Suppose for a moment that flow through the trap is in the opposite direction to that shown in *Figure 10.8,* so that the element and valve are on the inlet side of the seat orifice. The adjustment is then set so that the valve is just closed when steam at the particular working

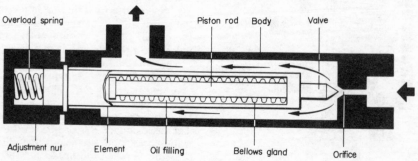

Figure 10.8 Liquid expansion trap

pressure and, therefore, temperature of the plant surrounds the element. If the pressure now falls, so that the steam temperature is reduced, the element will immediately contract because the temperature of the oil is lower and the trap will blow live steam.

When the element is on the outlet side of the orifice, as shown in *Figure 10.8,* the temperature surrounding it cannot exceed 100°C unless there is a back-pressure on the outlet of the trap, when it can rise to the temperature of saturated steam at that pressure, but no higher. As the condensate entering the trap approaches steam temperature, the valve will throttle the orifice until it is just closed when live steam arrives. The condensate around the element will then cool down and the valve will start to open. If live steam is still present, it will shut again immediately, otherwise it will open by an amount determined by the condensate temperature. A drop in steam pressure will not make the trap blow live steam and a rise in pressure will simply increase the amount of waterlogging.

Liquid expansion traps are rugged and will stand up to water hammer and superheat. They normally discharge condensate continuously and at a temperature below 100°C. They do not react as quickly to changes in temperature as do balanced-pressure traps and, because the condensate is held back while it cools down, a cooling leg is essential unless the plant can tolerate quite severe waterlogging.

Bimetal traps

An interesting development of the metallic-expansion thermostatic trap, which has become popular for certain applications, is the bimetal trap.

If two metals, having different coefficients of expansion, are bonded together and heated, the composite piece will take up a curved shape with the metal that has expanded most on the outside. On cooling down the original shape will be regained. This movement with changing temperature can be made to operate the valve of a steam trap.

One possible arrangement is shown in *Figure 10.9.* When cold, the bimetal strip is straight and the valve is wide open. Steam is turned on and air and cool condensate pass freely out through the wide-open valve. As the condensate warms up, the bimetal bends until the valve closes off the seat. When the condensate surrounding the bimetal cools, the strip straightens out and eventually pulls the valve off the seat against steam pressure.

Because, when the valve is closed, steam pressure is holding it onto the seat orifice, the

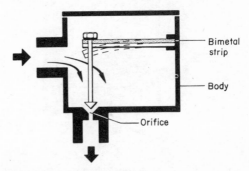

Figure 10.9   Simple bimetal trap

bimetal will find it much more difficult to open the valve than close it. Consequently the condensate must cool down well below the closing temperature before the trap will open and discharge it. Also the bimetal will close the valve at a certain fixed temperature even though the steam pressure, and hence temperature, is likely to vary quite widely when the plant is working. This means that under conditions other than those for which the trap is set, it will either waterlog the plant or blow steam.

To overcome this problem, bimetal traps normally have the valve on the outlet side of the orifice so that the force exerted by the steam pressure helps the valve to open. As the pressure (and therefore the temperature) varies there is a corresponding variation in the forces acting on the valve and the pressure versus temperature characteristic of the trap follows a straight line inclined to the axis. This is shown in *Figure 10.10* on which is also plotted the saturated steam curve which, ideally, the trap should match.

A typical trap giving this straight-line response is shown in *Figure 10.11.* The element consists of a stack of bimetal discs, arranged in opposed pairs, operating a valve on the outlet side of the seat orifice. When the discs are cold they are flat, allowing the valve to open wide. As the temperature rises, the pairs of discs bow in

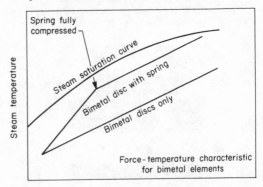

Figure 10.10 Characteristic of bimetal disc element

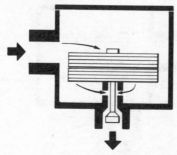

Figure 10.11   Bimetal trap with open downstream valve

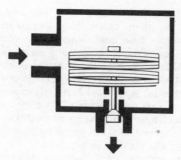

Figure 10.12   Bimetal trap with closed downstream valve

opposite directions and close the valve *(Figure 10.12).*

The simple bimetal disc trap can be improved by interposing a spring between the discs and the valve seat attached to the trap body *(see Figure 10.13).* The spring is arranged to compress and absorb some of the force of the bimetal in the lower part of the pressure range. Once the spring is fully compressed, the bimetal operates along its normal characteristic line and, as can be seen from *Figure 10.10,* the result is to make the trap follow the steam saturation curve along two straight lines. It can, therefore, be set to operate nearer to steam temperature without crossing the steam curve and blowing live steam.

The performance can be further improved by shaping the bimetal leaves in a variety of ways

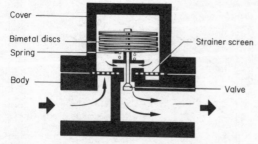

Figure 10.13   Bimetal trap with disc and spring element

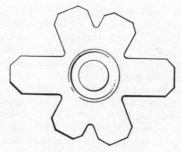

Figure 10.14 **Bimetal element in the form of a cross**

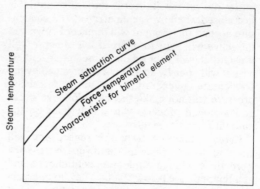

Figure 10.15   Characteristics of cross-shaped element

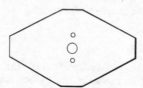

Figure 10.16 **Bimetal leaf**

and sometimes using them in combination with a characterized valve arrangement.

Figure 10.14 shows the plan view of an opposed pair of bimetal leaves shaped so that, when cold, they touch along only part of their perimeter. Because the arms are of different lengths and widths, they come into operation in sequence as the temperature rises to exert an increasing force on the valve. The effect on the trap characteristic is shown in *Figure 10.15.* Each time an additional pair of legs comes into contact the slope changes and, in this way, a good approximation to the steam curve is obtained.

Figure 10.16 shows another element, also in plan view. As before, the leaves are used in opposed pairs to operate a downstream valve. When cold the leaves are flat but, as they heat up, each pair deflects and starts to touch at the four corners. As deflection continues more of

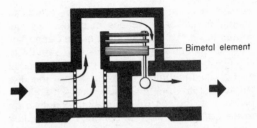

Figure 10.17 Cantilever bimetal element

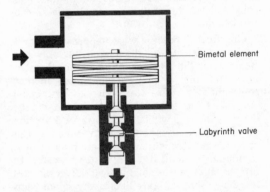

Figure 10.18 Bimetal labyrinth valve

the perimeter of each leaf comes into contact with its neighbour until, eventually, they are touching all around and exerting maximum force. In this way the trap characteristic is made to approximate to the steam saturation curve.

Another design is shown in *Figure 10.17*. Here the element consists of several bimetal strips of different thicknesses forming a cantilever and coming into operation in sequence, producing a force on the valve which increases in steps as the pressure and temperature rise. Elements of this type require quite a lot of bimetal to provide the required force and can be rather slow to react to varying conditions.

One final design of bimetal trap should be mentioned *(see Figure 10.18)*. The valve takes the form of an adjustable labyrinth, the position of which is varied by the bimetal element as the temperature inside the trap changes. This is really an automatically adjusted labyrinth trap, the latter type being described later in this chapter.

Because they can be set to discharge condensate well below steam temperature, thus reducing flash-steam problems, and can readily be constructed with steel bodies to resist freezing, thermal shock, water hammer and corrosive condensate, bimetal traps are frequently used on large exposed sites by the petrochemical industry. They are particularly suited to draining product tracer lines and jacketed pipes

when maximum heat output is not important and some waterlogging is permissible. It follows that they are not normally recommended for use on plant required to give maximum heat output at all times and where the pressure and load conditions can vary widely and rapidly. Condensate discharge is normally continuous but can be intermittent on light load.

10.4 Thermodynamic traps

Steam traps which use a freely moving disc, controlled by the forces generated by flashing condensate and steam flowing through orifices, are called 'thermodynamic traps'. As can be seen from *Figures 10.19 and 10.20,* this type of trap is mechanically very simple since only three components are required. The operating principle is, however, rather more complicated.

The body of the trap carries two circular seat rings or lands, which are concentric with the central inlet passage. The outlet connection is joined to the annular space between the two seat rings by one or more passages. A disc is free to move vertically in the space between the seat rings and a top cap attached to the body and there is an annular clearance between the edge of the disc and the side of the cap. The space between the top face of the disc and the top cap is called the *control chamber*. The bottom face of the disc and the seat rings are ground flat so that, when the disc touches the rings, it seals off both the inlet and the control chamber from the outlet, allowing the trap to shut tight. The surface of the disc facing the annulus between the two seat rings often carries one or more concentric circular grooves. Their purpose will be described later.

When steam is turned on, air and cold condensate are forced towards the trap. The pressure lifts the disc and the air, followed by the condensate, is discharged through the outlet, the flow taking place radially from the centre of the disc towards its edge.

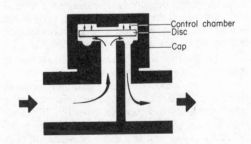

Figure 10.19 Thermodynamic trap

Figure 10.20 Interior of the thermodynamic trap

The condensate now starts to heat up and, because it drops in pressure as it passes through the trap, some of it flashes into steam and the velocity of the radial jet beneath the disc increases considerably. This radial flow obeys Bernoulli's theorem, which indicates that the sum of the static and dynamic pressures will remain constant. The nearer the condensate gets to steam temperature, the more flash steam is formed and the greater becomes the dynamic pressure. It follows from Bernoulli that the static pressure under the disc must fall and so the latter is drawn towards the seat rings. This reduces the flow through the inlet passage, the dynamic pressure falls, the static pressure rises and the disc will be pushed away from the seat rings again unless something is done to prevent it. This is the function of the control chamber.

When the radial jet hits the side of the top cap, some of it will be deflected up through the gap between the cap and the edge of the disc into the control chamber. Here it will be brought to rest and its dynamic pressure will be converted into static pressure. This will act on the whole top surface area of the disc and, eventually, produce sufficient force to seat the disc against the inlet pressure, which is able to act only on an area of the underside of the disc equal to that of the inlet passage. The trap is now shut and will remain so until the pressure in the control chamber has fallen far enough for the inlet pressure to lift the disc once more. The operating cycle then starts again.

The rate at which the flash steam in the control chamber loses pressure will vary with the temperature of the fluid at the trap inlet and the ambient temperature. If there is live steam at the inlet, heat will flow through the body of the trap to the flash steam in the control chamber, reducing the rate of condensation and making the trap cycle more slowly. If condensate collects at the inlet and starts to cool down, less heat will flow to the control chamber and the trap will open more quickly, which is just what is required.

So far as the effect of ambient heat loss is concerned, if thermodynamic traps are installed outside on exposed sites, insulating covers should be fitted over the top caps to prevent the traps from cycling too frequently. In some models, an additional cover is fitted over the normal top cap and the space between them is connected to the inlet port so that it becomes filled with steam and condensate. This acts as an insulating jacket to reduce heat loss but can sometimes make the operation of the trap rather sluggish so that it does not respond rapidly to changes in load. To overcome this a small radial groove is sometimes machined across the disc where it seats on the outer ring. This allows pressure in the control chamber to bleed slowly to the outlet and the trap operates more rapidly than it otherwise would. This can lead to excessive cycling on occasions and the disc and seats will wear quickly. The small groove can also become blocked by dirt.

One further point is what happens if there is no condensate to be discharged but only live steam when the pressure in the control chamber falls and the disc eventually lifts. In this comparatively rare situation, a very small amount of live steam will be sufficient to seat the disc and the trap will be open only for a fraction of a second. Because a thermodynamic trap can open when there is no condensate present, it is sometimes accused of being a steam waster. In fact, because of its small physical size, it radiates less heat from its body than many steam traps and tests have shown that, so long as it is maintained in good condition, it wastes less energy than comparable float, inverted bucket or bimetal types.

Earlier, reference was made to air reaching the trap on start-up, lifting the disc and passing through to the outlet. The air will pass freely so long as its velocity is insufficient to seat the disc. High-velocity air will act in a similar manner to flashing condensate and so thermodynamic traps can air bind. Consequently, if there is much air to be discharged, it may be necessary to fit a separate air vent in parallel with the trap.

As an alternative, to hold the disc open when the plant is starting up from cold, some thermodynamic traps are fitted with a strip of bimetal below the disc. Once the trap reaches working temperature, the bimetal changes shape and allows the disc to work normally. With such an arrangement, there is always the possibility that, owing to dirt for example, the bimetal will stick and prevent the disc from seating. The trap will then blow continuously and the seating faces will be quickly damaged.

Because thermodynamic traps depend for their operation on high fluid velocities and discharge with a distinct blast action, it is important that they are correctly installed and that the discharge pipework in particular is adequately sized and free from sudden changes in direction close to the trap.

Disadvantages of the thermodynamic trap are the tendency to air bind, which has already been discussed, the noise produced by the sudden blast action, especially if the trap is discharging to atmosphere, and limitations on the minimum inlet pressure and maximum back-pressure. The noise can be considerably reduced simply by fitting a metre or two of pipe to the outlet, but clearly this is not the type of trap to use in, for example, a hospital ward. The inlet and back-pressure limitations are due to the need to maintain sufficient velocity across the underside of the disc to generate the force necessary to seat it.

Thermodynamic traps have many good characteristics which include simplicity of construction, small size and the ability to withstand water hammer, superheat, vibration, freezing and corrosive condensate. They will also work over an exceptionally wide range of pressures without any alteration to the mechanism.

They discharge condensate with a blast action at a temperature which depends on the construction of the trap. The presence of concentric circular grooves on the underside of the discs in some traps has already been mentioned. These disturb the flow of the radial jet and delay the formation of the low-pressure area which draws the disc towards the seat rings. When these grooves are present, the trap discharges condensate closer to steam temperature than when the disc face is plain.

10.5 Impulse traps

The way in which an impulse trap works can be seen from *Figure 10.21*. The moving part is a hollow tube carrying a piston at the top and having a conical valve machined towards the bottom which closes a seat orifice carried by the body. The piston moves up and down in a tapered cylinder attached to the body by a screw thread, so that its position relative to the piston can be varied.

In its lowest position the valve rests on the seat

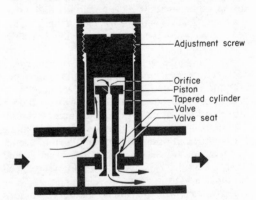

Figure 10.21 Impulse trap

but fluid can still pass through the trap via the clearance between piston and cylinder and the inside of the hollow tube. An orifice at the top of the tube restricts this passage.

This is the path taken by air and cold condensate when steam is turned on. As pressure builds up under the piston, it rises, opening the valve and allowing the trap to discharge. Some condensate continues to pass between the piston and cylinder and through the orifice in the hollow tube to the outlet. Pressure drops across the piston due to this flow, so that the pressure above it is less than that below, keeping the valve open. As the condensate nears steam temperature, some of it flashes into steam as it passes the piston and this collects in the space above the piston from where it tries to escape through the orifice in the tube. Because the steam has a much greater volume than the condensate, its flow is restricted by the orifice to a much greater extent and pressure builds up above the piston, forcing it down the taper. Eventually the piston takes up a position at which the pressures balance and the trap discharges continuously.

If live steam reaches the trap, it builds up enough pressure above the piston to shut the valve, but steam continues to pass down the hollow tube so that there is a continuous leak.

Impulse traps are simple and robust and can handle a large amount of condensate for their size. They cannot air bind, will work over a wide range of steam pressures without any change in valve size and can be used on superheated steam. They will leak steam if no condensate is present and, sometimes, on a light load will open and close rapidly, producing a chattering noise. They are liable to stick should dirt collect in the fine clearance between piston and cylinder.

10.6 Pilot-operated traps

The main valves of all the traps so far described are operated directly by the sensing mechanism, be it float, thermostatic element, bimetal or the like. This puts a limit on the valve size and, therefore, capacity unless the trap is made unreasonably large. To overcome this, traps are available having a large main valve which is opened and closed by the upstream pressure acting on a piston and controlled by a pilot valve which can be temperature- or buoyancy-operated. With this arrangement the sensing element has only to control a small pilot valve and the force required to operate the large main valve is provided by the steam pressure in the plant.

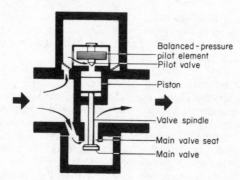

Figure 10.22 Pilot-operated trap

Figure 10.22 shows a trap of this type. The main valve is attached to a spindle which passes up through the valve seat. On top of the spindle is a piston working in a cylinder. Pressure from the inlet port acts on top of the piston which pushes down on the spindle and opens the main valve against the flow of condensate. The pressure on top of the piston is controlled by the pilot valve which, in this case, is a balanced-pressure trap element of the type already described.

When steam is turned on, air and condensate pass freely through the main valve, which has fallen open under its own weight. As pressure builds up it acts on top of the piston, through the open pilot valve, and keeps the main valve open against the force of the flow which will, eventually, try to close it. As the condensate nears steam temperature, the pilot valve element will expand and close its valve and the pressure on top of the piston will leak away to the outlet port via the clearance between piston and cylinder. The flow will now be able to lift the main valve and seat it. When the condensate cools, the pilot element will contract, opening the pilot valve and line pressure will once more act on top of the piston to open the main valve.

10.7 Labyrinth traps

Figure 10.23 shows a labyrinth trap, which consists simply of a series of shaped orifices increasing in size towards the outlet. Cold condensate flows through the trap relatively freely, but, as the temperature approaches that of steam, more and more flash steam is formed as the pressure drops through each stage. This flash chokes the orifices, reducing the flow of condensate and preventing live steam from passing.

An adjustment is provided so that the areas of the orifices can be varied to suit the plant conditions. If the latter change appreciably, the

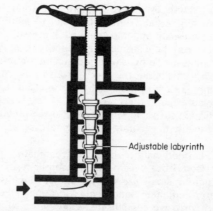

Figure 10.23 Labyrinth trap

trap will need resetting manually if it is not to blow steam or hold back condensate.

10.8 Orifice plates

Although the labyrinth trap is a very simple device, it would be even simpler if there were only one, non-adjustable orifice: in fact, an orifice plate. The main problem, of course, is that the orifice can be the correct size only for one set of conditions and for any others it will either be too large, wasting steam, or too small, holding back condensate. It was because of these shortcomings of the simple orifice, when it was applied to a wide variety of industrial plant, that the steam trap, which is simply an automatically variable orifice, was invented.

Nevertheless, if it so happens that a plant does run for long periods with nearly constant load and pressure conditions, an orifice plate can be used in place of a conventional steam trap and, because it has no moving parts to wear or stick, is likely to prove very reliable.

If the condensate load is small, the orifice, too, must be small with the possibility that it may become blocked with dirt or pipe scale. For this reason it is usual to protect it with a strainer screen.

To give some idea of the small size of orifice required, it is calculated that the drain point on a 200-mm saturated steam main working at a pressure of 10 bar and needing to pass 0.0088 kg/s would need an orifice of diameter 0.8 mm. The calculation includes a safety factor to allow for changes in operating conditions and, consequently, at the design load, this orifice would waste 0.000 13 kg/s, which would be reduced should the load increase or vice versa.

An orifice will, of course, give a continuous discharge of condensate.

10.9 Pumping traps

Pumping traps are not really steam traps at all.
They are displacement pumps operated by steam
or compressed air and are normally used for
lifting condensate or pumping other liquids, for
which reason they are commonly called
'automatic pumps.' Their application as condensate pumps will be referred to later in this
chapter but, because on occasion they can be
used in place of steam traps to remove condensate from steam spaces, their operation will be
described here.

Figure 10.24 shows one type of pumping trap.
Condensate flows into the body by gravity head
through the inlet non-return valve. As the water
level rises it lifts the float, which is loosely
guided by the exhaust valve spindle. Eventually
the float contacts the collar at the top of the
spindle and the latter starts to lift. This opens the
steam inlet valve by means of the lever, and
steam enters the body and starts to build up
pressure. When the pressure differential across
the exhaust valve is sufficient, the valve and
spindle move upwards and the exhaust valve
seats. Pressure in the body continues to rise until
it overcomes any back-pressure on the outlet of
the pump, and condensate is displaced through
the outlet non-return valve. The inlet non-return
valve closes to prevent flow back into the inlet
piping.

As the water level falls, so too does the float,
which eventually contacts the collar at the
bottom of the exhaust valve spindle and, by its
weight, pulls the exhaust valve off its seat, at the
same time closing the steam inlet valve. Any
steam left in the pump body is now vented
through the open exhaust valve, condensate
once again starts to fill the pump through the
inlet non-return valve and the operating cycle is
repeated.

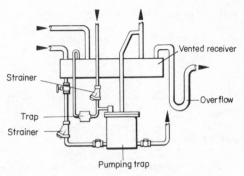

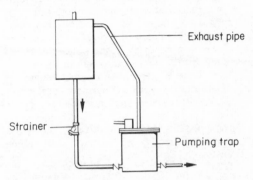

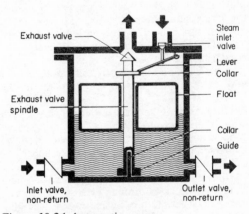

Figure 10.24 Automatic pump

Figure 10.25 Installation of automatic pump

*Figure 10.26   Pumping trap draining steam space
under vacuum pressure*

If compressed air is used as the operating
medium instead of steam, the method of working
is just the same. It is not normally advisable to
use compressed air when condensate is being
pumped because the latter may become aerated
and cause corrosion.

Because the pump fills and empties intermittently, it is necessary to provide a receiver in
which the condensate can collect while the pump
is discharging. This receiver should be vented to
atmosphere so that the pump is able to fill under
a gravity head only and the installation normally
recommended in shown in *Figure 10.25*. A steam
trap is used to drain the steam supply to the
pump to prevent the inlet valve from being
choked by condensate.

Pumping traps can, in some circumstances, be
used to drain steam spaces under vacuum or a
small positive pressure, in which case the
installation shown in *Figure 10.26* is used. The
pump is mounted below the unit being drained so
that there is a gravity-filling head and the
exhaust valve is connected to the top of the
steam space. This allows the pressures in the
steam space and pump body to equalize when the
exhaust valve is open so that the pump can fill
under the gravity head between the two units.
For this type of application to work satisfac-

torily, it must be correctly engineered and so it is advisable to consult the manufacturers of the pumping trap for their recommendations.

10.10 Selection of steam traps

When a steam trap is selected for a particular application, the following points need to be considered:

1. Do the operating characteristics of the trap match those of the plant?
2. Will the trap work up to the required maximum pressure and temperature?
3. Does it have the necessary condensate capacity under all operating conditions?
4. Are the materials from which the trap is made suitable for the conditions?
5. Will the trap stand up to water hammer, vibration, superheat, corrosive condensate or frost if any of these are likely to occur?

These questions are very important if the plant is to work efficiently and each of them merits discussion.

Operating characteristics

The characteristics of the traps most often met with in practice have already been described and it should be clear that there is no universal steam trap capable of dealing with all applications. It is now a matter of deciding which type matches the needs of the plant most closely.

For example, if it is essential to remove all the condensate from the steam space as soon as it forms, it would be better to use a mechanical type, such as a float or inverted bucket trap, rather than a thermostatic trap which would hold back the condensate while it cools down.

Another case is that of a high-duty concentrating vessel such as a brewing copper. This is best drained by a float trap because the heavy blast discharge of an inverted bucket trap can cause the boiling liquor to surge. Again, a noisy blast discharge trap would not be used in, for example, a hospital ward.

In many cases, several different types of trap can be used equally well and choice then becomes a matter of personal experience and preference.

Pressure and temperature limits

Pressure and temperature limits are generally straightforward; either the trap is suitable for the conditions or it is not. Perhaps it is worth mentioning that, when superheat is said to exist, the temperature quoted is very often that of the steam when it leaves the boiler. Unless the degree of superheat is considerable, it is most likely that any steam reaching the trap will be saturated.

Thermodynamic traps will not operate if the back-pressure is excessive and care should be taken to see that this type of trap is not used when the maker's limitations are likely to be exceeded.

Steam trap capacity

The condensate discharge capacity of a steam trap depends mainly on the size of the valve orifice, the differential pressure across it and the temperature of the condensate. Within obvious limits, it does not usually depend on the size of the pipe connections.

Clearly, the larger the diameter of the orifice the greater is the capacity of the trap, but the length and shape of the orifice are also important. In some cases, the flow resistance of the inlet and outlet passages in the trap body can also limit the capacity. It is because of these factors that traps with the same size of orifice can have different capacities.

In the discussion of mechanical traps, the point was made that although a larger orifice gave an increased capacity, it meant that the maximum working differential pressure would be lower unless the operating power and, therefore, the size of the trap was increased. Trap design is therefore a compromise between capacity, maximum pressure and size.

Next the differential pressure must be considered. This is the difference between the pressures at the inlet and outlet of the trap. It is most important to realize that the trap inlet pressure may be quite different from that of the steam supply to the plant. On start-up, when the unit is cold, the rate of condensation will be heavy, causing a considerable pressure drop between the supply main and the steam space. It may take quite a long time before the pressure at the trap has built up to anything approaching the line pressure and during this period it is essential that the trap should be able to discharge the condensate. Even when the plant is warm, any automatic temperature control on the steam inlet may throttle and reduce the pressure in the steam space.

The pressure at the trap outlet may be close to atmospheric but, if the trap is discharging into a condensate return system, it could well be appreciably higher for a number of reasons. The condensate pipe may not be big enough to carry all the condensate as well as the flash steam formed as it passes through the trap orifice to a lower pressure. Other steam traps discharging into the same pipe may be blowing steam, creating a high back-pressure. Finally the return line from the trap may rise so that there is a head of water over the outlet.

The pressure equivalent of a head of stationary water in a vertical pipe 1 m high is 0.098 bar but, in addition, there is the pipe friction when flow is taking place. It is, therefore, safer to allow 0.11 bar for each 1 m of vertical lift when calculating the back-pressure. Taking as an example a steam trap with a gauge pressure of 7 bar at its inlet and a vertical lift after the outlet of 8 m, the differential pressure across it will be 7–(8 × 0.11) = 6.12 bar.

It is also possible for a trap to discharge into a pressure below atmospheric because it is connected to a condenser or vacuum pump. In this case, the differential pressure will be increased by the vacuum and so will the trap capacity. If, in the example just quoted, instead of the condensate being lifted, the trap discharged into a space at an absolute pressure of 0.4 bar, the differential pressure would be 8.013–0.4=7.61 bar instead of 6.12 bar (7.00 bar gauge pressure = 8.013 bar abs).

The third factor affecting capacity is the condensate temperature. Because flash steam is formed when hot condensate passes through an orifice to a lower pressure and will choke the orifice, a steam trap always discharges less hot condensate than cold water. Therefore it is never safe to size a trap on cold-water capacity figures and most manufacturers now publish hot-condensate capacities.

As a general rule, traps should not be greatly oversized. There are some types, such as thermodynamic traps, whose cycling rate is increased, leading to rapid wear. The rate of operation of very lightly loaded inverted bucket traps is also increased, because steam passes through the vent hole in the bucket and condenses in the body and this is wasteful. Finally, oversized traps are often physically larger than they need be and the radiation loss from their bodies is consequently higher.

Materials

Steam trap bodies are usually made from steel, cast iron or brass, the choice normally depending on cost and the maximum working conditions. The petrochemical industry specifies steel for on-site applications regardless of pressure because of the very stringent safety precautions enforced in these plants.

Stainless steel is very widely used for internal components because of its resistance to corrosive condensate.

Adverse conditions

These must be borne in mind when choosing a steam trap. Water hammer, superheat, frost, vibration and corrosive condensate can occur singly or in combination in steam installations and will be dealt with in more detail later. Clearly, if severe water hammer or superheat is unavoidable, it is no use fitting a trap with a comparatively flimsy balanced-pressure bellows element. Instead a robust thermodynamic trap is likely to be a better choice. Float and bucket traps can be damaged if they are allowed to freeze, whereas thermodynamic and bimetal types are often constructed to resist this hazard.

So, before choosing a trap, one should note any adverse factors and take them into account.

10.11 Installing steam traps

More steam trapping troubles are caused by bad installation than by the choice of the wrong type or faulty manufacture. To ensure a trouble-free installation, careful consideration should be given to the following details.

The drain point

It may seem to be stating the obvious to say that the drain point should be arranged so that condensate can easily flow to the trap but this is not always appreciated. For example, it is useless to provide a 15-mm drain hole in the bottom of a 150-mm steam main because most of the condensate will simply be carried past it by the steam velocity. A proper pocket of at least 100 mm diameter is needed into which the condensate can fall.

A steam separator makes a very suitable steam main drain point. In addition to forming an ideal collecting pocket for the condensate, it will also remove water drops from the steam so improving its quality.

The drain point should be at the lowest part of the steam space, otherwise there will always be some condensate left behind and never discharged.

Pipe sizing

The pipes leading to and from steam traps should be of adequate size. This is particularly important in the case of thermodynamic traps because, as mentioned earlier in this chapter, their correct operation can be impaired by excessive resistance to flow in the connecting pipework.

In many instances it is satisfactory to use pipes of the same nominal size as the trap connections, but care should be taken when very large amounts of condensate have to be discharged. The discharge may be accompanied by substantial volumes of flash steam and, unless the discharge pipes are very adequately sized, a high back-pressure will result and the effective capacity of the trap reduced.

Pipe fittings such as globe valves, bends and tees close to the trap will also set up a back-pressure which may, in some circumstances, be excessive.

Air binding

This has already been mentioned when the operation of certain types, such as float traps, was being described. Steam plant will always fill with air when steam is off and this will have to be discharged when steam is turned on again. Air is also carried into the steam space by the steam while the plant is running. This is not the place to deal with the proper air venting of steam spaces, which plays such an important part in ensuring maximum heat output. However, some of the air will be pushed by the steam towards the condensate outlet and must be discharged, either by the trap itself or a thermostatic air vent fitted in parallel with the trap.

The inverted bucket type is an example of a trap which will not air bind completely but will release air only slowly and may need the help of a separate air vent, as shown in *Figure 10.27*. Float traps, on the other hand, are completely closed when the plant is shut down and the air, which cannot escape, will prevent condensate from reaching them to open the valve. For this reason most float traps are now fitted with an automatic air release.

Unless adequate provision is made for removing air, either by the steam trap or a separate air vent, the plant may take a long time to warm up from cold and never give its full output.

Steam locking

This is similar to air binding except that the trap

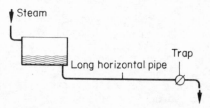

Figure 10.28 Steam locking

is locked shut by steam instead of air. *Figure 10.28* shows a piece of plant drained by a steam trap fitted some distance away on the end of a horizontal pipe. When steam is turned on, air is forced towards the trap and is discharged as is the condensate that follows it. Then live steam fills the pipe and reaches the trap, which closes. Condensate starts to build up in the steam space because it is prevented from reaching the trap by the steam in the connecting pipe. This will continue until the steam in the pipe loses heat to the atmosphere and condenses, which may take quite a long time. Meanwhile the plant is waterlogged and output suffers. This is steam locking.

In this case, the simplest remedy is to fit the trap close to the drain point, doing away with the long connecting pipe and, where possible, traps should always be installed in this way. There are times, however, when this is impossible.

Figure 10.29 shows a rotating drying cylinder from which condensate is removed by a stationary siphon pipe. The siphon pipe passes through the centre of the trunnion bearing in which the cylinder rotates and its lower end dips into the pool of condensate in the bottom of the cylinder. The steam trap is connected to its other end. If the level of condensate drops far enough to uncover the lower end of the siphon pipe, steam will pass up to the trap, which will steam lock. The situation is now even worse than that shown in *Figure 10.28* because most of the siphon pipe is surrounded by live steam and the loss of heat from the steam locked inside it will be very slow.

A further example is shown in *Figure 10.30*. Here the unit is a tilting jacketed pan such as is used in the food industry for boiling jam. As was the case with the drying cylinder, condensate must be raised from the bottom of the steam

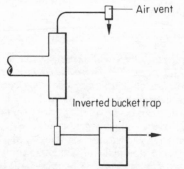

Figure 10.27 Air venting an inverted bucket trap

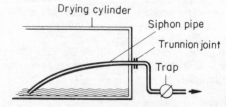

Figure 10.29 Steam locking of a drying cylinder

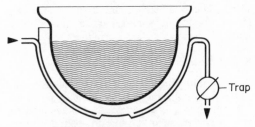

Figure 10.30 Steam locking of a jacketed pan

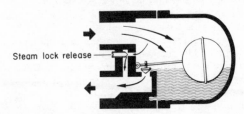

Figure 10.31 Float trap with steam lock release valve

jacket to the trap by some form of siphon pipe and steam locking can occur.

In neither of these examples can the trap be moved closer to the drain point which is, in effect, the lower end of the siphon pipe. It is, therefore, necessary to provide some means of removing the steam locked in the siphon pipe so that the trap can operate normally. This is done by a small bleed valve called a *steam lock release valve,* incorporated into the steam trap *(Figure 10.31).* The small, adjustable valve controls the passage of locked steam from the inside of the trap to the outlet connection. The valve is set under working conditions so that it is open just far enough to allow the trap to operate continuously without locking.

It may be thought that the steam lock release valve is wasting steam, but it should be realized that the steam, once it has entered the siphon pipe or other connecting pipe to the trap, can no longer do any useful work in the steam space. Unless it is removed, it will slow down the process and this will be even more wasteful.

The steam lock release valve will also pass air and prevent the trap from air binding but, correctly set, it will vent air only slowly. When the amount of air is considerable, a thermostatic air vent should also be used, either built into the trap or fitted in a by-pass around it.

Group trapping

It is tempting to try to save money by connecting several units to one steam trap as shown in *Figure 10.32.* This is known as group trapping and is rarely successful, normally causing water-

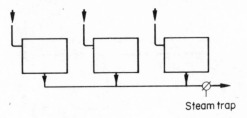

Figure 10.32 Group trapping

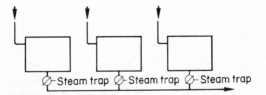

Figure 10.33 Individual trapping

logging and loss of output. The steam consumptions of a number of units are never the same at any particular moment in time and, therefore, the pressures in the various steam spaces will also be different. It follows that the pressure at the drain outlet of a heavily loaded unit will be less than in the case of one that is more lightly loaded.

If all the units are connected to a single steam trap, the condensate from the heavily loaded and therefore lower-pressure steam space is going to find it difficult to reach the trap against the higher pressure produced by the lightly loaded units. Indeed, the latter may even have allowed live steam to get to the trap, which is then effectively locked shut.

The only satisfactory answer is to drain each steam space with its own trap and then connect the outlets of the various traps to the common condensate return main *(see Figure 10.33).*

Dirt

Dirt is a common enemy of steam traps and the cause of many failures. New steam systems contain mill scale, casting sand, weld metal, swarf and pieces of packing and jointing materials. When the system has been in use for a while, the inside of the pipework and fittings may be attacked by corrosive condensate so that rust, in the form of a fine brown powder, is also likely to be present. All this dirt will be carried through the system by the steam and condensate until it reaches the steam traps. Some of it will pass through the traps into the condensate system without doing harm, but inevitably at some stage the dirt will jam the mechanism.

Sometimes the trap is preceded by a dirt pocket as shown in *Figure 10.34,* but not all the

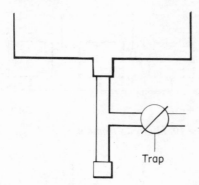

Figure 10.34 Dirt pocket

dirt will fall into the pocket and some will still be carried into the trap by the condensate. Because of this it is now common practice either to fit a strainer with a woven wire mesh or perforated metal screen immediately before the trap *(see Figure 10.35)* or to include a screen inside the trap itself *(see Figure 10.36)*. The latter arrangement is neat and does not involve extra installation costs, but very often the size of screen has to be severely reduced if it is to fit into the available space, nor is it so easily cleaned. There is no point in fitting a strainer unless it is cleaned regularly, otherwise it will simply block up and prevent the flow of condensate. The frequency with which strainers will need to be cleaned will vary with the amount of dirt in the system and this will soon be found from experience. New installations should, if possible, be blown through before the traps are finally

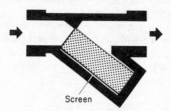

Figure 10.35 Strainer

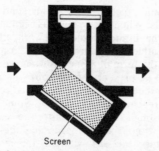

Figure 10.36 Thermodynamic trap with strainer screen

fitted. The strainers should then be inspected frequently until it is clear that the initial dirt has gone.

Water hammer

Water hammer in a steam system is caused by condensate collecting in the plant or pipework and being picked up by the fast-moving steam and carried along until it hits an obstruction such as a bend, valve, steam trap or some other pipe fitting. The resulting shock is likely to cause noise, damage to fittings and equipment and leaking pipe joints.

The cause of the water hammer should be eliminated by realigning the pipes so that there is a continuous fall in the direction of flow of at least 12 mm in every 3 m and providing an adequate number of drain points. Along a straight run of main the latter should occur every 30–50 m. It is particularly important to drain any low points in the system and to make sure that the steam traps do not hold back condensate in the main.

Water hammer may also occur in process plant if, at any time, the pressure in the steam space falls below that at the trap outlet so that condensate discharge stops. This will almost certainly happen if condensate is lifted after the trap into a high-level return line and the steam inlet to the plant is throttled by a temperature control valve. As condensate builds up in the steam space, the process temperature will fall, causing the temperature control valve to open wide and steam to rush into the waterlogged plant, producing severe water hammer.

With this type of system it is best to discharge the condensate by gravity from the steam trap to a receiver vented to atmosphere and lift it up to high level by means of a pump. Even so, it is still possible for the steam space to waterlog should the steam supply be throttled enough for a vacuum to form. This can sometimes be dealt with by fitting a vacuum-breaking valve to the plant but if, for some reason, this is not possible, the water hammer must be accepted as inevitable and a steam trap chosen which is capable of withstanding the shock.

Superheat

The main reason for superheating steam is to obtain the maximum amount of power from it when it is expanded in a steam turbine. Also on large factory sites it is often distributed in the superheated state so that it is still reasonably dry when it reaches the process plant, which may be a long way from the boilerhouse.

Although in theory condensate and super-heated steam cannot exist together and consequently there should be no need to drain a superheated steam main, in practice this is not so. Condensate will be formed when the main is started up from cold and, even when the main is up to temperature, it is possible for saturated steam to condense on the wall of the pipe although a core of superheated steam is passing down the centre.

It is, of course, necessary to ensure that any steam traps fitted to a superheated steam main are suitable for the temperature and pressure conditions.

Corrosion

The principal cause of corrosion in a steam system is incorrect treatment of the feedwater or even no treatment at all. Free oxygen and carbon dioxide may form and dissolve in the condensate, turning it into a dilute acid which will then attack the piping and fittings, including steam traps. In addition, priming and foaming may occur in the boiler so that water, carrying feed treatment chemicals and other impurities, may pass over into the steam system and attack it. Sometimes the correct feed treatment chemicals are misused when, to save time, a large quantity is added in a single dose instead of more gradually at shorter intervals.

Condensate can also become corrosive by coming into contact with chemicals used to carry out an industrial process. For example, steam coils may be used to heat tanks or vats containing corrosive liquors. If a coil perforates, liquid will be drawn in when the plant is shut down and the residual steam in the coil condenses, forming a partial vacuum. This corrosive liquid will eventually reach the steam trap and may even find its way back to the boiler. Again, steam may come into direct contact with the material being processed as happens when rubber is vulcanized in an autoclave and the resulting condensate will be corrosive.

At one time, because of the materials available, it was inevitable that steam traps used on these applications would corrode away sooner rather than later. Now, because of the increased use of stainless steels, there is a better chance of finding a trap to withstand the corrosion for a reasonable time except when very aggressive chemicals are used. These remarks apply equally to any thermostatic air vents used on this type of application.

Of course it is not only the steam traps and air vents that will suffer if the condensate becomes corrosive; pipework and other fittings may also be attacked. It is particularly important that corrosive chemicals should not get back to the boiler and, where there is any danger of this

happening, the condensate should not be returned for use as boiler feedwater. After the heat has been extracted it might, for example, be used in a washing or rinsing process.

Frost damage

If a steam trap contains condensate when steam is turned off and the surrounding temperature is low enough, the water will freeze and may damage the trap, depending on its construction. If freezing is likely to occur it is best to fit traps that will stand up to the resulting stresses. Thermodynamic, bimetallic or balanced-pressure traps with steel bodies are widely used on exposed sites for this reason.

In countries where the winters are particularly severe, it is common practice to prevent exposed steam traps, valves and similar equipment from freezing up by surrounding them with heated tracer lines.

By-passes

At one time it was common practice to fit by-passes, controlled by stop valves, around steam traps because it was found that plant performance could be improved if the by-pass valve was opened. This usually occurred during start-up and simply indicated that the installation was suffering from air binding or steam locking or that the traps had insufficient capacity to handle the starting load.

Over the years, by-passes have been responsible for a tremendous waste of live steam either because the valves leak when shut or operators have left them wide open. Fortunately with a better understanding of steam trapping techniques, the need for by-passes has greatly diminished and they are no longer fitted as a matter of course.

Now that energy conservation is so important, by-passes should be provided only on those applications where continuous operation is vital and it is impossible to shut the plant down even for a short time to attend to a faulty steam trap. In these cases it is advisable to lock the by-pass valves to prevent unauthorized operation and they should be regularly inspected to ensure they are not leaking.

If a by-pass is fitted around an inverted bucket trap, it is essential that it should be positioned above the trap to avoid the loss of the water seal in the trap body.

Lifting condensate

In the interests of energy and water saving, every effort should be made to recover and reuse condensate. Often this means that the

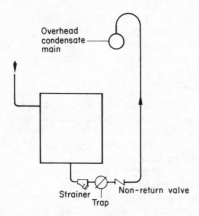

Figure 10.37 Lifting condensate

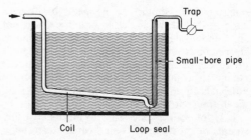

Figure 10.39 Coil-heated tank: correct layout

condensate must be lifted into a return main above the plant. There are also instances where the layout of the plant dictates that the steam traps must be fitted above the units being drained and wrong installation can lead to trouble.

Because of the back-pressure imposed on the steam trap, it is often better not to lift condensate directly from the trap but to let it flow by gravity to a pump or pumping trap which can do the lifting. However, if it is decided that the condensate can be lifted by the pressure at the trap, it is important that the installation is correctly arranged.

Figure 10.37 shows a typical example. The trap, protected by a strainer, should be fitted at the bottom of the lift, close to and below the drain outlet to prevent steam locking. A non-return valve follows the trap and from it the rising pipe is taken up into the top of the condensate main. The non-return valve will prevent condensate from running back into the trap and the steam space when steam is turned off. This is also a reason for leading the condensate into the top of the return main but, in addition, the condensate in the rising pipe will be accompanied by flash steam, which could well cause water hammer if it were discharged into the cooler condensate in the lower part of the return main.

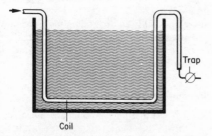

Figure 10.38 Coil-heated tank: incorrect layout

The non-return valve may also seat well enough to isolate the trap from back-pressure in the condensate system and allow it to be serviced, but it is probably safer to fit isolating valves on either side of the trap in case the non-return valve leaks.

Figure 10.38 shows a piece of plant where the layout makes it impossible to fit the trap at the bottom of the rising pipe. Many plating vats and metal treatment tanks are heated in this way by steam coils and, because of the corrosive nature of the contents, it is not possible to run the outlet of the coil through the wall of the tank. Instead it must rise up and pass over the top to the trap. If the trap is simply fitted to the end of the coil, as in *Figure 10.38,* it will be steam locked as steam passes over the condensate lying in the bottom of the coil and then up the rising pipe to the trap. When eventually the steam lock is broken and condensate starts to rise up to the trap, steam will again get into the rising column, breaking up the flow, and the process will be repeated.

Figure 10.39 shows a much better arrangement. At the bottom of the rising pipe the coil is looped to form a water seal. A small-bore pipe is then passed through a steam-tight joint in the top of the rising pipe and its end is pushed well down into the loop seal. The trap is fitted as close to the top of this pipe as possible. The water seal now makes it much harder for steam to enter the pipe leading up to the trap and the small bore of this pipe ensures that the water column rises steadily, unbroken by steam bubbles.

If an inverted bucket trap is fitted at the top of the small-bore pipe, it is important to drop down into the trap and fit a non-return valve immediately before the inlet to prevent loss of water seal from the trap.

General points

Steam traps should always be fitted in accordance with the maker's instructions. It is particularly important that mechanical traps of the float or bucket types are fitted the correct way up. Unless this is done, the mechanisms will not be able to operate and the traps will hold back condensate or, more usually, blow live steam continuously.

When planning the pipework, ensure that the trap is accessible for maintenance and there is sufficient clearance around it to allow it to be dismantled. Pipe unions fitted close to the inlet and outlet will permit the complete trap to be removed readily for repair or replacement.

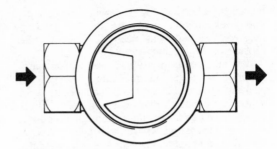

Figure 10.40 Sight glass

10.12 Steam trap maintenance

Steam traps generally work under arduous conditions, handling a mixture of steam and condensate, and are fitted in such a position that they form a natural repository for any dirt in the system. Because they contain moving parts, steam traps will eventually wear and, like any other mechanism, require regular maintenance if they are to continue working efficiently.

Unfortunately, all too often traps are neglected until they eventually fail and when this happens it is quite likely that live steam will blow to waste. In addition the material being processed may well be damaged. As an indication of the amount of energy that can be wasted by a blowing steam trap, an orifice of diameter 5 mm can pass 0.017 kg/s of steam at a pressure differential of 8 bar. This is equivalent to wasting about 25 tonnes of fuel oil in a working year of 6000 hours.

All steam traps should undergo regular scheduled maintenance. It is impossible to lay down any general period between inspections because operating conditions, even in the same plant, vary very widely. It is suggested that they should be checked at least annually and the screens of any associated strainers cleaned at the same time.

Checking steam traps

When there is a large number of steam traps in a plant, checking each of them for correct operation can be very tedious and time-consuming.

If the traps happen to discharge to atmosphere, it is usually possible to decide whether or not all is well by watching the end of the outlet pipe. Blast discharge traps should close off tight, leaving only a small wisp of steam as any remaining drops of condensate at the trap outlet evaporate. Continuous-discharge traps present a more difficult problem because the jet of condensate is accompanied by flash steam formed during passage through the valve orifice to a lower pressure. If, between the end of the discharge pipe and the visible jet of steam, there is a transparent zone with a hazy bluish appearance, it is likely that the trap is blowing

steam. However, in most cases the traps will discharge into a closed condensate return system, which makes the task of checking much more difficult. One solution is to fit a sight glass after each trap so that the discharge pattern can be studied through the glass window *(see Figure 10.40)*.

Another possibility is to use a stethoscope, rather like the medical variety, consisting of a metal rod joined to a diaphragm to which is connected a normal pair of earpieces. This is particularly useful in the case of blast discharge traps because each time the trap opens and closes the noise can be clearly heard.

Ultrasonic leak detectors can also be used on steam traps and have an advantage over stethoscopes because they can be set so that disturbances within very short distances of the traps do not interfere with the sound made by the traps themselves.

Quite a lot of practice is needed before the sounds heard through stethoscopes and ultrasonic leak detectors can be interpreted at all accurately. It is best to practise on a variety of traps arranged to discharge through open-ended pipes so that the sounds can be related to the visible evidence of operation.

The measurement of temperature in the line close to the trap is sometimes suggested as a way of deciding whether or not it is working correctly. Because it is difficult to measure pipe surface temperatures accurately and then to interpret the results, this method calls for great care and some experience, otherwise wrong conclusions can very easily be drawn.

Repairing steam traps

Faulty traps should be repaired as soon as possible for several reasons. First, if they are blowing steam, this is a direct waste of energy. Secondly, the performance of the plant may be adversely affected by a defective trap and expensive material spoiled. Finally, damage may be done to the trap itself, and, if the repairs are postponed, what would have been a simple matter of cleaning and renewing components may well involve replacing the whole trap because the body has been damaged by the erosion of the escaping steam.

It is important only to use replacement parts supplied by the trap manufacturer. Normally all gaskets should be renewed and joint faces properly cleaned. Valve seats and gasket joints should have a small amount of jointing compound applied to them and, where a particular torque is specified for tightening screwed components, this should be used on reassembly.

Finally the trap should be tested under working conditions to make sure that all the faults have been rectified.

It should be clear from this chapter that, despite their apparent simplicity, steam traps have a very important role to play in the efficient operation of steam plant. If they are to do this satisfactorily, they should be chosen carefully, bearing in mind that low cost is not always the most important factor, installed correctly and maintained regularly.

Reference

1. Northcroft, L.G. and Barber, W.M. *Steam Trapping and Air Venting*. London: Hutchinson Educational (1979)

11

Turbines and engines

11.1 Introduction

To use steam efficiently is not just a matter of getting high efficiency. It means getting a good return from any project — and efficiency is only one of the issues which go towards this.

Take a steam power-station, for instance. The money we pay to earn revenue from electricity includes:

1. first cost;
2. the fuel bill (affected by the efficiency and cost of fuel selected);
3. the maintenance bill;
4. the staff bill

and the amount of money we earn depends on the tariff, but also on:

5. running hours;
6. the average load, and
7. availability.

So in considering how efficiently we use steam in a power project, all seven factors have to be taken into account, and some are more important than others. To help appreciate which factors often matter most, here are some approximate figures for a small oil-fired power-station, say in North Africa or the Middle East. The absolute values do not matter and in fact could well mislead, because costs can change dramatically with time. What's more important is to pick out the significant factors by comparing the different amounts.

The station chosen has four 100-MW condensing steam turbo-alternators, and the steam is raised in oil-fired boilers. Mechanical and electrical works and civil works are included. The machines do not use reheat.

First cost

Take £300/kW as approximating to the world price for such a station:

First cost = £120 million = C

Fuel bill

| Take life as 100000 hours Take operating load factor as 50% | Total kWh = 50000 × 400000 = 2×10^{10} |

225

(operating load factor is $\dfrac{\text{average load carried}}{\text{full load}} \times 100\%$)

Take station heat rate as 9750 kJ/kWh at full load. (This is the common way of expressing efficiency. It is roughly inversely proportional to efficiency — just to make life difficult!). The heat rate will be higher most of the time because load is often less than full, so assume the heat rate is 9750/0.85 = 11 470 kJ/kWh.

Take fuel as 40 200 kJ/kg lower calorific value. Amount of fuel burnt is therefore 11 470/40 200 = 0.285 kg/kWh.

$$\frac{0.285 \times 2 \times 10^{10}}{1000} = 5.7 \times 10^6 \text{ t}$$

Take oil cost of £47/t

Fuel bill = £268 million = 2.2 × C

Note: Critics will most certainly say that fuel price will vary enormously over the life of the set, and we have ignored this; but note that we have also ignored the interest to be paid to borrow the money — as most authorities do — to pay for the station. We assume that the interest is written off by balancing it against increase in fuel cost — and this seems as accurate an assumption as many made in the industry!

Maintenance bill

The maintenance costs depend very much on plant selected, on how it is run and on how the maintenance is planned. Take a probably optimistic view and assume that the maintenance bill is only 20% of first cost of station. It could well be higher!

Maintenance bill = £24 million = 0.2 × C

Staff bill

The staff bill will vary greatly from country to country, but take total staff as 100 and average cost per person including vast overheads as £16000/year. Then

Total staff bill = 100 × £16000/year × 25 years
= £40 million = 0.3 × C

The total expenditure therefore includes for electricity at the station:

First cost	= £120 million	= C
Fuel bill	= £268 million	= 2.2C
Maintenance bill	= £24 million	= 0.2C
Staff bill	= £40 million	= 0.3C

It also includes many other things such as land cost and services, but note that distribution costs have been ignored. However, and even though several assumptions have been made, these figures begin to show the relative importance of different aspects.

If we take the money earned we have a simple sum:

Effective generating hours × average kW generated
(100000)   (200000)
× tariff £/kWh = total earnings
(0.05)   (£1000 million)

(Tariff is selected from current ones, all vastly different!). This may again exclude a number of issues but it is reasonable for present purposes. One is tempted to compare the outlay, which totals £452 million, with these earnings of £1000 million. This would mislead because many items such as distribution costs are ignored. The figures nevertheless help give a perspective to a number of issues and to emphasize the important factors which affect earnings such as:

1. life capability of plant;
2. load factor — the higher the load generated the more earned;
3. reliability — if availability is poor then other less efficient plant has to be run and the earning capacity of a project can be ruined.

Of course no one wants to make a loss, so the final adjusting factor to offset all sins and omissions or to glorify the success of a project, is the tariff. But if this is too high engineers are criticized so it is not really an adjusting factor after all, but an indication of success or failure.

Taking all these matters together and considering both expenditure and return it is clear that some points stand out as especially important in judging the form which a steam power project should take and the requirements of plant to use in it. They are:

1. first cost;
2. reliability;
3. efficiency;
4. load factor;
5. life;
6. ease of maintenance;
7. ease of handling, and
8. number and quality of staff required.

For the case taken, fuel bill stands out as a main expenditure — and obviously efficiency as such is the important issue here. The fuel, over the life of the plant, costs more than twice as much as the power-station itself. However, first cost of station is still a large and significant sum, and although the staff and maintenance bills together are much less than the fuel bill, they are still large amounts. Most important is reliability, or lack of it, which directly affects the earnings which as we have seen are several times as large as the fuel bill. Poor availability can ruin a project by turning a profit into a loss.

So efficiency in its strict thermodynamic sense, whilst very important, is not the only factor. It is amongst many which have to be considered. All of them go together to deserve attention when considering power plant and the efficient use of steam in it and by it. This fact is reflected in the sections which follow and in which we shall not only be examining means of making power plant work at higher efficiencies but also these other factors such as reliability and load factor; because they too have an influence on the efficient use of steam.

11.2 Power from steam: some facts about the cycle

This section deals briefly with how steam makes power. It aims to get the basic concepts right before going on to the later sections which go more deeply into how engines and turbines work and how we can best use them. Some mathematics and thermodynamics are given, but the important logic can still be understood without knowing much about these subjects.

The basic cycle

Power is produced by raising steam in a boiler and making it do work in an engine or turbine. The steam could be exhausted to the air — as it used to be in steam locomotives — but this is wasteful. Since much of the energy in steam is at pressures below atmospheric, it pays to exhaust the steam to a vacuum, unless there is good reason such as use of exhaust steam in a factory. So most machines exhaust to a condenser. Also, the water from con-

densed steam is valuable because it has to be pure so as not to corrode the steam plant, and it contains heat. For both reasons it is saved by returning it to the boiler after draining from the condenser; hence the classic steam plant ring as shown in *Figure 11.1*.

Fuel adds heat to the boiler to change water into steam, which drives the turbine or engine and thus loses much of its energy. The spent steam exhausts to a condenser where coolant takes out most of the heat and the steam reappears as water. This is then pumped back to the boiler, forming a continuous cycle.

The steam to the turbine is superheated in most plant, rather than being left almost wet. This is because it is more efficient to do so and also because neither engines, turbines nor piping like wet steam. They cannot use it efficiently and they suffer damage from the water.

The fluid goes round and round the ring of steam plant, always returning to the same state at each point in the plant — at each of points 1, 2, 3, 4, in *Figure 11.1* for instance. Thermodynamicists call this a 'cycle'. They use mathematical models to examine the merits of this cycle for steam plant and to compare it with other cycles such as diesel, petrol engines, gas turbines, etc. The most common cycle for steam is called the *Rankine cycle* after the famous Scottish engineer who did some of the early studies of it.

We can use diagrams to compare the merits of the various cycles. For those who wish to be reminded of them, *Figure 11.2* gives three diagrams for the Rankine cycle and with the state points 1, 2, 3 and 4 such that the fluid can be followed round the plant diagram of *Figure 11.1* and the same points seen in *Figure 11.2*.

Another tool used by thermodynamicists is called *Carnot efficiency*, which is a concept that

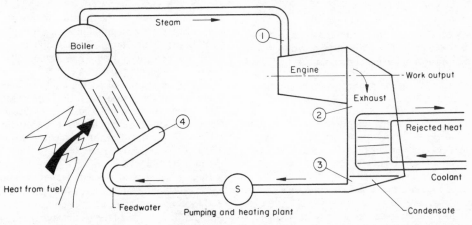

Figure 11.1   The basic plant of the steam cycle. (Follow the state-points through the diagrams of Figure 11.2: points 1, 2, 3 and 4 all correspond)

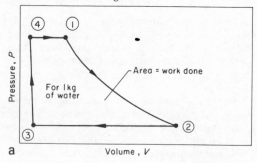

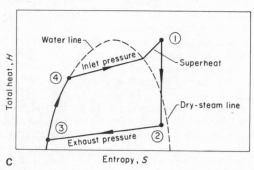

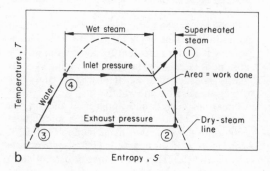

Figure 11.2   (a) Pressure–volume diagram for the steam cycle; (b) temperature–entropy diagram; (c) total heat–entropy diagram

helps them compare different types of engine. The idea is that a perfect engine is used as a datum and it can be shown to have an efficiency of

$$\eta_C = \frac{T_1 - T_2}{T_1} \times 100\% = \text{Carnot efficiency}$$

where T_1 is the absolute temperature at the engine inlet and T_2 is the absolute temperature at the exhaust. No engine using fluid at T_1 and exhausting at T_2 can have a higher efficiency than this. In practice they all have much lower ones.

To get a feel for the best the steam cycle can do let us work out its Carnot efficiency. Take 496°C as the steam inlet temperature as in a medium-sized power-station for the Middle East. Take 38.3°C as the exhaust temperature (this corresponds to

about 68 mbar back-pressure, which is a usual figure for such a plant).

$$T_1 = 769 \text{ K}$$

$$T_1 = 311.3 \text{ K}$$

$$\eta_C = \frac{769 - 311.3}{769} \times 100$$

$$= \frac{457.7}{769} \times 100$$

$$= 59.5\%$$

And here we have the depressing fact that we cannot convert more than 60% of the fuel energy into work no matter how hard we try — at least for the simple cycle.

Practical steam plant is even worse than this theoretical plant. A modern large power-station, with all its costly and crafty arrangements, barely achieves half this efficiency, and about two-thirds of the fuel energy is lost. Much of the careful thought and engineering that go into steam plant is to find ways of regaining this two-thirds.

A rough guide is that each tonne of fuel provided can be divided into three equal parts. The first goes to provide useful work. The second is wasted because the basic cycle is so inefficient and the third is also wasted because the plant we provide cannot even meet the efficiency of the basic cycle.

These figures show that there are great savings of money to be made by innovating to improve the cycle of the simple steam plant and by making the machinery itself work better. Such is the constant theme of steam engineering and of the next few sections on engines and turbines. First though, it is as well to look at some of the reasons why the steam cycle is far from perfect and why it fails to reach the ideal set by the thermodynamicists.

It is also quite reasonable to ask why we bother at all to use steam plant if it is so inefficient. In fact its rivals are often no better and steam plant has many advantages as will be seen.

The main source of inefficiency in the steam cycle is heat thrown away in the engine exhaust. Returning to the simple concept of Carnot efficiency, if the engine exhausted at absolute zero temperature, the Carnot efficiency would be 100%. Of course no engine can do this and even at the modest temperature of 38°C the exhaust takes with it a great deal of useful heat. Conditions commonly met with in industrial steam turbines and medium power-stations such as are found in the Middle East are of the order of 86.2 bar, 496°C at inlet and exhaust at 67.7 mbar and say 10% wet. (All pressures are given in bar absolute.) Steam tables will show that each kilogram of this steam contains 3382 kJ of heat and the exhaust steam contains 2311 kJ, which is mostly thrown away. The process is best demonstrated by calculating its efficiency. Here we use Rankine rather than Carnot efficiency because it has far more meaning for steam.

Rankine efficiency = η_R

where $$\eta_R = \frac{H_i - H_e}{H_i - h_e} \times 100\%$$

which for a simple plant means

$$\frac{\text{Work done}}{\text{Heat available}} \times 100\%$$

H_i is the total heat at the turbine inlet, H_e is the total heat at the turbine exhaust and h_e is the sensible heat of the condensate. For the figures given,

$$\eta_R = \frac{3382 - 2331}{3382 - 158} \times 100\%$$

$$= 32.6\%$$

i.e. 67.4% of the energy in the inlet steam is not used!

The main reason for this loss is the great amount of heat taken away by the exhaust and dumped in the sea or atmosphere. So, it is important to keep this loss down by choosing as low an exhaust pressure as possible, and sometimes, by making use of the exhaust heat for factory processes or even for district heating. It is certainly well worth thinking about such schemes when steam turbines are used in industry and there are other needs for heat or steam in the factory.

The steam cycle is not the worst cycle for throwing heat away in its exhaust. In fact it is one of the best because it can exhaust at a much lower temperature than the gas turbine, oil engine and petrol engine, which have very hot exhausts. They offset their high exhaust loss by using higher inlet temperatures than the steam turbine though it is at the expense of shorter life and other complications.

Apart from the exhaust loss there are many other sources of loss in practice and *Figure 11.3* shows what the various losses are for a typical simple steam plant of boiler and turbine and how they compare with each other and with the work done. Again it will be seen how important the exhaust loss is. This is partly because the steam temperature is fairly low — say 38°C. Thus the water or air used to cool and condense the exhaust leaves the condenser at a temperature even lower than 38°C, so it is difficult to make much use of the

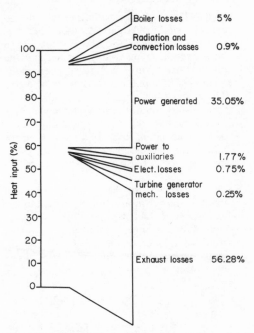

Figure 11.3   Analysis of the energy in a simple cycle of a steam power plant using a boiler, turbine and condenser

heat they take away. Still, various schemes are possible as will be dealt with in Section 11.6.

The other losses in the engine itself are much smaller but are often easier to reduce. For instance, keeping the turbine blades in good order, avoiding leaky glands and keeping the bearings in good condition are all means of saving energy. These and other factors are mentioned in Sections 11.3 - 11.5. They are matters of good design and good maintenance. There are also a number of very useful ideas to apply to make the basic cycle more efficient. Most steam plant uses one or other of them and later sections deal with them. They include feedheating, reheat, back-pressure arrangements to use exhaust heat, pass-out and the use of gas turbines and steam turbines together in a common cycle.

The advantages of steam plant must be recognized if we are to get a true, modern perspective of its place in power production. As against the disadvantages perhaps of size and complication, there are important merits and these are:

1. The enormous ability of steam turbines to produce power. Steam turbines are developed to larger and still larger sizes and far outstrip in potential the power capacity of gas turbines, oil engines, or petrol engines. Currently the output of a single-shaft turbine may be as

high as 1200 MW. It is technically possible to conceive of much larger sizes than 1200 MW whereas not long ago 30 MW was thought to be a large machine. All this is without the physical size of turbine increasing very much — far less than in the ratio of work increase. The reasons why this is so are inherent in the construction of the steam turbine and its simplicity and the modest temperatures it uses. In fact larger sizes often produce higher efficiencies because gland, bearing and other losses do not increase in step with power.

2. Another reason for the popularity of steam plant for power production is that it can use all types of fuel whereas other engines cannot. Steam power is currently produced from many sources including coal, oil (in many varieties), gas, nuclear energy, waste heat from processes (sugar, wood, nuts, oil

refining, etc), refuse and geothermal energy. This versatility is basically because an open cycle is used, the fuel and steam circuits being quite separate.

3. The steam cycle uses only modest temperatures and its parts can therefore last a long time. Power-station steam turbines are often designed to last 200 000 hours, which is many times the life of a gas turbine.

In comparison, internal-combustion engines burn the fuel within the engine and need a careful selection of fuel if they are not to be damaged by chemical attack. They most usually burn gas, petrol or specially distilled oil.

As against these facts in its favour, steam power plant tends to be dimensionally larger than gas turbines and other prime movers and more complicated. This is because of the boiler and various pumps and heat exchangers which go with it. Though it has little competition for the high-power

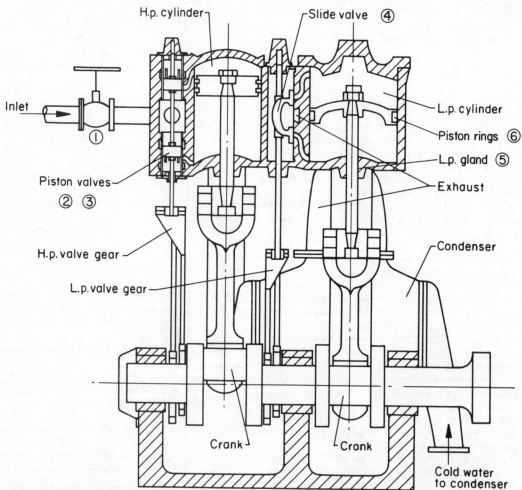

Figure 11.4   Section of a compound marine steam engine and condenser

range, it has fierce competition for small and medium powers. For instance warships once used steam exclusively but steam has mostly given way to gas turbines, because they are lighter, cheaper and more manoeuvrable.

In the end one realizes that there is no one prime mover which will dominate all uses. However, steam power plant has an important part to play and it is an asset for most engineers to know best how to use it. The next few sections should help.

11.3 The steam engine

General

Steam power was first produced by engines as opposed to turbines — apart from Hero's turbine which appears to have been just a toy. The early engines were slow and used very low pressures; they were used to operate pumps in mines and drove them by large swinging beams. This brought higher pressures and various innovations, chiefly the condenser (which greatly improved plant economy), the crankshaft drive and a succession of more useful valve and other mechanisms. Locomotives generally used atmospheric exhaust — no condensers — but the more modern engines in marine use and in factories used condensers. The steam engine is now rare and the description here is therefore brief. It centres on the condensing engine.

How the steam engine works

Figure 11.4 shows a marine steam engine. Steam from the boiler enters through valve (1) and goes to the cylinder and piston, usually through a control valve (2). Various sorts are used but the piston valve (3) and for the second cylinder the 'D' valve (4) shown are the most popular. These valves are driven by eccentrics and arrange for steam admission to cut off at points 'b' and 'g' in *Figure 11.5*. This means that the valve closes before the piston has completed its full stroke. The steam trapped in the cylinder then expands for the rest of the piston stroke. Unless steam is used expansively in this way, the engine will be inefficient.

When pressures of the order of say 7 and 14 bar are used, there is still considerable energy in the steam when it leaves the first cylinder, so a second cylinder is added and this is called 'compounding'. Marine engines commonly had a third and even fourth cylinder. Each has to be larger in diameter as the steam reaches lower and lower pressures and each has to have its own valve gear (4). Finally, the steam leaves the last cylinder and goes to the condenser.

There are great varieties of engines, for example Willans, Uniflow, Bauer Wach, and studying them makes interesting reading — if only

to show the ingenuity and resourcefulness of the engineers who designed them using the knowledge and materials which were then available. Most engines are now extinct, but it may be useful to mention briefly a few points to watch to save fuel, in case the reader happens to come across one of the survivors.

How to get the best use out of the engine

Valve timing

Unless the valves are set carefully to give the right cut-off and exhaust point the engine economy will be reduced. The plant is very sensitive to valve timing.

Vacuum

So much of the work is done at sub-atmospheric pressures (*Figure 11.5*) that it is necessary to get as high a vacuum as possible. The low-pressure (l.p.) glands (5 in *Figure 11.4*) need particular care to stop air leaks ruining the vacuum. Exhaust joints too need careful checking for tightness.

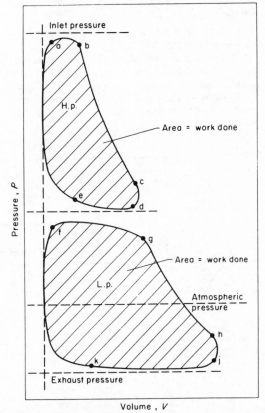

Figure 11.5   Pressure–volume diagram for a compound steam engine

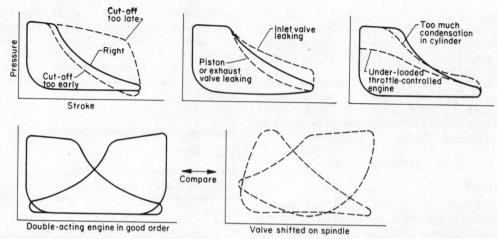

Figure 11.6   Disorders revealed in a steam engine by the study of indicator cards

Piston rings

Piston rings (6 in *Figure 11.4*) and cylinders wear in time and allow steam to blow past the piston, which reduces plant efficiency. Rings should be replaced to stop this.

Lubrication

The mechanism has a number of bearings and slides, all of which lose energy by friction and so need careful alignment and lubrication. In particular, one should make sure that the glands are in good condition, and are set properly (5 in *Figure 11.4*) because they can become stiff and waste energy. On the other hand they must not lose steam or admit air.

Indicator diagrams

These show pressure plotted against volume as in *Figure 11.5*. The shape of the diagrams reveals how healthy the engine is. *Figure 11.6* shows some common faults to watch for, to help save fuel. Indicator diagrams should be taken periodically as a check on engine performance.

Uses and limitations

The steam engine is a much more cumbersome mechanism than the turbine so it has a lower mechanical efficiency. Also it cannot readily use very high steam conditions because of the problem of sealing the pistons and yet allowing them to slide, and higher efficiencies are not easy to attain.

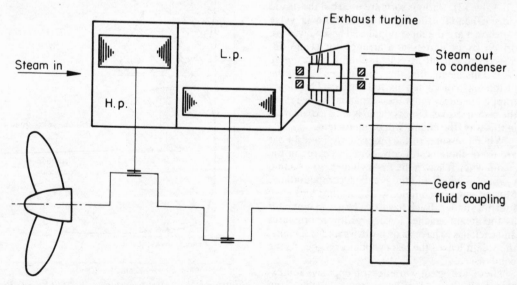

Figure 11.7   Bauer Wach principle of compounding of engine and turbine

Some arrangements improve efficiency by adding an exhaust turbine (e.g. the Bauer Wach principle) but at the expense of a gearbox and fluid coupling (*Figure 11.7*) and a higher first cost.

The engine is essentially low-speed compared with the turbine, because the mechanism becomes more highly stressed than a turbine rotor does at higher speeds. Both this and the complicated arrangement make it a very large machine for high powers, and it tends to be used only at low powers. At these low powers the diesel, gas turbine and petrol engines easily surpass it in economy and convenience of use. An awkward feature of the steam engine is that new hot steam entering the cylinder loses heat to the cylinder walls, which have been cooled by the previous charge of steam when it became spent. This is a significant heat loss.

The steam engine is almost extinct because it cannot produce great power and yet is inefficient and cumbersome for the low powers it can produce. However, it may yet survive. The pollution problem in cities and the scarcity of fuel have created new interest in the use of steam engines in cars and heavy transport. Boilers burn steadily whereas the flames in petrol and diesel engines go off and on at high frequency. For this and other reasons the steam cycle gives a cleaner exhaust. It can also burn less costly fuel than petrol and diesel oils and has quite a useful torque characteristic.

There are a number of engineers looking into steam plant for road transport. At the moment, the difficulty is not the engine itself, but the heat exchangers and overall control. Still, some developments may yet occur which will bring back the steam engine. Meanwhile, it remains a nearly extinct animal, except, perhaps, for the growing number being retrieved by engineers in their spare time for nostalgic reasons.

11.4 The steam turbine

How it works

The simplest turbine is the windmill (*Figure 11.8*). The wind blows and glances off the blades and its direction is changed so that there is a reaction. The force created by this change in momentum pushes the blades round.

Winds have low velocities by turbine standards and the windmill tends to be a slow-speed affair and quite large for its power. It is also very inefficient because the wind leaves the mill at a velocity not much less than it started with, so only a small part of the available energy is used. Besides, the wind is moody, so power is generated erratically.

The simple steam turbine has much the same basic elements as the windmill (*Figure 11.9*) but the velocities are much higher. The wind or driving jet is created by release of heat energy. Steam expands in nozzles from boiler pressure (P_i) to near exhaust pressure P_e. For pressure ratios P_i/P_e of more than about 2, the jet issues faster than the speed of sound, say at 450–600 m/s. These very high-velocity jets glance onto moving blades, whose curved surfaces deflect them. *Figure 11.10* shows how the jet is slowed down and how the momentum change creates a force to drive the blades.

Geometry of the practical turbine is such that blades rotate at almost half the steam velocity for best efficiency, but this is still a very high velocity and can be over half the speed of sound. This

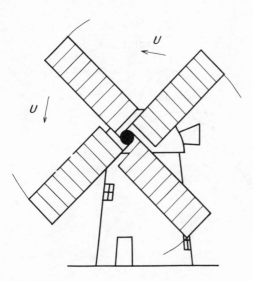

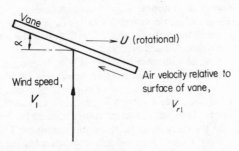

Figure 11.8   The windmill

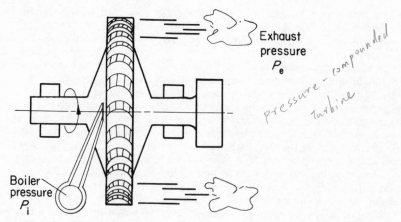

pressure-compounded Turbine.

Figure 11.9   The simple turbine

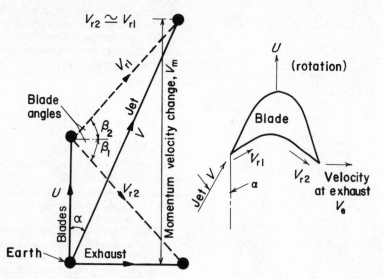

Figure 11.10   Principle of the simple turbine

$$Work = \frac{w}{g} \times U \times V_m$$

where w is the mass flow and g is the acceleration due to gravity

simple turbine therefore must run at very high rotational speeds, so high that it becomes difficult to use. The leaving steam also has quite a high velocity, as *Figure 11.10* shows, so it takes a lot of energy with it and throws it away.

This type of simple one-stage turbine is inefficient and difficult to use. It still is met with occasionally to drive auxiliaries and where simple compactness is wanted and energy can be lost; but almost all turbines are more elaborate and have more than one stage.

Multi-stage turbines are more efficient for various reasons, the main one being that later stages catch and make use of the fast steam which leaves the first stage. Also, the pressure is expanded down in a number of steps rather than in one and so the jets reach much lower velocities and hence are easier to use and give more efficiency. *Figure 11.11* shows a common way of compounding, while *Figure 11.12* compares the efficiency of the simple turbine shown in *Figure 11.9* with that of the pressure-compounded machine.

Use of a number of stages is usually done in the way shown in *Figure 11.11*, each row of blades being preceded by a row of nozzles. Another, less common, way is merely to guide the exhaust from the first row into a second row of moving blades — and this may be done three or four times. This is called a *Curtiss* or *velocity-compounded turbine (Figures 11.13 and 11.14)*. The pressure is mostly

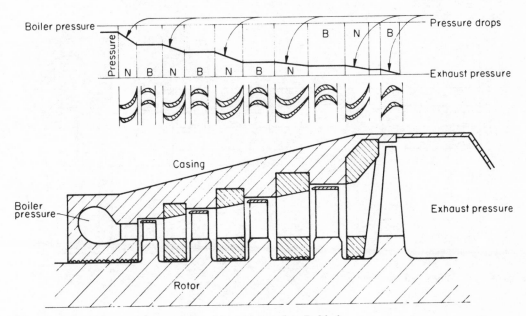

Figure 11.11   Pressure-compounded turbine. N, nozzles; B, blades

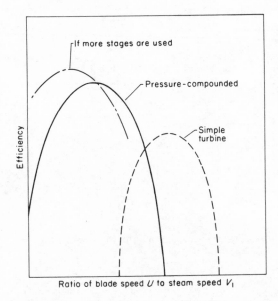

Figure 11.12   Efficiency of pressure-compounded and simple turbines

expanded to a high velocity in one row of nozzles, rather than in each succeeding stage as in the pressure-compounded turbine shown in *Figure 11.11*. The Curtiss turbine is not very efficient, one reason being that it is very difficult for the designer to judge the exact direction and velocity of the steam leaving each row of blades so his design tends to be inexact. It is particularly difficult to

design such a turbine to suit all the circumstances of pressure, load and speed which it will meet, say, in marine service. The machine has its uses though, as a means of getting power from a light, compact turbine and as a way of reducing temperature and pressure in a short length at the beginning of large turbines. It is also commonly used as an astern element in marine turbines, but it is more wasteful of fuel than the more usual turbine, viz. the pressure-compounded machine shown in *Figure 11.11*. The Curtiss often has only about two-thirds of the efficiency of pressure-compounded stages, though it has to be admitted that these latter make for a larger machine.

As mentioned in Section 11.1, a notable part of the work and economy of a turbine comes from exhausting to a vacuum. Now the expansion ratio can be enormous. Take for instance a machine with an inlet condition of 86 bar, 496°C and exhausting to 68 m bar and 10% wet. The inlet specific volume is 0.039 m³/kg but the exhaust specific volume is 19.2 m³/kg — an expansion ratio of almost 500 : 1. Strictly, if every pound of steam which entered the turbine reached the exhaust and if equal blade leaving velocities were used, the exhaust blades would need to be five hundred times as high as the inlet blades!

Often about a quarter of the steam is withdrawn for feedheating before it reaches the exhaust; also the low densities allow us to use much higher blade leaving velocities from the exhaust blades than from the inlet blades. The exhaust annulus is also made with a larger diameter than is the turbine

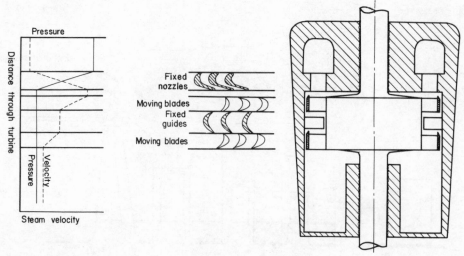

Figure 11.13   The Curtiss turbine

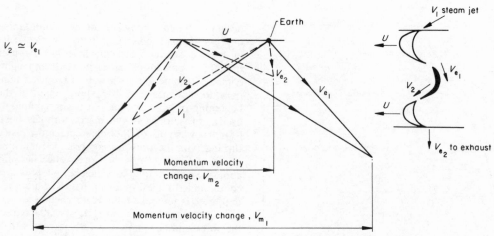

Figure 11.14   Principle of the Curtiss turbine $Work\ done = \dfrac{w}{g}\ (V_{m_1} + V_{m_2})\mu \quad w = mass\ flow$

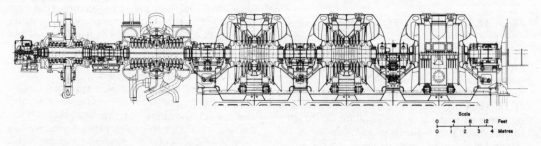

Figure 11.15   Section through a 500-MW GEC set. (Courtesy of GEC Ltd)

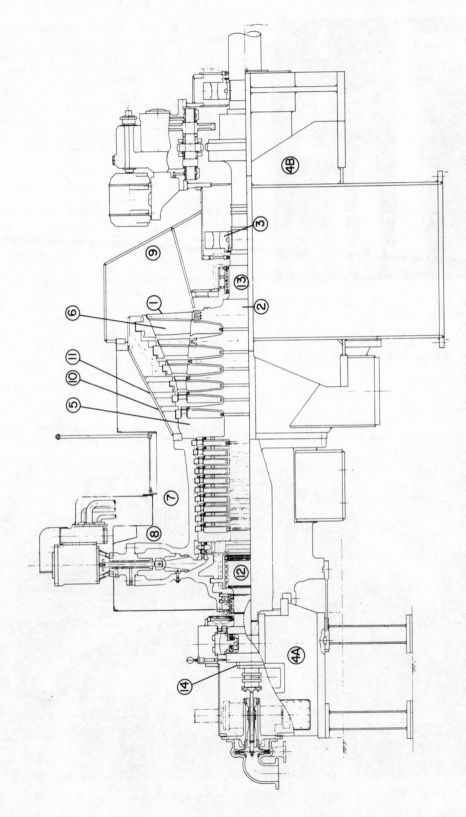

Figure 11.16 Section through a single-cylinder pressure-compounded turbine. (Courtesy of GEC Ltd)

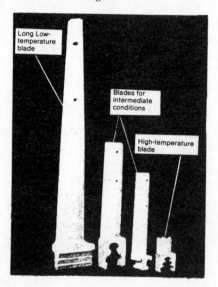

Figure 11.17   Large and small blades. Reproduced from Watson, H. 'Factors in the design of large steam turbines for high availability', originally presented at the Steam Plant Group Convention on Steam Plant Availability, Dublin, May 1965

inlet row, and all these effects tend to reduce the height of the last blades. Nevertheless about a hundred times the length of blade is commonly required compared with the first-stage blade.

In large turbines, blades long enough to achieve

this cannot withstand the centrifugal force, so more than one exhaust is used and the blade is brought down to a manageable height. Such a machine is shown in *Figure 11.15* representing a large central power-station turbine. It is obviously more complex and costly with its multi-exhaust, though of course it can produce extremely high powers. The benefits in the search for high power and low costs depends significantly on the problem of designing an adequately large, and yet a safe, last blade.

Most industrial and small power-station turbines have only one exhaust and this simpler machine (*Figure 11.16*) can be used to describe the basis of construction of a turbine since many of its features are common to the large machine too. The moving blades (1) are carried by a rotor (2) which is supported in bearings (3) inside pedestals (4A and 4B). In this type of machine, each blade row runs within a compartment at a particular pressure and whose ends are sealed by diaphragms (5). The diaphragms carry the pressure-reducing nozzles (6) which produce the driving jets. The diaphragms are supported within a casing (7) which, in turn, is supported on the pedestals (4). The casing is usually split along its horizontal joint and held together by bolts.

Steam enters by way of a stop valve which trips shut in emergency such as a risk of extreme overspeed, and then passes through control valves (8) whose opening is adjusted to suit the power required. After passing through the stages, steam

Figure 11.18   Turbine nozzles during manufacture. (Courtesy of GEC Ltd)

enters the exhaust (9) and goes hence to the condenser. Some steam is usually drawn off in the earlier stages such as (10) and (11) to heat the feedwater which is about to go to the boiler.

The glands (12) and (13) are a feature which can save or lose fuel because if they leak, steam escapes from the blade path without doing its share of work. In most designs the glands are of metal and are kept clear of the shaft by a small amount — say 0.5 mm. If there is much distortion of the cylinder or deflection of the shaft, the glands can rub and cause trouble, which, in its mildest form, means a loss of energy by steam leakage. Therefore glands are often sprung in segments so as to move back if they are hit by the shaft and do so causing least wear. Another way is to use glands which are sufficiently soft and low in friction as to be able to touch the shaft without trouble. They can be made of carbon but this is a design rarely used nowadays since such glands tend to be fragile.

The heart of the machine is the blading and nozzles; examples of these are shown in *Figures 11.17* and *11.18*. The blading in particular has a very arduous duty and the designer must needs devote more time to it than to any other feature. He has to make the blades produce work efficiently while withstanding the very difficult environment of centrifugal force, violent pulsing as the blade passes through the steam jets, vibration, corrosion and sometimes creep or erosion. Equally the user must take special care to ensure that the blades are kept in good order to avoid wastage of fuel or an enforced shutdown just when the plant is most needed.

Expansion arrangements differ from design to design. That used in *Figure 11.16* is quite common and is demonstrated in *Figure 11.19*, where the turbine is anchored against axial movement by keys A at the exhaust. The cylinder expands thermally and pushes the front pedestal, which slides

on a baseplate and is guided by a central key B. Transverse thermal expansion is allowed by movement on the keys A, and takes place without the turbine shaft moving from the central axis. Expansion and keying have to be carefully thought out and looked after, when it is realized that the whole turbine may weigh well over 100 t, have its inlet parts at a dull red heat, and still have to maintain clearances of as little as 0.5 mm between its rotating and static parts.

In the common arrangement described, the pedestal takes the rotor with it as it moves because it carries the thrust block (14 in *Figure 11.16*). So axial clearances between rotor and stator remain little changed as temperatures climb because the axial expansion of the rotor is almost matched by that of the casing and both use the common datum of the thrust block. This helps to keep gland leakage low because it allows easier and more efficient glanding than would otherwise be the case.

Why the steam turbine is so useful

The steam turbine is a useful prime mover for various reasons inherent in its principle:

1. It is simple.
2. It can be made more powerful without becoming too heavy or hungry for steam.
3. The cycle is not fussy over fuel.

So, with proper selection and careful application it can be a compact and cheap source of power.

It has its bad points too. It requires a lot of other plant such as boiler, feed pump and condenser and it is slow in starting compared with the gas turbine. Also it is not very competitive at low powers. Clearly, plant selection demands some judgement and there are many good features of a steam turbine which need to be clearly understood to aid the

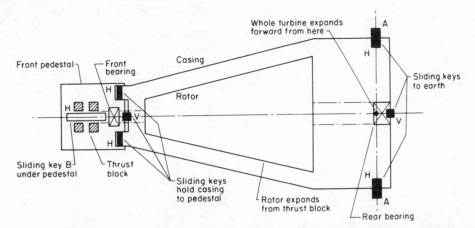

Figure 11.19 Typical expansion and keying arrangements. V, vertical keys; H, horizontal keys

selector in his task. The above three are the main ones.

Simplicity

The simplicity of the steam turbine is apparent if the simple rotating mechanism of the steam turbine is compared with the complicated reciprocating mechanism of a steam or oil engine. Of course, the boiler and other plant must be allowed for, but the steam turbine plant as a whole has advantages which tend to make it last longer than most other machines. The parts rotate steadily so most stresses do not cycle and cause fatigue, though there are important exceptions such as the cyclic stresses caused by blade vibration. Bearings are steadily loaded, if the rotor is well balanced instead of being cyclically loaded as in oil engines. The

furnace combustion is steady instead of cyclic as in an internal-combustion engine.

On the whole, the steam turbine has the advantage of simplicity though it must be appreciated that economics and the high centrifugal field persuade the designer to stress the metal highly.

Capacity for more power

The heart of the machine is the blading and an important factor in sizing it is the axial velocity of the steam. The steam is arranged to travel axially from the high-pressure blades at about the same velocity in small as in large turbines. In fact, the blade path can be looked on as a circular annulus (*Figure 11.20*) along which the steam travels at an average velocity whose value is fairly standard for most turbines though it can be higher in the low-pressure than in the high-pressure stages.

If now we need a turbine of twice the power, this means twice the throughput of steam, so we use twice the area of annulus. We can get this if we can increase the height of the blades by just less than twofold.

A little has to be added to the length of the machine to carry these heavier blades but even so the resulting turbine is less than twice the volume — and much less than twice the diameter of the original machine, yet it has twice the power. So the weight of metal increases at a much lower rate than does the power output, and this is a very significant factor in steam plant economics. It means that turbines of higher output cost less per MW than do small ones.

To demonstrate this important point with figures, take a turbine whose ratio $d/h = 10$ (typical of an intermediate stage). (For the meaning of the symbols *see Figure 11.20*.) It will be found from the formula in *Figure 11.20* that the blades need to be lengthened by 85% if the power is to be doubled. A 15% lengthening of rotor span should be allowed for to carry the longer blades. Then

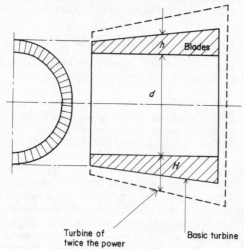

Turbine of twice the power   Basic turbine

Figure 11.20   Doubling the annulus of a turbine so as to give twice the mass flow and hence twice the power

$$\pi(d + 2H)^2 - \pi d^2 = 2\pi(d + 2h)^2 - 2\pi d^2$$
which gives

$$\frac{H^2 + Hd}{h^2 + hd} = 2$$

If d is much larger than h and H then

$$\frac{H}{h} \sim 2$$

If d is small in relation to h and H then

$$\frac{H}{h} \sim 1.4$$

So, to double the power, increase the blades by 40–100% depending on the diameter

$$\frac{\text{Volume of new machine}}{\text{Volume of old machine}}$$

$$= \frac{\pi(d + 2H)^2 \times 1.15}{\pi(d + 2h)^2}$$

$$= \frac{(10h + 3.7h)^2 \times 1.15}{(10h + 2h)^2}$$

$$= \frac{13.7^2 \times 1.15}{12^2} = 1.5$$

So the power has been doubled without adding more than 50% to the weight of the machine.

The relationship between power and weight is shown in *Figure 11.21*. The ratio power/weight increases as power is increased as shown in *Figure*

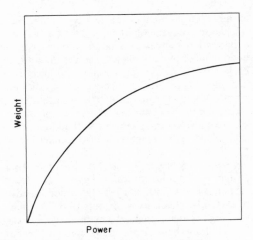

Figure 11.21 Weight of turbines of higher output

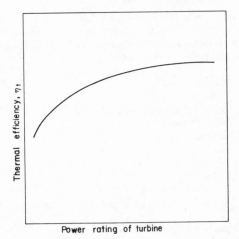

Figure 11.23 Trend of efficiency as outputs grow

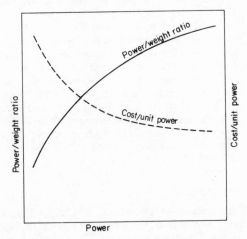

Figure 11.22 Power/weight and cost/unit power trends

11.22. For the same reasons weight/unit power comes down and so does specific cost, as *Figure 11.22* also shows, so the plant should cost less per MW if higher powers are selected.

Another important factor is that efficiency tends to rise if machines of larger power are chosen. Efficiency can be expressed as

$$\eta_t = \frac{\text{energy available} - \text{losses}}{\text{energy available}}$$

Turbine losses tend to be a function of diameter and we have seen that this does not change much as the plant becomes more powerful. For instance, steam leakage past a gland is proportional to shaft diameter and clearances — in other words steam leaks in proportion to the area of the gap. Clearances change little with diameter and diameter itself changes but little with power, as we have

seen. So, in going to more powerful turbines there should be little extra loss, hence the curve of efficiency against output rating is as in *Figure 11.23*.

So it seems that there is great attraction in going to machines of larger and larger output. Cost per MW comes down and efficiency goes up. However, these benefits are achieved only by a prodigious development effort. Inherent in this is the nature of *Figure 11.22*, which shows that larger turbines provide cheaper power but also that to achieve this the metal has to be worked harder and harder. This follows from the increasing power/weight ratio.

These fundamental facts are behind much of the massive effort put into the turbine development in the 1950s and 1960s. Blades and other turbine parts cannot always be doubled or trebled in size, yet not to do so would rob the user of enormous savings of money. The period 1950–1970 has therefore seen a race between designers to achieve the largest-output turbine and yet to do so without making the plant unreliable. Sooner or later there has to be a compromise and hence we see such features as the multiple exhaust of *Figure 11.15*. Six exhaust rows are used instead of the ideal single row because metals could not support the single-blade alternative with its enormous height and the resulting very strong centrifugal forces.

So there is compromise and some dilution of the gains to be got when going to larger outputs but the basic economic trend is still there. The steam turbine is remarkable in its ability to develop higher powers and in the money it can save in so doing.

Versatility of fuel

Because the combustion process occurs outside the steam circuit a great variety of fuels can be burnt. This is unlike the internal-combustion engine, which has to swallow the products of combustion and the poisons therein. To demonstrate the point, some of the fuels currently being fired in steam power-stations are

Hard coal
Soft coal
Oil — light, medium and heavy
Nuclear energy
Refuse
Gas
Wood pulp
Sugar waste
Nut waste
(Exhaust from gas turbines or oil engines)

Types of turbine

The many types of turbine differ mainly in their blading — how the steam does its work (whether by impulse or reaction) and whether the steam moves along the shaft axially or radially. All the various types have their advantages, their difficulties and their best applications.

Impulse

The basic impulse turbine has already been described on p 233 and in *Figure 11.9*. All the expansion of steam is in the nozzles and the high-velocity jets so created drive the blades around by impulse. In its simplest one-stage form, the machine is wasteful though compact. To reduce the wasted energy two arrangements are used, or a combination of them: pressure-compounding and velocity-compounding.

Pressure-compounded turbine (Figure 11.11). This

is the more popular of the two types. The basic operation was described on p 234: the steam is expanded in many rows of nozzles rather than one and a row of moving blades receives the jet from each expansion. The jet velocities are lower than in a single-stage turbine and easier to use efficiently and the energy thrown away by one stage is partly recovered in the next stage of nozzles and blades. The exhaust energy is much less than in a simple stage because the steam velocities are much lower.

Velocity-compounding. This is the other basic design of impulse turbine (*Figures 11.13* and *11.14*), called a Curtiss turbine (also mentioned on p 234). The steam expands only once to reach a very high velocity. Instead of a lot of energy being lost in the exhaust from the one row of blades, several rows are used. The steam leaving each is redirected by a fixed guide blade without much loss of pressure before it drives the next row of blades. The arrangement is not as efficient as the pressure-compounded machine because the multiple rows of blades and guides do not use the steam velocities very efficiently, but, as said earlier, the machine is very compact and much more economical than the single-stage impulse machine. It tends to be used to drive auxiliaries and as a pressure and temperature reducer at entry to some large machines, with some sacrifice of efficiency but a saving of first cost. It is also used as an astern element in marine sets.

Reaction turbine

The turbine developed by Sir Charles Parsons used the reaction principle and this is still the basis of many modern machines. The concept is that

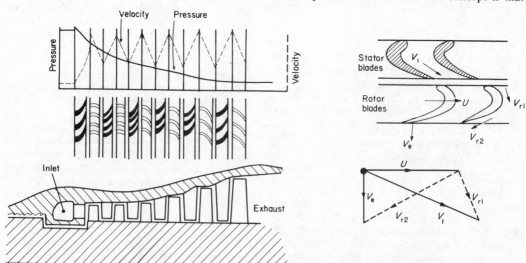

Figure 11.24   Reaction turbine. $V_{r2} > V_{r1}$ because of acceleration in the blade passage

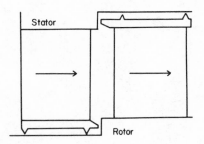

Figure 11.25 Reaction turbines require blade sealing

only about half the pressure drop occurs in the nozzles. The remainder occurs in the moving blades, whose passage shapes form nozzles (*Figure 11.24*). The jet from the fixed nozzle does work on the moving blade by impulse as before but work is also done by the jet created by the moving blades, which act like rotating nozzles. The reaction of this jet helps push the blades around, hence the name of the design.

Reaction turbines require sealing between the moving blade and the casing as well as between the fixed blades and the rotor (*Figure 11.25*), because, unlike the blades of impulse turbines, each blade has a substantial pressure drop across it. These seals must be kept in good order to prevent leakage and energy loss.

A typical single-cylinder reaction turbine is shown in *Figure 11.26*. This should be compared with *Figure 11.16*.

Impulse v. reaction

Turbine engineers have long argued about the respective merits of impulse and reaction machines, but in truth no turbine uses either principle exclusively. As has been seen, the 'reaction' turbine of *Figure 11.24* has an element of 'impulse' in its working principle in that the nozzle jet drives the blades by a change of momentum as well as by jet reaction. Also, the impulse machine (*Figure 11.11*) has some kinetic head developed in its moving blades as the steam squeezes through the passage. Designers of such machines reckon on a small amount of reaction in the early stages and a large amount in the later stages. In fact the low-pressure staging of so-called impulse and reaction turbines is very similar (*compare Figures 11.26 and 11.16*). The differences are mainly in the high- and the middle-pressure stages. Taken between them, these two types of turbine form most of the modern machines, and they are about equally popular. Both can give almost the same efficiency if carefully designed and properly looked after. Books could be written about the argued differences, but we need recognize only that they usually balance out.

Some less usual types of turbine

The Lungström turbine (Figure 11.27). This is less seen than it used to be. Steam moves radially away from the shaft and rotates the blades, which jut out from the discs. There are two sets of counter-rotating blades, set in alternate stages, and pressure is reduced in both sets of blades much as in the reaction machine.

A difficulty with the Lungström turbine is that the blades, being parallel to the shaft, suffer bending stresses from centrifugal force. As blades grow

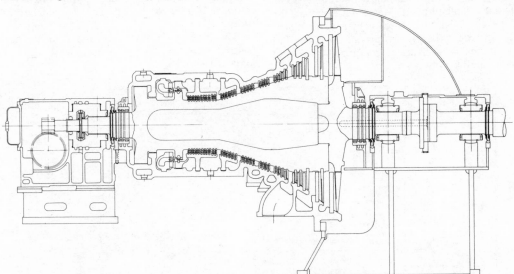

Figure 11.26 Longitudinal section through a single-cylinder 30-MW reaction turbine. (Courtesy of NEI Parsons)

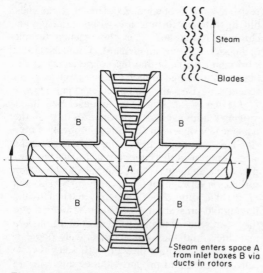

Figure 11.27 Diagram of a section through a Lungström turbine

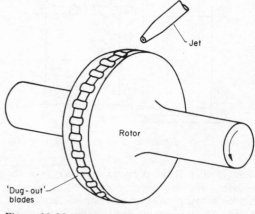

Figure 11.28   Terry turbine

in size to give more power, these stresses become prohibitive much more quickly than in machines such as that shown in *Figure 11.26*, which has radial blades and where the centrifugal field produces a simpler and less damaging tensile stress. So Lungström machines have tended to be used less and less as larger outputs are required. They are nevertheless useful for relatively small outputs.

The Terry turbine (*Figure 11.28*). This is a novel machine sometimes used where power demand is small and there is a need for a simple, compact and very robust unit, for instance for driving small standby auxiliary plant. Steam jets bombard the disc head and are turned away by depressions cut into the disc. The process produces a change of momentum and hence a rotational force, but rather inefficiently.

Where and why the different types are used

The machines which are most often used in power-stations, industry and in ships are the pressure-compounded impulse turbine and the reaction turbine. Occasionally these use velocity-compounding in their first stages of blading as in *Figure 11.16*. For smaller outputs, all the stages are mounted in a single cylinder as in *Figure 11.26* — say up to about 100 MW. The large central power-stations require the most powerful machines, up to 1200 MW and beyond, and these have multiple exhausts and a number of cylinders, as in *Figure 11.15*. Other forms of machine, which will be dealt with later, are the back-pressure machine (*Figure 11.46*), the pass-out machine (*Figure 11.48*) and the marine turbine. All these turbines may use impulse or reaction blading or a combination of both.

The Lungström turbine is limited to medium outputs and the Terry turbine is used only for small powers.

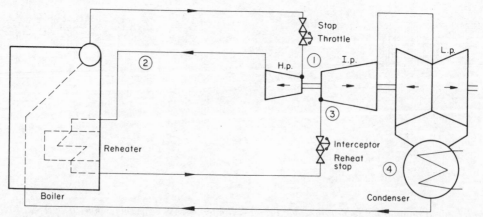

Figure 11.29   Reheat plant

Reheat

This is a way of getting a better efficiency and is currently used in most power-station turbines of over 100 or 200 MW output and occasionally in less powerful machines in industry or ships. Instead of expanding the steam right through all the blade stages at one go, it is taken so far, returned to the boiler to be reheated, and then expanded through the rest of the turbine. This technique is dealt with in more detail in Chapter 2.

Figures 11.29 and *11.30* show the process and how it is arranged: Inlet steam (1), say at 540°C, expands through a high-pressure turbine to about 340°C and is then taken back to the boiler (2). The hot gases heat the steam up to 540°C again, but of course it is then at a lower pressure than before (commonly the h.p. inlet is at 162 bar and the i.p. turbine inlet is at 31 bar). In this reheated state (3), steam expands through the i.p. and then through the l.p. turbine, then it goes to the condenser (4) and finally back to the boiler as feed-water.

By the use of this process the cycle efficiency can be improved by up to as much as 10% of what it was for a cycle without reheat — in other words it can save up to 10% of the fuel bill.

Reheat has another advantage, since the steam does more work per kilogram and so less steam has to be used. This eases the problem of the last row of blades, which as we have seen is a critical factor in the development of large turbines.

However, reheat is a complication and the saving of fuel has to be offset against the more costly plant and the extra care and effort required to operate it.

It also means that the inlet pressure has to be higher than for the simple cycle. Whereas the latter rarely goes higher than 100 bar, reheat machines use 160 bar or higher and sometimes have supercritical conditions of above 220 bar. (Supercritical steam is at pressures so high that there is no latent-heat phase. The heated water turns straight into steam without the dwell period required to make water boil at more normal pressures. This needs special plant.)

The reheat plant shown in *Figure 11.29* uses the boiler gases to do the reheating but there is another form. In some nuclear plants where pressurized-water or boiling-water reactors (PWR or BWR) are the source of energy, the form of the reactor makes it awkward to reheat by anything like the usual method. Live steam — (1) in *Figure 11.31* — is taken from the turbine inlet to heat the steam which leaves the h.p. turbine (2), and the reheated steam (3) then expands through the l.p. turbine.

Such reactors work at a fairly low pressure for large turbines (about 70 bar) and the steam they produce is barely dry, so a considerable amount of water forms when the steam expands through the h.p. turbine, most of it being removed by a drier before the steam is reheated (*Figure 11.31*).

Reheat is a useful way to save fuel but it complicates the plant. However, as fuel becomes more costly we can expect to see it used more and more and for smaller outputs than at present.

Choosing the right conditions

Selection of steam conditions and vacua

Higher inlet conditions give higher efficiencies —

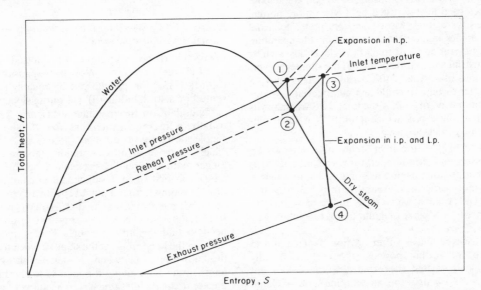

Figure 11.30   Mollier diagram for a reheat cycle

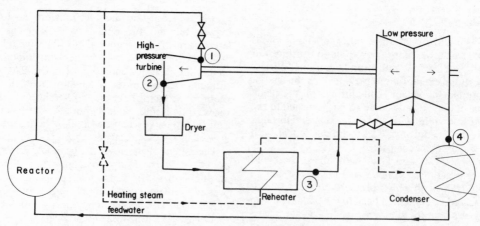

Figure 11.31   Live steam reheating as for pressurized-water reactors

but there are practical limits. First and foremost is the limit of temperature. Turbine inlets are subject to two forms of strain. The first occurs during steady long-term operation and is a time-dependent effect termed *creep*, which also depends on temperature and stress (*see* Chapter 3). The second type is *thermal strain* and this occurs especially when starting and stopping a machine.

If inlet temperatures much above 540°C are used, normal ferritic materials lose their creep-resistant properties and austenitic steels have to be used in parts of the boiler. Beyond 578°C these steels have to be used in the turbine inlet parts too, and they are very expensive. Further, while they are better than ferritic steels for creep resistance, they often have a low proof stress and so distort more easily under thermal stress. They also have other incidental properties such as not rusting — so nuts come loose which used to stay rusted tight when more normal steels were used. Most engineers prefer to avoid austenitics and so limit the turbine inlet temperature for generating plant to 540°C or even less, whilst industrial and marine plant and the smaller power-stations usually use 510°C or lower. This allows a simpler turbine. It could be that material development or ways of cooling the inlet parts will make us change these practices but until then such temperature limits are used.

The heat of the inlet steam also depends on pressure as well as temperature, and one goes to as high a pressure as one reasonably can in a search for more efficiency. Again there is a limit which depends on exhaust wetness and here we have to resort to a Mollier diagram again to explain why (*see Figure 11.32*).

Last-row blades suffer erosion damage and to keep this within bounds, the cycle is usually designed so that the exhaust wetness does not exceed 10% or — in an extreme case — 13%. Taking a simple non-reheat cycle, exhausting at

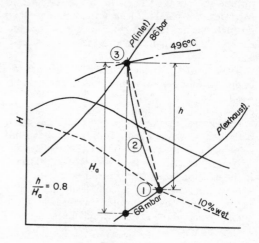

Entropy, *S*

Figure 11.32   Selecting inlet conditions for a chosen state of turbine exhaust

say 68 mbar, the end-point can be plotted and is point (1) in *Figure 11.32*. Now the expansion line (3)–(2)–(1) of the turbine can be roughly represented by a straight line (3)–(1) whose slope h/H_a is dependant on turbine stage efficiency. This is usually in the region such that $h/H_a = 0.8$ and a simple method gives a rough approximation from which to arrive at inlet conditions (accurate but longer methods would be used in a design office to adjust this first shot). Using a Mollier chart a line (3)–(1) is drawn from a point (1) with a slope such that h/H_a equals the assumed efficiency (say 0.8). Inlet temperature is known (say 496°C) and we need to find the inlet pressure. This is done by drawing the line (3)–(1) at the slope stated and from the known point (1) where it intersects the 496°C temperature line, giving the inlet state and hence the approximate inlet pressure. The answer for the case given is an inlet pressure of around 86 bar. The

Table 11.1 Various steam conditions to give same exhaust state

Case	1	2	3	4	5
Inlet temp. (°C)	538	510	496	482	454
Inlet pressure (bar abs)	121	96.6	86.2	75.9	60.3
Rankine thermal efficiency (%)	34.0	33.0	32.6	32.2	31.2
Equivalent increase in fuel burnt (% with case 1 as datum)	0	+2.9	+4.1	+5.3	+8.2

This table shows the approximate steam inlet conditions to give 10% wetness at 68 mbar exhaust pressure for non-reheat cycle without feedheating. The average stage efficiency is 80%. Comparative thermal efficiencies are also shown.

figure will vary depending on the efficiency, the selected wetness and inlet temperature and the finer points left out by this rough and ready method.

Table 11.1 gives a range of steam conditions which result from a series of such first approximations.

It also shows the comparative thermal efficiencies and how much can therefore be got from the change of conditions. (Thermal efficiency is calculated here simply as Rankine efficiency as given on p 229 and assuming a cycle without either reheater

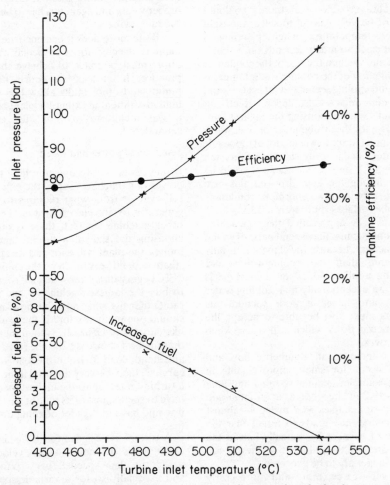

Figure 11.33 The effect on fuel rate of different steam conditions at the inlet for the same state at the exhaust. Exhaust pressure = 68 mbar; wetness = 10%; average stage efficiency = 80%

Table 11.2   Efficiency for a simple cycle at 86.2 bar, 496°C

	Back-pressure 85 mbar	Back-pressure 68 mbar	Back-pressure 51 mbar
Rankine efficiency	32.1%	32.6%	33.5%
Difference (%)	−1.5	0	+2.7

or feedheating.) *Figure 11.33* shows the results graphically.

Selection of vacuum is usually a matter of climate and economics. If the cooling water is warm, as in the tropics, one has to accept a poor vacuum and this brings with it a lower efficiency, whilst on the other hand cold water allows a good vacuum and saves fuel. Some approximate figures for efficiency at different vacua are given in *Table 11.2* for a simple cycle. These are very theoretical figures. For one thing they assume that the last blades can make use of any reduction in back-pressure — which is not always so. However, there is no doubt that one must be very careful to select the right cooling-water temperature when planning a turbine plant since so much depends on it. For a given output and vacuum the size of the condenser is mainly a function of the cooling-water temperature. Pump and cooling-water system costs — and they can be quite high — also depend greatly on this parameter. Simply choosing the highest temperature known for the available sea or river water when designing a plant can waste a lot of money. If this temperature occurs only say once every ten years and then for only a few hours, it could be worth while letting the load drop on this rare occasion rather than buy an enormous condenser whose full tube surface is but rarely used.

It should also be appreciated that a machine rated for a poor vacuum may spend most of its life at a higher vacuum, because the climate is usually more moderate than the cooling-water and vacuum rating implies. So, when a machine is designed for an exceptionally high cooling-water temperature, and hence a poor vacuum, its exhaust ducts must also be able to accept the higher volumetric flows which will occur when vacuum improves.

Quite large increases in volumetric flow and velocity can occur for small improvements in vacuum. For example, steam at 68 mbar and 10% wet occupies 19.2 m^3/kg whereas at 34 mbar and also 10% wet, it occupies 36.7 m^3/kg — almost double. Of course one tends to forget that the small change of vacuum has actually halved the absolute pressure of the exhaust, so these large volumetric changes are to be expected.

As water gets scarce, more and more costly cooling plant has to be used and in order of increasing cost and water scarcity these are:

1. sea water as coolant;
2. river water;
3. wet cooling towers;
4. an air-cooled condenser; and
5. an air-cooled cooling tower.

(More mention of these plants is made in Section 11.5.) The more expensive such plant is, the more one tends to accept a poorer vacuum, optimizing first cost against thermal efficiency. In all this, of course, it has to be accepted too that the turbine itself becomes more costly if it has to cope with higher vacua and again this has to be offset against the fuel saving.

All the more does it become true that once the plant is selected for a particular vacuum, every effort must be made to achieve that vacuum in practice. If air leaks or poorly maintained air pumps and other faults allow loss of vacua, the high investment in expensive plant and the money it was meant to save on fuel can easily be squandered.

Selection of power and speed

It may seem odd to question how to choose the power of a machine. Surely the power required is self-evident from what requires to be driven: a generator for the electricity grid, a compressor or other machine. In fact, there is quite an art in choosing the size of a turbine and how much money the plant will earn and its efficient use of steam depend very much on the choice.

To begin with we know that it is sound economics to buy the largest machine — one large turbine rather than five small ones; but how large a machine should one really ask for? If the load stays steady like curve A of *Figure 11.34* then there is no doubt that the best choice is a turbine rated up to the full and steady load X. But if the load varies, say like curve B, then it is very doubtful if the best choice is a turbine rated up to the highest load X. It would have to spend most of its time at part load and also it would have to do a lot of going up and down in load.

A turbine is designed for its highest load; at all lower loads the nozzle steam velocities do not match the blade speeds. This is so for all turbines and especially so for a variable-speed machine. When this mismatching occurs energy is lost in collision of steam and blade; also the valves have

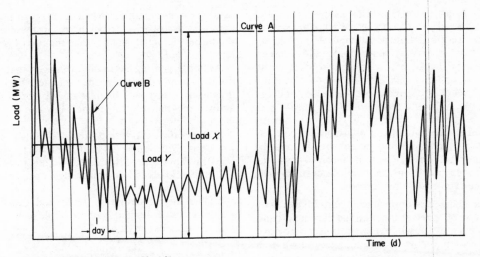

Figure 11.34   Different types of loading

to throttle to keep down the steam flow and this wastes useful energy because it makes the exhaust hotter than it need be.

So a turbine can waste quite a lot of energy if it is run at lower loads than it is designed for. Whilst there are ways of reducing the loss (*see the next section*), there is no way of avoiding it altogether. The loss at part load could well be enough to more than offset the money saved by going to a larger-output machine. Hence, the load curve B of *Figure 11.34* is probably better met by having, say, two turbines each half the power of that needed for curve A — or perhaps even better by having one turbine of output *Y* and carrying the peaking loads on a gas turbine.

Of course most industries and utilities gradually expand and a turbine which is big enough for this year is much too small in ten years' time. Thus one may have to choose the size to suit the projected future output rather than what seems sensible for the present. This is sound logic and new machines are often larger than currently necessary. Even so, one must not make a machine larger than is really needed and the facts centred on *Figure 11.34* and mentioned earlier can save a lot of money in the end.

Another point to remember when sizing turbines, relates to power generation to a system because if too large a machine is chosen and it trips out, the shock is such that the system may become unstable. It may even collapse completely by rejecting all its load, so a machine size has to be selected with this in mind too. In the English system the figure appears to have generally been kept down well below 5% of the total grid power demand, but some countries accept a greater risk and buy machines whose output exceeds 5% of the system.

The lesson of this section is to go for the largest machine appropriate, but to set the limit wisely, knowing that a machine running at part load wastes energy, and that with an electric grid there is a limit of machine size beyond which there is a risk of a complete black-out if the one large machine trips.

Selection of turbine speed

It usually pays to select a high speed for a steam turbine rather than a low speed. Most blades give best results if they move at a particular ratio of blade speed to jet velocity (*see Figure 11.12*), usually about 0.5. So, the faster the blades travel, the higher can be the jet velocity, which means that a turbine with high blade speeds will need fewer stages and so cost less than a turbine with slower blade speeds. High jet velocities require more pressure drop to produce them than do low jet velocities. This means that the boiler pressure can be broken down in fewer stages of blading. Thus higher rotational speeds produce a smaller and therefore a cheaper turbine.

There are limits to this argument. As higher and still higher speeds are used, a limit is reached where the more usual materials cannot hold the blades onto the rotor in the high centrifugal field. For this reason steam turbines rarely have speeds of over 10000 rev/min, and in fact most marine sets run up to only 4000–7000 rev/min. Power-station machines are a special case. The alternator cannot run faster than grid frequency, nor can the turbine unless gearing is used, so turbine speeds are usually either 3000 or 3600 rev/min. The very large turbines (e.g. 1200 MW) generally limit the centrifugal field by using 1500 or 1800 rev/min and four-pole generators. In fact speed tends to be set by whatever the turbine is driving rather than by the economics of the turbine itself.

For lower powers, gearing can be used, and there are many arguments as to what power gearing should be limited to. Most engineers would say that about 25 MW is a reasonable limit at present. Below this limit, the turbine speed is chosen to give low cost and good efficiency, and it does not have to equal the speed of the driven machine. For example, a turbine generator of say 20 MW may have a generator speed of 3000 rev/min but the geared turbine would run at a higher speed, say 6000 rev/min. This arrangement would usually be cheaper than one in which the turbine runs at the same speed as the driven members even allowing for the extra cost of the gearbox.

The higher-power turbines, then, drive directly at the same speed as the machine they are driving. They are mostly used for electric power or to drive large compressors. The compressor drive is a special case. The compressor usually likes high speeds just as do the turbines, and direct driving at up to 10000 rev/min or more is becoming normal practice at quite high powers — up to and even over 30 MW. Speeds of 7000 rev/min at say 25 MW are quite common. Compressors are rarely driven through gearing, since the engineers who buy compressors generally feel that gears are too great an extra risk to take with the exceptional demand for reliability, and — as stated — turbine and compressor speeds usually match well anyway. Gearing can be very reliable but, clearly, it can never be as reliable as a direct drive.

Power-station turbines of 25–1200 MW or more use direct drives. As stated, because of the economics of using high speed, they usually drive two-pole alternators to give 3000 rev/min at 50 Hz (or 3600 rev/min at 60 Hz). With very large sizes — say 800 MW or over — the blade and rotor designs become too difficult with such speeds and four-pole alternators are used so that speeds become 1500 rev/min (or 1800 rev/min). Dimensional size of turbine goes up considerably and so does cost. In some very special cases low speeds are chosen for other reasons. One is in geothermal steam turbines where the steam contains much water and putrid gases. Some designers aim to extend the blade life in this difficult environment by using low speeds.

The range below 25 MW covers most marine and industrial applications and not a few sets for small power-stations, and one has the choice of using a direct drive or gearing. Marine units have propellers which cannot work well above about 300 rev/min, and the turbine would be most uneconomic if it drove the propeller direct. Although this used to be done, nowadays all marine steam turbine drives are through gearing except for a few which are turbo-electric. With these small turbines gearing is also usual for electricity and industrial

uses. A direct-driven turbine generally costs more because the cost arising from increasing the size of the turbine is usually greater than the cost of gearing.

Although gearing has its disadvantages, they are usually accepted when money dictates, but the drawbacks must still be recognized and taken account of when selecting plant. They are:

1. A gearbox can lose power at about 2% per gear reduction at full load. Moreover — and this is not generally realized — a box working at part load can lose a much higher percentage of the power it receives.
2. The large number of teeth and bearings reduces the reliability of the whole plant.
3. Gearboxes can be noisy.

Selecting the method of control

This includes many topics, but the one that most influences the efficient use of steam is whether to have throttle control or nozzle control.

The throttle valves control the amount of steam going to the turbine and are positioned to suit the load. In throttle control, these valves open together progressively as load increases until they are almost fully open at 100% load. *Figure 11.35* shows one such arrangement. The characteristic of stage pressure v. load in a throttle-control machine is distinctive. It is the straight line AB of *Figure 11.37*. The arrangement is simple but it wastes energy when the machine is away from full load. When the turbine is on part load the valves throttle all the steam going to the machine and the stage inlet pressure becomes so reduced that the nozzles and blades work a long way from their design conditions. Of more importance, the machine exhausts more heat than it would were it to receive the full load pressure. This can be appreciated by studying the process on a Mollier chart. So, while the method is simple and is efficient at full load, it

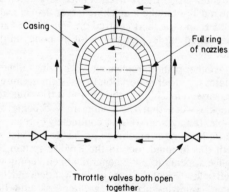

Figure 11.35   Steam inlet arrangement for throttle control

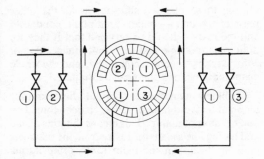

Figure 11.36   Steam inlet for nozzle control

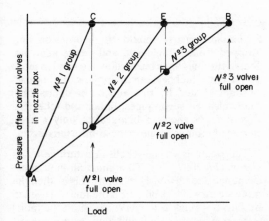

Figure 11.37   Nozzle supply pressure characteristic at the inlet to a throttle-controlled machine (A–B) and a nozzle-controlled machine (A–C–D–E–F–B)

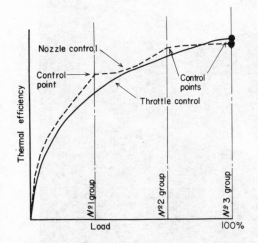

Figure 11.38   Efficiency comparison for throttle v. nozzle control

is wasteful at part load.

Some of the losses are avoided if nozzle control is used instead of throttle control. Here the first-stage nozzles are divided into separate groups, and each is controlled by one or more throttle valves as in *Figure 11.36*. These open in sequence to make each group of nozzles in turn achieve full pressure and to do so at progressively increasing fractions of full load. Eventually all are open and the machine is at full load. Instead of the stage inlet pressure curve of AB (*Figure 11.37*) we have the more complicated but higher curves of ACB, DEB and FB, each occurring as a new group of nozzles receives steam from its valve. These curves are distinctive for nozzle control. They give generally higher pressures than with throttle control — pressures which are nearer to those the machine was designed for, hence the efficiency is improved. Thus the dotted curve of efficiency against load (*Figure 11.38*) is achieved rather than the lower curve which throttle control would give (and shown as a full line). The gains are greatest when each valve is full open and it pays to run at or near these positions, which are called the control points.

There is fuel to be saved by using nozzle control if the machine has to run enough of its life at part load, but on the other hand the arrangement costs more and can lead to a less reliable turbine. The valve and nozzle box castings and the valve gear and nozzle arrangements are more complicated, the life of the first-row blades being especially arduous, and vibration failures can occur unless great care is taken in design. At part load some nozzles are active and some are idle, so the blade runs into and out of bands of steam jets and this can heavily excite vibration and cause blade fatigue, unless a very strong design indeed is used. Also, nozzle box arrangements can lead to trouble unless carefully designed and well proved. All this having been said, nozzle control is the usual practice, and many manufacturers and their machines are successful. The problem is not with these well proven sets, but in extrapolating the design upwards in size as sets become larger — a practice which may sometimes overstretch the design. So the benefits have to be weighed against the risks and the advice is that to benefit from fuel savings, make sure that the nozzle-controlled machine is of well proven design or is very carefully designed to avoid blade vibration failure and nozzle box and casting trouble. If the sets are to run at or near full load for most of their life, best use throttle control.

It should also be noted that a nozzle-controlled machine at full load is no more efficient (perhaps slightly less efficient) than a throttle-controlled machine when at full load, since the gap between the nozzle groups creates a source of disturbance and energy loss. So use of the device should be confined to machines which really will run for much of their lives at part load.

Getting the best from a turbine

No matter how good the concept, the return obtained from investment in a steam turbine depends on how the machine is looked after. This means taking care over how it is installed, how it is run, and how it is maintained. It also means keeping a check on its performance and using this as a guide to good maintenance and operation. Many things need watching but here are a few of the more significant ones. First, some general comments about availability and maintenance.

The steam turbine is very reliable and its high availability is vital to good economics. It is a long-life machine: typical figures for a large set, say 500 MW, are a life of 200000 hours spread over some 40 years and with say 200 cold starts and about 3000 hot starts; one shaft might rotate over 36×10^8 times before the turbine is scrapped. During all this time the machine should be producing its highest power and efficiency. It is at its best when doing so, since this is what it was designed for. Running at part load or manoeuvring is not economical. Nor does it make any sense to lose availability and money by being forced to shut down the turbine for repair when least expected.

Obviously the plant has to shut down sometimes for maintenance, but this should be preventative rather than forced by failure. It should be planned for wide intervals, as for example every four years.

During these planned shut-downs all the other parts of the unit — boiler, feed plant, condenser and the rest — should be serviced too. If they are done one at a time and such that outages do not coincide, costs become cumulative and the whole economic basis of a plant can be shattered.

Turbine maintenance should be carefully planned to avoid failure, rather than be forced on one because of failure. This means thinking ahead and basing one's plans on advice from the designers and on checks on the plant itself, often during operation. Much also depends on the early days of building and commissioning the plant when troubles should be found and cured rather than ignored in youth to fester in old age.

Installing the turbine

Steam-swept parts should be kept clean and stopped from going rusty, and debris kept out. Steam turbines have been known to need as much as 1% extra fuel because their blades and nozzles become blasted by rust and other debris from badly cleaned steam pipes, boiler and reheaters. *Figure 11.39* shows a blade after only a short period of running in one of these unfortunate sets.

The steam is virtually held in a turbine by its glands (*Figure 11.16*). They must all have some clearance and obviously the more this is, then the more steam will leak and the more fuel will need to be burnt. Taking a 100 MW set, if all the radial clearances between shaft and stator were increased

Figure 11.39   Blades peppered by debris

by as little as 0.15 mm, the fuel rate could increase by as much as 0.3%.

The right gland clearances must be achieved during building; if they are too large then more fuel will have to be burnt than is necessary. If they are too small, the shaft may strike the static glands and this will at least cause a very wide and wasteful clearance. It can also make the shaft bend to an unrunnable extent and so bring on a long and costly shutdown. Yet getting the clearances right is a very exacting business and allowances must be made for many factors such as the position of the journals in the bearings, the loaded state of the cylinder, whether the horizontal joint has been bolted when clearances are taken and many other things. It is an expert's job to set shaft clearances.

Turbines can lose useful energy if they are not lagged properly, first because bad lagging allows heat to leak away, and secondly because badly fitting lagging can cause distortion of a cylinder and this can cause loss of clearances and, perhaps, an expensive outage. Lagging blankets should be avoided, since they sag away at the bottom half of the machine and permit air gaps. The most effective lagging is that which fits closely to the hot part and permits no air gap. Nowadays it is recognized that asbestos is a health hazard, so the lagging should not contain this substance.

Running the machine

The machine should always be run at the highest load which the demand permits, since as seen earlier this leads to the highest efficiency. Load should not be altered unnecessarily, because transients waste fuel and it is best to keep the machine at a steady high load if good economy is to be achieved. The machine is designed for a particular set of steam conditions and it is wise to keep to them. Apart from the risk of damage, running at other than design conditions means that steam will not glide smoothly across the blades but strike them obliquely and lose energy. It also means that the cycle will lose efficiency, for instance by having too much heat in the exhaust. For a turbine in a typical industrial use or small power-station working at 86 bar, 496°C and exhausting at 68 mbar, *Table 11.3* shows the approximate changes in fuel burnt for the same load that

would be required if its steam conditions were changed from design by the amount shown.

A common source of efficiency loss is air leaking into the vacuum in the l.p. end and condenser through badly made joints. It must also be realized that, when at part load, the turbine has vacuum in the early blade stages which are usually above atmospheric pressure, and these can leak air too. It takes very little air to reduce the vacuum by a significant amount and even a pinhole aperture can damage the efficiency out of all proportion to the extra cost and care of avoiding it.

Another common fault, especially just after starting a machine, is to leave drains open much too long and waste steam and — more often — to have drain valves which have been worn in use by steam flashing, which leak and waste steam. Isolation, by fitting valves in series, is often advisable. One is used for throttling and the other is used only for isolation and so remains tight. Some machines have by-passes for starting purposes and these can be a source of loss too if the valves are not maintained to seal when the machine is on load. These various leaks can generally be checked by finding out which drain or by-pass lines are warm and whether they should be.

Maintenance

All the time the turbine is running, its maintenance should be under consideration. Thinking ahead enables everything to be done to make sure that the machine will complete its next spell of operation without interruption. In particular, any signs of distress should be noted — vibration, extra fuel being burnt, steam leaks, growth of noise and loss of vacuum. The section on testing gives some advice on how to do routine tests to check the continued economy of a running machine (*see* p 254).

Most maintenance is mechanical in the sense that it aims to avoid breakdown — but this is also a matter of efficiency since a failed machine loses revenue. Two features are usually especially important in this class:

1. Creep — the phenomenon of growth of metals in time when under stress and high temperature and which eventually may lead to metal breakdown and failure. Notable here is the relaxation of joint and other bolts

Table 11.3

Condition	Decrease	Change in fuel rate
86 bar inlet pressure	5%	0.6% extra fuel
496°C inlet temperature	25°C (5%)	0.9% extra fuel
68 mbar exhaust pressure	17 mbar (25%)	2.7% fuel saved

in high-temperature cylinders; these may need periodic retightening or replacement if leaks and even mechanical failure are to be avoided.

2. Balance — the turbine rotor has to be maintained at a very fine state of balance if rough running is to be avoided. Slight dimensional change and surface deposits can mar this. Money is saved by keeping rotor balance right.

A number of maintenance features have a more obvious or more direct effect on the efficient use of steam. Maintenance of clearances is a usual feature of any major overhaul; these clearances are sometimes badly increased by the running of the machine and restoring them can save a lot of fuel. It is also as well to find out and put right the cause of clearance changes — bad lagging, a slightly bent rotor, and so on. It also pays to check that each spring-back gland is free and not stuck solid.

In a major overhaul the blades, the nozzles and all steam-swept surfaces should be carefully examined. Bent edges due to particles passing through blades or nozzles are not uncommon and these will obviously affect efficiency and may even start a crack. An expert should be asked whether the edges should be straightened or the blade replaced. Straightening should always be followed by testing using crack detection.

Curing leaks is a standard task in any maintenance operation but particular attention must be paid to any defect causing air leakage to the condenser, particularly if there has been difficulty in getting vacuum.

Maintenance lists would usually include many more items than mentioned here, but the factors mentioned have been chosen because they are often important, especially as regards plant economy.

Testing

Development is essential to progress and ultimately to good economy, but the average user knows that most new designs have teething troubles. It is as well to realize what this might cost when buying a new turbine and to set the cost against the benefits which the new design may offer. *Figure 11.40* is drawn from statistics from a number of large turbines. It shows that on average a prototype has much poorer availability than a standard design, at least until lessons are learned and adjustments made after the first few years of running. Much of this trouble can be avoided by careful and imaginative testing of the prototype before ever it is installed — or at least by discerning which are the critical features and by putting them through exhaustive tests. So a good rule when buying a turbine

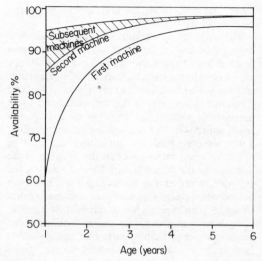

Figure 11.40   Curves showing the trend of availability for large steam turbines, constructed from results averaged for the following machines: 100 MW — six machines; 120 MW — seven machines; 200 MW — eight machines; 275 MW — two machines. Calculated according to the formula

$$Availability\ (\%) = 100 \left(1 - \frac{fault\ outage\ hours}{8760}\right)$$

Reproduced from Watson, H. 'Factors in the design of large steam turbines for high availability'. Inst. Mech. Eng., Rugby sub-branch, 1 December 1965

is to find out if there are any prototype features and to make sure that they are tested properly in the maker's works rather than waste fuel in doing so when the turbine is in service. Some buyers insist that all features must have been tried first by another user, but, of course, there would be no progress if everyone did this and the years have shown that design progress brings some very substantial rewards to the user. The risks are much reduced by proper testing.

A more usual type of testing is to check performance. Almost all turbines undergo such a test as part of the purchase, and this is a very standard and formalized procedure. Basically, the power is measured and the steam mass flow is assessed by measuring condensate flow and correcting it by a host of other measurements of bled steam flow, etc. Steam conditions are either brought to the design standard or corrections are made, and from such measurements at a selected range of loads the thermal efficiency of the machine is assessed.

The process is fairly easy to apply and is quite sensitive for power-station plant. However, it is not so easy for marine plant where power assessment has to be either derived back from the hull and propeller performance (a very inaccurate affair) or measured by use of torque-meters, which also can be inaccurate. Also, there is little space in a ship's engine room for the straight lengths of pipework which accurate flow meters require. Fortunately, marine turbines are smaller than most power-station plants and it becomes more practical to carry out full-scale tests before installation in the hull. The difficulties mentioned and the pressing need for fuel economy make such a practice more and more worth while as time goes by and fuel prices rise.

With plant which has been installed and running for some time, a deal of useful information can be acquired without going to the elaboration of the full and formal performance test. Measuring the pressure at a few stages in a turbine and logging it periodically can reveal blade damage, nozzle choking, and any general fall-off in efficiency. If the instruments are carefully installed and looked after, this simple method can be quite sensitive.

By Willan's law, the pressure in a turbine bears a straight-line relationship to load. For each particular load there is a particular pressure at each stage of the machine, and once values are established for normal running, any departure from the normal is evident. Moreover the cause of the trouble can sometimes be revealed by comparing readings down the length of the machine. Thus an increased fuel rate might occur and a high h.p. stage 1 pressure be noted, yet the i.p. inlet pressure might be unduly low. This combination would point to an increased resistance in the steam path within the h.p. stages, possibly because of deposits on the blades or damage to the nozzles.

It will be noted that temperature measurements by thermocouples or other instruments have not been mentioned, for these simple checks of a machine in service. They can be helpful but can also mislead unless they are used by an expert — and even then do mislead sometimes. The reason is that the very high velocities of steam involved and the complicated pattern of temperature of the metal surrounding the nozzles and blading make it very difficult to measure true steam temperature inside a turbine stage. Measuring pressure is much easier and is adequate in itself for many purposes, though a single check of steam temperature at supply to the turbine would be a wise supplement to the pressure checks.

Uses

This section is mainly for the student: to show the wide variety of uses of steam turbines so as to help put ranges of power and speed into perspective. The whole range of turbines is divided into six groups:

Group 1: power-stations

The turbines are usually about 150–700 MW for large central power-stations, but can go as high as 1300 MW from one shaft (1977). They are constant-speed machines and almost all have reheat.

Industrial and small power-stations use turbo-generators of up to about 150 MW, often non-reheat. Machines of less than 25 MW are often geared down to the speed of the alternator.

Group 2: total-energy sets

A turbine produces power, usually to drive an alternator, and passes its exhaust for further use. This may be used for district heating or for a factory process, or for desalination of impure water. Machines usually are 1–20 MW in size though they can be much larger, and drive generators through gearing for the smaller outputs.

A variant of this is the pass-out machine, which exhausts part of its steam from an intermediate stage and at a controlled rate to, say, a desalination plant or other process. The rest of the steam carries on to a condenser after passing through the l.p. blade stages (*see also* Section 11.6).

Group 3: mechanical drives (land)

Steam turbines are increasingly used to drive compressors or feed pumps, the turbines used being variable-speed sets of sometimes quite considerable power (30 MW–1977). They are used in the growing chemical industries for the compression of synthetic natural gas, ammonia, methanol, urea, ethylene, blast furnace gas, air and in coal gasification. The larger power-stations also tend to use steam turbines for driving the feed pumps, sometimes of powers of 20 MW or more (1977).

Group 4: mechanical drives (marine)

The marine field has always been a battleground where different engines contend for the market. Currently (1977) the steam turbine holds the high-power range for merchant vessels (plant of say around 30 MW) but has been almost ousted from naval vessels by the gas turbine. Exceptions are nuclear submarines, which are driven by steam turbines.

Group 5: combined cycles

It is likely that, in future, a growing number of applications of the steam turbine will occur in combination with the gas turbine; for instance, using the exhaust of the latter as a steam raiser. The high efficiencies possible are very tempting. More is said about this in Section 11.6.

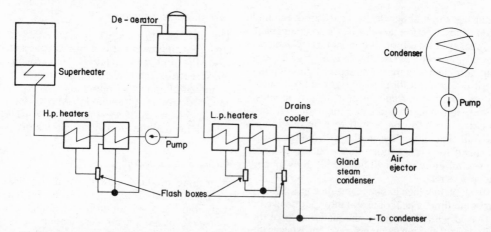

Figure 11.41   Simplified feed diagram for a small power-station

Group 6: small auxiliaries

Auxiliaries such as oil pumps, extraction pumps and the like are mostly driven by electric motors nowadays, but there are still a few cases where a small steam turbine is used. These often carry only a few stages of blading and are frequently of the Curtiss type. Running at quite high speeds and developing powers of a few hundred kW, they are notably compact.

11.5 Supporting plant and its influence on turbine economics

The turbine is supported by auxiliary plant, chiefly the condenser, feed plant and oil system. Some items are intended to improve the efficiency of the cycle — the feedheater for example — while others, such as the oil system, are there solely to enable the turbine to function. Even these can have a noteworthy effect on efficiency because they take power to operate. The object of this section is to consider some of the main items of auxiliary plant and their effect on plant efficiency and some other ways too in which they can save or lose money.

Feed plant

A typical arrangement for a small power-station is shown in *Figure 11.41*, and further examples will be found in Chapter 20. Condensate is taken from the hot well and pumped through the tube nests of low-pressure feedheaters which are fed by steam from the low-pressure stages of the turbine. The warmed water goes then to a de-aerator and then to the main feed pump, which raises the pressure high enough to inject the feedwater into the boiler, though it first goes through the tubes of high-

pressure heaters which take steam from the high-pressure stages of the turbine.

The feed plant is therefore in three parts: heating plant, de-aerator and pumping plant. The de-aerator has a dual role: first, to take enough oxygen from the water to prevent it from damaging the boiler, and secondly to act as another feedheater (*see* Chapter 7). In the de-aerator the water is atomized and heated by steam extracted from the turbine, the two effects of heating and de-aeration being simultaneous. Sometimes de-aeration is done in the condenser rather than in a special vessel.

The object of feedheating is to improve cycle efficiency. It also helps to make the water more acceptable for the boiler since cold water can promote acid deposits on the gas side of the boiler tubes. A further advantage, sometimes claimed, is that the turbine exhaust tends to be more lightly loaded because of the steam extracted — but the blade designer can rarely use this fact because he knows that the machine will sometimes run without the heaters, and the exhaust blades will then have to accept the full flow. The main use of feedheating therefore is to use less fuel and to help stop boiler corrosion.

Of course one pays extra money for these benefits and feedheating can be quite costly, especially if it is an elaborate arrangement. It also brings with it a risk which may put the turbine out of action for a long time if not properly guarded against, since if a fault occurs cool fluid from the feedheaters can return to the turbine by way of the bled-steam lines. This can so distort the machine that severe bending of the rotor and perhaps even more serious damage may occur. Non-return valves are often used to stop this happening (and also to prevent steam reflux whose energy may add to overspeed) but non-return valves are no complete answer and a number of costly extra measures are generally needed, such as automatic isolating valves. So, whilst there are useful gains, one has to realize the cost of a feedheating system and take care to counter the risks involved.

If the best balance of gains over losses is to be achieved, one should favour simplicity. For instance it is often wise to select fewer stages of feedheating than thermodynamics alone would indicate as a best choice. The simpler system may prove more reliable even though it is not quite so efficient and what matters in the end is total cost not theoretical efficiency alone.

The basis of the feedheating process is shown in *Figure 11.42*. A simplified diagram is used for demonstration. Steam is extracted from the turbine at three points (2), (3) and (4). The flow W_2 goes to h.p. heaters, W_3 to the de-aerator and W_4 to the l.p. heaters. The result is that the condensate is raised almost to the saturation temperature of the highest pressure of extraction, to give it a sensible heat of h_2 instead of h_5.

Of course, this is done at the expense of lost work in the turbine, but, on balance, an overall gain in efficiency is achieved with any reasonable selection of plant. For a typical cycle for a small station using 82 bar without reheat, a final feed temperature of 200°C and 68 mbar exhaust, the use of three stages of heating reduces fuel burnt by 9%.

One point to take special note of is the disposal of drains. If the heater drains are run straight to the condenser, useful heat is lost, and good practice is to cascade them as in *Figure 11.41*. The drains from each h.p. heater go to the shell of the next heater of lower pressure — and so in this way one can be sure that the heat in the drains goes into the boiler and not to the condenser cooling system.

The other main member of the feed plant is the feed pump. This can take considerable power — up to 15 MW in a 600-MW power unit. Much of the energy reappears in the feedwater as pressure energy or heat, but there is a useful amount of energy to be saved, particularly in the larger plants, given some ingenuity. To start with, constant-speed pumps are less efficient than variable-speed. These latter vary the speed to suit the load required, whereas a constant-speed pump always delivers at the highest pressure characteristic required and throws part of this head away when only lower presures are needed. A number of arrangements can be adopted to save fuel in larger installations (*see Figure 11.43*). One is to drive the feed pumps from the end of the main turbine by means of a fluid coupling and gearbox (*Figure 11.43c*). Another, more common arrangement is to use a driving turbine which takes steam from an intermediate stage of the main turbine and then exhausts it to feedheaters or returns it to the main turbine at a later stage (*Figure 11.43e*); yet a further variety is to exhaust this steam to a condenser (*Figure 11.43d*). All these methods save fuel. Whilst there is argument about which is the wisest to adopt in the large stations, the smaller stations tend to use the simpler yet less economic drive (*Figure 11.43a* or *11.43b*). This is probably good sense because if turbines were used to drive the pumps they would be so small as to be very inefficient, but there may be a case in principle for driving the pump of small units from the main turbine as in *Figure 11.43f*.

Condensers

The usual condenser is of the surface variety and much could be written about its design. Only one simple point will be mentioned however, and that is the importance of keeping the tubes clean. Layers of dirt collect inside the tubes in time and

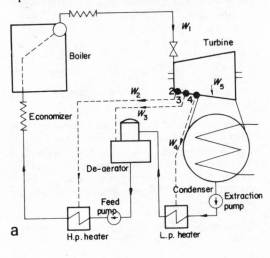

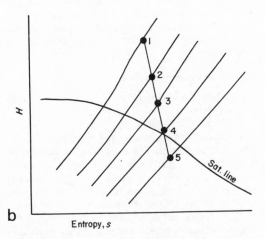

Figure 11.42 Basis of feedheating. $W_1 - W_5 = W_2 + W_3 + W_4$

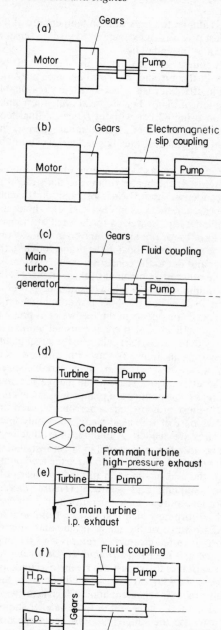

Figure 11.43 *Different ways of driving a feed pump to gain economy. (a) Constant-speed drive; (b) electric drive with some speed variation; (c) driven from the end of a turbo-generator — small speed variation but with coupling losses; (d) separate turbine drive, condensing — fully variable speed; (e) turbine drive integrated into the steam circuit of the main turbine — fully variable speed; (f) a marine arrangement*

raise their thermal resistance. Outside the tubes any oil or grease coming over with the steam will tend to leave a film on the tube surface and can more drastically affect the process of condensation.

The condenser is the end-point of the cycle and for every 1°C which these deposits cause the exhaust temperature to be raised, up to 0.5% goes onto the fuel rate which can mean 800 t of fuel extra per year in a 100-MW unit. Thus it pays to keep the tubes clean and probably to do so while the machine is on load.

As always there is a warning. If the cleaning process is too vigorous the ferrous sulphate and other naturally occuring and very thin protective layers may be lost and tube corrosion may occur. It is as well to get an expert to check that the cleaning process is safe.

If cooling water is scarce then cooling towers are used. These are usually of the direct-contact type where water is sprayed into the air, but if the water is really scarce air cooling can be used instead. There are several techniques and they are coming into increasing use as more power-stations are being constructed in dry areas. The three main methods of dry cooling are shown in *Figure 11.44*.

Dry cooling tower with jet condenser (Figure 11.44a)

This is a system in which steam is condensed by direct contact with atomized feedwater which then collects and is cooled in an air radiator at the base of a cooling tower, before coming back again to work in the jet condenser as a coolant. A small proportion of the returned water goes to feed the boiler.

Dry cooling tower with surface condenser (Figure 11.44b)

Here a surface condenser is used and the cooling water is kept in a closed circuit. It need not then be feedwater, which saves some money and complications but at the expense of a slight worsening in vacuum.

Air/steam condenser (Figure 11.44c)

Steam goes inside the tubes and air over the tubes to cool them.

Of these three choices, the third tends to be cheapest and tends to be used in the stations of lower power output. As larger outputs are required, the duct economics can weigh against this scheme — a long duct being necessary between turbine and condenser. One of the other two schemes would be usual in the larger stations where water is scarce. The first type is the more efficient though there are often practical preferences for the second.

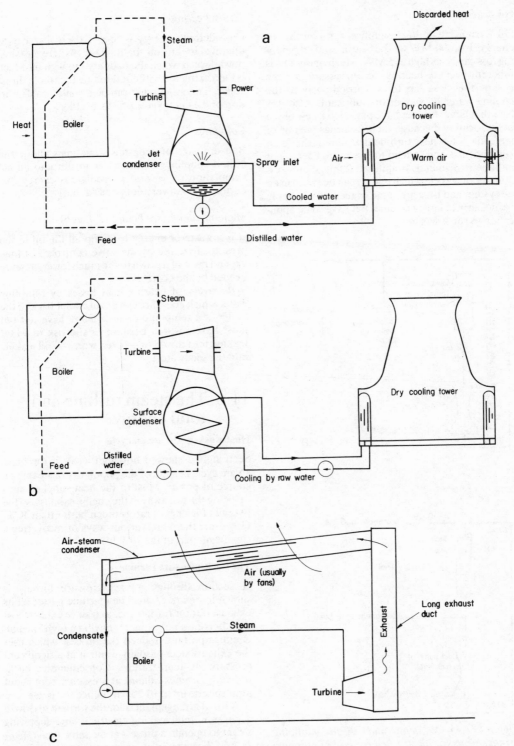

Figure 11.44 (a) Dry cooling tower with a jet condenser; (b) dry cooling tower with a surface condenser. (The cooling-water circuit is now separate from the feedwater circuit and so untreated water can be used.) (c) Air-cooled condenser

Oil systems

Oil systems can lose significant quantities of energy. In a 500-MW set the bearing and oil pumping loss can be as high as 5 MW. Much of this loss is inherent because bearings are necessary and the energy they lose has to be carried away to the cooling water by way of the lubricant. Also it is true that large turbines have passed to a new phase of lubrication because their bearings, being of large diameter, have turbulent oil films rather than laminar films and so tend to lose more energy per millimetre diameter. In spite of all this, there are a number of ways in which energy can be saved in an oil system and here are some of them. They apply particularly to large machines but have some application to small sets too.

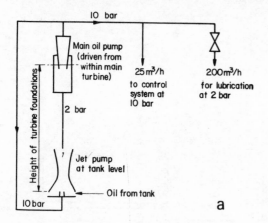

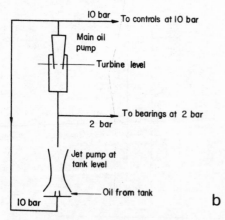

Figure 11.45 Wasteful and thrifty pumping arrangements for oil. (a) Bad method of pumping oil; most of the oil goes up to 10 bar only to be reduced then to 2 bar, a waste of the pump's power; (b) a better method of pumping oil using less power

Thrust bearings

Considerable energy is lost if the collar has to operate in an oil bath. Designs are feasible nowadays in which the pads are fed with oil which is then extracted without flooding the whole thrust collar. This saves what can be a considerable portion of the energy loss of a thrust block.

Couplings

Bad drainage of pedestals sometimes allows the bolted couplings of the rotor to dip into an accumulation of oil and a prodigious energy loss occurs — and a very hot pedestal too!

Main oil pumps (see Figure 11.45a, b)

It is a waste of energy to pump all the oil to the pressure required by the valve controls and then expand most of it down to the much lower pressure needed by the bearings.

Recovery of bearing heat losses by returning water which goes through an oil cooler back to the boiler is a temptation which many have felt but most have resisted because of the risk of water leaking into the oil or — even worse — oil leaking into the feedwater!

11.6 The steam turbine and total energy

Heat waste in the steam cycle

Section 11.2 showed how inefficient is the basic steam cycle in spite of the popularity of steam as a source of power. Most of the heat supplied ends up being thrown away in the engine exhaust, so the overall efficiency is rarely much better than 30%. However, there are various ways of recovering a significant part of the 70% loss.

The back-pressure turbine

A section through a back-pressure turbine is shown in *Figure 11.46*. The machine passes all its exhaust out for further use, and since exhaust loss then becomes no problem, having a high vacuum is not important. Indeed the process which uses the exhaust steam usually wants it at a significant pressure or temperature. Consequently, back-pressure turbines exhaust at pressures from about atmospheric up to 10-20 bar, hence the name.

A usual arrangement is for the turbine to drive a generator, thus making electricity and supplying steam to operate a process at the same time *(Figure 11.47)*. For the inlet conditions used in *Figure 11.47b* the Rankine efficiency *(see* Chapter 2) of the turbo-generator would be only 30% if the machine exhausted to waste at 68 mbar, but the

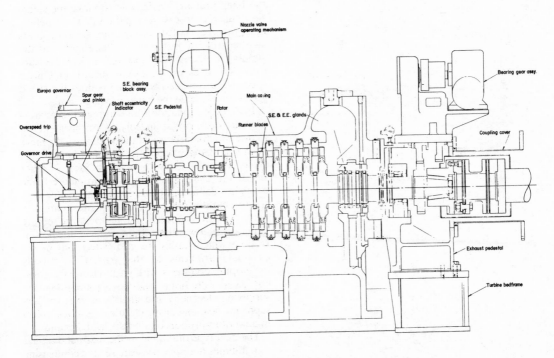

Figure 11.46   Section through a back-pressure turbine. (Courtesy of GEC Ltd)

back-pressure machine uses its exhaust heat even though it exhausts at a much higher pressure (in this case 3.5 bar). In fact a Rankine efficiency of 100% is theoretically possible if all the heat passed to the exhaust is used and only the sensible heat is discarded.

Of course, in practice heat is lost by the boiler flue and some is used to drive auxiliaries and to make up other losses. But effective thermal efficiencies of 60 to 70% from heat in fuel to used steam are possible whereas the condensing cycle shown in *Figure 11.47b* would reach only around 25% in practice, after the various losses had been deducted.

The efficiency of the back-pressure cycle will depend very much, of course, on the use that is made of the exhaust heat in the factory or district heating or desalination scheme.

One way of regarding back-pressure turbines is as a very efficient form of reducing valve. Instead of raising steam at 45 bar (for the case of *Figure 11.47b*) and then reducing it to suit a process at 3.5 bar, the pressure reduction is done in a turbine which does valuable work. Back-pressure turbines also generate electricity economically since the heavy losses associated with the exhaust of a normal power-station are now put to good use and so is much of the loss internal to the turbine. It reappears as exhaust heat and is mostly used in a

further process in the factory or wherever the exhaust heat is employed.

Back-pressure machines are quite small for their power because they have no great volume of exhaust to cope with, the density being high. They are usually single-cylinder, hence they are cheap in terms of cost per MW compared with condensing machines of the same power. Back-pressure sets are used to supply many processes, including:

1. desalination;
2. in factories, such as in the processing of wool and sugar and the manufacture of paper;
3. district heating;
4. petrochemical installations, and
5. gas production.

These machines do not always drive generators. They are often used to drive compressors and one special variety drives the main feed pumps in some of the latest large power-stations in the UK. The idea sounds so good, one asks why it is not more used. One answer is that its potential is not understood as well as it could be, but a more telling reason is that more power is often needed than exhaust heat. To explain this and to help understand why the next type of turbine to be described — the pass-out set — is often preferred, we first need to look at the control of the back-pressure set.

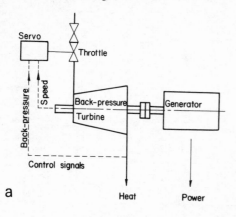

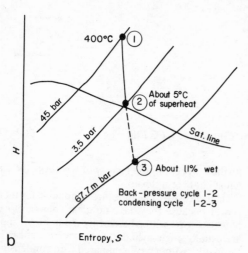

Figure 11.47   (a) Typical back-pressure arrange-ment; (b) typical back-pressure cycle and extension to condensing cycle

Figure 11.47a shows that the back-pressure set is usually controlled as for most turbines, by adjusting the inlet throttle valve. However, this is not done just by a speed-sensing device, but also by one which senses back-pressure. So, if speed is high, the valve is closed in and if speed is low, it is opened. The back-pressure device opens the valve if back-pressure is low and closes it if it is high. In fact the last two sentences can be incompatible. For instance, a shortage of electrical power would cause more steam to be let in, which the back-pressure process may not want. Also, an increase in steam demand by this process would cause an increase in electrical power which may not be wanted. The two devices — speed and back-pressure control — would, in fact, fight each other. Hence the turbine is often put under the control of

the back-pressure device and to make the steam flow suit the process demand only. The machine must then be used alongside other generating sets — the grid for instance — which make up the supply of electricity if too high a back-pressure causes the back-pressure set to throttle in. Only if speed goes outside certain limits does the speed governor override the back-pressure control.

It is, then, common sense to regard the back-pressure cycle not as an isolated arrangement but as one which works in parallel with a usually more powerful string of condensing sets which supply electricity only, often the national grid. In other words the usual arrangement is for there to be much less demand for exhaust steam than for electricity, and this presents a convenient situation so far as control is concerned. Back-pressure sets are generally of low output compared with the power-stations which supply the grid. There may be occasional variations to this pattern in rapidly developing countries with small electricity grids, but it generally holds true: large condensing sets supplying electricity and small back-pressure sets supplying heat and giving electricity as a by-product in quantities proportional to the heat demand.

The next type of turbine — the pass-out machine — combines the back-pressure set and condensing set into one engine.

Pass-out turbines

A pass-out turbine is shown in *Figure 11.48* and — more diagrammatically — in *Figure 11.49*. More steam is generally wanted for power than for heat, so this machine passes most of the steam it receives through all its h.p. and l.p. blades, but enough steam is drawn off part-way along the machine, to meet the heat demand — say to a desalination plant, or to a factory process. This may be up to as much as half of the total steam inlet flow, though in most machines it is much less, say a quarter of the total flow. The pass-out pressure is selected to suit the process.

The cycle efficiency of such a machine is higher than for a normal condensing set though it is obviously not as high as for a back-pressure arrangement such as the one shown in *Figure 11.47*, but it is often a simpler and neater arrangement. It also costs less than having a back-pressure set and a condensing set in parallel, since the pass-out machine does in a single unit what it takes both these other machines to do. If we take a case of say a 10-MW back-pressure set and a 90-MW condensing set, the same heat demand can be met at about the same efficiency using a pass-out set, so efficiencies are about matched if, as is common sense, the total network of turbines is considered rather than comparing the back-pressure set in isolation with a pass-out machine.

113 bar g
510°C

16 bar g   4 bar g   0.1 bar g

Figure 11.48   Section through a pass-out turbine. (Courtesy of GEC Ltd)

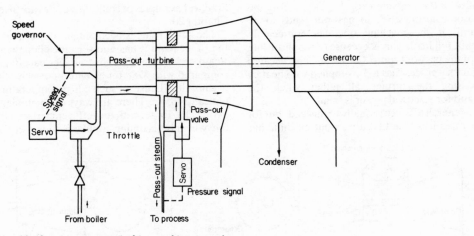

Figure 11.49   A pass-out machine and its control

We do, however, often pay something for the convenience of a pass-out machine in terms of cost of fuel and this is inherent in its control. *Figure 11.49* shows that the total steam flow is extracted at the pass-out stage, most of it being returned by the turbine through a pass-out control valve. This works by automatically closing if the back-pressure is too low and by opening if it is too high, hence too low a flow to the factory which needs the heat will bring the valve to a more closed position. This will raise the pass-out pressure to its right value and will also make less steam go through the l.p. stages of the turbine. The lower steam flow will make the turbine tend to reduce power, and its speed control will then make the turbine throttle valve open to compensate. So, a new balance is struck wherein process steam is increased and flow through h.p. stages is increased.

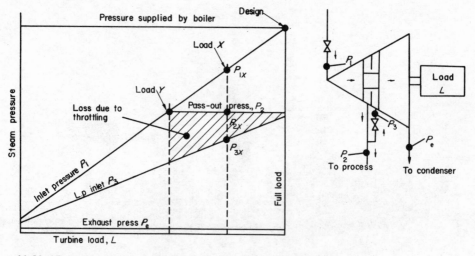

Figure 11.50   Principle of pressure control for a pass-out arrangement at varying load

The two control systems — speed control and pass-out control — are compatible and can share the overall task of control between them. The control principle is demonstrated further in *Figure 11.50*. This figure reveals two awkward features: first, that pass-out cannot be used below a certain load Y, because the pressure would not be high enough, and secondly that for the loads higher than Y but still lower than full load, a loss occurs because of the pressure drop $P_{2x}-P_{3x}$ across the pass-out control valve, so pass-out tends to be wasteful if the machine operates appreciably beneath full load. This is because of the throttling loss of the pass-out control valve, and also because the factory process has to be supplied with heat by by-passing the turbine altogether when the demand for electrical power is small.

To generalize is occasionally to mislead, but for most cases it is true that a pass-out machine has

something to offer over a combination of condensing and back-pressure sets even though the attraction disappears if the pass-out set spends long at part load. Both arrangements well deserve study when thinking out a scheme for the supply of energy.

Combined cycles

Practical examples of combined cycles are given in Chapter 20.

The gas turbine is becoming more reliable. On the other hand it has a lower efficiency than the steam cycle (about 29% overall thermal efficiency compared with 37% for a central power-station), because it exhausts at such a high temperature — typically 485°C. There are ways of combining the two cycles to get a better efficiency than either; one which is becoming popular is shown in *Figure*

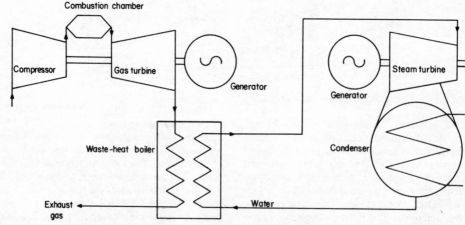

Figure 11.51   Combined cycle of steam and gas turbines

11.51. The case shown is for electricity supply but it can have other uses.

The fuel is burnt in the gas turbine, which drives its own compressor and a generator, and the hot exhaust raises steam in a waste-heat boiler. This supplies a steam turbine which drives a further electric generator, and thus the steam and gas turbines combine to supply power each from their own drive but by means of a common cycle whose efficiency is higher than it would be were either to operate alone.

The arrangement has attractions, a main one being that it should reach overall thermal efficiencies of over 40%. In addition, the gas turbine can supply power much quicker than a steam plant could (and in the cycle shown it provides from half to two-thirds of the total power). The steam turbine lags behind during start-up, so the cycle as a whole gives a more rapid response than steam plant alone would do, at least for a significant part of the intended load. There is sometimes another advantage because the gas turbine, being usually a standard article, can be supplied more quickly than steam plant can and this may be a useful way of meeting an urgent power demand. The steam turbine can follow later and then provides the extra power and efficiency, after the gas turbine has been put to use to meet the pressing need for power. The combined plant is generally expected to be lighter than conventional steam plant of the same power output. The disadvantages are mainly that the gas turbine can lower the reliability of the plant as a whole and this can affect and may destroy the increased cycle efficiency. The gas turbine is sensitive to type of fuel and this could cause significant reduction in availability if oil is used — at least until the machine is developed beyond its present state (1978). Of course this whole matter is relative to what can be achieved with conventional steam plant and the statements made here should not be misunderstood to imply any vast unreliability of gas turbines using oil, but the effect is there and significant enough in comparison, though not very large. The risk of unreliability may well be reduced when gas (methane for instance) is used as a fuel supply. There is some evidence that this is so and that combined cycles supplied with gas may be attractive. However, they may have the disadvantage of a somewhat heavy fall-off of efficiency at part load.

The trend appears to be to use the combined cycle for cases where fuel supply — probably gas — enables acceptable availability figures to be achieved for the combined plant or where oil is so readily available as to compensate for the somewhat poorer availability figures given by the plant which uses it. Experience may, of course, evolve machines that are adequately reliable with oil.

They are not as yet (1978) able to use coal, but even here there is a possibility that means of converting coal into gas may make the combined cycle attractive. The whole picture is developing in an interesting way and it appears that the combined cycle has possibilities. Even at present, it appears that using steam and gas turbines together in a combined cycle may have value in some applications.

11.7 Steam turbine troubles

If plant is damaged it loses money through being idle and it costs money to repair, so the efficient way of using steam plant is to keep it out of trouble.

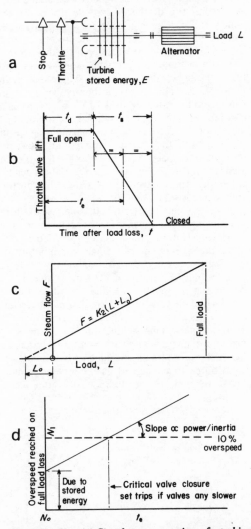

Figure 11.52 (a) Simple representation of a turbine; (b) equivalent closure time of valves; (c) Willans line; (d) basic overspeed characteristic (t_e as in Figure 11.52b)

This section gives brief notes on some important hazards and how they can be recognized and avoided.

Overspeed

The most lethal destroyer of turbines is overspeed. If the steam valves stay open after load has been removed from a turbine, the blades will accelerate until they almost catch up with the steam. Nozzle jet velocities are usually about twice as high as the velocity of the blades, or thereabouts, so a machine with open valves and no load will ultimately reach almost twice normal speed (in most designs about 1.8 times normal speed).

Few turbines can be designed to withstand this, and either the discs will explode or the blades come off before such a speed is even approached. The result is a wrecked turbine and — if disc explosions occur — the wreck could be disastrous.

To understand the problem more deeply and the safeguards, consider a very simple case as in *Figure 11.52*. The energy of the revolving system when running normally is $K_1 IN^2$, where K_1 is a constant (as are $K_2, K_3 \ldots$), I is the moment of inertia of the rotors and N is the rated speed in rev/min, and the energy supplied to cause an ultimate overspeed N_1 is $K_1I(N_1^2 - N^2)$. When load is removed the speed increases. If the machine is healthy, the control system closes the throttle valves but it takes time to do so. *Figure 11.52b* shows that some time (if only 0.1 s) elapses before the valves start to move. Also they take some time t_s to stroke (often of the order of 0.2 s). These two times are expressed by a single combination of $(t_d + {}^1/_2 t_s)$ to give t_e, the equivalent valve closing time. It may be as little as 0.1 s or as high as 1 s depending on the turbine and the valve duties. Even when the valves have closed, some steam has already passed them but has not yet gone through all the blades. This steam, trapped in the loop pipes, steam chests and various internal spaces of the turbine, contains stored energy E and this contributes to overspeed as the steam expands down through the turbine stages after valve closure.

Hence speed rise is obtained from:

$$K_1I(N_1^2 - N^2) = K_3(L + L_0)t_e + E$$

$$K_1IN_1^2 = K_3(L + L_o)t_e + E + K_1IN^2$$

$$N_1 = \left[(K_3Lt_e + K_3L_0t_e + E + K_1IN^2)\frac{1}{K_1I}\right]^{1/2}$$

This plots as a simple curve as in *Figure 11.52d*. It tells us that to prevent excessive overspeed, the valves must close quickly. If the machine is not to trip, the throttle valves must close in less than a

certain time (*see Figure 11.52d*) and it is a prime object of the governing system to ensure that this speedy action is achieved. The critical closing time should be known for each turbine and it is good practice to exercise the valves regularly, to measure the actual stroke times achieved and to correct any tendency to slow down.

Note also that even were the valves to close in zero time, stored energy would still be active and would create some overspeed — a point of some importance to the designer, who must aim to reduce steam storage spaces.

Reheat machines are a special case because of the vast amount of steam which can be stored in the reheater and the potential it has for overspeeding the turbine. Special valves called *interceptors* are fitted to prevent this happening. Their health is vital to machine security.

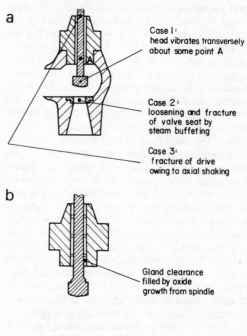

a

Case 1:
head vibrates transversely about some point A

Case 2:
loosening and fracture of valve seat by steam buffeting

Case 3:
fracture of drive owing to axial shaking

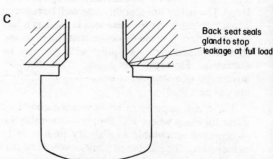

b

Gland clearance filled by oxide growth from spindle

c

Back seat seals gland to stop leakage at full load

Figure 11.53   (a) Some valve vibration troubles; (b) sticking of spindle caused by oxide; (c) back-seating

Valve failure

The last section showed why it is important to have healthy control valves. The present one mentions briefly some of the things that can go wrong.

Head and drive vibration

The throttle valve has a more arduous duty than most parts of the turbine, the only exception being possibly the last blade. When the turbine is at part load, the throttle valve reduces the steam pressure by a mixed process of expansion and reconversion of the resulting velocity to thermal energy. The amounts of energy released can be enormous compared with the size of the valve, consequently the valve structure must be immensely strong or it may be prone to translatory vibration as in case 1 of *Figure 11.53a*. This may even cause bending fatigue of the spindle or other damage.

The violently disturbed conditions sometimes produce a loosening and fracture of the valve seat (case 2), and trouble may also occur as an axial vibration of the drive (case 3), usually at a point of mechanical connection. In this case fractures sometimes occur at the mechanical connections within the valve and spindle drive.

These and other valve failures are fortunately not common but are by no means unknown. They can be avoided by good design even though it is a fact that designers do not yet know all they would like to about the aerodynamic instabilities involved. Even if the design is good or average, and more so if it is bad, it pays to look out for any evidence of valve vibration during running by watching the driving gear and the spindle and to look carefully for evidence whenever the valve chest is opened. If it is found that there are parts of the load curve where the valves vibrate, it could be wise to avoid them until the situation can be corrected.

Valve sticking

Oxides form on the valve spindle, particularly when steam temperatures are high. These may take various forms depending on the spindle material and descriptive names occur such as 'blue blush'. In a severe form, the coating is very adherent and can take up the clearance in the spindle gland (*Figure 11.53b*), which causes stickiness and jamming. These are a hazard because the valves will close slowly, if at all, and the machine may seriously overspeed. The trouble can be contained by good selection of materials and it is also important that hard surfaces be used for rubbing contact, for instance for the spindle and for the bush it slides in. The valves should be frequently exercised, since this can reveal any tendency to jam, if closing times are measured, and it also offers a possible way of scraping off the oxide

without shutting the machine down and opening up valve chests.

A further cause of valve jamming is distortion of the valve chest and parts. Bent valve spindles can be a particular source of trouble, and valve alignment should be checked very carefully on overhaul and ways found of taking the valve chests apart without applying high lateral forces to the spindles, which may bend them.

Running for long with a throttle valve just off its seat should be avoided since this is a risky position: it can easily promote vibration and is difficult for the governor to control. Such a valve can too easily strike the seat during slight instability, and repeat the process in a damaging form of hammering. The slightly open position also produces very high steam velocities which can damage the sealing surfaces and are a common source of noise.

A further design feature of control valves concerns steam saving. Since steam leaks along the valve spindles, some designs are provided with a back-seat (*Figure 11.53c*) which does two things: first, it closes the path to steam leakage, and secondly, it helps to hold the head firmly in position against vibration. The feature is obviously effective only when the valve is fully open. It becomes more important to prove freedom of movement by frequent testing when a back-seated valve is fitted. Without a back-seat the valves would move slightly, which gives a degree of exercise not present when a valve operates held firm against its back-seat.

Blade failure

The object here is to mention some of the basic points concerning blade and nozzle vibration so that an engineer will know better what to look for during maintenance of plant and so help avoid the worst results of vibration failure.

Blades become longer as the steam proceeds through the turbine stages, of which there are often twenty or more. Each blade has a series of natural frequencies, the lowest frequency being the simplest. The mode of resonance becomes more complicated the higher is the frequency, so if we plot the blade resonance for each stage of the machine we get a descending curve for each type and then a further curve above it for the next more complex type and so on. This may go on indefinitely with ever-increasing frequencies but, fortunately, the high-frequency complex resonances are very difficult to excite so we can usually forget them.

Now it takes not only a resonance to cause vibration but also an exciting force of the same or nearly the same frequency. A potential source is the nozzle wakes. Each blade passes through a number of bands of steam each time it rotates and may receive a considerable shaking if the nozzle

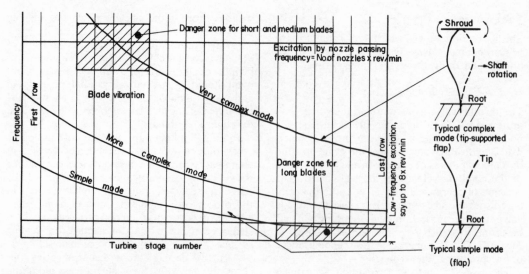

Figure 11.54   Blade vibration

wakes are pronounced. For an impulse turbine there are usually between 50 and 200 and often around 100 nozzles per stage. The number of nozzles — generally near equal for most stages — multiplied by the running speed gives the frequency of the exciting force and this is plotted in *Figure 11.54*. Note that it cuts the blade resonance lines for only the short and medium length of blades and for each such case the designer has to juggle the design to give a suitable margin of safety against resonance. He usually alters the number of nozzles to avoid coincidence of frequency of excitation and blade resonance.

The type of resonance which is often most dangerous for these early and middle-stage blades and excited at a very high frequency — say a value in the range of 5000–13000 Hz — is the tip-supported flap mode shown in the sketch at the top right-hand side of *Figure 11.54*. Note that it is for a shrouded blade and that the shroud is put under a severe form of flexure, so that during inspection particular attention should be paid to the state of the shrouding. Also, the tips and the roots of all middle and early stages of blading should be checked. Of course, the risks are highest with a machine of new design and can be reduced by crack-detecting. Failures ought to be very rare but it generally pays to take no chances. Well proven machines are, of course, quite another matter and such checks should be unnecessary.

The longer blades have lower natural frequencies so the vibration resonances to be concerned with in practice are in turn excited by lower frequencies. These may be anything up to say eight times normal running speed for the medium and large machines. The higher-order exciting force does exist though it tends to be very weak for the larger

machines. For instance an excitation at one times running speed is easy to conjecture, with the blade passing the exhaust ducting once per revolution. Aerodynamics of exhaust can lead one to contrive two or three times running-speed excitation. But much higher numbers are not so easy to imagine so far as exhaust blading is concerned.

It is good practice to prove each prototype blade, preferably by test, to show it is clear of resonances up to an appropriate excitation frequency.

Machine vibration

Being high-speed machines, steam turbines need to be finely balanced, and if the balance is disturbed, vibration will result. This is important in itself because vibration can cause damage — bearing hammering, coupling fret and other troubles — but vibration is often more important as an indicator of other trouble — shaft vibration caused by blade failure is one such case. ('Fret' here means wear by rubbing of parts together when either or both vibrate. It is often seen as 'fretting corrosion', which leaves a brown powder between the parts.) There are many others so it pays to investigate machine vibration and to find out its cause. It is advisable to get to know the vibration characteristics of a particular machine and to note and investigate any change which may occur. This is good practice, inherent in the efficient use of steam plant. To ignore it may be to cause a costly and untimely breakdown rather than a planned maintenance at a time when outage costs little.

Some simple sums show how sensitive a turbine can be to a shift of balance (*Figure 11.55*). Say a turbine rotor is bent slightly to have a throw of

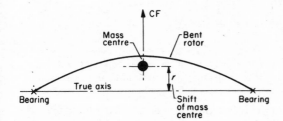

Figure 11.55 Mass shift in a bent rotor. W is the weight of the rotor, ω is the rotational speed, r is the throw of the mass centre and g is the acceleration due to gravity.

$$Centrifugal\ force = \frac{W}{g}\omega^2 r$$

mass centre of r. It runs in two bearings, and we assume that these are perfect constraints, which means they have zero clearance and massive rigidity. The centrifugal force of rotating mass is $(W/g)\omega^2 r$ (symbols are as in *Figure 11.55*). How large will r have to be to make the rotor lift off its bearings each time it rotates?

This is when

$$W = \frac{W}{g}\omega^2 r$$

Then

$$r = \frac{g}{\omega^2} = \frac{9.815 \times 10^3}{(50 \times 2\pi)^2}$$

(assuming a rotor speed of 3000 rev/min)

$$= 0.1\ mm$$

Take a rotor of 20 t and bearing span of say 6 m. (This is typical of the l.p. rotor of a medium to large turbine.) A bend that would move the mass centre by only 0.1 mm would cause these violent forces, and the rotor would lift off its bearings once each revolution and then thump down on them with twice the normal force — and this for a mass centre radial shift dimensionally equal to less than 0.002% of the bearing span.

Of course the assumptions made to simplify the analysis are far from right. In actual practice, the bearings have clearance and their supports and the oil films have significant flexibility. The rotor tends to rotate about its new mass centre and to waggle the bearings. In other words, the motion is far more complex than our simple sums assume and most rotors are accordingly somewhat less sensitive. However, it is still true that it takes only

a small radial change of mass to produce some quite violent results, so vibration is a notable indicator of change of position or shape of turbine rotating parts. It should not be ignored both because of the direct harm it may do and because it may signify internal damage. Vibration may take many forms and have a great variety of causes, some of the more common cases and a few notes on each one being given in *Table 11.4*.

Water ingress

This is probably the most important cause of breakdowns in large turbines. Its effect can vary from a loss of efficiency due to rubbing of rotating parts because of loss of clearance, to heavy outage due to rotor and casing distortion. There have even been extreme cases where severe water ingress has caused enough damage to require the turbine to be rebuilt from new parts.

The trouble occurs when the steady running state is disturbed by water or cool steam suddenly entering a hot turbine. The usual source is the bled-steam lines and the feedheaters they are connected to, but a drain choked or closed in error or a split tube in a heater or the act of connecting a flooded line to the machine by opening a valve — all these and other things too can cause water or cool steam to go back to a running turbine. Once inside the machine the stuff cools and distorts the cylinder and diaphragms and this may cause interference between the static glands and the spinning rotor. The latter bends and so makes the interference progressively more massive, and thus the rub becomes worse and may be catastrophic.

The danger is often (though not always) well recognized by plant design engineers. The answer is to design the heater system, its bled-steam lines and their drains so that water or cool steam cannot return to the turbine. This means:

1. selection of feed plant which has least risk of flooding;
2. arranging the plant and pipes in a sensible way; for instance, it can be arranged to self-drain and so that the water runs away from the turbine;
3. fitting non-return and automatic isolating valves, and making sure they are of good design and automatically close should water try to get into the turbine along bled-steam lines;
4. making sure that the action of the protection equipment can be readily and safely checked, even with the turbine on load.

It is also wise to make sure that the turbine has glands which are relatively insensitive to shaft interference. It is common practice to use spring

Table 11.4

Cause	Evidence
Bent rotor — often caused by water ingress	Radial vibration of bearings at running speed. Gets worse as the machine runs up and makes most critical speeds more prominent.
Blade failure	Radial vibration of bearings at running speed. Gets worse as the machine runs up and makes most critical speeds more prominent.
Change of machine alignment	Vibration at bearings, and can be axial and/or radial. Some shaft critical speeds may be made much worse if the load is taken off the bearings. Vibration is mostly at once per revolution but there may be some half shaft-speed vibration because of bearing unloading.
Gear errors	Axial vibration of pedestals may occur in geared sets because of errors in cutting or aligning the main wheel. Usually the frequency is that of the driven component.
Running on or too near to a shaft critical speed	If rotors need an undue amount of attention to balancing, such as a periodic need to balance *in situ*, it may be that a natural frequency of the rotor system is too near to running speed.
Electrical imbalance	If bearing vibration occurs only when a turbogenerator is synchronized this suggests that electrical imbalance within the alternator and its circuitry is the reason.
Oil whip	Half shaft-speed vibration at bearings, if met, is often caused by the phenomenon termed 'oil whip'. This is usually associated with a bearing which is very lightly loaded. Bearing experts will advise how to get over it. Alignment may also be at fault.
Valve stem vibration, pipe vibration, condenser tube vibration, guide vane vibration and many others	Cases where vibration is not at shaft or half shaft frequency are not uncommon inside steam space. Excitation is usually aerodynamic.

supports and material which will not readily damage the rotor surface if it rubs.

Water ingress, this arch-enemy of turbines, is being more and more understood and as time goes by, design and operating practices should overcome it, but some plants still attract trouble and it is as well to check the precautions and reduce the risk which may cause waste of fuel, loss of plant operation and loss of money.

Erosion

The classic case of erosion is that of the last row of blades (*see Figure 11.56*). This is not the only place where erosion can strike, since use of low-steam conditions in some modern nuclear plant makes erosion in the intermediate-pressure stages a matter of some concern too.

Erosion of exhaust blades

Turbines usually run with wet steam at the exhaust stage, around 10% and sometimes as high as 13%

wet. Most of the water in the steam passes through the turbine without doing any damage. It often appears as a mist of very fine drops carried along with the steam and passing the blades without much impact, and it is not this, the majority of the water, which causes the trouble, but the small amount which appears as big drops.

At various positions in the nozzles and casings pools of water collect. Steam howls across these miniature lakes like a gale and snatches water from the surface. This spindrift is formed of drops which are quite massive compared with the average small ones which the steam already contains. Further, they travel much slower than the steam, hence when a blade is reached, they will not glide onto its surface as the steam does, but slam into it at an angle and — because of their mass and the high relative velocity — the impact is enormous. Given time, the surface of the blade is torn away, as in *Figure 11.56*, and new blades may have to be fitted.

Figure 11.56   Eroded blades. (Courtesy of GEC Ltd)

There are many equations which portray this process though few of them are accurate. Research still has to reach firm conclusions on some aspects but several factors are known to have significance:

1. The mass of droplet is important — and this grows inherently as steam pressure falls. So a high vacuum can cause more erosion than a low vacuum partly because of the larger droplet size. (It also, of course, tends to give higher efficiency.)
2. Blade tip speeds are important. There is a threshold tip velocity beneath which little damage occurs and the amount of damage is a function of the difference between this and the actual service velocity.
3. Degree of wetness obviously matters but may not be as significant as was once thought.
4. How the nozzles are positioned relative to the blades and the casing can have a significant effect on erosion. It pays to keep the likely points of water formation such as in the nozzles at some distance from the blades by using a large clearance between blades and nozzles. This allows any heavy drops time to acquire steam velocity and for the steam and static parts to break them into smaller, less harmful drops, before they reach the blades.

5. Material properties, particularly hardness, are significant.
6. Most turbine designers recognize that it pays to have a high heat drop across the last row of nozzles to 'bash the water into a fine mist'.

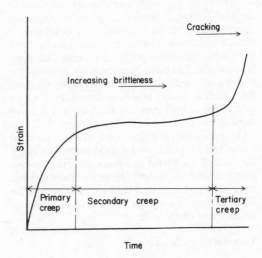

Figure 11.57   Creep curve

Creep

As *Figure 11.57* shows, if a metal is held at a particular stress for long enough at a high temperature, it first relaxes fairly rapidly (primary creep) then steadies to a more moderate rate (secondary creep). Finally tertiary creep sets in and the metal breaks down rapidly.

For practical purposes of turbine engineering, creep occurs for most metals above about 400°C. In time, bolts and other fixtures at higher temperatures may become slack and therefore need planned attention. Important bolts such as for horizontal joints need adjustment at each overhaul (every two to four years say) and less important bolts may even need replacement — if for no other reason than the growth of their thread pitch which makes them impossible to remove except by cutting.

Blade roots should, of course, have been designed allowing for creep, but in case the designer is wrong it pays to take a look at the high-temperature roots by crack-detecting when the machine is opened up on its major overhaul. The same applies to valve stems and to valve chests, and in fact to all high-temperature parts — say at above 400°C.

By paying this attention and generally by getting to know more about creep and its effects on steam plant, money can be saved not just by reducing outages but by keeping joints tight and so avoiding leakages. This is especially so inside a machine where quite high leakages may go undetected for a long time and can cause a prodigious waste of steam and fuel.

Bearing damage

Bearing damage is generally one form or another of melting of the white metal or its extrusion or fatigue. It may, more seriously, be accompanied by damage to the shaft surfaces. The result is extra outage and to some extent loss of efficiency. Both go to make the plant a poorer investment. A bearing may even fail so badly that the rotor contacts the stator and causes serious damage to the machine itself such as loss of blades or distortion of major parts. The object must be to catch any bearing trouble and correct it before this occurs.

An adequate and clean supply of oil is a must for steam turbines. It is also a good routine to check the state of the thrust and journal bearings in any overhaul and ask oneself why any items of damage have occurred. This may lead not just to a cure for the damaged bearing but point to some more significant and costly fault.

Thermal stress failure

The steam turbine is not good at fast load changes — it is nothing like so swift in run-up, for instance, as the gas turbine or diesel engine. It can be brought up to speed quite quickly, but only provided its designer and the operator know what they are doing as regards thermal stress. Steam transfers its heat very readily, especially when it is condensing on a surface, so when steam is admitted to a cold turbine it can heat up the inner surface of the metal parts more rapidly than the heat can spread through the metal to the extremities. Hence part of, say, the steam valve chest can be at the steam temperature of 370°C while much of the rest of the chest is near to room temperature and the relative expansion is restrained, causing very high stresses. Steam has to be applied in moderation when heating (or cooling) a machine and sudden changes to steam condition should be avoided. This is not to say that one must treat the machine gently; but at least the more violent shocks should be avoided by careful control of steam conditions and by carefully thinking out the warming through and shutdown procedures.

The operating instructions should give guidance and normally a reference instrument is quoted. Steam admission is controlled to maintain a specified difference of temperature from a given datum. If a reasonable degree of care is not exercised, cracking may result owing to repeated severe thermal cycling, or parts may distort as a result of severe thermal stress.

As part of a major overhaul, crack detection applied to high-temperature surfaces can pay dividends (*see* Chapter 3). It can reveal the start of cracks in time for new parts to be procured before the next major overhaul and before the cracks become serious, and can also point to the need to adjust operating procedures. However unpopular and dramatic at the time, such discipline is a wise policy if the plant is to pay its way.

So far as the designer is concerned, there is no doubt that most designs would benefit from having their high-temperature static parts of a much simpler shape and in structural forms of less redundancy. Cracks which have occurred in steam chests, for instance, often just show up the ungainly shapes given to the structure by the designer. If he uses a complicated structure whose stress analysis would be difficult, then the chances are that thermal stress will break it — if not at once, then later.

Final

Reading this chapter may make one cautious about buying steam plant, having seen all the things that might go wrong with it, and having heard a little about its shakes, cracks and seizures; but this would be quite wrong. The reliability of the steam turbine is immense compared with that of other plant. In a way it suffers from a virtue of being so useful and lucrative to its owner that the occasional troubles are made much of. The attitude of always looking out for trouble is not a bad one. At least it is sensible engineering to know the worst that can happen and plan to avoid it even though the plant may well complete its 200 000 hours of life without incident. Better this than be a disappointed optimist, and lose the plant in the process!

12 Heat transfer

12.1 Introduction

Heat transfer, particularly heat transfer by convection, is not simple, and engineers often want simplified formulae to solve their problems. This is not because they do not understand the subject, but because they are very aware at times of the order of accuracy of their basic data, involving as it does many properties of fluids, pipes and vessels, which often may not warrant an exact formula. For this reason a number of approximate, sometimes empirical, formulae and tables have been presented in this chapter and in Chapter 14. However, it is important when using these to be aware of any assumptions which have been made in the simplification.

This chapter attempts to describe the conditions which govern heat transfer, both for the reader who needs to know the full picture and for anyone using the tables and simplified formulae so that they can assess the importance of any assumptions which have been made.

A list of symbols used in this chapter and Chapter 14 is given on p 292.

12.2 Heat transfer

It is an everyday experience that heat is transferred in three different ways: by conduction — for example touching a hot metal surface will cause a burn; by convection — contact with a hot vapour (steam) or a liquid will scald; by radiation — basking in sunshine or the heat from a fire will produce a pleasant warming sensation.

For the purposes of what follows, radiation will generally be ignored and steady-state heat flow assumed.

12.3 Conduction

Conduction usually involves heat transfer within a material, usually solid, which has well defined boundaries. Pure conduction is difficult to achieve in gases and liquids because temperature differences cause fluid motion.

The rate of heat transfer by conduction within a solid material is proportional to the area available for heat transfer and to the temperature gradient across the material (*see Figure 12.1*).

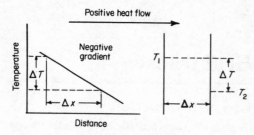

Figure 12.1   *Conduction through a plane wall*

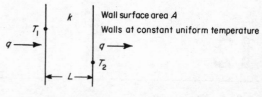

Figure 12.2   *Conduction within a plane wall*

$$q = k A \frac{(T_1 - T_2)}{L} \qquad (12.2)$$

The statement usually takes the form

$$q = - k A \frac{\Delta T}{\Delta x} \qquad (12.1)$$

where q is the rate of heat flow in watts, A is the area in m^2 across which heat flow takes place, $\Delta T / \Delta x$ is the temperature gradient normal to area A in K/m (ΔT being the drop in temperature over a distance Δx) and k is the thermal conductivity of the material in W/m K. The minus sign is included because heat flows from a high to a low temperature; k is a constant of proportionality called the *thermal conductivity*. The conductivity is dependent on the nature of the material, the direction of heat flow within the material and its temperature. In practice it is usually assumed constant and evaluated at the arithmetic mean temperature of the material. It has the units of W/m K and some typical figures for metals are given in *Table 12.1*. It should be noted that conductivity for pure metals decreases, and for alloys it increases, with increasing temperature.

Conduction within a plane wall

Consider a plane wall of thickness L as indicated in *Figure 12.2*. The wall temperatures are fixed at T_1 and T_2 and the material has conductivity k. The rate of heat transfer through the wall is

$$q = - k A \frac{\Delta T}{\Delta x} = - k A \frac{(T_2 - T_1)}{L}$$

Use of this equation is shown by the following example:

A reaction vessel has a carbon steel (0.5% C) wall which is 12 mm thick. The inside wall temperature is 140°C and the outside wall temperature is 20°C. What is the heat flux (flow per unit area per unit time) through the vessel wall?

Equation (12.2) can be used to find the heat flux q/A (W/m^2):

$$q = k A \frac{(T_1 - T_2)}{L}$$

or heat flux

$$q/A = \frac{k(T_1 - T_2)}{L}$$

where $T_1 = 140$°C and $T_2 = 20$°C with $L = 0.012$ m. The value of the thermal conductivity k is obtained from *Table 12.1* for a mean temperature of 80°C and is 52.6 W/m K, so that

$$q/A = \frac{52.6 \times (140-20)}{0.012}$$

Heat flux $q/A = 526$ kW/m^2

Composite walls

When a wall is composed of several layers of material, for example firebrick, insulating brick

Table 12.1   Thermal conductivity of metals

Metal	Thermal conductivity (W/m K)			
	0°C	*100°C*	*200°C*	*300°C*
Aluminium	236	240	238	234
Cast iron (3% C)	28.5	32.4	35.8	37.2
Copper (pure)	401	393	389	384
Aluminium bronze (90% Cu : 10% Al)	49	57	66	
Carbon steel (1.0% C)	43	42.8	42.2	41.5
Carbon steel (0.5% C)	55	52	48	45
Stainless steel (18% Cr : 8% Ni)	14.7	16.6	18.0	19.4

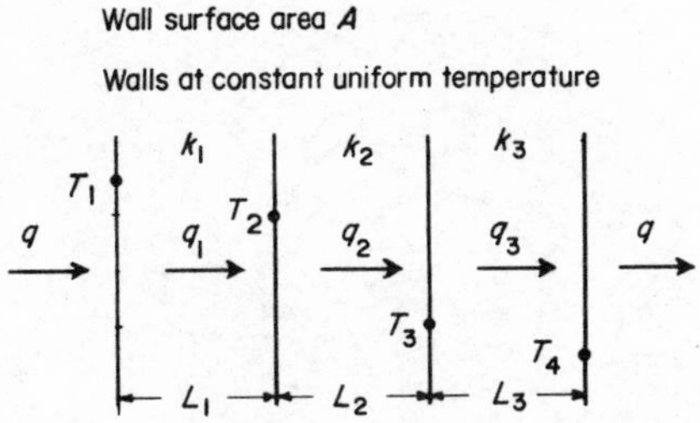

Wall surface area A

Walls at constant uniform temperature

Figure 12.3   Conduction in a composite wall

and plain brick, the situation is as indicated in *Figure 12.3*. For steady flow

$$q = q_1 = q_2 = q_3$$

and

$$q_1 = k_1 A \frac{(T_1 - T_2)}{L_1}$$

$$q_2 = k_2 A \frac{(T_2 - T_3)}{L_2}$$

$$q_3 = k_3 A \frac{(T_3 - T_4)}{L_3}$$

Now

$$(T_1 - T_4) = (T_1 - T_2) + (T_2 - T_3) + (T_3 - T_4)$$

or

$$(T_1 - T_4) = q\left\{\frac{L_1}{k_1 A} + \frac{L_2}{k_2 A} + \frac{L_3}{k_3 A}\right\}$$

Rearranging, we obtain the following expression for the rate of heat flow q (W):

$$q = \frac{(T_1 - T_4)}{\left\{\dfrac{L_1}{k_1 A} + \dfrac{L_2}{k_2 A} + \dfrac{L_3}{k_3 A}\right\}} \tag{12.3}$$

The terms $L_i/k_i A$ may be regarded as the thermal resistance of each layer of the wall, and the rate of heat flow q is the total temperature drop across the composite wall divided by the total wall resistance. Thus the equation may be extended to any number of layers.

A heated, lagged reaction vessel is an example of heat flow through a number of layers in series, as can be seen from the following example:

The reaction vessel in the previous example is lined with 3 mm of stainless steel (18% Cr : 8% Ni) and is insulated with 85% magnesia 50 mm thick. The inside and outside surface temperatures remain unchanged. We can recalculate the heat flux and determine the temperature of the lagging in contact with the vessel wall if the insulating material has a conductivity of 0.050 W/m K. Here equation (12.3) may be used:

$$q = \frac{(T_1 - T_4)}{\left\{\dfrac{L_1}{k_1 A} + \dfrac{L_2}{k_2 A} + \dfrac{L_3}{k_3 A}\right\}} \tag{12.3}$$

where $T_1 = 140°C$, $T_4 = 20°C$, $A = 1 \text{ m}^2$, $L_1 = 0.003$ m, $L_2 = 0.012$ m and $L_3 = 0.050$ m. From *Table 12.1*, assuming no temperature drop across the metal, $k_1 = 17.16$ W/m K, $k_2 = 50.4$ W/m K and $k_3 = 0.050$ W/m K. Thus

$$\frac{L_1}{k_1} = \frac{0.003}{17.16}; \quad \frac{L_2}{k_2} = \frac{0.012}{50.4}; \quad \frac{L_3}{k_3} = \frac{0.05}{0.05}$$

$$= 0.00017 ; \quad = 0.00024 ; \quad = 1 \quad \frac{\text{m}^2\,\text{K}}{\text{W}}$$

Thus

$$q/A \text{ (W/m}^2) = \frac{140-20}{1.0004}$$

Heat flux $q/A = 120$ W/m^2.

Compare this figure with that given by the previous calculation for the same vessel, unlagged, namely 526 kW/m^2, i.e. nearly 4400 times greater.

The assumption of negligible temperature drop across the metal may be checked as follows (*Figure 12.3*):

$$\frac{T_1 - T_3}{T_1 - T_4} = \left\{\frac{L_1/k_1 + L_2/k_2}{L_1/k_1 + L_2/k_2 + L_3/k_3}\right\}$$

$$= \frac{0.00017 + 0.00024}{1.0004}$$

$$= 0.00041$$

so that $T_1 - T_3 = 0.00041 \times 120 = 0.05$ K. Thus the total temperature drop across the metal and lining is a negligible 0.05 K so that the inside surface of the lagging may be taken to be 140°C.

Cylindrical wall

Conduction through cylindrical walls is commonly met with in the process industry, which relies heavily on cylindrical pipes for the transfer of fluids, both hot and cold.

The main difference between a plane wall and a cylindrical wall is that as heat passes through a cylindrical wall the area available for its flow increases and under steady conditions the heat flux must decrease.

Consider a cross-section of a cylindrical pipe (*Figure 12.4*). The rate of heat flow q may be expressed as

$$q = -k A_\text{m} \frac{\Delta T}{\Delta r}$$

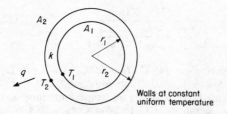

Figure 12.4   *Conduction in a cylindrical wall*

where A_m is an appropriate mean or average area to compensate for the increase of area with radius (r), k is the thermal conductivity and $\triangle T/\triangle r$ is the radial temperature gradient. Textbooks on heat transfer indicate that the appropriate area is the log mean area A_m.

$$A_m = \frac{A_2 - A_1}{\ln(A_2/A_1)} = \frac{2\pi L(r_2 - r_1)}{\ln(r_2/r_1)}$$

L being the tube length. Thus for a single cylindrical wall

$$q = \frac{2\pi kL(r_2 - r_1)}{\ln(r_2/r_1)} \frac{(T_1 - T_2)}{(r_2 - r_1)}$$

$$= \frac{2\pi kL(T_1 - T_2)}{\ln(r_2/r_1)} \qquad (12.4)$$

This expression may be recast into the form

$$\text{Heat flow} = \frac{\text{temperature drop}}{\text{resistance}}$$

i.e.

$$q = \frac{(T_1 - T_2)L}{\ln(r_2/r_1)/2\pi k}$$

from which the thermal resistance of a cylindrical wall is seen to be $(\ln(r_2/r_1)/2\pi k)$ per metre of pipe run.

Composite cylindrical walls

Process pipes carrying hot fluids are usually lagged to preserve heat, so that they must be considered as composite cylindrical walls. Heat flow through these walls is arrived at in exactly the same way as for plane walls, i.e.

$$\text{Rate of heat flow} = \frac{\text{total temperature drop}}{\text{total resistance}}$$

For the insulated steam pipe indicated in *Figure 12.5,*

$$q = \frac{(T_1 - T_3)L}{\left\{\dfrac{\ln(r_2/r_1)}{2\pi k_1} + \dfrac{\ln(r_3/r_2)}{2\pi k_2}\right\}}$$

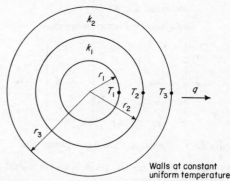

Figure 12.5   *Conduction in a composite cylindrical wall*

The heat loss in the practical case of a lagged 300 mm pipe can be calculated as follows:

A carbon-steel pipe (0.5% C) has an internal diameter of 300 mm and an outside diameter of 325 mm. The outside of the pipe is covered with a layer of 85% magnesia which is 50 mm thick and has a conductivity of 0.05 W/m K. The inside pipe wall is at a temperature of 140°C and the outer surface of the lagging is at 20°C. Calculate the heat loss per metre length of pipe run.

Equation (12.5) may be used for this purpose:

$$q/L = \frac{(T_1 - T_3)L}{\left\{\dfrac{\ln(r_2/r_1)}{2\pi k_1} + \dfrac{\ln(r_3/r_2)}{2\pi k_2}\right\}} \quad \text{(W/m)} \quad (12.5)$$

where $T_1 = 140°C$, $T_3 = 20°C$, $r_1 = 150$ mm, $r_2 = 162.5$ mm and $r_3 = 212.5$ mm.

From *Table 12.1*, $k_1 = 50.4$ W/m K. For 85% magnesia, $k_2 = 0.05$ W/m K.

$$\frac{\ln(r_2/r_1)}{2\pi k_1} = \frac{\ln\left(\dfrac{162.5}{150}\right)}{2\pi \times 50.4} = 0.00025 \text{ m K/W}$$

$$\frac{\ln(r_3/r_2)}{2\pi k_2} = \frac{\ln\left(\dfrac{212.5}{162.5}\right)}{2\pi \times 0.05} = 0.853 \text{ m K/W}$$

The thermal resistance of the pipe (0.00025) is small compared with that of the lagging (0.853) and may be neglected.

The heat flux per metre of pipe run (q/L) is therefore

$$q/L = \frac{140 - 20}{0.853} = 141 \text{ W/m}$$

12.4 Convection

Heat transfer by convection involves a fluid (gas or liquid) flowing over a surface. The rate at which heat is transferred to or from the surface depends on many factors, the most important of these being the fluid velocity, the fluid's physical properties (thermal conductivity, specific heat, density and viscosity) together with the shape and orientation of the surface and the temperature difference between fluid and surface.

The rate of heat transfer is proportional to the area of the surface A and the average or mean temperature difference $\triangle T_m$, i.e.

$$q \propto A \times \triangle T_m$$

or

$$q = h \times A \times \triangle T_m \qquad (12.6)$$

where h is the heat transfer coefficient ($W/m^2 K$).

Heat transfer coefficients can be calculated for many simple situations, notably those involving laminar flow, but in other situations they must be determined empirically. It is common practice to present such experimentally determined coefficients in dimensionless equations produced by dimensional analysis.

If equation (12.6) above is compared with the equation

$$\text{Rate of heat flow} = \frac{\text{temperature difference}}{\text{thermal resistance}}$$

it is seen that the thermal resistance associated with a heat transfer coefficient is $1/hA$. Such thermal resistances may be added to the conduction thermal resistances, so that in a steam main, heat will be transferred from the steam to the pipe wall, through this pipe wall and lagging and then lost by convection to the surrounding atmosphere.

The heat transfer resistances are as follows:

Steam to inside of wall $\quad 1/h_i A_i$

Through wall and
lagging (from previous $\quad (\ln(r_2/r_1)/2\pi k_{wall})$
section p 278) $\quad + (\ln(r_3/r_2)/2\pi k_{lagging})$

Outside lagging to $\quad 1/h_o A_o$
surroundings

The total resistance to heat transfer between the steam at a temperature T_s and the surroundings at a temperature T_a is therefore

$$\frac{1}{h_i A_i} + \frac{\ln(r_2/r_1)}{2\pi k_{wall}} + \frac{\ln(r_3/r_2)}{2\pi k_{lagging}} + \frac{1}{h_o A_o}$$

This cumbersome expression is used to define an overall heat transfer coefficient H_o so that the rate of heat transfer is

$$q/L = H_o A_o (T_s - T_a) \qquad (12.7)$$

where T_s is the temperature of the saturated steam and T_a is the ambient temperature.

$$\frac{1}{H_o A_o} = \frac{1}{h_i A_i} + \frac{\ln(r_2/r_1)}{2\pi k_{wall}}$$
$$+ \frac{\ln(r_3/r_2)}{2\pi k_{lagging}} + \frac{1}{h_o A_o}$$

From equation (12.7),

$$\frac{q}{L H_o A_o} = (T_s - T_a)$$

$$\therefore q = \frac{L(T_s - T_a)}{1/H_o A_o}$$

Since $A_i = 2\pi r_1$ and $A_o = 2\pi r_3$, we have

$$\frac{1}{H_o A_o} = \frac{1}{2\pi r_1 h_i} + \frac{\ln(r_2/r_1)}{2\pi k_{wall}}$$
$$+ \frac{\ln(r_3/r_2)}{2\pi k_{lagging}} + \frac{1}{2\pi r_3 h_o}$$

so that

$$q = \frac{2\pi L (T_s - T_a)}{\dfrac{1}{r_1 h_i} + \dfrac{\ln(r_2/r_1)}{k_{wall}} + \dfrac{\ln(r_3/r_2)}{k_{lagging}} + \dfrac{1}{r_3 h_o}}$$

This overall heat transfer coefficient H_o is based on the outside area A_o. It is possible to use the inside area of the pipe (A_i) to define an overall heat transfer coefficient H_i such that

$$H_o A_o = H_i A_i$$

Values of H are useful for design purposes and again must be determined experimentally.

The use of equation (12.7) is shown in the following example, which is a more accurate calculation of the previous example on p 278. The carbon-steel pipe referred to in that calculation contains steam and has an internal heat transfer coefficient of 5000 $W/m^2 K$. The outer surface of the lagging loses heat by convection and radiation to surroundings at 20°C. The lagging surface heat transfer coefficient is 10 $W/m^2 K$. Calculate the heat loss per metre run of pipe.

Equation (12.7) may be used:

$$q/L = H_o A_o (T_s - T_a) \qquad (12.7)$$

where

$$\frac{1}{H_o A_o} = \frac{1}{h_i A_i} + \left[\frac{\ln(r_2/r_1)}{2\pi k_{wall}}\right]$$
$$+ \left[\frac{\ln(r_3/r_2)}{2\pi k_{lagging}}\right] + \frac{1}{h_o A_o}$$

i.e. total thermal resistance = inside thermal resistance + wall thermal resistance + lagging thermal resistance + outside thermal resistance. The pipe wall and lagging thermal resistances may be taken from the example on p 278. The remaining resistances are calculated as follows:

Inside thermal resistance:

$$\frac{1}{h_i A_i} = \frac{1}{h_i 2\pi r_1} = \frac{1}{5000 \times 2\pi \times 0.15}$$

$$= 0.000212 \text{ m K/W}$$

Outside thermal resistance:

$$\frac{1}{h_o A_o} = \frac{1}{h_o 2\pi r_3} = \frac{1}{10 \times 2\pi \times 0.2125}$$

$$= 0.0749 \text{ m K/W}$$

Therefore

$$\frac{1}{H_o A_o} = 0.000212 + 0.00025 + 0.853 + 0.0749$$

$$= 0.9284 \text{ m K/W}$$

$$H_o A_o = 1.077$$
and
$$(q/L) = 1.077 \times (140-20) = 129.2$$

Heat loss per metre of pipe = 129.2 W/m. This figure is for steam condensing within the main. Good distribution practice would have steam at a temperature above saturation to reduce losses and in these circumstances the internal heat transfer coefficient would be approximately 500 W/m²K. Reworking the problem with this value of the

internal heat transfer coefficient produces a calculated heat loss of 129 W/m.

Note that the internal thermal resistance and that due to the wall are small and could safely be neglected. Neglecting these resistances produces the value 129.3 W/m.

In the case of the steam main referred to above, if the steam is superheated the internal heat transfer mechanism is that of convection due to the flow of the steam over the surface (forced convection). If the steam is saturated, any heat loss will cause the steam to condense on the surface, and in these conditions the internal heat transfer coefficient is very high and the internal resistance is often neglected when calculating the total resistance. The heat loss from the outside of the pipe to the surroundings is said to produce 'free' or 'natural' convection, and any flow of fluid over the surface is entirely due to the heat transfer. There are three main types of heat transfer by convection: *forced* convection, *free* or *natural* convection, and convection due to *condensing vapours*, and these will be discussed further, together with heat transfer from boiling liquids.

There are also a number of cases of condensation which have to be considered, namely: turbulent film condensation; condensation inside vertical tubes; condensation inside horizontal tubes; and condensation outside vertical tubes.

Table 12.2 shows a range of approximate convective heat transfer coefficients for various conditions.

Forced convection

Forced convection exists when a fluid (liquid or

Table 12.2   Individual (film) heat transfer coefficients (W/m²K) (approximate)

Forced convection	
Gases and dry vapours	10–1000
Liquids	100–10000
Free convection	
Gases and dry vapours	0.5–1000
Liquids	50–3000
Condensation	
Steam condensing (film)	500–25000
Steam condensing (dropwise)	20000–45000
Boiling	
Water	3000–10000
Organic liquids	500–2000

Overall heat transfer coefficients (W/m²K) (approximate)

Hot fluid	Cold fluid	
Steam	Water	2000–4000
Steam	Organic liquids	500–1000

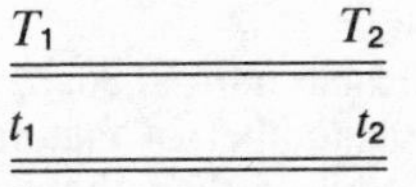

$$T_1 \overline{\overline{}} T_2$$

$$t_1 t_2$$

Figure 12.6   Temperature differences

gas) is pumped along a duct or channel or stirred in a tank. Analysis of forced-convection problems is very difficult except for a few cases of laminar flow in simple situations. As a result of this, recourse has to be made to experimental methods, interpreting the results by means of dimensional analysis.

The rate of heat transfer is expressed as

$$q = h \times A \times \triangle T_m$$

where h is the heat transfer coefficient, A the area over which heat transfer takes place and $\triangle T_m$ is the appropriate mean temperature difference. In the case of forced convection with turbulent flow this is usually the log mean temperature difference, but for laminar-flow situations the use of the arithmetic mean temperature difference is common. It is essential to establish the correct mean temperature difference before using any correlation.

Temperature differences

Figure 12.6 shows a simple situation of forced convection in a pipe. Now

$$\triangle T_1 = T_1 - t_1 \quad \text{and} \quad \triangle T_2 = T_2 - t_2$$

The arithmetic mean temperature difference is defined as

$$\triangle T_{am} = \frac{\triangle T_1 + \triangle T_2}{2}$$

and is commonly used for free convection.

The logarithmic mean temperature difference is defined as

$$\triangle T_{lm} = \frac{\triangle T_1 - \triangle T_2}{\ln(\triangle T_1/\triangle T_2)}$$

This expression is commonly used for turbulent heat transfer. The *bulk fluid temperature* is $\frac{1}{2}(t_1 + t_2)$, while the film temperature, T_f, is defined as

$$\frac{1}{2}\left[\left(\frac{T_{w1} + T_{w2}}{2}\right) + \left(\frac{t_1 + t_2}{2}\right)\right]$$

i.e. the arithmetic average of the mean wall temperature and the bulk fluid temperature.

When the temperature drop across the tube wall is neglected, the film temperature may be defined as

$$T_f = \frac{1}{2}\left[\left(\frac{T_1 + T_2}{2}\right) + \left(\frac{t_1 + t_2}{2}\right)\right]$$

We can look at a practical case of steam on the outside and water flow through the tube in *Figure 12.6*. Steam at 140°C condenses on the outside of a condenser tube containing cooling water which enters at 20°C and leaves at 50°C. Calculate (a) the arithmetic mean temperature difference; (b) the logarithmic mean temperature difference; (c) the bulk fluid temperature; and (d) the average film temperature, neglecting temperature drop across the tube wall.

(a) Referring to *Figure 12.6*,

$$\triangle T_1 = T_1 - t_1 = 140 - 20 = 120°C$$

$$\triangle T_2 = T_2 - t_2 = 140 - 50 = 90°C$$

The arithmetic mean temperature is defined as

$$\triangle T_{am} = \frac{\triangle T_1 + \triangle T_2}{2} = \frac{120 + 90}{2} = 105°C$$

(b) The logarithmic mean temperature is defined as

$$\triangle T_{lm} = \frac{\triangle T_1 - \triangle T_2}{\ln(\triangle T_1/\triangle T_2)} = \frac{(\triangle T_1 - \triangle T_2)}{2.303\log(\triangle T_1/\triangle T_2)}$$

$$= \frac{120 - 90}{\ln(12/9)} = \frac{30}{0.288} = 104.3°C$$

When $(T_1/T_2) < 2$, the arithemtic mean temperature difference is within 4% of the logarithmic mean temperature difference. $\triangle T_{lm}$ is always smaller than $\triangle T_{am}$.

(c) The bulk fluid temperature is $\frac{1}{2}(t_1 + t_2) = 35°C$.

(d) The average film temperature is defined as

$$\frac{1}{2}\left[\left(\frac{T_1 + T_2}{2}\right) + \left(\frac{t_1 + t_2}{2}\right)\right]$$

$$= \frac{1}{2}(140 + 35) = 87.5°C$$

Convective heat transfer depends upon a number of dimensionless groups or numbers, the chief ones of which are explained below.

Reynolds, Prandtl and Nusselt numbers

The Reynolds number (Re) may be regarded as a measure of the ratio of inertia forces to viscous forces within the flowing fluid. The value of the Reynolds number decides whether a given flow is streamline (laminar) or has a turbulent velocity distribution.

$$Re = \frac{VD\rho}{\mu}$$

where V is the velocity of flow, D is the tube diameter, ρ is the density of the fluid and μ is the viscosity evaluated at bulk temperature.

Values of the Reynolds number below 2100 indicate a fluid undergoing streamline flow, while a value above 10^4 indicates a fluid with turbulent flow.

For values intermediate between 2100 and 10^4 the flow is in a transition region and its heat transfer performance is difficult to predict.

The Prandtl number (Pr) is the ratio of the diffusivity of momentum to the diffusivity of heat within the fluid.

$$Pr = \frac{C_p\mu}{k}$$

where C_p is the specific heat capacity at constant pressure (J/kg K), μ is again the viscosity of the fluid and k is the thermal conductivity of the fluid.

Low values of the Prandtl number occur with liquid metals; for example, mercury at 293 K has a Prandtl number of 0.0249. High values are associated with heavy oils — engine oil at 293 K has a Prandtl number of 10400. Intermediate values are associated with water and other mobile fluids: water at 293 K has a Prandtl number of 6.74 while Freon at the same temperature has a Prandtl number of 3.5. The Prandtl number for dry steam and gases is approximately 1; steam at 380 K and 1 bar pressure has a Prandtl number of 1.06; air at 350 K and 1 bar pressure has a Prandtl number of 0.697.

The Prandtl number is a property of the fluid and is a function of temperature. For example, the Prandtl number for water at 1 bar pressure and 293 K is 6.74, but at 1 bar pressure and 363 K it has dropped to 1.96.

The Nusselt number (Nu, equal to hD/k) can be regarded as a dimensionless heat transfer coefficient. Alternatively, the heat flux may be written as $h \times \triangle T$, where h is a heat transfer coefficient and $\triangle T$ is the temperature difference between the pipe wall and the fluid. If the fluid were at rest the heat flux could be written as $k \times (\triangle T/r)$, where k is the fluid's thermal conductivity and r is the pipe radius. Dividing these two values for heat flux yields hr/k. The Nusselt number is hD/k $(= 2hr/k)$ and therefore can be regarded as a measure of the ratio of the heat transfer to a flowing fluid to the heat transfer to the same fluid at rest.

The value of the heat transfer coefficient is likely to depend upon a number of factors. In forced convection in a pipe or duct these may be the diameter D, pipe length L, pipe surface condition, fluid velocity V, fluid density ρ, fluid specific heat C_p, fluid conductivity k and fluid viscosity μ. Dimensional analysis indicates the following arrangement of variables:

$$\frac{hD}{k} = f\left(\frac{VD\rho}{\mu}, \frac{C_p\mu}{k}\right) \tag{12.8}$$

viz.

$$Nu = f(Re, Pr)$$

that is, the Nusselt number is a function of the Reynolds and Prandtl numbers. For non-circular pipes D is replaced by D_e, the hydraulic mean diameter, defined as

$$D_e = \frac{4 \times \text{cross-sectional area}}{\text{channel perimeter}}$$

It should be noted that this relationship does not contain any mention of pipe or duct length or surface condition. The variation of duct length is usually accounted for by quoting a range of length to diameter ratios over which a given experimental correlation may be applied. However, surface condition is much more difficult to assess. One simple method is to quote heat transfer coefficients for 'clean' and 'dirty' surfaces.

Simplified equations exist for a number of simple situations. Typical examples, for pipe flow, are as follows:

Water flowing in pipes. For heat transfer to water in turbulent flow, equation (12.9) (below) may be modified to

$$h = 1063\,(1 + 0.00293t_w)\,V^{0.8}/D^{0.2}$$

where h is the heat transfer coefficient in W/m² K, t_w is the absolute temperature of the bulk water, D is the pipe diameter in metres and V is the fluid velocity in m/s. Some data calculated from this equation are presented in *Table 12.3*.

Air in long smooth pipes. For gases, the Prandtl number can be regarded as constant over a wide range of conditions and equation (12.9) may be written as

$$Nu = 0.02\,(Re)^{0.8}$$

Taking properties for air at approximately atmospheric temperature and pressure produces the equation

$$h = \frac{3.7\,V^{0.8}}{D^{0.2}}$$

Table 12.3 Results of applying the Dittus–Boelter equation (12.9) to water at 293 K flowing, with various velocities, through tubes of different diameters

Water velocity (m/s)	Tube diameter (mm)	Heat transfer coefficient (W/m² K)
1	20	4137
	25	3962
	36	3691
	50	3456
1.5	20	5738
	25	5484
	36	5084
	50	4772
2.0	20	7218
	25	6910
	36	6426
	50	6016
2.5	20	8637
	25	8263
	36	7667
	50	7187
3.0	20	9966
	25	9543
	36	8875
	50	8311

Superheated steam in pipes. In this case the heat transfer coefficient h (W/m² K) is given by

$$h = (4.07 + 3.13 \times 10^{-3} T_s)\, V^{0.79} / d^{0.16}\, l^{0.5}$$

where V is the velocity of flow in m/s at STP, T_s is the absolute temperature of the saturated steam, and l and d are the pipe length and diameter, respectively, in metres.

Typical experimental relationships, for turbulent flows, are obtained by assuming that the equation

$$Nu = f(Re, Pr)$$

takes the simple form

$$Nu = B.\, Re^a\, Pr^b$$

where the constants B, a and b are determined experimentally.

A classic example of this type of correlation is the Dittus–Boelter equation, applied to the inside of straight circular pipes:

$$Nu = 0.023\,(Re)^{0.8}\,(Pr)^n \qquad (12.9)$$

which is used with a log mean temperature differ-

ence and has the following restrictions: $0.7 < Pr < 120$, $10^4 < Re < 1.2 \times 10^5$, $L/D > 60$, and $n = 0.4$ for heating and 0.3 for cooling of the fluid. All properties are evaluated at bulk fluid temperature.

This equation may be used with non-circular pipes if D is replaced by D_e, the hydraulic mean diameter.

We can take the condenser in the previous example (p 281) and calculate the heat transfer coefficient. The tube has an internal diameter of 0.015 m and an outside diameter of 0.019 m. The water flowing through the tube has a velocity of 1.25 m/s.

Equation (12.9) may be used:

$$Nu = 0.023\,(Re)^{0.08}\,(Pr)^{0.4} \qquad (12.9)$$

where the exponent 0.4 is chosen because the water in the tube is being heated. The physical properties at the bulk fluid temperature of 35°C are: density (ρ) = 993.9 kg/m³; thermal conductivity (k) = 0.625 W/m K; specific heat capacity (C_p) = 4178.5 J/kg K; dynamic viscosity (μ) = 720.3 × 10⁻⁶ kg/m s. The Reynolds number (Re) is defined as

$$Re = \frac{VD\rho}{\mu} = \frac{1.25 \times 0.015 \times 993.9 \times 10^6}{720.3}$$

$$= 25\,872$$

$$(Re)^{0.8} = 3390$$

The Prandtl number (Pr) is defined as

$$Pr = \frac{C_p\,\mu}{k} = \frac{4178.5 \times 720.3 \times \cdot10^{-6}}{0.625} = 4.81$$

$$(Pr)^{0.4} = 1.87$$

The Nusselt number, defined as (hD/k), is evaluated from

$$Nu = 0.023\,(Re)^{0.8}\,(Pr)^{0.4}$$

$$= 0.023 \times 3390 \times 1.87 = 145.8$$

The internal heat transfer coefficient is obtained from the relation

$$h = Nu \times \frac{k}{D}$$

$$= \frac{145.8 \times 0.625}{0.015}$$

$$= 6075 \text{ W/m}^2 \text{ K}$$

The Dittus–Boelter equation contains no term

which accounts for variation of viscosity with temperature. An equation that attempts to do this is that of Sieder and Tate, which applies to turbulent flow in straight pipes — that is, with a Reynolds number $> 10^4$ and $0.6 < Pr < 100$:

$$Nu = 0.027 \, (Re)^{0.8} \, (Pr)^{0.33} \left(\frac{\mu}{\mu_w}\right)^{0.14} \qquad (12.10)$$

where μ is the bulk viscosity and μ_w the viscosity at the wall temperature. Equations of this form are also used to predict heat transfer in jacketed vessels.

Equations for use in predicting heat transfer coefficients with laminar flow are usually empirical representations of analytical solutions which are themselves very complicated in form. Typical equations are, for straight circular pipes,

$$Nu = 1.86 \, (Re)^{1/3} \, (Pr)^{1/3} \left(\frac{D}{L}\right)^{1/3} \left(\frac{\mu}{\mu_w}\right)^{0.14} \qquad (12.11)$$

for laminar flows in short tubes where $Gz > 10$, and

$$Nu = 3.66 \qquad (12.12)$$

for laminar flows in long tubes where $Gz < 10$. Gz is the Graetz number:

$$Gz = \left(\frac{\pi}{4} \cdot \frac{D}{L} \cdot Re \cdot Pr\right)$$

When these equations are used, the arithmetic mean temperature difference should be taken. The fluid properties are evaluated at the bulk fluid temperature, with the exception of viscosity, which is evaluated at both bulk fluid temperature and the wall temperature.

If, taking the previous example, we reduce the water velocity in the condenser tube to 0.05 m/s, we shall then have laminar flow to which equation (12.11) will apply. We can calculate the internal heat transfer coefficient assuming that the physical properties are unaltered and the pipe is 3 m long. Equation (12.11) may be used:

$$Nu = 1.86 \, (Re)^{1/3} \, (Pr)^{1/3} \left(\frac{D}{L}\right)^{1/3} \left(\frac{\mu}{\mu_w}\right)^{0.14} \qquad (12.11)$$

as will be seen below. The value of the Reynolds number is now

$$Re = \frac{25\,872 \times 0.05}{1.25}$$

$$= 1035$$

This is well below 2100 and laminar flow will occur.

Equation (12.11) is used when the Graetz number is greater than 10:

$$Gz = \frac{\pi}{4} \times \frac{D}{L} \times Re \times Pr$$

$$= \frac{\pi}{4} \times \frac{0.015}{3} \times 1035 \times 4.81$$

$$= 19.5$$

This is greater than 10 and hence equation (12.11) is valid.

$$Nu = 1.86 \, (Re)^{1/3} \, (Pr)^{1/3} \left(\frac{D}{L}\right)^{1/3} \left(\frac{\mu}{\mu_w}\right)^{0.14} \qquad (12.11)$$

$Re = 1035$, $\therefore (Re)^{1/3} = 10.12$; $Pr = 4.81$, $\therefore (Pr)^{1/3} = 1.68$; $D/L = 0.015 \div 3$, $\therefore (D/L)^{1/3} = 0.17$. $(\mu/\mu_w)^{0.14}$ is assumed to be equal to 1.

$$Nu = 1.86 \times 10.12 \times 1.68 \times 0.17 \times 1$$

$$= 5.37$$

The internal heat transfer coefficient is calculated from

$$h = Nu \times \frac{k}{D}$$

$$= 5.37 \times \frac{0.625}{0.015}$$

$$= 224 \, W/m^2 \, K$$

Compare this with the calculation on p 283 where the heat transfer coefficient was 6075 W/m² K.

Free convection

Free convection occurs from furnace walls exposed to colder air, in unstirred vessels (or in stirred vessels if the stirrer fails) and in some slow-moving pipe flows. The movement which causes the convection is due entirely to density differences produced by the transfer of the heat itself.

The heat transfer coefficient in free convection is a function of a characteristic dimension of the surface, L, temperature difference between surface and surrounding fluid ΔT, fluid conductivity k, fluid specific heat capacity C_p, fluid density ρ, fluid viscosity μ, and fluid coefficient of thermal expansion β.

Dimensional analysis gives the following suitable form:

$$\frac{hL}{k} = f\left(\frac{\beta g \, L^3 \rho^2 \, \Delta T}{\mu^2}, \, \frac{C_p \mu}{k}\right) \qquad (12.13)$$

where g is the acceleration due to gravity (m/s²),

i.e. the Nusselt number is a function of the Grashof and Prandtl numbers. The Grashof number is the ratio of buoyancy and inertia forces to viscous forces in free convection. It may be regarded as the equivalent of the Reynolds number in forced convection.

$$Gr = \frac{\beta g L^3 \rho^2 \Delta T}{\mu^2}$$

For vertical surfaces of sufficient length the fluid flow over the surface may start as laminar and become turbulent, but for horizontal surfaces and horizontal cylinders laminar flow is usual.

For use with laminar flow the equation

$$Nu = f(Gr, Pr)$$

may be simplified to

$$Nu = f(Gr \times Pr) \qquad (12.14)$$

Some useful equations are as follows:

For laminar flow

Vertical surface:

$$Nu = 0.59(Gr \times Pr)^{1/4} \qquad (12.15)$$
$$\text{for } 10^4 < (Gr \times Pr) < 10^9$$

where the height is the characteristic dimension.

Horizontal cylinder:

$$Nu = 0.53(Gr \times Pr)^{1/4} \qquad (12.16)$$
$$\text{for } 10^4 < (Gr \times Pr) < 10^9$$

where the diameter is the characteristic dimension.

For turbulent flow

Vertical surface:

$$Nu = 0.13(Gr \times Pr)^{1/3} \qquad \text{for } (Gr \times Pr) > 10^9 \qquad (12.17)$$

Horizontal cylinder:

$$Nu = 0.13(Gr \times Pr)^{1/3} \qquad \text{for } (Gr \times Pr) > 10^9 \qquad (12.18)$$

For values of $(Gr \times Pr) < 10^3$, free convection may be ignored. Properties are evaluated at the mean of surface and bulk temperature.

The coefficient of cubical expansion for gases may be obtained from the relation $\beta = 1/T_g$, where T_g is the temperature of the gas in K.

When a heated surface loses heat to surrounding air, a common occurrence, the use of simplified equations is possible. These are given at the foot of the page.

A calculation of the heat loss by natural convection from a lagged steam main shows how Grashof and Prandtl numbers are used.

Supposing a lagged steam main has an outside lagging diameter of 0.25 m. The lagging has a surface temperature of 80°C and is surrounded by air with a temperature of 20°C. Calculate the heat loss from a 3 m length of pipe if it is mounted (a) horizontally, and (b) vertically.

(a) The first step is to evaluate the Grashof number for the horizontal pipe. The Grashof number is defined by

$$Gr = \frac{\beta g D^3 \rho^2 \Delta T}{\mu^2}$$

where the physical properties are those of air at an average temperature of 50°C. β, for gases, may be taken to be the reciprocal of the absolute temperature of the gas, i.e. 1/293. The air may be taken to have the following properties at 50°C: specific heat capacity $C_p = 1.007$ kJ/kg K; density $\rho = 1.087$ kg/m³; thermal conductivity $k = 0.028$ W/m K; viscosity $\mu = 1.96 \times 10^{-5}$ kg/m s. Thus

$$Gr = \frac{(0.25)^3 \times (1.087)^2 \times 9.81 \times 60}{(1.96 \times 10^{-5})^2 \times 293}$$

$$= 9.65 \times 10^7$$

	Streamlined, $10^4 < Gr < 10^9$	Turbulent, $10^9 < Gr < 10^{12}$
Vertical plate or cylinder with height L	$h = 1.42\left(\dfrac{\Delta T}{L}\right)^{1/4}$	$h = 1.31\Delta T^{1/3}$
Horizontal cylinder with outside diameter d	$1.32\left(\dfrac{\Delta T}{d}\right)^{1/4}$	$1.25\Delta T^{1/3}$
Horizontal plate (heated plate facing upwards or cooled plate facing downwards)	$1.32\left(\dfrac{\Delta T}{L}\right)^{1/4}$	$1.52\Delta T^{1/3}$
Horizontal place (cooled plate facing upwards or heated plate facing downwards)	$0.59\left(\dfrac{\Delta T}{L}\right)^{1/4}$	

Table 12.4   Heat loss from a lagged horizontal pipe to still air at 291 K

Surface temperature (K)	Radiation heat transfer coefficient (W/m² K)	Convection heat transfer coefficient	Total heat transfer coefficient	Total heat loss (q/A) (W/m²)
293	5.1	1.6	6.7	13
298	5.2	2.4	7.6	53
303	5.3	2.8	8.1	97
308	5.5	3.2	8.7	148
313	5.6	3.5	9.1	200
323	5.9	4.0	9.9	317
333	6.2	4.3	10.5	441
343	6.5	4.6	11.1	577
353	6.9	4.9	11.8	732
363	7.2	5.2	12.4	893
373	7.6	5.4	13.0	1066

The Prandtl number is now evaluated from

$$\text{Pr} = \frac{C_p\mu}{k} = \frac{1.007 \times 10^3 \times 1.96 \times 10^{-5}}{0.028} = 0.7$$

The product Gr × Pr is

$$9.65 \times 10^7 \times 0.7 = 6.755 \times 10^7$$

This is less than 10^9, therefore we use equation (12.16), which is

$$\text{Nu} = 0.53 \,(\text{Gr} \times \text{Pr})^{\frac{1}{4}} \qquad (12.16)$$

$$= 0.53 \,(6.755 \times 10^7)^{\frac{1}{4}}$$

$$= 48$$

The heat transfer coefficient is obtained from the expression

$$h = \text{Nu} \times \frac{k}{D} = \frac{48 \times 0.028}{0.25}$$

$$= 5.4 \text{ W/m}^2\text{K}$$

The total heat loss is obtained by multiplying h by the area available for heat transfer and the temperature difference between the lagging surface and its surroundings.

$$\text{Heat loss} = 5.4 \times \pi \times 0.25 \times 3 \times 60$$

$$= 763 \text{ W for 3 m of pipe}$$

Clearly this is a large, unacceptable loss of energy, indicating that the lagging thickness was insufficient.

(b) For the vertical pipe, the Grashof number is defined as

$$\text{Gr} = \frac{L^3\rho^2 g \,\beta\Delta T}{\mu^2}$$

where L is the height of the vertical surface. Using the same physical properties as before,

$$\text{Gr} = \frac{3^3 \times (1.087)^2 \times 9.81 \times 60}{(1.96 \times 10^{-5})^2 \times 293}$$

$$= 1.67 \times 10^{11}$$

The product Gr × Pr is

$$1.67 \times 10^{11} \times 0.7 = 1.17 \times 10^{11}$$

This is greater than 10^9, therefore equation (12.17) should be used. This is

$$\text{Nu} = 0.13 \times (\text{Gr.Pr})^{\frac{1}{3}} \qquad (12.17)$$

$$= 0.13 \times (1.17 \times 10^{11})^{\frac{1}{3}}$$

$$= 635.8$$

Thus

$$h = \frac{635.8 \times 0.028}{0.25}$$

$$= 71.2$$

and the heat loss is

$$71.2 \times \pi \times 0.25 \times 3 \times 60 = 10065 \text{ W}$$

This heat loss is several times larger than that for the corresponding horizontal pipe and is clearly unacceptable. The lagging should be much thicker.

12.5 Radiation

Natural convection is not the only source of heat loss from surfaces; heat loss by radiation is also significant and can exceed that by convection. This heat loss is calculated from the equation

$$q = \sigma. \,\epsilon.A(\,T_s^4 - T_a^4)$$

where q is the rate of heat loss in watts, σ is the Stefan–Boltzmann constant, i.e. 5.67×10^{-8} $W/m^2 K^4$, ϵ is the emissivity of the surface losing heat, T_s is the surface absolute temperature, and T_a is the absolute temperature of the surroundings.

A radiation heat transfer coefficient can be defined by the equation

$$h_r = \sigma \cdot \epsilon \left(\frac{T_s^4 - T_a^4}{T_s - T_a} \right)$$

h_r can be added to h_c, the natural convection coefficient, to produce a combined radiation and convection coefficient. h_c for still air (e.g. indoors) may be conveniently calculated from the simplified equation

$$h_c = 1.25(T_s - T_a)^{1/3}$$

Table 12.4 shows the results of radiation and convection calculations for a horizontal pipe losing heat to the surroundings, which have a temperature of 291 K. The surface is assumed to have an emissivity of 0.9.

12.6 Boiling

In discussing heat transfer associated with boiling, use is made of the heat flux q/A at the heating surface rather than the heat transfer coefficient h. From equation (12.6) we can see that

$$q/A = h \, \Delta T$$

where q is the rate of heat flow from the surface of area A in m^2, q/A is the surface heat flux in W/m^2, h is the heat transfer coefficient in $W/m^2 K$ and ΔT is the temperature difference between the heating surface and the bulk temperature of the boiling liquid (K).

Pool boiling

A typical plot of q/A against ΔT for a pool of boiling liquid is shown in *Figure 12.7* for the case when the wall temperature is controlled. The region OA represents a region in which heat

transfer is essentially by natural convection. The region AB is the 'nucleate boiling region' where heat transfer is much enhanced by the action of bubbles formed on the heating surface. This region is one of stable boiling in the sense that as the surface temperature is increased, the heat flux also increases up to a maximum value at point C. The region CD beyond this point is unstable — an increase in the driving force ΔT causes a reduction in the heat transfer coefficient. The reason for this is that large volumes of vapour are produced, causing a vapour blanket to form over the heating surface. The final region from D to E is a region of stable film boiling where again heat transfer coefficient increases with ΔT. Heat is transferred by convection and radiation across the layer of vapour which blankets the heating surface. The point E is often referred to as the 'burn-out' point. The region AB is of paramount importance. Nucleate boiling heat transfer coefficients are extremely difficult to predict theoretically. Values of the maximum heat flux and critical temperature difference are given in *Table 12.5* for a number of liquids.

The *critical temperature difference* is that temperature difference between the boiling liquid and the heating surface at which the maximum heat flux occurs. The value of the critical temperature difference for water is about 25 K. The temperature difference between boiling liquid and the heating surface in most boilers is of the order 3–6 K, hence the heat flux is well below the maximum value.

The ability to predict the value of $(q/A)_{max}$, i.e. point C in *Figure 12.7*, is also useful as this represents an upper limit in nucleate boiling heat transfer. A fairly simple formula, due to Rohsenow and Griffith, is, in SI units:

Table 12.5 Maximum heat flux and critical temperature difference for boiling liquids (approximate)

Liquid	Surface	$(q/A)_{max}$ (kW/m²)	ΔT (K)
Water	Nickel-plated copper	1100	29
Water	Chrome-plated copper	550	25
Water	Steel	1200	83*
Methanol	Copper	380	67*
Methanol	Steel	380	58*
Benzene	Copper	170	44*
Benzene	Steel	250	55*

* Overall temperature difference from heating medium to boiling fluid. Adapted from McAdams[4].

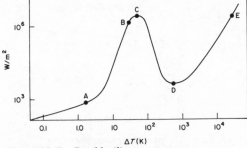

Figure 12.7 Pool boiling

$$\frac{(q/A)_{\max}}{\rho_v \lambda} = 0.0121 \left(\frac{\rho_L - \rho_v}{\rho_v}\right)^{0.6} \quad (12.19)$$

where ρ_L and ρ_v are the densities of liquid and vapour respectively, and λ is the latent heat. For water at atmospheric pressure this becomes

$$\frac{(q/A)_{\max}}{0.597 \times 2257} = 0.0121 \left(\frac{957.8 - 0.597}{0.597}\right)^{0.6}$$

i.e.

$$(q/A)_{\max} = 1365 \text{ kW/m}^2$$

For particular situations involving either especially clean surfaces, very dirty surfaces, specially treated surfaces, liquid metals or high pressures, the reader is referred to specialized texts on heat transfer.

Forced-convection boiling

The generation of vapour by passing liquid through a tube heated by condensing steam is a common occurrence in the process industries. The flow system within the boiling tube is complex and consists of some or all of the following regions:

1. A sub-cooled boiling region where bubbles are formed at the tube surface but subsequently collapse within the liquid;
2. A nucleate boiling region, where bubbles formed at the tube wall persist;
3. an annular region where the liquid is situated at the tube walls and the core is vapour that will contain a small amount of entrained liquid which if the tube is long enough will turn to vapour, thus leading to
4. a region of pure vapour.

The first and fourth of these regions are extremes consisting respectively of liquid only and vapour only and here the Dittus–Boelter equation (12.9) may be applied. Intermediate regions may be considered to have the forced-convection heat transfer enhanced by the nucleate boiling process. A simple approximate estimate of the heat transfer coefficient may be obtained by calculating the forced-convection coefficient and adding it to that estimated for pool boiling.

12.7 Condensation

The process of heat transfer by condensation is of paramount importance in steam utilization in all process industries. The latent heat of water is large (1320 kJ/kg at a pressure of 100 bar abs (311°C)) and increases with decreasing pressure to 2257 kJ/kg at 1 bar abs pressure (100°C). Unfortunately, lowering the pressure to increase the amount of available heat also causes a reduction in the temperature at which condensation occurs, leading to a smaller temperature difference and hence a loss of driving force.

The heat transfer coefficients obtained with condensing steam are large, of the order of 5000–15000 W/m² K, and usually the heat transfer in the material being heated controls the rate at which heat enters this material. To increase rates of heat transfer, therefore, attention should be given to the improvement of the heat transfer within the heated material by agitation, increase of velocity of flow, or alternatively increasing the area available for heat transfer by the use of finned surfaces.

Condensation is generally regarded as taking place in one of two ways. These are (a) film condensation, in which vapour condenses to form a continuous film on the cooling surface, and (b) dropwise condensation, in which the vapour condenses to form discrete droplets on the surface leaving part of it uncovered by liquid. This mode of condensation gives rise to high heat transfer coefficients but is difficult to achieve with steam unless it is contaminated.

The classic theoretical solution to the problem of film condensation is due to Nusselt, and makes the following assumptions (*see Figure 12.8*):

1. Vapour at its saturation temperature condenses on a vertical surface at constant temperature to produce a film of condensate in which flow is streamline and steady.
2. The vapour exerts no drag at the vapour–liquid interface.
3. There is no temperature drop at the vapour–liquid interface.

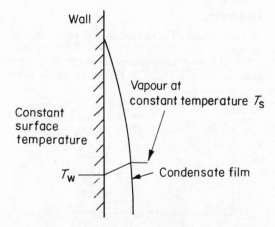

Figure 12.8   Temperature profile in film condensation

4. The temperature distribution across the laminar condensate film is linear.
5. Physical properties are constant.

In spite of the large number of assumptions, the analysis produces a useful design equation for use with most fluids on short tubes or on long tubes if the rate of condensation is low.

The result of the analysis for vertical surfaces, i.e. flat plates or the inside and outside of vertical tubes where the film is thin compared with the tube diameter, is the Nusselt equation:

$$\frac{h_m L}{k} = Nu_{m,L} = 0.943 \left(\frac{g \rho^2 \lambda L^3}{\mu k \triangle T} \right)^{1/4} \quad (12.20)$$

A corresponding equation for the horizontal tubes is

$$\frac{h_m D}{k} = Nu_{m,D} = 0.725 \left(\frac{g \rho^2 \lambda D^3}{\mu k \triangle T} \right)^{1/4} \quad (12.21)$$

The Nusselt value of the constant is 0.725, but later computer simulations suggest 0.728.

These equations may be rewritten as follows:

For vertical surfaces:

$$h_m \left[\frac{\mu^2}{k^3 \rho^2 g} \right]^{1/3} = 1.47 \left[\frac{4 \Gamma}{\mu} \right]^{-1/3} \quad (12.22)$$

where Γ is the mass rate of flow of condensate per unit length of perimeter.

For horizontal tubes:

$$h_m \left[\frac{\mu^2}{k^3 \rho^2 g} \right]^{1/3} = 1.51 \left[\frac{4 \Gamma'}{\mu} \right]^{-1/3} \quad (12.23)$$

where Γ' is now the mass rate of flow of condensate per unit length of tube. On comparing the two equations it is seen that provided the length is more than three times the diameter, the horizontal tube will give a higher heat transfer coefficient for the same temperature conditions. It should be noted that if the constant is taken as 1.5, the same equation may be used for both cases.

From a study of experimental results McAdams[4] suggests that the Nusselt equation (12.20) under-predicts and for vertical surfaces should be multiplied by 1.2 if $4 \Gamma /\mu$ is less than 1800, i.e.

$$Nu_{m,L} = 1.13 \left[\frac{g \rho^2 \lambda L^3}{\mu k \triangle T} \right]^{1/4} \quad (12.24)$$

When using the equation, the physical properties are evaluated at the mean film temperature, $\frac{1}{2}(T_w + T_s)$, with the exception of the latent heat λ, which is evaluated at the saturation temperature.

An empirical equation for steam condensing on a vertical tube is

$$h = 13.8 \times 10^5 L^{-1/4} (\triangle T)^{-1/3}$$

A similar equation may be used for horizontal tubes, i.e.

$$h = 1.07 \times 10^5 D^{-1/4} (\triangle T)^{-1/3}$$

where h has units of $W/m^2 K$, L is the height of the vertical surface, D is the tube diameter in metres, and $\triangle T$ is the temperature difference in °C between the steam and the condensing surface.

An example of the calculation of the heat transfer coefficients for condensing steam follows, for both vertical and horizontal tubes:

Steam flowing at a rate of 10000 kg/h and at 120°C is condensed using cooling water at an average temperature of 20°C. The condenser contains 800 tubes which have an outside diameter of 18 mm. Estimate the heat transfer coefficient (a) if the condenser is vertical, and (b) if the condenser is horizontal with tubes 3 m long and condensation takes place outside the tubes.

(a) Equation (12.22) may be used for this purpose.

$$h_m \left[\frac{\mu^2}{k^3 \rho^2 g} \right]^{1/3} = 1.47 \left[\frac{4 \Gamma}{\mu} \right]^{-1/3} \quad (12.22)$$

In this equation the physical properties are evaluated at the average temperature of the condensate film, i.e. 70°C. These properties are: density = 977.8 kg/m^3; thermal conductivity = 0.66 W/m K; viscosity = 404.7 × 10^{-6} kg/m s; Γ is the mass rate of flow of condensate per unit length of perimeter, i.e.

$$\Gamma = \frac{10000}{3600} \bigg/ (800 \times \pi \times 0.018)$$

$$= 6.14 \times 10^{-2} \text{ kg/s per metre of perimeter}$$

The Reynolds number of the flow is given by

$$\frac{4\Gamma}{\mu} = \frac{4 \times 6.14 \times 10^{-2}}{404.7 \times 10^{-6}}$$

$$= 607$$

Thus the flow in the film is streamlined and equation (12.22) is valid. Substituting the appropriate values into equation (12.22),

$$h_m \left[\frac{(404.7 \times 10^{-6})^2}{(0.660)^3 \times (977.8)^2 \times 9.81} \right]^{1/3}$$

$$= 1.47 \times (607)^{-1/3}$$

$$h_m (3.931 \times 10^{-5}) = 1.47 \times 0.118$$

$$h_m = \frac{0.174}{3.931 \times 10^{-5}} = 4426$$

Thus the average heat transfer coefficient is 4426 $W/m^2 K$.

(b) For horizontal tubes equation (12.23) may be used, i.e.

$$h_m \left(\frac{\mu^2}{k^3 \rho^2 g}\right)^{1/3} = 1.51 \left(\frac{4\Gamma'}{\mu}\right)^{-1/3} \qquad (12.23)$$

where Γ' is defined as the mass rate of flow per unit length of tube, i.e.

$$\Gamma' = \frac{10000}{3600 \, (3 \times 800)}$$

$$= 1.15 \times 10^{-3} \text{ kg/s per metre}$$

The flow parameter is

$$\frac{4\Gamma'}{\mu} = 11.44$$

and the flow is clearly streamlined. Substituting the appropriate values into equation (12.23), and remembering that the physical properties are the same as part (a), produces

$$h_m \times 3.931 \times 10^{-5} = 1.51 \times (11.44)^{-1/3}$$

i.e.

$$h_m = \frac{0.670}{3.931 \times 10^{-5}}$$

$$= 17048$$

Thus the average heat transfer coefficient is 17048 $W/m^2 K$.

This illustrates very well the advantage of using horizontal rather than vertical condensers.

Turbulent film condensation

The motion of the condensate film undergoes a transition from laminar to turbulent flow when the film Reynolds number $4\Gamma/\mu$ is greater than 2000 for vertical surfaces and greater than 4000 for horizontal surfaces. The latter condition is rarely reached but turbulence is common in vertical films.

The local heat transfer coefficient for turbulent vertical condensation is given by

$$\frac{h_x}{k} \left[\frac{\mu^2}{\rho^2 g}\right]^{1/3} = 0.056 \left(\frac{4\Gamma_x}{\mu}\right)^{0.2} (Pr_L)^{1/3} \qquad (12.25)$$

where h_x is the local coefficient a distance x from the top of the condensing surface where the mass flow rate is Γ_x. Pr_L refers to the Prandtl number of the liquid film.

A mean value of the heat transfer coefficient is obtained by integration of h_x over the surface, using the Nusselt equation:

$$h_x = \left[\frac{k^3 \, \rho^2 g \lambda}{4\mu \Delta T x}\right]^{1/4} \qquad (12.26)$$

for regions where the Reynolds number $(4 \, \Gamma/\mu)$ is less than 1600. When $(4 \, \Gamma/\mu)$ is greater than 1600, equation (12.25) should be used. The result of this procedure is shown in *Figure 12.9*. This diagram should be used for condensation outside vertical tubes and for condensation inside vertical tubes with downward flow of vapour.

Condensation inside vertical tubes

If the vapour velocity is assumed to be zero (as in the Nusselt equation), the vapour is stagnant and exerts no drag on the vapour surface. With downward flow in a vertical tube, however, the effect of the vapour drag will be to thin the condensate film and increase the heat transfer coefficient. With high-velocity downward flow, the heat transfer coefficient may be up to ten times greater than that predicted by the Nusselt equation.

Upward flow in a vertical tube tends to thicken the condensate film and reduce the heat transfer coefficient. If the velocity is low enough to prevent flooding, caused by the upward vapour flow preventing the condensate from draining down the tube, then shear stress, or the effect of vapour velocities, may be neglected. High vapour velocities may drag, or blow the condensate out of the top of the tube, thus designs involving upward flows should be avoided. A simple experimental correlation for downward flow inside tubes is:

$$h_m = 0.065 G_v \left[\frac{C_p \, \rho k (\tau_w / \rho \, V^2)}{\mu \rho_v}\right]^{1/2}$$

$$= 0.065 G_v \left[\frac{C_p \, \rho k f}{2\mu \, \rho_v}\right]^{1/2} \qquad (12.27)$$

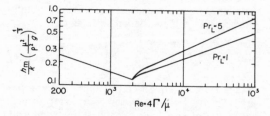

Figure 12.9 Plot of $(h_m/k) \, (\mu^2/\rho^2 g)^{1/3}$ versus Reynolds number for vertical condensation

where C_p, ρ, k and λ refer to the condensate and ρ_v and G_v refer to the vapour.

τ_w is obtained by using the shear-stress equation for dry pipes:

$$\tau_w = f \cdot \tfrac{1}{2} \rho V^2$$

where f is the Fanning friction factor (*see* Chapter 9) and τ_w is calculated from the mean mass flow rate of the vapour:

$$G_v = \left(\frac{G_1{}^2 + G_2{}^2 + G_1 G_2}{3} \right)^{1/2}$$

where G_1 and G_2 are the inlet and outlet mass velocities.

For complete condensation $G_2 = 0$ and $G_v = 0.58 G_1$. All physical properties except ρ_v are evaluated at a film temperature $T_f = T_s - 0.75(T_s - T_w)$.

Condensation inside horizontal tubes

Condensation inside horizontal tubes is of considerable industrial importance, but analysis is difficult. Both axial and circumferential flow of condensate may occur, resulting in complicated flow patterns. In addition, the effect of vapour shear stress is at right angles to the gravity force.

The Nusselt equation for condensation on the outside of a horizontal tube can be applied in the modified form

$$\text{Nu} = 0.555 \left[\frac{D^3 \rho_L (\rho_L - \rho_v) g \lambda k^3}{k_L \mu_L (T_s - T_w)} \right]^{1/4}$$

(12.28)

when either short tubes are used or the Reynolds number of the inlet vapour is low, i.e. $\text{Re}_v < 3.5 \times 10^4$. For long tubes or when the vapour velocity is high, use the equation

$$\text{Nu} = 0.0265 \left(\frac{D \, G_E}{\mu} \right)^{0.3} \left(\frac{C_p \mu}{k} \right)^{1/3}$$

(12.29)

when $D G_E / \mu > 5 \times 10^4$, $D G_E / \mu$ being a Reynolds number based on the tube diameter and an 'equivalent mass velocity' defined as

$$G_E = G_L + G_v \left(\frac{\rho_L}{\rho_v} \right)^{1/2}$$

G_L and G_v are the mass velocities of the liquid and vapour phases respectively.

Condensation outside horizontal tubes

Equations based on a Nusselt-type analysis have already been presented as equations (12.20) and (12.21). This analysis has been extended to condensation on a vertical row of horizontal tubes by replacing D by $N_T D$, where N_T is the number of tubes in a vertical row. This is to say that

$$h_{m, N_T} = h_{m, 1} N_T{}^{-1/4}$$

(12.30)

where h_{m, N_T} is the mean heat transfer coefficient for a vertical row of tubes and $h_{m, 1}$ is the mean heat transfer coefficient for a single tube. This assumes that the liquid film remains laminar and that the film falls from one tube to the next in an orderly manner as a continuous sheet which is uniform along the tube length. This is at variance with the practical situation in which the condensate falls as droplets producing splashing and turbulence within the liquid film, and the equation must be regarded as conservative.

The flow situation in tube banks is extremely complex. At entry to a tube bundle the vapour velocity is likely to be high and the resulting shear forces will cause the heat transfer coefficient to be much greater than the Nusselt prediction (possibly up to 20 times greater).

As the outlet of the condenser is reached, vapour velocities are likely to be low and the Nusselt equation (12.21) is likely to hold.

Effect of superheated vapour

When the vapour is superheated and the temperature of the cold surface is above the saturation temperature, no condensation occurs, the vapour is cooled and becomes less superheated. Heat transfer follows the same pattern as single-phase gas heat transfer.

When superheated steam is introduced into a situation where it has easy access to a large amount of condensate, desuperheating is likely to be rapid and the effect of the superheat will quickly disappear. In a confined-flow situation – as in plug flow down a pipe – there will be an entrance region in which desuperheating takes place and the heat transfer coefficient will be very small followed by a second region in which heat is transferred by the normal process of condensation.

Non-condensable gases

The presence of non-condensable gases is common in industrial equipment in which steam is condensed.

Condensation of steam mixed with air will occur only if the steam's partial pressure exceeds the vapour pressure at the temperature of the cold surface. If film-type condensation occurs then the surface temperature of the film assumes a saturation value corresponding to the local partial pressure of the steam. A 'blanket' of air collects at the vapour–liquid interface and the process of condensation may be controlled by diffusion of

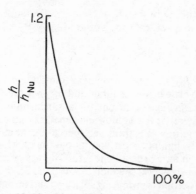

Figure 12.10   Plot of h/h_{Nu} versus composition of steam–air mixture. (Adapted with permission from ref. 9. Copyright 1964 American Chemical Society)

the steam through the air 'blanket'. The net result is a lower temperature difference across the condensate film, causing a lower heat flux and a reduced rate of condensation.

A small proportion of air causes a significant reduction in the heat transfer coefficients, as indicated in *Figure 12.10*. This diagram shows a typical plot of the ratio of heat transfer coefficient for the steam–air mixture to the heat transfer coefficient predicted by the Nusselt equation for condensation on a vertical surface, plotted against the percentage by volume of air in the steam–air mixture.

In addition to causing the build-up of a blanket of air at the condensing surface, which causes a reduction in heat transfer, owing to increased thermal resistance, the presence of air lowers the

partial pressure and hence the temperature of the steam (*see Table 12.6*). This reduction in steam temperature reduces the temperature difference between the condensing steam and the cooled surface, leading to a reduction in the driving force for heat transfer.

The effect on the temperature of the steam–air mixture can be calculated for any particular case by using partial pressures. If, for example, we take a steam–air mixture at 4 bar absolute pressure which contains 20% by volume of air, then the partial pressure of steam $= 0.8 \times 4$, or 3.2 bar abs, and the temperature corresponding to this pressure, taken from steam tables, would be 135.8°C, instead of 143.6°C which it would be if there was no air mixed with the steam. *Table 12.6* shows the effect of air on steam temperature.

List of symbols

a	Constant exponent on the Reynolds number
A	Surface area (m²)
b	Constant exponent on the Prandtl number
B	A constant
C_p	Specific heat capacity at constant pressure (J/kg K)
D	Tube diameter (m)
D_e	Hydraulic mean diameter (m)
f	Fanning friction factor
g	Acceleration due to gravity (9.81 m/s²)
G	Mass flow rate per unit area (kg/m² s)
G_E	Equivalent mass flow rate per unit area (kg/m² s)

Table 12.6   Effect of air on the temperature of a steam–air mixture

Steam pressure (bar abs.)	Temperature (°C) of a steam–air mixture						
	0% air*	5% air	10% air	20% air	30% air	40% air	50% air
0.2	60	59	58	55	53	50	46
0.4	76	75	73	71	68	64	60
0.6	86	85	83	80	77	73	69
0.8	94	92	90	88	84	80	76
1.0	100	98	96	94	90	86	81
2.0	120	118	117	113	109	105	100
4.0	144	142	140	136	131	126	120
6.0	159	157	155	150	145	140	134
8.0	170	168	166	162	156	150	144
10.0	180	178	175	170	165	159	152
15.0	198	196	193	188	182	175	168
20.0	212	210	207	201	195	188	180

* Percentages are by volume.
A comprehensive review of the subject is available in National Engineering Laboratory Reports Nos. 114, 219 and 281.

G_L Mass flow rate of liquid per unit area $(kg/m^2 s)$

G_v Mass flow rate of vapour per unit area $(kg/m^2 s)$

Gr Grashof number ($\beta \triangle T g \rho^2 L^3/\mu^2$)

Gz Graetz number ($\frac{1}{4}\pi.(D/L).Re.Pr$)

h Heat transfer coefficient (film) $(W/m^2 K)$

h_m Mean heat transfer coefficient (film) $(W/m^2 K)$

$h_{m,1}$ Mean heat transfer coefficient unit for a single horizontal tube (film) $(W/m^2 K)$

h_{m, N_T} Mean heat transfer coefficient for a vertical row of N_T tubes (film) $(W/m^2 K)$

h_{Nu} Heat transfer coefficient (film) derived from the Nusselt equation

h_x Heat transfer coefficient at point x (film) $(W/m^2 K)$

H Overall heat transfer coefficient $(W/m^2 K)$

k Thermal conductivity (W/mK)

L Thickness of a plane wall; length of pipe run, characteristic dimension, height of condensing surface (m)

Nu Nusselt number (hL/k or hD/k)

Nu_m Nusselt number based on h_m ($h_m L/k$, where L is a characteristic length)

$Nu_{m,L}$ Nusselt number based on h_m and L ($h_m L/k$, where L is height)

$Nu_{m,D}$ Nusselt number based on h_m and D ($h_m D/K$)

n Constant exponent in equations (12.9) and (12.19)

N_T Number of tubes in a vertical row

Pr Prandtl number ($C_p\mu/k$)

Pr_L Prandtl number (liquid)

q Rate of flow of heat (W)

q/A Heat flux (W/m^2)

r Radius (m)

Re Reynolds number [($VD\rho/\mu$) for pipe flow; ($4\Gamma/\mu$) for condensate flow]

t_w Water temperature (K)

T Temperature (K)

$\triangle T$ Temperature difference (K)

T_g Gas temperature (K)

T_s Temperature of saturated steam (K)

T_w Temperature of wall (K)

V Velocity (m/s)

x Distance (m)

$\triangle x$ Distance (m)

β Coefficient of cubical expansion (K^{-1})

Γ Condensate flow per unit perimeter of a vertical tube (kg/m s)

Γ_x Condensate flow per unit perimeter of a vertical tube or surface a distance x below the top of the surface (kg/m s)

Γ' Condensate flow per unit length of a horizontal tube (kg/m s)

λ Latent heat (J/kg K)

μ Viscosity evaluated at bulk temperature $(kg/m s = N s/m^2)$

μ_w Viscosity evaluated at wall temperature $(kg/m s = N s/m^2)$

ρ Density (kg/m^3)

ρ_L Liquid density (kg/m^3)

ρ_v Vapour density (kg/m^3)

σ Stefan–Boltzmann constant

τ_w Shear stress at pipe wall (N/m^2)

ϵ Surface emissivity

References and further reading

1 Butterworth, D. and Hewitt, G. F. *Two-phase Flow and Heat Transfer*. London: Oxford University Press (1977)

2 Collier, J. G. *Convective Boiling and Heat Transfer*. London: McGraw-Hill (1972)

3 Perry, J. H., Perry, R. H., Chilton, C. H. and Kirkpatrick, S. D. *Chemical Engineer's Handbook*, 4th edn. New York: McGraw-Hill (1963)

4 McAdams, W. H. *Heat Transmission*, 3rd edn. New York: McGraw-Hill (1954)

5 Kern, D.Q. *Process Heat Transfer*. New York: McGraw-Hill (1950)

6 Rohsenow, W. M. and Hartnett, J. P. *Handbook of Heat Transfer*. New York: McGraw-Hill (1973)

7 Dryden, I. G. C. (Editor) *The Efficient Use of Energy*. Guildford: IPC Science and Technology Press (1975)

8 Coulson, J. M. and Richardson, J. F. *Chemical Engineering*, 3rd edn. (SI units), Vol. 1. Eds J. R. Backhurst and J. H. Harker. Oxford: Pergamon Press (1977)

9 Stewart, P. B. *et al*. 'Condensing heat transfer in steam–air mixtures in turbulent flow'. *Industrial and Engineering Chemistry — Process Design and Development*, Vol. 3, No. 1, p. 48 (1964)

13

Steam heating by direct contact

13.1 Direct-contact steam heating

Basic principles of steam injection

Almost complete utilization of sensible and latent heat can be achieved by direct-contact injection of steam into liquids or solids. Steam can be finely dispersed as small vapour bubbles into most liquids. The condensate formed will dissolve into the heated material if miscible whilst incondensable gases present in the steam may need to be separated and vented. The temperature of the material can be raised ultimately to the steam saturation temperature or possibly higher if the steam is superheated.

Direct steam heating may be required in order to cook, sterilize, cure, bleach, hydrolyse or dissolve materials according to the chemical reactions which arise at the temperatures achieved. Most chemical reactions are exothermic so that steam may be required only in order to reach some desired initiation temperature. The quantity of steam used is determined by the maximum temperature, mass and heat capacity of the batch together with the rates of heat loss and any steam losses present. Where chemical reactions must be completed, the required residence or holding time at the desired temperature together with the heat of reactions taking place will significantly affect the quantity of steam required.

Direct-contact steam heating is an efficient and cheap method requiring little factory space and relatively simple equipment owing to the rapid dispersal of steam into liquids which is possible by means of jets and diffuser nozzles, together with the high heat transfer coefficients associated with condensing steam. The excessive noise often associated with injection and condensation of steam bubbles in cold liquids can be avoided by correct choice and design of the injector. Venturi-nozzle-type steam injectors achieve good, thorough circulation of liquor together with intimate dispersal of steam. The rate of steam condensation will be controlled by the surface area of steam bubbles, the temperature of liquor surrounding the steam bubbles and its associated thermal resistance. An intimate dispersion of fine bubbles with efficient recirculation and mixing of the liquid phase will therefore ensure rapid heating with minimum loss of uncondensed steam.

A variety of efficient and silent steam injectors are commercially available to cover a wide range of heating duties, high turndown ratios being possible if required. The use of steam jet heaters as liquid pumps and mixers is dicusssed on p 309.

Operational control and economic aspects of direct steam heating

Direct-contact steam heating may be used only when wetting and dilution of the process material with relatively small amounts of condensate are permissible. The steam used for heating may rarely be superheated but is usually at or near saturation and at relatively low pressure (approaching 2 bar) as required for satisfactory control of injection dispersion and mixing in the process stream. Exhaust steam from non-condensing power-generating turbines is suitable for many process heating duties and contains more than 70% of the heat initially supplied for steam generation and superheating. Such low-pressure steam may be available at very low cost relative to steam generated specifically for process heating; however, the quantities of boiler feedwater required are greatly increased (*see* Chapter 11).

A well-designed direct-contact steam heating system will ensure that virtually all the injected steam is condensed for heating purposes; however, as the process material approaches the steam saturation temperature, at the system pressure, the temperature difference for condensation and liquor heating will approach zero and an increasing escape of uncondensed steam will occur. These losses can be minimized by reducing the steam flow as the saturation temperature is approached, and by imposing good mixing and bulk circulation on the process material, so that maximum temperature differences are ensured.

If the steam injection rate is reduced too much, the mixing and condensation may become very noisy owing to the formation and collapse of isolated bubbles. Many injectors are provided with suction holes where atmospheric or compressed air can be bled into the steam jet, greatly increasing the liquid circulation rate, preventing the complete collapse of bubbles and thus achieving silent operation.

Countercurrent flow of the injected steam with the process steam being heated will also help to reduce the steam losses and increase condensation efficiency. This flow pattern can be achieved in steam stripping towers and, though less conveniently, in tanks or pipelines, where co-current flow is to be expected. In this case the injected steam bubbles are initially present with a maximum temperature difference which falls rapidly to

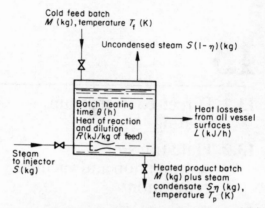

Figure 13.1 Heat balance quantities for batch heating by direct steam injection

a final equilibrium value as determined by the steam saturation temperature and the maximum temperature reached by the liquid according to the heat balance for the batch heating tank shown in *Figure 13.1*.

For the system shown, if the feed steam enthalpy is H kJ/kg, the steam condensate enthalpy is h kJ/kg and the average heat capacity of the batch is c kJ/kg K, then the appropriate heat balance equation is

$$\eta S H + McT_f + MR = \\ \eta S h + S(1-\eta)H + McT_p + L \qquad (13.1)$$

where η is the fractional steam condensation efficiency and R is the heat of reaction plus dilution in kJ/kg K, assumed to be positive and exothermic. From equation (13.1), the amount of steam required is given by the expression

$$S = \frac{Mc(T_p - T_f) + L - MR}{(\eta - 1)H + \eta \ (H-h)} \qquad (13.2)$$

Available systems and equipment for direct steam heating

Although simple steam sparging pipes with multiple injection holes along their length can be used, they are not so silent or thermally efficient as the nozzle and venturi type shown in *Figure 13.2*. This type also acts as an efficient internal liquid circulation pump by drawing in relatively cold liquid from behind the nozzle and ejecting a fine dispersion of condensing steam bubbles from the venturi outlet.

The nozzle and venturi type may be installed internally, externally, or in the walls of batch heating tanks as shown in *Figure 13.2*. Careful positioning of the venturi nozzle heater will help in achieving good mixing and uniform temperatures throughout the vessel. These devices have been developed

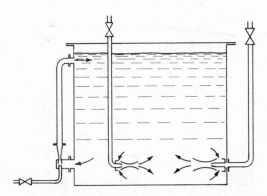

Figure 13.2 Alternative arrangements for installing venturi nozzle steam injectors to tanks and vessels

empirically by specialist manufacturers who can offer a wide range of designs and sizes to cover all the normal heating situations.

Similar designs of venturi-nozzle-type steam heaters are available for pipeline installation in continuous-flow processes, or in external recirculation lines to process vessels.

Where internal fluid recirculation is not required, as for example in a countercurrent flow contactor, then a simple steam injection pipe with single or multiple orifice jets may be employed. Care must be taken to ensure that there is an approach to plug flow (no back-mixing) in both streams by provision of baffles, trays or packings, or by having a large ratio of contactor length to diameter. Countercurrent heating of solids with steam can readily be achieved in screw conveyors and transfer pipes as well as in baffled towers.

Specification and design methods

A simple heat and mass balance on the process system to be heated will reveal the quantity or flow rate of steam required for a given batch or continuous heating duty. If enthalpy functions for the liquid or solid materials being heated are not available, their average specific heats and temperatures should be used together with the heats of dilution or reaction arising from the steam condensation and residence time. For the case of batch heating the maximum or minimum time allowable must be specified in order to calculate the required steam flow rate. An allowance for inefficiency due to steam losses arising from poor mixing and heat transfer can be made, although this should not need to be more than a few per cent for well designed and operated systems.

For purposes of the heat balance, the feed steam enthalpy should be taken at the temperature and pressure in the service main and the exit steam or condensate enthalpy at the steam pressure and corresponding saturation temperature. An equip-

ment supplier would require knowledge of the steam heating rate derived from the mass and heat balances, of the flow characteristics of the process material (viscosity, density, etc.), and of the vessel in which the heating will take place, such as whether the process is batch or continuous, its size, shape, internal fittings, feed and exit branches, etc. The initial and final temperatures required and the pressures or pressure drops to be overcome by the heated stream must also be specified.

13.2 Fluid transfer compression and vacuum generation

Basic principles of steam jet vacuum pumps and compressors

One of the most important uses of live steam is for the transfer of fluids against a pressure difference to achieve a pumping action. This is done by expanding steam through a convergent–divergent nozzle to generate a supersonic jet having a very low static pressure which is then recovered by deceleration in the diverging section of a venturi tube. This device, shown diagrammatically in *Figure 13.3*, is known as a *steam-driven ejector* and has the ability to entrain large volumes of gas or vapour into the venturi throat and compress them to a much higher exit discharge pressure. Momentum transfer occurs between the suction gas and the high-velocity steam jet in the mixing section and is followed by static pressure recovery in the divergent diffuser section, thus achieving an overall compression of suction gas. Thermodynamic

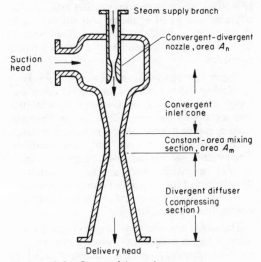

Figure 13.3 Steam-driven ejector pump

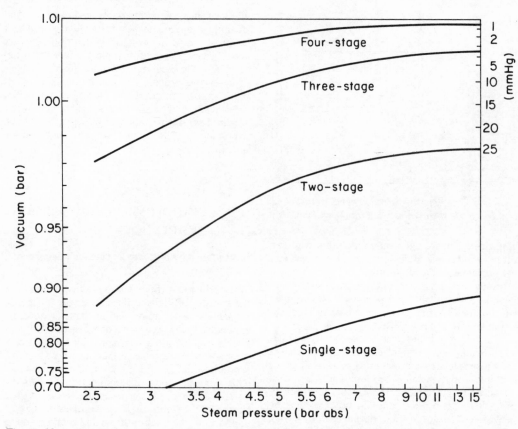

Figure 13.4 Recommended optimal number of ejector stages for varying vacuum and steam pressures

efficiency of an ejector is the ratio of work required for ideal adiabatic compression to the heat energy of the driving steam used by the ejector, and although the device has a relatively low thermodynamic compression efficiency (20–30%), quite large compression ratios can be obtained (up to 10 or more) without the use of moving parts, whilst volumetric flow rates of suction gas can be very high especially at vacuum pressures.

There are many advantages to be gained by employing ejector pumps, and these often out-weigh the relatively high energy consumption compared with mechanical pumps; for example: simple, compact construction, minimum mainten-ance, corrosion resistance and high reliability. Their rather low capital cost favours rapid inter-mittent operations such as the evacuation of vessels, whilst their ability to pump large volumes of low-pressure gases makes them suitable for continuous vacuum pumping.

The steam and compressed gases require separ-ation in an after-condenser, which can often be of the direct-contact type if contamination of cooling water is permissible. Otherwise indirect-contact surface condensers must be used.

A single ejector pump can achieve quite large compression ratios (up to 10); however, the optimum is about 6. It is often necessary to couple several pumps in series to achieve low suction pressures, for example two stages to obtain a press-ure of 0.04 bar and three stages to obtain 0.013 bar*. Interstage steam condensers are used to remove the steam and thus reduce the pumping load on the next ejector with important resulting savings of steam. The minimum pressures which can be achieved with interstage condensation are limited by the vapour pressure and temperature of the condenser cooling water, e.g. 0.056 bar is the minimum at 35°C and 0.043 bar at cooling-water outlet temperatures of 30°C. Any suction pressures below 0.13 bar are more economically achieved using two or more stages with inter-condensers. *Figure 13.4* shows the approximate optimum number of stages required to achieve a given vacuum pressure using an available steam supply pressure. At suction pressures up to 0.006 bar the saturated water vapour temperature lies

---

* All pressures are absolute except where otherwise stated.

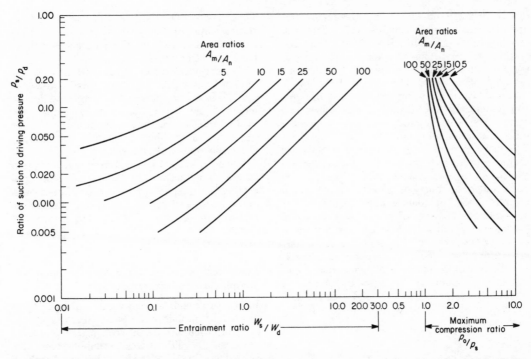

Figure 13.5   Ejector pump performance chart recommended by DeFrate and Hoerl. Note: for dissimilar molecular weights and temperatures, and for empirical corrections of entrainment and compression, see text. (From L. A. DeFrate and A. E. Hoerl, Chem. Eng. Prog. Symp. Series **55**, *21, p 43 (1959))*

below 0°C and ice can form in the suction head and mixing section of the venturi, which should therefore be provided with a steam-heated jacket.

By making certain simplifying assumptions concerning the expansion, mixing and compression processes, it is possible to formulate thermodynamic expressions for calculating the performance of steam jet ejectors. The computed results for various ratios of mixing section to expansion nozzle areas (A_m/A_n) are expressed as plots of expansion ratio (suction gas to driving gas pressure, p_s/p_d) against both the entrainment ratio (suction gas to driving gas flow rates, W_s/W_d) and the compression ratio (exit gas to suction gas pressure ratio, p_o/p_s) as shown in *Figure 13.5*. These curves are claimed to predict the true performance within a maximum 15% error and can be corrected for the effects of varying molecular weight and gas temperature. Although their accuracy is somewhat limited for design purposes, they are useful for preliminary evaluation of geometrical design and operating conditions when approaching an equipment supplier. Theory also predicts the mass flow rate W_s of gas moved by a given ejector to be dependent on ratios of the molecular weights and temperatures (K) of the driving and driven gases according to the expression

$$\left(\frac{W_s}{W_d}\right)_{\text{corrected}} = \left(\frac{W_s}{W_d}\right)_{\text{uncorrected}}$$
$$\times \left(\frac{M_s}{M_d} \times \frac{T_d}{T_s}\right)^{1/2} \qquad (13.3)$$

The mass rate of pumping is therefore increased by increases in the molecular weight M_s of the suction gas and increases in the driving-gas temperature T_d.

It is important when selecting and operating a steam ejector system to appreciate clearly its operating characteristics. Increasing the steam pressure to the jet nozzle increases the compression ratio but reduces the entrainment ratio. This usually results in a higher vacuum being produced with a small increase in suction gas flow rate. The steam ejector or thermocompressor should be regarded essentially as a pump of constant volumetric capacity whereby the suction gas mass flow rate at constant driving steam pressure increases in direct proportion to the suction gas pressure. If, however, the delivery pressure is increased whilst the suction pressure and driving steam pressure are held constant, then the suction gas flow rate remains constant up to a maximum delivery pressure. Beyond this it falls rapidly to zero, when the ejector becomes unstable. This maximum compression ratio p_o/p_s increases with decreasing expansion ratio p_s/p_d but this results in a decreased entrainment ratio. Thus an optimum set of operating conditions exists for each ejector where the thermodynamic compression efficiency rarely exceeds 25%. This is significantly less than for equivalent-duty mechanical compressors and pumps; however, thermodynamic efficiency is not the sole criterion for pump selection.

Expansion ratios p_s/p_d approaching 0.05 are required to achieve compression ratios above 3 and the steam ejector pump is therefore a device more suited for pumping gases from a vacuum chamber than for compression of gases above atmospheric pressure. For compression above barometric pressure both high driving steam pressures and flow rates are required to achieve only moderate compression ratios approaching say 3. For these reasons, most of the commercial applications of steam ejector pumps have been concerned with producing and maintaining vacuum in process vessels for a wide variety of purposes.

Applications of steam jet ejectors

The main application is to establish and maintain vacuum in order to achieve evaporation of liquids, usually water, for purposes of concentration and drying. Vaporization of liquids under reduced pressure lowers the boiling point and thus increases the available temperature differences for heating. Vacuum evaporation (*see* Chapter 15) also enables the economical use of low-pressure steam for heating and the employment of multiple-effect evaporators, even where the solutions have significant boiling-point elevations. Vacuum drying of solids allows the moisture to be reduced to lower bound-moisture contents approaching complete dryness.

If external heat is not supplied to the evaporator, then vacuum evaporation results in refrigeration and air-conditioning is widely practised employing single or multistage vacuum evaporators in conjunction with steam vapour condensers and vacuum ejectors. An application utilizing both vacuum evaporation and refrigeration is the concentration and crystallization of solids from solutions where very favourable conditions arise under vacuum, with both low temperature and maximum concentration at liquid-vapour interface.

In some applications, steam jet ejectors are used to compress steam or other vapours rather than moist air, as for example in booster ejectors compressing water vapour, from low pressures (<0.04 bar) to pressures capable of condensation at normal cooling-water temperatures (>0.11 bar).

This is also practised in thermocompressors compressing waste or flash steam at around 1 bar to pressures suitable for condensation heat transfer above 3 bar.

Steam-driven vacuum ejector systems are also used for degassing and deodorizing liquids and solids. Additional steam may be injected directly into the liquid, to assist the desorption and stripping of dissolved or absorbed gases from the solution phase, by raising the temperature and reducing the partial pressure of the gases.

Steam jet vacuum systems can be used to transfer liquids as in vacuum filtration, pump priming or establishing a liquid siphon. De-aeration of water and degassing of molten steel are especially important applications of the steam jet vacuum system.

Equipment and systems available for vacuum pumping and vapour compression

In order to obtain a given vacuum pressure there exists an optimum number of ejector stages to achieve minimum overall cost. *Figure 13.4* is an approximate guide to the optimal system. This should be compared with equipment suppliers' data. Intermediate condensers are usually installed between the later stages in order to remove ejector steam which would otherwise need to be compressed along with the gases being evacuated. The available cooling-water temperature decides the optimum interstage pressures in a multi-stage design having indirect-contact surface condensers. The acceptable range of cooling-water feed temperatures is 10–24°C whilst outlet temperatures may be up to 40°C on intercondensers and 60°C on after-condensers.

In general, greater steam pressures will enable higher vacuum to be economically achieved employing fewer stages, but the benefits which arise become small at pressures above 21 bar. The lowest operable driving steam pressures are about 2 bar although successful operation of booster ejectors at very low suction pressures has been claimed using 1.1 bar steam. The most desirable steam pressure range for ejectors is 8–15 bar, whilst minimum suction pressures of 6.6×10^{-5} bar can be achieved using a four-stage ejector system.

In order to evacuate a process system during plant start-up, it may be necessary to provide multiple parallel ejectors in order to handle the large initial pumping load rapidly and efficiently. An alternative for large incondensable duties is the use of a multi-nozzle ejector known as an *augmentor*. Rapid-evacuation charts of the type shown in *Figure 13.6* can be used to calculate the time required for a given ejector system to establish

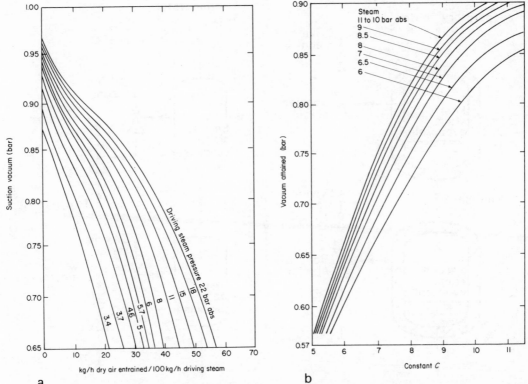

Figure 13.6 (a) A typical dry-air performance curve for a single-stage ejector under varying operating steam pressures. (b) Typical rapid-evacuation curve for a single-stage ejector; time in minutes = V × C × 15.7/S, where V is the volume to be evacuated in m³, S is the steam consumption of the ejector in kg/h and C is a constant. Both graphs relate to a Hick-Hargreaves type 10 ejector. (Courtesy of Hick Hargreaves, Bolton)

a particular vacuum pressure in a known volume of plant.

Figure 13.7 and *Figure 13.8* illustrate the use of steam ejectors as thermocompressors to achieve both evaporation and recovery of low-pressure steam for recycling or other process heating purposes. A high-pressure steam supply is necessary to achieve sufficient vapour recompression for steam recovery at pressures which

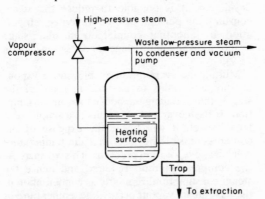

Figure 13.7 Use of a thermocompressor and high-pressure steam to reduce the steam consumption of a vapour recompression evaporator. Condenser and vacuum pump required

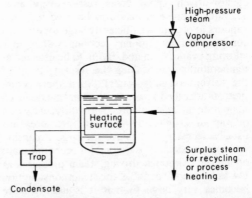

Figure 13.8 Use of a thermocompressor with high-pressure steam to recover and recycle low-pressure steam from a vapour recompression evaporator. Condenser and vacuum pump not required

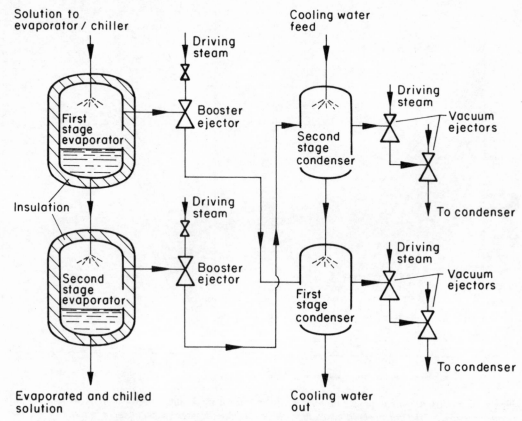

Figure 13.9   Multi-stage evaporation and condensation system for chilling and evaporation

allow an adequate-temperature driving force for subsequent condensation and heating. A surplus of low-pressure steam (which must be subsequently condensed or compressed, to avoid releasing to the atmosphere) will always be produced by an ejector-driven vapour recompression evaporator. Thermocompressors may also be used to pump vapours to pressures sufficiently large for efficient condensation by ordinary cooling water, thus allowing evaporation and drying to be effected at temperatures approaching the freezing point of the solvent (usually water). Such thermocompressors are called *booster ejectors* and are designed to operate on large volumes of low-pressure steam or vapour. High driving steam pressures are usually necessary to achieve the large expansion and compression ratios needed for economic plant operation. Although driving steam pressures as low as 1.1 bar are possible, the steam consumption becomes very large so that it is usually more economical to use driving steam at around 8 bar for thermocompression applications. Driven-steam flow rates of up to several thousand kg/h are readily achieved with relatively compact and simple thermocompressors. It should be noted

that secondary ejectors for air removal will require steam at a pressure greater than 3.2 bar to operate satisfactorily with an adequately large expansion ratio.

Since the steam usage of a vapour booster ejector is proportional to the compression ratio developed, it is possible to reduce the steam consumption per unit of evaporation or refrigeration by adopting countercurrent multi-stage evaporation and multi-stage condensation (*Figure 13.9*).

Multi-stage evaporation enables lower vapour compression ratios to be used in some of the stages, thus reducing the booster steam consumption. If flash evaporation occurs in a simple insulated vessel, it will be at the expense of the contents' sensible heat, so that the temperature will fall as evaporation proceeds. This will increase the compression ratio required and hence the steam consumption. Similarly as condensation of the flash steam vapour occurs, the temperature of the cooling water will rise, thus also increasing the compression ratio and steam consumption. High cooling-water rates, low cooling-water feed temperatures and multi-stage condensation will all reduce the condensation temperatures and vapour pressures, and consequently the unit steam consumption.

Thus to minimize the overall cost of steam jet refrigeration, it is necessary to choose the optimum number of evaporation and condensation stages, and cooling-water rate, for a given capital equipment, steam and cooling-water cost structure, cooling-water temperature, and driving steam pressure.

Operational, control and economic aspects

Steam-driven ejectors for vacuum production and vapour compression are thermodynamically less efficient than mechanical compressors; however, they have no moving parts and can have relatively low capital cost even when made from corrosion-resistant materials. There are many applications where their choice can be justified on sound economic grounds but care is needed to optimize the system design and the operational control of the ejector, in order to achieve maximum efficiency with a minimum steam consumption. Where large quantities of surplus waste steam are available, the use of ejectors is almost always justified.

After an ejector system has been designed and installed, it is possible to achieve maximum efficiency only by varying the steam supply pressure to the jet, or less readily by changing the jet nozzle size. The operation may become less efficient when higher delivery or suction pressures than intended by the design are present.

Automatic control of steam jet pressure can be provided to maintain minimum steam consumption with constant delivery pressure under moderate fluctuations in suction pressure; the thermodynamic efficiency may however be reduced.

In steam ejector systems with inter- and after-condensers, the cost of cooling water may be quite significant and should be included in the economic analysis. An optimization of the design may be necessary to ensure that the consumption of cooling water is optimal, relative to the condenser outlet temperature, ejector compression ratio and desired rate of driving steam.

The refrigeration chilling capacity of a steam ejector vacuum evaporator is not easily controlled by varying the steam pressure to a single booster ejector, since its volumetric capacity is constant above a minimum steam jet pressure below which it fails to pump. Capacity control in this case is best achieved by installing multiple parallel ejectors, which can be shut down progressively to obtain the desired pumping capacity. Some degree of automatic control can be achieved by regulating the steam and cooling-water rates in order to obtain the desired chilled water temperature at a given throughput. This may not be possible if the

cooling-water temperature increases too much because of an ejector design which is basically unsuitable.

Steam jet refrigeration units are most efficient and economical when large volumes of cold cooling water are cheaply available whilst substantial steam economies may also be achieved by adopting multi-stage chilling evaporators and condensers to meet a given duty. As stated earlier, a steam jet ejector operates best and most efficiently at its design capacity under steady conditions. If the suction pressure tends to vary, it is possible to control it by adjusting the steam pressure to the ejector but this technique frequently leads to instability and thermal inefficiency. Steady control is frequently achieved in practice by running the ejector at its design capacity and automatically admitting air on the suction side to keep the desired suction pressure constant.

Capacity of a vacuum ejector system

A necessary step in the design of any vacuum system, whatever its application, is to estimate the amount of air leaking into it. A simple and practical method is based on an estimation or measurement of the rate of pressure rise J when a system is evacuated and isolated. There should be an acceptable value of J which depends on the size of plant and the desired operating pressure. The actual value of J depends on the size of plant and type of construction, as evident in *Table 13.1* for three categories of construction: A (common practice), B (better practice) and C (best practice for minimum air leakage).

It can readily be shown that the required volumetric capacity C_j of the vacuum pump at suction inlet conditions in m³/min is

$$C_j = 1.32 \frac{VJ}{p} \tag{13.4}$$

where V is the volume of the vacuum system (m³) and p is the vacuum pressure (mbar). The time in minutes required to establish a given vacuum pressure p in a system of volume V with pump capacity C and leakage rate J is given by the

Table 13.1 Value of J for three categories (A, B, C) of construction (*see text*)

Operating pressure (bar)	Pressure rise rate J (mbar/min)		
	A	B	C
<0.013	0.6	0.3	0.07
0.013–0.04	1.3	0.7	0.07
0.04–0.13	2.6	0.7	0.07

following equation, where J is in mbar/min and p is in mbar:

$$t = 2.3 \frac{V}{C} \log \left(\frac{1000 \frac{C}{V} - J}{\frac{pC}{V} - J} \right)$$

It is also possible to estimate roughly the air leakage rate from a knowledge of the total perimeter length of large-bore flange connections using a figure of 200–400 g/h of air leak rate per metre of seal length. This figure may be reduced to 50–100 g/h if specially designed flange connections with special gaskets and accurately finished sealing surfaces are used.

For plants with typical numbers of flange connections, inspection glasses, cocks, valves, stuffing boxes, etc., the air leakage rates to be expected according to the volume of plant under vacuum and the quality of the vacuum seal connections are given in *Table 13.2*.

The main additional source of incondensable gases is dissolved air or other gases (usually CO_2) entering the vacuum system in a continuous liquid or vapour stream. Cooling water normally contains 10–20 g/m^3 of air dissolved. To allow for these further sources of incondensable gas the following empirical equations are recommended.

Table 13.2 Typical leakage rates for vacuum plant

Volume under vacuum (m^3)	Air leakage rate (kg/h)
0.2	0.2–0.5
1	0.5–1
3	1–2
5	2–4
10	3–6
25	4–8
50	6–12
100	9–18
200	12–25
500	30–60

Surface condensers

$$\text{Air (kg/h)} = \frac{\text{steam to condenser}}{2000} \text{(kg/h)} + 1.36$$

Jet condenser

$$\text{Air (kg/h)} = \frac{\text{steam to condenser}}{2000} \text{(kg/h)} + 1.36$$
$$+ \frac{\text{cooling water (m}^3\text{/min)} \times 100}{[1.8 \times \text{inlet temp. (K)}] - 460}$$

Deodorizing plants

$$\text{Air (kg/h)} = 4.5 + \frac{\text{stripping steam}}{100} \text{(kg/h)} \times 1.2$$
$$+ \frac{\text{cooling water (m}^3\text{/min)} \times 100}{[1.8 \times \text{inlet temp. (K)}] - 460}$$

Vacuum refrigeration plants

$$\text{Air (kg/h)} = 4.5 + \frac{\begin{array}{c}\text{mixture air + water vapour}\\\text{from booster ejector (kg/h)}\end{array}}{1000}$$
$$+ \frac{\text{cooling water (m}^3\text{/min)} \times 100}{[1.8 \times \text{inlet temp. (K)}] - 460}$$

The total quantity of air entering the system, as calculated above, will need to be increased by an estimate of the associated water vapour content. In most cases it is assumed to be saturated at the temperature present and the appropriate humidity may be obtained from psychrometric charts for air–water vapour mixtures.

The total air–water vapour mass flow rate is divided by the entrainment ratio to obtain the required driving-steam flow rate and hence also the ejector capacity.

Examples of specification and design of steam ejector systems

Single-stage vacuum ejector (vacuum pressure 0.203 bar)

Ejector sizes range in capacity from 40 to 5230 kg/h steam consumption. According to the chart for Hick-Hargreaves type 10 ejectors (*see Figure 13.6*), for a suction pressure of 0.203 bar delivering to atmosphere and using a driving steam pressure of 7.9 bar the air to steam ratio will be 26 kg/h per 100 kg/h steam, giving an entrainment ratio of 0.26.

$$\text{Compression ratio} = \frac{1.013}{0.203} = 5.0$$

$$\text{Steam expansion ratio} = \frac{0.203}{7.9} = 0.0256$$

$$T_s = 15°C \quad \text{and} \quad T_d = 170°C$$

Entrainment ratio = 0.26 on the DeFrate and Hoerl chart (*see Figure 13.5*) assuming

$$\left[\frac{W_s}{W_d} \right]_{\text{corrected}} = 0.26 = \left[\frac{W_s}{W_d} \right]_{\text{uncorrected}}$$

$$\times \left(\frac{29}{18} \times \frac{443}{288} \right)^{1/2}$$

then

$$\left[\frac{W_s}{W_d}\right]_{\text{uncorrected}} = 0.26 \times \left(\frac{18 \times 288}{29 \times 443}\right)^{1/2}$$

$$= 0.165$$

Using the steam expansion ratio of 0.0256 we get (from *Figure 13.5*) an ejector with a mixing throat to nozzle area ratio of

$$\frac{A_m}{A_n} = 14.0$$

The maximum compression ratio predicted by the DeFrate and Hoerl chart is seen to be 5.0, which is in agreement with the actual performance chart.

Two-stage vacuum ejector (capacity range 45–875 kg/h steam without intercondenser)

For a pressure of say 0.138 bar using 7.9 bar steam (T_{sat} 170°C), the air to steam ratio from the performance chart (type 20) is 13 kg/h air per 100 kg/h steam.

$$\text{Compression ratio} = \frac{1.013}{0.138} = 7.35$$

for two stages, and

$$(7.5)^{1/2} = 2.71$$

for each identical stage. As before, the correction factor for molecular weight and temperature is 0.63.

$$\left[\frac{W_s}{W_d}\right]_{\text{uncorrected}} = 0.63 \times \left[\frac{W_s}{W_d}\right]_{\text{corrected}}$$

For the first-stage ejector, the suction pressure is 0.135 bar.

$$\text{Steam expansion ratio} = \frac{0.135}{7.9} = 0.0171$$

Compression ratio required = 2.71

This requires

$$\frac{A_m}{A_n} = 50$$

and gives an uncorrected entrainment ratio of 0.6, for which the corrected entrainment ratio is $0.6/0.63 = 0.95$. For the second-stage ejector, the suction pressure is $0.138 \times 2.74 = 0.378$ bar.

$$\text{Steam expansion ratio} = \frac{0.378}{7.9} = 0.0478$$

Compression ratio required = 2.71

This requires

$$\frac{A_m}{A_n} \simeq 15$$

and gives an uncorrected entrainment ratio of 0.45.

Since the mean molecular weight of the air–water vapour mixture from the first-stage ejector is 24, the correction factor is now

$$\left(\frac{18}{24} \times \frac{443}{443}\right)^{1/2} = 0.87$$

and the corrected entrainment ratio is $0.45/0.87 = 0.52$. The total steam consumption for 100 kg/h air moved is

$$\frac{100}{0.95} + \left(\frac{100}{0.95} + 100\right)\frac{1}{0.52}$$

$$= 105 + 395 = 500 \text{ kg/h steam}$$

hence 20 kg/h of air requires 100 kg/h steam, which is rather optimistic in comparison with the actual performance claimed by the manufacturers.

Design calculations for a single-stage vacuum refrigeration plant

The system under discussion is shown in *Figure 13.10*. Assume that refrigeration equivalent to a water evaporation rate of 1000 kg/h is required. The latent heat of water vapour in the temperature range 21–25°C is 2490 kJ/kg, so the refrigeration load is then 2.49×10^6 kJ/h. If it is assumed that a water stream is being chilled from 25°C to 4°C then the feed stream flow rate is:

$$\frac{2.49 \times 10^6}{4.19 \times (25 - 4) \times 1.0} + 1000 = 39300 \text{ kg/h}$$

The contents of the vacuum chilling evaporator are taken to be well mixed at 4°C. The vapour pressure of water at 4°C is 0.0080 bar. Exploratory calculations suggested that the evaporated water vapour plus incondensable gas should be compressed to a pressure of 0.107 bar to enable satisfactory condensation by direct contact with cooling water at 21°C. The vapour pressure of cooling water at 21°C is 0.025 bar, which the partial pressure of water vapour in the steam and air mixture from the booster ejector must exceed for condensation to occur.

The flow of cooling water is adjusted so that it leaves the condenser at 40°C, having a vapour pressure of 0.073 bar and a sensible heat content of 167.5 kJ/kg. The booster ejector is assumed to be driven by 7.9 bar steam from the control valve. A 3°C temperature approach at the cold end of the

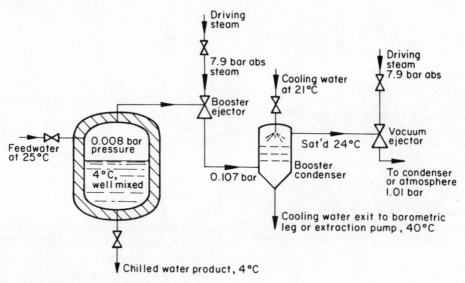

Figure 13.10 Single-stage steam ejector water chilling system

condenser is assumed so that the incondensable gases are leaving saturated with water vapour at 24°C.

Specification of booster ejector

The preliminary calculation above gives 0.107 bar as the delivery pressure and taking the vapour pressure of water at 4°C as 0.008 bar we get the compression ratio required as

$$\frac{0.107}{0.008} = 13.4$$

Steam jet driving pressure = 7.9 bar

Steam expansion pressure ratio $= \dfrac{0.008}{7.9} = 0.001$

According to the ejector performance chart (*Figure 13.5*), this can be achieved using an ejector with a mixing throat to nozzle area ratio A_m/A_n of 100 giving an entrainment ratio of 0.07 kg of suction gas per 1 kg of driving gas.

No correction need be applied for differences in specific heat ratio of driving and suction gases. Therefore the uncorrected driving-steam flow rate to the booster ejector is

$$\frac{1000}{0.07} = 14300 \text{ kg/h (neglecting air leaks)}$$

According to DeFrate and Hoerl, the calculated steam flow rate must be corrected for the effects of differences in molecular weights and temperatures of the driving and suction gases.

$$\left[\frac{W_s}{W_d}\right]_{\text{corrected}} =$$

$$\left[\frac{W_s}{W_d}\right]_{\text{uncorrected}} \times \left(\frac{M_s}{M_d} \times \frac{T_d}{T_s}\right)^{\frac{1}{2}} \qquad (13.3)$$

$M_s \simeq M_d = 18$

$T_d = 167°C$ i.e. 440 K

$T_s = 4°C$ i.e. 277 K

$$\left(\frac{M_s}{M_d} \times \frac{T_d}{T_s}\right)^{\frac{1}{2}} = \left(\frac{440}{277}\right)^{\frac{1}{2}} = 1.28$$

The quantity of driving steam required is therefore reduced by a factor 1.28 to

$$\frac{14300}{1.28} = 11200 \text{ kg/h}$$

Steam to be condensed in the booster condenser = 11200 + 1000 kg/h. The sensible plus latent heat of steam to be transferred in the booster condenser at a saturation pressure of 0.107 bar is $2586 - 167.5 = 2418.5$ kJ/kg. The sensible heat content of steam condensate at 40°C is 167.5 kJ/kg. The cooling water required is

$$\frac{12200 \times 2418.5}{4.18 \times (40 - 21)} = 372000 \text{ kg/h}$$

taking the specific heat of water as 4.18 kJ/kg.

Gas–vapour load on vacuum ejector system

In order to calculate the gas–vapour load on the vacuum ejector system, it is necessary to estimate the amount of air entering the system and to be pumped out by the final vacuum ejector.

The rate of cooling-water flow to the booster after-condenser has been established at 372 m³/h. For vacuum evaporation chilling plants the recommended empirical equation is

Air to be removed (kg/h)

$$= 4.5 + \frac{\text{mixture discharge rate}}{\text{from booster ejector (kg/h)}} \over 1000$$

$$+ \frac{\text{cooling water (m}^3\text{/min)} \times 100}{[1.8 \times \text{inlet temp. (K)}] - 460}$$

$$= 4.5 + \frac{12200}{1000} + \frac{100 \times 6.21}{(1.8 \times 294 - 460)}$$

$$= 25.5 \text{ kg/h}$$

The first two terms give the air entering the booster ejector as 16.7 kg/h and therefore the mean molecular weight of the steam–air mixture entering the booster is about 18.1.

Total air to be pumped out of the booster ejector condenser at 0.107 bar = 25.5 kg/h saturated with water vapour at 24°C. The vapour pressure of water vapour at 24°C is 0.03 bar, and the mole fraction of water vapour at 24°C is 22.4/80 = 0.28.

Mole fraction of air = 1.0 − 0.28 = 0.72

The mean molecular weight of moist air from the condenser is 0.28 × 18 + 0.72 × 29.9 = 26.5. The mass flow rate of wet air to be ejected from the booster condenser is given by

$$\text{Mass flow rate} = 25.5 + \frac{25.5}{29.9} \times \frac{0.28}{0.72} \times 18$$

$$= 25.5 + 6.0 = 31.5$$

Hence the water vapour plus air flow to be pumped out of the booster condensers is 31.5 kg/h.

Specification of vacuum ejector after booster ejector condenser

For a one-stage vacuum ejector the compression ratio required is 1.01/0.107 = 9.45. The expansion ratio using 7.9 bar steam is 7.9/0.107 = 74.0 and the suction to driving pressure ratio is therefore 1/74 = 0.0135. Using the ejector performance chart (*Figure 13.5*) shows that an ejector with an

area ratio A_m/A_n of 10 is required, having an entrainment ratio W_s/W_d of 0.02. The first uncorrected estimate of steam flow required is therefore

$$\frac{31.5}{2.2} \times \frac{1}{0.02} = 718 \text{ kg/h}$$

The correction factor for temperature and molecular weight differences is as calculated before:

$$\left(\frac{26.5}{18} \times \frac{440}{297} \right)^{1/2} = 1.21$$

The corrected steam flow rate required is

$$\frac{718}{1.21} = 592 \text{ kg/h}$$

After-condenser to vacuum ejector

The latent plus sensible heat of steam from the vacuum ejector at 1.01 bar to be removed in the condenser is 2674.0 − 167.5 = 2506.5 kJ/kg of steam condensed. Cooling water enters at 21°C and leaves at 40°C.

$$\text{Cooling water required} = \frac{592 \times 2506.5}{19 \times 4.18}$$

$$= 18\,700 \text{ kg/h}$$

Design specification for a vapour recompression evaporator employing a steam-ejector-type thermocompressor

The evaporator is of the single-effect shell and tube climbing-film type with a vapour–liquid cyclone separator (*see Figure 13.11*). For simplicity it is assumed to be evaporating an aqueous solution with negligible elevation of boiling point and the sensible heat contents of the feed and concentrated solutions are omitted from the heat balance. The vapour recompression evaporator system must be designed to suit the temperatures and pressures of the steam and of the solution being evaporated. These may be varied arbitrarily by the designer, or may be found by an optimization procedure based on the combined running and capital cost of the system in relation to the rate of evaporation required. The conditions assumed here are as follows: (a) The steam pressure required from the thermocompressor to the evaporator is 0.38 bar having a condensation temperature of 75°C. (b) The required temperature for evaporation of solution is 60.1°C corresponding to an evaporator body vapour space pressure of 0.20 bar. (c) This allows an overall temperature driving force for heat transfer of 14.9°C. (d) Driving steam is available at an absolute pressure of 5 bar.

It is desired to specify the capacity and size of the thermocompressor to meet this duty.

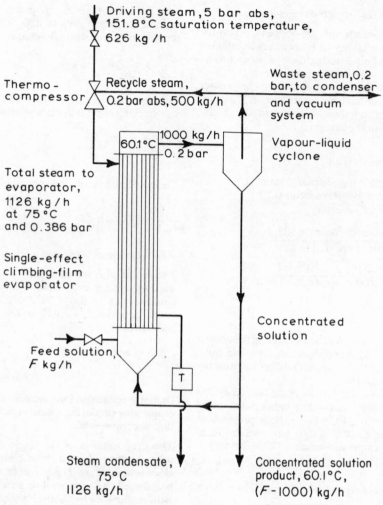

Figure 13.11   Single-effect vapour recompression evaporator system

Suction to driving pressure ratio required $= \dfrac{0.20}{5.00}$

$= 0.04.$

Compression ratio required $= \dfrac{0.38}{0.20} = 1.93.$

According to the steam ejector performance chart (*Figure 13.5*), this duty would be met by an ejector with an area ratio (mixing throat to nozzle) of 25 operating with an entrainment ratio of 0.8.

It is now possible to solve the material balance on the steam and vapour condensing and evaporating. If x is the recycled vapour from the evaporator to the thermocompressor the driving steam required is $x/0.8 = 1.25x$. The steam passing to the evaporator is then $x + 1.25x = 2.25x$.

If the evaporator is required to evaporate 1000

kg/h of water with a total heat of 2610 kJ/kg corresponding to a pressure of 0.2 bar, the quantity of steam required at 0.38 bar with a latent heat of 2322 kJ/kg is given by a simple heat balance assuming the enthalpies of the feed and concentrated solutions are zero or identical.

$$2322 \times 2.25x = 2610 \times 1000 \text{ kJ/h}$$

from which $x = 500$ kg/h of recycled steam and the driving steam required is $500/0.8 = 626$ kg/h.

Total steam to evaporator body $= 1126$ kg/h

Overall steam economy $= \dfrac{626}{1000}$

$= 0.626$ kg steam/1 kg evaporated

Evaporation efficiency $= \dfrac{1000}{626}$

$= 1.6$ kg evaporated/1 kg steam

By employing a steam jet thermocompressor to recycle part of the steam produced by evaporation it is possible to reduce the fresh (5 bar) steam consumption by 44% relative to a single-stage evaporator without recycle.

The temperature difference available for heat transfer falls from 91.7°C to 14.9°C so that the heat transfer area required for evaporation must be increased at least sixfold to achieve the desired evaporation rate.

A practical application of a thermocompressor in a whisky distillery is given in Chapter 20.

Steam jet liquid pumping

The pumping and transfer of liquids may also be effected by means of high-velocity steam jets in devices similar in design and operation to the vacuum ejector or thermocompressor. The steam jet pump consists of a steam expansion nozzle, suction chamber and venturi tube having a mixing throat and divergent cone diffuser for maximum pressure recovery. The high-velocity steam jet will suck both gases and liquids into the mixing throat, hence the pumps are self-priming. The kinetic energy of the steam jet is transferred to the liquid in the mixing section, where steam condensation and liquid heating also occur. The condensation helps to increase the suction and delivery heads produced by the pump and they are consequently more efficient when handling cold liquids. The liquid pumping rate and the suction and delivery pressures fall progressively from maximum values at 20°C to zero at liquid inlet temperatures of above 60°C. Although steam jet liquid pumps have in general low thermodynamic efficiencies down to 20%, they can be supplied to meet quite large volumetric duties against substantial delivery and suction pressures. The con-

densation of driving steam must be completed, resulting in both dilution and heating of the liquid being pumped and should be either desirable or acceptable. For example, an efficient jet pump could be expected to produce a 3% dilution with a temperature rise of about 15°C.

The jet pump is simple and reliable with a low initial cost, and is widely used for transferring liquids between tanks. It is especially suitable for intermittent duties on corrosive or erosive solutions and slurries, where it requires little or no maintenance.

A special type of jet pump is the boiler feedwater injector, which is driven by the boiler steam being generated and is designed to deliver feedwater into the boiler at the same pressure as the driving steam. In order to achieve this, the injector has a high steam consumption relative to water pumped, but all the heat energy is returned to the boiler so that the injector is virtually 100% efficient.

Choice and specification of steam jet liquid pumps

There are two main types of steam jet pump available from suppliers such as Wiegand. First, there is a type suitable for large suction heads of up to 7 m of water but with low delivery heads of up to 10 m of water depending on the driving steam pressure.

Figure 13.12 shows both suction and delivery head curves against volumetric flow rate of liquid for various pump sizes and steam driving pressures. As an example of its use, a size 4 pump will deliver 5 m³/h of water from a suction head of 6 m of water against a delivery head of 4.5 m of water using steam at a pressure of 4 bar. From the graph it is apparent that as the suction head is reduced, the maximum delivery head increases a little, but the volumetric flow rate increases rapidly. Increasing the driving steam pressure increases the maximum delivery pressure at which the pump will operate. Steam jet delivery pumps have delivery characteristics similar to those of ejectors and

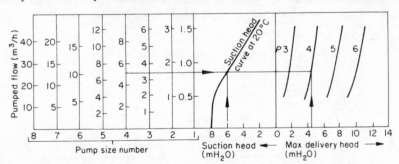

Figure 13.12 Performance chart for steam jet liquid pumps with low delivery or high suction heads. P is the pressure of the driving steam (bar abs)

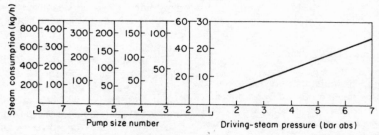

Figure 13.13   Steam consumption chart for steam jet liquid pumps with low delivery or high suction heads. P is the pressure of the driving steam (bar)

thermocompressors in that the volumetric pumping rate is constant up to a maximum delivery pressure, which is determined by the pressure of the driving steam.

At pressures above this maximum, the pumps fail to deliver. *Figure 13.13* shows that the steam consumption for each size of jet pump increases in proportion to the driving steam pressure. From this graph the steam usage required for the size 4 pump example cited above is 80 kg/h, which causes a 1.6% dilution and 9°C temperature rise in the water being pumped.

The second type of steam jet pump is designed for low suction heads and high delivery heads. Suction heads may be up to 2 m of water whilst delivery heads may be up to 35 m of water using 6 bar driving steam, as is apparent from *Figure 13.14*. As with all other jet pumps, the volumetric

flow rate is constant up to the maximum delivery pressure and is determined by the size of the ejector. Steam consumption is proportional to driving steam pressure, as shown in *Figure 13.15*, whilst the volumetric pumping rate falls from a maximum at 20°C to zero at 60°C according to *Figure 13.16*.

An increase in the specific gravity of the liquid being pumped also reduces the performance and capacity.

Although the thermodynamic efficiency of steam jet liquid pumps is much lower than that of mechanical-type pumps, which usually exceeds 60%, they are most suitable for intermittent pumping duties on difficult liquid transport problems where trouble-free, reliable performance is required.

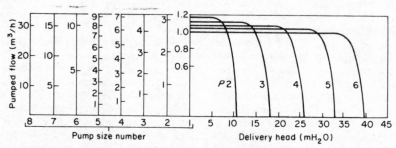

Figure 13.14   Performance chart for steam jet liquid pumps with high delivery and low suction heads. P is the driving steam pressure (bar). (1 mH₂O = 0.098 07 bar)

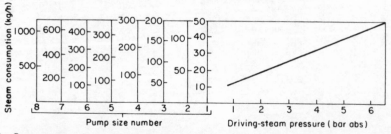

Figure 13.15   Steam consumption chart for steam jet liquid pumps with high delivery and low suction heads. (Courtesy of Wiegand Karlsruhe GmhH)

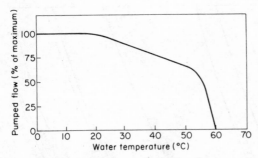

Figure 13.16 Fall in pumping rate of a steam jet liquid pump with increasing temperature

13.3 Steam distillation and stripping

Basic principles of steam distillation

There are a number of closely related unit operations employing steam in direct contact with liquid or solid phases. When applied to the separation of water-immiscible liquid mixtures, the process is known as *steam distillation*; otherwise it is known as *steam stripping*. The liquid or solid mixtures may themselves be miscible or immiscible and contain two or more components varying widely in volatility. A separation is achieved when the more volatile components evaporate under the mass transfer concentration gradients existing between the liquid or solid interface and the bulk steam flow, whilst the less volatile impurities remain in the residue passing through the still.

The stripping steam flow must be brought into intimate contact with the liquid or solid phases in order that there should be a close approach to thermodynamic equilibrium between the two phases. Under such conditions the steam will tend to become saturated with the volatile non-aqueous components at their equilibrium vapour pressures and these will be swept continuously away from the liquid or solid phase, thus achieving vaporization and separation.

The equilibrium vapour pressures of the volatile components present in the liquid or solid mixture will depend on the vapour pressures of the components when pure and hence indirectly on the temperature. If the components are mutually soluble and thermodynamically ideal then Raoult's law* will be applicable. The amount of a component distilled or stripped from a mixture will also depend on the volumetric steam flow rate at

---

* Raoult's law states that the equilibrium vapour pressure exerted by a volatile liquid in thermodynamically ideal solution is equal to the product of its pure vapour pressure and its mole fraction in solution.

the system pressure. Less steam will be required for distillation or stripping at low system pressures since the equilibrium mole fraction of vaporizing component will be larger. Long contact times, high mass transfer coefficients and large interfacial areas will help to establish the maximum possible concentrations of volatile components in the steam phase and thus reduce the steam required for a given quantity of distillate. It is important to note that the vapour pressure exerted at a liquid surface is independent of the amount of any other immiscible liquid or solid phases which may be present, including water. Whilst the previous discussion has not assumed that liquid water is present, this is often the case owing to condensation of steam when providing sensible and latent heat to the various component vapours and of course for heat losses. In this case the partial pressure of steam present in the vapour phase must be identical with the equilibrium vapour pressure of the water at the temperature present. This may introduce constraints on the phases present so that only temperature (and not pressure) can be independently varied without changing the number of phases present.

By Dalton's law of partial pressures,

$$P = p_s + Ep_v = p_s + p$$

where P is the system pressure (present in the evaporator or still); p_v is the equilibrium vapour pressure of a volatile component at the specified temperature, and may be calculated from the Clausius–Clapeyron equation for pure components and Raoult's law for ideal solutions knowing the mixture mole fraction; p_s is the partial pressure of steam; p is the partial pressure of a volatile component, and E is the stripping or steam distillation efficiency, which is defined as the molecular concentration of a volatile component expressed as a fraction of the maximum molar concentration in equilibrium with the liquid phase.

If y_s and y_v are the mole fractions of steam and a single volatile component in the gas phase, then

$$y_s = \frac{p_s}{P} \quad \text{and} \quad y_v = \frac{Ep_v}{P}$$

$$\therefore y_s + y_v = 1$$

according to Dalton's law. If the steam injection rate is S kg/h, the rate of distillate production D is given by the equation

$$D = \frac{y_v}{y_s} \times \frac{S}{18} \times M = \frac{Ep_v}{(P - Ep_v)} \times \frac{S}{18} \times M \text{ kg/h}$$

where M is the molecular weight of the distillate.

This equation also enables the amount of distillate per unit steam consumption to be calculated and

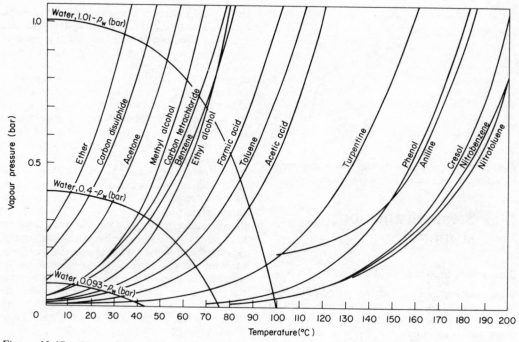

Figure 13.17   Vapour pressure curves for various organic liquids and water at three system pressures.
p_w = *vapour pressure of water* (bar). (*From* Hausbrand Verdampfen Kondensieren und Kuhlen, *6th ed.*
p 44, (1918))

indicates that minimum steam consumption will
result when P is small, p_v is large and the distillation
efficiency is large.

In order to distill with steam in the absence of
liquid water it is necessary to provide an indirect
heat source, usually from steam-heated surfaces
such as reboiler tubes, U-tubes or coils. The partial
pressure of steam in the still will then be less than
the saturated vapour pressure of water at the temperature present in the still.

At equilibrium between gas and liquid phases,
$E = 1$ and $P = p_s + p_v$.

If water is present in the still, the temperature is
determined by the above equation, which can be
found by a trial and error calculation to satisfy it.
The relationship can be expressed in a plot of
vapour pressure v. temperature for the distillate
and water at various system pressures (*see Figure
13.17*). This chart, originally due to Hausbrand, is
useful in determining the temperature required to
distill a known immiscible volatile substance in the
presence of water at a given system pressure. The
distillation temperature may be considerably
reduced below the normal boiling point of the
distillate at the system pressure owing to the partial
pressure of steam present in the still. If water is not
present then the still temperature must be
maintained above the saturation temperature of
steam, corresponding to the partial pressure of
steam in the system. This requires the use of

superheated steam injection or indirect heating.
The apparent reduction in boiling point which can
be achieved by steam distillation is useful in
separating and purifying substances having a high
normal boiling point, with a tendency to
decompose, or which may be hazardous to distill
in the conventional manner using a high-
temperature heat source, or under vacuum.

As an example of the use of the simple equation
for one-component steam distillation, one can
calculate the rate of toluene distillation when
sparging with 1000 kg/h of steam under a system
pressure of 1.01 bar.

Using *Figure 13.17* shows that at a temperature
of 85°C the vapour pressure of water is 0.57 bar
and that of toluene (p_v) is 0.44 bar, so that

$$P = p_s + p_v = 0.57 + 0.44 = 1.01$$

The efficiency of steam distillation E will depend
on the geometrical design of the steam sparging
system and on the molecular weight and viscosity
of the liquid phases present. One can expect E up
to 90% for a well-designed steam–liquid contacting system with liquids of low molecular
weight and viscosity; however, much lower values
of around 60% have been observed in poorly
designed systems with high-viscosity liquids
($> 0.1\,\mathrm{N\,s/m^2}$). The molecular weight of toluene is
92. Assuming $E = 0.90$, then

$$D = \frac{Ep_v}{(P - p_v)} \frac{SM}{18} = \frac{0.90 \times 0.44}{(1.01 - 0.44)} \times \frac{1000 \times 92}{18}$$

$D = 3550$ kg/h toluene distillate

If the system pressure is reduced, the rate of toluene distillation at the same steam rate will increase as follows:

If $P = 0.4$ bar, the temperature of steam distillation falls to 61°C, at which $p_v = 0.19$ bar. Then

$$D = \frac{0.90 \times 0.19}{(0.40 - 0.19)} \times \frac{1000 \times 92}{18}$$

$$= 4160 \text{ kg/h toluene distillate}$$

This shows that in this case a 60% reduction in system pressure increases the distillate production by 17%.

Batch steam distillation

If there are several volatile components present, or if the volatile component is soluble in a non-volatile component, there will be a depression of the vapour pressure approximated closely by Raoult's law if the system is near-ideal. For these systems the steam distillation of batches as depicted in *Figure 13.18* follows an unsteady state behaviour with the vapour pressure of the more volatile components falling steadily during the period of distillation. The batch steam distillation problem for a volatile component soluble in a non-volatile component can be solved by integrating the differential form of the appropriate mass balance equation.

If the distillation pressure P and temperature are held constant then p_v is also constant; however, during the course of a batch distillation there

is a continuous decrease in the concentration and partial pressure of the volatile component. The partial pressure of steam p_s will correspondingly increase and approach P closely towards the completion of the batch cycle. It is clear therefore that a distillation temperature at which the saturation pressure of steam is greater than the system pressure will ensure that no condensation of direct-contact steam occurs.

Integration of the differential equation for batch distillation boundary conditions gives the following equation for the steam required to reduce the number of moles of volatile component in the batch from N_{v1} to N_{v2}.

$$N_s = \left(1 - \frac{P}{EP_v}\right)(N_{v2} - N_{v1}) + \frac{PN_I}{EP_v} \ln\left(\frac{N_{v1}}{N_{v2}}\right)$$

where P_v is the vapour pressure of the pure volatile component, N_s is the number of moles of steam required and N_I is the number of moles of non-volatile component. If the concentration of non-volatile component is negligibly small so that $N_I \ll N_v$, then $p_v = P_v$ and $p = EP_v$. The differential mass balance equation is simply

$$\frac{dN_s}{dN_v} = \frac{-p_s}{p} = 1 - \frac{P}{EP_v}$$

Integration over the same boundary conditions gives the result

$$N_s = \left(1 - \frac{P}{EP_v}\right)(N_{v2} - N_{v1})$$

or

$$\frac{N_s}{N_{v1} - N_{v2}} = \frac{P - EP_v}{EP_v}$$

The mass ratio of steam to distillate collected is

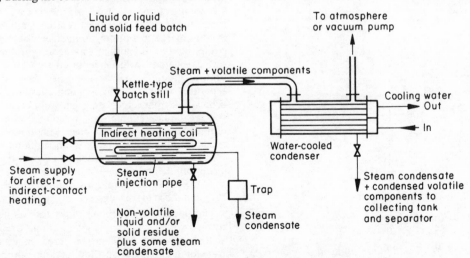

Liquid or liquid and solid feed batch

To atmosphere or vacuum pump

Steam + volatile components

Kettle-type batch still

Cooling water Out

In

Indirect heating coil

Water-cooled condenser

Steam supply for direct- or indirect-contact heating

Steam injection pipe

Trap

Steam condensate

Steam condensate + condensed volatile components to collecting tank and separator

Non-volatile liquid and/or solid residue plus some steam condensate

Figure 13.18   Single-stage batch-type steam distillation or stripping system

then

$$\frac{W_s}{W_v} = \frac{P - EP_v}{EP_v} \times \frac{M_s}{M_v}$$

where M_s and M_v are the molecular weights of steam and volatile component respectively. This is equivalent to the equation for the rate of steam distillation of a single volatile component previously presented. This equation is also applicable to the case of steam distillation in the presence of involatile components having no influence on the vapour pressure of volatile components. In general, however, if a high-boiling component is being removed by batchwise distillation from a non-volatile solvent, then as the recovery proceeds to high efficiencies the unit steam consumption will also increase and a point will be reached where further distillation is uneconomic. This must be found by repeated calculation and optimization of the batch cycle time.

Continuous steam distillation and stripping

Continuous countercurrent steam distillation, or *stripping* as it is usually called, enables a higher recovery efficiency of volatile components to be achieved with minimum steam consumption. The operation may be carried out in multi-stage-type plate columns as shown in *Figure 13.19* or in differential-type packed towers although the

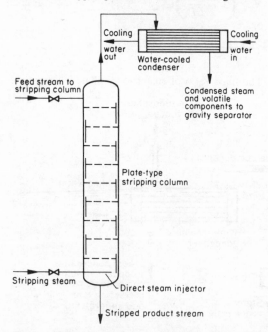

Figure 13.19 Continuous multi-stage plate-type steam distillation and stripping column

choice of which system to employ is not always obvious.

The design and analysis of multi-stage plate-type strippers is based on the graphical or numerical solution of sets of mass and heat balance equations and of vapour–liquid equilibrium equations for each plate in the tower, according to the feed compositions and flow rates present.

As the liquid being steam-stripped passes down the tower its volatile component is reduced in steps to the level desired in the exit stream. Steam injected directly to the bottom of the tower desorbs and entrains the dissolved volatiles from the liquid phase according to the concentrations present and the steam distillation efficiency on each plate. The steam leaving the top plate will contain volatiles at concentrations close to equilibrium with the feed liquid. An economic balance should be established when designing or operating a continuous-stripping tower, between the steam required to reduce the volatiles to a desired concentration and the capital cost of providing the required number of plates for the given throughput of material.

For stripping operations there will exist a maximum liquid to steam ratio above which the desired efficiency of volatile-component recovery cannot be achieved. This minimum steam consumption will also correspond to the necessity of an infinite number of plates, so that the economic optimum design of stripping tower and operating conditions corresponds to some lower liquid to steam ratio, which should be determined in each case.

If water is miscible or partly miscible with the mixture of volatile and non-volatile components then the steam stripping process becomes one of continuous fractional distillation employing direct steam injection in place of the conventional reboilers. If water is the least volatile component, it will emerge as bottom product, whilst volatile components will leave as vapour top product. A few extra plates will be required to achieve the same degree of separation as when employing a separate reboiler, the column design being achieved by plate to plate calculation employing vapour–liquid equilibrium relations and tray efficiencies in the usual manner. Minimum steam consumption would require an infinitely tall column whilst minimum tower height requires maximum steam consumption. An optimum design and reflux ratio (liquid to vapour ratio) lies between these two extremes.

Continuous steam stripping may also be effected using towers packed with metal, ceramic or plastic shapes offering high surface area, high mass transfer coefficients and low pressure drops. A well-irrigated bed of packing offers true countercurrent stripping with high mass transfer rates for desorption of volatiles.

Capital costs are often less than for equivalent plate towers whilst steam usage can be at a very economical level. Dirty liquid streams containing suspended solids can in general be steam-distilled more conveniently in packed towers than in plate towers. Packed-tower strippers are designed by integration of the mass transfer differential rate equations employing overall mass transfer coefficients and material balances.

13.4 Steam for cleaning and firefighting

High-pressure steam can be used to produce a high-velocity jet with some superheat by expansion through a suitable nozzle to atmospheric pressure. The high velocity is effective in removing dirt and loose scale from solid surfaces, whilst the temperature encourages the melting or vaporization of oil and grease deposits, thus releasing the solid deposits for mechanical blast removal. Some condensation of steam on the initially cold surfaces also takes place, which may help to dissolve and release dirt and scale from surface crevices.

The steam jet can be directed at high velocity from a conveniently long or angled lance, thus allowing safe, wide-ranging access to large or awkwardly shaped areas. Internal and external cleaning of vessels, buildings and vehicles has been practised using steam jet lances where convenient steam supplies are available; however, some of this work is now done with high-velocity water jets containing powerful detergents delivered by mobile high-pressure pumps. Steam cleaning reduces fire hazards but care must be taken to handle the steam lances safely and to extract or disperse the steam vapours without obscuring visibility. It is advisable to wear suitable protective clothing.

Steam can also be used for cleaning and re-generating heat exchanger surfaces and reactor catalyst beds.

Saturated-steam temperatures will vaporize or melt oils and greases to achieve surface cleaning; however, if steam is used in reactor tubes or beds at temperatures above 500°C, the water gas reaction with carbon becomes active and carbonaceous deposits must be removed by chemical reaction. This is a specialized application suited to relatively few processes where it is safe and convenient to use.

13.5 Steam displacement of liquids and gases

Liquids and gases may be evacuated or displaced from tanks and vessels using steam either directly or indirectly. Where vacuum or pressure is applied to vessels in order to transfer or replace fluids, care must be taken to ensure that the pressures and stresses for which the vessel was designed are not exceeded. Suitable relief devices must be fitted and set in accordance with these requirements, or the practice of pressure or vacuum transfer should not be attempted.

If suitable pressure or vacuum can be safely applied to a vessel or tank then liquids may be sucked in or forced out by the static pressure differences which are set up. Batch displacement of liquid from one vessel to another can be effected by applying steam pressure to the vapour space. Whilst liquid is being displaced, steam will be condensing on any cold liquid or vessel wall surfaces, thus increasing steam consumption above that required to displace the liquid volume at the required pressure. Some heating and dilution of the liquid batch will occur but need not be significantly large provided the liquid surface layers are undisturbed. The empty vessel may finally be rapidly purged with steam before refilling with another batch of liquid. This method of liquid transfer can be thermodynamically efficient but is necessarily intermittent in operation and requires suitably strong vessels with over- and underpressure protection devices together with either operator attention or sophisticated control systems. One or more of these reasons usually makes the practice unattractive so that other methods which are more efficient, safer and easier to operate are usually chosen. Vessels which have been purged with steam should not be isolated and allowed to cool down unless they are suitably designed or protected against the vacuum which will develop. Purging of air from vessels and systems can be done using a sufficient throughflow of live steam, but this leaves the vessel filled with steam, which

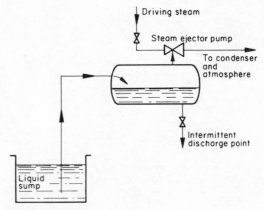

Figure 13.20 Steam-driven vacuum system for liquid elevation and transfer

may be undesirable for the reasons mentioned above. It is now considered better practice to purge vessels with inert incondensable gases such as nitrogen or carbon dioxide when this is necessary. However, if the purging steam can be put to a condenser, the steam can be removed and the residual gases or vapour can then be condensed or absorbed and safely recovered.

An attractive alternative to the use of pressure steam for displacement and transfer of liquid from vessels is the elevation of liquids under vacuum applied from a steam ejector system. *Figure 13.20* shows a simple system for raising and transferring liquid by vacuum suction from a lower to a higher vessel. Incondensable gases (usually air) and vapour from the liquid must both be pumped out of the higher vessel to apply sufficient vacuum for the necessary static pressure gradients required to drive the liquid being transferred. This method is quite frequently adopted for safe liquid transfer, where it appears to be especially convenient for reasons other than efficient energy utilization.

14

Heat exchangers and steam heating in coils and jackets

14.1 Heat exchange equipment

Any piece of equipment in which material of any sort receives or gives up heat may be called a heat exchanger. The whole field is both vast and complex. In this section attention will be confined to equipment in which condensing steam is used as a heating medium, and this means essentially annular heat exchangers, shell and tube heat exchangers and plate heat exchangers. Evaporators are dealt with in a separate section. The detailed mechanical design of heat exchangers is outside the scope of this text and reference should be made to specialist texts, such as BS 5500, BS 3274 and the Tubular Exchange Manufacturers' Association Standards (1978).

The annular or double-pipe type of heat exchanger is one of the simplest designs, being simply two concentric tubes or pipes (*see Figure 14.1*). One stream, usually the process fluid, flows inside the inner tube while the other (condensing steam) flows in the annular space between the tubes. For two liquid streams flow can be arranged as parallel flow (both streams in the same direction) or countercurrent flow (the two streams in opposite directions). When the heating medium is condensing steam only, the difference in flow arrangements does not exist.

The shell and tube type of exchanger is the one most commonly used in the process industries. As its name suggests, it consists of a large tube called the *shell* which contains a bundle of smaller tubes (*see Figure 14.2*). One fluid stream, which is often condensing steam, flows inside the shell and outside the tubes (shell-side fluid), the other, usually the process stream, flows inside the tubes (tube-side fluid). The tube-side fluid may flow once through the exchanger (single-pass) in parallel or countercurrent flow or may be directed to flow through the shell more than once (multipass) (*see Figure 14.3*).

The change in direction of the tube-side fluid is achieved using a header at the end of the exchanger. In the case of a single-shell and two-tube pass exchanger the use of U-tubes is often preferable to the use of a header.

The single-shell two-tube pass exchanger is commonly used because of its cheapness and simplicity, although multi-tube pass and multi-shell pass exchangers are available to cope with a

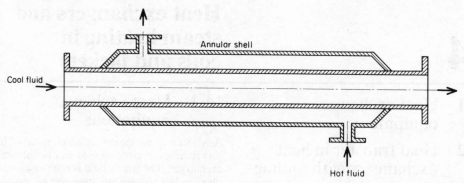

Figure 14.1   Annular heat exchanger in counterflow

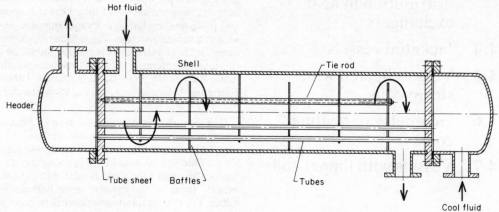

Figure 14.2   Simple shell and tube heat exchanger with one tube pass and one shell pass in counterflow. (From BS 3274, courtesy of the British Standards Institution)

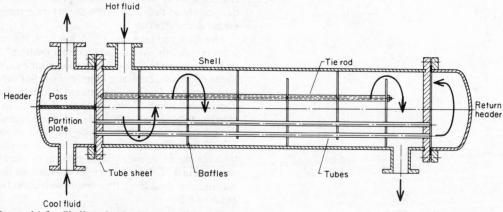

Figure 14.3   Shell and tube heat exchanger with one shell pass and two tube passes. (From BS 3274, courtesy of the British Standards Institution)

variety of special problems.

When one is condensing large volumes of steam, use is frequently made of a cross-flow exchanger in which steam enters the shell at several points (*Figure 14.4a*) or sometimes only at the mid point (*Figure 14.4b*). The tube-side fluid usually makes one or more passes through the

exchanger to give an average velocity of 1.5–3 m/s.

To generate process vapour for use in a distillation column, a kettle-type boiler is frequently used. This type of exchanger has a bundle of tubes (often U-tubes) immersed in a large volume (or pool) of liquid (*Figure 14.5*)

The shell of a shell and tube exchanger usually

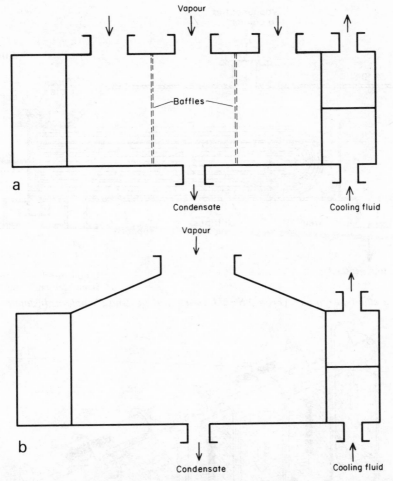

Figure 14.4   (a) Cross-flow condenser with multiple vapour inlets; (b) cross-flow condenser with external vapour belt

contains a number of baffles, which are plates at right angles to the tube bundle, and these partly block the cross-sectional area of the shell. Their two main functions are to act as tube supports and to direct the shell-side fluid so that it flows at right angles to the tubes. Their use is often advocated in steam condensers (where steam is in the shell) although in horizontal condensers they usually act only as tube supports; in vertical condensers they cause the tubes to shed their condensate at regular intervals. In addition, baffles in condensers are useful in ensuring that any non-condensable gases present are directed to the air vent.

Plate heat exchangers (*Figure 14.6*) are occasionally used as an alternative to shell and tube exchangers. In this type of heat exchanger the two fluid streams are separated by plates which are held together in a press or frame, the edges being sealed with a gasket. Plates are available with various patterns of corrugation which serve to improve the heat transfer coefficient, improve the rigidity of the plates and increase the area available for heat transfer.

As a result of the narrow gap width between the plates and because of the turbulence promoted by the corrugated surface, high heat transfer coefficients in plate heat exchangers can be achieved with low liquid velocities and a moderate pressure drop. Overall heat transfer coefficients can be two or three times those in a shell and tube exchanger with the same duty; with suitable plates turbulence can occur with Reynolds numbers below 20, and as a result, plate heat exchangers are useful for high-viscosity liquids. Also, high overall heat transfer coefficients enable a high rate of heat transfer to be obtained with small temperature differences.

A disadvantage of plate heat exchangers is that their use is limited to pressures below 25 bar and temperatures below 250°C. At high temperatures

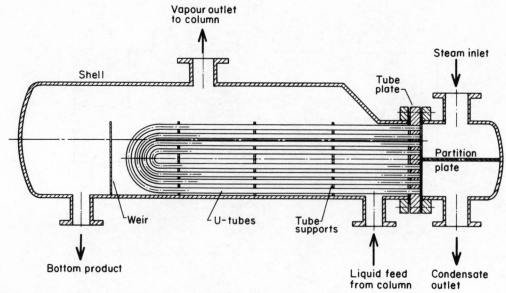

Figure 14.5   Kettle-type reboiler. (From BS 3274, courtesy of the British Standards Institution)

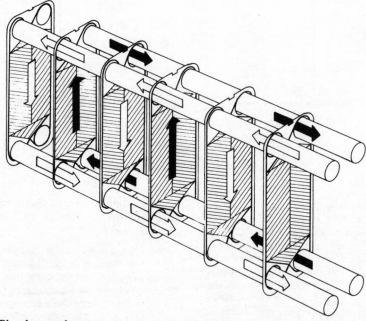

Figure 14.6   Plate heat exchanger

the choice of gasket material is limited, which restricts the number of fluids that can be handled. One advantage is that they can be opened up easily for inspection and cleaning.

14.2 Heat transfer in heat exchangers with fouling

Equations have already been presented in Chapter

12 which enable heat transfer coefficients to be calculated for liquids flowing inside tubes and for condensation both inside and outside tubes. These equations are for clean tubes, but in practice, surfaces in heat exchangers usually become 'fouled'; that is to say, they become covered or coated with a variety of substances dependent on the material being handled: for example, scale in boilers, dirt in cooling water, crystallization and polymerization

products, and similar deposits.

The effect of this is to cause heat transfer to be reduced, in practice, because of the thermal resistance of the surface coating. These thermal resistances are often referred to as *fouling factors* and have units of $m^2 K/W$ or $m^2 K/kW$.

In heat exchanger design, the prediction of fouling factors is difficult especially in the absence of experience of exchanger operation for different duties in particular areas; as a result the choice is often arbitrary.

A number of factors are likely to influence the fouling but detailed information on these is often lacking. Some of these factors are:

1. Temperatures of the streams will determine the solubility of some deposits.
2. Tube wall temperatures will determine the rate of some sludge deposition as well as the rate of the polymerization process, which may also cause fouling.
3. Tube surface roughness and the degree of turbulence will have an effect on fouling.
4. Fouling will vary with the age of the equipment.
5. The most important variable in many fouling situations is the flow velocity. High velocities will reduce fouling at the expense of increased pressure drop.
6. Operating conditions and the actual design of the heat exchanger.

Present methods of assigning fouling resistances rely to a large extent upon published values, particularly those produced by the Tubular Exchanger Manufacturers' Association of America. A number of typical values are given in *Table 14.1*.

The tabulated fouling factors are usually included to make sure that the heat exchanger will not deliver less than the required process heat load for about one year in service. In a process plant containing many heat exchangers, the use of tabulated fouling factors should enable all the exchangers to be shut down for maintenance and cleaning at the same time. For most processes with liquid/liquid heat transfer only, or when clean fluids are being condensed, low fouling factors are assumed. Fouling factors of 0.1–0.2 $m^2 K/kW$ will require heat exchangers 10–30% larger than those needed for clean surface rating depending upon the influence of the other heat transfer resistances in the exchanger.

In steam-heated reboilers subject to fouling on both sides, a 50–75% greater area is often provided.

When relatively high heat transfer coefficients can be achieved in both shell and tubes of a heat exchanger, the effect of fouling on the size and therefore initial costs is very significant.

Table 14.1   Fouling factors ($m^2 K/kW$)

Water (1 m/s, temperature < 323 K)	
Distilled	0.09
Sea	0.09
Clean river	0.21
Cooling tower (untreated)	0.58
Cooling tower (treated)	0.26
Steam	
Good-quality oil-free	0.052
Poor-quality oil-free	0.09
Exhaust from reciprocating engines	0.176
Liquids	
Treated brine	0.264
Organic liquids	0.176
Fuel oils	1.056
Tars	1.76
Gases	
Air	0.26–0.53
Solvent vapours	0.14

From Coulson and Richardson (ref. 8 of Chap. 12)

It can be seen that wherever possible, fouling factors should be carefully selected on the basis of operating experience. Haphazard or random guessing can be costly.

The overall heat transfer coefficient, H_o, for a heat exchange tube without fouling is calculated from the equation

$$\frac{1}{H_o A_o} = \frac{1}{h_i A_i} + \frac{y_w}{k_w D_w \pi} + \frac{1}{h_o A_o}$$

where H_o is the overall heat transfer coefficient based on A_o, A_o is the outside surface area of the tube πD_o per metre length, A_i is the inside surface area of the tube πD_i per metre length, y_w is the tube wall thickness $\frac{1}{2}(D_o - D_i)$, D_o and D_i are the outside and inside tube diameter, D_w is the average tube diameter, i.e. $(D_o - D_i)/\ln(D_o/D_i)$; for thin-walled tubes this can be replaced by $D_w = \frac{1}{2}(D_o + D_i)$; k_w is the thermal conductivity of the tube wall, and h_o and h_i are the outside and inside heat transfer coefficients.

Overall heat transfer coefficients calculated from this equation may be regarded as 'clean' coefficients.

To obtain 'dirty' or service coefficients, the above equation must be modified as follows:

$$\frac{1}{H_o A_o}$$

$$= \frac{1}{h_{if} A_i} + \frac{r_i}{A_i} + \frac{y_w}{k_w A_w} + \frac{r_o}{A_o} + \frac{1}{h_o A_o}$$

where r_o and r_i are the external and internal fouling factors.

As an example of the use of this equation, consider steam condensing on the outside of horizontal brass tubes having an outside diameter of 0.0254 m and an inside diameter of 0.0203 m. The tube wall conductivity is 130 W/m K. The outside and inside heat transfer coefficients are 6000 and 4000 W/m² K respectively. The corresponding fouling factors are 0.0001 and 0.00026 m²K/W.

Wall thickness $y_w = \frac{1}{2}(D_o - D_i)$

$= \frac{1}{2}(0.0254 - 0.0203) = 0.0025$ m

$D_w = \frac{1}{2}(D_o + D_i)$

$= \frac{1}{2}(0.0254 + 0.0203) = 0.0228$ m

$$\frac{1}{H_o} = \frac{1}{h_o} + r_o + \left(\frac{1}{h_i} + r_i\right)\frac{D_o}{D_i} + \frac{y_w}{k_w}\frac{D_o}{D_w}$$

$$= \frac{1}{6000} + 0.0001 + \left(\frac{1}{4000} + 0.00026\right)$$

$$\times \frac{0.0254}{0.0203} + \left(\frac{0.0025}{130}\right)\left(\frac{0.0254}{0.0228}\right)$$

$$= 9.26 \times 10^{-4}$$

i.e. $H_o = 1080$ W/m² K

This should be compared with a value for the 'clean' coefficient of 1997 W/m² K.

14.3 Temperature distribution in heat exchangers

Consider a simple annular heat exchanger (*Figure 14.1*) in which one fluid is exchanging heat with a second fluid without change of phase. The shape of the temperature distribution curves will depend upon the heat capacities of the flowing streams and whether they are in parallel or counter flow, as shown in *Figure 14.7*.

If the hot fluid can be considered to have an infinite heat capacity, as can for example condensing steam, the diagrams can be simplified to give the temperature gradients shown in *Figure 14.8*.

Similar plots of temperature distribution are obtained for simple one-tube pass, one-shell pass heat exchangers, but plots for multi-pass exchangers are more complex. The temperature difference between the hot and cold fluids, which is the driving force for heat transfer, varies along the length of the exchanger. For design purposes an average temperature difference is desirable, and for simple parallel-flow and counter-flow exchangers an appropriate choice is the logarithmic mean temperature difference $\triangle T_{lm}$.

$$\triangle T_{lm} = \frac{\triangle T_1 - \triangle T_2}{\ln(\triangle T_1/\triangle T_2)} = \frac{\triangle T_1 - \triangle T_2}{2.303 \log(\triangle T_1/\triangle T_2)}$$

where $\triangle T_1$ is the larger terminal temperature difference and $\triangle T_2$ is the smaller terminal temperature difference.

The total heat transfer in the exchanger may be expressed as

$$Q = HA\triangle T_{lm}$$

where Q is the heat transferred (in watts), H is the overall heat transfer coefficient and A is the area available for heat transfer.

If the hot fluid is superheated at entry to the exchanger and subcooled at the exit, the temperature distribution is more complicated, as shown in *Figure 14.9*. It can be seen that the exchanger consists of three zones: a desuperheating zone, a condensing zone and a subcooling zone. The total area in the exchanger can be evaluated by considering each zone separately and then adding the individual areas together.

Additional complications arise when multi-pass exchangers are considered, for example a one-shell pass, two-tube pass condenser. Here a typical temperature distribution is given in *Figure 14.10*.

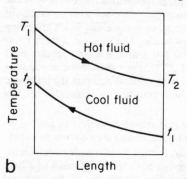

Figure 14.7   Temperature distribution in simple heat exchangers. (a) Parallel flow; (b) counterflow

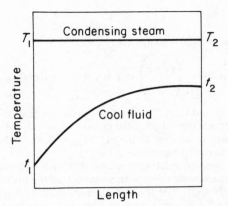

Figure 14.8 Temperature distribution in a simple condenser

The calculation of an average temperature difference is not easy; usually the log mean temperature difference is calculated using the four stream temperatures T_1, T_2, t_1 and t_2 as if the heat exchanger were a simple counter-flow exchanger and multiplying this value by a correction factor F so that

$$\Delta T_{ave} = F \times \Delta T_{lm}$$

Values of F have been published for a large number of heat exchangers.

14.4 Jacketed vessels

Jacketed vessels have been used in the process industry for many years, and are made in volumes of up to 20 m³. There are two kinds of jacketed vessel: those with a removable jacket and those with a fixed jacket.

Removable jackets are used where the expected life of the inner vessel is limited, where the inner vessel is a casting or where it is not practicable to weld the jacket to the inner vessel for other reasons. In general a vessel with a welded-on jacket is cheaper than a bolted system.

In jacketed vessels, steam is admitted into the annular space between the inner vessel and the jacket, and condensate is removed from the bottom of the jacket. Frequently, the jacket is also used for cooling the vessel and in this case cooling water is admitted at the bottom of the jacket and removed at the top.

Jacketed vessels are preferred to coil-heated ones in applications where provision of coils presents problems, as in cases where the process demands special materials like enamel, or where the minimum surface area is required for contact with the contents, on account of cleanliness or corrosion. Where these constraints do not apply, a coil-heated vessel is the more economic choice.

As the pressure of heating steam is increased, the cost of a jacketed system increases considerably. The inner vessel must be capable of withstanding the collapsing pressure of the jacket steam, and the scantlings of the jacket become heavy, particularly if a bolted system is used. Thus it is unusual to find jacketed vessels operating with a jacket steam pressure above 10 bar gauge.

Condensing steam has a high heat transfer coefficient of the order of 5000–6000 W/m² K, so the overall heat transfer coefficient is governed by the coefficient on the batch side. This in turn depends on the viscosity and level of agitation on the batch side. For all practical purposes this agitation can be provided by either an anchor agitator or a flat-disc, flat-bladed turbine.

In a well-designed agitated jacketed vessel, heat transfer coefficients of the order of 500–600 W/m² K may be expected when water is being heated, but the value may fall to 100–200 W/m² K when one is heating viscous materials (*Table 14.2*). The best correlation for heat transfer in an anchor-agitated vessel on the batch side is

$$\frac{h_w D_T}{k} = K_1 \left(\frac{D_i^2 N \rho}{\mu}\right)^a \left(\frac{C_p \mu}{k}\right)^{1/3} \left(\frac{\mu}{\mu_w}\right)^{0.18} \quad (14.1)$$

where h_w is the heat transfer coefficient at the wall of the heated vessel in W/m² K, D_T is the inside

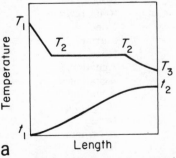

a

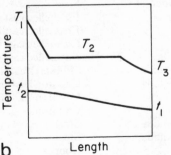

b

Figure 14.9 Temperature distribution in a simple condenser with in-tube condensation. (a) Parallel flow; (b) counterflow

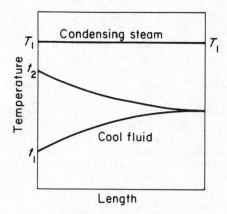

Figure 14.10   Temperature distribution in a one-shell pass, two-tube pass condenser

diameter of the jacketed vessel in metres, k is the thermal conductivity in W/m K, D_i is the diameter of the agitator impeller in metres, N is the number of revolutions per second of the agitator, ρ is the density of the fluid, μ is the viscosity evaluated at the bulk temperature, μ_w is the viscosity evaluated at the wall temperature and C_p is the specific heat capacity at constant pressure.

$K_1 = 1.0$ and $a = \frac{1}{2}$

for $10 < \left(\dfrac{D_i^2 N\rho}{\mu} \right) < 300$ (laminar flow)

while

$K_1 = 0.36$ with $a = \frac{2}{3}$

for $300 < \left(\dfrac{D_i^2 N\rho}{\mu} \right) < 4 \times 10^4$ (turbulent flow)

Uhl and Gray[3] suggest that maximum heat transfer is achieved when the ratio of anchor wall clearance to anchor diameter, c/D_i, is 0.08 for heat transfer to Newtonian fluids.

Anchor agitators are used with viscous liquids, for example those with viscosities of the order of 1 N s/m². For low- or medium-viscosity liquids (10^{-4}–1 N s/m²), turbine agitators are to be preferred. The batch-side heat transfer coefficient is then given by

$$\frac{h_w D_T}{k} = K_2 \left(\frac{D_i^2 N\rho}{\mu} \right)^{2/3} \left(\frac{C_p \mu}{k} \right)^{1/3} \left(\frac{\mu}{\mu_w} \right)^{0.14} \tag{14.2}$$

where K_2 is a function of the impeller geometry. For a flat-disc, flat-blade turbine

$K_2 = 0.54$

for unbaffled tanks with $40 < (D_i^2 N \rho/\mu) < 3 \times 10^5$; and

$K_2 = 0.74$

for one, two or four baffles with $300 < (D_i^2 N\rho/\mu) < 3 \times 10^5$. The following calculation shows how equation (14.2) can be used.

Table 14.2   Overall heat transfer coefficient H (W/m²K) for jacketed vessels. The fluid inside the jacket is steam in all cases

Fluid in tank	Wall material	Agitation	H
Water	Copper	None	840
Water	Copper	Simple Stirring	1380
Boiling water	Copper	None	1420
Water	Cast iron + loose lead lining	Agitated	22–50
Water	Cast iron + loose lead lining	None	17
Boiling water	Steel	None	1060
Water	Enamelled cast iron	0–400 rev/min	540–680
Milk	Enamelled cast iron	None	1130
Milk	Enamelled cast iron	Stirring	1700
Boiling milk	Enamelled cast iron	None	2840
Organic liquids	Mild steel lead-lined	Agitation	275
Organic liquids	Cast iron lead-lined	Agitation	165
Water	Cast iron lead-lined	Agitation	155
Water	Cast iron	40 rev/min	350
Organic liquids	Steel	None	520
Organic liquids	Steel	20 rev/min	570
Water	Copper	None	1232

Adapted from ref. 2 and other sources.

Example

A stainless-steel cylindrical flat-bottomed tank may be fitted with a steam-heating jacket on the cylindrical portion only. The tank is 1.2 m in diameter and is equipped with a flat-disc, flat-bladed turbine agitator which is 0.4 m in diameter. The tank is filled to a depth of 1.2 m with an aqueous liquor. The tank wall is 3 mm thick, is clean and free from fouling and has a thermal conductivity of 16 W/m K. The agitator rotates at 2 rev/s. How long will be required to raise the temperature of the charge from 40°C to 80°C using steam at 120°C?

The heat transfer from the vessel wall to the charge can be calculated using equation (14.2):

$$\frac{h_w D_T}{k} = 0.54 \left(\frac{N D_i^2 \rho}{\mu} \right)^{2/3} \left(\frac{C_p \mu}{k} \right)^{1/3} \left(\frac{\mu}{\mu_w} \right)^{0.14}$$

$$(14.2)$$

where μ and μ_w are the viscosities of the charge at the bulk temperature and wall temperature respectively. The physical properties may be taken to be the same as those of water. At 60°C these are density (ρ) 983.2 kg/m³; viscosity (μ) 467.3 × 10^{-6} N s/m² = kg/m s; thermal conductivity (k) 0.654 W/m K; specific heat capacity (C_p) 4184 J/kg K; speed of rotation (N) 2 rev/s; agitator diameter (D_i) 0.4 m; tank diameter (D_T) 1.2 m; liquid depth (H_L) 1.2 m.

$$\frac{\rho . N D_i^2}{\mu} = \frac{983.2 \times 2 \times 0.4 \times 0.4}{467.3 \times 10^{-6}}$$

$$= 6.732 \times 10^5$$

The maximum value of $\rho N D_i^2 / \mu$ for which equation (14.2) applies is 3×10^5. A conservative estimate of the time of heating will be achieved by taking this value in evaluating the wall heat transfer coefficient. Thus

$$\left(\frac{\rho N D_i^2}{\mu} \right) = 3 \times 10^5$$

$$\left(\frac{\rho N D_i^2}{\mu} \right)^{2/3} = 4481.4$$

$$\frac{C_p \mu}{k} = \frac{4184 \times 467.3 \times 10^{-6}}{0.654} = 2.99$$

$$\left(\frac{C_p \mu}{k} \right)^{1/3} = 1.441$$

Assume

$$\left(\frac{\mu}{\mu_w} \right)^{0.14} = 1$$

Then

$$h_w = \frac{0.54 \times 4481.4 \times 1.441 \times 0.654}{1.2}$$

$$= 1900 \text{ W/m}^2\text{K}$$

the heat transfer coefficient from the vessel wall to the charge. The value of the heat transfer coefficient on the steam side (h_s) may be taken to be 5000 W/m²K.

These heat transfer coefficients are used to check the assumption that $(\mu/\mu_w)^{0.14} = 1$.
The thermal resistances are:

1. Steam side: $1/h_s = 1/5000 = 2.000 \times 10^{-4}$

2. Wall resistance is $\dfrac{\text{thickness}}{\text{thermal conductivity}}$

$$x/k = (3 \times 10^{-3})/16 = 1.875 \times 10^{-4}$$

3. Tank wall surface to charge

$$1/h_w = 1/1900 = 5.262 \times 10^{-4}$$

Total resistance = 9.137×10^{-4}

Now check whether the assumption that $(\mu/\mu_w)^{0.14} = 1$ was sound.

$$\frac{T_s - T_b}{\text{Total resistance}} = \frac{T_s - T_w}{\text{Steam} + \text{wall resistance}}$$

where T_s is the steam temperature (120°C) and T_b is the average charge temperature (60°C). T_w is the temperature at the inside of the tank wall. Thus

$$\frac{120 - 60}{9.137} = \frac{120 - T_w}{3.875}$$

i.e.

$$120 - T_w = 25.4$$

or

$$T_w = 94.6$$

From tables of data on water,
$$\mu_{94.6} = 299.7 \times 10^{-6}$$
and
$$\mu_{60} = 467.3 \times 10^{-6}$$
Thus
$$\left(\frac{\mu}{\mu_w}\right)^{0.14} = \left(\frac{467.3}{299.7}\right)^{0.14} = (1.559)^{0.14} = 1.06$$

This is sufficiently close to 1 for the assumption to be acceptable.

The overall heat transfer coefficient H is the reciprocal of the total resistance, i.e.

$$H = 1/(9.137 \times 10^{-4}) = 1095$$

For heating with a constant-temperature heating medium, equation (14.8)(p 329) is used. Thus the time (in seconds) required to raise the charge from 40°C to 80°C will be

$$\theta = \frac{MC_p}{HA} \ln\left(\frac{T_s - t_1}{T_s - t_2}\right)$$

The heating area A is given by
$$A = \pi . D_T . H_L = \pi \times 1.2 \times 1.2$$
$$= 4.52 \text{ m}^2$$

The charge volume $\frac{1}{4}\pi D_T^2 \times H_L$ is given by

$$\frac{\pi D_T^2 \times H_L}{4} = \frac{\pi \times 1.44 \times 1.2}{4}$$
$$= 1.355 \text{ m}^3$$

The charge mass M is calculated from charge volume × density, i.e.

$$M = 1.355 \times 983.2 = 1332$$
$$\ln\left(\frac{T_s - t_1}{T_s - t_2}\right) = \ln\left(\frac{120 - 40}{120 - 80}\right)$$
$$= \ln\left(\frac{80}{40}\right) = \ln 2 = 0.693$$

$$C_p = 4184 \text{ J/kg K}$$

Finally

$$\theta = \frac{1332 \times 4184 \times 0.693}{1095 \times 4.52} \text{ seconds}$$
$$= 780 \text{ s} = 13 \text{ min}$$

Unless the vessel is used part full, a central position is recommended when installing turbine propellers.

The difficulty with heat transfer in jacketed vessels lies with cooling, since the velocity of cooling water in the annular space is low, resulting in low Reynolds numbers and low heat transfer coefficients of the order of 500–600 W/m²K or less on the water side.

For water with a linear velocity below 0.03 m/s, the heat transfer coefficient inside a plain jacket space h_j is given by

$$\frac{h_j}{k} = 0.11 \left(\frac{C_p \mu}{k}\right)^{1/3} \left(\frac{\rho^2 \beta g \triangle T}{\mu^2}\right)^{1/3} \quad (14.3)$$

where β is the coefficient of cubical expansion in K^{-1} and g is the acceleration due to gravity in m/s².

At higher velocities of flow, no satisfactory correlation exists and experimental values should be used.

When steam is condensing in the jacket, the heat transfer coefficient is very high and is not a controlling factor. For design purposes a figure of 5000 W/m²K may be used.

Thus the question of whether cooling is also required influences the designer's decision on whether to use a jacket for heating with steam. Indeed, he may consider pumped recirculatory water, which is in turn heated with live steam and cooled by addition of cooling water, in situations where heating and cooling cycles frequently alternate.

It is important to be conscious of where the resistance to heat transfer lies. The heat transfer coefficient on the condensing-steam side is very good and constitutes only a small percentage of the overall resistance. The metal wall's resistance is generally appreciable: it may be 10–30% of the overall resistance. The batch-side resistance is very sensitive to the effect of temperature, primarily because of the reduction in viscosity: the higher the temperature, the lower the viscosity, and hence the lower the resistance. Thus for a range of temperatures the batch resistance has been found to vary from 75% at 50°C to 40% at 130°C.

It must also be remembered that piping and valve systems become complicated when switching is required from steam to water and vice versa.

In order to be able to use jacketed vessels with cooling water in the jacket and obtain a heat transfer coefficient as high as possible, the velocity of the cooling water should be kept as high as possible consistent with economy of water use. To achieve this, the annular clearance between the outside wall of the inner vessel and the jacket wall should be as small as possible. There is a lower limit to what this clearance can be, because large cast or fabricated vessels made commercially must have reasonable dimensional tolerance in manufacture and the suggested acceptable annular clearance should be approximately 25 mm.

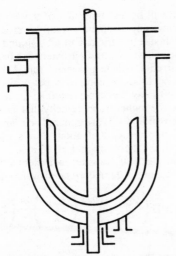

Figure 14.11 Jacketed vessel with bottom outlet and bolted-on jacket. Note that a closely fitting anchor agitator is possible

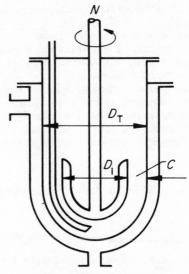

Figure 14.13 Jacketed vessel with blow pipe and bolted-on jacket fitted with anchor impeller

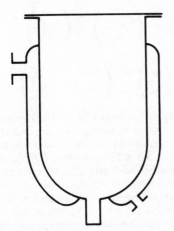

Figure 14.12 Jacketed vessel with welded-on jacket

If the inner vessel requires a bottom outlet (*Figure 14.11*), a design with a removable jacket presents more problems than a welded-on jacket (*Figure 14.12*). A seal of some sort, generally a stuffing box, is required at the bottom and this adds to the cost, presents a potential leakage hazard and adds to maintenance requirements. On the other hand the existence of a bottom outlet solves some other problems. In particular, the need for a blow-over pipe (*Figure 14.13*) is eliminated, a piece of equipment which is vulnerable and needs considerable maintenance. Furthermore, if an anchor agitator is required for stirring viscous materials, heat transfer considerations demand that the outer edge of the anchor should pass at a distance from the vessel wall which is about 8% of

the anchor diameter. This is difficult if a fixed blow pipe is used and heat transfer consequently suffers. It is, of course, possible to design a retractable blow pipe, which would permit a close-fitting anchor, but this is quite costly and introduces more operational and maintenance problems.

A steam jacket is a pressure vessel and therefore subject to statutory regulations concerning pressure vessels. Currently this involves a pressure vessel inspection every two years. A welded-on jacket, unlike a bolted-on one, cannot be inspected visually, but a hydraulic test of 1½ times working pressure is acceptable to the authorities. It is an advantage nevertheless to have an inspection branch through which the condition of the outer wall of the inner vessel may be observed. Such a provision is probably an unnecessary luxury in the case of a jacket that is used only for steam heating, but if cooling water is also used, then corrosion or solid deposits may be found, depending on the quality of the cooling water. Chemical cleaning is sometimes used to remove solid deposits and improve heat transfer and this in turn may cause corrosion. An inspection opening is then useful to assess the nature of the deposits as well as to inspect the walls of the annular space for possible corrosion.

If heating steam is admitted at a high velocity into the jacket space, its impingement on the wall of the inner vessel may cause erosion, which may go undetected for a long time. This phenomenon should be guarded against by provision of wear plates or by a large inlet branch to reduce the velocity of the impinging steam. In the latter case the designer should aim at keeping the inlet velocity below 15 m/s. The maximum velocity, of course, occurs when the jacketed vessel is being heated up from cold.

There is nothing special about condensate removal, air venting and steam trap selection for jacketed vessels; the advice given in other chapters should be followed.

At low speeds, or when the agitator is stationary, natural convection is the main cause of heat transfer within the vessel. The value of the heat transfer coefficient can be estimated from the natural convection equation for a single horizontal coil:

$$\frac{hd}{k} = \text{Nu} = 0.53(\text{Gr} \times \text{Pr})^{1/4} \quad \text{for } (\text{Gr} \times \text{Pr}) > 10^4$$

$$(14.4a)$$

and

$$\frac{hd}{k} = \text{Nu} = 0.13(\text{Gr} \times \text{Pr})^{1/3} \quad \text{for } (\text{Gr} \times \text{Pr}) > 10^9$$

$$(14.4b)$$

where

$$\text{Gr} = \frac{\beta g \Delta T \rho^2 d^3}{\mu^2} \quad \text{and} \quad \text{Pr} = \frac{C_p \mu}{k}$$

Nu, Gr and Pr are the Nusselt, Grashof and Prandtl numbers respectively, they are dealt with in Chapter 12.

These equations will normally underestimate the natural convection coefficient. There is evidence that for small coils the heat transfer coefficient may be 50% greater than that estimated, so that these equations are conservative.

14.5 Vessels heated with steam coils

Heat transfer

In the previous section it was stated that unless there are special factors, perhaps relating to corrosion or cleanliness, coil heating is a more economical choice than jackets; the larger the vessel the more true this is.

The overall heat transfer coefficient from a coil-heated vessel will be more favourable than from a jacket, because the metal resistance of the thinner

coil wall will be less than that of the vessel wall. Also, some improvement should be expected to the batch-side coefficient in an agitated vessel, since the coil will act to some extent as a baffle and eddy currents will be produced round it. If the coil is also used for cooling, a better water-side coefficient may be expected than in a jacket, owing to the higher water velocity that using a coil makes possible. Coils are generally designed for a linear water velocity of about 2 m/s while the velocity in the jacket might be 0.05 m/s.

The inside heat transfer coefficient for a coil carrying cooling water is correlated by the equation

$$\frac{hd_i}{k} = 0.021\left(\frac{Vd_i\rho}{\mu}\right)^{0.85}\left(\frac{C_p\mu}{k}\right)^{0.4}\left(\frac{d_i}{D_c}\right)^{0.1}$$

$$(14.5)$$

where d_i is the inside diameter of the tube which forms the heating coil and D_c is the diameter of the heating coil. For a flat-disc, flat-blade turbine the batch-side coil coefficient is correlated by

$$\frac{h_c d}{k} = 0.17\left(\frac{D_i^2 N\rho}{\mu}\right)^{0.67}\left(\frac{C_p\mu}{k}\right)^{0.37}$$

$$(14.6)$$

$$\times \left(\frac{\mu}{\mu_w}\right)^{0.24}\left(\frac{D_i}{D_T}\right)^{0.1}\left(\frac{d}{D_T}\right)^{0.5}$$

where h_c is the heat transfer coefficient on the outside surface of the heating coil and D_T is the inside diameter of the tank, and where $2.3 < (C_p\mu/k) < 6.3 \times 10^3$ and $400 < (D_i^2 N \rho/\mu) < 1.5 \times 10^6$. Baffles have little effect on this heat transfer coefficient. (d is the o.d. of the tube).

If a coil of the same surface area as the wetted wall of the jacket is used, it is reasonable to expect an improvement in heat transfer of 110–140%.

The heat loss from large storage tanks to the surrounding air may be calculated using natural convection coefficients estimated from the equations

$$h = 0.0014 (\Delta T/L)^{0.25} \quad \text{for } (\text{Gr.Pr}) > 10^4 \quad (14.7a)$$

and

$$h = 0.0013 (\Delta T)^{0.33} \quad \text{for } (\text{Gr.Pr}) > 10^9 \quad (14.7b)$$

Table 14.3

	V < 5.0 m/s			V > 5.0 m/s		
	A	B	n	A	B	n
Smooth surfaces	5.57	3.73	1	0	7.2	0.78
Rolled surfaces	5.79	3.73	1	0	7.2	0.78
Rough surfaces	6.19	4.10	1	0	7.5	0.78

From Dryden (ref. 7 of Chap. 12)

Table 14.4 Overall heat transfer coefficient H (W/m^2 K) for coils immersed in liquids

Fluid inside coil	Fluid inside tank	Coil material	Agitation	H
Steam	Water	Lead	Agitated	390
Steam	Boiling aqueous solution			3400
Steam	Sugar and molasses solution	Copper	None	280–1360
Steam	Vegetable oil	Steel	Various	220–400
Steam (7–10 bar g)	Vegetable oil	Steel	None	130–165
Steam	Water	Steel		1600
Water	Organic solution			1700
Steam	40% H$_2$SO$_4$	Lead-lined copper	None	425
Water	Organic solution	Steel	20 rev/min	440
Water	Organic solution	Steel	Agitation	410
Water	Water–oil mixture	Steel	None	480
Steam	Fatty acid	Copper pancake coil	None	300–560

Adapted from Perry and other sources.

Typical values for indoor tanks are in the range 8–10 W/m K (including radiation). Values for outside storage tanks will depend upon the wind velocity; a typical figure for a 5 m/s wind with a 50 K temperature difference is 35 W/m K.

The effect of wind velocity on convection from plane walls can be estimated from *Table 14.3*, which gives values of the heat transfer coefficient h in W/m^2 K as a function of wind velocity V using the formula

$$h = A + B V^n$$

The heat transfer coefficient h (W/m^{2}K) from the heating coils can be estimated using the equation for a single horizontal tube already quoted as equations (14.4). Some data are presented in *Table 14.4*.

Heating and cooling agitated batches

The time required for heating and cooling batches of liquid in stirred tanks may be estimated from the following equations:

Case 1. Coil-in-tank or jacketed vessel with constant-temperature heating medium, e.g. steam:

$$\theta = \frac{MC_p}{HA} \cdot \ln\left(\frac{T_1 - t_1}{T_1 - t_2}\right) \quad (14.8)$$

where θ is the time required for heating the charge from temperature t_1 to temperature t_2 (s), M is the mass of the charge (kg), H is the overall heat transfer coefficient (W/m^2 K) from heating medium to charge, A is the area available for heating (m^2),

T_1 is the temperature of the heating medium (°C), t_1 is the initial temperature of the charge (°C), t_2 is the temperature of the charge after time θ (°C) and C_p is the specific heat capacity of the charge (J/kg K).

Case 2. Coil-in-tank or jacketed vessel, non-isothermal cooling medium, e.g. cooling water:

$$\theta = \frac{MC_p}{WC_{pc}}\left(\frac{K}{K - 1}\right) \cdot \ln\left(\frac{T_1 - t_1}{T_2 - t_1}\right) \quad (14.9)$$

where θ is the time required for cooling the charge from temperature T_1 to temperature T_2 (s), M is the mass of the charge (kg), C_p is the heat capacity of the charge (J/kg K), W is the coolant's mass flow rate (kg/s), C_{pc} is the specific heat capacity of coolant, t_1 is the coolant inlet temperature and $K = e^z$, where $z = HA/WC_{pc}$.

These equations are based on the following assumptions:

1. The overall heat transfer coefficient is constant and does not vary over the heating surface.

2. Liquid flow rate and specific heat capacities are constant.

3. The batch has a uniform temperature and the heating or cooling medium has a constant inlet temperature.

4. No phase changes occur in the batch.

5. Heat losses are neglected.

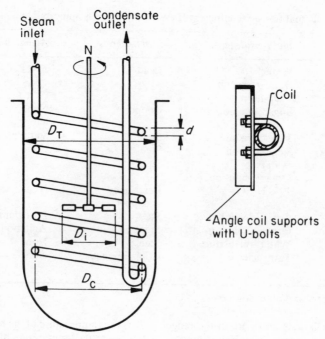

Figure 14.14   Vessel with cylindrical spiral coil and turbine agitator

14.6 Geometry of heating coils

The metal thickness of the coil wall is small compared with the vessel wall. The coil wall is also at a higher temperature than the vessel's contents and may be subject to corrosion, so it is highly desirable to be able to remove the coil for maintenance or replacement.

Welded-in coils, although not unknown, are very rarely used in the chemical industry, thus the design of both vessel and coil is influenced by the desirability of being able to take out the coil and replace it. In a cylindrical agitated vessel heated with a cylindrically wound spiral coil (*Figure 14.14*), this means having a detachable cover with consequently a significant extra expense for flanges, particularly if the vessel is a pressure vessel. Naturally, a detachable cover may be required in any case, for example if it is necessary to use anchor agitators.

Cylindrical spiral heating coils are preferred to pancake spiral coils, since the former are easier to make and support. Heating coils are generally made of tube with a bore of 25–50 mm. The smaller the bore, the greater the surface area per unit weight of metal and indeed the better the heat transfer coefficient (*see* equation 14.5). On the other hand, for the same metal thickness, the larger-bore coil is much more rigid, less prone to vibration and requires fewer vertical supports.

Also, smaller-bore coils may not have sufficient cross-sectional area for adequate flow of steam, condensate or cooling water and will require several 'starts', complicating the coil design and that of the vessel where the coil enters and leaves.

It is a good rule to have as few welds as possible inside the vessel, therefore complicated coil shapes should be avoided and the coil made from pipe stock which is as long as possible. If welds are required, these should be of the straight butt type and located in a readily accessible part of the coil.

Steam should be admitted at the top of the spiral so that condensate always travels downhill. The condensate outlet may go out of the vessel bottom but this presents jointing problems. Mostly condensate is taken out at the top from a vertical riser from the lowest point in the coil. *Figure 14.15* shows a method of connecting the coil through a branch in the cover; this design is aimed at allowing removal of the cover without the coil having to be taken out at the same time.

Earlier in this section it was stated that a spiral cylindrical coil is preferable to a pancake helix, but this is not always acceptable in cases where the heating area must be provided at the lowest point in the vessel, because it is dangerous for reasons of thermal decomposition to expose any of the heating surface to the gas phase. In other cases, the batch would be evaporated to a low level in the vessel and a cylindrical coil would start to be exposed above

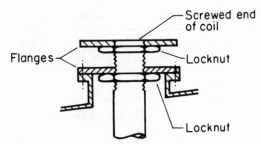

Figure 14.15 *Design permitting removal of cover leaving the coil behind*

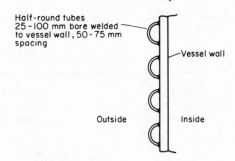

Figure 14.17 *Limpet coils*

the liquor level and become progressively ineffective.

Another way of heating vessels with coils is to use heating elements inserted from the side (*see Figure 14.16*). This technique is commonly used with unagitated storage vessels or distillation stills. It will be seen that the design is based on U-tubes expanded or welded into a tube plate with its own header for steam inlet and condensate outlet. It has the advantage that a removable cover is not required, only a branch to accept the tube bundle. The tube bundle can be easily removed for cleaning the heating element or the vessel. U-tubes are used so that thermal expansion does not produce mechanical stresses.

Vessels may be heated with built-in callandrias. This is common in evaporation practice (*see* Chapter 15).

14.7 Vessels with limpet coils

Instead of having an external jacket embracing the whole vessel, or internal heating coils, heating or cooling systems can be designed so that the vessel is heated by a spiral half-round tube welded to the outside of the vessel (*see Figure 14.17*). This is a limpet coil system, a type which has become more popular over the past ten years since initial troubles with leaking welds have been overcome. The design, if made by a reputable firm, can be regarded as technically well established.

Limpet coil systems are in direct competition with jacketed systems although there are still fields for both.

The limpet coil systems become more attractive

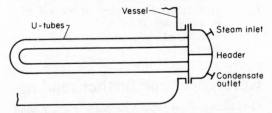

Figure 14.16 *Removable tube bundle inserted through vessel wall*

than the jacketed systems where the pressure of the heating steam is high. In a jacketed system, the jacket and vessel scantlings would be affected by high-pressure steam, whereas limpet coils and indeed the vessel remain virtually unaffected.

If the vessel also has to be cooled, limpet coils permit a high cooling-water velocity and the water-side heat transfer coefficient is correspondingly greater.

The heat transfer coefficient for limpet coils may be estimated using the Dittus–Boelter equation in the form

$$\frac{hD_e}{k} = 0.023 \left(\frac{V\rho D_e}{\mu}\right)^{0.8} \left(\frac{C_p\mu}{k}\right)^{0.4} \quad (14.10)$$

where D_e, the hydraulic mean diameter, is defined as (4 × flow area/channel perimeter), and V is the velocity of flow. For a semicircular passage of diameter D over the curved position this is

$$D_e = 4 \times (\pi D^2/8)/(D + \pi D/2)$$
$$= 0.611D$$

The area available for heat transfer is the area in contact with the vessel wall, given by $\pi D_T \times D \times$ number of turns. However, it is usually quite unnecessary to place the coils very close together. Conduction through the wall can render the entire jacket surface up to 90% efficient in transferring heat. For details *see* ref. 4.

There are several over advantages in using limpet coils compared with the conventional jacketed vessel:

1. The volumetric hold-up in the coils is small in comparison with the volume of the jacket, and consequently the change-over from one heating medium to another is faster.
2. It is possible to have several coils in parallel, which is useful when the heat load is sufficiently large that the exit temperature of the coolant from a single coil becomes excessive.
3. With more than one coil it is possible to sep-

Table 14.5　Approximate overall heat transfer coefficients for shell and tube equipment

Hot side	Cold side	Overall heat transfer coefficient (W/m² K)
Condensers		
Steam (pressure)	Water	2000–4250
Steam (vacuum)	Water	1700–3400
Heaters		
Steam	Water	1420–4250
Steam	Light oils	300– 850
Steam	Heavy oils	60– 455
Steam	Organic solvents	570–1140
	Gases	30– 300
Evaporators		
Steam	Water	2000–4250
Steam	Organic solvents	570–1140
Steam	Light oils	455–1020
Steam	Heavy oils (vacuum)	140– 425
Heat exchangers (no change of state)		
Water	Water	850–1700
Organic solvents	Water	280– 850
Gases	Water	17– 280
Light oils	Water	340– 910
Heavy oils	Water	60– 280

From Coulson and Richardson (ref. 8 of Chapter 12)

arate heating and cooling duties without emptying. This is particularly useful when exotic heating or cooling media are used, and is something which is quite impossible in a jacket.

4. In larger vessels, limpet coil construction is cheaper than jacket. A saving of around 50% is claimed by some manufacturers for stainless steel vessels of capacity 10 m³, but for smaller vessels of capacity less than 2.5 m³, particularly with a low-pressure heating or cooling medium, this advantage disappears.

The choice is between (i) a bolted-on-jacket; (ii) a welded-on jacket; (iii) a limpet coil, or (iv) an internal coil. An *internal coil* should always be the first choice unless corrosive conditions or cleanliness demand that internal surfaces be kept to a minimum. A *welded-on jacket* is the second choice unless (a) the life expectancy of the inner vessel is low; (b) the material of the inner vessel does not lend itself to welding (e.g. cast iron); (c) the pressure of the heating steam is high, i.e. above 7–10 bar gauge; (d) cooling takes an appreciable part of the time cycle; or (e) the vessel is very large. A *bolted-on jacket* should be chosen if condition (a) or (b) prevails and a *limpet coil* would be chosen if conditions (c), (d) or (e) prevails.

List of symbols

The symbols used in this chapter are the same as those from Chapter 12, with the addition of the following items:

C	Wall clearance for anchor agitator (m)
d	Outside diameter of tube forming heating coil (m)
D_c	Diameter of heating coil (m)
D_i	Diameter of agitator impeller (m)
d_i	Inside diameter of tube forming heating coil (m)
D_T	Inside diameter of tank or jacketed vessel (m)
h_c	Heat transfer coefficient on outside surface of heating coil (W/m² K)
h_w	Heat transfer coefficient at the wall of a heated vessel (W/m² K)
N	Number of revolutions/second of an agitator (s⁻¹)

References and further reading

1　Holland, F. A. and Chapman, F. S. *Liquid Mixing and Processing in Stirred Tanks*. New York: Reinhold (1966)

2 Perry, J. H. *Chemical Engineer's Handbook*, 3rd edn. New York: McGraw-Hill (1950)

3 Uhl, V. W. and Gray, J. B. *Mixing — Theory and Practice*, Vol. 1. New York: Academic Press (1966)

4 Kneale, M. 'Design of vessels with half coils'. *Trans. Inst. Chem. Engnrs.*, Vol. 47, p. T279 (1969)

5 Rogers, G. F. C. and Mayhew, Y.R. 'Heat transfer and pressure loss in helically coiled tubes with turbulent flow'. *Int. J. Heat Mass Transfer*, Vol. 30, p. 387 (1963)

15

Evaporation and distillation

15.1 Introduction

Although evaporation and distillation are treated as distinct processes, this is principally because it is a matter of convenience in describing the mode of operation of equipment rather than a fundamental difference in the physicochemical nature of the operations. Both make use of heat as a means of changing the composition of liquid mixtures by vaporization of one or more components. Evaporation can be regarded as a special case in that pure solvent is removed from a liquid containing an involatile solute, that is, a component which does not appear in the vapour phase. Often the solute is a dissolved solid, which may be recovered in a subsequent crystallization stage. However, since the division is somewhat arbitrary and primarily one of convenience, it does include systems where the 'involatile' component is a liquid with a very low volatility. In either case, the desired product may be either the vaporized component, which is recovered as a condensate, as in desalination processes or the residual liquor during the concentration of sulphuric acid.

Distillation involves the relative enrichment of the lower-boiling components of a liquid mixture by partial vaporization. The distinction is that all components are present in both the liquid and vapour, and this distinction results in a significantly different arrangement of equipment compared with evaporation, despite the basic similarity of the governing physicochemical processes. To achieve an acceptable change in composition of the mixture usually requires the vaporization process to be carried out several times, with corresponding heating and cooling of liquid and vapours.

Both processes use large amounts of heat, and design and operating policies reflect a balance between capital and running costs, particularly with respect to the most appropriate arrangement of equipment. Clearly, this will depend on the appropriate balance between capital and operating (energy) costs at any time. Consequently, schemes for reducing energy requirements which formerly were unattractive some years ago when fuel costs were cheap are now attracting more attention. For example, heat pumps in distillation processes are being reappraised[1-3], and vapour recompression in evaporation can be attractive[4,5].

Separation principles

Except in very special circumstances, the equilibrium vapour in contact with a liquid mixture has a different composition, being richer in the more volatile components. Hence, vaporization of a mixture by the application of heat results in a vapour being produced which has relatively a greater amount of the component(s) with lower boiling point(s). The factors which govern the quantitative relationship are derived from thermodynamics, and represent the maximum change which can occur at equilibrium. For actual processes, the changes occur at finite rates and this limiting condition will not be reached.

The relationships are usually complicated and it is difficult to derive general formulae for anything but the ideal case. Nevertheless, the limiting cases are useful in suggesting the patterns of behaviour found in other situations.

Ideal mixtures

For ideal mixtures, with the vapour behaving as an ideal gas, it is possible to use Raoult's law[7] to relate vapour and liquid pressure (p_i) of component i in a liquid mixture in terms of the composition (x_i) and vapour pressure (p_i^∞) of the pure component at the temperature of the solution (T) by

$$p_i = x_i p_i^0 \qquad (15.1)$$

where x_i is the mole fraction of component i in the liquid, and the vapour pressure is a function of temperature $(p_i(T))$. This is true for each of the components. If the vapours are ideal gases, then

$$\sum_{i=1}^{n} p_i = P = \sum_{i=1}^{n} x_i p_i^0 \qquad (15.2)$$

where P is the total pressure of the system and n is the number of components. For a given liquid mixture, i.e. one in which the x_i values are known, the temperature of the solution will be such that equation (15.2) is satisfied. Thus the computational procedure involves guessing various values of temperature until this condition is met. The value of temperature satisfying this will be that of the liquid and the vapour composition y_i given by

$$y_i = \frac{p_i}{P} \qquad (15.3)$$

where y_i is the mole fraction of component i in the gas phase.

Evaporation

Commonly, the system can be regarded as being binary, so that $n = 2$. By definition, one of the components (say $i = 1$) is involatile and so is not present in the vapour phase. This means that the total vapour pressure of the solution is

$$p_2 = x_2 p_2^0 \qquad (15.4)$$

where subscript 2 refers to the volatile solvent.

The manner in which vapour pressure changes with temperature is given by the Clausius–Clapeyron equation[7]:

$$\frac{dp^0}{dT} = \frac{L_v p^0}{RT^2} \qquad (15.5)$$

where p^0 is the vapour pressure, T is the absolute temperature (K), L_v is the latent heat of vaporization of the liquid and R is the gas constant. Rewriting this for the vapour pressure of the solutions at temperature T gives

$$\frac{d \ln p}{dT} = \frac{L_v}{RT^2} \qquad (15.6)$$

and assuming L_v is constant:

$$d \ln p = \frac{L_v}{R} \frac{dT}{T^2}$$

Integrating between solution vapour pressure p_2 (temperature T) and vapour pressure of pure solvent p_2^0 (temperature T_0) gives

$$\ln\left(\frac{p_2^0}{p_2}\right) = \frac{L_v}{R}\left(\frac{1}{T} - \frac{1}{T_0}\right)$$

or using equation (15.4),

$$-\ln x_2 = \frac{L_v}{R} \frac{(T_0 - T)}{T_0 T}$$

For small changes in temperature $T_0 = T$,

$$\therefore -\ln x_2 = \frac{L_v}{RT_0^2}(T_0 - T)$$

For a binary system,

$$x_2 = 1 - x_1$$

where x_1 is the mole fraction of the solute in the liquid, so that

$$\ln(1 - x_1) = \frac{L_v}{RT_0^2}(T - T_0) \qquad (15.7)$$

If x_1 is small, $\ln(1 - x_1) = x_1$ and

$$x_1 = \frac{L_v}{RT_0^2}(T - T_0) \tag{15.8}$$

This may be expressed as

$$T = Kx_1 + T_0 \tag{15.9}$$

where $K = RT_0^2/L_v$ is a constant. This implies that the vapour pressure of the solution is a linear function of the mole fraction of the solute. It provides a means of correlating the boiling point of solutions of fixed compositions (Dühring's rule). Usually this is given as a linear plot relating boiling point of the solution to that of the pure component, as shown in *Figure 15.1*.

Depending on the pressure, this enables the boiling point of a solution having a given composition to be determined providing the boiling point of the pure solvent is known. The resulting graphs are known as Dühring lines. For a pure solvent boiling at temperature T_B, a solution containing a mole fraction of solute $x = 0.1$ would boil at a higher temperature T_{Bi}. The temperature difference $(T_{Bi} - T_B)$ is termed the *boiling point rise* (BPR), and becomes greater the higher the concentration of the solute. It is an important consideration in evaporators.

Figure 15.2 gives a nomogram for a number of solutes. While this method of correlating data is useful, it is nevertheless an approximation applying to limiting concentrations and must be used with a recognition of the limitations. This can be seen by reference to *Figure 15.3*, which gives more complete information for the system sodium hydroxide (NaOH) – water.

Distillation

For a binary system, both components appear in the vapour phase and there is a relative enrichment in the more volatile component. In the case of a binary mixture, it is possible to obtain an explicit solution, but for $n > 2$ a trial and error procedure is necessary. Nevertheless the general characteristics can be identified by considering a two-component system. By equation (15.3),

$$y_1 = \frac{p_1}{P} \quad \text{and} \quad y_2 = \frac{p_2}{P} \tag{15.10}$$

and using equation (15.1),

$$y_1 = \frac{x_1 p_1^0}{P} \quad \text{and} \quad y_2 = \frac{x_2 p_2^0}{P} \tag{15.11}$$

Hence

$$\frac{y_1}{y_2} = \frac{x_1 p_1^0}{x_2 p_2^0} = \alpha \frac{x_1}{x_2} \tag{15.12}$$

where $\alpha = p_1^0/p_2^0$ and is termed the 'relative volatility' (of component 1 with respect to component 2). When 1 is the more volatile component, $\alpha > 1$. Despite the fact that vapour pressures (p_i^0) are strong functions of temperature, if the latent heats of vaporization are approximately equal, then α is practically constant and independent of temperature. For a binary system, since $x_1 + x_2 = y_1 + y_2 = 1$, it is convenient to let $x_1 = x$ and $x_2 = 1 - x$; similarly, $y_1 = y$ and $y_2 = 1 - y$. Then

$$\frac{y}{1-y} = \alpha \frac{x}{1-x} \tag{15.13}$$

or

$$y = \frac{\alpha x}{1+(\alpha -1)x} \tag{15.14}$$

Thus, if the liquid composition is known, the corresponding vapour composition at equilibrium can be determined directly. For more than two components the same approach can be used, but a trial and error procedure is necessary to determine the vapour composition.

If α is constant, in the case of a binary mixture, plotting y v. x gives a curve of the type shown in *Figure 15.4*. Comparing with the line $y = x$ shows that for a given liquid composition the vapour contains more of component 1 ($\alpha > 1$). This means that vaporizing the liquid increases the fraction of the more volatile component in the vapour. By separating the vapour, condensing it and vaporizing some of the liquid, a further enrichment of the more volatile component occurs. Repeating this gradually enables a separation of components to be achieved. Distillation columns are designed to

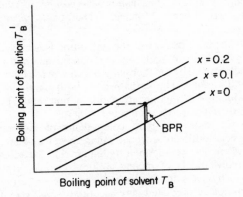

Figure 15.1   Dühring lines for an ideal system

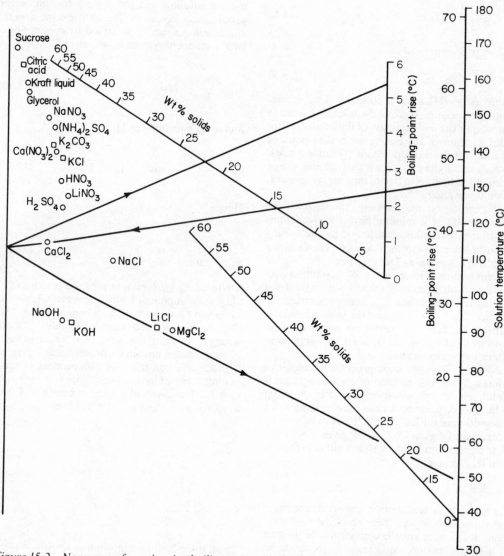

Figure 15.2   Nomogram for estimating boiling-point rise (BPR) of various solutions. Example: At 132°C a 22% CaCl₂ solution has a BPR of 5.38°C. Note: points shown as □ are based mainly on atmospheric boiling point. (Adapted from Perry, R. H. and Chilton, C. H. (Eds.) Chemical Engineers' Handbook, 5th edn. New York: McGraw-Hill (1973))

bring this about in the most convenient fashion. Many systems exhibit non-ideal behaviour[7], but the same general principle applies.

In both evaporation and distillation, the vapour pressure plays an important part. It is strongly dependent on temperature and the latent heat, as indicated by equation (15.6). This equation also suggests that the vapour pressure of a liquid can be conveniently represented by a plot of $\ln p$ v. $1/T$ where, assuming L_v is constant, only two points are necessary to establish the (straight) line. If L_v is temperature-dependent, then the line will be curved.

For both processes, the separation is achieved by an input of heat, and the amount required is determined by the thermal properties of the liquid and vapour. The enthalpies of both pure components and vapours are required, and should be referred to a consistent standard state.

Enthalpies of pure components present no special difficulties. In particular, the steam-water system is well-defined (Chapter 1). Mixtures involve heats of mixing, volume change, etc., which means that for many systems the properties cannot be predicted very accurately. *Figure 15.5* gives typical enthalpy data for the sodium hyd-

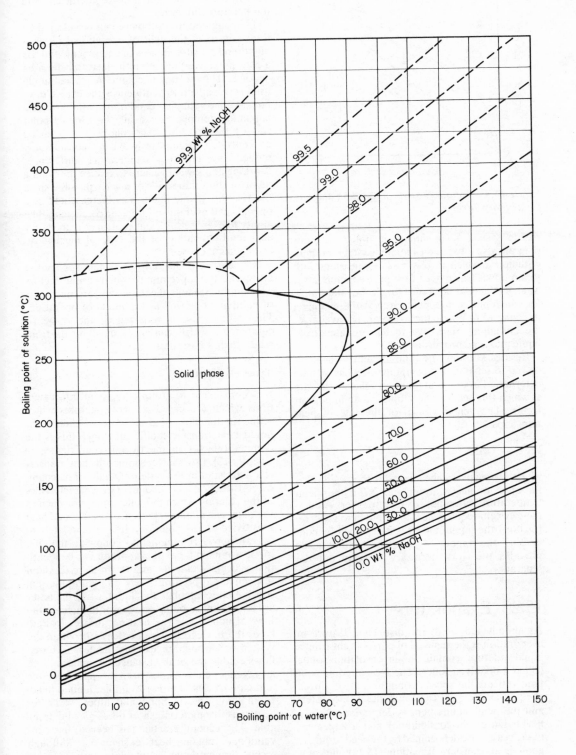

Figure 15.3   Boiling-point rise for solutions of NaOH–water. *Adapted from ref. 8*

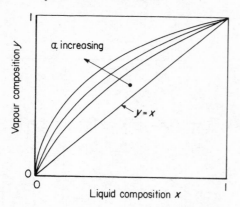

Figure 15.4   Vapour–liquid composition diagram for a binary mixture

roxide system [8]. It should be noted that this diagram also is based on a reference state for these enthalpies, which in this case is consistent with steam tables (since one of the pure components is water). A similar diagram [9] for alcohol and water, for which both components are volatile, is shown in *Figure 15.6*. Where these data are not available, the enthalpies may have to be estimated from liquid and solid properties.

Besides knowing the total amount of heat required to separate the components, which can be determined from a heat (energy) balance, the rate at which this heat can be supplied is an important factor. The general form for the rate of heat transfer is

$$\text{Rate} = UA \, \triangle T \qquad (15.15)$$

where U is an overall heat transfer coefficient, A is the area for heat transfer and $\triangle T$ is the mean temperature difference for heat transfer. A complete system requires heat to be put in to vaporize (or boil) the liquid and heat is removed by condensing the vapour. It is this which basically provides the work necessary to carry out the separation.

15.2   Evaporators

As already indicated, the distinctive feature in evaporation is the removal of pure solvent from a liquid mixture containing an involatile solute (often a dissolved solid). The type of equipment used reflects the special conditions arising from the physicochemical characteristics of the system and the heat requirement is determined from a heat balance. The configuration and arrangement of the vessels are determined by the need to ensure good heat transfer. Equation (15.15) indicates that three factors need to be considered, namely

heat transfer area, heat transfer coefficient and temperature difference.

The temperature difference can be selected by the designer in the light of operational requirements and possible choices of equipment, and has a considerable influence on the heat transfer area needed. The heating medium most commonly used is steam and this influences the choice in so far as the supply conditions establish the maximum temperature available. Boiling-point rise of the solution, particularly if it is being concentrated significantly, can considerably reduce the effective temperature difference. Working at a lower pressure to reduce the boiling point of the solution is not always possible since the viscosity of the liquor may increase and give only a small overall heat transfer coefficient. The ability to exercise sufficient control over the latter also tends to influence the type of mechanical arrangement chosen.

It is apparent that any particular application represents a compromise between various factors which influence both the design and arrangements of equipment as well as the mode of operation. This compromise is reflected in the range of equipment, which can meet most needs from relatively few basic designs.

Types of evaporator

It is convenient to group equipment into categories which are based on those features which influence the flow of conditions and hence the liquid heat transfer coefficient. Since this is the dominant factor in the overall coefficient (*see* Chapter 12), this also determines the heat transfer characteristics of the system. Details of mechanical construction take account of the characteristics of the solution which influence operation such as foaming, entrainment, presence of solids and heat sensitivity of the solution. It is also related to overall power requirements. Following this division, two main types of evaporator can be identified, using *natural* and *forced circulation* respectively. The former rely on natural thermal convection to circulate the liquid, while the latter use a mechanical pump or agitator to increase the flow of liquid over the heating surface. In both types the induced flow can be entirely within the system or through an external heater. External flows enable the heat exchange equipment to be arranged for convenience, both for space available and ease of cleaning. For example, limited headroom may indicate horizontal tubes, while for heat-sensitive material, short tubes may be desirable. The general practice has been to use conventional tubular heat exchangers, although recent designs have found plate exchangers to have some advantages [10].

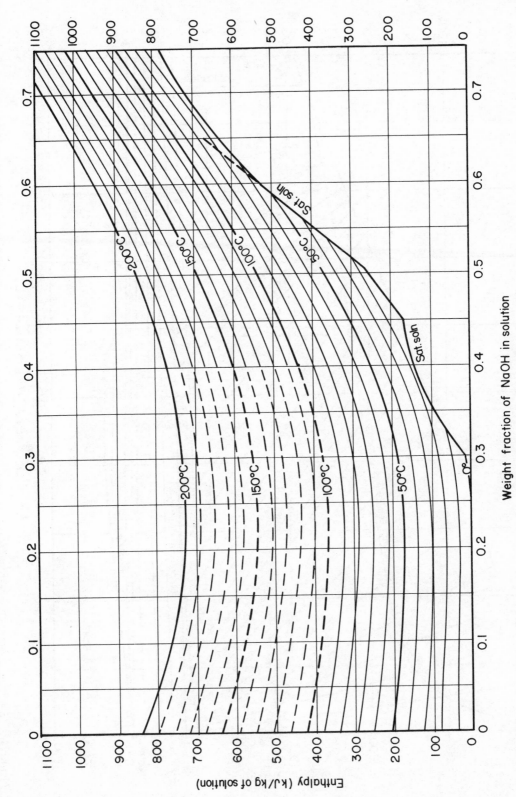

Weight fraction of NaOH in solution

Figure 15.5   Enthalpy–total pressure–composition diagram for NaOH–water. Adapted from ref. 8

342

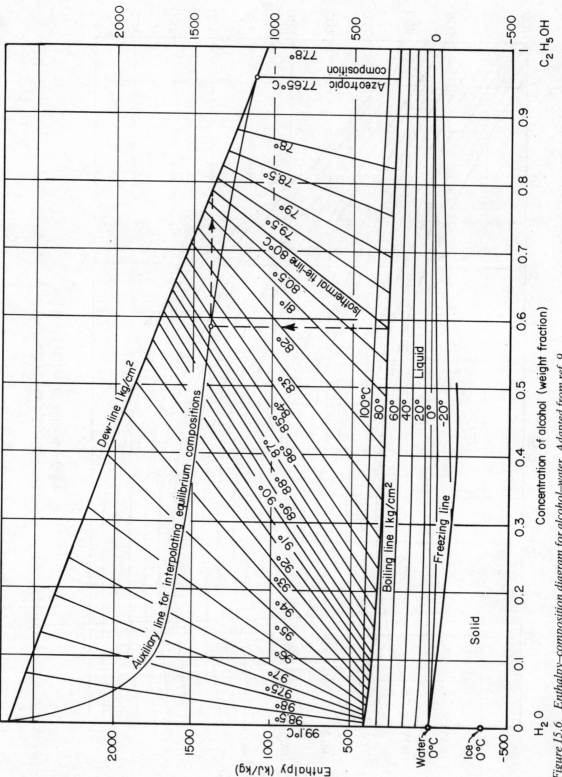

Figure 15.6 Enthalpy–composition diagram for alcohol–water. Adapted from ref. 9

Natural-circulation evaporators

The movement of liquid in this class of equipment relies on natural convection induced by heating. As cold liquid is heated, its density decreases and the hydrostatic forces cause it to rise. With more heat input and as the solution begins to boil, the vapour bubbles formed also rise and tend to drag the surrounding liquid. If the liquid is in tubes, a central two-phase region of vapour and liquid tends to rise, accelerating as it moves upwards, and forms along a film of liquid on the tube heating surface. No pump for recirculation is required, and if the viscosity of the solution is not too high, the rate of heat transfer can be good. The mixture of vapour and liquid is discharged into a disengagement space to separate vapour and liquid.

Various mechanical configurations can be used to take advantage of this, as illustrated in *Figures 15.7–15.10*. The vertical-tube arrangement shown in *Figure 15.9* is a variation termed a *climbing-film evaporator*. It has the particular advantage of having a low retention time with high heat transfer coefficients. Satisfactory operation of natural-circulation evaporators is dependent on an adequate temperature between heating medium and liquid, and hence influences the design in

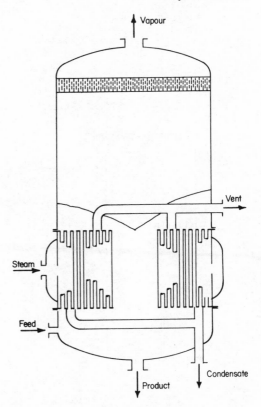

Figure 15.8   Basket-type evaporator

selecting $\triangle T$ of equation (15.15).

Where only limited temperature differences are available, and short contact time is desirable, falling-film evaporators (*Figure 15.10*) have advantages which can enable high concentrations to be achieved. Here, the liquid and vapour flow downwards, and care must be taken with the liquid distribution to the tubes. For good performance, the tubes tend to be rather long. Designs based on plate heat exchangers, but using the climbing- and falling-film concepts in sequence, are used and are reported as having good performance characteristics.

Forced-circulation evaporators

In some cases, particularly where concentrated solutions are produced, the viscosity of the liquid can result in low values of the film coefficient with natural convection, and hence poor heat transfer (unless large temperature differences are used). By promoting the liquid circulation with mechanical pumping, it is possible to ensure high velocities which give large heat transfer coefficients. Taking advantage of this enables boiling to be suppressed in the heating tubes by using an adequate hydrostatic head, which is

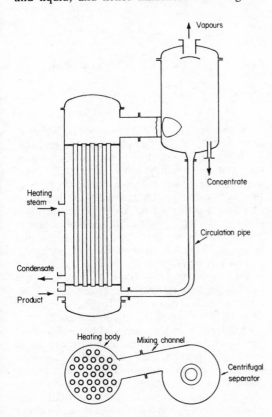

Figure 15.7   Natural-circulation evaporator

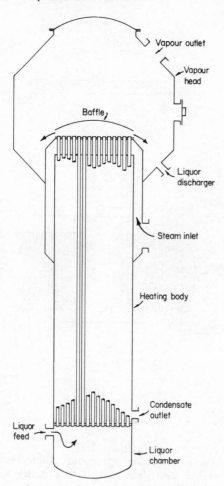

Figure 15.9   Long-tube vertical rising-film evaporator

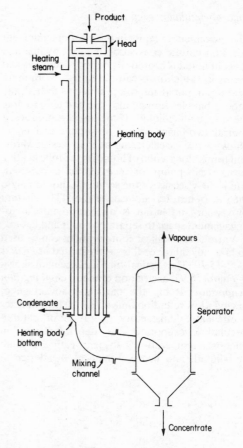

Figure 15.10   Falling-film evaporator

desirable with concentrated liquids if solids deposition can occur. In addition, it is possible to ensure that there is only a small temperature rise in the heating section, by relying on the high re-circulation rates. Typical equipment is shown in *Figures 15.11 – 15.13*. Depending on the site requirements, as well as operational considerations, the heating tubes can be either vertical or horizontal. The superheated liquid flash vaporizes as it enters the separator. If the liquid tends to foam, modified heat exchangers and separators may be necessary.

Using forced circulation enables special heat exchange surfaces to be designed. The heat transfer coefficient is independent of the temperature difference. In addition, by allowing the use of horizontal heating tubes, a more uniform hydrostatic pressure can be maintained, as well as saving headroom if the tubes are long.

A disadvantage of the conventional arrangement is that the liquid hold-up tends to be large. With liquids having high viscosities and where contact time should be short, alternative designs are necessary. One approach, based on a wiped film, is to employ a rotor to sweep the liquid as a film over the heating surface[12]. By employing a slotted rotor it is possible to agitate the film to ensure good heat transfer and enable vapour and liquid to be easily separated. This permits a compact design where the vapours can be condensed internally. It is possible to have a high throughput with relatively compact units and this type of design can handle thermally sensitive material of high viscosity with little difficulty.

Mechanically agitated tanks, either with internal cooling coils or external jackets, have been used for evaporation. They rely on the general agitation caused by the stirrer and the boiling process to give good film heat transfer. Such equipment can be used for small batch operations and offer some advantages for highly viscous liquids such as food products. While good control of product quality is

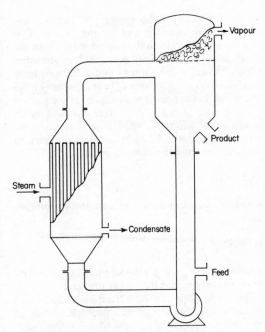

Figure 15.11   Forced-circulation evaporator with external heat exchange

possible, the productivity is low because of the low ratio of heat transfer area to volume of liquid.

15.3   Single-effect evaporation

For continuous operation, whichever type of evaporator is employed, the overall factors governing performance depend on the material balance and heat balance being simultaneously satisfied. These equations give a quantitative description of the changes taking place, and relate them to the operating conditions and the heat transfer characteristics of the equipment. The schematic relationship in *Figure 15.14a* shows the factors involved. The vapour is removed and condensed externally. The heating medium, usually steam, is supplied at pressure P_{s0} and temperature T_{s0} and for most cases, this will be the saturation condition. Where this is so, neglecting any subcooling or flashing of the condensate, this will mean that T_{s1} is the same as T_{s0}.

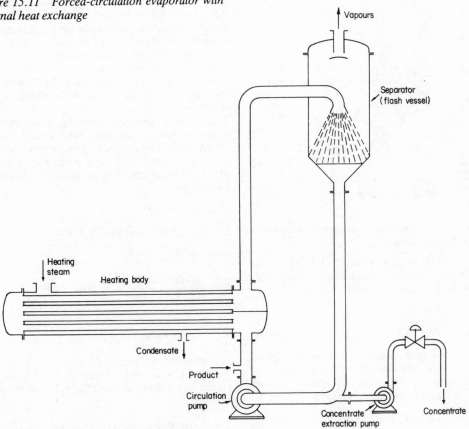

Figure 15.12   Forced-circulation evaporator with horizontal heating body

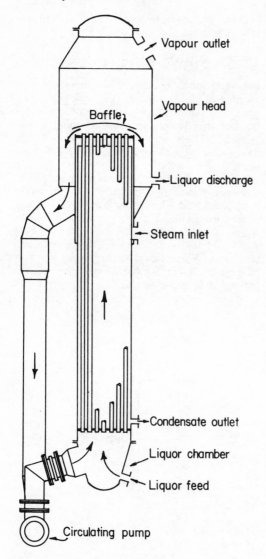

Figure 15.13   Forced-circulation evaporator with internal heat exchange

The changes in concentration of the liquor are described by an overall mass balance together with that of the involatile component, namely

Overall: $F = V + P$ (15.16)

Solute: $Fc_0 = Fc_1$ (15.17)

assuming no solute is carried over in the vapour, where F, V, P, are mass flow rates and c_0, c_1 are mass fractions of the solute. The heat balance, neglecting heat losses, takes the form

$$Fh_F + SH_s = VH_v + Ph_p + Sh_s   \quad (15.18)$$

where h_i refers to the enthalpy of the liquid i, and

H_i the enthalpy of the vapour. 'F' denotes the feed, 'p' the product and 's' the steam. This equation involves both the contributions from the steam and the solution. A further relationship which identifies the contribution is derived from an equation giving the rate of heat transfer Q from the steam to the solution, as required by equation (15.15), i.e. $Q = UA \, \triangle T$. Here $\triangle T$ is a mean temperature difference which is determined by the type of equipment. In addition, the heat given to the solution from the steam is given by

$$Q = S(H_s - h_s)$$

which for condensate at the saturation condition gives

$$Q = S\lambda_s$$

where $\lambda_s \, (= H_s - h_s)$ is the latent heat of vaporization of the steam at the supply pressure.

The equations can be solved simultaneously, given a specification of the problem. Thus, if existing equipment is being used, the overall heat transfer coefficient U and area A, will be known. Also, the condition of the feed will be specified, so that by setting the pressure in the evaporator and knowing the conditions of the steam supply, the production rate can be determined.

More commonly, however, it is desired to calculate the area for a given duty. To illustrate the procedure, consider an example where a 5% solution of NaOH at 70°C is being concentrated to 55% in an evaporator operating at atmospheric pressure. For convenience, take a feed rate of 10 000 kg/h. This imposes no restriction since any other flow rate would result in the size of equipment (A) being scaled proportionately. The mass balance gives

Overall: $10\ 000 = P + V$

Solute: $10\ 000 \times 0.05 = 0.55P$

from which

$$P = \frac{10\ 000 \times 0.05}{0.55} = 909.1 \text{ kg/h}$$

and

$$V = 9090.9 \text{ kg/h}$$

At atmospheric pressure, a 55% solution of NaOH boils at 149°C *(Figure 15.3)*. If saturated steam is available at 160.1°C, 6.2 bar, the heat balance is

$$SH_s + 10\ 000h_F = 9090.9H_v + 909.1h_p + Sh_s$$

and the rate of heat transfer is

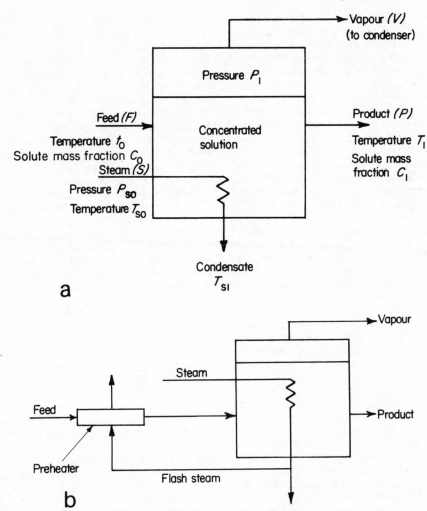

Figure 15.14   (a) Relationship between variables in a single-effect evaporator. (b) Arrangements for preheating of the feed by vapour

$$S(H_s - h_s) = UA \, \triangle T$$

where it is assumed $\triangle T$ is given by $160.1 - 149 = 11.1°C$. *Figure 15.5* gives $h_F = 279$ kJ/kg and $h_p = 756$ kJ/kg. The vapour is at 1 bar, 149°C, so $H_v = 2776.08$. The other enthalpies can be obtained from steam tables, so that

$$S(2756.9 - 676.0) = $$
$$9090.9 \times 2776.08 + 909.1 \times 756 - 10\,000 \times 279$$

hence

$$S = 11\,117.5 \text{ kg/h}$$

The product UA can be obtained as:

$$UA = \frac{S(H_s - h_s)}{\triangle T}$$

$$= \frac{11\,117.5 \times 2080.9}{11.1} \text{ kJ/K h} = 578.9 \text{ kW/K}$$

The heat transfer area will depend on the evaporator design, but to illustrate the method, assume $U = 1200$ W/m² K. Then $A = 482$ m².

Clearly, some refinement will be necessary as more detailed information on the final design becomes available, not least on how $\triangle T$ must be revised, but the procedure is the same. Note that if the boiling point rise had been ignored, $\triangle T$ would have been 60.1°C and this would give a predicted heat transfer area of 99 m². Hence, it is apparent that this effect is very important, and should not be neglected. It effectively reduces the overall available temperature difference by the boiling point rise, and will always be important where there is a significant increase in concentration, as can be seen by reference to *Figure 15.2*. Reducing the pressure will lower the boiling point, but since the BPR will be almost unaffected, it will mean that the available $\triangle T$ will be increased and hence the heat transfer area reduced. However, the lower operating temperature tends to make the solution more viscous which in turn reduces the heat transfer coefficient. Clearly a compromise must be made in the use of the extra energy for operating under vacuum and possibly for agitation of the liquid.

If the feed had been available at 35°C, some of the steam supplied would be required to heat the solution. For these conditions, the steam requirement would be 11 724 kg/h (5.5%). Where preheating is a problem, it is useful to consider taking advantage of the flash steam produced from the condensate which is at 6.2 bar abs. On reducing the pressure to atmospheric, 11.4% of the condensate will flash to produce saturated steam which can be condensed in a preheat exchanger for the feed. If this is done, as shown in *Figure 15.14b*, the steam requirement is reduced to 10 437 kg/h. By failing to take advantage of this, approximately 12% more steam is required. Offsetting this is the need to provide an additional heat exchanger.

Another possibility would be to use the hot condensate to preheat the feed, but this would require a larger heat exchanger because the mean temperature difference would be reduced and advantage would not be taken of the latent heat.

The two factors which are specified as a result of these calculations are the steam requirement and the size of the evaporator, i.e. the heat transfer area. For the single-effect evaporator, the steam requirement is directly linked to the amount of liquid to be evaporated. There is very little scope for reducing this requirement directly, but there is scope for using the vapour produced by employing it as a heating medium for the evaporator. This removes the need for additional condensers and obviously will reduce the net amount of steam requirement for the system. The vapour from the boiling solution will be at the temperature of the solution and pressure of the system. If there were no BPR this would mean that it could be condensed at the same temperature and so could not produce an effective temperature driving force ($\triangle T$). Where there is a BPR, the vapour produced from the solution would be superheated and so condensed at a *lower* temperature so that it could not be used. In order to bring the vapour to a condition which will enable it to be used, it must be compressed, which will further superheat it. If it is then desuperheated, it can be used as part of the evaporator steam supply. The process is conveniently described using the graph in *Figure 15.15*, based on a temperature–entropy plot for water. For simplicity, it is assumed that the vapour produced from the evaporation is at a condition illustrated by point A. If this is on the phase equilibrium line as shown, it implies that the vapour is saturated. A superheated condition would mean that it would be located somewhere to the right of the phase equilibrium, say A'. However, the remaining arguments would be unaffected by this. By compressing the vapour reversibly and adiabatically, i.e. isentropically, the entropy remains constant, so that the final state, depending on the pressure p_2, will be vertically above C, say at point B (or B') which represents a superheated vapour. By adding a sufficient quantity of liquid water, the vapour (at the same pressure, p_2) can be desuperheated so as to bring it to the saturated state, at the condition shown at point C. The appropriate amount of water to be added can be determined by a heat balance. At this new condition, the temperature is T_2 and the vapour can be condensed to produce water at temperature T_2 and at a state corresponding to point D.

The compression has thus resulted in the vapour being condensed at a higher temperature, which will provide the driving force for transfer of heat. This can be achieved by either mechanical recompression, or by use of a steam ejector (*see* Chapter 13). Consequently, the reuse of the vapour for heating has been made possible only by the expenditure of further energy in compressing it so that the resulting condensation temperature gives an acceptable $\triangle T$. The magnitude of the $\triangle T$ is essentially dependent on the compression ratio.

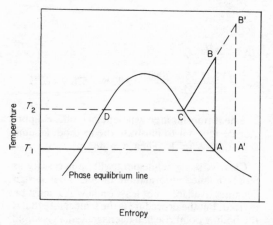

Figure 15.15 Thermodynamic diagram for a vapour recompression cycle

Increasing $\triangle T$ not only tends to save more steam, but will also reduce the heat transfer area.

Operational considerations

The work of compression, and therefore the amount of energy to be supplied, is determined essentially by the pressure ratio. Mechanical compressors usually use electrical drives and this tends to be expensive compared with steam jet compression, as well as requiring more maintenance. Sometimes it is possible to use pass-out turbines to drive a compressor if a suitable steam supply is available from other parts of the site, and the steam can be conveniently used or condensed elsewhere. In this case, the economies can be considerable. Where electrical drives are used, it is desirable that the pressure ratio should be as low as possible if mechanical compressors are being used. To ensure an adequate temperature driving force, a minimum compression ratio of about 2 : 1 is necessary if the vapour produced is not superheated. When the BPR is significant, then the required ratio must be greater, but should preferably not exceed about 2.5 : 1, otherwise steam jet compression tends to become more attractive if a sufficiently high-pressure steam supply is available.

Positive-displacement compressors as an alternative to centrifugal compressors would only be considered for flow rates of less than about 7 kg/h. Commonly, two or more centrifugal units in series are employed (external-flow compressors are not suitable for evaporators because they are vulnerable to corrosion and and solid deposition) and can handle the volume of vapour with no difficulty.

Calculations for a vapour recompression evaporator

For the evaporator considered on p 347, the effect of using vapour recompression can be examined where the operating pressure is (a) atmospheric, and (b) 0.067 bar abs. The resulting configuration is shown schematically in *Figure 15.16*.

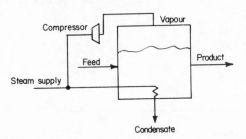

Figure 15.16 Schematic arrangement of equipment for vapour recompression evaporator

(a) It is assumed that the vapour is to be compressed to 6.2 bar abs and desuperheated. In this case a large compression ratio of 6.12 is required.

Assuming isentropic compression, steam at 1 bar, 149°C has an enthalpy of 2774 kJ/kg and this increases to 3208 kJ/kg, and the temperature is 370°C. If water is available at say 30°C to desuperheat the resulting vapour, the amount required is determined by an enthalpy balance.

Let x be the mass of water to be added for each kilogram of vapour. At 30°C the enthalpy of the water is 125.7 kJ/kg, and the enthalpy of saturated steam at 6.2 bar is 2756.9 kJ/kg. Then

$$125.7x + 3208 = 2756.9 (1 + x)$$

from which x = 0.171. Thus for each kilogram of vapour produced, there is available 1.17 kg of saturated steam at the supply pressure.

$$
\begin{aligned}
\text{Total steam available} &= 1.17 \times 9090.9 \\
&= 10\,636.3 \text{ kg/h}
\end{aligned}
$$

The steam required (*see* p 347) is 11 117.5 kg/h. There is therefore a deficiency of 481.2 kg/h of steam.

Obviously, at start-up there must be an adequate supply of steam to bring the system to operating conditions, but thereafter, only a fraction of the total amount required has to be supplied.

The energy necessary to supply the steam is derived from the work of compression which for isentropic compression is equal to the enthalpy change. For each kilogram, the work is 3208 – 2774 = 434 kJ/kg. If all the vapour is compressed, this is 9090.9 × 434 = 3.945 GJ/h but if only sufficient to meet the net steam supply is sent to the compressor, i.e. the excess is not included, this will be 3.818 GJ/h. With an electrical drive of 60% efficiency, this is equivalent to electrical power supply of 1.768 MW.

Using thermocompression, with high-pressure steam available at 15 bar, the net amount of steam required would be 10 630.9 kg/h compared with 11 117.5 kg/h at 6.2 bar. Of the vapour produced, 8612.9 kg/h would have to be condensed. Thus, the reduction in steam would be modest, leaving comparatively large amounts of vapour to be condensed separately.

(b) With an operating pressure of 0.067 bar abs, the boiling point of the solution is 85°C (*Figure 15.3*) and the corresponding boiling point for water would be 38°C. The vapour produced (0.067 bar, 85°C), has an enthalpy of 2660 kJ/kg. Operation at reduced pressure means that a lower-temperature (pressure) steam supply can be used. For convenience, take this pressure to be 1 bar. Compressing the vapour isentropically to this pressure raises its temperature to 400°C and results in an enthalpy of 3278 kJ/kg. The required pressure ratio is 1/0.067 = 15, which is much larger than for case (a).

The water at 30°C required to desuperheat the vapour is given by

$$125.7x + 3278 = 2676\,(1 + x)$$

which gives x as 0.236.

The amount of steam required is found to be 9392.9 kg, which means that the excess steam if all the vapour is compressed would be

$$9090.9 \times 1.236 - 9392.9 = 1843.5 \text{ kg/h}$$

This means that only 7600 kg/h of the vapour needs to be compressed.

The energy requirement, assuming the same efficiency for the drive, is 2.189 MW, which is 26% more than for case (a). It should also be noted that if the value of U were the same, the heat exchanger area for evaporation would be 327 m². At these much lower temperatures,

however, the increased viscosity would probably result in appreciably smaller values of U, say 800 W/m² K. Then the area would be 492 m².

The direct energy costs could be reduced by operating with smaller temperature driving forces across the heat exchanger surfaces, but this would be at the cost of larger equipment. Generally, vapour recompression is used in systems with a low BPR (i.e. less than about 5°C) and hence for fairly dilute solutions (refs 6, 13, 14).

In this case, thermocompression is even less favourable. Assuming steam is available at 5 bar, 9251 kg/h would be required and 8952 kg/h of vapour must be condensed separately, i.e. only about 140 kg/h of the vapour is actually compressed, the steam source providing the rest.

In both the above examples, a very heavy penalty is paid in exploiting the potential economy because of the BPR. Where it is only a few degrees, the picture changes dramatically. For example, in (a), if the boiling point rise were negligible (i.e. solution is at 100°C), the vapour need only be compressed sufficiently to a saturation 11.4°C above the liquid, which implies a compression ratio of 1.50/1.013 = 1.48. Then the enthalpy change is 2756.9 – 2676.0 = 80.9kJ/kg and the energy for compression is 7600 × 80.9 = 614 MJ/h. For a drive of 60% efficiency, this

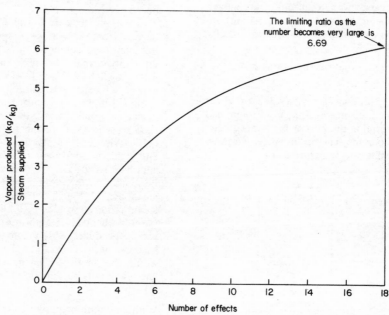

Figure 15.17 Approximate amounts of vapour produced per kilogram of steam supplied, in multiple-effect evaporation

is equivalent to 284 kW, which is much less than the 1.736 MW when the boiling point is significant. To desuperheat the compressed vapour, 0.026 kg water/kg vapour is required which will provide 9329.9 kg steam/h. This means that some make-up steam might be required.

15.4 Multiple-effect evaporation

Instead of compressing the vapour from the evaporator and feeding it back as the heating medium, an alternative approach would be to condense it in another evaporator directly. To make this effective, the boiling point of the solution in this second effect would have to be lower than the condensation temperature of the vapour. This can be achieved by operating the second evaporator at a lower temperature. The vapour from this can be similarly used for another evaporator. Such a procedure is referred to as *multi-effect* evaporation, each evaporator being called an 'effect'. This repeated use of the vapour results in economic use of the steam since, as a first

approximation, 0.9 kg of vapour is produced from the solution for each kilogram of steam condensed. *Figure 15.17* illustrates the benefits which can be realized by employing several stages to reduce the overall steam consumption.

One possible arrangement to take advantage of this is shown in *Figure 15.18*, where the feed and steam are introduced to the same (first) effect and move in the same direction. This is termed 'forward' (or sometimes 'parallel') feed. An alternative arrangement termed 'backward feed' is shown in *Figure 15.19*. The reduced pressure is obtained by applying a vacuum to stage 3 for forward feed and stage 1 for backward feed. When the system settles down to stable operating conditions, all the intermediate stages settle down to reduced pressures and temperatures resulting from the mass and heat balance of the system being satisfied.

Examples of multiple-effect evaporation in industry are given in Chapter 20.

Multiple-effect calculations

Double-effect evaporator

The double-effect forward-feed evaporator shown

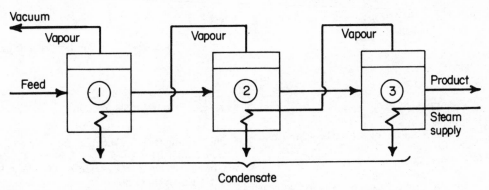

Figure 15.18   Forward-feed multi-effect evaporation

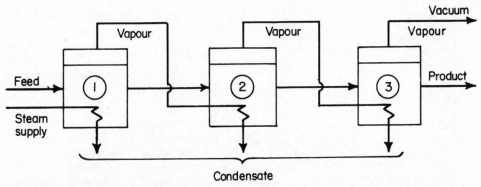

Figure 15.19   Backward-feed multi-effect evaporation

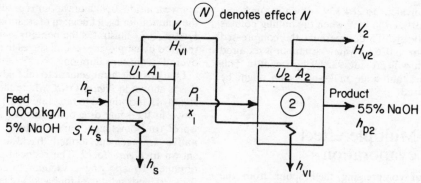

Figure 15.20   Double-effect evaporators

in *Figure 15.20* can be used to illustrate the method of calculation for the above cases. As before, the procedure is based on material and heat balances, but now there is one for each effect. The mass balances become:

Overall $10\,000 = V_1 + V_2 + P_2$

Solute $10\,000 \times 0.05 = 0.55P_2$

$$V_1 + V_2 = 9090.9$$

and $P_2 = 909.1$

Assume that $U_1A_1 = U_2A_2$, and consider the mass balance for each.

For the first effect

Overall $P_1 = V_2 + P_2$

Solute $0.05P_1 = 0.55P_2 = 500$

The heat balance for this effect can be written as

$$10000h_F + SH_s = V_1H_{v1} + P_1h_{p1} + Sh_s$$

In addition, the rate equation for heat exchange is

$$Q_1 = U_1A_1 \, \Delta T_1 = S(H_s - h_s)$$

Similarly, for the second effect

$$P_1h_1 + V_1H_{v1} = V_2H_{v2} + P_2h_{p2} + V_1h_{v1}$$

and

$$Q_2 = U_2A_2 \, \Delta T_2 = V_1(H_{v1} - h_{v1})$$

assuming all the vapour condenses.

If a vacuum is applied to the second effect so that the vapour space is maintained at 0.067 bar abs (saturation temperature 38.7°C), then the boiling point of the solution (from *Figure 15.3*) will be 85°C. From *Figure 15.5*,

$$h_{p2} = 558.2$$

and the boiling-point rise (BPR) is $85 - 38.7 = 46.3°C$.

To proceed further, it is necessary to make some assumption regarding the amount of vapour produced in each effect. Subsequent calculations will then enable this to be checked. As a first guess let:

$$V_1 = V_2 = V = 4545.45$$
$$(\text{since } V_1 + V_2 = 9090.9)$$

hence

$$P_1 = V_2 + P_2 = 4545.45 + 909.1 = 5454.55 \text{ kg/h}$$

and

$$x_1 = \frac{500}{P_1} = 0.092 \text{ mass fraction}$$

From this, the BPR for the first effect is 2.8°C, so that the total BPR = 46.3 + 2.8 = 49.1°C. The maximum available temperature difference for heat transfer is therefore

$$\Delta T_a = T_s - 38.7 - 49.1$$

Assume that saturated steam is supplied at 4.6 bar, 148.9°C. Then $\Delta T_a = 61.1°C$. Since it has been assumed that $V_1 = V_2$, it is reasonable to assume further that $\Delta T_1 = \Delta T_2 = \Delta T = 30.55°C$.

With this information, the temperature of the solution in the first effect must be $148.9 - 30.55 = 118.35°C$, and the equivalent boiling point of water is 2.8°C lower, that is, 115.6°C with a vapour pressure of 1.724 bar abs. Using appropriate charts and tables, the enthalpies of all the streams can be determined and the heat balance on each effect completed.

For the first effect, the steam supply can be calculated:

$$S = \frac{V_1 H_{v1} + P_1 h_{p1} - 10000 h_F}{(H_s - h_s)}$$

$$= \frac{4545 \times 2699.6 + 5454 \times 453.6 - 10000 \times 279}{2744 - 627.3}$$

$$= 5647 \text{ kg/h}$$

Also, from the rate equation

$$U_1 A_1 = \frac{S(H_s - h_s)}{\Delta T} = 391\,260$$

In addition, in effect 2, the rate equation predicts the heat transfer to be $V_1(H_{v1} - h_{v1}) = 10065367$ and $U_2 A_2 = 329471.6$, so that

$$\frac{U_1 A_1 \Delta T_1}{U_2 A_2 \Delta T_2} = \frac{S(H_s - h_s)}{V_1(H_{v1} - h_{v1})} = 1.187 = \frac{\Delta T_1}{\Delta T_2}$$

But $\Delta T_1 + \Delta T_2 = 61$, so that

$$\Delta T_1 = 33 \quad \text{and} \quad \Delta T_2 = 28$$

The adjustments necessary to the BPR are negligible and using the new temperatures, the heat balances can be repeated until the values of $U_1 A_1$ and $U_2 A_2$ agree. Following this iterative procedure, using the adjusted values of ΔT_1 and ΔT_2, results in

$$U_1 A_1 = 3.6 \times 10^5$$

and

$$U_2 A_2 = 3.6 \times 10^5$$

Consider again the heat balances. Effect 1 can be written as

$$10000 h_F + S(H_s - h_s) = P_1 h_{p1} + V_1 H_{v1}$$

$$= V_2 H_{v2} + \overline{P_2 h_{p2}} + V_1 h_{v1} - P_1 h_{p1} + P_1 h_{p1}$$

Also, $V_2 = 9090.9 - V_1$ and substituting for this gives

$$10000 h_F + S(H_s - h_s)$$
$$= (9090.9 - V_1) H_{v2} + P_2 h_{p2} + V_1 h_{v1}$$

Solving for V_1 gives 4582.2 so that

$$V_2 = 4508.7$$

With these revised values for the amount evaporated in each effect, the calculation must be repeated. Thus, the mass balance for the first effect becomes

$$10000 = 4582.2 + P_1$$

$$P_1 = 5417.8$$

and

$$x_1 = \frac{10000 \times 0.05}{5417.8} = 0.092$$

Proceeding as before shows that the revised values for the amounts evaporated in each stage are satisfactory, namely

$$V_1 = 4560 \text{ kg/h}$$

$$V_2 = 4531 \text{ kg/h}$$

and the intermediate concentration of solute is 9%.

The corresponding values of the area–heat transfer factors are

$$U_1 A_1 = 3.6 \times 10^5 \text{ and } U_2 A_2 = 3.6 \times 10^5$$

and

$$S = 5612 \text{ kg/h}$$

In view of the uncertainties of values read from charts, this agreement is satisfactory.

Using backward feed, the corresponding values are

$$V_1 = 4297 \quad \text{and} \quad V_2 = 4794$$

and

$$U_1 A_1 = 4.2 \times 10^5 \quad U_2 A_2 = 3.1 \times 10^5$$

$$S = 5406 \text{ kg/h}$$

which is less than the 5612 kg/h for forward feed. It should be noted that the effect receiving the steam supply benefits from this by evaporating most liquid, as might be anticipated. There is also a marginal gain in using forward feed in terms of reducing the size of units required.

The calculation must proceed by trial and error because no explicit relationships are available for the properties. Having specified the pressure in effect at the opposite end from the cascade, the remaining variables automatically take up values which cause the mass and energy balances to be satisfied.

As noted earlier, the BPR has a very important influence on the heat transfer processes. *Figure 15.21* illustrates how it affects the overall available temperature driving force for the parallel-feed case. It can severely limit the number of effects which it is feasible to use. With more effects, the method of calculation remains the same, but obviously becomes more involved. It involves nested trial and error loops which must be progressively

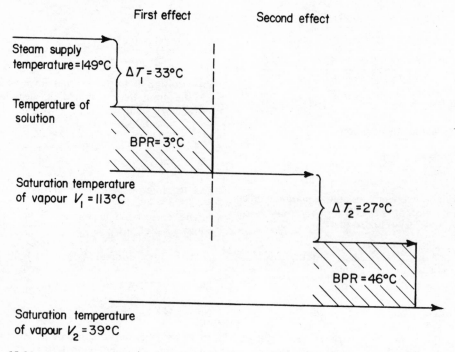

Figure 15.21   Influence of boiling point rise on overall available temperature difference

satisfied. Computer solutions can easily automate this procedure, although there can be problems in representing the data satisfactorily. For manual calculations, the following procedure is convenient if the heat transfer area and the amount of steam are required; it will also give the stage compositions.

The data to be specified are:

(i)   the feed conditions (temperature and composition);
(ii)   product specification (composition);
(iii) configuration of the equipment, including the number of stages;
(iv)   temperature and pressure of the steam supply;
(v)   vacuum pressure; and
(vi)   the desired distribution of (U_iA_i) — not necessarily the absolute values.

1. Determine the temperature, BPR and enthalpy of the last stage, N. For some arrangements, initial guesses may have to be made, e.g. for backward feed.
2. Estimate the amount of vapour produced in each effect.
3. From the mass balance, calculate the interstage flow rates and composition.
4. Calculate the BPR for each effect.
5. Determine the total available temperature difference for heat transfer $\Delta T_a = \Delta T_{ov} -$

BPR_i, where ΔT_{ov} = temperature of steam supply minus the condensation temperature of vapours from the vacuum stage; BPR_i is the boiling point rise in effect i.

6. Assign ΔT_i to each effect such that $\Delta T_a = \Sigma \Delta T_i$.
7. Calculate the temperature of the solution in each effect.
8. Use the heat transfer rate equations and energy balances to calculate V_i.
9. Compare V_i values with the previous estimate. If they disagree, adjust the values and return to step 3, otherwise continue.
10. Calculate U_iA_i from the rate equations.
11. Compare with the specified distribution for U_iA_i : if they do not agree, modify the method of selecting T_i and return to step 6. Otherwise calculate the amount of steam required, S.

If the final values of ΔT_i are not satisfactory, because some of them are unacceptably small, then changes must be made to the original specification, as in the distribution of the (U_iA_i) values or the steam supply pressure. Other variations in the data supplied and information required can easily be accommodated.

Calculations for a triple-effect parallel-feed arrangement for the same general specifications as the double effect give

$V_1 = 3200 \text{ kg/h}$ $V_2 = 2989 \text{ kg/h}$ $V_3 = 2902 \text{ kg/h}$

$\triangle T_1 = 22°C$ $\triangle T_2 = 18°C$ $\triangle T_3 = 19°C$

$S = 3805 \text{ kg/h}$

$U_1 A_1 = U_2 A_2 = 3.9 \times 10^5$ $U_3 A_3 = 3.4 \times 10^5$

As expected, the amount of steam has been reduced, but the capital costs will be higher. Part of this is due to the smaller temperature differences.

A modification of this general approach, making use of flash vaporization after heating the liquid, has been used very successfully in the production of fresh water [15, 16]. Instead of allowing the solution to boil, the liquor is heated and then discharged to a vessel at lower pressure, when some of the liquid flashes off (as occurs during blowdown of condensate).

General comments

Multiple-effect evaporation makes use of the latent heat in the vapours for further heating. The enhanced vaporization is at the cost of additional stages. Using vapour recompression, a compressor will be required to increase the pressure of the vapour produced so that it condenses at a temperature $\triangle T$ degrees higher, where $\triangle T$ is the temperature driving force for heat transfer. A suitable value for $\triangle T$ is determined by balancing the work of compression against the agitation necessary to ensure a reasonable heat transfer coefficient and hence a small heat exchanger area. As the BPR becomes greater this becomes less attractive since vapour pressure increases exponentially with temperature and hence results in large pressure ratios. Bearing in mind the equivalent power input to the compressor, although it may be roughly equivalent to 30 or more stages of a multi-effect cascade, because of the difference in cost of steam and electrical power, it tends to be reduced to approximately 10–15. Thermo-recompression has operational advantages in not requiring moving parts and is easily maintained. However, it does require a high-pressure steam supply and consideration

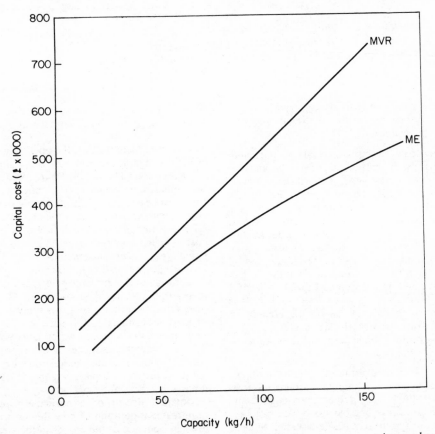

Figure 15.22   Typical capital cost v. capacity for mechanical vapour recompression and multiple-effect evaporator systems

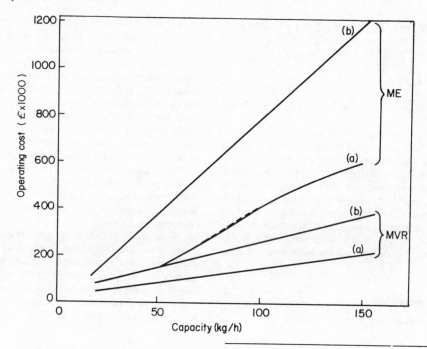

Figure 15.23 Operating costs for mechanical vapour recompression (MVR) and multiple-effect (four-stage ME) evaporators. The 1973 costs are given opposite

	(a)	*(b)*
Steam (£/t)	1.35	2.80
Electricity (£/MWh)	7.50	12.50
Water ((£/m³) × 10⁻²)	1.1	1.75

needs to be given to alternative approaches such as driving a turbine and using the exhaust steam as the heating medium.

It is important to emphasize that each particular problem must be considered separately, and it is not possible to draw general conclusions. Nevertheless, it is useful to examine a case study to gain some insight as to the comparison between the different approaches. Clearly, any such comparison will depend on relative costs, and in order to illustrate this, it is useful to consider the influence of these costs. *Figure 15.22* shows the capital cost of vapour recompression (MVR) and multiple-effect (ME) evaporators for various capacities at 1973 prices[13], where the duty can justify MVR. It is obvious that the capital charges are greater for MVR and increase linearly, whereas there is less than a proportionate increase for ME cascades as the capacity increases.

In terms of total plant requirements, multiple-effect evaporation may require a cooling tower in addition to the process and ancillary equipment, which occupies considerable space. A vapour recompression system requires less steam, hence a smaller boiler (to start up) and no cooling tower. The principal disadvantage of MVR, however, is

that compressors are very expensive, and this tends to make the overall capital cost higher than multi-effect systems.

To compensate for this, the operating costs for MVR are significantly smaller, especially at high capacities, as can be seen in *Figure 15.23*. In order to emphasize how relative costs influence the picture, two cases are illustrated which show the consequences of increases in energy prices. It is apparent that the rate of increase in operating costs is higher for multiple-effect systems as well as being greater in absolute value.

While it is not possible to generalize these results, it does suggest that for large plants, as energy costs increase, MVR should be considered. Clearly, the question of whether or not it is suitable will also depend on technical factors such as BPR and the viscosity of the solution, which does not favour MVR, although it can be used for preliminary concentration. Thermocompression is best used in conjunction with ME plant (*Figure 15.24*) because it has a low thermal efficiency.

Detailed design of a particular application requires consideration of how the most effective use can be made of the energy in the steam. Not only does this mean that the supply pressure is important, but the use of heat exchangers to re-

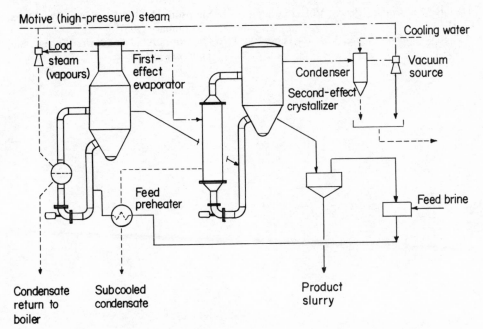

Figure 15.24 Typical arrangements of multiple-effect evaporation with thermocompression

cover heat from vapours or hot product streams should be examined. For high-pressure supplies, there is the possibility of using turbines to drive a mechanical compressor or provide steam for a thermocompressor. This latter can be useful where heat-sensitive materials are being processed. Normally, simply throttling the steam does not make the best use of the energy in it.

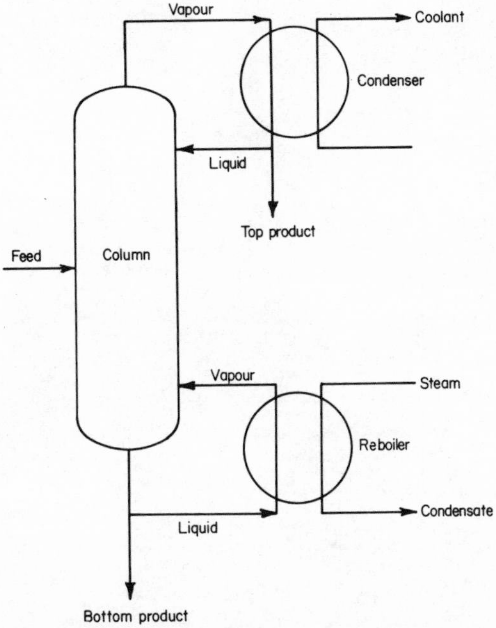

References

1 Patterson, W. C. and Wells, T. A. *Chem. Engng,* Vol. 79, Sept. 26 (1977).
2 Null, H. R. *Chem. Eng. Progr.,* Vol. 56, July (1976).
3 O'Brian, N. A. *Chem. Eng. Progr.,* Vol. 65, July (1976).
4 Bennett, R. C. *Chem. Eng. Progr.,* Vol. 67, July (1978).
5 Casten, J. W. *Chem. Eng. Progr.,* Vol. 61, July (1978).
6 Rozycki, J. *Chem. Eng. Progr.,* Vol. 69, May (1976).
7 Dodge, B. F. *Chemical Engineering Thermodynamics.* New York: McGraw-Hill (1944).
8 McCabe, W. L. *Trans. Am. Inst. Chem. Engrs.,* Vol. 31, p. 129 (1935).
9 Bosnjakovic. *Technische Thermodynamik.* Leipzig: T. Steinkopff (1935).
10 Usher, T. D. *NEL Report No. 329,* Section 3.3, January (1969).
11 Usher, T. D. *NEL Report No. 329,* Sections 3.1, 3.2, January (1969).
12 Coulson, J. M. *NEL Report No. 329,* p.6, January (1967).

Figure 15.25 Schematic arrangement for vapour recompression in a distillation column

13 Gray, R. M. *Chem. Proc.*, Vol. 35, Sept. (1974)

14 Cole, J. W. *Chem. Engng*, Vol. 76, February (1975).

15 Simpson, H. C. *NEL Report No. 329*, Section 4.2, January (1967).

16 Dickson, A. N. *Chem. Engng*, Vol. 79, February (1976).

16

Steam as a process material

16.1 Introduction

Steam is used in a wide range of industrial chemical processes as a reactant, as a diluent or moderator, and as a reaction heat transfer medium. Examples of such processes are the steam cracking of light oils for ethylene manufacture, partial oxidation of heavy fuel oils to produce hydrogen or synthesis gas, and coal and oil gasification processes. However, its most widespread current use as a reactant is in the catalytic steam reforming of petroleum refinery products for the manufacture of gas mixtures for fuel or for chemical synthesis. Steam reforming processes are used throughout the world in the chemical, oil refinery and gas industries.

In any gasification process, the hydrogen/carbon ratio of the product gas is higher than that of the oil or coal feedstock. Gasification therefore involves the increase of this ratio by the addition of hydrogen, the removal of carbon, or both. Steam is the cheapest and most readily available source of hydrogen for this purpose; in addition, upon decomposition, its oxygen content combines with part of the carbon from the feedstock to form carbon dioxide. This compound can subsequently be removed from the gas mixture by a number of well-known processes, thereby achieving partial removal of carbon.

16.2 Steam reforming processes

In the steam reforming process, light hydrocarbon feedstock such as natural gas, liquefied petroleum gas, naphtha, or in some cases heavier distillate oils, after being purified from sulphur compounds, are reacted with steam over a nickel-containing catalyst to produce a mixture of hydrogen, methane and carbon oxides. Essentially total decomposition of compounds containing more than one carbon atom per molecule is obtained.

Steam reforming in industrial practice falls into two main classes, according to the catalyst type and reactor equipment used: hydrogen production by high-temperature reforming, generally at above 700°C, and methane manufacture by low-temperature reforming at below 550°C.

The amount of steam consumed by reaction in the overall process depends upon the choice of product gas. Taking the formula of a petroleum naphtha, per atom of carbon, as approximately CH_2 (such hydrocarbons would typically have about six to eight carbon atoms per molecule), the extreme cases are:

$$4\,CH_2 + 2\,H_2O \rightarrow 3\,CH_4 + CO_2 \qquad (16.1)$$

Steam reacted = 0.5 mol/atom carbon
(0.64 kg/kg naphtha)

$$4\,CH_2 + 8\,H_2O \rightarrow 12\,H_2 + 4\,CO_2 \qquad (16.2)$$

Steam reacted = 2.0 mol/atom carbon
(2.6 kg/kg naphtha)

In practice, total consumption of steam by reaction as indicated by equations (16.1) and (16.2) is never achieved (despite total decomposition of the hydrocarbon), because both the methane reforming (16.3) and carbon monoxide shift (16.4) reactions approach a thermodynamic equilibrium instead of proceeding to completion:

$$CH_4 + H_2O \rightleftharpoons CO + 3\,H_2 \qquad (16.3)$$

$$CO + H_2O \rightleftharpoons CO_2 + H_2 \qquad (16.4)$$

Steam is a reactant in both of these reactions, which are reversible over the catalyst. The equi-librium composition of the product gas mixture can be altered by choice of suitable temperature, pressure and steam/feedstock ratio (*see Figure 16.1*) to produce a gas mixture consisting largely of methane or largely of hydrogen with varying proportions of carbon monoxide, in each case with some carbon dioxide which can subsequently be removed.

It is often convenient to use more than one reaction stage, to modify the gas mixture produced from the primary gasification step towards the desired composition.

The need for excess steam

As noted above, some excess of steam over that indicated by reactions (16.1) or (16.2) will always be required because, at equilibrium, some steam remains unreacted in the product gas mixture. At equilibrium, if additional (excess) steam is added, reactions (16.3) and (16.4) will proceed in the direction of consumption of steam. Thus if it is desired to produce mixtures of H_2 and CO, with little CH_4, further excess steam is added to force reaction (16.3) to the right.

A further reason for the addition of excess steam is the need in all cases to force reaction (16.4) to the right so that the concentration of carbon monoxide is lowered to a level below which carbon deposition will not occur at equilibrium

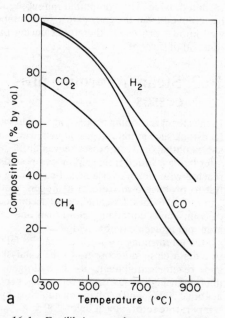

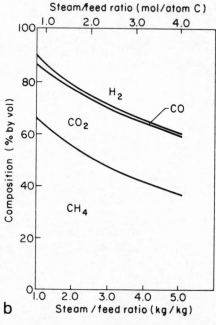

a

b

Figure 16.1   Equilibrium product gas compositions (dry basis) from steam reforming of light naphtha at 24.1 bar. (a) Varying temperature, steam/feed ratio 1.6 kg/kg; (b) varying steam/feed ratio, temperature 550°C

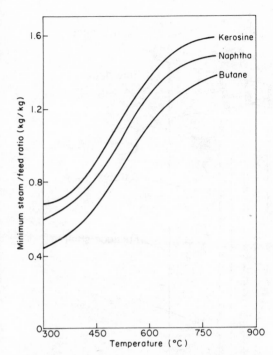

Figure 16.2   Variation with temperature of minimum steam/feedstock ratio to avoid carbon deposition. Pressure 25 bar

according to the Boudouard reaction:

$$2\,CO \rightleftharpoons CO_2 + C \qquad (16.5)$$

There is therefore a certain minimum amount of steam required and this quantity depends on temperature, as shown in *Figure 16.2*.

Finally, with the catalysts currently available for either high- or low-temperature reforming, excess steam is required to maintain a good catalyst life by avoiding the deposition of carbonaceous materials on the catalyst owing to side reactions.

Disadvantages of excess steam

The necessary use of excess steam leads to high running costs of the process because of the fuel required to supply its sensible and latent heat. Although the latent heat of the excess steam is subsequently released upon cooling the product gases, the temperature of condensation is lower than the original boiler temperature because the steam is diluted with other gases, so the heat cannot be recycled by raising high-pressure process steam. Excess steam also leads to increases in equipment costs because of increased boiler capacity and increased volume of all the process vessels to handle the larger volumetric flow rate of the gas–steam mixture.

Steam generation

Steam for process use must be generated at a pressure at least as great as the process pressure, typically 20–50 bar. The process steam can be used as a power source by generating at higher pressures, up to 100 bar, and supplying to the process via pass-out or back-pressure turbines. At these pressures, very high-quality feedwater is required, of similar specification to that for electric power-station boilers, to ensure trouble-free boiler operation. Also certain contaminants need to be removed to very low levels, to prevent deterioration of the catalysts when the steam is used in the reforming process. The quantities of steam involved can be very great: for example, a typical large plant, as used in the USA, producing $3.4 \times 10^6\,Nm^3/d$ of methane as a supplement for natural gas (SNG), requires about 250000 kg/h of high-pressure process steam. Since this is an essential reactant and is also required to protect the catalyst from carbon deposition, a secure supply of process steam is essential for safe and reliable operation and the best boiler practice has to be observed.

16.3 High-temperature reforming

Operation of the steam reforming process at high temperatures, low pressures and high steam/feedstock ratios favours the production of hydrogen and carbon oxides according to the equilibria of reactions (16.3) and (16.4). At high temperatures, a catalyst of relatively low activity can be used, containing a low percentage of nickel metal. The high-temperature reforming process and catalyst was pioneered by Imperial Chemical Industries (ICI) Ltd, and the first commercial plant, reforming a mixed-gas feedstock at atmospheric pressure, was built in 1936. Later catalyst and process developments have enabled operation at progressively higher pressures, up to about 30 bar, and on heavier feedstocks, from ethane to petroleum naphtha. The process is now used widely for the manufacture of hydrogen, synthesis gases for the production of ammonia, methanol and higher alcohols, and fuel gas. It can also be used for the production of reducing gas for steelmaking. The ICI steam–naphtha process is the most widely used for naphtha feedstocks, boiling up to 220°C.

The steam/feedstock ratio is determined largely by the desired product composition and ranges from about 2 kg/kg (1.8 mol/atom C) to 7 kg/kg (6.2 mol/atom C). The reformer outlet temperature is usually in the range 750–850°C. At these temperatures, the overall reactions taking place require a net supply of heat, and it is conventional to operate with reactant preheat temperatures below the outlet temperature, requiring an ad-

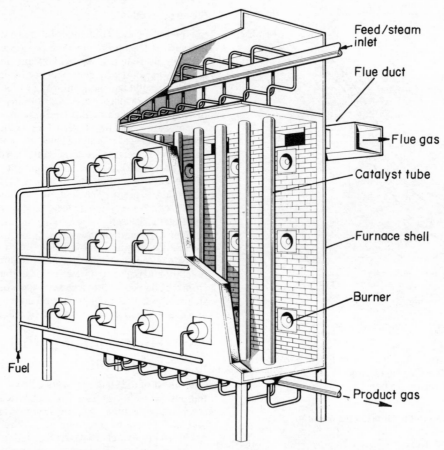

Figure 16.3   Simplified diagram of a small, side-fired high-temperature tubular reformer

ditional heat input. The reactor design evolved to supply this heat into the reaction zone consists of a series of catalyst-filled tubes suspended or supported in a furnace (*see Figure 16.3*). The tubes are made of high-alloy stainless steels, typically about 100 mm in diameter and up to 12 m long. The largest reformers have over six hundred such tubes. The metallurgical limits of the tube material set a limit to the combination of pressure and outlet temperature that can be achieved.

At the steam/feed ratios normally used, the initial product gas from the reformer contains a substantial amount of carbon monoxide, which is not wanted if hydrogen or ammonia is the desired final product. If the gas is subsequently contacted with reforming catalyst at reduced temperature, reaction (16.3) will proceed to the left with an undesirable net consumption of hydrogen. However, catalysts are available which will promote reaction (16.4) but not reaction (16.3). Thus in the commercial process, the gas is passed over one or more beds of such catalyst at temperatures in the range 250–550°C, resulting in conversion of much

of the carbon monoxide by reaction with steam already present in the mixture and the production of additional hydrogen. Additional steam may be added to maximize the carbon monoxide conversion. The carbon dioxide can then be readily removed to leave a hydrogen-rich product gas. Final traces of carbon oxides may be converted to methane, if required, by carrying out the reverse of reaction (16.3) over a catalyst at about 300°C. A simplified diagram of a complete plant is shown in *Figure 16.4*.

Steam balance and heat recovery

In the main reformer furnace, the catalyst tubes are relatively widely spaced to provide reasonably uniform heat flux, and the reaction outlet temperatures are high. Thus the flue gases emerge at high temperature and heat utilization of the fuel burnt in the furnace is only about 50% of the gross heating value. Furthermore, the product gas leaving the reforming tubes at up to 900°C will release large quantities of sensible heat, in addition to

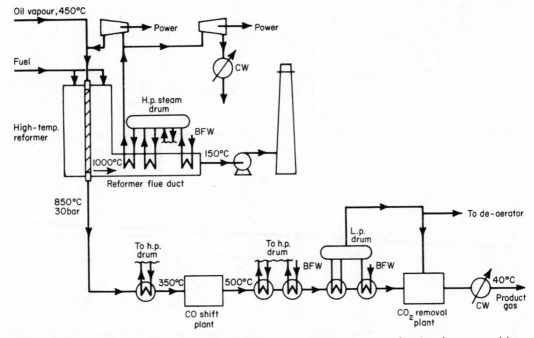

Figure 16.4 Simplified flowsheet for a high-temperature reforming process, showing the steam-raising system. BFW, boiler feedwater; CW, cooling water

heat of condensation of the unreacted excess steam, as it is cooled towards ambient temperature. The process will have a very low overall efficiency unless these large quantities of heat are efficiently recovered; the raising of steam at various pressures, superheating and feedwater heating are excellent means of recovering this heat, as shown in *Figure 16.4*. In particular, the above duties are the preferred method for heat recovery from the reformer flue gas because, compared with the heating of hydrocarbon streams, they avoid the danger of fire if there is any leakage in the flue bank heat exchangers. Because of the high temperatures and low fuel efficiency, the amounts of high-pressure steam that may be generated from waste heat are normally in excess of the process requirements; any surplus may be used in condensing turbines for power generation or exported from the plant for other uses. In some applications, there are large power requirements for gas compression because the reformer pressure is restricted to about 30 bar but the product gas may be required at much higher pressures — for example, hydrogen for refinery hydrocracking of heavy oils at 100–140 bar or for ammonia synthesis at 150–350 bar; the total power requirements for a 1000 t/d ammonia plant are about 30 MW. As much steam as possible is raised at 70–100 bar and used to generate shaft or electric power in back-pressure or pass-out turbines before being supplied

as reformer process steam or at lower pressures for other uses, such as in the carbon dioxide removal unit. A simplified steam balance for a plant based on high-temperature reforming is shown in *Figure 16.5*.

The overall high-temperature steam reforming process is thus a classic example of the efficient utilization of steam within the constraint of a fixed steam requirement, by careful design of the steam-raising system and multiple use of the steam.

16.4 Low-temperature reforming

Operation of the process at low temperatures, high pressures and low steam/feedstock ratios favours the production of methane via the equilibria (16.3) and (16.4). Operation at lower temperatures requires a much more active catalyst than is used in high-temperature reforming; a catalyst containing a high percentage of nickel is usually employed. The most successful process of this type is the British Gas Catalytic Rich Gas (CRG) Process, based on catalyst and process development by Dr F. J. Dent of the Gas Council in the 1950s. Petroleum distillates as heavy as kerosine (boiling range 150–250°C) can be used as feedstock. CRG-based processes have been widely used in the UK and are currently used in Europe,

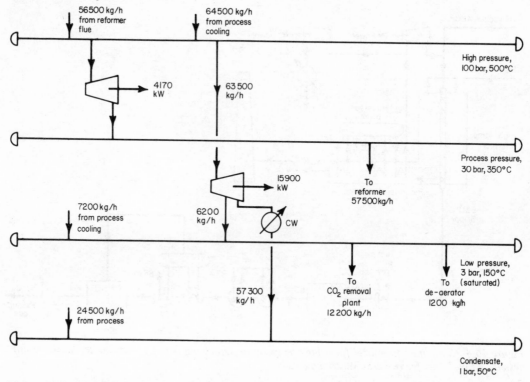

Figure 16.5   Simplified steam and power balance for a high-temperature reforming process

Japan and the USA as the basis of the production of fuel gases of calorific value about 19 MJ/m³ and substitute natural gas (SNG) of calorific value 37–39 MJ/m³. Since the product gas from a primary CRG stage is an ideal feedstock (in place of natural gas) for the high-temperature reforming process described above, a CRG-based step can also be used for the primary oil gasification in synthesis gas manufacture, exploiting the ability of the process to handle heavier distillate feedstocks than can be economically used directly in high-temperature reforming.

The dry product gas from a CRG reactor has a calorific value of about 25 MJ/m³. Conventional town gas (19 MJ/m³) can be made by high-temperature reforming of part of the CRG product gas and mixing the resulting product gas with the remaining methane-rich CRG gas; this overall route is known as the CRG Series 'A' process.

The primary CRG reactor is usually operated at 400–550°C and at pressures up to 70 bar, depending on feedstock. Under these conditions, the gasification reactions involve a moderate net production of heat, which causes a small rise in temperature across the reactor. A very simple and inexpensive reactor design can therefore be used, consisting of a single pressure vessel, containing a fixed bed of catalyst of up to about 4 m in diameter.

To increase the methane content in the product gas, equilibrium (16.3) requires the steam/feedstock ratio to be as low as possible, consistent with complete gasification of the feedstock.

The minimum steam/feedstock ratio is limited in practice with liquid feedstocks to 1.3–2.0 kg/kg, depending on the feedstock (compared with the reaction requirement of 0.64 kg/kg shown in equation (16.1)), jointly by the need to obtain good catalyst performance and to avoid carbon deposition on the catalyst by the Boudouard reaction (16.5). There is, however, scope for further reduction of steam/feedstock ratios by careful process design and by catalyst development, as shown later.

For good catalyst life with naphtha feedstocks, the minimum temperature for oil gasification is normally about 400–500°C. Under these conditions of excess steam and temperature, the product gas, while rich in methane, contains substantial amounts of hydrogen and carbon monoxide, quantities which are not normally acceptable in SNG. These gases can be subsequently largely converted to additional methane and carbon dioxide by simultaneously forcing the equilibria (16.3) to the left and (16.4) to the right over further beds of similar catalyst, by the use of lower temperatures. The reverse of reaction (16.3) is also favoured by lower

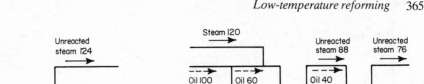

(a) CRG only
Overall steam/feed ratio 2.0 kg/kg

(b) CRG plus hydrogasification
40% of oil to hydrogasification
Overall steam/feed ratio 1.2 kg/kg

Basis: 100 kg/h oil (total). Steam/feed ratio in CRG stage 2.0 kg/kg

Figure 16.6   The effect of hydrogasification on overall steam utilization in the British Gas CRG process

steam/gas ratios. Such process steps, called methanation, are possible because in the absence of oil, the catalyst can convert the gas mixture at temperatures down to 250°C. One or two stages of methanation can be used depending on the methane content required in the final gas. The steam/gas ratio can be reduced if required by partial condensation by cooling the gas mixture to 120–150°C prior to methanation. The steam rate can be reduced without incurring carbon deposition because of the lower temperature of operation, as shown in *Figure 16.2*.

The minimum temperature for the initial oil gasification is limited to the above values if steam is used as the sole gasifying agent. This limits the minimum steam/feedstock ratio as shown in *Figure 16.2*. However, the important discovery was made that additional oil feedstock could be gasified, and at lower temperatures, in the product mixture of gas and unreacted steam from the primary CRG reactor without the need to add extra steam. This process variant is called *hydrogasification*. When considering an overall combination of CRG and hydrogasification, where up to half of the total oil can be supplied to the hydrogasification stage, the total steam used (*see Figure 16.6*) is only equivalent to that needed in the CRG stage, i.e. as little as half that required if all the oil were to be gasified in the CRG stage alone at an acceptable catalyst performance.

The overall steam/carbon ratio thus approaches more closely the minimum limit set by the onset of Boudouard carbon deposition at the hydrogasifier conditions, which at the lower temperatures of hydrogasification will be less than that in the CRG stage, as shown in *Figure 16.2*.

A similar effect to hydrogasification can be achieved within the initial CRG reactor by recirculation of hot product gases around the reactor. The

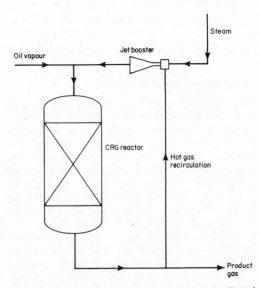

Figure 16.7   Hot gas recirculation around a British Gas CRG reactor driven by a steam jet booster

reaction steam, generated at higher than process pressure, can be used as a source of motive power for this. Although a combination of back-pressure turbine and compressor is an obvious choice, a more elegant solution which eliminates the need to cool the recirculated gas can be adopted, namely the use of a steam-driven jet booster — a large, high-pressure version of a steam ejector (*see Figure 16.7*). This has the great advantages of low cost and absence of moving parts, minimizing maintenance requirements, and further acts as an excellent steam/gas mixing device for introducing the process steam to the reaction system. The operation of steam jet boosters is explained in more detail in Chapter 13.

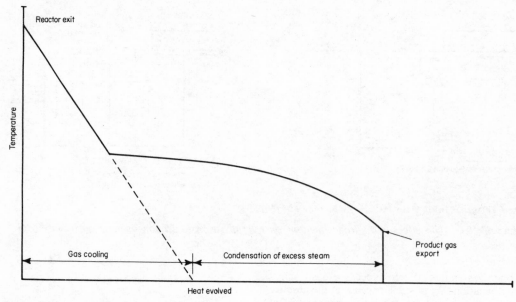

Figure 16.8   *The effect of condensation of excess steam on the heat release from cooling process gas*

Steam balance and heat recovery

Because of the lower temperatures of operation, less fuel is burned in the low-temperature reforming process and the overall process is thus inherently more efficient than high-temperature reforming. Although there is therefore much less waste heat recoverable from hot process gases and furnace flues, heat recovery by steam-raising from waste heat is still an important feature, recovering up to 11% of the total thermal input, up to 7% in the form of high-pressure process steam. The overall thermal efficiency thereby achieved by a CRG-methanation process is an impressive 90–92%. The steam generated from these sources is less than the process requirement and is supplemented from a fuel-fired boiler. There is therefore a direct benefit in fuel and boiler costs if the overall process steam requirement can be reduced, and the further reduction in boiler fuel possible with hydrogasification increases the overall efficiency to up to 95% — a classic example of the efficient use of steam by modifying the process to reduce the steam requirements.

16.5 Heat recovery using low-pressure steam

In both high- and low-temperature reforming processes, the unreacted process steam condenses from the product gas at relatively low temperatures, typically below 200°C (*see Figure 16.8*). The latent heat of condensation can be recovered, but at temperatures too low for process steam raising and in amounts in excess of those required for feedwater heating. However, this heat can be used for raising low-pressure steam (at 1–3 bar and boiler temperatures of 130–150°C), which is required by the CO_2 removal plant at the rate of 1–2 kg steam/kg CO_2 removed. As the excess steam used in the gasification process is reduced, this source of heat is reduced and ultimately for low-temperature reforming, the low-pressure steam demands for CO_2 removal can limit the overall efficiency by requiring supplementary boiler fuel. However, steam is not consumed by reaction in this step but merely used as a heating and stripping medium, after which it is discarded at a slightly reduced temperature. It is possible to recycle the associated latent heat within the process by systems such as heat pumps, and such techniques are being pursued by the developers of CO_2 removal processes.

16.6 Summary

Steam is the key process reactant of both high- and low-temperature steam reforming processes. The heat demands for steam raising determine the fuel requirements, and hence overall efficiency, of the process. Thus the efficient use of steam has been a major goal in the development of steam reforming processes. The high-temperature reforming process is a classic example of how, in a situation where the quantity of steam required is fixed by other considerations, efficiency may still be improved by multiple use of the steam at several pressure levels. The low-temperature reforming process is a classic example of how careful process design can significantly improve the efficiency of an already efficient process by reducing the net steam requirements.

17

Steam demand and production

17.1 The pattern of steam demand

No industrial demands for steam are absolutely constant, whether they are for process steam or for power generation. Steam flow recorders commonly show great fluctuations in both the short and the long term. There are moment to moment variations in demand, often of high magnitude and occurring very rapidly, but the steam boiler is a relatively sluggish piece of equipment, since the heat input cannot be increased sufficiently rapidly to follow rapid changes in steam demand.

However, a boiler and its steam pipework contain much steam and hot water in which fluctuations of pressure provide a reservoir of steam from which the peaks of demand can be supplied. The size of this reservoir can be deliberately increased if this is desirable. There will be slower variations (which the boiler can follow) during the day, particularly if the factory does not operate three shifts, because with daily operation load has to be built up each morning. Even for three-shift factories working a five-day week there will be weekly variations. There will also be annual variations, particularly where steam is used for space heating, and in some industries there are seasonal variations. The latter are particularly prominent in factories working in connection with agricultural processes where the harvest may determine the demand. There are some cases, particularly in canning factories, in which the product can be stored in some intermediate state, as for instance in canning peas where 'garden peas' may be canned very shortly after picking and 'processed peas' may be stored for off-peak canning. In other cases, for instance beet sugar making, the factory works a 'campaign' to treat the harvest quickly since the sugar content falls after a while, and in such cases much plant may be idle before the harvest. It is vital that all the plant needed to process a crop like this should be available when required, since delay may lead to ruin of the crop. Thus good use must be made of the off-load season to ensure availability when steam is needed.

Typical daily and annual steam demand patterns are shown in *Figures 17.1* and *17.2*.

The proportion of total costs represented by steam production and distribution (including overhead costs) varies widely with the production

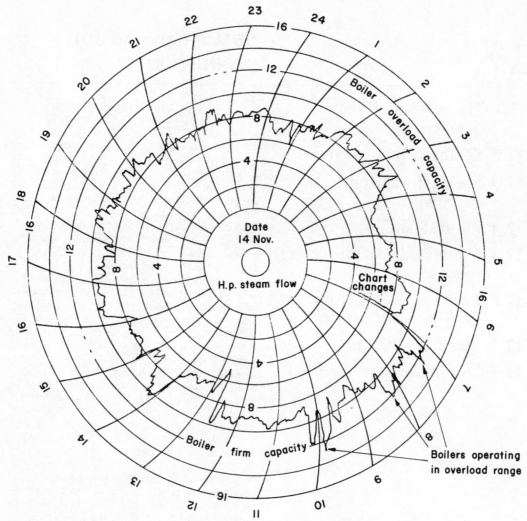

Figure 17.1   Typical steam load variation in a normal production day at a brewery

process in the factory concerned, but in most cases it is far from being the largest factor and frequently is very small. Whilst therefore economy in steam supply is important, measures to reduce steam costs must always be considered in the wider context of works costs as a whole. Economies in steam plant installation leading to a considerable reduction in product output during steam plant outage will in most cases lead to increases in total costs, and thus the steam engineer should always consult his colleagues dealing with the whole range of the factory's activities before making decisions concerning plant installation and operation. It is often forgotten that the factory exists to make its products, not steam. It is only when steam is not available when required that its cost may be high; in this situation lack of steam leads to loss of product output. Thus availability tends to

be more important than heat, and ability to plan maintenance is more important to the works engineer than familiarity with the niceties of thermodynamics.

Steam-using processes in factories fall into two main classes, continuous processes and batch-type processes, and the difference between them must be taken into account when deciding the amount of boiler plant to be installed. In continuous processes the steam requirements will be substantially constant once the plant is up to temperature, and thus the boiler plant needed must be adequate for this continuous load together with the requirements of the initial warming up in a reasonable time. If operation is for seven days a week for long runs, then the warming-up time will be relatively small and since it is in any case likely that spare boiler plant will be provided to cover breakdowns

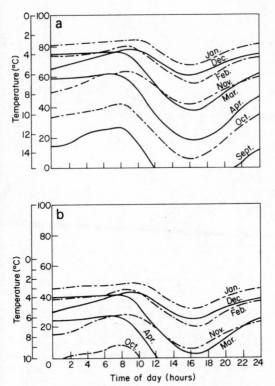

Figure 17.2   *Typical factory space heating demand over the course of a year. (a) Weekdays; (b) weekends (works heated only to 10°C)*

and maintenance, this spare plant should be available to provide for extra steam to speed the warming-up process. When a factory works a five-day week the warming up will be a weekly matter and the time it takes becomes of greater importance. Moreover it is less likely that the spare plant will be available every week. It will be necessary therefore for the factory manager to judge whether or not extra boiler capacity is justified by the extra production it makes possible. Nice judgement is needed when planning a steam installation, and this is discussed in Section 17.7.

In batch-type processes the fundamental difference is that the time cycle is faster. There will be a warming-up period, during which the steam demand will be high so as to get the production process going as quickly as possible, a reaction time of constant demand, and a discharge/recharge time in which the demand is virtually zero. Most batch-type processes involve a number of batches being processed simultaneously. The curve of steam demand against time will not be a regular shape but it will be repeated, and if all the batches are started at the same time there will be a period of high demand, followed by a period of lower

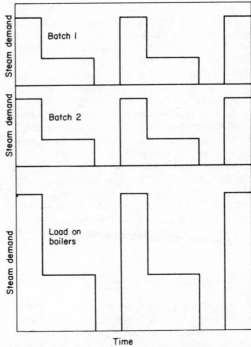

Figure 17.3   *Total steam demand for a two-batch process, not staggered*

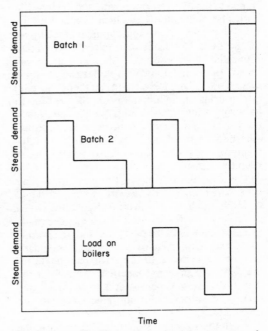

Figure 17.4   *Total steam demand for a staggered two-batch process*

demand and a period of zero demand, loads which are inconvenient and expensive to supply. *Figure*

17.3 shows the addition of two such batches while *Figure 17.4* shows that if the batches are staggered in time the load is more constant. The figures are, of course, smoothed and it is unlikely that a completely uniform demand will result, but even if there are short peaks above the constant-demand curve the fact that they are likely to be short means that it will be possible to supply them. This can be done by allowing some fluctuations of steam pressure, thus using the steam and water spaces of the boiler and the steam pipes as a steam accumulator, instead of having to install more boilers to carry longer peaks and risking blow-off during the zero-demand periods. The greater the number of batches being processed simultaneously, the greater the chance of being able to programme operations and to smooth out the boiler load, and therefore the greater fuel economy.

17.2 Steam storage in boilers

No boiler that supplies saturated steam can follow changes in the demand for steam while maintaining the steam pressure absolutely constant. Nor can a boiler supplying superheated steam maintain constant temperature and pressure. When the load is increased, the boiler heat supply does not rise immediately to keep pace with the increase in load, and momentarily the heat supplied by the boiler as steam exceeds that supplied to the boiler by the fuel. This leads to a fall in temperature within the boiler, causing a fall in pressure of the steam. In a hand-controlled boiler the operator notices the fall in pressure and can then adjust the rate of firing of the fuel to restore the pressure to its normal value. If the load falls, the steam pressure will rise and he will reduce the rate of firing. Alternatively the changes can be made by an automatic control system. If the control system tries to keep the pressure very close to normal then there will be continuous changes in firing and while close control of firing is possible with gaseous or liquid fuels it is much more difficult with solid fuels. The control system is therefore designed so that no action is taken until the deviation from the normal value exceeds a certain value, which should be based on experience of the error reasonable for the particular process concerned. The closer the control the more expensive it is likely to be, and there is no substitute for informed judgement on such matters.

When the steam pressure falls, the water in the boiler water space will be temporarily at a temperature greater than saturation temperature and so water will be evaporated ('flashed') until the temperature again reaches saturation temperature. The water content of the boiler is in effect a store

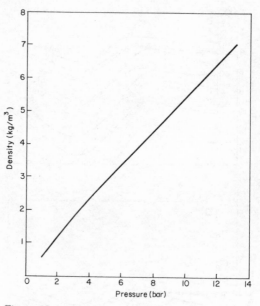

Figure 17.5   Density of saturated steam

of heat, and so of steam, and this cushions the boiler until the rate of firing can again keep pace with the demand for steam. A boiler has a steam space as well as a water space; if the pressure falls this reduces the density of the steam, and hence reduces the mass of steam that can be contained in the steam space. The difference is a further cushion for changes in steam demand. *Figure 17.5* plots the density of saturated steam v. pressure. If we take a fall in temperature of 5°C as being the effect of a certain increase in load (and it is the temperature rather than the pressure change which is fundamental) then the amount of steam produced by flashing of the water is given in *Table 17.1*. Thus the proportion of water flashed for a given temperature fall varies little with operating pressure.

In the case of the steam space the relation of steam pressure to saturation temperature is a fundamental property of water substance, and so the mass of steam in the steam space is almost proportional to the steam pressure. Thus the amount of heat stored by the steam in the steam space is almost proportional to pressure, and so for every cubic metre of steam in the steam space the steam made available by a fall of saturation temperature of 5°C is given by *Table 17.2*. It can be seen that there is a substantial increase as the boiler pressure is increased. The steam space concerned is not only the steam space above the water in the boiler, but includes the pipework, any steam receivers and other steam vessels.

If we take practical figures for a shell-type boiler, containing 25 tonnes (t) of water and taking a total steam space of 20 m³, then the amount of

Table 17.1 Amount of steam produced by flashing of water (*see text*)

Boiler pressure (bar)	Proportion of water flashed to steam for a temperature drop of 5°C
5	0.010
10	0.013
20	0.012

This table is derived from the formula

(Specific enthalpy at higher temp. minus specific enthalpy at lower temp.) divided by latent heat at lower temp.

and the same formula has been used for *Tables 17.2* and *17.3*.

Table 17.2 Amount of steam made available by a fall in saturation temperature (*see text*)

Boiler pressure (bar)	Steam made available per cubic metre by a fall in saturation temperature of 5°C (kg)
5	0.35
10	0.59
20	0.77

Table 17.3 Amount of steam made available by a fall in saturation temperature (*see text*)

Boiler pressure (bar)	Steam made available by a fall in saturation temperature of 5°C (kg)		
	From flashing water	From steam space	Total
5	250	7	257
10	325	12	337
20	300	15	315

steam made available is as shown in *Table 17.3*. Thus because of its density, the water in the boiler provides a much greater reserve of steam (as heat) than does the steam space.

The figures for the steam available may seem small, but it must be remembered that they are only a reserve to be used pending the re-establishment of an equilibrium between load and firing. If the reserve were needed to cover a five-minute peak it would suffice to cover an increase of load of 3000–4000 kg/h for the five minutes, which is quite a significant quantity in most process plants. For a

boiler operating at 20 bar the pressure would drop to about 18.8 bar at the end of five minutes or to some intermediate pressure if corrective action is taken to increase boiler output before the pressure reaches its lowest value.

The above argument on energy storage is applied directly to the steam storage capacity effectively available in a boiler. If this is judged to be inadequate then it can be increased by storing further hot water under pressure in a separate vessel. This is the principle of the steam accumulator. The water in such a vessel is not usually heated by circulation in a boiler but by the water in the accumulator absorbing steam, by which means the water can be stored at a temperature up to the saturation temperature of the available steam. It is necessary in steam accumulators (or boilers) to make the change in pressure sufficiently slowly to avoid excessively violent ebullition which could cause damage, for instance by carrying water over into the blades of a steam turbine. The use of steam accumulators is dealt with more fully in Chapter 18.

17.3 Steam storage and carryover

A spherical drop of liquid will fall through a gas at a speed corresponding to Stokes's law, which states that the steady-state (or terminal) velocity of fall v is given by

$$v = \frac{KSD^2}{\mu}$$

where K is a constant, S is the specific gravity of the liquid, D is the diameter of the drop and μ is the absolute viscosity of the gas. For very small drops, below 1 μm in diameter, and for very large drops over about 1000 μm, or in very turbulent flow, the law is somewhat different, but these very small and very large drops are not important in the present case. The significant thing is that these terminal velocities are low relative to the velocities common in steam pipes. Thus when steam carrying droplets of water is flowing upwards in a vertical pipe, the water droplets cannot fall relative to the pipes and so are carried forward. In horizontal pipes they may fall onto the pipe surface but can be sheared off again by friction from the flowing steam.

In boiler plant the bubbles of steam coming off the water surface carry some water along with them from the 'skin' of the bubble, and this water is of course boiler water, containing whatever substances are dissolved in the water. If this water is evaporated, as in a superheater, the solids are in most cases deposited on metal surfaces since whilst they are soluble in water they are not soluble in steam. As the thermal conductivity of films of salts is very much lower than that of metals, a very thin film of deposit may lead to a large temperature difference across the tube wall of a superheater element, and this overheating may be high enough to damage the metal or even to lead to a tube burst. There are a number of steam scrubbers available which catch the water droplets, causing them to merge into larger drops whose terminal velocity may exceed the steam velocity, so that they can drop out of the flow of steam. A common method of doing this is to pass the steam through stainless-steel mesh in a properly designed scrubber where the mesh is adequately retained, the water droplets falling into a part of the scrubber which is drained back to the water space.

In process vessels, such as evaporators, a fluid being boiled by the steam may carry dissolved solids over, and again this may cause troubles or loss of product.

Where steam accumulators are used to provide a store of steam to cover peaks, too high a rate of fall of pressure will cause the hot water in the accumulator to boil so vigorously that water is carried forward. This is particularly so when the steam accumulator is too small, so that an inadequate accumulator can lead to serious trouble.

Carryover depends on the rate at which steam bubbles leave the water surface, so that it is necessary to limit the rate of steam released from the water surface to about 200 kg/m²h times the absolute pressure in bars.

Where steam passes through a nozzle the steam velocity may be very high. Where the absolute pressure upstream of the nozzle is more than about twice the downstream pressure, the steam velocity through the throat of the nozzle will approach supersonic (300 m/s or more) and the flow of steam will tend to speed up any water droplets to a velocity approaching that of the steam. Water droplets at such speeds can cause severe erosion to steam turbine blades.

17.4 Flash steam

As is shown in *Figure 17.6*, the greater part of the enthalpy or total heat in steam as used for industrial processes is in the form of latent heat, which is given up on condensing. Unless superheated steam is used, and provision is made for a contra-flow desuperheating section of a process heater, the maximum temperature available in the heater is the temperature of condensation or saturation temperature of the steam supplied to the heater. Many industrial heating processes, both physical processes (such as evaporation) and chemical reaction processes, call for a more or less constant temperature and it is one of the many advantages of steam as a heating medium that it inherently provides such a temperature, and that most of the heat supplied to the steam is given up at that temperature. The curve of variation of steam saturation temperature with pressure shows that the variation of pressure is greater than the variation of temperature. For instance, at a pressure of 15 bar g the saturation temperature is approximately 200°C. A variation of pressure of ±10%, to between 13.5 and 16.5 bar, gives saturation temperatures from 196 to 205°C, so that a substantial change in pressure, involving a substantial change in stored heat, gives a comparatively small change

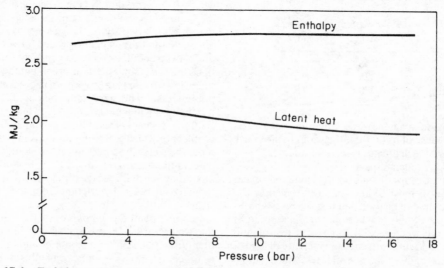

Figure 17.6   Enthalpy and latent heat of saturated steam

in process temperature, and so makes its control easier and the industrial process that much more stable.

It carries the penalty however that the condensate on the steam side of the heater is at saturation temperature, and that at full steam pressure the heat in the condensate cannot be recovered in the heater without addition of a contraflow drain cooler section, which heats the process feed before it enters the process vessel. The greater part of the heat is latent heat in the steam but the sensible heat in the condensate is not negligible. For the same example the heat content of the steam supplied is 2.8 MJ/kg while the heat content of the condensate is 0.83 MJ/kg, both above water at 0°C. Above water at atmospheric temperature of say 20°C, which is about the limit to which condensate can be cooled and also the normal intake temperature of water, these figures become 2.72 and 0.75 respectively, so that nearly a quarter of the usable heat is in the condensate. In most cases, therefore, it is necessary to recover the heat in the condensate. This can be done expensively, as mentioned above, by a contraflow drain cooler supplying preheat to the process feed material. However, this has the disadvantage that the heat transfer coefficient from water to feed is much lower than from steam to feed, so that the surface area per joule second °C in the drain cooler section has to be much greater than in the main condensing heater, with correspondingly high cost. This disadvantage can be substantially overcome by passing the condensate through an orifice, or other throttle device, to reduce its pressure, or through a trap, usually to near atmospheric pressure. The water temperature will then be reduced to 100°C and its heat content above 20°C will be 0.35 MJ/kg. The merit of the arrangement is that the steam flashed off, when the water pressure and temperature fall, will then be condensed to water at 100°C at the high heat transfer coefficient of condensing steam. The 0.35 MJ/kg will be lost but more than half of the heat in the original condensate will have been recovered. The maximum temperature to which the process material can be raised by flashing in a single stage to atmospheric pressure is, of course, 100°C. In a factory using steam at more than one pressure, then the drain from the highest pressure can be flashed at one or more intermediate pressures before reaching atmospheric pressure. This is shown in *Figure 17.7*. If the factory has any sub-atmospheric plant then the 100°C water can be flashed to the vacuum process. Condensate at 100°C can be used as boiler feed, and the heat in it is then recovered automatically. If because of contamination or for other reasons it cannot be used as feed, part of it can be recovered in a water/process material heat ex-

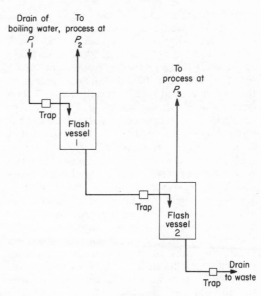

Figure 17.7   Two-stage flashing of drains

changer but like other liquid/liquid heat exchangers this is likely to be expensive and in many cases it would be cheaper to lose the heat in the factory drainage system. When hot water is rejected to the drains it is necessary to do so safely, taking precautions against injury both to staff and to the general public, and to comply with any local authority requirements on temperature, usually by quenching with cold water. If the factory drains are of plastics material it may be necessary to quench the condensate to protect the drains. A similar problem may arise with cast-iron or earthenware drains, where sudden heating may lead to uneven expansion with risk of cracking. A local authority may rule, for example, that water should not be rejected to their drains at a temperature above 50°C, depending on quantity, type of sewage treatment and other factors. If a drain from blowdown is at 100°C and quench water is available at 15°C then 1.33 t of quench water will be needed for every tonne of blowdown.

17.5 Combined heat and power schemes

Most process steam requirements call for steam at a modest pressure, often determined by the process temperature setting the required saturation temperature and so the pressure of the steam. If the steam were generated at a higher pressure than that required by the process, the size of pipework required to distribute the steam to the various process plant users would be correspondingly reduced. The saving thereby might be adequate to pay for the extra cost of boiler plant needed for the higher pressure, and for the reducing valves needed to lower the pressure to the process requirement. There are many older factories where this is the case, and others in which uncertainty about future process pressure requirements, at the time the plant had to be ordered, made the cost of the higher pressure a risk worth taking. When energy was cheap the wastefulness of pressure-reducing valves was unimportant. Where the difference in pressure is sufficient, and the amount of steam adequate, pressure-reducing valves can be replaced by steam engines or turbines. This can reduce the cost of purchased electricity and at current higher energy costs may become attractive. Electricity bought from an outside supplier will in almost all cases, where thermal generation is concerned, be generated by condensing steam turbines, and will incur losses in transmission and distribution which will give an effective efficiency of electricity generation of the order of 30% or less. If the electricity is generated by back-pressure engines or turbines the efficiency of generation will effectively be only a little less than that of the boiler, possibly as high as 75% or even more, so that back-pressure generation of this kind has more than twice the efficiency of a public supply system, and will save a substantial proportion of the energy used in producing the electricity for the supplying authority. The difference may be sufficient to pay all the costs incurred, including capital charges, and leave a profit on the capital cost involved, but any proposal for a scheme of this kind needs to be carefully engineered and costed to ensure that all the considerations involved have been fully taken into account. The major problems usually arise in connection with the non-coincidence of the maximum demands for steam and electricity, since while some limited storage of steam can be provided (for instance in accumulators and boiler drums) there is no practicable and economic way of storing a significant amount of electricity.

Back-pressure generation has been dealt with more fully in Chapter 11.

When planning a combined heat and power scheme any diversity in time between power demand and power generation must be taken into account when assessing the economic benefits of the scheme. *Figure 17.8* shows a much simplified case, in which the steam demand curve shows full demand for half of the time, and half of full demand for the remainder, while the pattern of power demand is quite different. By a suitable choice of scales the steam demand and power generation curves in the figure are made to coincide. The figure illustrates three things. First, the hatched area represents power generation for which there is no demand, so that either the excess

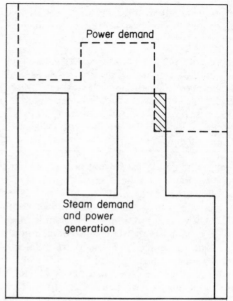

Figure 17.8[1]   Steam demand curve as compared with the pattern of power demand in a combined heat and power scheme

must be sold, if a market can be found, or the steam demand must be supplied partly through a reducing valve/desuperheating station rather than through the turbine. Secondly, the remainder of the area between the power demand and generation curves represents energy which must be purchased. Thirdly, the power demand which must be purchased is the maximum difference between the power demand and generation curves. Thus, given such data, self-generation makes a clear and simply calculated difference in energy purchase (kWh) but may lead to a much smaller reduction in the power demand (kW).

A factory will almost certainly have to meet its own requirements for steam since, except in a small number of industrial or trading estates, there is no widespread distribution of steam and any such supply would be available only at one pressure, which might not be the pressure required by the process. Steam must be produced as and when required, smoothed out to some extent by the steam storage capability of the system as already referred to. Electricity is almost always sold under a multi-part tariff, comprising at least a charge for the kilowatt hours of energy bought, determined mainly by the cost of fuel used to produce this energy, and also a charge for the maximum number of kilowatts of power bought (i.e. the maximum rate of taking energy), determined mainly by the capital cost of the generating, transmission and distribution plant required to supply the maximum demand. If the purchaser takes a supply from the supply authority in addition to his own generation he will have to pay for both the energy and power taken, and if he relies on the supply authority to provide standby capacity in the event of an outage of the purchaser's generating plant, then in most cases there would be a charge for this service also. Electricity supply authorities have a variety of tariffs to cover various eventualities and these need to be studied carefully before embarking on a combined heat and power project. Electricity generated by the user himself will certainly reduce his purchase costs, but if he generates more than he needs himself he is likely to find that the price a supply authority will pay for any surplus is very substantially less than what the same authority will charge for electricity that it supplies, and the appropriate rates need to be ascertained before money is spent. In many cases the supply authority will not take the surplus, particularly at night when the system load is low and the supply authority has plenty of plant of its own.

It is in connection with the kilowatt charge that the difficulties usually arise. This charge will not necessarily be reduced by the maximum amount of power generated, but only by the amount generated at the time of the user's maximum demand on the supply undertaking. This cannot be greater than the amount actually generated and may well be substantially less, and possibly zero if the generating plant happens to be out of service, as is bound to happen during the life of the plant. The factory owner can, of course, install spare plant but this is often more costly than buying a standby supply. If the charge for kilowatts is based on the annual maximum demand and the generator happens to be out of service at that time, then the generator will have contributed nothing. If the kilowatt charges are made monthly, then it will have contributed nothing that month. If the demand for steam happens at the time to be less than the full-load steam flow of the generating set, then only the electricity that can be generated at the time of maximum demand will help to reduce the bill. In particular, if the demand for steam is very 'peaky' then it is unlikely that generating plant able to swallow the whole of the steam will pay for itself, and such peaks are best taken by suitable pressure-reducing equipment. Careful study of the power and steam requirements of the factory will give guidance in choosing the best amount of generating plant to install. Where the steam available always exceeds the full-load steam demand of the generating plant and the electrical load always exceeds the capacity of that plant, then in principle the generating plant can run at a very high load factor and is most likely to pay. Even then, allowance should always be made for the risk of plant outage at some time during the life of the plant.

Where the electrical load exceeds the kilowatt hours generated from the available demand for back-pressure steam, then in principle the shortfall can be made up by the use of condensing machines or possibly by pass-out condensing machines which are in effect a combination of a back-pressure and a normal condensing machine in the same frame. However, these are likely to be much more expensive than back-pressure machines, since condensing plant and cooling water or air-cooled condensers will be required, and the efficiency of such plant is almost certain to be less than that of large plant on an electricity supply system. Usually the efficiency of back-pressure generation is twice that of the public supply while the condensing part of the plant has an efficiency half that of the public supply. Only very large users are likely to find that condensing plant will pay.

When one is considering such plant, of course, account should be taken of any advantage which accrues from a reduction in the risk of loss due to outage of the public supply system. There are many industries where an interruption in power supply, even for a fairly short period, can do much damage and the supply authority is unlikely to be prepared to recompense the purchaser for such a loss. In such cases private supply, even if of much less capacity than the purchased supply, can often help to ensure a safe and controlled shutdown which would prevent such damage and thus justify its cost.

It will be seen that consideration of the installation of generating plant is by no means straightforward, and is likely to be outside the experience of many of those responsible for taking decisions on the matter. The smaller users of steam plant would be well advised to take outside expert advice on the matter.

17.6 Power available from back-pressure generation

The power which can be generated by back-pressure generation is dealt with in more detail in Chapter 11. It may be useful, however, to refer to *Figure 17.9*, which shows the power that can be generated for a given flow (t/h) of process steam expanding from the steam conditions stated on the three curves to the conditions stated on the abscissa. The range of steam conditions shown covers the most common conditions for both boiler plant and process plant for small and medium-size users. Large users may find that higher supply pressures and temperatures are economic but such large users are more likely to have the technical staff able to design and appraise combined heat and power systems.

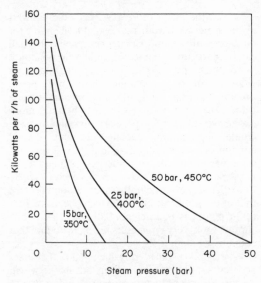

Figure 17.9   Back-pressure generation from the conditions shown on the curves to pressure as shown on the abscissa

17.7 Steam production

Introduction

When a new factory is being built, or extensions to an existing factory call for extra supplies of steam, a decision has to be taken about the right size of boiler, or boilers, to install. It is a decision which has many factors, and it may be instructive to look at some of these.

The first decision on boiler size must be whether additional steam-raising plant is really needed. Although it is not common, sharing of boiler capacity between two quite separate factories is not unknown as a commercial operation, and it can be quite satisfactory. The factory supplying the surplus steam naturally becomes the dominant partner, but given the right approach between the two participants a reasonable working arrangement can exist for a number of years. Some of the disadvantages of common steam supply have been briefly mentioned on p 376.

For a factory which must have its own boilers, the considerations are different for different factory work patterns. Manufacturing processes fall into three broad groups:

1. continuous manufacture throughout the year — whether it is on a daily, shift or continuous shift system;
2. continuous manufacture throughout seasons of the year, with long idle periods. The food processing industry is an obvious example (*see* p 369); and

3. manufacturing processes which are basically continuous, but in which periods of inactivity of a few days can be tolerated.

Boiler pressure and temperature

Before considering boiler capacity — although capacity and steam conditions are to some extent interdependent since it is unusual to have a larger boiler producing low-pressure steam and vice versa — let us look at the steam conditions.

An existing factory will have an existing set of steam conditions. It might be right simply to copy these for any new boiler, but it is worth looking at the arrangement to find whether it is really the most suitable one.

Elsewhere in this book — particularly in Chapter 11 and earlier in the present chapter — the influence of private generation on initial and final steam conditions is discussed, and the choice of steam conditions for generation needs a complex and detailed investigation, requiring information on pattern of steam demands and electricity demands, fuel costs, and electricity supply tariffs. These are the principal factors, but a number of other considerations apply, and there is no simple answer.

When steam is required for process use only, a number of outside factors, such as electricity usage and supply tariffs, can be omitted from the considerations since these are not now relevant.

Pressure

Assuming a carefully designed distribution main, which can carry the steam without excessive pressure drop, the pressure of steam leaving the boilers must be based on process demands. It is unusual for all processes to require the same steam temperature, which of course depends on the saturation pressure, and it is important to be cautious. There may appear to be a need for high-pressure (high-temperature) steam but if this is only a small amount, other and better ways may exist of supplying the required heat than by a high-pressure boiler. Electric heating can be used, or high-temperature heating fluids can be circulated from a separate heating unit using suitable fuel. Clearly some judgement must be made as to when to accept the demand as being a reasonable one for the boilers to meet, and when it is too small to impose its presence on the normal factory boiler plant.

The lower the factory steam pressure the simpler the installation. The pressure must, of course, be high enough to give a saturation temperature adequate for the process, but since the steam is being used as a heat transfer medium it does not matter, in theory, what the boiler pressure is so long as it is above this minimum

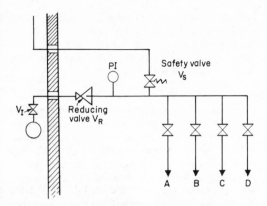

Figure 17.10 Reduced-pressure installation

requirement; in other words, the enthalpy in the steam is not, within limits, particularly important. In practice the boiler pressure does make a significant difference to costs. High-pressure boiler plant costs more to purchase and to maintain, and auxiliary plant such as feed pumps and feed-heaters would also be more expensive; the increased cost could also be reflected in steam piping for the distribution main, steam traps and supports.

Any user not requiring the full steam pressure produced at the boiler plant would need a pressure-reducing, and also perhaps a desuperheating, station to avoid the effect of too high process temperature. Pressure-reducing valves, although basically simple and reliable pieces of plant, are not really understood by many process operators and can waste a lot of steam, as shown in *Figure 17.10*. A high-pressure steam main supplies four units A, B, C and D inside a manufacturing plant. There is an isolating valve V_I on the steam main, a reducing valve V_R and a safety valve V_S, to protect plant against excessive pressures.

Whilst some steam is being used, all goes well, but at some stage A, B, C and D will all be shut down. Now, a pressure-reducing valve is not designed as a shut-off valve, and it cannot be expected to stop all the steam flow. As a result of this, pressure builds up in the steam main inside the plant and the safety valve, whose discharge is almost always outside the plant, can be blowing for a long time before anyone inside knows about it. There is no perfect way of avoiding this — the best thing that can be done is to have the isolating valve V_I where it can be easily operated from inside the plant, so that it can be shut off when there is no demand for steam.

The need for a desuperheater, as well as a pressure-reducing valve, depends on the amount of pressure reduction and the subsequent wire-drawing (*see* Chapter 1). Desuperheaters must be well designed in order to operate with minimum trouble. Sometimes, with spray-type desuper-

heaters, the importance of water quality is over-looked; if it is not satisfactory, deposits from dis-solved solids in the water can build up on valve faces and other places where small clearances are important. In some cases, premature failure of specialist equipment, such as pipe bellows, may be a consequence of poor water quality. The operation of desuperheaters is discussed starting on p 384.

Thus it really is important to choose the best boiler operating pressure and to avoid, as far as possible, the problems associated with pressure and temperature reduction.

Temperature

When the operating pressure of the boiler plant has been settled, the steam temperature can be chosen. Clearly, this temperature can be anything greater than the saturation temperature, depending on the degree of superheat required, if any.

It is simpler to raise only saturated steam from the boiler, because it will not then need a super-heater. This, however, would be unwise except in the simplest installation. As will be clear from most of the preceding chapters, steam starts to lose heat the moment it leaves the boiler stop valve, and continues to do so until it finally condenses. If it starts as saturated steam, then as soon as it loses heat it becomes wet. This wet steam will probably cause trouble with steam pipe joints, and the trouble will be worse in and around the boiler plant than anywhere else, for two reasons. First, the steam supply will have to be isolated at its source for repairs to be carried out, which is likely to affect everyone, and secondly, the flange joints will be larger than anywhere else and thus more difficult to repair.

The desirable amount of superheat is difficult to establish. One could look at the theoretical ideal of making sure that the user at the furthest point receives saturated steam under the worst conditions. This would be a counsel of perfection that would leave most other users with highly super-heated steam, which is not a good heat transfer medium, and could also cause trouble with steam traps.

A reasonable figure for a medium-sized factory with distribution mains longer than ½ km would be to have 50–80°C of superheat in the steam from the boiler plant. This is sufficient to ensure that the steam is reasonably dry for most of the consumers, although users at the end of the line will inevitably get rather poor steam. Calculations of the likely temperature at any using point, starting with a certain level of superheat, are not reliable because the temperature of the steam at a given place depends on the heat loss in the steam main which is affected by weather conditions, such as ambient temperature and wind velocity, and on factory steam demands at any place. It is better to make an informed judgement as to the desirable superheat temperature at the boiler plant.

Boiler pressure and temperature do not really depend on the character of the factory, but this can be important when considering boiler capacity, and the next section deals with this.

Boiler capacity

The broad grouping of factories according to their pattern of production gives some guidance into the matters which are important when choosing boiler capacities. These groups are:

1. daily production, but not rigidly tied to continuous operation;
2. continuous seasonal operation; and
3. continuous operation throughout the year.

Before we look at these three cases, we should consider the circumstances which can make a boiler or boilers unavailable — here lumped together under the general term 'maintenance'.

Maintenance

Maintenance operations are significant when looking at boiler capacity, since they result in either:

1. unscheduled loss of manufacture due to breakdown of the boiler;
2. a planned fall in production whilst the maintenance work is being carried out; or
3. a decision to install a spare boiler so that enough steam is always available irrespective of maintenance work.

In fact these are not quite the only three choices since, given the right set of circumstances, maintenance work can be carried out without losing production. This is discussed when looking at the case of the continuously operated factory.

In order to put the problem of boiler maintenance in its right place, one should realize that it has three elements: cleaning, inspection and repairs.

Boiler cleaning.
Cleaning is necessary to enable the boiler to continue to operate safely and with reasonable efficiency, since all the usual fuels contain carbon (and most fuels contain a number of other substances, as is discussed in Chapter 5). There will therefore be deposits of carbon and other compounds in the boiler passes and on tubes and brickwork, and in ancillary parts such as economizers, superheaters and air heaters. Although these deposits can be kept at bay, for a time, by the judicious use of sootblowers, they will eventually

have to be removed. The deposits build up most quickly in coal-fired boilers, more slowly in oil-fired boilers, and are least troublesome with gas firing. Thus the frequency of cleaning could vary from six months with coal to two years or more with gas.

Inspection. Chapter 3 gives a full description of the statutory inspections which must be carried out on steam boilers. The frequency of the inspections depends on the character of the boiler — whether used for electricity generation, factory steam processes or as a waste-heat boiler as part of a manufacturing process. The agreed period for inspections must be settled with the insurance company concerned.

Inspection cannot be carried out without first cleaning the boiler, whereas cleaning can be done as a separate operation. Common sense tells us that these two activities should be planned together.

Repairs. Repairs are particular maintenance operations concerned with putting faults right, and affect every part of the boiler. When one is looking at the effect of boiler maintenance — as discussed in Chapter 19 — it must be remembered that the amount of maintenance which needs to be done can vary appreciably from year to year, and this must be allowed for when looking at possible out-of-service periods.

Resources. The resources needed to carry out these three operations must be found either wholly within the factory, wholly outside the factory, or from a mixture of the two. There are a large number of ways of combining these, but *Table 17.4* gives a few possibilities.

Repairs can, of course, be carried out separately from the other two operations, although in the case of major repairs some cleaning will have to be done first.

The importance of keying in these three operations, to give the minimum shutdown period,

Table 17.4 Possible ways of organizing maintenance

Cleaning	Inspection	Repairs
Works boiler cleaning section	Insurance inspector	Works mainten-ance team
Contract cleaners	Insurance inspector	Works mainten-ance team
Contract cleaners	Insurance inspector	Contract work for major repairs, works mainten-ance team for minor repairs

should be clear from what has been said. The time the boiler is out of service depends upon the resources which can be made available, and both imagination and good planning need to be applied to give a good operation.

Waste-heat boilers. These are described in Chapters 4 and 5, and some examples of their use in industry are given in Chapter 20. Before looking at the factors which are important in deciding what size of boiler to install, we should be clear about the role of waste-heat boilers. They are part of a manufacturing process, and the fuel which they use is also part of this process. The steam output of the boiler can thus be lost if there is no demand for the product which is being made, if the raw material for the process ceases to be available, if the labour which runs the plant can be more usefully employed elsewhere, or for a number of other reasons.

The output from such a boiler is clearly not dependable, and should not normally be taken into account when doing the sums, except perhaps as a help if a calculated risk has been taken about the margin of supply over demand for a short period.

Most waste-heat boilers are a part of a works in which many varied manufacturing processes are carried out, and it is to this type of installation that the above comments apply. However, there are some cases where the boiler is an integral part of a single-product works, so that if the boiler is shut down beause the process is shut down, the steam demand will also have disappeared — no manufacture, no production of steam, no demand for steam. In this case the output from the waste-heat boiler can be considered as a reliable contribution towards the total steam demand.

Having discussed some of the factors which can affect decisions on boiler size, let us now look at the pattern of the works. The first step is to get some measure of steam demand, and since this comes naturally in the consideration of a works operating continuously, it is dealt with later on p 382, but of course the principles apply to any kind of factory.

Daily production

Cases where production is on a daily basis are probably the easiest to settle. Important production takes place every day — which might be 5, 6 or 7 days in a week — but it can be assumed that some minor interruption is no more than annoying, and can be made up again when steam supplies have been restored.

Assuming a reliable boiler of proven design, the repairs which are needed with any unplanned shutdown should not take more than 3–4 days to carry out, and so the factory load could be carried by one boiler, which must have reasonable capacity to deal with peak loads. Provided the boiler is reliable — and modern boilers, competently operated, *are* reliable, unless they have some radical design feature — a single boiler would be the cheapest installation. Major cleaning and overhauls could be planned for a holiday shutdown.

It should be realized, when deciding the type of boiler to install, that the controls of an unattended boiler (Chapter 3) cannot usually exercise judgement and when things go wrong it will — rightly — shut itself down and ask questions afterwards, whereas an experienced boiler operator might be able to avoid such a shutdown by intelligent anticipation. Again, when considering the disturbance caused to production by an unplanned boiler shutdown, the type of fuel is important. A bed of coal on the grate provides a reserve of heat which can be valuable when the feed of fuel to the boiler is temporarily lost, whereas an oil- or gas-fired boiler would shut down, if not with a bang, at least with distressing finality, and should not be relit until a carefully designed purging sequence had been carried out.

So, there are a number of points to be considered when choosing a single boiler to carry the steam load. They are not as significant if two boilers are installed to carry the load, and this is clearly a line of action which carries less risk, and gives more freedom over matching boiler output to factory steam demand. A single boiler large enough to supply peak demands could, at times, be operating at an undesirably low load bringing a number of problems ranging from acidic smuts in the chimney to air heater fires.

Economies of scale are important, since the unit cost of steam is less from large boilers, and good basic information and judgement help not only in matching a new boiler plant to the needs of the factory, but also in making an intelligent guess as to future needs when considering the plant layout.

Computers will analyse a mass of data, and can be invaluable in assessing future demands on the basis of past experience, assuming that no disturbing elements arise which could vitiate the assumptions.

Continuous seasonal operation

Continuous seasonal operation is largely related to food and material processing, which are based on seasonal requirements, usually requiring high reliability for a definite period followed by a long (to most boiler plant managers) period of complete shutdown. This is of course the period when cleaning, statutory inspections and maintenance overhauls can be done.

The same factors — fuel, reliability and maintenance — as were considered in the previous section apply, with perhaps a greater importance on reliability and a less demanding maintenance schedule. The reliability of the plant is more significant because of the probably greater scale of operations and the loss of money which could arise from a major enforced shutdown.

A food-processing plant is likely to be a large enough operation to justify several boilers and with the reliability of medium-sized modern boilers there should be little risk in matching boiler output to steam demand without carrying any spare boilers.

Factory on continuous operation

A works which requires steam for 168 hours a week, and for most weeks in the year, is likely to have an appreciable steam demand. It could thus be supplied either by a very few large boilers, or by more boilers of a smaller size, and we should now look at advantages and disadvantages of large boilers. Their capital cost per tonne of steam produced is less, and they probably have a slightly higher thermal efficiency. When considering how a steam load below the maximum installed capacity of the boilers is going to be met, we come to a difference in operation. At reduced steam loads the larger boilers would be operated at less than maximum continuous rating (MCR) whereas if the steam load was met by a number of smaller boilers one of them would probably be taken off range.

Working efficiency does not vary much with boiler output (*see* Chapter 4) until we get to about 50% MCR, but below that it could fall off significantly.

We could probably find which of these two methods of operation gave the more economical usage if we carried out careful measurements under close supervision, but in the rough and tumble of everyday operation there is not likely to be much difference.

If a large boiler is suddenly shut down the effect is much more dramatic than if the works loses the steam from a smaller boiler.

So the judgement rests on capital cost versus flexibility — although the final decision might well have to be made on the basis of the size of site or boilerhouse available.

In order to put in the right size of additional boiler (in an existing factory) or total boiler plant (in a new factory), the best possible information is necessary. With a new factory the most reliable basic data must be used — plus a dash of intuition — to get the best answer, but it is easier to decide the size of boiler needed on an existing factory because there should be much information on the steam output from the existing boiler plant.

The *weekly* output should be taken: daily steam demands will be too variable and monthly figures too general. It is an advantage if these demands can be set against some figure which represents the amount of production achieved in that week, and over a period a series of curves will be obtained showing steam demand for a range of factory outputs. The results will look like *Figure 17.11*, which shows average weekly steam output against pro-

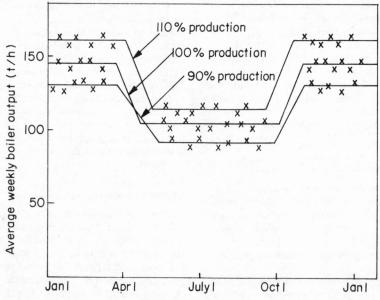

Figure 17.11   Steam demand at a factory throughout the year

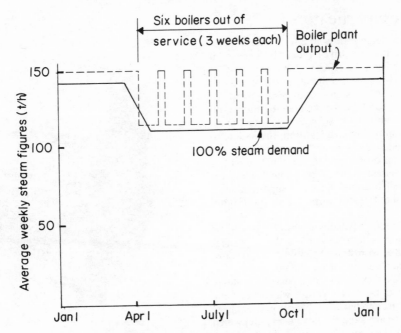

Figure 17.12   Steam demand and supply throughout the year

duction for each week in the year. The summer months naturally show a smaller amount of steam used for a given production than in the winter, because heat losses from the steam mains both inside and outside buildings will be less, and less direct space heating will be needed in offices and similar buildings.

The periods at the end of the winter and at the end of summer are areas of uncertainty, being very dependent on the weather conditions, and not too much credence should be placed on these, as far as the pattern of subsequent years is concerned.

The lines have of course been drawn to give the best approximation to the points plotted for each production percentage, and there will be some rogue figures which do not fit into the trend. Nevertheless a reasonable series of curves can usually be drawn from reliable data.

This diagram has been extended in *Figure 17.12* to show the 100% production line steam demand against the output from six 25-t/h boilers, using all six in the winter, but only five in summer, and it demonstrates the flexibility given by a number of smaller boilers. The diagram shows the available output from the boiler plant, and it will be seen that the 100% demand of 140 t/h can be met in winter by all six boilers, but when summer conditions have arrived only five boilers are needed.

Thus a boiler programme could be arranged with this in mind with each of the boilers in turn being taken off for maintenance during the period

mid-April to mid-October. Assuming a three-week duration for each boiler with one week overlap, six boilers could be overhauled in this period without losing any production, and all the boilers would be available in the winter. It may be thought that this would involve some risk of boilers being out of service when they are badly needed in the winter, but it is surprising how long a boiler can be kept on if it just cannot be spared. This risk is minimized by a planned summer overhaul. Some help towards meeting the rather stringent production/availability pattern can also be obtained in two ways. Statutory holiday periods can be used, when production is almost certain to be lower, to carry out essential maintenance — or even minor cleaning — on boilers. The other possibility, which depends entirely on production pattern, is to try to find a manufacturing plant with an appreciable steam demand whose production can be postponed in a real emergency.

The example given is naturally an ideal one, but the principle is worth looking at since it avoids having to install a spare boiler and is a good way of using capital to the best advantage.

Clearly there is no simple way of ordering exactly the right size and type of boilers to serve a new factory, or to allow for the extension of an existing factory. The ideas which have been mentioned are only guides to the correct decision, but they are all significant factors in getting the best solution, and should be considered when reviewing factory extensions.

17.8 Desuperheaters

Superheated steam is desirable for power generation and for turbine drives generally, because it increases the Rankine efficiency, but nevertheless it has disadvantages once it gets into a steam distribution system. In some instances its temperature could be too high for the system, and would be bad for components such as cast-iron valves, and expansion bellows. In addition, the high temperature could give too much expansion in the steam distribution system, or at least in that part of it which is nearest to the boiler plant. It may also be undesirable because, since it is superheated, it has poorer heat transfer properties than saturated steam.

For a number of reasons it has at times to be desuperheated, either to reduce the superheat temperature or to restore it to its saturated state, and there are a number of ways of doing this.

The simplest way is to leave a part of the steam main unlagged, but this is a crude way of reducing the temperature and has a number of disadvantages. It creates a hazard from the hot steam pipe, which would have to be carefully guarded. The heat produced from the unlagged pipe could be unwelcome at times, and the siting of the pipe would have to be carefully considered; this feature of desuperheating using a bare pipe also emphasizes the major objection to it, that it is wasteful and serves only to heat the surrounding air. Another disadvantage is that it is imprecise — the degree of superheating depends upon the steam flow through the pipe, and to some extent upon weather conditions.

As an example let us assume a crude desuperheater which has been made by leaving thermal insulation off a length of 150 mm pipe. The steam in the pipe is at a pressure of 10 bar abs and a temperature of 300°C, although the saturation temperature is only 180°C.

From *Table 6.6* (Chapter 6), we can get useful values of heat loss from a bare pipe, with different wind speeds, for an ambient temperature of 20°C. Assuming that the bare pipe is inside the building, the wind velocity is zero, and the rate of heat loss will be 3970 W per metre length.

Let us assume a reasonable steam flow velocity of 50 m/s, then the volume of steam flowing will be $50 \times \frac{1}{4}\pi \times (0.15)^2$ m³/s, and with a specific volume of 258 dm³/kg the mass flow will be

$$\frac{50 \times \pi \times (0.15)^2 \times 1000}{4 \times 258} = 3.42 \text{ kg/s}$$

If we leave 10 m of pipe unlagged then the heat loss will be 39 700 J/s, and the heat loss per kilogram of steam will be 39.7/3.42 or 11.6 kJ/kg.

Figure 17.13   Desuperheater

Now steam at 10 bar, 300°C has an enthalpy of 3052.1 kJ/kg, and the loss of 11.6 kJ/kg will leave it with 3040.5 kJ/kg corresponding to steam at 10 bar with a temperature of about 295°C.

If the steam demand now falls to 1.2 kg/s, the heat lost from the bare pipe will be 33.1 kJ/kg and the enthalpy will be 3019 kJ/kg, corresponding to steam at 10 bar, 285°C. The final steam temperature clearly cannot be controlled.

If the steam main is outside, the wind velocity could be significant and the desuperheating process becomes even more variable.

The size of steam main, in this example, has been chosen because the data in *Table 6.6* were available, but the use of a bare 150-mm pipe as a desuperheater would in fact be a deplorable practice. It is also inefficient, because 10 m of bare pipe produces only an insignificant temperature drop.

Pipeline desuperheaters

If superheat has to be removed from steam, then a correctly designed superheater should be used. In pipeline desuperheaters, superheated steam is passed through a section of pipe into which is fitted one or more spray nozzles depending upon capacity. These inject a fine spray of feedwater into the steam which is itself converted into steam, absorbing the heat from the steam and reducing the quantity of superheat. As the water is absorbed the steam supply is augmented.

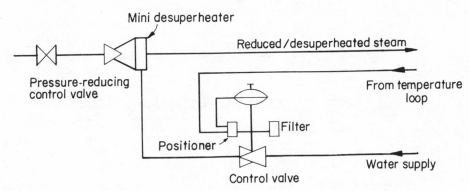

Figure 17.14   Arrangement of a mini-desuperheater

For small duties, desuperheaters have been designed which fit into the pipeline, as shown in *Figure 17.13*. Temperature reduction is achieved by injecting cooling water into the steam through the desuperheater body, which may be bolted directly onto the control valve outlet flange or installed using a tapered distance piece as shown.

Cooling water is supplied to an annular chamber created between the desuperheater body and a centrally located stainless-steel bush. The water is then forced under pressure into the steam main through a series of very small holes drilled radially through the wall of the bush.

The outlet steam temperature is controlled by regulating the flow of cooling water. The temperature controller senses variations in the steam temperature and relays a proportional pneumatic signal direct to the diaphragm of the water control valve which governs the quantity of water passing into the desuperheater body. These desuperheaters are quite short, being only 76 mm in length for a pipe of diameter up to 50 mm and about twice as long for an 80-mm pipe. The pipework arrangement for such a desuperheater is shown in *Figure 17.14*.

For larger duties a more flexible design is needed, and a variable-orifice spray nozzle provides one solution. High differential pressures — up to 30 bar — between the feedwater and steam can be accommodated by the unit. Since the spray nozzle also acts as a control element, the separate water control valve can frequently be dispensed with, making a significant contribution to cost reduction.

A turn-down capability (the ratio between maximum and minimum working conditions) in excess of 25 : 1 is available with this design of nozzle. A swirl chamber gives efficient atomization of the spray water; in this chamber injection holes are drilled tangentially round the body of the nozzle which together with the profile of the control element create a rotating conical spray pattern

easily absorbed by the steam.

The quantity of spray water injected is controlled by automatically varying the area of the discharge orifice. Full water/steam pressure differential is maintained at all flows for maximum efficiency. The nozzle is operated by a pneumatic actuator complete with positioner which is remotely controlled by a pneumatic controller.

The variable-orifice spray nozzle is shown in *Figure 17.15,* and *Figure 17.16* shows the pipeline arrangement of this desuperheater.

Figure 17.15   Desuperheater with a variable-orifice spray nozzle

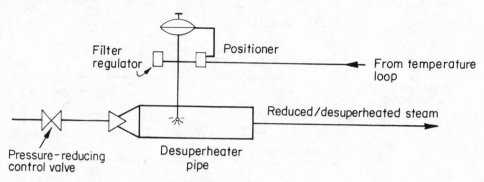

Figure 17.16   Arrangement of a pipeline desuperheater

Desuperheater installation

A desuperheater should be installed so that the spray nozzle is located at the steam inlet of the tube.

Owing to the severe expansion strains which may be imposed on the joints when starting up, it is essential that all flange joint bolts are manufactured from high-tensile alloy steel irrespective of the steam pressure. The joints should be made with a compressed asbestos gasket or sheet 0.80 mm thick. The joint faces should be machined to a gramophone finish. These remarks also apply to the water joint flanges, which are also subject to sudden temperature changes.

The fact that a desuperheater is a device for reducing the steam temperature sometimes leads to the mistaken impression that the lagging of steam and water pipes is not important. Unlike the absorption of heat by the spray water, any loss of heat should be avoided. Unless the pipework can be maintained at the proper temperature, successful desuperheating may not be possible and a preliminary trial of a plant before it has been lagged may prove disappointing.

Efficient drainage of the pipework following the desuperheater is essential. To ensure that water cannot accumulate at any point, the pipe should be arranged to fall in the direction of flow approximately 20 mm per metre under actual working conditions and be provided with an efficient large-capacity trap at the lowest point. To prevent the trap from becoming airbound the drain pipe should have ample capacity to deal with the drainage and be fixed as near to vertical as possible. There must be sufficient space in the drain pipe for water to flow down and air to pass up the pipe.

When the plant is started up it is advisable to open the trap by-pass valve to deal with any excess water. If a by-pass valve is not fitted the trap should be inspected to ensure that it is passing water and has not become airbound. When the pipework has warmed through to the working temperature and a reasonable amount of steam is flowing, the drainage of water should practically cease and the trap by-pass valve can then be closed.

Successful operation of a desuperheater depends to a large extent on the injection water being hot, preferably near to the saturation temperature of the steam to be cooled so that it is mainly the latent heat which is extracted from the steam to evaporate the injection water. This minimizes the time that the water particles are suspended in the steam so that all the water is evaporated and none falls to the inside walls of the pipework. As mentioned previously, the pipes connecting the water supply to the injection nozzle should be efficiently lagged to minimize the loss of heat.

The quality of the spray water is important. The dissolved-solids content of this water should be as low as possible since all these solids will come out of solution and will be deposited on the faces of valves and will also tend to block up small passages.

Other types of desuperheater

There are, of course, other ways of cooling superheated steam, as in surface desuperheaters. In these, no mixing takes place between the water and the steam. Attemperators, which are used to control the final steam temperature from a boiler, are a type of surface desuperheater although really they are acting as heat exchangers between the superheated steam and the cooler boiler water, as mentioned in Chapter 5. They can be used economically only if a use can be found for the heated water.

Desuperheater calculations

Steam tables can be used to calculate how much spray water will be required for a given installation, and how much additional steam will be produced.

If we take the steam from the previous example, with a flow rate of 3.42 kg/s at 10 bar, 300°C, and use a properly designed desuperheater, we can produce saturated steam — 180°C at the same pressure — using spray water at 15 bar abs, 150°C.

The enthalpy of saturated steam at 10 bar is 2776.2 kJ/kg so we must remove 3052.1 − 2776.2 = 275.9 kJ/kg or 275.9 × 3.42 = 943.58 kJ/s.

The spray water must be heated from 150°C to 180°C and then evaporated to saturated steam at 10 bar, for which it must receive the latent heat quantity of 2013.6 kJ/kg.

Water at 180°C has an enthalpy of 763.1 kJ/kg

Water at 150°C has an enthalpy of 632.1 kJ/kg

so altogether we must supply 2013.6 + 131 = 2144.6 kJ for each kilogram of water.

Thus the water flow rate will be 943.58/2144.6 = 0.44 kg/s, and the original steam flow will be increased from 3.42 to 3.86 kg/s.

Clearly this is a much more satisfactory way of desuperheating than removing a part of the lagging of the pipe.

18   Steam storage

This chapter deals with the storage of steam in industry and power-stations. Storage systems used purely for space heating or domestic purposes are not included. The purpose of steam storage[1] is to accept steam when demand is low and to keep it until such time as there is an additional or unexpected requirement.

18.1 Importance of steam storage

Steam stored in an accumulator is immediately available to the consumers and can be used for a variety of types of steam demand. For short periods, the accumulator can discharge steam at very high rates and reduce the size of the boiler plant required. Where steam is subject to regular cycles or predictable fluctuations, the load can be balanced for hours or even days. In every case, there will be a more steady load on the boiler plant[2], whereby losses are reduced and fuel savings achieved.

Thus steam storage gives the project or operating engineer an additional tool to ensure that steam supply is adequate and efficient at any time. The possible effects and advantages deserve to be more generally known in order to bring about the most efficient use of steam.

18.2 Development

The first steam accumulators were installed by Rateau at the beginning of this century for balancing the waste-steam flow from winding engines and ensuring a constant supply to the low-pressure turbine. The basic principles of steam storage were applied to higher pressures, and automatic operation was added by Ruths in 1913. This was followed by similar developments of the feedwater storage system by Marguerre and others, especially in connection with the displacement type.

For applications in power-stations, special storage turbines were developed and pressures up to 150 bar used by Gilli in 1938. At present, new systems are being developed for nuclear power and for solar and other unconventional sources of energy, aiming at storage volumes of several thousand cubic metres per unit.

18.3 Definitions

The following definitions of important terms related to steam storage will be found useful in connection with the further explanations.

Storage capacity, S, is the amount of steam or heat stored between the limits of the fully charged and the fully discharged conditions, expressed either in kg (t) of steam or kJ (MJ) of heat.

Specific storage capacity, s, is the storage capacity S divided by the volume V (or weight) of the storing medium, expressed in kg/m^3 (kg/kg) or kJ/m^3 (kJ/kg).

Charging rate, L, is the rate of steam (heat) flow into the accumulator in kg/h (t/h) or kJ/h (MJ/h).

Discharging rate, D, is the steam (heat) flow rate out of the accumulator in kg/h (t/h) or kJ/h (MJ/h).

Efficiency, η, is the quantity of steam or heat discharged during a full cycle expressed as a percentage of the quantity of steam or heat charged during the same period.

18.4 Equipment

Storage vessel

The storage vessel is the most important part of an accumulator installation, and usually the most costly. It is designed to hold the storage medium, normally water and/or steam. At temperatures which are usually required, the vessel must be suitable for the corresponding saturation pressure. For industrial purposes, the maximum operating pressure for which the vessel has to be designed varies between 5 and 30 bar, and for power-stations, between 20 and 150 bar.

Most accumulators are of cylindrical form with elliptical, or for larger units spherical, ends, as can be seen from a typical industrial installation shown in *Figure 18.1*. To obtain optimal conditions, the ratio of diameter to total length should be between 1:4 and 1:6, but if site conditions require it, the ratio can be varied between wide limits.

Most storage vessels are manufactured from boiler-quality steel plate. However, there are limitations to the plate thickness, which means that, for instance, in the case of a maximum pressure of 20 bar, the volume of the vessel will normally be limited to about 500 m^3, and correspondingly less for higher pressures. Larger storage volumes can be obtained only by employing several vessels.

A new development is intended to avoid this disadvantage by using prestressed cast-iron pressure vessels[3], expected to reach volumes of up to 8000 m^3 at pressures between 60 and 120 bar (*see Figure 18.2*). Alternatively, the use of caverns for containing the storage medium has been suggested, similar to those already employed for compressed-air storage[4].

Figure 18.1   Horizontal pressure vessel of a pressure-drop accumulator with connecting pipework placed outside a chemical factory. (Courtesy of Steam Storage Co., Leeds)

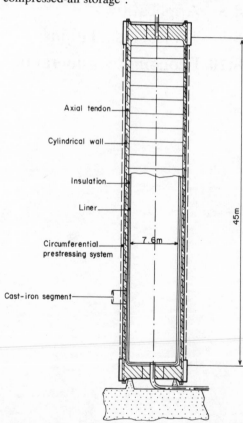

Figure 18.2   Prestressed cast-iron pressure vessel steam accumulator, capacity 2000 m^3, pressure 60 bar. (Courtesy of Siempelkamp Giesserei kG, Krefeld)

In view of the importance of keeping vessel cost as low as possible, various other methods have been tried, such as using existing boiler shells for small installations. Special attention has to be given to the thermal expansion of the vessel, especially when operating in the higher pressure range. Foundations and pipelines have to be designed to allow for these changes in length.

It is of the greatest importance to keep heat losses as low as economically possible, as they have a marked influence on both efficiency and storage capacity. As accumulators usually operate in the temperature range between 200 and 300°C, this means that the heat insulation is an essential part of any accumulator installation. For further information *see* Chapter 6.

Charging and discharging equipment

The equipment required for charging and discharging varies in accordance with the storage system, as described on p 392 under the heading 'Systems'. The charging process involves the condensation of the steam, which has to be accepted by the accumulator. This can be effected either by introducing the steam into the water used as a storing medium, or by mixing it with the water.

For the pressure-drop accumulator (*see* p 392), charging nozzles are used and are arranged over the whole length of the accumulator, so that the steam is evenly distributed throughout the water volume. The nozzles have a great number of small holes of diameter about 10 mm through which the steam enters the water in an upward direction. In cases where the water depth is great or the pressure range small, tubing round the nozzles is provided to ensure a good circulation and even temperatures at all levels of the water content, with the nozzles close to the water surface.

For the constant-pressure system (*see* p 393), the mixing of steam and water can be carried out by a system of cascades in the top part of the accumulator, with the water flowing downwards and meeting an upward flow of steam. Alternatively, a separate cascade mixer can be employed or, if direct contact of steam and water has to be excluded, a heat exchanger, designed to heat the water to the desired temperature.

Discharging in the case of the pressure-drop system requires no special equipment, except that in vertical vessels and for high discharge rates, circulation tubing may be necessary to ensure that the evaporation is spread over the whole height of the accumulator. For the constant-pressure system, discharging means that the preheating of feedwater is reduced or stopped completely. Thus here too, no special provisions need to be made.

Other equipment

Accessories on the accumulator vessel — similar to those in boiler plants — include indicators to show the pressure and the water level, as well as valves to blow off steam at maximum pressure, to blow down water at maximum level, to feed water at minimum level and to release air. The pipelines to and from the accumulator must be fitted with stop valves and, in the charging pipe, non-return valves to prevent accumulator water from flowing back into the steam supply line.

Automatic control forms an essential part of any accumulator installation, as it is one of its main functions to keep the operating conditions permanently constant throughout the steam plant. In most cases, this means pressure regulators which control the boiler, the accumulator and the consumer pressures. In addition, regulators to control steam temperatures or the water level in the accumulator may be required for completely automatic operation. (*See also* Chapter 8.)

Effective metering equipment is of decisive importance, including recorders for boiler, accumulator and consumer pressures. It is particularly important to record continuously the state of accumulator charging, which is reflected in either the pressure, the temperature or the water level in the accumulator, or in the case of a displacement system, by the dividing level between hot and cold water.

18.5 Storage media

Steam or heat is stored in a medium at increasing temperature. Any rise or fall in temperature is due to the addition or extraction of heat. The specific storage capacity s, defined opposite, can easily be calculated, if the specific heat c of the medium is known, from the equation

$$s = H_2 - H_1 = c(T_2 - T_1) \qquad (18.1)$$

where H is the heat content in kJ/kg and T the absolute temperature, while '1' and '2' indicate the discharged and the charged condition respectively.

Thus, heat storage exists in every steam plant, whether by intention or not. Without some storage effect, no thermal process can take place.

For the purpose of planned thermal storage, an accumulator plant usually has to be added and water is used as a storage medium. Water has many advantages over other media: it is everywhere plentifully available and thus very cheap; it has no toxic, corrosive or otherwise detrimental effects, and it has a relatively high specific storage capacity s. On the other hand, it has the disadvantage that it requires a pressure vessel to keep it at temperatures above 100°C, with the pressure rising steeply at increasing temperatures. For this reason, other media have been considered, mostly chemical compounds. They have higher boiling points and can operate over a higher temperature range at much lower, or even at atmospheric pressure, but are relatively expensive. For effective steam storage they also involve using a far more complicated installation and are sometimes toxic and/or corrosive. Thus their application has so far been within a very restricted range.

18.6 Systems

There are, in principle, two different systems possible for the storage of thermal energy;

1. the pressure-drop accumulator, operating on the principle of a constant volume of water, whilst pressure and temperature are allowed to vary; and
2. the constant-pressure accumulator, operating on the principle of a constant pressure or temperature of the water, whilst its volume is allowed to vary.

There are various ways and means of applying these basic systems to solve a given storage problem for a particular type of installation. However, in most cases the methods used are on the following lines:

Pressure-drop accumulator

Pressure-drop accumulators can be called simply 'steam accumulators', as they discharge steam. The accumulator, usually arranged horizontally, consists of the pressure vessel with insulation, the necessary accessories and the charging equipment, as described on p 391 under the heading 'Charging and discharging equipment'. When fully charged, it is normally about 90% full of water.

During the charging operation, the surplus steam is blown into the water through the charging equipment. The steam condenses quickly, as its temperature is higher than that of the surrounding water. Thereby, heat is added to the water content and with the higher temperature, the pressure rises correspondingly until it reaches the maximum, that is, the pressure for which the vessel was built.

When discharging takes place, steam is allowed — by opening a valve — to leave the steam space of the accumulator and the pressure drops accordingly. This causes the water, being at a somewhat higher temperature than now corresponds to the resulting pressure in the steam space, to boil and

thereby replace the discharged steam by evaporation. This process continues until the minimum is reached, that is, the pressure required for the consumers.

During charging, the condensing steam entering the water content is added to it, and thus the water level rises. It drops again during discharging when water is lost by evaporation, and thus the water level varies in accordance with the state of charging. If the steam charged is saturated, some water will be added permanently, namely the amount of condensate corresponding to the heat losses. On the other hand, if the steam charged is superheated, there will be a surplus of heat, as the steam discharged is always dry and superheated. Therefore, more condensate will be evaporated, and it may even be necessary to feed the accumulator, since if steam temperatures are high it may supply more steam than it had received.

The arrangement of a steam accumulator has to suit the existing steam plant and the intended purpose. Owing to its method of operation, it always has to be charged at a higher pressure than that at which it is discharged; thus it has to be arranged so that it can be charged from a supply line of higher pressure and discharged into a line of a lower pressure.

It is important to realize that a steam accumulator can have a balancing effect on both the high-pressure (h.p.) line and the low-pressure (l.p.) line, as shown schematically in *Figure 18.3*, the inserts indicating the type of load. The direct-balance type (*Figure 18.3a*) is used if the load fluctuations occur at the l.p. consumers, whilst the demand of the h.p. consumers is constant. In this case, a charging regulator can balance the boiler load by controlling the flow of steam into the accumulator according to its charging state, opening more as less steam is left in the accumulator. The indirect-balance type (*Figure 18.3b*) is used if demand from the h.p. consumers fluctuates. A surplus regulator, also called an overflow valve, maintains a constant pressure at the h.p. line by opening more, as the h.p. load is reduced.

Another important application is connected with combined heat and power installations, where the steam accumulator has to provide a balance between differing demands for heat and power. Here again there are, in principle, two possible ways of arranging the accumulator. In *Figure 18.4a* a parallel arrangement is shown, in which the accumulator is in a by-pass to the back-pressure engine which supplies the base-load to the heat consumers, whilst any additional steam demand comes from the accumulator. *Figure 18.4b* shows a series arrangement, with all steam passing through the back-pressure engine, and the accumulator providing a balance by accepting

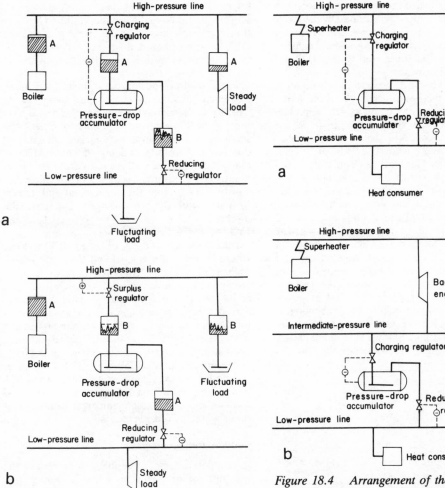

Figure 18.3   Balancing effect of the pressure-drop accumulator. (a) Direct balance of fluctuating low-pressure demand; (b) indirect balance of fluctuating high-pressure demand. A, Steady flow; B, fluctuating flow

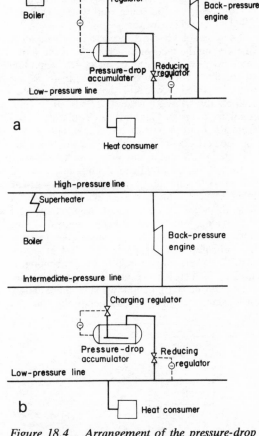

Figure 18.4   Arrangement of the pressure-drop accumulator with back-pressure engine. (a) Parallel arrangement; (b) series arrangement

steam as supplied by the engine and discharging it again, as required by the heat consumers. The series method has the advantage of using all the steam for power generation but at a reduced pressure range, as the exhaust pressure has to be higher in order to leave the pressure range necessary for the accumulator to operate.

Constant-pressure accumulator

Constant-pressure accumulators can be called 'feedwater accumulators', as they discharge feedwater. The accumulator consists of the pressure vessel with necessary insulation and accessories, and also charging equipment, as described on p

391. The vessel is usually arranged in a vertical position, so that the hot water in the top part and the cold water in the bottom part can both be stored in the same vessel.

During the charging operation, the surplus steam enters the steam space, where it is mixed with cold feedwater. The steam is condensed and the feedwater heated to the saturation temperature corresponding to the steam pressure. As more hot feedwater is produced, less cold feedwater remains in the bottom part of the accumulator; thus the dividing line moves downwards, until the whole accumulator is filled with hot feedwater, that is, it is fully charged.

During discharging, on the other hand, less feedwater is preheated than is required for boiler feed, and this means that the boiler can supply a corresponding amount of additional steam to the consumers. In the event that no preheating takes place at all, the discharge rate reaches its maximum as the boiler output is increased by the whole amount of steam which is otherwise used for preheating. The accumulator will gradually come to contain less hot and more cold water, until it is filled with cold feedwater.

The principles behind the two different methods of charging the feedwater accumulator are shown in *Figure 18.5*. Charging by mixing feedwater and steam, as shown schematically in *Figure 18.5a*, has been described above, and is mostly used in industrial plants. During low-load periods, the surplus regulator opens further and more cold water taken from the bottom part of the accumulator enters the top part. By contact with the steam, this water is heated to the saturation temperature and stored in the top part, so that the dividing line between hot and cold water moves downward. During peak loads, less cold water is preheated, some hot water from the top of the accumulator is discharged, and the dividing line moves upwards again. Charging hot water which is produced from extraction steam in preheaters (*Figure 18.5b*) is used in power plants[4], where this method of preheating is applied to increase the efficiency of the power cycle. During charging at low loads, more extraction steam is used for feedwater preheating. At

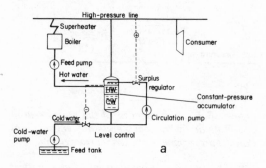

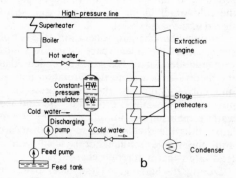

Figure 18.5   Arrangement of constant-pressure accumulator (displacement type). (a) Preheating by steam and water mixing; (b) preheating by extraction steam. HW, hot water; CW, cold water

high load, less steam is extracted, leaving more for power generation in the turbine. It should be mentioned that it is possible to design the accumulator for a lower pressure than the boiler pressure, either to obtain optimal conditions or to use back-pressure steam.

Pressure-drop and constant-pressure accumulators each have their specific field of application. The steam accumulator can be discharged very quickly, within a period of minutes or even a few seconds, thus reaching extremely high rates of discharge, quite independently of the actual boiler load. It can also be situated away from the boiler plant. The feedwater accumulator, on the other hand, is linked with the boiler plant and its performance with the boiler output. The maximum discharge rate is restricted to between 10% and 15% of the actual boiler steaming rate, where extraction steam is used, or up to 20% or 30%, where boiler steam is used and there is no feed-preheating by an economizer. However, the feedwater accumulator also has great advantages, as its specific storage capacity s is in most cases considerably greater than for the steam accumulator, so that the storage volume required is less and costs are considerably reduced. This advantage is even more important in power plants, as the feedwater accumulator supplies additional steam at full boiler pressure and temperature, whilst the steam from steam accumulators is at a reduced pressure and at saturation temperature only, unless superheated by outside means.

Combination accumulator

It is, of course, possible to arrange the accumulator in such a way that it can operate according to a combination of the two systems, though it cannot then achieve either storage effect fully[5]. One part of the storage capacity can be used according to the pressure-drop system, allowing a high discharge rate, whilst the remainder operates according to the constant-pressure system, ensuring a greater storage capacity. The method of charging consists of a combination of the operations described above, whereby l.p. steam is used to preheat the inflowing water, and then h.p. steam to bring it up to full pressure.

18.7 Basic design

Storage capacity

Storage capacity is the first requirement to be determined, if a storage plant is to work successfully. In the case of a steam accumulator, the specific storage capacity s depends only on the pressure range. It can be calculated by a rather complicated formula, as the pressure changes

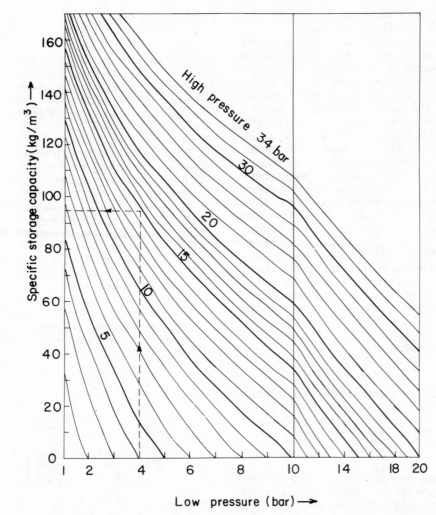

Figure 18.6   Capacity chart for pressure-drop accumulator. Example: high pressure 15 bar, low pressure 4 bar; this gives a specific storage capacity of 95 kg/m³

during the discharging operation affect the specific heat content (enthalpy) of the water, as well as its specific gravity and the latent heat of the evaporated water, and finally the amount of water left in the accumulator[1]. For exact calculation, *Figure 18.6* shows the amount of steam discharged per cubic metre of water volume, if the accumulator pressure is reduced from a given high pressure to a given low pressure. To obtain the accumulator volume required, V (m³), the storage capacity necessary, S (kg steam), has to be divided by the specific storage capacity, s (kg/m³) and the water content expressed as a fraction f of the vessel's total volume (m³/m³):

$$V = \frac{S}{s \cdot f} \qquad (18.2)$$

In the case of the feedwater accumulator, the storage capacity s can be worked out from the heat added by preheating in relation to the total heat for preheating and evaporation, multiplied by the specific gravity of the hot water stored, γ_h (kg/m³):

$$s = \frac{H_h - H_c}{H_s - H_c} \gamma_h \qquad (18.3)$$

where the subscript 'h' refers to the preheated feedwater, 'c' to the cold feedwater and 's' to steam. The accumulator volume V is then found by using equation (18.2).

Charging and discharging rate

The required rates for charging and discharging determine the equipment needed for the two operations, as well as the dimensions of the piping leading to and from the accumulator.

For the steam accumulator, the charging rate L required can be ensured by providing sufficient charging nozzles for obtaining a permissible outflow velocity of steam into the water, so that the charging operation remains without noise and vibration. The maximum discharging rate D is related to the volume of steam in the accumulator, which must be large enough to avoid the carrying over of water droplets with the discharged steam.

For the feedwater accumulator, the charging rate L determines the output of the pump supplying the cold water to the accumulator so that all the steam charged is condensed. If extraction steam is used for preheating, the charging rate is limited by the maximum rate which can safely be obtained from the preheaters. The discharging rate D, on the other hand, cannot be freely chosen, as it is determined not by the equipment, but by a factor relating it to the actual boiler output. The percentage of additional boiler output is limited by the heat added to the feedwater $(H_h - H_c)$ related to the heat added in the boiler:

$$D_{max} = \frac{H_h - H_c}{H_s - H_h} \times 100 \qquad (18.4)$$

If extraction steam is used, the additional turbine output is dependent on the increase in performance that can be obtained by closing the supply of extraction steam to the preheaters.

Efficiency

Finally, it may be useful to consider the efficiency figures which can be expected in accumulator plants. Irrespective of the system employed, there are only two kinds of loss involved: radiation losses and thermodynamic losses. Where steam from the accumulator is used for heat supply, only radiation losses occur. By effective insulation they can be kept at a very low level, and especially where frequent alternations of charging and discharging take place they are quite negligible, when related to the total amount of steam passing through the accumulator. The losses increase, of course, with the duration of the complete cycle, and must be considered seriously if each cycle lasts a day or longer. Excessive radiation losses may render thermal storage uneconomic.

The thermodynamic losses are due to the pressure drop and the loss of superheat in the steam accumulator; they do not occur in a feedwater accumulator. These losses considerably reduce the adiabatic drop for power generation in an engine or turbine, and thereby increase the amount of steam required for 1 kWh. (*See* p 403 under the heading 'Economic considerations'.)

18.8 Application

Steam storage is mainly used where the demand is subject to heavy fluctuations. Generally speaking, there are three different types of steam demand, irrespective of whether it concerns a single consumer, machine or process, or a whole factory, as illustrated in *Figure 18.7*.

1. *Steady demand:* Perfectly constant load conditions are very rare; they exist where continuous processes require steam at unchanging rates over long periods. (*Figure 18.7a* shows a load that is practically steady.)
2. *Predictable variations:* More often, consumers are subject to regular working periods with known times of starting and finishing, as well as of high and low loads (*Figure 18.7b*).
3. *Unpredictable variations:* These are typical for single consumers, as well as for whole factories that carry out a great number of processes with varying characteristics, and where diversification may sometimes smooth out the load and on other occasions make the demand more acute (*Figure 18.7c*).

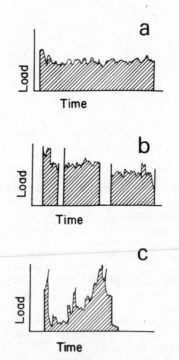

Figure 18.7 Characteristic types of steam demand. (a) Steady demand; (b) predictable fluctuations; (c) unpredictable fluctuations

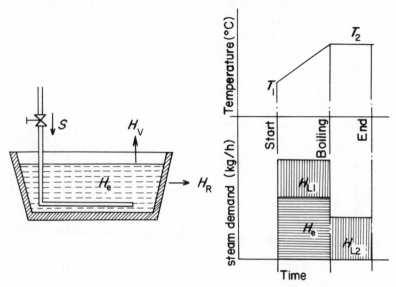

Figure 18.8   Heat balance of a dye-vat.

$$S = H_e + H_R + H_V$$

S, Steam demand; H_e, useful heat; H_R, radiation loss; H_V, vapour loss; H_{L1}, losses during heating-up period; H_{L2}, losses during boiling period

If a storage system is being considered, an extensive study of load conditions is most valuable, and is often essential to determine the need for and the optimal size and layout of the accumulator. If at all possible, the steam meter charts of boiler plant and main consumers should be carefully investigated to arrive at typical load charts for the works or the project.

If there is no flow recorder available or if a new process or plant is to be supplied, the heat or steam requirements have to be calculated. For instance, the steam demand of a dye-vat may be determined[6], as illustrated by *Figure 18.8*. The heat required to increase the temperature of the liquid from T_1 to T_2 may be considered as the useful heat H_e. The heat supplied with the steam, S, must also cover the losses H_R due to radiation and H_V due to evaporation which occur partly during the heating-up period (H_{L1}) and partly while the liquid is being kept on the boil (H_{L2}). Such consumers are typical for many industries, such as dyeworks, breweries, laundries and chemical works where large quantities of liquid have to be heated and/or boiled, causing extreme load fluctuations.

The duration of such periodic cycles is of decisive influence on the design of a storage plant. The type of demand described above usually involves fluctuations over periods of say one to four hours. This is the range where steam storage can be applied most effectively, for instance in the steel and paper industries and in sugar and other food factories, as well as the examples already mentioned.

There are many factories with only a few distinct peak loads daily, usually a heating-up peak in the morning and a second after a midday break. This kind of steam load, for which *Figure 18.9* represents a typical chart, is characteristic of many industries including a variety of steam-using departments, such as scouring, dyeing and drying machines, or a space-heating load in a textile works. The complete balance indicated by the dotted line considerably reduces the boiler load and thus may eliminate the need for a new boiler, and hence capital savings may exceed the cost of an accumulator. (*See also* p 403 under the heading 'Economic considerations'[7].)

Steam storage may sometimes be installed for balancing longer cycles, extending over periods of more than 24 hours. However, radiation losses must then seriously be taken into consideration, even with extensive insulation. Accumulators have, for instance, been effectively used for supplying requirements at weekends, such as for space heating, but heat losses will normally prevent the complete balance over full weekly periods.

On the other hand, there is practically no limit as regards shorter periods of minutes or even seconds, especially for steam accumulators. Discharging can be designed for extremely high rates, corresponding to ten times or more than the charging rate, as shown in *Figure 18.10*. The accumu-

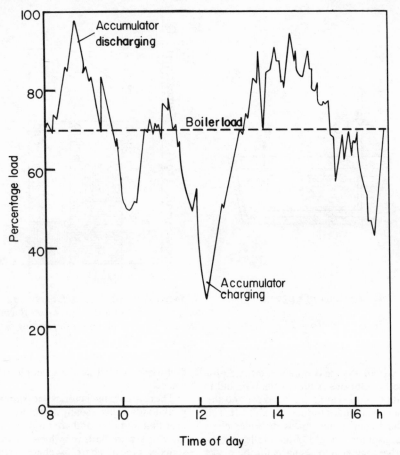

Figure 18.9   Typical industrial steam demand chart showing the balancing effect of a steam accumulator

lator plant can supply steam at the extremely high rate of 500 t/h for a short period of 7–8 minutes to ejectors required for jet engine testing, whilst recharging over longer periods[7] needs only about 20 t/h. In some cases, as for instance in connection with steam catapults on aircraft carriers, the accumulators[8] may even be discharged in a few seconds; steam supply rates as high as that could not possibly be obtained from a boiler plant without steam storage.

A distinctly different kind of application is the use of steam storage for instantaneous standby, and where no balancing effect is required. Its purpose is to supply steam, if there is a sudden and unexpected demand, such as in the case of a boiler breakdown. The discharging period is determined by the time required for bringing other supply installations into operation, that is, starting a boiler or increasing its steaming rate. Usually, this can be done within about 20–30 minutes, therefore the storage capacity and the volume of the accu-

mulator can be relatively small. Here too, only the pressure-drop system is suitable.

18.9 Typical installations

Steam accumulator supplying peaks in process demand

The plant shown in *Figure 18.11* indicates the conditions in a carpet factory, including oil-fired boilers working at 10 bar pressure and supplying 6 t/h steam each. Sharp peaks in the dyehouse's demand are caused by large vats holding some 30 m³ of liquid, each of which has to be brought to the boil in less than 30 minutes. The other consumers, drying machines and the h.p. hot-water system for space heating have a fairly steady heat requirement. If a steam accumulator of diameter 3 m and length 10 m is installed, working in the pressure range between 10 and 2 bar, it can cope with the peaks in steam demand that occur when the dye vats are heated up. In addition to a substantial fuel saving, the accumulator ensures

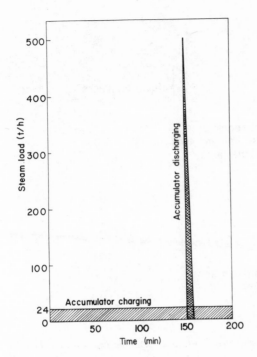

Figure 18.10   High rate of steam supply achieved by discharging a pressure-drop accumulator for very short periods

adequate steam supply, even for an additional dye vat which would otherwise require the installation of a further boiler, involving capital costs that would exceed the total costs of the storage plant.

Feedwater accumulator balancing load fluctuations

Three Economic-type boilers at a steelworks, each producing about 10 t/h at a steam pressure of 12 bar, could not maintain the normal working pressure during peak periods caused by the load fluctuations of the steam hammers and presses (*see Figure 18.12*). As full boiler pressure is required for this type of steam consumer, only a constant-pressure storage system could be applied. In view of the fact that there were no economizers for feed-preheating, the low feedwater temperature of 40°C resulted in a high storage capacity of 4.5 t of steam and a maximum additional steaming rate of about 6 t/h. An existing flue-tube boiler was converted into an accumulator by blanking the flue tubes and adding a mixing cascade preheater. The almost complete load balance achieved was very effective, in view of the relatively small water content of the boilers, providing a permanently constant steam pressure at the hammers and presses.

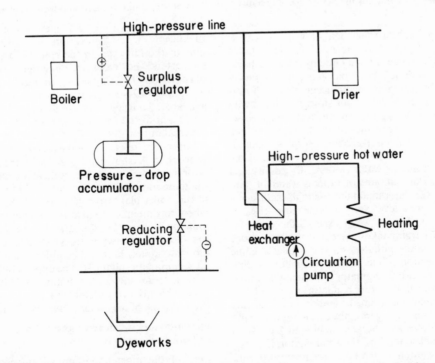

Figure 18.11   Pressure-drop accumulator supplying high peaks in process demand when heating-up large dye-vats in a carpet factory

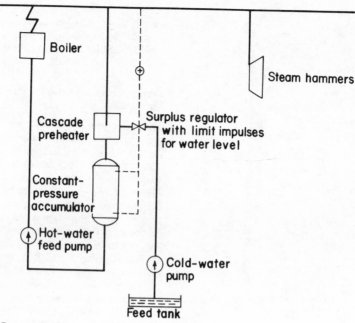

Figure   18.12   Constant-pressure   accumulator   balancing   load   and   maintaining   constant   boiler pressure at a steelworks

Hot-water accumulator for better use of exhaust steam

As shown by the arrangement drawing of a textile factory in *Figure 18.13*, steam for process is taken from the l.p. line supplied mainly from the back-pressure turbine. To avoid reducing its power output by using a steam accumulator, it was decided to install hot-water storage charged with steam from the l.p. line. The vertical storage vessel has a height of 12 m and a diameter of 3 m. When surplus l.p. steam is available, a surplus regulator opens and the steam enters at the bottom of the vessel, heating its water content. By admitting a corresponding amount of process water, a temperature regulator maintains the temperature at a predetermined level and the water level rises. If the demand for hot water exceeds the water intake, discharging takes place and the level drops again. Limiting impulses on the regulator come into operation when the accumulator is full, closing the surplus regulator, or when it is empty, opening the temperature regulator, irrespective of their normal operation. In addition to balancing the l.p. steam supply from the turbine and demand at the dyeworks, thereby maintaining constant operational conditions, the accumulator, in providing hot water at nearly boiling temperature without delay, eliminated the waiting time necessary when cold water was supplied to the dyeworks.

Steam accumulator for waste-heat recovery

Recovery of waste heat may often not be practicable, if the heat is not continuously available at the full rate. In the case of oxygen steel converters[9], hot gases are discharged during the blast period of 10–30 minutes' duration, followed by periods of 20–30 minutes when no waste heat is available. To bridge this gap and assist in supplying steam to the works at a steady rate, a steam accumulator of diameter 2.5 m and length 12 m was installed, operating in the pressure range from 18 to 5 bar. As shown in *Figure 18.14*, the accumulator discharges steam to a preheater which raises the temperature of the constant flow of feedwater to the boiler plant from 40 to 150°C. At the time when maximum waste heat is available, the accumulator is charged at the rate of 55 t/h steam. As the steam generated by the waste heat would be blown to atmosphere and completely lost without an accumulator, all the steam supplied by it represents a steam saving, amounting to 30 000 t per year, which is a considerable saving to set against the total cost of the accumulator installation.

High-pressure steam accumulator for instantaneous reserve

One of the most important advantages of the pressure-drop system is that the steam reserve is immediately available at a very high rate. In the

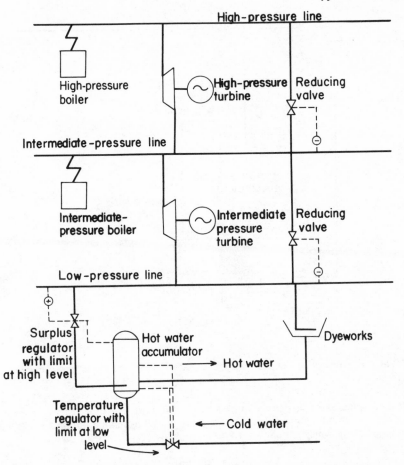

Figure 18.13   Hot-water accumulator for better use of exhaust steam for preheating process water at a textile factory

case of the installation at a power-station in Vienna[10], this was essential for uninterrupted electricity supply, which depended heavily on long-distance transmission lines from hydropower stations in the Alps. Even quick-starting boilers required 15 minutes to reach full-load conditions. The accumulator plant was designed to supply sufficient steam for bridging this gap, so that there was no drop in the grid voltage. The plant consisted of eight forged-steel drums with a total volume of 82 m^3 and discharged 14.8 t of steam at a pressure drop from 120 to 30 bar, whereby superheating to between 240 and 300°C was effected in the two upper drums of the superheat accumulator (*see Figure 18.15*). As the accumulator was kept ready for operation at maximum pressure over long periods, heat insulation was of the greatest importance. It consisted of 200-mm aluminium foil, which over 10 hours' duration restricted the pressure drop to about 10 bar, equivalent to a loss of approximately 1000 kg of steam or 6% of the

storage capacity of approximately 15 t of steam. The steam from the accumulator plant was used in a normal turbine, and could produce 4000 kWh, or an output of 16 MW for 15 minutes' duration. The accumulator was normally recharged by a heat exchanger within 12–24 h.

Expansion-type accumulator for power-station peaks

Owing to the rapid increase of output and steam conditions, the use of steel pressure vessels in power-stations has been uneconomic since the 1930s. A new system[11] is based on prestressed cast-iron pressure vessels which have been designed for sizes up to 8000 m^3 at pressures of 100 bar and over (*see Figure 18.2* on p 390). At the same time, a new method of discharging steam accumulators is suggested (*Figure 18.16*), whereby hot water is taken from the accumulator, pro-

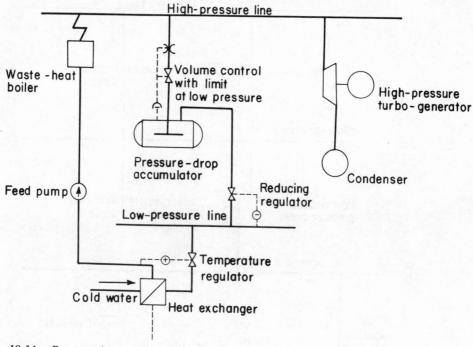

Figure 18.14   Pressure-drop accumulator for recovery of waste heat from exhaust gases at an oxygen–steel works

ducing steam in evaporators at reduced constant pressures. The evaporators are arranged in series and can supply steam which enters a turbine at different pressure stages. The steam is super-heated from an additional superheat accumulator which is charged by passing boiler steam through

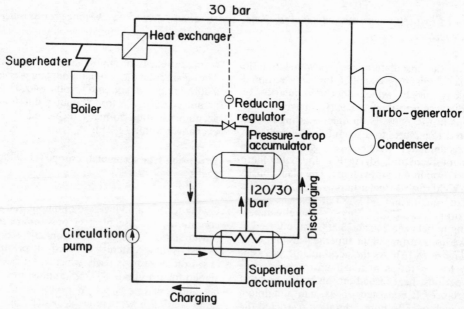

Figure 18.15   High-pressure steam accumulator for instantaneous reserve in case of a breakdown in the grid supply at a power-station

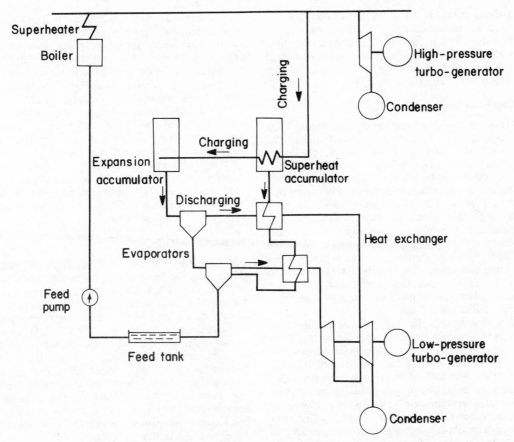

Figure 18.16 Expansion-type steam accumulator for supplying steam for peak-load requirements at power-stations

its water content before it is charged into the expansion accumulator. It is suggested that for a storage capacity sufficient for maintaining an output of 400 MW over a period of 2 hours, a storage plant of four 7500-m³ vessels working between 60 and 1.5 bar for steam supply and one 4000-m³ vessel operating at 65 bar for superheating would be required.

18.10 Economic considerations

Steam storage installations must be justified by operational advantages and financial savings, which under normal conditions may be determined quite accurately. However, there are some advantages that cannot be assessed in terms of accountancy, such as reliability of steam supply and maintenance of optimal steam conditions, but which have a favourable influence on production. Sir Oliver Lyle probably had these additional benefits in mind when he wrote, 'In case of doubt, the decision should be taken in favour of installing

accumulators which can bring attendant intangible advantages.'

Fuel savings

The additional fuel losses due to rapidly changing boiler firing vary greatly with the type, size and flexibility of the boiler plant, with the kind of fuel, standards of supervision and maintenance, etc., so that it is very difficult to state definite figures for the fuel savings that thermal storage may bring. Comparative tests have resulted in figures sometimes exceeding 10%, but normally nearer 5%. Oil firing, although more flexible, usually produced lower savings in tests than did coal firing. There is, however, no doubt that the highest boiler efficiency — for otherwise equal circumstances — can be obtained only at continuously constant operation at full load. Additional fuel losses may arise from operation at part load, since radiation losses are not less than at full load, and there may also be losses from rapid changes in load condition and from periods of standing, as well as stopping and starting the boiler plant. As fuel costs are now so greatly increased, it is obvious that more attention should be given to the maintenance of a high boiler efficiency by eliminating such additional losses, and thermal storage is one of the effective means to achieve this.

Capital savings

However important fuel savings are today, their financial effect is usually secondary to the capital savings which were the main reason for the installation of most accumulators.

In other words, if steam requirements exceed boiler capacity, it may be less expensive to install a storage plant to cover the peaks than to install a boiler plant which must include the auxiliaries and buildings. Accumulators are usually placed outside, and require only simple foundations. Another factor, which is often overlooked, is that in comparing cost figures it is not the total expenditure which counts, but the yearly cost. Here the accumulator has the great advantage of longer life, less maintenance, and practically no repairs. Whilst it is true that cost of maintenance and repairs for steam storage plant is almost negligible — compared with, for instance, boiler plant where tube failures and similar defects are not uncommon — it is still of the greatest importance that the plant is kept in proper condition and that its operation is permanently checked. Therefore, it is strongly recommended that a specialist firm with long-term experience in the accumulator field is not only employed for the design and construction of the storage plant, but also that it undertakes to start it up and service it, at least for an initial period of six months. With accumulators this servicing is not less important than the correct supply of the equipment.

Cost of storage plant

Whilst no definite figures can be given, as they change with time, locality and requirements, there are certain factors which have an influence on the price level. First of all, the pressure vessel to contain the storage medium is by far the biggest single item. For normal industrial conditions, the vessel accounts for about 65–85% of the total installation costs, whilst for power-station conditions it may be nearer 75–90%. This means that all the other items, such as heat insulation, accessories, automation and piping, may add only between 1/5 and 1/2, or 1/10 and 1/3, to the cost of the vessel. As the vessel costs depend on the storage capacity, whilst the additional costs depend mainly on the charging/discharging rates, it follows that long periods of discharging will tend to bring the vessel costs nearer to the upper limits mentioned above.

For the pressure vessel there is a definite relation between cost and the factor of volume times pressure (m^3 bar) which applies generally, except for small units. For steel vessels this lower limit is approximately 50 m^3, whilst for prestressed cast-iron pressure vessels it is about 500 m^3. Below this limit, the cost per m^3 bar goes up very quickly.

The ratio of diameter to length or height, respectively, is also of considerable influence, as larger diameters result in greater wall thickness and greater length results in larger surface area, both influencing the weight and thus the cost of the vessel. A larger surface will also mean increased cost for heat insulation. The optimum ratio for steel vessels lies between 1 : 4 and 1 : 5, whilst for prestressed CI it is nearer 1 : 6.

Economic limitations

The importance of the time factor (usually, the duration of the accumulator discharge) cannot be over-emphasized. It has a decisive influence on the size of the storage plant required to achieve the desired balancing effect. In many cases this is not sufficiently appreciated; often the size and output of the boiler are the sole factors considered and the time factor hardly enters the calculation of installation costs. Requirements for storage capacity are often inflated (to be 'on the safe side') and the extra cost for a correspondingly larger accumulator (which may not really be necessary) has killed many projects which otherwise would have proved effective and economic.

In general, steam storage plant will be less expensive than the comparable boiler plant for a duration of up to 4 hours, if the peak load takes the normal, approximately triangular, form. In power-stations, this figure may go up to about 6 hours, as recent investigations have shown[12].

References

1 Goldstern, W. *Steam Storage Installations*, 2nd edn. Oxford; Pergamon Press (1970) (includes 96 references)
2 Goldstern, W. 'Development, importance and application of steam storage' (in German). *VDI Conference Report 223, Stuttgart* (1974)
3 Schilling, F. E., Beine, B. and Gross, H. 'The prestressed cast-iron pressure vessel'. *Nucl. Eng. Design*, **25**, 315 (1973)
4 Bitterlich, E. 'Generation of storage heat by extraction steam at low loads for use during peak-load periods.' *BWK 2* (1977) (in German)
5 Marguerre, F. 'Heat storage in conventional and nuclear power stations' *World Power Conference, Madrid* (1960)
6 Goldstern, W. 'The steam demand for dyeing'.

Soc. Dyers Col., 301 *(1946)*

7 Goldstern, W. 'Three Economic boilers and accumulators can produce steam at the rate of 1 000 000 lb/h. *Power W. Engr.*, 86 (1956)

8 Plummer, G. A. 'Wet accumulator for naval steam catapult'. *Engineer*, 741 (1959)

9 Woolley, E. M. 'Waste heat boiler'. *Iron and Steel*, **11**, 65 (1965)

10 Mokesch, R. '120 atm steam storage at Vienna Power Station'. *Arch. Wärmew.*, 87 (1938) (in German)

11 Beckmann, G. and Gilli, P. V. 'Thermal energy storage for peak-load supply'. *VDI Convention Report 236, Düsseldorf* (1975) (in English)

12 Gilli, P. V. and Beckmann, G. 'The nuclear steam storage plant'. *9th World Energy Conference, Detroit, 1974.* Paper 4.1–10

19 Steam costing

Steam should always be costed, the complexity of the costing method depending on the amount of steam used. It might be enough to add up the cost of fuel, water and a bit of Joe's time, and divide this by the amount of steam sent out, or thought to be sent out, from the boiler plant. Where appreciable amounts of steam are used, particularly by a number of different users, a more detailed costing is necessary. Only by knowing the cost of steam can a manager see the value of using steam efficiently, and set this against the cost of doing so, or be able to make comparisons with alternative heat sources. It is no use saving steam by putting in new equipment, if the annual cost of servicing the equipment — operation, maintenance, interest on capital cost — exceeds the value of steam saved.

There can be several costs of steam, but most managers will be adequately served by three: the *budget* cost (or bogey, or normal cost — choose your own word for it), the *actual* cost, and the *marginal* cost.

Whatever cost is chosen, the cost of steam (and electricity) may be significant in the final cost of a product, be it chemicals, food or oil, and an efficient boiler plant will contribute to the overall profitability of a commercial operation.

The whole costing structure depends upon the use of reliable steam meters (or possibly, on the boiler plant, of water meters) and upon their accuracy. Steam from boiler plants should always be metered, but the decision as to further metering depends upon several factors. There is no clear rule about this, only a number of pros and cons. If steam to users is metered, a check can be kept on the efficiency of the process; any abnormal consumptions show up and data which will go towards realistic product costing can be built up. On the other hand the initial cost of the meter and installation must be found, as must the cost of reading the meter, changing the charts on recording instruments, and the maintenance costs with the eventual cost of modifying or replacing the meter. This may outweigh the cost advantage of having accurate measurement of steam usage in the first place. Perhaps on further consideration experienced estimates might suffice.

19.1 Budget cost

The *budget cost* is an estimate of the cost of

producing a given amount of steam, based on the best estimates of the various costs which go into steam production. The estimates are usually deliberately kept low by the management, abetted by accountants, whilst the boiler plant manager, by exercising low cunning and his undoubted technical superiority, attempts to increase them substantially; the result is usually a fair compromise.

For reasons which will appear later, the budget cost should be worked out for an annual steam output, using estimated annual costs.

19.2 Actual cost

The *actual cost* is what its name suggests, and indicates the deviation from the budget cost arising from seasonal factors, unrealistic estimating, abnormal weather conditions, good (or bad)

operation, changes in fuel costs and many other factors. How often this cost is worked out depends mostly on how the works accounting system is organized, but a monthly figure is a good one to aim at. What this figure tells interested parties may be a shock, a pleasant surprise, a cause of worry or gratification, but it is always of value. There may be — there will be — factors within the cost which are outside the control of the immediately interested parties; there will be others which are very much controllable, and regular costing is important because it shows these up.

Frequency should be such that figures can be used to monitor operations, and not become merely 'history'.

Table 19.1 shows a suitable sheet which can be used to record monthly the actual steam costs against a budget cost.

Table 19.1   Steam costing chart

	Budget	Actual		
		Jan	Feb	March etc.
Salaries	£			
Operating wages				
Direct wages	£			
Overheads	£			
Maintenance				
Materials	£			
Contractors	£			
Direct wages	£			
Overheads	£			
Fuel	£			
Internal steam	£			
Water	£			
Electricity	£			
Other services	£			
Operating materials	£			
Total (A)	£			
Depreciation	£			
Insurance	£			
Boiler output, B (t)				
Steam charged, C (t)				
Mains loss, B − C (t)				
Distributed steam cost A/C £/t				

19.3　Marginal cost

Marginal cost is the real cost of producing a given additional amount of steam, and marginal saving is the money return for not producing a certain specified quantity of steam. In its simplest form it is built up from the variable elements in the steam cost, but accountancy is rarely simple and other considerations do intrude. For instance, the marginal cost of producing an extra 10 t/h from a boiler plant designed for, and running continuously at, 50 t/h, could include the capital and operating cost of a new boiler. This is an extreme case, but one could imagine a situation where reduced demands, because of saving, could lead to a reduction in manning levels of one man per shift. Whilst it is important to know about marginal costs, and how they are built up, it is as well to leave it to accountants to calculate these as a preliminary to a reasoned discussion.

19.4　Costing factors

Quantity of steam

The quantity of steam is clearly the basic start to the exercise; if we do not know how much steam we are discussing, we cannot work out a cost per unit. It is best to work on the basis of the total amount of steam as measured on the steam meters — or water meters, after allowing for blowdown — on all the boilers. It is quite practicable to use, instead of the steam produced, a figure for the steam distributed (that is, the steam leaving the boilerhouse) to the customers. This has the disadvantage that steam used (or wasted) inside the boiler plant is not accounted for, and that is not really desirable. This figure might be embarrassing for the boiler manager, but he ought to know what it is.

The amount of steam which appears in the budget cost is not easy to estimate because it depends on the demands of production which may be many months ahead when the estimate is made, and only several years' experience of varying production demands can give a reasonably accurate figure.

Because both fixed and variable costs go into the steam account, the cost of steam produced varies with the output, though not directly. This does not produce any appreciable problems in working out the cost of steam, but it does distort the efficiency of steam production, as measured in monetary terms, since the cost per unit of steam goes up quite sharply as output falls.

In a rather similar way the actual usage of steam, as measured to a manufacturing unit, is not directly proportional to manufacturing output, and just as a boiler plant has fixed and variable costs, so does a consuming unit have fixed and variable usages. Even on the lowest output, steam mains have to be kept charged up, and unattended leaks will still be supplied with steam — and it is surprising how many fixed usages can be found once an investigation is carried out. A realistic approach to product costing would then be to charge the production unit with a fixed amount of steam, plus another amount which is proportional to output. The way the total usage is split can be subject to considerable error, but this method recognizes facts and is an attempt to show them in the costing system. In a complex situation computer technology can be used with advantage.

Salaries

This figure is the total cost of the salaries of all the people directly concerned with steam production and distribution, and should include attendant costs such as overtime payments, bonus payments and expenses. In many cases the production of steam may not be the only responsibility of the engineer, and a reasonable estimate must be made of the proportion of his effort which is directly concerned with steam production.

Operating wages

This is usually easier to determine since it will not be as common for operators' time to be divided amongst several different functions as is the case for salaried staff, although in small, well-controlled boiler plants the operator may have other duties. Overheads such as national insurance, sickness pay, holiday payments and similar fringe expenses must be included unless it is company policy to carry these in a separate account. It is best to include, amongst this cost, the wages of men concerned with fuel handling, ash removal, water treatment and laboratory testing, since the expense of maintaining separate costs for fuel and treated water is rarely justified — although it might be if either of these were used additionally in another part of the factory that has nothing to do with steam raising.

Maintenance charges

The total cost of maintaining the boiler plant and its fuel handling system, auxiliary plant, buildings, steam mains and supports should be a charge on the cost of steam. The total cost will be made up of materials and labour, including those overheads which were mentioned under 'operating wages'. The cost of outside contracts for repair work should be included, and these can be items of considerable expense.

As discussed previously, the only accurate cost is that which is built up on an annual basis. Major maintenance expenditure on boiler plant tends to appear irregularly month by month, since major boiler overhauls have to fit in with production patterns and the statutory requirements for inspection, and can cause gross distortion of a month's figures. Annual costs show much less variation.

Fuel

The major operating cost of any boiler plant is the cost of fuel, and this is fairly readily obtained on a monthly basis, once allowance has been made for any change in bunker stocks. It has become much more difficult over the last few years to estimate accurately the price of the fuel which is going to be burned in the coming year, and this can only be based on past experience with a dash of political and commercial acumen. The varying calorific values of coal can introduce unwelcome discrepancies between estimated and actual cost, but in the UK at least, this is somewhat mitigated by the National Coal Board's current (1978) policy of basing their price largely on calorific value, even though there are other factors affecting the price such as the grade, ash content and sulphur content. Transport costs must, of course, be included, and these can be an important factor in choosing the best buy from several fuels.

Steam

Steam used within a boiler plant should be charged, just like any other expense. The amount used can be quite small: steam loss from drains, leaks, boiler sampling, steam lancing. If there is much feedheating of raw water, or if steam-driven auxiliaries are used, then the amount could be appreciable, sometimes as much as 20% of the total steam produced from boilers, and so must be charged to the boiler-house account. The arithmetic used to calculate the monthly unit cost of steam, when this itself contains an appreciable steam component, may be more involved than can be justified by the accuracy of other factors, and it is often better to use a nominal cost for steam used internally — perhaps the previous month's steam cost.

Water

The water cost is a straightforward cost of the raw water delivered to the boiler plant for steam raising, back-washing and rinsing of ion exchange plant, ash quenching and sluicing and other incidental uses. Any materials used in an ion exchange plant, or for boiler water dosing, would usually be included in the operating materials cost, which is discussed on p 411.

Electricity

Electricity is usually one of the easiest usages to meter, and the only problem which arises is the cost of the electricity if supplies purchased from the supply authority are supplemented by private generation. It can also be complicated by tariff structures which carry seasonal maximum demand payments, power factor penalties and other charges which may not be known until some time later. Here again there is much to be said for using a nominal value for electricity, and the best possible estimate must be made of the total annual cost of electricity — whether all purchased, all generated, or a combination of the two, which appears in the forward annual budget for steam.

Other services

Other services are likely to be small — perhaps only a nominal charge for gas and compressed air. However, it is important to keep this item in the budget in case unusual circumstances arise.

Mains losses

Steam is always lost in the distribution system outside the boiler plant. A theoretical calculation of the steam loss in a typical medium-sized factory would show a figure of perhaps 4% of the boiler output, but the actual discrepancy between steam from the boiler plant and all the steam which can be accounted for on the factory would probably be double that amount.

Mains loss can be treated in several ways, but a practical assessment of loss, as distinct from simply a heat transfer calculation, should include:

1. condensation of steam in distribution mains between the boiler plant and each consumer;
2. errors in the steam meters together with possible arithmetical errors in calculating steam usage;
3. the inevitable errors in assessment of steam used by smaller consumers for whom the expense of steam metering is not justified;
4. steam poaching — unauthorized and undeclared steam usage on the works; and
5. inevitable steam leaks — often difficult to stop promptly in a complicated distribution system.

The steam losses represent an expenditure which has to be paid for by someone: either the producer of the steam, or the users of the steam. If we take a fictional factory we can see how this works. Let us assume an annual steam production from the boilers of 150000 t with total operating expenses of £800000 giving a cost of production of £5.33 per tonne, and that throughout the year only 140000 t can be accounted for from consumers (that is, only 140000 t can be charged).

If the consumer pays for the loss, then we have

$$\text{Cost per tonne} = \frac{\text{Total cost}}{\text{steam charged to users}}$$

$$= \frac{800\,000}{140\,000} = £5.71 \text{ per tonne}$$

If the cost of this unaccounted 10000 t is charged back to the boiler plant in a rather spurious way by adding the value of this steam to the boiler expenses, we have

Total operating cost = £800000 + 10000 t

at an approximate cost of £5.33 per tonne

Total operating cost = £800000 + £53300
for 150000 t

or an overall cost of £5.68 per tonne, which is almost the same figure as before, the difference being caused by assuming a cost of £5.33 per tonne. Note that the spurious charge arises because the cost of the lost steam has been charged back to the boiler plant, without a corresponding increase in steam output from the boilers. This creates an artificial system which is difficult to justify, and it is better to divide the total operating costs by the steam which can be accounted for.

Operating materials

The cost of materials — other than the water and fuel used for steam raising — should be included. Most engineering materials which find their way onto the boiler plant will be included in maintenance costs, but allowance must be made for other things which are not directly concerned with maintenance. The principal cost will be of chemicals for direct dosing of the boilers, and those materials used with ion exchange plants, including the cost of eventual replacement of the ion exchange resin.

A good principle is to charge the materials which are used by operating staff to this account, and to allocate other materials to the maintenance costs.

Depreciation

Depreciation should probably be left out of periodic steam costs. Although the eventual cost of replacing the boiler plant and its buildings is a real charge on the cost of steam raising, it is not, in periods of high inflation, easy to be sure of including a valid figure, particularly since this could be influenced by financial policy decisions. It is best to build up a cost of steam excluding this figure, but to keep a notional figure which can be added if the overall cost of steam, including depreciation, is needed at any time.

Insurance

All boiler plants must carry insurance cover, but since this may only be a part of a much greater overall insurance charge, it is advisable to deal with this as with depreciation and to exclude it, unless it is specially required.

19.5 Steam and electricity costing

If there is no electricity generation from steam, the costing system is simple, since each consumer is charged at a price which reflects the cost of producing and distributing the steam. Even if it is produced at a higher pressure for a few users and then reduced in pressure for the rest, it is scarcely worth charging at two different prices, since in this case the high-pressure steam has no greater commercial worth than that at a lower pressure.

Similarly, if all the steam is used for electricity generation, it is being used only as a medium for transferring the energy from the fuel to the generator, and its value in pence per tonne is not important as such, but only as one of the costs of producing electricity.

However, when steam is used for heating, and for power, a simple charging scheme will not give effective cost control. Nearly all the steam which goes through a back-pressure turbine or comes from the pass-out stages of an extraction turbine has been unchanged in quantity, but changed in quality. A small amount has, of course, been used for gland sealing and eventually lost. This must be accounted for, but is only a small percentage of the total amount of steam to the turbine.

A straightforward cost on the amount used could only result in all the steam being charged to the turbine — giving expensive electricity and free steam — or all being charged to the process use — giving free electricity and steam charged at boiler plant cost; neither of these is desirable.

There are two main costing systems in general use, based either on the heat available to the steam user, or on the energy available. The terms are somewhat anomalous, since heat is a form of energy, but the essential difference in the approach will be clear from the theoretical treatment of steam in Chapters 1 and 2.

Heat basis

The cost of steam to a consumer on a heat basis is calculated on that proportion of the total heat in the steam (above some arbitrary base temperature) which is available to the consumer. If we look at the simple system shown in *Figure 19.1*, and taking a base temperature of 39°C (the reason for choosing this temperature will be apparent from the next section entitled 'energy basis'), then the calculation is as follows:

Enthalpy of steam at 15 bar, 270°C	=	2970.7 kJ/kg
Enthalpy of steam at 2 bar, 150°C	=	2768.5 kJ/kg
∴ Heat taken out by turbine	=	202.2 kJ/kg
Enthalpy of steam at 2 bar, 150°C	=	2768.5 kJ/kg
Enthalpy of water at 39°C	=	163.3 kJ/kg
Heat available for manufacturing process	=	2605.2 kJ/kg

So on a heat basis, the charge to the generation of electricity by the turbine would be

$$\frac{202.2}{(2970.7 - 163.3)} \times 5.30 = £0.38 \text{ per tonne}$$

and the charge to the manufacturing unit would be

$$\frac{2605.2}{(2970.7 - 163.3)} \times 5.30 = £4.92 \text{ per tonne}$$

It should be noted that the steam has remained as steam through the turbine — as back-pressure steam or from an extraction stage — but has condensed to water in the manufacturing process. This does not affect the relevance of the method since in both cases we are dealing only with the heat which could be abstracted. It also assumes that the process can extract heat condensate down to 39°C, because the basis of the charge is the heat available, not what is used. Drain coolers could be used to extract more heat, as mentioned in Chapter 17, if it were economical to do so.

From this reasoning it follows that any user of steam at 15 bar for heating, or for power production in which the exhaust steam is not reused, should be charged the full steam cost of £5.30 per tonne.

In the example based on *Figure 19.1* a turbine efficiency of 100%, giving an exhaust pressure of 2 bar and a temperature of 150°C, was assumed. With a normal turbine efficiency the temperature would be somewhat lower than this. In the second example, which involves double generation (*Figure 19.2*) from 40 bar → 15 bar → 2 bar, a turbine adiabatic efficiency of 100% has been assumed. Without any change of entropy, the exhaust steam from the 40-bar turbine would be at 15 bar and 264°C, and if this was passed to the 15-bar turbine without any temperature drop between the two turbines the exhaust steam at 2 bar would be saturated at 120°C with about 6.3% wetness fraction. These values have been used in the calculations.

The method of determining the various steam costs is the same as for the system shown in *Figure 19.1* as follows:

Enthalpy of steam at 40 bar, 400°C	=	3215.7 kJ/kg
Enthalpy of steam at 15 bar, 264°C	=	2957.2 kJ/kg
∴ Heat taken out by 40-bar turbine	=	258.5 kJ/kg
Enthalpy of steam at 15 bar, 264°C	=	2957.2 kJ/kg
Enthalpy of water at 39°C	=	163.3 kJ/kg
∴ Heat taken from steam for process use at 15 bar	=	2793.9 kJ/kg
Enthalpy of steam at 15 bar, 264°C	=	2957.2 kJ/kg
Enthalpy of wet steam at 2 bar sat.	=	2567.6 kJ/kg

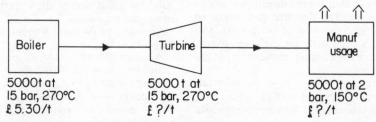

Figure 19.1 Calculation of steam cost on a heat basis

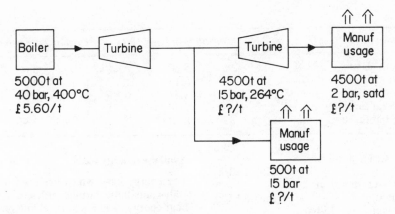

Figure 19.2 Calculation of steam cost for a system involving double generation

∴ Heat taken out by 15 bar
turbine = 389.6 kJ/kg
Enthalpy of wet steam at 2
bar sat. = 2567.6 kJ/kg
Enthalpy of water at 39°C = 163.3 kJ/kg
∴ Heat taken from steam
for process at 2 bar = 2404.3 kJ/kg
The full heat availability of the 40-bar steam, to a final temperature of 39°C, would be 3215.7 − 163.3 = 3052.4 kJ/kg.

So, for the various costs of steam, we have:

Process steam at 40 bar = £5.60 per tonne

which is the cost of production and distribution.

Charge to generation for 40-bar turbine =

$$\frac{258.5}{3052.4} \times 5.60 = \text{£0.47 per tonne}$$

so the charge to process steam at 15 bar is

$$\frac{2793.9}{3052.4} \times 5.60 = \text{£5.13}$$

The charge to generation for the 15-bar turbine is

$$\frac{389.6}{3052.4} \times 5.60 = \text{£0.72}$$

Charge to process steam at 2 bar is

$$\frac{2404.3}{3052.4} \times 5.60 = \text{£4.41 per tonne}$$

Summarizing these costs, we have

(a) Charge for process
steam at 40 bar = £5.60 per tonne
(b) Charge for process
steam at 15 bar = £5.13 per tonne
(c) Charge for process
steam at 2 bar = £4.41 per tonne

(d) Charge to 40-bar
turbine for generation = £0.47 per tonne
(e) Charge to 15-bar
turbine for generation = £0.72 per tonne

It should be noted that (b) + (d) add up to the cost of steam from the high-pressure boilers of £5.60 per tonne and (c) + (e) to the cost of steam at 15 bar.

Energy basis

There are a number of variants on the energy basis, but to illustrate how it is used we will take a system assuming turbines of 100% adiabatic efficiency. The heat energy abstracted at each stage is taken from a Mollier chart, and these values are then used to determine the cost of the steam. The method of doing this is given in greater detail in Chapters 1 and 2.

The base or sink condition for the exhaust steam from the 15-bar turbine is taken as 0.07 bar, which is a turbine exhaust pressure that can reasonably be achieved under most conditions. The corresponding temperature is 39°C, the temperature that was used for the previous cost assessment on the heat basis, thus making the two methods comparable.

Enthalpy of steam at 40 bar,
400°C = 3215.7 kJ/kg
Enthalpy of steam at 15 bar,
264°C = 2957.2 kJ/kg
Energy taken by 40-bar
turbine = 258.5 kJ/kg
Enthalpy of steam at 15 bar,
264°C = 2957.2 kJ/kg
Enthalpy of steam at 39°C
(0.07 bar) = 2102.8 kJ/kg
Energy from steam at 15 bar
taken for process = 854.4 kJ/kg

Table 19.2

Steam condition	Cost on heat basis (£/t)	Cost on energy basis (£/t)
Process steam, 40 bar	5.60	5.60
Process steam, 15 bar	5.13	4.30
Process steam, 2 bar	4.41	2.34
Charge to 40-bar turbine	0.47	1.30
Charge to 15-bar turbine	0.72	1.96

Enthalpy of steam at 15 bar,
264°C $= 2957.2$ kJ/kg
Enthalpy of wet steam at 2
bar (saturated) $= 2567.6$ kJ/kg
Energy taken by 15-bar
turbine $= 389.6$ kJ/kg
Enthalpy of wet steam at 2 bar
(saturated) $= 2567.6$ kJ/kg
Enthalpy of steam at 39°C
(0.07 bar) $= 2102.8$ kJ/kg
Energy from steam at 2 bar
taken for process $= 464.8$ kJ/kg

The full energy availability of the 40-bar steam to a final exhaust temperature of 39°C (0.07 bar) would be $3215.7 - 2102.8 = 1112.9$ kJ/kg. Using the same method of calculation as in the heat basis gives

(a) Charge for process
steam at 40 bar $= $ £5.60 per tonne

(b) Charge for process
steam at 15 bar $= $ £4.30 per tonne

(c) Charge for process
steam at 2 bar $= $ £2.34 per tonne

(d) Charge to 40-bar
turbine for
generation $= $ £1.30 per tonne

(e) Charge to 15-bar
turbine for
generation $= $ £1.96 per tonne

Again, the steam costs add up at the various stages.

Available-energy basis

The energy basis which has been used assumes 100% adiabatic turbine efficiency, so that the heat energy drop is a vertical line on the Mollier diagram, and no change of entropy takes place.

This method can be modified by using the actual turbine efficiency to find the available energy, and can be further refined, if desired, to allow for some pressure and temperature drop between the two turbines. The calculation is similar to the one which has just been shown on p 412, but it is not really necessary to do this unless some small reduction in the cost of steam for electricity generation is thought to be desirable.

Comparison of costs on heat and energy basis

Table 19.2 shows the effect of using either a heat basis or an energy basis. The heat basis gives cheap electricity, at least in so far as the steam passing through the turbines is a major part of this cost; the energy basis charges more to electricity, and the steam becomes correspondingly cheaper.

There is no 'best' method; it depends on the circumstances and the policy which is being adopted, whether one should encourage the use of electricity (heat basis), or make this a more expensive service in the factory costing system (energy basis). Whichever method is adopted, it should be made part of a continuous costing operation, and where major decisions have to be taken, the marginal costs involved should be calculated, and the financial decisions should be based on these costs.

20

Steam in industry

This chapter deals with the practical production and use of steam in modern industry. The examples have been chosen to cover as wide a range as possible, and to illustrate, from present-day industrial practice, some of the theoretical aspects of steam production and use which have been dealt with in other parts of the book. A further example appears in Chapter 16 showing the installation of steam reformers.

20.1 Steam in a chemical works

An industrial installation in a chemical works, which makes use of both conventional and waste-heat boilers, is shown in *Figure 20.1*. The use of waste-heat boilers to produce process steam at once brings out a major problem in deciding on the true steam availability at all times. Although the use of waste-heat boilers is an admirable development which saves fuel, they are, in most cases, a part of the manufacturing process and not of the central boiler plant; as such they are unlikely to be under the control of the boiler plant manager.

Since they are part of the process, they are subject to shutdowns because of limited demand for the product, plant maintenance outages and perhaps even shortage of labour. Although the boiler plant manager can plan for — and be answerable for — his own plant performance, he can hardly do it for a chemical process not under his own control.

Another feature of waste-heat boilers is that they are often operated by plant process labour, and are looked upon as an appendage — not always a welcome one — to the manufacture. To ensure safe and efficient operation, such plant should be under the benevolent eye of an experienced boiler operator or even boiler plant manager. Particularly careful scrutiny is necessary if there is some common link with the central boiler plant over steam exported, raw or treated water, blowdown systems or other common feature. These considerations were in fact fully appreciated in this works, and a satisfactory arrangement was made for the conventional and waste-heat boilers to be under the control of one manager.

Figure 20.1 indicates the form of the steam/turbo-generator system which has been developed in stages with the growth of the

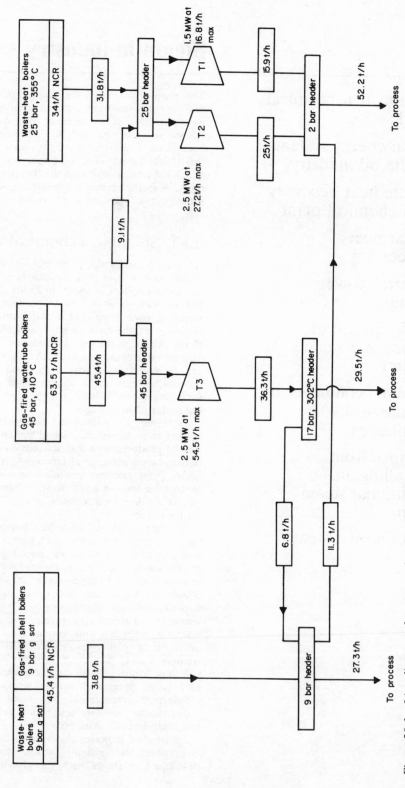

Figure 20.1   Line diagram of a steam turbo-alternator system in a chemical works. NCR, normal continuous rating

process manufacturing plant over a period of twenty-five years. It should not, therefore, be looked upon as the optimum system for the current steam demand. It represents a system which exists and has been installed in stages; for example, turbo-alternator T2 was installed four years after T1, and T3 some seven years later.

Turbo-alternators T1 and T2 were installed to generate power from the steam produced from waste-heat boilers installed in exothermic processes. At this time there was a demand for 2 bar gauge steam from a manufacturing process and it was expected that additional exothermic processes would be installed to increase the amount of 25 bar g steam to the maximum throughput of T1 and T2. In the event this did not materialize and in fact the situation began to reverse in that a demand for 17 bar g steam was created and further exothermic processes with waste-heat boilers were not installed.

This led to the installation of conventional boilers generating at 45 bar g and turbo-alternator T3 exhausting at 17 bar g. This particular expansion took place later when the electricity to fuel cost ratio was approximately 12 : 1. Later the electricity to fuel cost ratio at this particular works was approximately 3.5 : 1 and much of the attractiveness of this back-pressure generation of electricity using conventional boilers had been lost, particularly as the process requirements pressure had risen from 2 bar g to 17 bar g and could in the future rise even higher.

Some time after the installation of the final turbine (T3), there was a review of the economics of the system in conjunction with a proposed expansion of the manufacturing plant which called for an increase in requirements for 17 bar g steam. The conclusions were that with then current fuel and electricity costs and the capital cost of a high-pressure boiler plant and turbo-alternators, there was not a sufficiently attractive return on investment to proceed further with the development of the power generation system at the works. This conclusion, of course, would not affect the situation for exothermic processes where waste-heat boilers could be used.

This shows the difficulty of planning major steam and power extensions, particularly when they are associated with a complicated industrial process. Many combinations of capital plant and operating conditions have to be assessed before a scheme can be found which will, unless major factors intervene, give a reliable supply to the factory and show a reasonable return on capital investment.

An important consideration which arose, and which affected the economics of the scheme, was the demand for steam at 17 bar g for process usage, and this illustrates the importance of critical examination of such requirements — including, if necessary, the alternatives to using steam at such a pressure, or at least restricting the use to essential cases. It is not inconceivable for a supply to be piped to a process at a relatively high pressure, to be used also by other processes which would have been satisfied with a much more modest supply.

The 29.5 t/h of steam at 17 bar g and 302°C shown in *Figure 20.1* would have been able to generate at about 2200 kW if expanded to a pressure of 2 bar g. Whatever the relative cost of fuel and electricity this would be a significant gain in electricity generation.

20.2 Total-energy systems in the oil industry

Conditions in the oil industry are often quite similar to those in the chemical industry, with the same opportunities for using waste heat and the same problems of determining the best steam and power plants for a particular set of circumstances. This example, which has been taken from the oil industry, deals particularly with the overall efficiencies which can be expected from conventional power plant and from gas turbine systems.

The oil and petrochemical industries use large quantities of steam mainly for heat exchange, machinery prime movers, gas stripping and assisting reactions in process plants. Where possible the steam is raised in the process units, using either waste heat which has been generated in a furnace for process requirements, or by heat exchange with high-temperature process streams. Obviously the quantity of steam which can be generated will depend on the quantity of surplus heat available. Often this is insufficient to satisfy the steam demands of the unit so it follows that in most chemical works and refineries some form of independent steam generation is necessary.

Besides producing waste heat, process units often produce combustible by-products and, where practicable, these are used as fuel for both process heaters and boiler plant. The quantity and quality of such fuels which can be made available for boiler plant will vary, depending on their value as a feedstock or as a fuel in the process units, and on the types of process installed in the plant. Nevertheless, when available these by-products are used in preference to commercial fuels so contributing to energy conservation and the overall efficiency of the whole plant.

Where an independent steam supply is required, conventional boiler plant may be used, designed to supply steam directly to process units at the conditions required by them (normally between 10 and 35 bar g). However, in large refineries and chemical works where an appreciable amount of electric power is required it is often advantageous to adopt total-energy techniques combining steam and power generation. These, if properly engineered, can be very efficient and will improve the overall efficiency of the whole plant. In some remote areas where an external electric power supply is unavailable there is of course no alternative but to adopt the total-energy principle.

The oil industry shows good examples of the use of total-energy systems, as mentioned previously in Chapter 11. The combined boiler and back-pressure turbine plant, which embodied total-energy principles long before that phrase came into current use, is the most common type of installation, but there are many circumstances where gas turbine systems are put forward as a better solution. Each case has to be carefully worked out on the basis of capital and operating costs, with a sideways look at reliability — perhaps an assessment of the cost of being without steam or power because of unplanned breakdowns.

The following examples show:

1. A typical system using high-pressure boilers and back-pressure turbo-alternator (*Figure 20.2*).

2. A typical alternative system with a gas turbine driving an alternator and exhausting its gases to a waste-heat boiler (*Figure 20.3*). (Waste-heat boilers are described in Chapter 5.)

Boiler and steam turbine system

Plant extensions at a large refinery/petrochemical complex called for peak steam loads of 300 t/h at 14 bar g and 45 MW of electricity. The existing plant receives steam and power from a number of high-pressure boilers supplying steam to a combination of back-pressure and pass-out/condensing turbo-alternators. Auxiliary plant such as fans and feed pumps is normally driven by back-pressure steam turbines, using steam at 14 bar g and exhausting to the de-aerators. The steam consumption of such auxiliary plant normally amounts to around 20–22% of the gross boiler output for systems of this type.

The system installed is shown in *Figure 20.2*. The three boilers are each rated at 136 t/h, superheater outlet conditions being 128 bar g and 516°C. They are designed to burn heavy fuel oil, light distillate fuel and refinery gas, also a combination of heavy fuel oil and refinery gas, at a thermal efficiency of 86%. Steam from the boilers is directed to three back-pressure turbo-alternators via a common header. In providing such a system, sufficient spare capacity must be installed to permit planned overhauls. The three turbo-alternators are each rated at 17 MW, exhausting to the refinery 14 bar g distribution system. In the event of a turbo-alternator's being out of service, steam can be supplied direct to

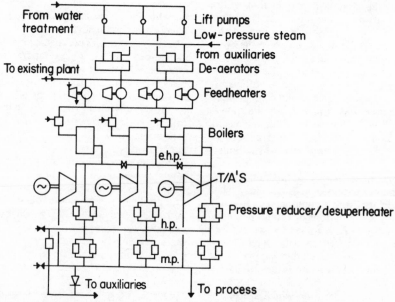

Figure 20.2   Example of boiler/steam turbine system in the petrochemical industry

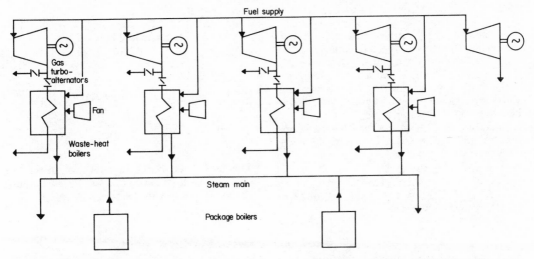

Figure 20.3   Example of a gas turbine/waste-heat boiler system in the petrochemical industry

the distribution system via pressure-reducing/desuperheating stations.

Steam for auxiliary plant is normally taken off the 14 bar g main but, should this system fail, a separate pressure-reducing/desuperheating station is provided to feed the auxiliaries direct. Exhaust steam from auxiliary drives is used in the de-aerators for removing oxygen and for heating boiler feedwater. Boiler feedwater is demineralized and supplied to the boilers via the two de-aerators, four boiler feed pumps (one spare) and individual feedheaters. A cross-connection to the existing system is provided at the feed pump suction header so that use can be made of spare de-aerator capacity in the existing system. The overall thermal efficiency of this type of system is high, since the losses outside the boiler are minimal, amounting mainly to mechanical and windage losses in the turbo-alternator, and heat losses in pipework. Energy exported from the system is in the form of electrical power and

steam which is used in the process areas. It is not ususual therefore to obtain overall efficiencies greater than 80% based on lower calorific value.

The example in *Figure 20.4* shows the system layout and quantities of a power plant similar to, but slightly larger than, that in *Figure 20.2*. A summary of the main items is as follows: three boilers, each with an output of 159 t/h at 126 bar g, 516°C using 13 t/h of fuel oil with a calorific value (CV) of 42 300 kJ/kg, and three turbo-alternators, each with an output of 19.6 MW using the above steam and exhausting at 12.2 bar g, 249°C. Auxiliary plant, de-aerators, feedheaters and certain boilerhouse items use 22% or 35 t/h of gross steam output, leaving 124 t/h available for process use from each boiler.

This shows one of the advantages of feedheating steam, since for a process requirement from each boiler of 124 t/h, the boiler plant raises an extra 35 t/h which generates about 4 MW of electricity. In fact, not all of this 35 t/h is

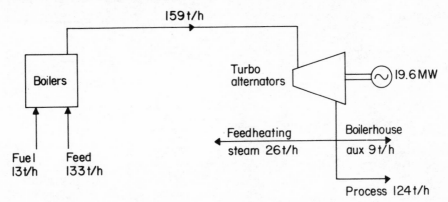

Figure 20.4   System layout with fuel, water and steam quantities for a boiler /turbo-alternator

used for feedheating, about 9 t/h being used for heating combustion air and oil storage tanks. The remaining 26 t/h drives fans and compressors before being used for feedheating.

The production of extra steam for feedheating does not call for any additional fuel, since the fuel which provides the extra 26 t/h would, without feedheating, be used within the boiler to heat the raw feedwater from, say, a hot well temperature of 23°C to the final feed temperature of 150°C. The heat usage would be as follows:

(a) *Feedwater at 150°C*

Enthalpy of steam 125 bar, 510°C	=	3370 kJ/kg
Enthalpy of water at 150°C	=	632 kJ/kg
		2738 kJ/kg

The heat added per kilogram would thus be 2738 kJ, or more conveniently 2738 MJ/t. Thus heat input to feedwater for a gross demand of 159 t/h = 159 × 2738 = 435 300 MJ/h.

(b) *Feedwater at 23°C*

Enthalpy of steam 125 bar, 510°C	=	3370 kJ/kg
Enthalpy of water at 23°C	=	97 kJ/kg
		3273 kJ/kg

Thus heat added per tonne is 3273 MJ, and heat input to the feedwater at 23°C, for a gross demand of 133 t/h = 133 × 3273 = 435 300 MJ/h, so the heat input in both cases is the same. The heat balance is as follows:

Heat input:

Fuel: 13 t/h with a CV of 42 300 kJ/kg, less	=	549 900 MJ/h
Feedwater: 133 t/h with enthalpy 97 kJ/kg	=	12 900 MJ/h
		537 000 MJ/h

Heat output:

Power:	19.6 MJ/s for 1 h	70 600 MJ/h
Steam:	133 t/h at 12.2 bar, 249°C (enthalpy 2932 kJ/kg)	390 000 MJ/h
		460 600 MJ/h

$$\text{System efficiency} = \frac{460\,600}{537\,000} \times 100$$

$$= 85.8\%$$

This does not account for blowdown losses and other minor losses but these will be low because of the high-quality feedwater which is used.

Gas-turbine-based systems

In the previous case the steam to power ratio is in the region of 8 kg/h per kilowatt so the high-pressure (h.p.) boiler and back-pressure turbo-alternator system can be economically and practically applied.

However, when the steam required is low compared with the electric power demand, say in the region 2–4 kg/h per kilowatt, the gas turbine with waste-heat boiler principle is more appropriate and generally of lower initial capital cost than the 'all steam' arrangement.

A typical installation is shown in *Figure 20.5*, the main plant items being one gas-fired turbine driving an alternator, using fuel with a calorific value of 45 700 kJ/kg at the rate of 6.8 t/h and producing 23.5 MW electricity; and one waste-heat boiler in the exhaust ducting producing steam at the rate of 50 t/h at 29 bar g, 343°C with an enthalpy of 3098 kJ/kg. The feedwater temperature is 146°C, with an enthalpy of about 615 kJ/kg.

The rough heat balance is as follows:

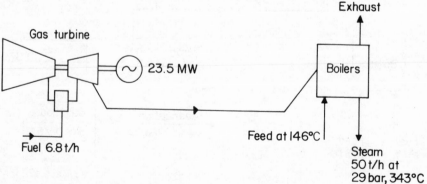

Figure 20.5   System layout with fuel, water and steam quantities for a gas turbine/boiler

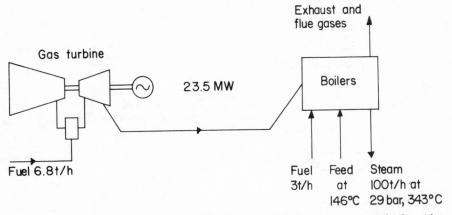

Figure 20.6 System layout with fuel, water and steam quantities for a gas turbine/boiler with auxili-ary firing

Heat input:
Fuel:	6.8×45700	$=$	310800 MJ/h
Feedwater:	50×615	$=$	30 800 MJ/h
			341 600 MJ/h

Heat output:
Power:	23.5×3600	$=$	84 600 MJ/h
Steam:	50×3098	$=$	154 900 MJ/h
			239 500 MJ/h

$$\text{System efficiency (\%)} = \frac{\text{Heat output}}{\text{Heat input}} \times 100$$

$$= \frac{239\,500}{341\,600} \times 100 = 70\%$$

If auxiliary firing is included on the waste-heat boiler to increase steam output, the fuel in the boiler is used with nearly 100% efficiency. This is because the combustion air is in the form of hot exhaust gases from the turbine, therefore the fuel has to impart much less heat into the air than would be the case if air of ambient temperature was used. The resultant flue gas temperature will not be much different from the final temperature of the waste-heat exit flue gases and the resultant effect on system efficiency can be an improve-ment of up to 10%

The previous arrangement is modified by using fuel oil of calorific value 40800 kJ/kg on the waste-heat boiler, and, by burning 3 t/h, the steam output of the boiler is raised to 100 t/h (*Figure 20.6*). The heat balance is as follows:

Heat input:
Fuel to turbine	$6.8 \times 45\,700$	$= 310800$ MJ/h
Fuel to boiler	$3 \times 40\,800$	$= 122400$ MJ/h
Feedwater	100×615	$= 61\,500$ MJ/h
		494 700 MJ/h

Heat output:
Power	23.5×3600	$=$	84 600 MJ/h
Steam	100×3098	$=$	309 800 MJ/h
			394 400 MJ/h

$$\text{System efficiency} = \frac{394\,400}{494\,700} \times 100\%$$

$$= 79.7\%$$

20.3 Waste-heat recovery in a chemical plant

Figure 20.7 shows a typical unit which takes advantage of energy recovery from chemical processes, many of which are exothermic, that is, they give out heat. The recovery comes from gas turbine exhaust gases, exothermic chemical reactions, heat exchange from high-temperature off-gases, expansion of off-gases and incineration of acid residues.

Oxidation of hydrocarbon feedstock gives a high-temperature reaction mixture and hot off-gases, and steam is produced from both of these. The heat of reaction is removed from the reaction mixture in a heat exchanger, from which low-pressure steam is separated in a steam drum, and the heat from the off-gases is removed in waste-heat boilers. These cooled off-gases then pass through a turbo-expander which generates electricity, and the cooled gases, at about $-60°C$, act as primary coolant in later stages of the process.

Air for the hydrocarbon oxidation is supplied by gas-turbine-driven compressors, and their exhaust gases raise high-pressure steam in waste-heat boilers. In addition to the recovery of process heat in this way, acid residues are burned in modified coal-fired boilers to provide more

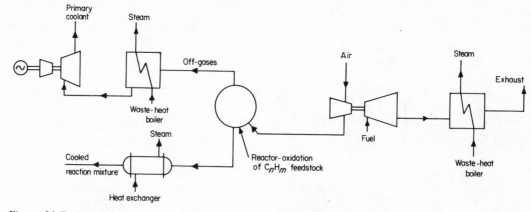

Figure 20.7 Waste-heat recovery system in a chemical plant

steam for electricity generation in conventional turbines and other plant uses.

The overall steam balance is shown below. The units used are arbitrary ones, steam output from the gas turbine waste-heat boilers being taken as 100.

Production		Usage	Balance
Gas turbine waste-heat boilers	100		
Reactor heat exchangers	135		
Waste-heat boilers	67		
	302	235	67

The balance is exported to other parts of the petrochemical complex.

The plant start-up presents no great problems, since electricity is available either from the works power-station or from the grid, and once the reaction has been started, steam is produced from the plant.

When the reactor is operating at design rate, a substantial quantity of heat is generated. The reactor heat exchanger removes about 50% of this, and process waste-heat boilers another 25%, with a final 6% recovery from the off-gases in the gas-turbine-driven alternator.

Because of the nature of the waste gases, maintenance problems had to be carefully considered in the design of the plant, and all waste-heat boilers were fabricated as tubular heat exchangers with tubes, tube plates and end boxes made from corrosion-resistant material, although naturally the waste-heat boiler shells, which hold only water or steam, were made from carbon steel.

The economic considerations of a plant of this nature depend largely on local conditions: the availability of reasonably priced fuels, plant load factors, predicted maintenance costs, initial capital costs and many other considerations. The same considerations applied to the choice of prime mover to drive the main air compressors, whether to choose electric motor, gas turbine or steam turbine. A brief summary of the chief advantages and disadvantages in this particular case is given in *Table 20.1*. As a result, gas turbine drive was chosen for these compressors.

Table 20.1

	Electric motor	Gas turbine	Steam turbine
Relative capital cost	1.00	1.69	1.31
Advantages	Ease of control, reliability	Waste-heat steam produced	
Disadvantages	Additional boilers needed to meet process demands	High capital cost	H.p. boiler needed for turbine and process steam

$0.9 \times 4.2 = 3.78$ kJ/kg.

The conditions in the various stages can be summarized as in *Table 20.2*. In the first part of stage 1, the steam at 3 bar has a latent heat of 2163.2 kJ/kg, and it gives up this latent heat to the sugar solution $= 33.9 \times 2163.2 = 73333$ kJ. However, the sugar solution is heated from 118°C to 127.3°C, thus receiving $125 \times 9.3 \times 3.78 = 4394$ kJ, leaving 68939 kJ for evaporation, and since the latent heat of the vapour in the body, at 2.4 bar, is 2184.9 kJ/kg the amount of vapour produced is $68939/2184.9 = 31.6\%$.

In the second effect, 28.7% of steam at 2.4 bar (latent heat $= 2184.9$ kJ/kg) gives out $28.7 \times 2184.9 = 62707$ kJ but in this effect the feed (75.9%) is cooled from 127.3°C to 118.2°C and gives out $75.9 \times 9.1 \times 3.78 = 2611$ kJ, so the total heat producing vapour is $62707 + 2611 = 65318$ kJ. The vapour is produced at a pressure of 1.8 bar with a latent heat of 2210.8 kJ/kg, and the amount is thus $65318/2210.8 = 29.6\%$. A similar calculation can be done for the succeeding stages.

All electricity needed to run the factory is generated by a back-pressure turbo-alternator, and the turbine exhaust at 3 bar is condensed in the main first body, and only the condensate from this one goes to the boilers. A gland leakage condenser on the turbine condenses any steam coming from the h.p. and l.p. glands, and this water is collected and passed to boiler feed. It is considered more economic to collect this steam as boiler feedwater than to use it for process heating.

The quality of boiler feedwater is all-important. Any losses should be made up either by a demineralization plant or by a distillation unit.

As a result of a study carried out at the factory, it was found that demineralization would be completely satisfactory but expensive in initial cost and running costs. A distillation unit was more efficient and could be designed to give good-quality water. This conclusion was, of course, valid only for this particular set of conditions.

The scheme shown takes second-effect calandria condensate, which is generally of excellent quality, and boils it in a small evaporator vessel supplied with live steam at reduced pressure. The steam produced is passed to the exhaust system feeding the evaporators. Condensate from the still calandria is taken to boiler feed. The quantity of make-up water produced is regulated by changing the pressure of the steam to the still calandria, and a small blowdown is arranged from the water side of the still to prevent build-up of solids. Virtually the only losses from this system are from radiation.

Some h.p. steam always has to by-pass the turbine to balance out fluctuating process loads, and the steam feed to the still forms part of this requirement. The boiling off of undesirable gases is prevented by chemically dosing the still feed and maintaining a pH in excess of 8.0.

The evaporator system used is a standard five-effect type with the vapour draw-off from each effect so arranged that virtually only flash steam goes to the condenser. The condensers are arranged with two connected in series. Almost all the vapour passing to the first condenser is condensed there by the water supply, but just a little is allowed to pass to the second condenser, where a surplus of water results in total condensation. The vacuum pump to remove air and incondensable gases is connected to the second condenser only.

This system allows the tail leg water in the first or 'hot' condenser to be at, say, 45°C and it can be used as feed to the process while the 'cold' condenser tail leg might be at only 25°C.

Each evaporator effect has, below it, a condensate receiving tank balanced back to its own pressure, and the water is passed down from stage to stage by controlling float valves operating on pressure differential. The various juice heaters operating at selected pressures return their condensate to the appropriate receiver. There are thus no traps in the factory other than those in the boilerhouse on h.p. mains. The flash from each condensate receiver is recovered and used at the appropriate pressure.

The collected condensate, in this case at 100°C, is used in heat exchangers to provide hot water for the tower diffuser and then as a heating medium for fuel oil storage tanks and space heating generally. The remaining unwanted surplus water passes to the condenser cooling tower system to supply a make-up for losses due to evaporation to the atmosphere.

20.5 Central power-stations

Although this book deals, in general, with smaller steam and power installations and steam distribution systems, the following account of the details of a 500-MW power-station has been included to show the most advanced techniques available to industry, if a particular scale of operations justifies this.

Whilst the CEGB* scale of operations can rarely be matched in industry, their system of analysis of plant efficiency and losses could be useful even to the smaller industrial installations.

---

* *The UK's Central Electricity Generating Board.*

Introduction

Nearly half of the installed capacity of British power-stations consists of 500–660-MW turbine generators and much larger units are currently being manufactured. These large units reduce significantly the installation costs for a given overall capacity and fewer power-stations are required to meet the continuously increasing load demand. Whilst installation costs are reduced by this means, operational costs can be significantly reduced only by increasing the efficiency of energy conversion and the possibility for this is limited by thermodynamic considerations.

Thermal cycle efficiency

Thermal cycle efficiency is the ratio of the work done by the fluid to the heat supplied in the fluid. This cycle can be represented on a temperature/entropy (T–s) diagram where the total area of the cycle is proportional to the heat supplied, and the area of the upper part of the cycle represents the work done. The aim of any thermal cycle efficiency improvement therefore is to maximize the area of the upper part of the cycle and to keep the width of the cycle to a minimum.

Figure 20.10 shows the approximate operating thermal cycle of a modern power-station plant. High design thermal cycle efficiencies are obtained by employing high initial steam pressures and temperatures, reheating the steam part-way through the cycle, and bleeding steam from the main part of the cycle to heat the condensed steam before returning it to the boiler. The employment of even higher steam pressures and temperatures to improve the cycle efficiency further is limited by the non-availability of metals which can withstand such parameters for extended periods, and the unavoidable increase in complexity with the associated cost penalty.

Typical steam conditions for currently employed thermal cycles on 500-MW turbine generators are 160 bar and 565°C for the initial steam, reheating from 42 bar, 365°C to 39 bar, 565°C, condensing at a back-pressure of 50 mbar (equivalent temperature 33°C) and heating the water to 252°C using bled steam prior to returning it to the boiler. The thermal cycle efficiency under these conditions is 52.13%, as shown in *Figure 20.10*.

Practical efficiency

In practice, turbine generators cannot achieve the above cycle efficiency because of irreversible losses caused by blading friction, interstage gland leakages, mechanical losses, etc. A typical maximum thermal efficiency for the turbine generator part of the cycle is 44.95% as compared with the cycle efficiency of 52.13%. This is further reduced by the need to convert the energy in the fuel into steam, which is presently carried out with boiler efficiencies of approximately 90%.

The following list summarizes the data for a 500-MW unit operating at full load.

Boiler losses:

dry flue gas	4.5%
moisture and hydrogen	4.5%
unburnt carbon in refuse	0.5%
radiation, etc.	0.5%
Corresponding boiler efficiency	90.0%

Turbine conditions:

initial steam pressure	159.6 bar
initial steam temperature	565.0°C
h.p. cylinder exhaust steam pressure	42.1 bar
h.p. cylinder exhaust steam temperature	365.5°C
reheated steam pressure	39.0 bar

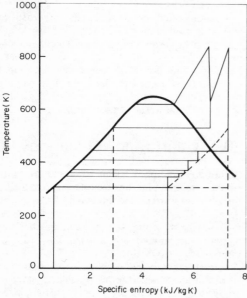

Figure 20.10   Temperature–entropy diagram showing the Rankine cycle efficiency for a 500-MW unit. Efficiency = 52.13%

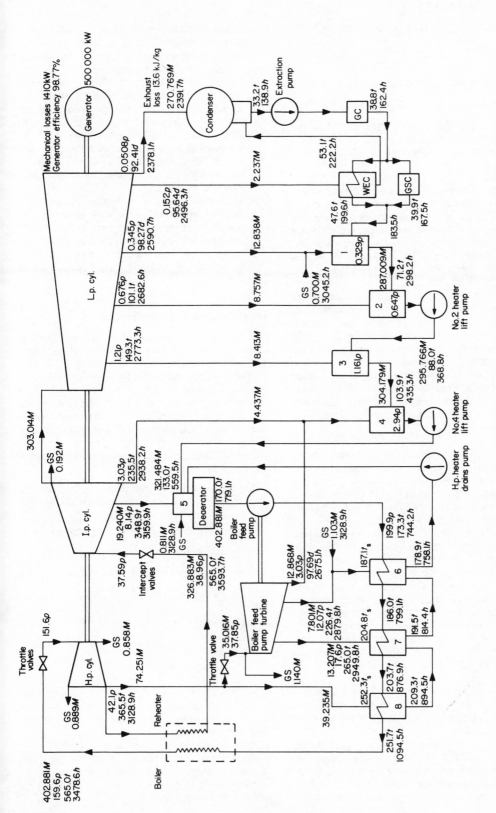

Figure 20.11 Heat balance diagram for a 500 MW unit. Heat rate 8010 kJ/kWh; efficiency 44.95%; mechanical losses 1410 kW; generator efficiency 98.77%. Mass flow rate M kg/s; pressure p bar; temperature t°C; enthalpy h kJ/kg; dryness fraction d%; saturation temperature t_s °C. WEC, water extraction condenser; GSC, gland steam condenser; GS, gland steam; GC, generator cooler

reheated steam temperature 565.0°C

L.p. cylinder exhaust steam
pressure   50.8 mbar

Final feedwater temperature 251.7°C

Steam flow rate at 500 MW 402.9 kg/s

Turbine generator heat rate 8009 kJ/kWh

Turbine generator thermal
efficiency   44.95%

Figure 20.11 shows a heat balance diagram for a turbine generator employing the above cycle. The main feed pump is driven by an auxiliary turbine which takes steam from the h.p. cylinder exhaust and returns it to the fourth, sixth and seventh feedheaters. This particular plant has four direct-contact l.p. feedheaters, a de-aerator/direct-contact feedheater, and three h.p. surface feedheaters. At the l.p. end of the feedheating train there is a water extraction condenser which takes wet steam from the last rows of turbine blades and this reduces slightly the wetness of the exhaust steam and hence limits blade erosion damage.

In a power-station there are various other thermal losses which must be taken into account before a maximum operating thermal efficiency can be derived. These losses can be summarized as follows:

1. Generator transformer — this transformer is used to increase the voltage of the generated electrical power to a level suitable for connecting to the transmission system (national grid) and it has a typical efficiency of 99.5%.
2. Auxiliary plant — most of the auxiliaries are driven by electric motors, but because of the high energy requirements of the boiler feed pump it has become conventional to drive it with a turbine using steam bled from the main turbine, which gives an overall improvement in thermal efficiency. The electrically driven auxiliaries for the typical 500-MW unit quoted consume some 17 500 kW (3.5% of main electrical output), the principal items of which are:

   coal milling plant   5 200 kW ≃ 1.0%
   boiler draught fans   3 900 kW ≃ 0.8%
   circulating water pumps 4 100 kW ≃ 0.8%

3. Make-up — water make-up requirements vary according to the particular design of plant and the tightness of the system, but a representative value is 5.5 kg/s, which is a combination of 1.2 kg/s for boiler blow-down purposes and 4.3 kg/s for steam and water leakages. In this particular example, boiler sootblowing has been assumed to be carried out using compressed air, but if steam were used then the make-up requirements would increase by about 1.5 kg/s. The equivalent heat loss due to make-up requirements is about 1.1% (including sootblowing). Make-up is supplied from a demineralization plant as this is less expensive than the equivalent evaporating plant for providing water of the high purity required.
4. Radiation losses — radiation losses from the interconnecting pipework between the boiler and turbine generator are not included in the individual thermal efficiency values. An allowance for these radiation losses should be made, and a typical value is 0.15%.

Overall station thermal efficiency

Various definitions are used in determining the overall thermal efficiency of power-station plant. The Central Electricity Generating Board currently define this as the heat equivalent of the electrical energy supplied to the grid system divided by the heat input in fuel to the boiler based on the gross calorific value, expressed as a percentage. Measurement of electrical output at another point, such as the generator terminals, or use of net calorific value will lead to an increase in the calculated efficiency value.

On this basis the overall thermal efficiency for the 500-MW unit at full load conditions is:

(Turbine × transformer × boiler) efficiencies ×

heat loss in make-up × allowance for auxiliary

power × heat loss from pipework radiation × 100

$= 0.4495 \times 0.995 \times 0.900 \times (1 - 0.035)$

$\times (1 - 0.011) \times (1 - 0.0015) \times 100$

$= 38.36\%$

This efficiency applies to a unit operating continuously at full load and at design thermal cycle parameters. In practice, the actual operating efficiency will be lower, owing to operation at partial loads and with operating parameters which cannot be maintained at their optimum values on a continuous basis.

Monitoring of performance is carried out as shown in the next section.

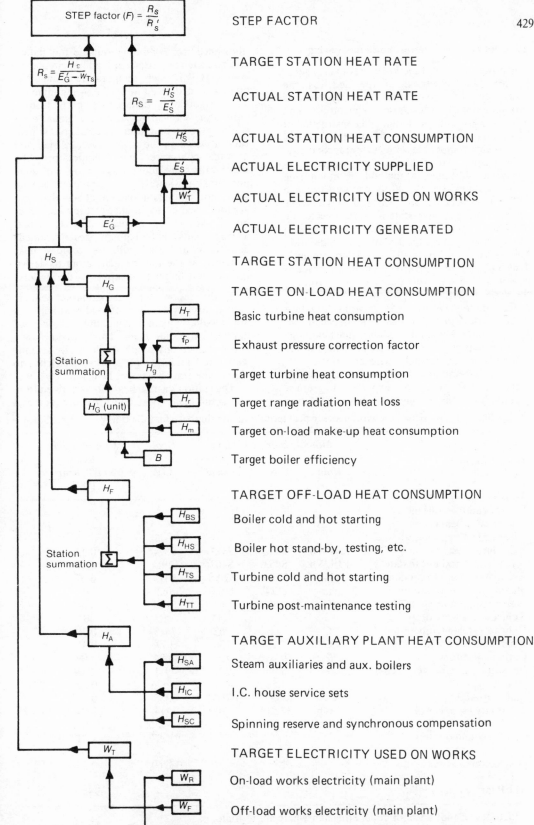

STEP factor $(F) = \dfrac{R_S}{R'_S}$

STEP FACTOR

$R_S = \dfrac{H_c}{E'_G - W_{Ts}}$

TARGET STATION HEAT RATE

$R_S = \dfrac{H'_S}{E'_S}$

ACTUAL STATION HEAT RATE

H'_S — ACTUAL STATION HEAT CONSUMPTION

E'_S — ACTUAL ELECTRICITY SUPPLIED

W'_T — ACTUAL ELECTRICITY USED ON WORKS

E'_G — ACTUAL ELECTRICITY GENERATED

H_S — TARGET STATION HEAT CONSUMPTION

H_G — TARGET ON-LOAD HEAT CONSUMPTION

H_T — Basic turbine heat consumption

f_P — Exhaust pressure correction factor

Station summation Σ

H_g — Target turbine heat consumption

H_G (unit)

H_r — Target range radiation heat loss

H_m — Target on-load make-up heat consumption

B — Target boiler efficiency

H_F — TARGET OFF-LOAD HEAT CONSUMPTION

H_{BS} — Boiler cold and hot starting

H_{HS} — Boiler hot stand-by, testing, etc.

Station summation Σ

H_{TS} — Turbine cold and hot starting

H_{TT} — Turbine post-maintenance testing

H_A — TARGET AUXILIARY PLANT HEAT CONSUMPTION

H_{SA} — Steam auxiliaries and aux. boilers

H_{IC} — I.C. house service sets

H_{SC} — Spinning reserve and synchronous compensation

W_T — TARGET ELECTRICITY USED ON WORKS

W_R — On-load works electricity (main plant)

W_F — Off-load works electricity (main plant)

W_S — Station services works electricity

Figure 20.12   STEP flow chart for a 2000-MW power-station

Thermal efficiency performance monitoring

The power-station's function is to convert energy in fuel into electrical energy and, as the efficiency of conversion directly affects production costs, considerable expenditure and effort are given to the design and construction of plant in order to provide the highest thermal efficiencies compatible with current technology.

To ensure that all plants are operated efficiently at all times, a method of monitoring power-stations' thermal efficiency performance (STEP) has been devised. This provides a means of measuring power-station performance by comparing the actual thermal performance obtained with that expected of it, consideration being given to the particular operational regime. This STEP factor is calculated monthly for each power-station, by a very detailed procedure, but the general method is as follows:

The *station thermal efficiency performance factor* is defined as the ratio between the station target heat rate and its actual heat rate, and is expressed as a percentage (this ratio is the inverse of thermal efficiency ratio).

The station target heat rate is the heat rate the station would be expected to return assuming optimum operation but making due allowances for conditions outside the station control, such as pattern of loading, circulating water (CW) inlet temperature, and fuel quality. It is derived in the following manner. The target heat demand of each turbine generator is calculated from the actual electricity generated and the acceptance test heat rate adjusted to the actual average load and average cold-water inlet temperature. To these values are added target heats for range and make-up losses, giving for each turbine generator its total on-load target heat demand. Again, based on acceptance test results, target boiler efficiencies corresponding to actual average loads and fuel quality are determined, and these are used with the on-load heat demands of the turbine generators to derive the on-load target heat inputs to the boilers.

To the station's total on-load target heat are added target values for off-load heat and heat for auxiliary plant, giving the station total target heat requirement. This is divided by a 'target' electricity supplied (electricity actually generated minus target works electricity) to derive the station's target heat rate.

The station's actual heat rate is derived from the actual heat consumed for generation and

Table 20.3   A typical breakdown of losses in heat terms on a monthly basis for a 2000-MW power-station

Losses due to:	Monthly average values			Heat loss* (GJ)	Contribution to loss of STEP factor (%)
	Units	Target	Actual		
Deterioration in turbine generator heat rates					
(a) from acceptance to latest test	kJ/kWh	8442	8453	9874	0.13
(b) from latest test to date	kJ/kWh	8453	8467	12911	0.17
Exhaust pressure to condenser	mbar	57.01	57.68	5315	0.07
Steam pressure to turbine	bar	159.8	160.0	162	0
Steam temperature to turbine	°C	566	563	2810	0.04
Reheater pressure drop	%	7.40	7.45	256	0
Reheater steam temperature	°C	566	562	7443	0.10
Final feedwater temperature	°C	241	236	11398	0.15
Carbon-in-refuse	%	0.43	0.52	6684	0.09
Moisture and hydrogen in coal	%	5.24	5.23	−911	−0.01
Dry flue gas	%	4.58	4.90	24576	0.32
Make-up water	GJ	133572	140913	8355	0.11
Electricity used on works	GWh	37.213	37.425	3114	0.04
Total accounted losses				91987	1.21
Unaccounted losses				13760	0.18
STEP factor achieved					98.61

* Includes an allowance for boiler efficiency where appropriate.

the actual electricity supplied by the station.

It must be emphasized that accuracy is essential in measuring the station's actual heat consumption for the production of a reliable STEP factor, and continual attention is required to maintain adequate accuracy of fuel weighing, determination of calorific value and periodic assessment of coal stocks.

The flowchart shown in *Figure 20.12* shows the basic steps in the calculation procedure for determining the STEP factor for a 2000-MW power-station with 'unit'-type plant (i.e. an individual boiler feeding each turbine generator).

This STEP factor is supplemented by a breakdown of losses, in order to identify which parts of the plant are contributing to any shortfall in thermal performance and to provide a guide to what remedial actions are required. A typical set of values is shown in *Table 20.3*.

20.6 Efficient use of steam in a sugar melter

This example, taken from the sugar industry, was supplied by the author of the original book, Sir Oliver Lyle, and is given, as nearly as possible, in his original words. The calculations have been changed to SI units, but 'pre-SI' phrases such as latent heat, specific heat, total heat have been left.

The process of melting consists of dissolving the affined sugar in water. We want the melter liquor to be at say 70% and 70°C. When sugar is asked to dissolve in water it resists the change from the solid state to the dissolved state by calling for a supply of heat. It takes up this heat by cooling the dissolving slurry, and, as less sugar will dissolve in a cool solution than in a hot one, slows down the dissolving. In order to produce melter liquor at 70°C, sufficient heat must be supplied to make good this 'heat of solution' and then to heat the solution up to the desired final temperature. The melting water consisted almost entirely of process condensate and was hot, say, 90°C; it could therefore provide some of the heat needed. A typical flow diagram is shown in *Figure 20.13*.

The total heat in liquor at 70% and 70°C is found, from a standard graph, to be 193.4 kJ per kg of liquor. The ingredients of 1 kg of melter liquor at 70% were:

Washed sugar	0.7 kg at 40°C
Moisture in sugar	0.01 kg at 40°C
Water ⎱ Steam ⎰	0.29 kg

The average specific heat of sugar between 10°C and 40°C is found from tables to be 0.3, so that the heat in sugar before melting is (at 40°C, with a sensible heat of 167.5 kJ/kg)

$$0.7 \times 0.3 \times 167.5 \ = \ 35.18 \text{ kJ in sugar}$$
$$0.01 \times 1 \times 167.5 \ = \ \underline{\ 1.68 \text{ kJ in moisture}}$$
$$\text{Total} \ = \ \overline{\underline{36.86 \text{ kJ}}}$$

Now the extra water to be added is 0.29 kg, which will be partly made up of the condensed steam blown into the melter. Water and steam together have got to supply the extra heat required to bring the ingredients from 36.86 kJ to the liquor heat of 193.4 kJ. The steam and water must therefore provide 193.4 − 36.86 = 156.54 kJ per kg of liquor. If we assume that the steam supply to the melter is at 1.4 bar g, and that its quality has been measured and found to be 6.4% wet, the total heat* in each kg of such steam is:

The sensible heat in 1 kg of steam at 1.4 bar, which is	527.2 kJ
The latent heat in 93.6% of 1 kg at 1.4 bar, or $2186.5 \times 0.936 =$	2046.6 kJ
Total heat in 1.4 bar-6.4% wet steam	$\overline{2573.8 \text{ kJ/kg}}$

The water for melting was at 90°C and contained 376.9 kJ/kg.
If we call the weight of steam x, the weight of water will be $0.29 - x$.
The heat to be provided is 156.54 kJ.
The heat in steam plus the heat in water must equal 156.5 kJ, so we can write

$$2574x + 376.9(0.29 - x) \ = \ 156.5$$
$$2574x + 109.3 - 376.9x \ = \ 156.5$$
$$2197x \ = \ 47.3$$
$$x \ = \ 0.0215 \text{ kg of steam}$$
$$0.29{-}x \ = \ 0.2685 \text{ kg of water}$$

Let us check this.
0.0215 kg of steam containing 2574 kJ/kg gives 0.0215×2574	55.34 kJ
0.2685 kg of water containing 376.9 kJ/kg gives 0.2685×376.9	$\underline{101.19 \text{ kJ}}$
	$\overline{156.5 \ \text{ kJ}}$

The calculated amount of steam is 0.0215 kg for melting 0.7 kg of sugar. This represents $0.0215 \times$

---

*Editor's note
This is not the way the enthalpy of wet steam is calculated in Chapter 1 (p 15) but in fact

$$x.h_g + (1 - x)h_f = x(h_{fg} + h_f) + (1 - x)h_f$$
$$= x.h_{fg} + x.h_f + h_f - x.h_f$$
$$= x.h_{fg} + h_f$$

which is just what Sir Oliver has done.

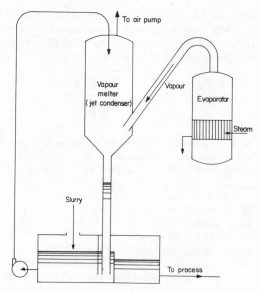

Figure 20.13   Flow diagram for a sugar melter

$100 \div 0.7 = 3.1$ kg of steam per 100 kg of sugar. In practice, the measured amount of steam was 5.1 kg so that there must have been a loss of 2 kg, or 40%. This is a high figure, because the liquid surface loses a lot of heat which is ducted away and the radiation loss is considerable.

It is impossible to do without some steam, unless the washed sugar could be a lot hotter and the melting water hotter. Suppose we say the water could be at 98°C. Then the water could provide $0.29 \times 410.6 = 119$ kJ. This leaves 193.4 – 119 = 74.4 to be in the washed sugar. We found that the moist sugar at 40°C contained 36.86 kJ, so that to contain 74.4 kJ the moist sugar would have to have a temperature of $40 \times 74.4/36.84 = 81°C$. This is quite out of the question as it would mean heating the raw magma to about 90°C. So we must assume that some steam will be needed for melting.

Now there is no reason why the melting steam should be live steam. The mixture of washed sugar and water can be pumped through one or two jet condensers attached to pans or evapora-tors. We have for some years been operating such a plant on a semi-full-sized scale with good results. We saw above that 70%, 70°C liquor contained 193.4 kJ/kg, and that at 60°C a liquor of 70% contains 165.8 kJ/kg. We found that at 70°C we should have to add 193.4 – 36.86 = 156.54 kJ, so that at 60°C we should have to add 165.8 – 36.86 = 128.94 kJ.

If we can use heat in the form of vapour to supply the heat to the melter it is clearly wasteful to use hot distilled water for melting. If the distilled water is hot, sweet-free process conden-sate it is a perfect boiler feed. If we melt with town water and send the hot distilled water to the boilers we save the cost of softening and distilling town water for boilers. On balance we are that much better off. So we will assume that we melt with town water, heated by pan vapour to 60°C, and therefore containing 251.1 kJ/kg.

Using the same method as in the previous section, we can find the amount of warm town water and the amount of vapour required.

Vapour at 60°C contains 2609.7 kJ/kg⎫ Average
Vapour at 70°C contains 2626.7 kJ/kg⎰ 2618.3 kJ/kg

If x is the weight of vapour per kg of liquor, we can write

$$2618x + 251(0.29 - x) = 156.5$$
$$2618x + 72.3 - 251x = 156.5$$
$$2367x = 84.2$$
$$x = 0.035$$

Water = $0.29 - 0.035 = 0.255$ kg
containing $0.255 \times 251 = 64$ kJ
The vapour must supply $128.9 - 64 = 64.9$ kJ at 60°C
and $156.5 - 128.9 = 27.6$ kJ at 70°C.

So we shall need $\dfrac{0.035 \times 64.9}{64.9 + 27.6}$ kg of vapour at 60°C

to melt 0.7 kg of sugar

and $\dfrac{0.035 \times 27.6}{64.9 + 27.6}$ kg of vapour at 70°C to heat 0.7 kg of liquor solids

or $\dfrac{0.035 \times 64.9 \times 100}{92.5 \times 0.7} = 3.5$ kg of vapour at 60°C

per 100 kg of refined solids output (RSO)

and $\dfrac{0.035 \times 27.6 \times 100}{92.5 \times 0.7} = 1.49$ kg of vapour at 70°C per 100 kg of RSO.

It would seem quite permissible therefore to pump the unmelted slurry through a jet condenser, at 60°C or 0.2 bar absolute, attached to a white sugar pan, and then to pump the almost completely melted liquor through another condenser at 70°C , or 0.32 bar absolute, attached to the second effect of a sweet-water evaporator. It is possible that each of these two vacua could be a little higher if we took account of boiling point elevation (BPE), since the BPE of 70% liquor is about 4½°C. It has been found, on crude experimental apparatus, that the part-melted slurry often leaves the vapour melter 1° or 2°C higher than the vapour temperature, but in practice we seldom get a measurable temperature elevation because the condenser cannot be fitted with baffles, to delay the flow, lest they get clogged with trash, whereas in a conventional heater baffles delay the syrup and a temperature elevation is secured.

We can confidently say there is no theoretical need for any live steam for melting.

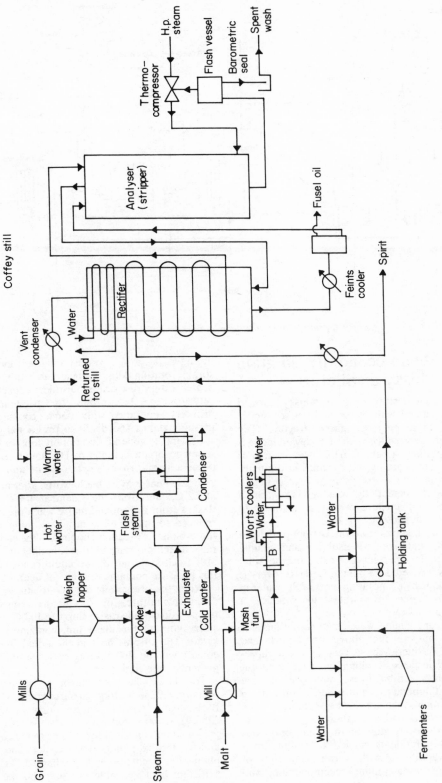

Figure 20.14   Flowsheet for a grain whisky distillery — part 1

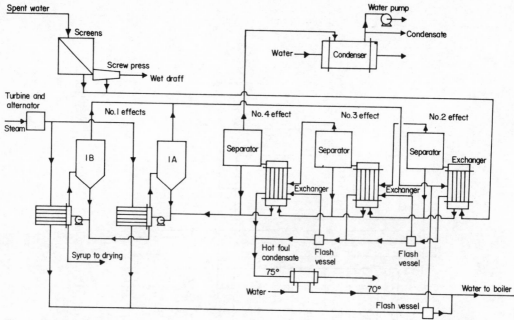

Figure 20.15   Flowsheet for a grain whisky distillery — part 2

20.7 Steam economies in grain whisky distilleries

For the manufacture of grain whisky, ground maize is mixed with water and cooked under pressure to simplify the starch structure. The cooked maize then has malted barley added to it and is mashed at about 62°C when starch is converted to sugar by the enzymes in the malt. This mixture, or worts, is then cooled to 20–25°C and fermented by yeast giving wash, a dilute alcohol mixture which is distilled to produce grain whisky.

Spent wash leaves from the bottom of the still containing unfermented insoluble and soluble matter, and is passed to waste, or the solid matter is recovered for animal feed. Recovery is usually done by evaporating most of the water in a multiple-effect evaporator to produce a concentrate followed by drying.

There are many ways and conditions for carrying out all the above operations, and different distilleries have very different capacities. For instance, cooking can be carried out continuously, or batchwise, and over a wide range of temperatures and times. A proportion of husk might or might not be separated in the mashing stage, and distillation can be done in traditional Coffey stills or in other continuous stills. Evaporation is carried out in multiple-effect evaporators with various numbers of effects, or using vapour recompression, and

drying is done in a variety of driers including spray, rotating kiln, vertical tube and steam-heated rotary disc driers. Distillery capacity can vary from 5×10^3 to 25×10^3 l per hour. One distillery operates with batch cooking and mashing stages and distils in traditional Coffey stills, and a general description follows of the steam economies practised. The flowsheet of the process is shown in *Figures 20.14 and 20.15*.

Waste heat is available in worts, after mashing at 62°C, and from the steam at 100°C which flashes from the cooked maize when pressure is reduced to atmospheric in a separating vessel, the exhauster. Steam is supplied to the cooker to raise its temperature until it is boiling at 4.4 bar abs. Each kilogram of the liquid condensate at this pressure contains 619.6 kJ of heat.

When the pressure is reduced to atmospheric, steam evaporates or flashes to reduce the temperature of the maize slurry to 100°C and this slurry goes to the mash tun, containing 419.1 kJ/kg. The surplus heat in the liquid from the cooker will be 200.5 kJ/kg which is therefore present in the flash steam.

The latent heat of steam at atmospheric pressure is 2256.9 kJ/kg, giving the percentage of flash steam from the maize slurry as (200.5/2256.9) × 100 = 8.9%.

Hot water is needed for feeding to the cookers and to sterilize piping, worts coolers and other plant after each cooker is discharged. There is sufficient heat available in worts and the flash steam to heat the total requirement of process water to 93 – 96°C by heat exchange, first in the worts coolers, when the water is heated to about 55°C, and secondly in the flash steam condenser. This is thus a simple two-stage heat transfer process, and the calculation can be done in the same way as in the example of a sugar refinery (*see* p 423).

Because of the variation in water supply temperature, part of the water from worts cooler A is fed to worts cooler B in winter and in summer a large flow of water is needed in A to cool worts for fermentation while fresh water is fed directly to worts cooler B. Such heat recovery makes a considerable reduction in the steam required to heat the cookers and to sterilize piping. The value of the steam saved by these means far outweighs the cost of the heat exchange equipment.

Distillation

Fermented wash containing some 5% of ethanol by weight at about 16°C is distilled in Coffey stills, the rectifying sections of which contain 33 perforated plates. The boiling point of the liquid mixtures increases from 78°C at the top of the rectifier to 93°C at the bottom. Banks of piping are fitted in the vapour spaces between plates and the feed is heated to about 88°C as it passes through these pipes from the top of the rectifier to the bottom, by heat transferred from the vapour. By this means the full requirement of reflux is produced. In more conventional distillation practice, the feed would be preheated in an overhead condenser where ethanol would be condensing at 78°C and it would be impractical to heat much above 70°C. Utilizing the higher temperatures of the vapours in the lower sections of the still to preheat the feed saves some 13 000 t/yr of steam in a distillery handling 10^5 l/h of wash for 6000 hours per year. External heat exchangers could replace the internal pipes, of course, and more plates are needed because of the low reflux ratios on the upper plates. The stills will, therefore, cost more than conventional units but the savings are considerable.

Operation of thermocompressor

Steam is supplied to the still at 11/15 bar abs, and is reduced to the pressure at the base of the still, 1.27 bar abs, in passing through a thermocompressor which subjects the stripped wash to an absolute pressure of 0.6 bar. The performance of the thermocompressor can be approximately calculated from the chart *Figure 13.5* in Chapter 13. The steam expansion ratio p_s/p_d is $0.6/13 = 0.046$, and the compression ratio p_d/p_s is $1.27/0.6 = 2.1$. These two values give a suitable

ejector with an area ratio A_m/A_n of 25, from which it follows that the entrainment ratio W_s/W_d is approximately 1. That is, 1 kg of driving steam entrains 1 kg of vapour from the still and provides 2 kg of steam to the still.

The use of the thermocompressors gives an annual saving of four to five times their cost.

The theoretical treatment of a thermocompressor, similar to this one, is developed further in Chapter 13.

Vacuum plant

The comparative operating economics of vacuum pumps as against steam ejectors can be seen from this plant, where ejectors were replaced by rotary stainless-steel vacuum pumps.

Steam ejector usage	0.7 t/h
Cost of steam	£4.00/t
Annual operating hours	4000
Total annual operating cost	= 0.7×4 × 4000
	= £11 200

Vacuum pump motor	11 kW
Cost of electricity	£0.025/kWh
Annual operating hours	4000
Total annual operating cost	= 11×0.025×4000
	= £1100

This is an oversimplified picture of the advantages of a vacuum pump over a steam ejector, because the capital cost of the motor-driven pump and its auxiliaries would be much more than that of the ejector. Maintenance would also cost more, although this should be kept as low as possible by the correct choice of material for the pump body to minimize corrosion. Thus the fixed charges would be higher, and the vacuum pump becomes a clear favourite only for reasonably long operating periods.

Multiple-effect evaporators

A quadruple-effect evaporation plant is shown to recover animal feed from the spent wash and economies practised include:

1. Condensate from the effects heated by fresh steam is allowed to flash into the next stage of evaporation and is then returned as boiler feedwater.
2. Condensate is allowed to flash into each subsequent stage.
3. Hot foul condensate from the fourth effect at 75°C is used to pre-heat boiler feedwater to about 70°C.

The pattern of feed flow to the evaporators is different from that in the sugar beet process (*see* p 427), again for very good reasons. The feed goes first to effect 2, then on to 3, 4, 1A and 1B. The purpose of doing this is to operate the effect handling the maximum concentration of material at the highest temperature so that the viscosity is as low as possible. It can be seen that the effects 1A and 1B are fitted with forced-circulation pumps, again because the viscosity is too high to allow the utilization of natural-circulation heaters as in the other effects. The heaters on 1A, 1B are horizontal with large pumps circulating the liquid through them, but the steam and circulating liquid from them are separated in separators which are almost identical with those of the other effects. It is more economical to operate such a system as nearly co-current as possible so that final streams leave at as low a temperature as possible, hence the use of co-current flow in effects 2, 3 and 4. The stream from No. 4 to 1A and 1B has to be raised in temperature, and this involves a loss of thermal efficiency but it is a smallish stream as some three-quarters of the liquid has been evaporated.

Turbo-alternators

There are several turbo-alternators which generate electricity for the distillery and also provide steam at sufficient pressure for process use. Average conditions are: steam pressure 14.25 bar abs, temperature 225°C, exhaust pressure 1.68 bar abs.

The available heat drop cannot easily be abstracted from steam tables, since with the low back-pressure the exhaust steam will be wet. The heat drop has to be worked out by following the procedure explained in Chapter 1.

Enthalpy of steam at 14.25 bar, 225°C is 2865 kJ/kg

Entropy of steam at 14.25 bar, 225°C is 6.618

Saturation temp. of steam at 1.68 bar is 115°C

Interpolating from the steam tables (Appendix 2, *Table A2*) we get

Entropy of saturated steam (s_g) at 1.68 bar is 7.1857

Entropy of water (s_f) at 1.68 bar is 1.4710

The entropy of the wet steam, assuming isentropic expansion at 100% efficiency, will be the same as the initial steam conditions, 6.618, and if the dryness fraction of the exhaust steam is x, then

Entropy = $x s_g + (1 - x) s_f$

so 6.618 = $7.1857x + (1 - x) \times 1.4710$

6.618 = $5.7147x + 1.4710$

$x = 0.9$

Hence the steam has a dryness fraction of 0.9.

so the enthalpy of this steam will be

$x h_g + (1 - x) h_f$

Interpolating from the steam tables gives

$h_g = 2698.4 \text{ kJ/kg}$ $h_f = 481.6 \text{ kJ/kg}$
and

Enthalpy = $2698.4 \times 0.9 + 481.6 \times 0.1$
= 2428.6 + 48.2
= 2476.8 kJ/kg

The theoretical heat drop from inlet to exhaust conditions is thus $2865 - 2477 = 388$ kJ/kg.

However, for reasons given in Chapter 11, 100% efficiency is never achieved, and the probable efficiency would be nearer 80%. So actual heat drop = $0.8 \times 388 = 310.4$ kJ/kg giving actual enthalpy of exhaust steam = $2865 - 310 = 2555$ kJ/kg. The exhaust pressure will still be the same, so that, going back to steam tables, h_g and h_f are as before, and we have

2555 = $2698.4 x_1 + (1 - x_1)\, 481.6$
2555 = $2698.4 x_1 - 481.6 x_1 + 481.6$
$2216.8 x_1 = 2073.4$
$x_1 = 0.935$, the actual dryness fraction

The actual heat energy extracted by the turbine will be 310.4 kJ for each kilogram of steam.

If we assume that the turbine mechanical efficiency (*see* Chapter 11) and electrical efficiency are both 90% — a reasonable figure, since the turbo-alternators are comparatively small machines — then the performance figure for the turbine will be $0.9 \times 0.9 \times 310.4$ kJ/kg = 251.4 kJ/kg, or if we want to express it in terms of steam consumption, it is

$$\frac{1}{251.4} \text{kg/kJ} \rightarrow \frac{1}{251.4} \text{ kg/kWs}$$

$$= \frac{3600}{251.4} \text{ or } 14.32 \text{ kg/kWh}$$

This is the performance we could reasonably expect from the machine operating continuously at full load. In practice, the load will rarely be full and almost certainly will vary, and the steam consumption will be appreciably higher than this figure.

20.8 Savings from installing an additional steam main

Previous examples in this chapter have concentrated on major power units and on integrated industrial processes, but the following example shows how savings can be made by a critical examination of existing steam distribution systems.

A combined heat and power system serving a number of factories in an area of some 10 km² had two power-stations. The newer oil-fired high-pressure back-pressure station had 44 to 16 bar turbines and 16 to 7.5 bar turbines. The older coal-fired station, which produced steam at 16 bar, had a 16 to 3.4 bar turbine and condensing plant used for electrical peak lopping in the winter, to avoid excessive maximum demand charges. On one section of the system a 16-bar interconnecting steam main between the two stations also served a factory adjacent to the older station. The arrangement is shown in *Figure 20.16*.

The 16-bar main, which supplied steam to the condensing plant as well as the factory at 16 bar, and also through reducing stations at 7.5 and 3.4 bar, was overloaded in winter, and the relatively inefficient coal-fired boilers had to be operated to relieve the situation.

A study of the problem showed that, since there was spare capacity in the 16 to 7.5 bar turbine plant at the high-pressure station, the best solution would be to install a 7.5-bar steam main to serve the factory. The distance was

about 2 km and the factory could utilize about 80 000 t/yr of steam at the pressure.

The resulting savings showed a 27% return on capital cost, as follows:

1. Additional electrical generation by expanding steam to 7.5 bar instead of 16 bar   18%
2. Savings in operating cost at the coal-fired power-station (wages and coal)   8%
3. Reduced operating costs in the factory resulting from improved steam conditions   1%

This is a good example of the way in which capital can be spent to save operating and other costs. Looked at as an energy-saving project it reduced the national usage by about 900 tonnes oil-equivalent per year.

These examples have been chosen to give a reasonable spread amongst modern industry, which is always looking for ways to adapt new ideas and discoveries to produce and use steam as economically as possible.

A comparatively new development has been the harnessing of geothermal energy in those parts of the world where this occurs in any appreciable amount. The following brief account gives the principal features of geothermal operation.

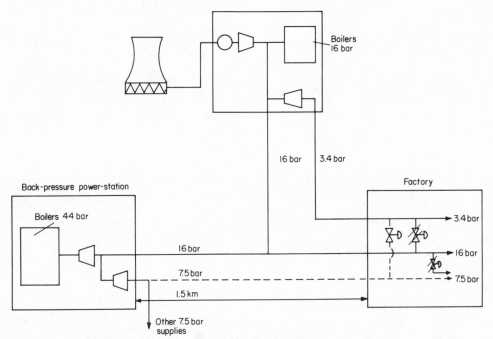

Figure 20.16 Condensing/back-pressure power-station and factory steam mains. (———) Existing steam mains; (————) new steam mains. N.B. The factory 16/7.5 bar and 16/3.4 bar reducing valves were removed when the 7.5 bar main was installed

20.9 Geothermal steam

In some parts of the world, steam rises from below ground level or warm springs are known. Many such places have been known for centuries or even millenia. The steam issuing from the earth is usually at atmospheric pressure or only sufficiently above it to provide the velocity head at which it emerges. However, it has been found in many places that by drilling, steam can be tapped at a useful pressure. Examples are Lardarello in Italy, Wairakei in New Zealand, The Geysers in California and a number of places in Iceland and the USSR, and power-stations of up to 250 MW capacity have been built to use geothermal steam. Investigations have been made in Ethiopia, Kenya, St Lucia and other places. The Department of Energy in the UK (and other government departments elsewhere) are looking into the possibility of extracting heat from hot rocks to generate steam.

Natural steam tends to have a very high moisture content (up to 90% in places) and a high content of solids such as borax, and of incondensable substances including corrosive and toxic gases such as hydrogen sulphide. The exploration and development of a geothermal steam field are expensive things and the choice of plant to use the steam involves difficult technology. Recent work has been mainly by governments and it is highly unlikely that development in future will be left to unrestrained private enterprise or that indiscriminate drilling will be permitted.

The pressure at the top of a steam well is highest when the wellhead valve is shut, the pressure in such a case being roughly the pressure in water gauge corresponding to the depth of the well. There is of course no flow. With the valve fully open the flow is a maximum and the pressure falls to a value depending on the flow into the well. The power available from the steam is zero at shut valve, and when the valve is wide open and flow is unrestricted power will again be zero or small while the flow is maximum. Thus there is some wellhead pressure at which the available power is a maximum. The flow/pressure characteristic of a well can be measured to determine this maximum and this is part of the exploration of a field. Efficiency has no clear meaning when applied to geothermal development and what is meant is usually development to obtain the highest available power from a well or field.

21 Reference list of British Standards

21.1 Introduction

21.2 List of Standards

21.1 Introduction

The British Standards Institution is the recognized body in the UK for the preparation and promulgation of national standards in all fields. It originated in 1901 as the Engineering Standards Committee, set up by the Institution of Civil Engineers and other professional bodies, and later became the British Engineering Standards Association. A Royal Charter was granted in 1929 and a Supplemental Charter in 1931, when the present name was adopted.

The BSI is an independent body and its main function is to draw up voluntary standards by agreement among all the interests concerned and to promote their adoption.

Standards are not intended to inhibit design or restrict technical development. They should essentially be regarded as reflecting what is economically best, to bring out fundamental uniformity when it is desirable, to reduce costs of manufacture, to increase production, and to protect life, health and the environment.

For information and guidance, references to British Standards relevant to the subject matter of a number of chapters are given below. Whilst the list of standards is not exhaustive, many of those listed contain further references to other standards which may be required to provide a completely definitive specification.

21.2 List of Standards

Chapter 1 — 'Properties of water and steam'

BS 350 Conversion factors and tables
  Part 1. Basis of tables. Conversion factors
  Part 2. Detailed conversion tables
  Supplement No 1: 1967 (PD 6203) to BS 350: Part 2 Additional tables for SI conversions

BS 1991 Letter symbols, signs and abbreviations
  Part 1. General
  Part 2. Chemical engineering, nuclear science and applied chemistry
  Part 3. Fluid mechanics
  Part 5. Applied thermodynamics

BS 3763 The International System of Units (SI)

BS 3812 Recommendations for estimating the dryness of saturated steam

PD 5686 The use of SI Units

Chapter 3 — 'The safe use of steam'
Noise

BS 2750 Recommendations for field and laboratory measurement of airborne and impact sound transmission in buildings

BS 3489 Sound level meters (industrial grade)

BS 3593 Recommendation on preferred frequencies for acoustical measurements

Pressure and temperature hazards

BS 2646 Copper laboratory autoclaves

BS 5410 Code of practice for oil firing
Part 1. Installations up to 44 kW output capacity for space heating and hot-water supply purposes
Part 2. Installations of 44 kW or above output capacity for space heating and hot-water supply purposes
Part 3. Installations for furnaces, kilns, ovens and other industrial purposes

Chapter 4 — 'Shell boilers'

BS 1971 Corrugated furnaces for shell boilers

BS 2790 Shell boilers of welded construction (other than watertube boilers)
Part 1. Class I welded construction
Part 2. Class II and Class III welded construction

Chapter 5 — 'Watertube boilers'

BS 749 Underfeed stokers

BS 799 Oil-burning equipment

BS 845 Acceptance tests for industrial type boilers and steam generators

BS 1113 Watertube steam generating plant (including superheaters, reheaters and steel tube economizers)

BS 1474 Recommendations on the use of British Standard log sheets for steam and hot-water boiler plants

BS 2885 Code for acceptance tests on stationary steam generators of the power-station type

BS 3285 Method of sampling superheated steam from steam generating units

CP 300 Installation and maintenance of underfeed stokers

Chapter 6 — 'Thermal insulation'

BS 874 Methods of determining thermal insulating properties, with definitions of thermal insulating terms

BS 2972 Methods of test for inorganic thermal insulating materials

BS 3533 Glossary of terms relating to thermal insulation

BS 3958 Thermal insulating materials
Part 1. 85% magnesia preformed insulation
Part 2. Calcium silicate preformed insulation
Part 3. Metal-mesh-faced mineral wool mats and mattresses
Part 4. Bonded preformed mineral wool pipe sections
Part 5. Bonded mineral wool slabs (for use at temperatures above 50°C)
Part 6. Finishing materials; hard-setting composition, self-setting cement and gypsum plaster

BS 4508 Thermally insulated underground piping systems
Part 1. Steel cased systems with air gap
Part 2. Asbestos-cement cased systems with air gap
Part 3. General requirements for cased systems without air gap
Part 4. Specific testing and inspection requirements for cased systems without air gap

BS 5422 Specification for the use of thermal insulating materials

CP 3005 Thermal insulation of pipework and equipment (in the temperature range of −73°C to +816°C)

CP 3009 Thermally insulated underground piping systems

Chapter 7 — 'Water treatment'

BS 1170 Methods for treatment of water for marine boilers

BS 1328 Method of sampling water used in industry

BS 2455 Methods of sampling and examining deposits from boilers and associated industrial plant
Part 1. Water-side deposits

BS 2486 Treatment of water for land boilers

Chapter 8 — 'Instruments and controls'

BS 1041 Code for temperature measurement
Part 2. Expansion thermometers
Part 3. Industrial resistance thermometry
Part 4. Thermocouples
Part 5. Radiation pyrometers
Part 7. Temperature/time indicators
Section 2.1 Liquid-in-glass expansion thermometers

BS 1042 Methods for the measurement of fluid flow in pipes
Part 1. Orifice plates, nozzles and venturi tubes
Part 2A. Pitot tubes, Class A accuracy

BS 1704 General-purpose thermometers

BS 1780 Bourdon tube pressure and vacuum gauges

BS 1904 Industrial platinum resistance thermometer elements

BS 3512 Method of evaluating the performance of pneumatic transmitters with 3 to 15 lbf/in^2 (gauge) output

BS 4151 Method of evaluating pneumatic valve positioners with 3 to 15 lbf/in^2 (gauge) input signal

BS 4575 Hydraulic power, transmission and control systems for industrial equipment

BS 4740 Method of evaluating control valve capacity
Part 1. Incompressible fluids
Part 2. Gases or vapours

BS 5235 Dial-type expansion thermometers

BS 5558 Methods of evaluating the performance of controllers with analogue signals for use in industrial process control

Chapter 9 — 'Steam piping systems'

BS 21 Pipe threads for tubes and fittings where pressure-tight joints are made on the threads

BS 759 Valves, gauges and other safety fittings for application to boilers and to piping installations for and in connection with boilers

BS 806 Ferrous piping systems for and in connection with land boilers

BS 1306 Copper and copper alloy pressure piping systems

BS 1560 Steel pipe flanges and flanged fittings for the petroleum industry

BS 1710 Identification of pipelines

BS 1740 Wrought-steel pipe fittings (screwed BSP thread)

BS 1965 Butt-welding pipe fittings for pressure purposes

BS 2779 Pipe threads where pressure-tight joints are not made on the threads

BS 3606 Specification for steel tubes for heat exchangers

BS 3974 Pipe supports
Part 1. Pipe hangers, slider and roller type supports
Part 2. Pipe clamps, cages, cantilevers and attachments to beams

BS 4504 Flanges and bolting for pipes, valves and fittings. Metric series
Part 1. Ferrous
Part 2. Copper alloy and composite flanges

BS 4865 Dimensions of gaskets for pipe flanges to BS 4504
Part 1. Dimensions of non-metallic gaskets for pressures up to 64 bar
Part 2. Dimensions of metallic spiral wound gaskets for pressures 10 bar to 250 bar

BS 5150 Cast-iron wedge and double-disk gate valves for general purposes

BS 5152 Cast-iron globe and globe stop and check valves for general purposes

BS 5153 Cast-iron check valves for general purposes

BS 5154 Copper alloy globe, globe stop and check, check, and gate valves for general purposes

BS 5160 Specification for flanged steel globe valves, globe stop and check valves and lift type check valves for general purposes

BS 5383 Specification for material marking and colour coding of metal pipes and piping system components in steel, nickel alloys and titanium alloys

Chapter 11 — 'Steam turbines and engines'

BS 132   Steam turbines

BS 752   Test code for acceptance of steam turbines

Chapter 13 — 'Steam heating by direct contact'

BS 3219 Horizontal cylindrical hospital sterilizers: pressure steam type

BS 3220 Horizontal rectangular hospital sterilizers: pressure steam type

BS 3233 Pressure steam sterilizers of small size (with independent steam supply) for unwrapped instruments and utensils

BS 3970 Steam sterilizers
Part 1. Sterilizers for porous loads
Part 2. Sterilizers for bottled fluids
Part 5. Electrically heated steam generators for use with hospital sterilizers

Chapter 18 — 'Steam storage'

BS 5500 Unfired fusion-welded pressure vessels

Appendix 1: Money values

The contributors to the book have been conscious of the rapidly changing value of money, and the ephemeral nature of any costs and prices quoted. Much thought has been given to the problem, but no ready solution could be found, and it was decided to face the fact of changing values and to provide a base from which these values could be assessed.

The various monetary values given opposite are those ruling at the end of 1978. By the very nature of the complexity of the money system, none is exact, but they will be accurate enough to enable future readers to do their own calculations, where money values appear in the book.

Values at the end of 1978

Retail price index	204 (100 in Jan. 1974)
Exchange rate	US$2 = £1
Energy costs:	
Coal to power-stations	£25.60 per tonne
Natural gas to domestic consumers (average)	£0.18 per therm (1 therm is approximately 105 MJ)
Crude oil (OPEC price)	US$14.5 per barrel
Electricity to domestic consumers (24-hour usage)	£29 per MWh

Appendix 2: Steam tables

Table A1: Saturation line (temperature)

Temp (°C) t_g	Abs press (bar) f_s	Specific enthalpy (kJ/kg)			Specific entropy (kJ/kgK)			Specific volume (dm³/kg)	
		h_f	h_{fg}	h_g	s_f	s_{fg}	s_g	v_f	v_g
0.01	0.00611	0.00	2501.6	2501.6	0.0000	9.1575	9.1575	1.0002	206163.1
2.5	0.00731	10.49	2495.7	2506.1	0.0382	9.0533	9.0916	1.0001	173934.8
5.0	0.00872	21.00	2489.7	2510.7	0.0762	8.9507	9.0269	1.0000	147163.3
7.5	0.01036	31.50	2483.8	2515.3	0.1138	8.8499	8.9637	1.0001	124941.2
10.0	0.01227	41.98	2477.9	2519.9	0.1510	8.7510	8.9020	1.0003	106429.9
12.5	0.01448	52.46	2472.0	2524.5	0.1879	8.6537	8.8416	1.0005	90956.2
15.0	0.01704	62.93	2466.1	2529.1	0.2243	8.5582	8.7826	1.0008	77978.0
17.5	0.01998	73.39	2460.2	2533.6	0.2605	8.4644	8.7248	1.0012	67057.2
20.0	0.02337	83.86	2454.3	2538.2	0.2963	8.3721	8.6684	1.0017	57838.4
22.5	0.02724	94.31	2448.4	2542.7	0.3319	8.2813	8.6132	1.0023	50032.0
25.0	0.03166	104.8	2442.5	2547.3	0.3670	8.1921	8.5592	1.0029	43401.8
27.5	0.03670	115.2	2436.6	2551.8	0.4020	8.1043	8.5063	1.0036	37753.9
30.0	0.04241	125.7	2430.7	2556.4	0.4365	8.0180	8.4546	1.0043	32928.9
32.5	0.04889	136.1	2424.8	2560.9	0.4708	7.9331	8.4039	1.0051	28795.5
35.0	0.05622	146.6	2418.8	2565.4	0.5048	7.8495	8.3543	1.0060	25244.9
37.5	0.06447	157.0	2412.9	2569.9	0.5386	7.7672	8.3058	1.0069	22186.8
40.0	0.07375	167.5	2406.9	2574.4	0.5721	7.6861	8.2583	1.0078	19546.1
42.5	0.08416	177.9	2400.9	2578.8	0.6053	7.6064	8.2117	1.0088	17260.1
45.0	0.09582	188.4	2394.9	2583.3	0.6383	7.5278	8.1661	1.0099	15276.2
47.5	0.1088	198.8	2388.9	2587.7	0.6711	7.4503	8.1214	1.0110	13550.5
50.0	0.1234	209.3	2382.9	2592.2	0.7035	7.3741	8.0776	1.0121	12045.7
52.5	0.1395	219.7	2376.9	2596.6	0.7357	7.2990	8.0346	1.0133	10730.7
55.0	0.1574	230.2	2370.8	2601.0	0.7677	7.2248	7.9926	1.0145	9578.9
57.5	0.1773	240.6	2364.7	2605.4	0.7995	7.1518	7.9513	1.0158	8567.9
60.0	0.1992	251.1	2358.6	2609.7	0.8310	7.0798	7.9108	1.0171	7678.5
62.5	0.2234	261.6	2352.5	2614.0	0.8622	7.0089	7.8711	1.0185	6894.7
65.0	0.2501	272.0	2346.3	2618.4	0.8934	6.9388	7.8322	1.0199	6202.3
67.5	0.2794	282.5	2340.2	2622.7	0.9242	6.8697	7.7940	1.0214	5589.6
70.0	0.3116	293.0	2334.0	2626.9	0.9548	6.8017	7.7565	1.0228	5046.3
72.5	0.3469	303.5	2327.7	2631.2	0.9852	6.7345	7.7197	1.0244	4563.6
75.0	0.3855	313.9	2321.4	2635.4	1.0155	6.6681	7.6835	1.0259	4134.1
77.5	0.4276	324.4	2315.2	2639.6	1.0454	6.6027	7.6481	1.0275	3751.1

Table A1 *(continued)*: Saturation line (temperature)

Temp (°C) t_g	Abs press (bar) f_s	Specific enthalpy (kJ/kg)			Specific entropy (kJ/kgK)			Specific volume (dm³/kg)	
		h_f	h_{fg}	h_g	s_f	s_{fg}	s_g	v_f	v_g
80.0	0.4736	334.9	2308.8	2643.8	1.0752	6.5380	7.6132	1.0292	3409.1
82.5	0.5236	345.4	2302.5	2647.9	1.1048	6.4742	7.5790	1.0309	3103.1
85.0	0.5780	355.9	2296.1	2652.0	1.1342	6.4112	7.5454	1.0326	2828.8
87.5	0.6371	366.5	2289.6	2656.1	1.1635	6.3488	7.5123	1.0344	2582.6
90.0	0.7011	376.9	2283.2	2660.1	1.1924	6.2875	7.4799	1.0361	2361.3
92.5	0.7704	387.5	2276.7	2664.2	1.2213	6.2266	7.4480	1.0380	2162.0
95.0	0.8453	398.0	2270.1	2668.1	1.2501	6.1665	7.4166	1.0399	1982.2
97.5	0.9261	408.5	2263.6	2672.1	1.2786	6.1072	7.3857	1.0418	1819.9
100.0	1.013	419.1	2256.9	2676.0	1.3069	6.0485	7.3554	1.0437	1673.0
102.5	1.107	429.6	2250.2	2679.9	1.3350	5.9905	7.3255	1.0457	1540.0
105.0	1.208	440.2	2243.5	2683.7	1.3630	5.9332	7.2962	1.0477	1419.3
107.5	1.316	450.7	2236.8	2687.5	1.3909	5.8764	7.2673	1.0498	1309.7
110.0	1.433	461.3	2230.0	2691.3	1.4185	5.8203	7.2388	1.0519	1209.9
112.5	1.557	471.9	2223.1	2695.0	1.4459	5.7649	7.2108	1.0540	1119.1
115.0	1.691	482.5	2216.2	2698.7	1.4733	5.7099	7.1832	1.0562	1036.3
117.5	1.833	493.1	2209.2	2702.4	1.5005	5.6555	7.1560	1.0584	960.67
120.0	1.985	503.7	2202.3	2706.0	1.5275	5.6018	7.1293	1.0606	891.52
122.5	2.148	514.4	2195.1	2709.5	1.5544	5.5486	7.1029	1.0629	828.24
125.0	2.321	525.0	2188.0	2713.0	1.5811	5.4958	7.0769	1.0652	770.23
127.5	2.505	535.6	2180.8	2716.5	1.6078	5.4435	7.0513	1.0676	717.02
130.0	2.701	546.3	2173.6	2719.9	1.6344	5.3917	7.0261	1.0700	668.14
132.5	2.910	557.0	2166.3	2723.3	1.6607	5.3405	7.0012	1.0725	623.19
135.0	3.131	567.7	2158.9	2726.6	1.6868	5.2897	6.9766	1.0750	581.81
137.5	3.365	578.4	2151.4	2729.9	1.7131	5.2392	6.9524	1.0775	543.67
140.0	3.614	589.1	2143.9	2733.1	1.7390	5.1894	6.9284	1.0801	508.49
142.5	3.877	599.9	2136.3	2736.2	1.7648	5.1400	6.9048	1.0827	476.01
145.0	4.155	610.6	2128.7	2739.3	1.7905	5.0911	6.8815	1.0853	445.98
147.5	4.449	621.4	2121.0	2742.4	1.8161	5.0424	6.8585	1.0880	418.19
150.0	4.760	632.2	2113.2	2745.4	1.8416	4.9942	6.8358	1.0908	392.45
155.0	5.433	653.8	2097.4	2751.2	1.8922	4.8989	6.7911	1.0964	346.44
160.0	6.181	675.5	2081.2	2756.7	1.9424	4.8051	6.7475	1.1022	306.76
165.0	7.008	697.3	2064.8	2762.0	1.9924	4.7124	6.7048	1.1082	272.40

Table A1 *(continued)*: Saturation line (temperature)

Temp (°C) t_g	Abs press (bar) f_s	Specific enthalpy (kJ/kg)			Specific entropy (kJ/kgK)			Specific volume (dm³/kg)	
		h_f	h_{fg}	h_g	s_f	s_{fg}	s_g	v_f	v_g
170.0	7.920	719.1	2047.9	2767.1	2.0415	4.6215	6.6630	1.1145	242.55
175.0	8.924	741.1	2030.7	2771.8	2.0906	4.5315	6.6221	1.1209	216.54
180.0	10.027	763.2	2013.1	2776.3	2.1393	4.4426	6.5819	1.1275	193.80
185.0	11.233	785.3	1995.1	2780.4	2.1875	4.3549	6.5424	1.1344	173.86
190.0	12.551	807.6	1976.7	2784.3	2.2356	4.2680	6.5036	1.1415	156.32
195.0	13.987	830.0	1957.8	2787.8	2.2832	4.1822	6.4654	1.1489	140.84
200.0	15.549	852.4	1938.5	2790.9	2.3306	4.0972	6.4278	1.1565	127.16
205.0	17.243	875.0	1918.7	2793.8	2.3776	4.0130	6.3906	1.1644	115.03
210.0	19.077	897.8	1898.4	2796.2	2.4245	3.9295	6.3539	1.1726	104.24
215.0	21.060	920.7	1877.6	2798.3	2.4711	3.8465	6.3176	1.1811	94.625
220.0	23.198	943.7	1856.2	2799.9	2.5177	3.7640	6.2817	1.1900	86.038
225.0	25.501	967.0	1834.2	2801.2	2.5639	3.6822	6.2461	1.1992	78.349
230.0	27.976	990.4	1811.6	2802.0	2.6101	3.6007	6.2107	1.2087	71.450
235.0	30.632	1013.8	1788.5	2802.3	2.6561	3.5195	6.1756	1.2187	65.246
240.0	33.478	1037.7	1764.5	2802.2	2.7019	3.4387	6.1406	1.2291	59.655
245.0	36.523	1061.7	1739.9	2801.6	2.7478	3.3579	6.1057	1.2399	54.606
250.0	39.776	1085.9	1714.5	2800.4	2.7933	3.2775	6.0708	1.2513	50.038
255.0	43.246	1110.3	1688.4	2798.7	2.8391	3.1968	6.0359	1.2632	45.896
260.0	46.943	1135.0	1661.4	2796.4	2.8843	3.1166	6.0010	1.2756	42.134
265.0	50.877	1159.9	1633.6	2793.5	2.9302	3.0356	5.9658	1.2887	38.710
270.0	55.058	1185.4	1604.5	2789.9	2.9759	2.9545	5.9304	1.3025	35.588
275.0	59.496	1210.9	1574.6	2785.5	3.0222	2.8725	5.8947	1.3170	32.736
280.0	64.202	1237.0	1543.5	2780.4	3.0680	2.7907	5.8586	1.3324	30.126
285.0	69.186	1263.3	1511.1	2774.5	3.1141	2.7079	5.8220	1.3487	27.733
290.0	74.461	1290.2	1477.5	2767.6	3.1610	2.6238	5.7848	1.3659	25.535
295.0	80.037	1317.4	1442.4	2759.8	3.2077	2.5392	5.7469	1.3844	23.513
300.0	85.927	1345.2	1405.8	2751.0	3.2548	2.4534	5.7081	1.4041	21.649
305.0	92.144	1373.8	1367.3	2741.1	3.3024	2.3661	5.6685	1.4252	19.927
310.0	98.700	1402.6	1327.4	2730.0	3.3512	2.2766	5.6278	1.4480	18.334
315.0	105.611	1432.3	1285.3	2717.6	3.3999	2.1859	5.5858	1.4726	16.856
320.0	112.891	1462.6	1241.0	2703.7	3.4495	2.0928	5.5424	1.4995	15.480

Table A1 *(continued)*: Saturation line (temperature)

Temp (°C) t_g	Abs press (bar) f_s	Specific enthalpy (kJ/kg)			Specific entropy (kJ/kgK)			Specific volume (dm³/kg)	
		h_f	h_{fg}	h_g	s_f	s_{fg}	s_g	v_f	v_g
325.0	120.556	1494.3	1193.7	2688.0	3.5004	1.9965	5.4969	1.5289	14.195
330.0	128.625	1526.9	1143.3	2670.2	3.5527	1.8963	5.4490	1.5615	12.990
335.0	137.117	1560.6	1089.2	2649.8	3.6066	1.7913	5.3979	1.5978	11.854
340.0	146.052	1595.5	1030.6	2626.2	3.6610	1.6818	5.3428	1.6387	10.781
345.0	155.454	1632.7	966.1	2598.8	3.7194	1.5632	5.2826	1.6858	9.7606
350.0	165.351	1672.4	895.2	2567.6	3.7798	1.4378	5.2176	1.7411	8.7984
355.0	175.772	1716.6	813.8	2530.4	3.8489	1.2953	5.1442	1.8085	7.8593
360.0	186.751	1764.2	721.3	2485.4	3.9210	1.1390	5.0600	1.8959	6.9399
362.5	192.461	1789.9	668.9	2458.8	3.9598	1.0522	5.0120	1.9505	6.4805
365.0	198.326	1818.0	610.0	2428.0	4.0021	0.9558	4.9579	2.0160	6.0116
367.5	204.350	1850.1	540.8	2390.9	4.0505	0.8440	4.8944	2.0985	5.5192
370.0	210.540	1890.2	452.6	2342.8	4.1108	0.7036	4.8144	2.2136	4.9728
372.5	216.903	1951.2	316.5	2267.7	4.2031	0.4902	4.6934	2.4209	4.2746
374.15	221.200	2107.4	0.0	2107.4	4.4429	0.0	4.4429	3.1700	3.1700

Table A2: Saturation line (pressure)

P_s (bar)	t_s (°C)	h_f	h_{fg}	h_g	s_f	s_{fg}	s_g	v_f	v_g
		Specific enthalpy (kJ/kg)			**Specific entropy (kJ/kgK)**			**Specific volume (dm³/kg)**	
0.01	6.983	29.32	2485.1	2514.4	0.1061	8.8706	8.9767	1.0001	129207.5
0.02	17.513	73.44	2460.2	2533.6	0.2607	8.4639	8.7246	1.0012	67005.2
0.03	24.100	101.0	2444.6	2545.6	0.3544	8.2241	8.5785	1.0027	45666.2
0.04	28.983	121.4	2433.1	2554.5	0.4225	8.0530	8.4755	1.0040	34801.4
0.05	32.898	137.8	2423.8	2561.6	0.4763	7.9197	8.3960	1.0052	28193.8
0.06	36.183	151.5	2416.0	2567.5	0.5208	7.8104	8.3312	1.0064	23741.4
0.07	39.025	163.4	2409.2	2572.6	0.5592	7.7175	8.2767	1.0074	20530.6
0.08	41.534	173.9	2403.3	2577.1	0.5926	7.6370	8.2296	1.0084	18104.9
0.09	43.787	183.3	2397.8	2581.1	0.6224	7.5657	8.1881	1.0094	16204.0
0.10	45.833	191.8	2392.9	2584.8	0.6492	7.5018	8.1511	1.0102	14674.5
0.12	49.446	206.9	2384.3	2591.2	0.6964	7.3908	8.0872	1.0119	12361.8
0.14	52.574	220.0	2376.7	2596.7	0.7367	7.2967	8.0334	1.0133	10694.4
0.16	55.341	231.6	2370.0	2601.6	0.7720	7.2148	7.9869	1.0147	9433.2
0.18	57.826	242.0	2363.9	2605.9	0.8036	7.1423	7.9460	1.0160	8445.4
0.20	60.086	251.4	2358.4	2609.9	0.8321	7.0774	7.9094	1.0172	7649.9
0.22	62.161	260.1	2353.3	2613.5	0.8581	7.0184	7.8765	1.0183	6995.3
0.24	64.082	268.2	2348.6	2616.8	0.8820	6.9644	7.8464	1.0194	6446.7
0.26	65.871	275.7	2344.2	2619.9	0.9041	6.9147	7.8188	1.0204	5980.3
0.28	67.547	282.7	2340.0	2622.7	0.9248	6.8685	7.7933	1.0214	5578.7
0.30	69.124	289.3	2336.1	2625.4	0.9441	6.8254	7.7695	1.0223	5229.3
0.32	70.615	295.6	2332.4	2628.0	0.9623	6.7851	7.7474	1.0232	4922.2
0.34	72.029	301.5	2328.9	2630.4	0.9795	6.7470	7.7265	1.0241	4650.3
0.36	73.374	307.1	2325.5	2632.6	0.9958	6.7112	7.7070	1.0249	4407.8
0.38	74.658	312.5	2322.3	2634.8	1.0113	6.6772	7.6884	1.0257	4190.0
0.40	75.886	317.7	2319.2	2636.9	1.0261	6.6448	7.6709	1.0265	3993.4
0.42	77.063	322.6	2316.3	2638.9	1.0401	6.6141	7.6542	1.0273	3815.0
0.44	78.194	327.3	2313.4	2640.7	1.0537	6.5846	7.6383	1.0280	3652.3
0.46	79.282	331.9	2310.6	2642.6	1.0667	6.5564	7.6232	1.0287	3503.4
0.48	80.332	336.3	2308.0	2644.3	1.0792	6.5295	7.6086	1.0294	3366.5
0.50	81.345	340.6	2305.4	2646.0	1.0912	6.5035	7.5947	1.0301	3240.3
0.6	85.954	359.9	2293.6	2653.6	1.1454	6.3873	7.5327	1.0333	2731.7
0.7	89.959	376.8	2283.3	2660.1	1.1921	6.2883	7.4804	1.0361	2364.7

Table A2 (*continued*): Saturation line (pressure)

Temp (°C) P_s	Abs press (bar) t_s	h_f	h_{fg}	h_g	s_f	s_{fg}	s_g	v_f	v_g
			Specific enthalpy (kJ/kg)			Specific entropy (kJ/kgK)		Specific volume (dm³/kg)	
0.8	93.512	391.7	2274.0	2665.8	1.2330	6.2022	7.4352	1.0387	2087.0
0.9	96.713	405.2	2265.7	2670.9	1.2696	6.1258	7.3954	1.0412	1869.2
1.0	99.632	417.5	2257.9	2675.4	1.3027	6.0571	7.3598	1.0434	1693.7
1.1	102.317	428.9	2250.7	2679.6	1.3329	5.9948	7.3277	1.0455	1549.3
1.2	104.808	439.3	2244.1	2683.4	1.3608	5.9376	7.2984	1.0476	1428.1
1.3	107.133	449.2	2237.8	2687.0	1.3867	5.8848	7.2715	1.0495	1325.1
1.4	109.315	458.4	2231.8	2690.3	1.4108	5.8358	7.2466	1.0513	1236.3
1.5	111.372	467.1	2226.2	2693.4	1.4336	5.7898	7.2234	1.0530	1159.1
1.6	113.320	475.4	2220.9	2696.2	1.4550	5.7467	7.2017	1.0547	1091.1
1.7	115.170	483.2	2215.8	2699.0	1.4751	5.7062	7.1813	1.0563	1030.9
1.8	116.933	490.7	2210.9	2701.5	1.4944	5.6678	7.1622	1.0579	977.23
1.9	118.617	497.9	2206.1	2704.0	1.5126	5.6314	7.1440	1.0594	929.01
2.0	120.231	504.7	2201.6	2706.3	1.5301	5.5967	7.1268	1.0608	885.44
2.1	121.780	511.3	2197.2	2708.5	1.5467	5.5637	7.1105	1.0623	845.90
2.2	123.270	517.7	2192.9	2710.6	1.5627	5.5322	7.0949	1.0636	809.83
2.3	124.705	523.8	2188.9	2712.6	1.5780	5.5020	7.0800	1.0650	776.82
2.4	126.091	529.7	2184.9	2714.5	1.5929	5.4728	7.0657	1.0663	746.45
2.5	127.430	535.4	2181.0	2716.4	1.6072	5.4448	7.0520	1.0675	718.45
2.6	128.727	540.9	2177.3	2718.2	1.6209	5.4180	7.0389	1.0688	692.51
2.7	129.984	546.2	2173.7	2719.9	1.6341	5.3921	7.0262	1.0700	668.44
2.8	131.203	551.5	2170.0	2721.5	1.6470	5.3670	7.0140	1.0712	646.04
2.9	132.388	556.5	2166.6	2723.1	1.6595	5.3428	7.0023	1.0724	625.12
3.0	133.540	561.5	2163.2	2724.7	1.6716	5.3193	6.9909	1.0735	605.56
3.5	138.873	584.3	2147.3	2731.6	1.7274	5.2118	6.9392	1.0789	524.00
4.0	143.623	604.7	2132.9	2737.6	1.7763	5.1180	6.8943	1.0839	462.23
4.5	147.917	623.2	2119.7	2742.9	1.8202	5.0345	6.8547	1.0885	413.76
5.0	151.844	640.2	2107.4	2747.4	1.8604	4.9588	6.8192	1.0928	374.67
5.5	155.468	655.8	2095.9	2751.7	1.8969	4.8901	6.7870	1.0970	342.48
6.0	158.838	670.5	2085.0	2755.5	1.9308	4.8267	6.7575	1.1009	315.47
7.0	164.956	697.1	2064.9	2762.0	1.9917	4.7134	6.7052	1.1082	272.68
8.0	170.415	721.0	2046.5	2767.5	2.0456	4.6140	6.6596	1.1150	240.26
9.0	175.358	742.7	2029.4	2772.1	2.0940	4.5252	6.6192	1.1213	214.81

Table A2 *(continued)*: Saturation line (pressure)

Abs press (bar) P_s	Temp (°C) t_s	Specific enthalpy (kJ/kg) h_f	h_{fg}	h_g	Specific entropy (kJ/kgK) s_f	s_{fg}	s_g	Specific volume (dm³/kg) v_f	v_g
10.0	179.884	762.7	2013.5	2776.2	2.1379	4.4449	6.5828	1.1274	194.29
11.0	184.067	781.2	1998.5	2779.7	2.1786	4.3711	6.5497	1.1331	177.39
12.0	187.961	798.5	1984.2	2782.7	2.2160	4.3034	6.5194	1.1386	163.20
13.0	191.609	814.8	1970.6	2785.4	2.2509	4.2404	6.4913	1.1438	151.13
14.0	195.042	830.1	1957.7	2787.8	2.2835	4.1816	6.4651	1.1489	140.72
15.0	198.289	844.7	1945.2	2789.9	2.3144	4.1262	6.4406	1.1539	131.66
16.0	201.372	858.6	1933.1	2791.7	2.3436	4.0739	6.4175	1.1586	123.69
17.0	204.307	871.8	1921.5	2793.4	2.3712	4.0246	6.3957	1.1633	116.62
18.0	207.111	884.6	1910.2	2794.8	2.3976	3.9775	6.3751	1.1678	110.32
19.0	209.797	896.8	1899.3	2796.1	2.4225	3.9329	6.3554	1.1723	104.65
20.0	212.375	908.7	1888.5	2797.2	2.4467	3.8899	6.3366	1.1766	99.536
22.0	217.244	931.1	1868.0	2799.1	2.4922	3.8093	6.3015	1.1850	90.652
24.0	221.783	952.0	1848.4	2800.4	2.5343	3.7347	6.2690	1.1932	83.199
26.0	226.037	971.8	1829.5	2801.4	2.5734	3.6654	6.2387	1.2011	76.857
28.0	230.047	990.6	1811.4	2802.0	2.6107	3.5997	6.2104	1.2088	71.388
30.0	233.841	1008.4	1793.9	2802.3	2.6456	3.5381	6.1837	1.2163	66.626
32.0	237.445	1025.5	1776.9	2802.3	2.6786	3.4799	6.1585	1.2237	62.440
34.0	240.881	1041.8	1760.3	2802.1	2.7096	3.4248	6.1344	1.2310	58.727
36.0	244.164	1057.7	1744.1	2801.7	2.7403	3.3712	6.1115	1.2381	55.415
38.0	247.311	1072.9	1728.3	2801.1	2.7686	3.3210	6.0896	1.2451	52.438
40.0	250.333	1087.5	1712.9	2800.3	2.7962	3.2723	6.0685	1.2521	49.749
42.0	253.241	1101.7	1697.7	2799.4	2.8232	3.2250	6.0482	1.2589	47.307
44.0	256.045	1115.5	1682.7	2798.3	2.8486	3.1800	6.0286	1.2657	45.080
46.0	258.753	1128.8	1668.2	2797.1	2.8731	3.1366	6.0097	1.2725	43.039
48.0	261.373	1142.0	1653.7	2795.7	2.8973	3.0940	5.9913	1.2792	41.162
50.0	263.911	1154.5	1639.7	2794.2	2.9204	3.0531	5.9735	1.2858	39.429
55.0	269.932	1185.0	1604.9	2789.9	2.9755	2.9554	5.9309	1.3023	35.629
60.0	275.550	1214.0	1571.0	2785.0	3.0273	2.8635	5.8908	1.3187	32.438
65.0	280.820	1241.4	1538.1	2779.5	3.0758	2.7768	5.8527	1.3350	29.719
70.0	285.790	1267.6	1505.9	2773.5	3.1219	2.6943	5.8162	1.3513	27.373
75.0	290.496	1292.7	1474.2	2766.9	3.1656	2.6154	5.7810	1.3677	25.327

Table A2 *(continued)*: Saturation line (pressure)

Temp (°C) t_s	Abs press (bar) P_s	Specific enthalpy (kJ/kg)			Specific entropy (kJ/kgK)			Specific volume (dm³/kg)	
		h_f	h_{fg}	h_g	s_f	s_{fg}	s_g	v_f	v_g
80.0	294.968	1317.2	1442.7	2759.9	3.2078	2.5393	5.7471	1.3842	23.525
85.0	299.231	1341.0	1411.5	2752.5	3.2482	2.4660	5.7141	1.4009	21.926
90.0	303.306	1363.8	1380.8	2744.6	3.2865	2.3956	5.6820	1.4179	20.495
95.0	307.211	1386.3	1350.1	2736.4	3.3241	2.3265	5.6506	1.4351	19.208
100.0	310.961	1408.3	1319.4	2727.7	3.3602	2.2596	5.6198	1.4526	18.041
105.0	314.568	1429.9	1288.9	2718.7	3.3957	2.1938	5.5895	1.4704	16.979
110.0	318.045	1450.8	1258.5	2709.3	3.4304	2.1291	5.5595	1.4887	16.006
115.0	321.402	1471.5	1227.9	2699.5	3.4641	2.0657	5.5298	1.5075	15.111
120.0	324.646	1492.2	1196.9	2689.2	3.4975	2.0027	5.5002	1.5268	14.283
125.0	327.785	1512.0	1166.3	2678.4	3.5295	1.9411	5.4706	1.5466	13.514
130.0	330.827	1532.3	1134.7	2667.0	3.5615	1.8794	5.4408	1.5672	12.798
135.0	333.777	1552.2	1102.8	2655.0	3.5928	1.8180	5.4108	1.5885	12.126
140.0	336.641	1571.8	1070.6	2642.4	3.6239	1.7563	5.3803	1.6106	11.495
145.0	339.425	1591.6	1037.6	2629.1	3.6546	1.6948	5.3494	1.6337	10.902
150.0	342.131	1611.2	1003.8	2615.0	3.6858	1.6320	5.3178	1.6579	10.340
155.0	344.764	1631.0	969.3	2600.3	3.7161	1.5697	5.2858	1.6834	9.8103
160.0	347.328	1650.9	934.0	2584.9	3.7468	1.5063	5.2532	1.7103	9.3081
165.0	349.827	1670.7	898.2	2568.9	3.7777	1.4423	5.2201	1.7390	8.8325
170.0	352.262	1691.7	859.9	2551.6	3.8107	1.3748	5.1855	1.7695	8.3712
175.0	354.638	1713.3	820.0	2533.3	3.8438	1.3060	5.1498	1.8031	7.9264
180.0	356.957	1734.8	779.1	2513.9	3.8765	1.2362	5.1128	1.8399	7.4977
185.0	359.220	1756.5	736.6	2493.1	3.9094	1.1647	5.0741	1.8806	7.0827
190.0	361.431	1778.7	692.0	2470.6	3.9429	1.0903	5.0332	1.9260	6.6775
195.0	363.591	1801.8	644.2	2446.0	3.9777	1.0116	4.9893	1.9775	6.2777
200.0	365.701	1826.5	591.9	2418.4	4.0149	0.9264	4.9412	2.0370	5.8768
202.0	366.533	1837.0	569.2	2406.2	4.0308	0.8897	4.9204	2.0639	5.7139
204.0	367.356	1848.1	545.2	2393.3	4.0474	0.8510	4.8984	2.0931	5.5486
206.0	368.173	1859.9	519.5	2379.4	4.0651	0.8099	4.8750	2.1252	5.3794
208.0	368.982	1872.5	491.7	2364.2	4.0841	0.7657	4.8498	2.1609	5.2052
210.0	369.784	1886.2	461.4	2347.6	4.1048	0.7175	4.8223	2.2015	5.0236
212.0	370.580	1901.5	427.4	2328.9	4.1279	0.6639	4.7918	2.2489	4.8314
214.0	371.368	1919.0	388.4	2307.4	4.1543	0.6026	4.7569	2.3061	4.6240

Table A2 (*continued*): Saturation line (pressure)

Temp (°C) P_s	Abs press (bar) t_s	Specific enthalpy (kJ/kg)			Specific entropy (kJ/kgK)			Specific volume (dm³/kg)	
		h_f	h_{fg}	h_g	s_f	s_{fg}	s_g	v_f	v_g
216.0	372.149	1939.9	341.6	2281.6	4.1860	0.5294	4.7154	2.3793	4.3921
218.0	372.924	1967.2	280.8	2248.1	4.2276	0.4347	4.6622	2.4832	4.1154
220.0	373.692	2011.1	184.7	2195.8	4.2946	0.2855	4.5801	2.6711	3.7287
221.0	374.150	2107.4	0.0	2107.4	4.4429	0.0	4.4429	3.1700	3.1700

Table A3: Properties of sub-saturated water and superheated steam

p (bar abs)		t (°C) : 0.01	20	50	100	150	200	250	300	400	500	600
0.01	h	0.00	2538.6	2594.6	2688.6	2783.7	2880.1	2977.7	3076.8	3279.7	3489.2	3705.6
	s	−0.0000	9.0611	9.2430	9.5136	9.7527	9.9679	10.1641	10.3450	10.6711	10.9612	11.2243
	v	1.0002	135228.0	149092.6	172186.7	195271.7	218352.2	241430.7	264508.1	310661.3	356813.6	402965.5
0.05	h	0.00	83.86	2593.7	2688.1	2783.4	2879.9	2977.6	3076.7	3279.7	3489.2	3705.6
	s	0.0000	0.2963	8.4981	8.7698	9.0094	9.2248	9.4211	9.6021	9.9283	10.2184	10.4815
	v	1.0002	1.0017	29783.0	34416.7	39041.3	43661.5	48279.5	52896.5	62128.9	71360.4	80591.5
0.10	h	0.01	83.87	2592.7	2687.5	2783.1	2879.6	2977.4	3076.6	3279.6	3489.1	3705.5
	s	0.0000	0.2963	8.1757	8.4486	8.6888	8.9045	9.1010	9.2820	9.6083	9.8984	10.1616
	v	1.0002	1.0017	14869.2	17195.4	19512.5	21825.1	24135.6	26445.1	31062.4	35678.8	40294.8
0.50	h	0.05	83.91	209.31	2682.6	2780.1	2877.7	2976.1	3075.7	3279.0	3488.7	3705.2
	s	0.0000	0.2963	0.7035	7.6953	7.9406	8.1587	8.3564	8.5380	8.8649	9.1552	9.4185
	v	1.0002	1.0017	1.0121	3418.1	3889.3	4356.0	4820.5	5283.9	6209.1	7133.5	8057.4
0.75	h	0.08	83.93	209.33	2679.4	2778.2	2876.6	2975.3	3075.1	3278.6	3488.4	3705.0
	s	0.0000	0.2963	0.7035	7.5014	7.7500	7.9697	8.1681	8.3502	8.6773	8.9678	9.2312
	v	1.0002	1.0017	1.0121	2269.8	2587.3	2900.2	3210.9	3520.5	4138.0	4754.7	5370.9
1.0	h	0.10	83.95	209.35	2676.2	2776.3	2875.4	2974.5	3074.5	3278.2	3488.1	3704.8
	s	0.0000	0.2962	0.7035	7.3618	7.6137	7.8349	8.0342	8.2166	8.5442	8.8348	9.0982
	v	1.0002	1.0017	1.0121	1695.5	1936.3	2172.3	2406.1	2638.7	3102.5	3565.3	4027.7
1.5	h	0.15	84.00	209.39	419.12	2772.5	2872.9	2972.9	3073.3	3277.5	3487.6	3704.4
	s	0.0000	0.2962	0.7035	1.3068	7.4194	7.6439	7.8447	8.0280	8.3562	8.6472	8.9108
	v	1.0001	1.0017	1.0121	1.0437	1285.2	1444.4	1601.3	1757.0	2066.9	2375.9	2684.5
2	h	0.20	84.05	209.44	419.16	2768.5	2870.5	2971.2	3072.1	3276.7	3487.0	3704.0
	s	0.0000	0.2962	0.7034	1.3068	7.2794	7.5072	7.7096	7.8937	8.2226	8.5139	8.7776
	v	1.0001	1.0016	1.0120	1.0437	959.54	1080.4	1198.9	1316.2	1549.2	1781.2	2012.9
3	h	0.31	84.14	209.52	419.23	2760.4	2865.5	2967.9	3069.7	3275.2	3486.0	3703.2
	s	0.0000	0.2962	0.7034	1.3067	7.0771	7.3119	7.5176	7.7034	8.0338	8.3257	8.5898
	v	1.0001	1.0016	1.0120	1.0436	633.74	716.35	796.44	875.29	1031.4	1186.5	1341.2
4	h	0.41	84.24	209.61	419.31	2752.0	2860.4	2964.5	3067.2	3273.6	3484.9	3702.3
	s	0.0000	0.2962	0.7033	1.3066	6.9285	7.1708	7.3800	7.5675	7.8994	8.1919	8.4563
	v	1.0000	1.0015	1.0119	1.0436	470.66	534.26	595.19	654.85	772.50	899.19	1005.4

Table A3 (continued): Properties of sub-saturated water and superheated steam

p (bar abs)	t(°C)	0.01	20	50	100	150	200	250	300	400	500	600
5	h	0.51	84.33	209.69	419.38	632.22	2855.1	2961.1	3064.8	3272.1	3483.8	3701.5
	s	0.0000	0.2962	0.7033	1.3066	1.8415	7.0592	7.2721	7.4614	7.7948	8.0879	8.3526
	v	1.0000	1.0015	1.0119	1.0435	1.0908	424.96	474.43	522.58	617.16	710.78	803.95
6	h	0.61	84.42	209.78	419.46	632.28	2849.7	2957.6	3062.3	3270.6	3482.7	3700.7
	s	0.0000	0.2961	0.7032	1.3065	1.8414	6.9662	7.1829	7.3740	7.7090	8.0027	8.2678
	v	0.9999	1.0015	1.0119	1.0434	1.0907	352.04	393.91	434.39	513.61	591.84	669.63
8	h	0.82	84.61	209.95	419.61	632.41	2838.6	2950.4	3057.3	3267.5	3480.5	3699.1
	s	0.0001	0.2961	0.7031	1.3063	1.8412	6.8148	7.0397	7.2348	7.5729	7.8678	8.1336
	v	0.9998	1.0014	1.0118	1.0433	1.0906	260.79	293.21	324.14	384.16	443.17	501.72
10	h	1.02	84.80	210.12	419.76	632.53	2826.8	2943.0	3052.1	3264.4	3478.3	3697.4
	s	0.0001	0.2961	0.7031	1.3062	1.8410	6.6922	6.9259	7.1251	7.4665	7.7627	8.0292
	v	0.9997	1.0013	1.0117	1.0432	1.0904	205.92	232.75	257.98	306.49	353.96	400.98

p (bar abs)	t(°C)	50	100	150	200	250	300	350	400	450	500	600
15	h	210.56	420.13	632.84	2794.7	2923.5	3038.9	3148.7	3256.6	3364.3	3472.8	3693.3
	s	0.7028	1.3058	1.8404	6.4508	6.7099	6.9207	7.1044	7.2709	7.4253	7.5703	7.8385
	v	1.0114	1.0430	1.0901	132.38	151.99	169.70	186.53	202.92	219.05	235.03	266.66
20	h	210.99	420.51	633.15	852.61	2902.4	3025.0	3138.6	3248.7	3357.8	3467.3	3689.2
	s	0.7026	1.3054	1.8399	2.3299	6.5454	6.7696	6.9596	7.1296	7.2859	7.4323	7.7022
	v	1.0112	1.0427	1.0897	1.1560	111.45	125.50	138.56	151.13	163.42	175.55	199.50
30	h	211.85	421.26	633.77	853.02	2854.8	2995.1	3117.5	3232.5	3344.6	3456.2	3681.0
	s	0.7021	1.3046	1.8388	2.3283	6.2857	6.5422	6.7471	6.9246	7.0854	7.2345	7.5079
	v	1.0108	1.0422	1.0890	1.1550	70.551	81.159	90.526	99.310	107.79	116.08	132.34
40	h	212.71	422.01	634.39	853.43	1085.9	2962.0	3095.1	3215.7	3331.2	3445.0	3672.8
	s	0.7017	1.3038	1.8377	2.3267	2.7932	6.3642	6.5870	6.7733	6.9388	7.0909	7.3680
	v	1.0103	1.0417	1.0883	1.1540	1.2512	58.833	66.446	73.376	79.958	86.341	98.763
50	h	213.57	422.76	635.02	853.85	1085.9	2925.5	3071.2	3198.3	3317.5	3433.7	3664.5
	s	0.7012	1.3030	1.8366	2.3252	2.7908	6.2105	6.4545	6.6508	6.8217	6.9770	7.2578
	v	1.0099	1.0412	1.0877	1.1530	1.2494	45.301	51.941	57.791	63.250	68.494	78.616

Table A3 (*continued*): Properties of sub-saturated water and superheated steam

p (bar abs)	t(°C)	50	100	150	200	250	300	350	400	450	500	600
60	h	214.42	423.51	635.64	854.27	1085.9	2885.0	3045.8	3180.1	3303.5	3422.2	3656.2
	s	0.7007	1.3023	1.8355	2.3236	2.7884	6.0692	6.3386	6.5462	6.7230	6.8818	7.1664
	v	1.0094	1.0406	1.0870	1.1519	1.2476	36.145	42.222	47.379	52.103	56.592	65.184
70	h	215.28	424.26	636.27	854.69	1085.9	2839.4	3018.7	3161.2	3289.1	3410.6	3647.9
	s	0.7003	1.3015	1.8344	2.3221	2.7860	5.9327	6.2333	6.4536	6.6368	6.7993	7.0880
	v	1.0090	1.0401	1.0863	1.1510	1.2458	29.457	35.233	39.922	44.131	48.086	55.590
80	h	216.14	425.02	636.89	855.12	1085.9	2786.8	2989.9	3141.6	3274.3	3398.8	3639.5
	s	0.6998	1.3007	1.8333	2.3205	2.7837	5.7942	6.1349	6.3694	6.5597	6.7262	7.0191
	v	1.0086	1.0396	1.0856	1.1500	1.2441	24.264	29.948	34.310	38.145	41.704	48.394
90	h	217.00	425.77	637.52	855.55	1086.0	1344.7	2959.0	3121.2	3259.2	3386.8	3631.1
	s	0.6993	1.3000	1.8322	2.3190	2.7813	3.2529	6.0408	6.2915	6.4894	6.6600	6.9574
	v	1.0081	1.0391	1.0850	1.1490	1.2423	1.4022	25.792	29.929	33.480	36.737	42.798
100	h	217.86	426.52	638.15	855.98	1086.0	1343.5	2925.8	3099.9	3243.6	3374.6	3622.7
	s	0.6989	1.2992	1.8311	2.3175	2.7790	3.2484	5.9489	6.2182	6.4243	6.5994	6.9013
	v	1.0077	1.0386	1.0843	1.1480	1.2406	1.3979	22.421	26.408	29.742	32.760	38.320
110	h	218.72	427.27	638.78	856.42	1086.0	1342.4	2889.6	3077.8	3227.7	3362.2	3614.2
	s	0.6984	1.2984	1.8301	2.3160	2.7767	3.2440	5.8571	6.1483	6.3633	6.5432	6.8499
	v	1.0073	1.0381	1.0837	1.1470	1.2389	1.3936	19.610	23.512	26.676	29.503	34.656
120	h	219.58	428.03	639.41	856.86	1086.1	1341.3	2849.7	3054.8	3211.4	3349.6	3605.7
	s	0.6979	1.2977	1.8290	2.3145	2.7745	3.2397	5.7636	6.0810	6.3056	6.4906	6.8022
	v	1.0068	1.0376	1.0830	1.1461	1.2373	1.3895	17.206	21.084	24.116	26.786	31.603
140	h	221.29	429.54	640.68	857.75	1086.2	1339.4	2754.2	3005.6	3177.4	3323.8	3588.5
	s	0.6970	1.2961	1.8269	2.3115	2.7700	3.2314	5.5618	5.9513	6.1978	6.3937	6.7159
	v	1.0060	1.0366	1.0817	1.1442	1.2340	1.3817	13.211	17.227	20.075	22.509	26.804
160	h	223.00	431.05	641.95	858.65	1086.4	1337.6	2620.8	2951.3	3141.6	3297.1	3571.0
	s	0.6961	1.2946	1.8248	2.3086	2.7657	3.2234	5.3109	5.8240	6.0972	6.3054	6.6389
	v	1.0051	1.0356	1.0804	1.1423	1.2308	1.3743	9.763	14.275	17.025	19.293	23.204

456

Table A3 *(continued)*: Properties of sub-saturated water and superheated steam

p (bar abs)		t (°C) 100	200	250	300	350	400	450	500	550	600	650
170	h	431.80	859.10	1086.5	1336.7	1668.2	2921.7	3123.1	3283.5	3427.0	3562.2	3693.5
	s	1.2939	2.3072	2.7635	3.2196	3.7718	5.7599	6.0489	6.2636	6.4435	6.6031	6.7493
	v	1.0351	1.1414	1.2293	1.3707	1.7283	13.034	15.763	17.966	19.918	21.721	23.428
180	h	432.56	859.56	1086.6	1335.9	1660.3	2890.3	3104.0	3269.6	3416.1	3553.4	3686.1
	s	1.2931	2.3057	2.7614	3.2158	3.7563	5.6947	6.0015	6.2232	6.4069	6.5688	6.7166
	v	1.0346	1.1405	1.2278	1.3673	1.7043	11.913	14.636	16.785	18.670	20.403	22.037
190	h	433.31	860.02	1086.8	1335.2	1653.5	2856.7	3084.4	3255.4	3405.2	3544.5	3678.6
	s	1.2924	2.3043	2.7593	3.2121	3.7428	5.6278	5.9549	6.1839	6.3716	6.5360	6.6854
	v	1.0342	1.1396	1.2262	1.3639	1.6839	10.889	13.623	15.726	17.554	19.223	20.792
200	h	434.07	860.49	1086.9	1334.4	1647.6	2820.5	3064.3	3241.1	3394.1	3535.5	3671.1
	s	1.2916	2.3029	2.7572	3.2084	3.7306	5.5585	5.9089	6.1456	6.3374	6.5043	6.6554
	v	1.0337	1.1387	1.2247	1.3606	1.6662	9.9470	12.707	14.771	16.548	18.161	19.672
210	h	434.82	860.95	1087.0	1333.8	1642.4	2781.3	3043.6	3226.5	3382.9	3526.5	3663.6
	s	1.2909	2.3014	2.7551	3.2049	3.7195	5.4863	5.8633	6.1082	6.3043	6.4737	6.6265
	v	1.0332	1.1378	1.2233	1.3574	1.6503	9.0714	11.874	13.907	15.638	17.201	18.658
220	h	435.58	861.42	1087.2	1333.1	1637.6	2738.8	3022.3	3211.7	3371.6	3517.4	3656.1
	s	1.2902	2.3000	2.7530	3.2014	3.7092	5.4102	5.8179	6.0716	6.2721	6.4441	6.5986
	v	1.0327	1.1369	1.2218	1.3543	1.6361	8.2511	11.113	13.119	14.810	16.327	17.737
240	h	437.09	862.36	1087.5	1331.9	1629.3	2641.2	2977.7	3181.4	3348.7	3499.1	3641.0
	s	1.2887	2.2972	2.7490	3.1945	3.6907	5.2430	5.7275	6.0003	6.2101	6.3876	6.5456
	v	1.0318	1.1352	1.2189	1.3482	1.6111	6.7392	9.7683	11.737	13.359	14.798	16.125
260	h	438.61	863.32	1087.8	1330.8	1622.2	2511.7	2930.2	3150.2	3325.3	3480.6	3625.7
	s	1.2872	2.2944	2.7450	3.1879	3.6741	5.0326	5.6364	5.9311	6.1508	6.3340	6.4957
	v	1.0308	1.1334	1.2161	1.3424	1.5896	5.2812	8.6160	10.565	12.132	13.505	14.762
280	h	440.12	864.28	1088.2	1329.8	1616.0	2330.7	2879.5	3118.1	3301.5	3461.9	3610.4
	s	1.2858	2.2917	2.7410	3.1815	3.6591	4.7503	5.5440	5.8636	6.0937	6.2829	6.4484
	v	1.0299	1.1317	1.2134	1.3369	1.5708	3.8219	7.6145	9.5566	11.078	12.397	13.594
300	h	441.64	865.26	1088.6	1328.9	1610.5	2161.8	2825.6	3085.0	3277.4	3443.0	3595.0
	s	1.2843	2.2890	2.7371	3.1752	3.6453	4.4896	5.4495	5.7972	6.0386	6.2340	6.4033
	v	1.0289	1.1301	1.2107	1.3316	1.5540	2.8306	6.7353	8.6808	10.166	11.436	12.582

Table A3 (continued): Properties of sub-saturated water and superheated steam

p (bar abs)	t (°C)	100	200	250	300	350	400	450	500	550	600	650
320	h	443.16	866.24	1089.0	1328.1	1605.5	2065.5	2768.2	3051.0	3252.9	3423.9	3579.5
	s	1.2829	2.2863	2.7333	3.1692	3.6325	4.3389	5.3526	5.7318	5.9851	6.1870	6.3603
	v	1.0280	1.1284	1.2081	1.3264	1.5389	2.3903	5.9581	7.9130	9.3674	10.597	11.698
340	h	444.67	867.23	1089.4	1327.3	1601.2	2011.8	2707.7	3016.0	3228.0	3404.7	3563.9
	s	1.2814	2.2836	2.7296	3.1633	3.6204	4.2525	5.2534	5.6670	5.9330	6.1416	6.3189
	v	1.0271	1.1268	1.2055	1.3215	1.5251	2.1795	5.2697	7.2351	8.6636	9.8572	10.918
360	h	446.19	868.23	1089.9	1326.7	1597.2	1977.5	2644.5	2980.3	3202.8	3385.4	3548.3
	s	1.2800	2.2810	2.7258	3.1575	3.6091	4.1953	5.1524	5.6028	5.8821	6.0976	6.2791
	v	1.0262	1.1252	1.2030	1.3168	1.5123	2.0558	4.6609	6.6329	8.0391	9.2007	10.226
380	h	447.71	869.24	1090.4	1326.1	1593.5	1953.0	2579.1	2943.8	3177.3	3365.9	3532.7
	s	1.2786	2.2783	2.7222	3.1519	3.5984	4.1528	5.0497	5.5392	5.8323	6.0549	6.2407
	v	1.0253	1.1236	1.2005	1.3122	1.5006	1.9717	4.1238	6.0958	7.4816	8.6145	9.6082
400	h	449.23	870.26	1090.9	1325.6	1590.1	1934.1	2515.6	2906.8	3151.6	3346.4	3517.0
	s	1.2771	2.2757	2.7186	3.1465	3.5882	4.1190	4.9511	5.4762	5.7835	6.0135	6.2035
	v	1.0244	1.1220	1.1981	1.3077	1.4896	1.9091	3.6748	5.6155	6.9815	8.0884	9.0530

Index

Units: Explanatory Notes

Symbols for SI units and factors are printed in ordinary roman type. Conversion factors have been rounded off for convenience. For more exact factors sometimes desirable in computer calculations. the official documents such as (1) below should be consulted. The 'factor' symbol precedes the unit symbol with no space. Unit symbols are separated in this book by a full space (a dot is also permissible).

The solidus is used in this book to distinguish numerator and denominator in compound units. Positive and negative powers are frequently used as alternative.

The following example illustrates the rule regarding the powers of (factor + unit):

$$km^2 \text{ signifies } (km)^2 = 10^6 \ m^2$$

References

1. Conversion factors and Table BS 350: Part 2: 1962 (Supplement No.1, 1967). From British Standards Institution, 2 Park Street, London W1A 2BS

A fuller selection of units (though not complete), at the same level of approximation as used here, may be found in:

2. SI and related units: quick-reference conversion factors (50p each + 25% of order for surface mail) from Dr I. G. C. Dryden, 112 Sandy Lane South, Wallington, Surrey SM6 9NR, UK